COMPLETE GUIDE
TO FRESH AND SALTWATER
FISHING

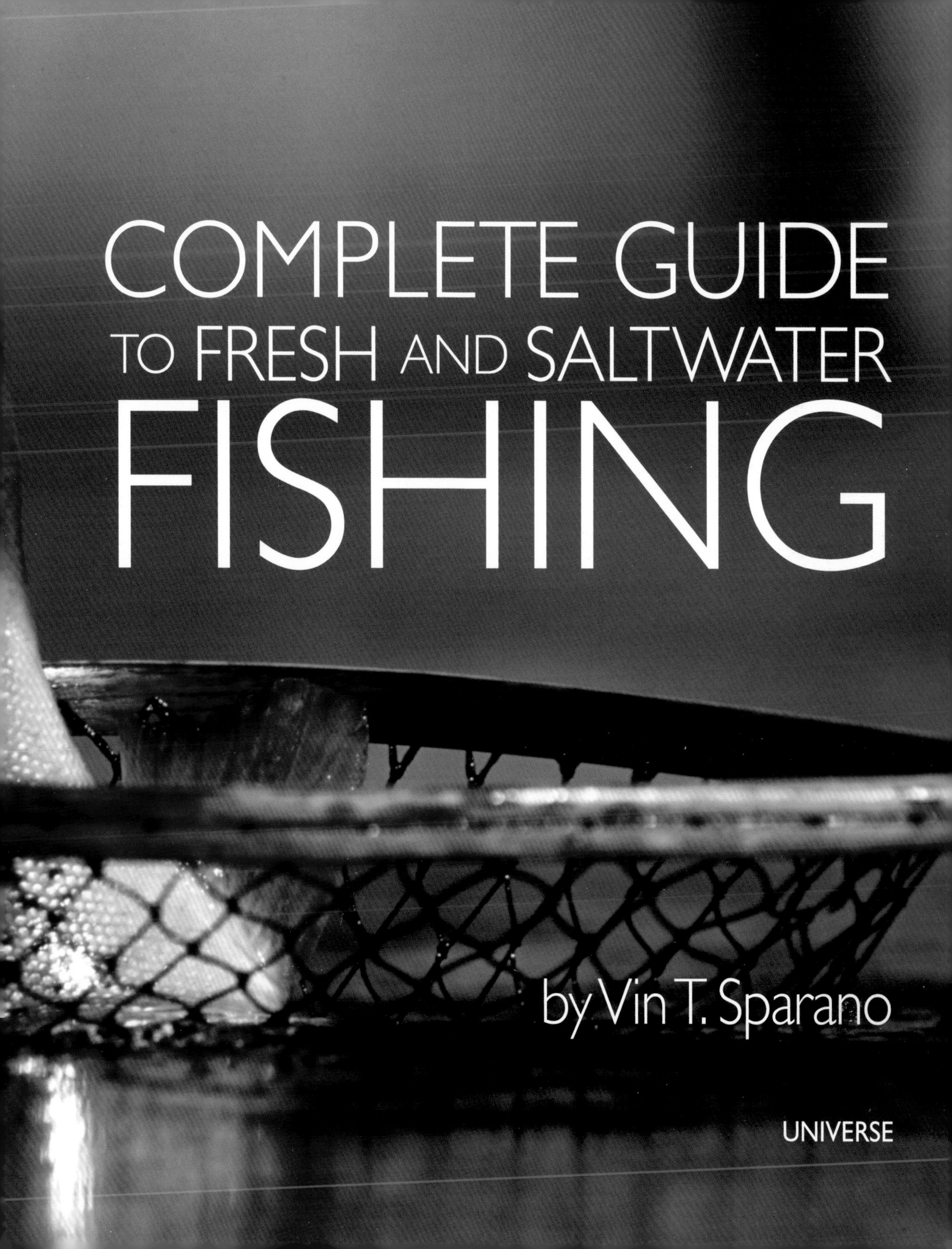

COMPLETE GUIDE
TO FRESH AND SALTWATER
FISHING

by Vin T. Sparano

UNIVERSE

Published by Universe Publishing
A Division of Rizzoli International Publications, Inc.
300 Park Avenue South
New York, NY 10010
www.rizzoliusa.com

Disclaimer: While all of the information in this book—both in text and illustrations—has been fact
checked and field tested, the publisher and author make no warranty, express or implied, that the
information is appropriate for every individual, situation, or purpose, and assume no responsibility
for errors or omissions. All information in this book is presented for entertainment value only, and
for an adult audience. Before attempting any new activity, make sure that you are aware of your own
limitations and all applicable risks. This book is not intended to replace sound judgment or professional
advice from an experienced instructor or outdoor guide.

Always follow any and all manufacturer's instructions when using any equipment featured in
this book. If the manufacturer of your equipment does not recommend the use of the equipment in the
manner herein described or depicted, you should comply with the manufacturer's recommendations.
You assume all risk and full responsibility for all of your actions, and the publisher and author will
not be held responsible for any loss, damage, or injury of any sort, whether consequential, incidental,
special, or otherwise, that may result from the information presented in this book.

In addition, masculine pronouns were used throughout the text in this book. This was done for
the sake of simplicity only, and was not intended to exclude female outdoors enthusiasts.

Project Editor: Candice Fehrman
Book Design: Lori S. Malkin
Text: Vin T. Sparano

2015 2016 2017 2018 / 10 9 8 7 6 5 4 3 2 1

Printed in China

ISBN-13: 978-0-7893-2925-7

Library of Congress Catalog Control Number: 2014952740

*In loving memory of
my grandson, Joey*

Contents

Preface

I hope you don't really think that fishing is simply a matter of putting a worm on a hook, casting it into a pond, and waiting for a red-and-white bobber to suddenly disappear. We have all heard stories about a kid with a cane pole outfishing a well-equipped angler. Well, it's just not true. A fisherman today who takes the time and effort to learn about fishing tackle and techniques and the eating habits of the species he wants to catch will not only outfish the cane-pole kid, but also most of his buddies.

That said, the array of constantly evolving and changing tackle, lures, and techniques could baffle even an experienced and dedicated fisherman. Imagine this scenario: A man walks into a tackle shop and says, "I'd like to try fishing."

"Fresh or salt water?" the salesman asks.

"Fresh water," the man answers.

"Spinning, casting, or fly fishing?"

"What's the easiest to learn?"

"Spinning," the salesman answers, but then continues with more questions. "What are you fishing for? Bass, trout, walleyes, or crappies? Do you want a light-, medium-, or heavy-action rod? One piece or two pieces? Do you want monofilament, fluorocarbon, or braided line for your reel? What lures? Spoons, crankbaits, spinners, bucktails, plastic lures, or buzz baits? How about hooks, swivels, and leaders?"

"Sounds complicated," the wannabe angler confesses. "Maybe I'll try fly fishing instead."

"OK," says the salesman. "Fresh or salt water?"

Unless you get a knowledgeable salesman to walk you through the different types of tackle available today and he is willing to take the time to match your tackle to the fish you're after, you may change your mind and take up golf instead! When I decided to write this book, my goal was to guide fishermen—both beginners and experienced anglers—through the various mazes of tackle, techniques, and types of game fish (both in fresh and salt water).

I have spent a lifetime fishing in both fresh and salt water in locations stretching from Alaska to Cuba and the Bahamas. I've fished with many superb guides and I've learned their techniques and methods. Throughout these pages, I have shared with you advice and many valuable tips from these fishing professionals.

In these pages, from start to finish, you will learn how to choose the best tackle for you, as well as which baits and lures to use on various game fish. Equally important, you will learn what to do after the catch, from filleting to cooking your fish. There's even a special section including some of my favorite recipes, as well as recipes from nationally recognized expert anglers who have mastered cooking their catches. Rounding out the book are chapters on first aid for fishermen and boating.

Books of this scope can never be the job of one person. Candice Fehrman, my editor at Rizzoli/Universe, and Lori S. Malkin, my book designer, were the engineers who took this enormous amount of information and designed a book that will make it easy for you to quickly find, learn, and absorb the fishing advice you seek. I also want to thank Jim Muschett, my publisher at Rizzoli/Universe, who was always there with advice and guidance throughout this project. And special thanks to my son, Matt, and Sheila Hassan from the Wulff School of Fly Fishing for all the instructional casting photos.

When I needed illustrations of any kind, I could also depend on the fishing industry, especially Isaiah James at Windsor Nature Discovery, Katie Mitchell and Jenna Kendall at Bass Pro, Mac McKeever at L.L. Bean, Tom Rosenbauer at Orvis, Joe Arterburn at Cabela's, and many others who answered my requests for photos and information.

You are now holding the complete and ultimate guide to fishing in fresh and salt water. Study it and I guarantee you will become a better fisherman. I wish you good fishing wherever you make that first cast.

—Vin T. Sparano
Editor Emeritus and Senior Field Editor
Outdoor Life

FISHING

FISHING

SPINNING

Spinning became popular in America in the late 1940s. It is unique because the reel is mounted on the underside of the rod—rather than on top, as in other methods—and because the reel spool remains stationary (does not revolve) when the angler is casting and retrieving.

In operation, the weight and momentum of the lure being cast uncoils line (usually monofilament, fluorocarbon, or braid) from the reel spool. Unlike conventional revolving-spool reels, in which the momentum of the turning spool can cause backlashes, the spinning-reel user has no such problem, for the line stops uncoiling at the end of the cast. A beginner can learn to use spinning gear much faster than conventional tackle. Still another advantage of spinning gear is that it permits the use of much lighter lines and smaller, lighter lures than can be cast with conventional equipment.

▨ The Reel

On a standard open-face spinning reel, the pickup mechanism is usually of a type called the bail—a metal arm extending across the spool's face. To cast a lure or bait, the angler opens the bail by swinging it out and down. This frees the line, which, as a rule, the angler momentarily controls with his index finger. He casts and then cranks the reel handle—not a full turn but just a small fraction of a turn. This snaps the bail closed, engaging the line.

Other devices on a spinning reel include the drag and the antireverse lock. The drag, an adjustable mechanism usually consisting of a series of discs and friction washers, is fitted on the outer (forward) face of the spool or at the rear of the gear housing in most reels. The drag permits a hooked fish to take out line without breaking off, while the reel handle remains stationary. The anti-reverse lock, usually a lever mounted on the gear-housing cover, prevents the reel handle from turning in reverse at such times as when a hooked fish is running out or when you are trolling.

Spinning reels are designed for all types of fishing. How does the beginner select the right one for his particular needs? A reel's weight and line capacity are the major determining factors. For ultralight fishing with tiny lures ($\frac{1}{16}$ to $\frac{5}{16}$ ounce), a reel weighing 5 to 8 ounces and holding about 100 yards of 2- to 4-pound-test line is the ticket. Reels for light freshwater use weigh 8 to 10 ounces and hold up to 200 yards of 6- to 8-pound-test line. Reels for general freshwater and light saltwater use weigh 12 to 16 ounces and hold up to 250 yards of 8- to 15-pound-test line. Heavy offshore and surf-spinning reels weigh upwards of 25 ounces and hold a minimum of 250 yards of 15-pound-test line. These yardage capacities are for monofilament or fluorocarbon line. Smaller-diameter braid line will usually increase these capacities on most reels.

In addition to the open-face spinning reel, there is a closed-face design. This type, too, is mounted under the rod. Its spool and working parts are enclosed in a hood, with the line running through an opening at the front. The pickup mechanism is normally an internal pin, and there's no need for a bail since the line control is accomplished by other means. In some of these reels, which were fairly common at one time, line was disengaged from the pickup by backing the handle a half turn. In others, it was accomplished by pushing a button, working a lever or disc, or pressing the front reel plate. Closed-face reels are still available, but are no longer common.

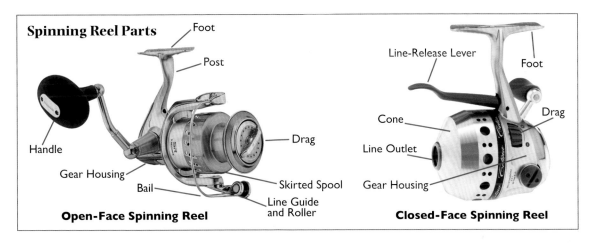

Spinning Reel Parts

Foot

Post

Handle

Gear Housing

Bail

Drag

Skirted Spool

Line Guide and Roller

Open-Face Spinning Reel

Line-Release Lever

Foot

Cone

Drag

Line Outlet

Gear Housing

Closed-Face Spinning Reel

Besides eliminating the bail, closed-faced reels give the spool and other parts some protection from the elements and help to keep out sand, dirt, and the like. Some fishermen, however, dislike the fact that the line is choked through the constriction at the point of the cone, feeling that this arrangement somewhat limits casting range and accuracy. Another drawback is that the hood enclosing the spool hides the line from the angler's view, preventing him from seeing line tangles and whether or not the line is uncoiling smoothly.

Mainly because of the simplicity of spinning reels, there has been little gadgeteering by manufacturers. However, some unusual features have appeared over the years. These have included bails that open automatically, self-centering (self-positioning) bails, rear drags,

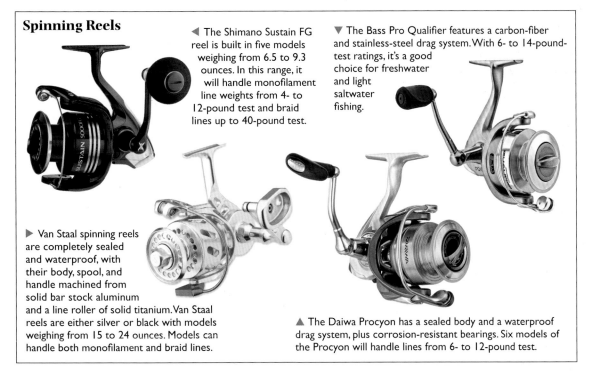

Spinning Reels

◄ The Shimano Sustain FG reel is built in five models weighing from 6.5 to 9.3 ounces. In this range, it will handle monofilament line weights from 4- to 12-pound test and braid lines up to 40-pound test.

▼ The Bass Pro Qualifier features a carbon-fiber and stainless-steel drag system. With 6- to 14-pound-test ratings, it's a good choice for freshwater and light saltwater fishing.

► Van Staal spinning reels are completely sealed and waterproof, with their body, spool, and handle machined from solid bar stock aluminum and a line roller of solid titanium. Van Staal reels are either silver or black with models weighing from 15 to 24 ounces. Models can handle both monofilament and braid lines.

▲ The Daiwa Procyon has a sealed body and a waterproof drag system, plus corrosion-resistant bearings. Six models of the Procyon will handle lines from 6- to 12-pound test.

How to Match Up Spinning Tackle

This chart is meant only as a general guide aimed at helping you put together, in proper balance, the basic elements of a spinning outfit tailored for fish of a particular weight category. Specific conditions—and your ability and personal preferences—should also be considered.

Species of Fish	Reel	Rod Action, Length (feet)	Line (pound test)	Lure Weights (ounces)
Trout, small bass, grayling, panfish	Ultralight	Ultralight, 4 to 6	2, 3	$\frac{1}{16}$ to $\frac{5}{16}$
Smallmouth, largemouth, and white bass, pickerel, trout, grayling	Light	Light, 5½ to 6½	4 to 8	$\frac{1}{4}$ to $\frac{3}{8}$
Large bass and trout, walleye, pickerel, pike, snook, landlocked salmon	Medium	Medium, 6 to 7½	6 to 10	$\frac{3}{8}$ to $\frac{5}{8}$
Salmon, lake trout, muskellunge, pike, bonefish, tarpon, striped bass, bluefish	Heavy	Heavy, 7 to 8½	10 to 15	½ to 1½
General saltwater use (surf and boat)	Extraheavy	Extraheavy, 9 to 13	12 and up	1 and up

and skirted spools, which prevent line from getting behind the spool.

▌ The Rod

There are spinning rods designed for every conceivable kind of sport fishing. They come in lengths from 4 to 13 feet and weigh from 2 to 30 ounces. Most are constructed of fiberglass, graphite, carbon, or Kevlar. Construction is usually one, two, or three pieces; however, some spinning rods designed for backpackers may have as many as a half-dozen sections.

Spinning rods fall into five general categories: ultralight, light, medium, heavy, and extraheavy. They are further broken down according to the type of reel and design of the hand grip.

Traditional Spinning Rod Designs

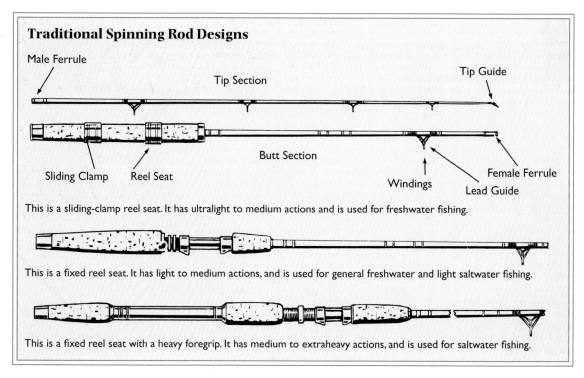

Male Ferrule

Tip Section

Tip Guide

Sliding Clamp   Reel Seat

Butt Section

Windings

Female Ferrule

Lead Guide

This is a sliding-clamp reel seat. It has ultralight to medium actions and is used for freshwater fishing.

This is a fixed reel seat. It has light to medium actions, and is used for general freshwater and light saltwater fishing.

This is a fixed reel seat with a heavy foregrip. It has medium to extraheavy actions, and is used for saltwater fishing.

How to Cast with Spinning Tackle

The Grip • Proper grip for open-face spinning reels puts two fingers on each side of the reel's supporting post. The index finger holds the line until the cast is made. With a closed-face spinning reel, the grip is similar except the index finger is used to control and release the line with a trigger release.

The Straightaway Cast • Here are the three steps in making a straightaway cast with an open-face spinning reel. Starting with your rod at a 45-degree angle, with your index finger holding the line, bring the rod backward smoothly until you feel the rod loaded with the weight of your lure or bait. The rod is powered forward, the line is released, and the rod is held at the angle shown, while the lure or bait sails to the target. A sidearm cast, generally used to avoid overhead foliage, is similar to the straightaway cast, except the rod is held parallel to the ground during the cast.

How to Cast with Spinning Tackle *(continued)*

The Underhand Lob • The underhand lob or underhand cast, usually used to clear brush or to cope with the wind, starts with the rod tip low to the ground and high on the upward swing. A lure with the underhand lob will sail in a high, soft arc *(right)* and will hit the water gently. It is a good cast for clear, shallow runs, where a splashy cast would scare fish.

The Bow-and-Arrow Cast • This is a trick that anglers use to shoot a lure through holes in streamside brush. The photos show the same cast from two different positions. Holding the rod low and parallel to the water will clear the cast from overhead brush. Holding the rod high will clear low brush and likely give you more distance. The technique is the same. Grasp the bend of the lowest hook on the lure so that it will clear your fingers smoothly and safely. Then, release the line, shooting the lure like an arrow.

Coping with Wind • When casting into the wind, keep your cast low and let the line shoot forward and down to minimize the wind as the lure shoots low over the water. With the wind at your back, let the line shoot forward with the rod tip high. This way the wind can carry the lure the additional distance.

Sidearm Cast • The sidearm cast is a good wind bucker, and useful when overhead foliage makes a conventional forward cast difficult. The cast starts with the rod low, and then comes the backswing and forward sweep that ends with the rod pointing to the target. The line is released just before the rod points toward the target. The rod's follow-through motion curves the lure to the target. Sidearm casts are particularly useful when wading narrow, tree-lined streams or in boats holding two or more anglers. There's plenty of room for casts with sidearm motion.

Retrieve • Hold the rod at a 45-degree angle or less during the retrieve. Keep the rod in a position for hook setting. The rod should also be in a position to absorb the shock of a hard strike from a big fish.

FLY FISHING

The art of fly fishing dates back to at least the third century AD and so is one of the oldest forms of sport fishing. Its adherents—and they are legion— say that it is also the most artistic form of the sport.

Fly fishing is unique in two basic ways. In all other forms of fishing, the weight of the lure or bait is what enables the angler to cast; in fly fishing, the weight of the line itself enables the cast. In spinning, spincasting, and baitcasting, a natural bait or a lure or plug imitating a natural bait is offered to the fish; a fly fisherman's offering is a near-weightless bit of feathers and hair that imitates an insect in one of its forms of life (though some flies—streamers and bucktails—imitate baitfish).

▨ The Reel

It is generally agreed that the reel, with the exception of saltwater fly fishing, is the least important item of fly-fishing tackle, and yet without it, the angler would find himself amid a tangle of line and leader. The fly reel is mounted below the rod grip and close to the butt end of the rod. In most kinds of fishing, the reel's main function is to store line that is not being used. In handling large fish, however, the workings and drag of the fly reel come into play.

There are two basic types of fly reels: the single action and the automatic.

The single-action reel, which is best when the quarry is either small or quite heavy fish, is so named because the spool makes one complete turn for each turn of the handle. The spool is deep and narrow. A beginner should make sure that the reel has a strong click mechanism to prevent the line from overrunning, and if he'll be tangling with sizable, strong-running fish, such as striped bass, tarpon or salmon, he should get a reel with a good smooth adjustable drag.

The standard (trout size) single-action fly reel weighs 3 to 5 ounces and has a spool diameter of 3 to 4 inches. The spool should be filled with enough line (the fly line itself, usually 30 yards, plus sufficient "backing" line) to reach within about ⅜ inch of the reel's cross braces. Many of the best fly fishermen like 15- to 30-pound-test braid or monofilament line as backing. For most freshwater fishing, 20-pound-test braid backing is fine, but 30-pound test is recommended for species such as striped bass, bonefish, and salmon. The chief advantages of the single-action fly reel are that it weighs considerably less than the automatic and it can hold much more backing, an important factor in handling large fish.

The automatic fly reel has a spring-operated spool

How to Match Up Fly Tackle

This chart is meant only as a general guide aimed at helping you put together, in proper balance, the basic elements of a fly-fishing outfit tailored for fish of a particular weight category. Specific conditions—and your ability and personal preference—should also be considered. The line sizes below are meant only as a general guide, and a newcomer to fishing should note that there is a wide range of conditions and circumstances that determines the correct line weight for a given rod. Level and double-taper fly lines may still be available, but the best advice for easy casting is to use weight-forward lines.

Species of Fish	Reel	Rod Length (feet)	Lines		
			Level	Double Taper	Weight Forward
Trout, small bass, grayling, panfish	Single-action, automatic	6½ to 7½	L4 or L5	DT4F or DT5F; DT6S	WF4F; WF6S
Smallmouth, largemouth, and white bass, pickerel, trout, grayling	Single-action, automatic	7½ to 8½	L6 or L7	DT6F or DT7F; DT8S	WF6F; WF8S
Large bass and trout, landlocked salmon, walleye, pickerel, pike	Single-action	8½ to 9	L8 or L9	DT8F or DT9F; DT9S	WF9F; WF10S
Salmon, lake trout, muskellunge, pike, bonefish, tarpon, striped bass, bluefish	Single-action	9½	L10	DT10F	WF10F; WF10S

KEY TO LINE DESIGNATIONS: L—LEVEL   DT—DOUBLE TAPER   WF—WEIGHT FORWARD   F—FLOATING   S—SINKING

Basic Types of Fly Reels

◀ The Orvis Battenkill Bar Stock is a typical fly reel design. Depending on the Orvis model, the Battenkill can handle any species from trout to billfish with line weights of I to II.

▶ The Pflueger Automatic fly reel has a spring-operated spool that retrieves line automatically when an angler activates the lever. A one-time favorite with some fly fishermen, it has decreased in popularity.

▲ The World Wide Sportsman Gold Cup is a fly reel designed for big fish. Two models are built for fly lines up to WF12F with 300 yards of 30-pound-test backing. It features a heat-resistant carbon drag.

▲ The Sage 1600 is an all-aluminum fly reel with a quick-release spool change and a sealed graphite drag. It is built for line weights of 4 to 9. In the model with a line weight range of 4 to 6, the Sage 1600 weighs only 5⅞ ounces. It is a good freshwater choice.

▲ The White River Kingfisher fly reel, machined from cold-forged aluminum with a sealed drag system, has an open-frame design and offers a wide range of models for freshwater and saltwater fishing. These models handle fly line weights from 3 to 10 with room for backing.

that retrieves line automatically when the angler activates the spool-release lever. The spring is wound up as line is pulled from the reel, but line may be stripped from the reel at any time, even when the spring is tightly wound.

Though heavier than the single action (the weight range is 5 to 10 ounces), the automatic greatly facilitates line control. Instead of having to shift the rod from the right to the left hand (assuming the user is right-handed) to reel in line—as the user of the single-action reel must do—the automatic user simply touches the release lever with the little finger of his right hand.

Fly Rod Parts

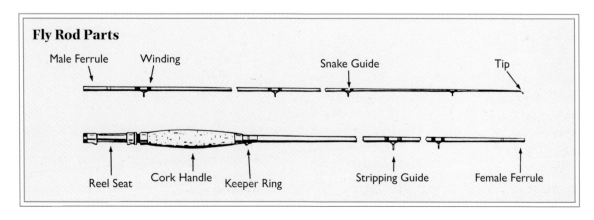

Male Ferrule   Winding   Snake Guide   Tip

Reel Seat   Cork Handle   Keeper Ring   Stripping Guide   Female Ferrule

How to Wade a River

Wading looks easy enough, but it can turn into a dangerous situation if you are swept off your feet in the swift current. The rules for safe wading are simple. First, never take a step in any direction unless your rear or anchor foot is firmly planted. Next, slide your lead foot forward until it is secure. When your lead foot is firmly planted, then slide your anchor foot ahead. Never try to wade by lifting your feet. The current will swing your leg out from under you and throw you off balance. Avoid wading big, wide stretches of river. It is safer to wade from pool to pool, taking advantage of slower current to rest.

Losing balance in a fast current can be frightening, but you can always use your fishing rod to keep from going down in the current. When you feel yourself falling, lower your rod into the river and push it underwater. Its buoyancy will often be enough to help you regain your balance. Don't worry. You won't break the rod.

If you fall, don't panic. Always ride downstream feetfirst until you can grab a branch or rock and get yourself back on your feet. Never ride the current headfirst. There is always the danger of striking your head. Make the current work for you. Use your arms and pick a course toward shore and safe ground.

Plan a route before you step into any stream. Always wade at an angle, quartering upstream as much as possible. When you stop to fish, stand sideways to the current, which is safer than taking the full force of the current against your front or back. Use a wading staff as a third leg to keep your balance and check depth. A wader belt is literally a lifesaver in streams and rivers. If you fall, the belt will trap air in your waders and give you buoyancy.

▨ The Rod

The rod is of paramount importance to the fly caster. It must be suited to the kind of fishing he does (saltwater, trout, bass bugging, and so on), and it must be matched with the proper fly line.

Fly rods can be made of fiberglass, graphite, or bamboo. Graphite fly rods are faster and more sensitive than fiberglass rods. And, ounce for ounce, graphite is twice as strong as glass. What length rod should the beginner select?

According to the recommendations of several casting instructors and tackle manufacturers, a good all-purpose length is 8 to 8½ feet with a weight of about 5 ounces. Such a rod should have fast action.

Action, briefly, is a measure of a rod's flexibility, and it determines the use for which the rod is suited. In fast-action rods, best suited for dry-fly fishing, most of the flex (or bend) is at the tip. Medium-action rods bend down to the middle and are designed to perform over a wide range of conditions. They are probably the best choice for an all-purpose fly rod. Slow-action rods, a traditional design that works well for fishing streamers, bass bugs, and the like, bend well down to and even into the butt.

Good fly rods have a screw-lock reel seat, which holds the reel securely. Line guides are usually made of stainless steel, except that the tip guide and sometimes the stripper guide (the one nearest to the reel) may be chrome or highly durable carboloy steel. The largest fly rods, those designed for taking tarpon and other large saltwater fish, have an extension butt or a fore-end grip, which gives the angler more leverage.

How to Use Fly Tackle

Sheila M. Hassan (*right*) is a Federation of Fly Fishers Master Certified casting instructor. She is the director at the Wulff School of Fly Fishing and an IGFA world-record holder for bonefish and bluefish. Joan Wulff (*left*) is a fly-fishing legend and a National Casting Champion with a record distance cast of 161 feet. Joan, elected to the IGFA Hall of Fame, is the founder of the Wulff School of Fly Fishing. The photos and techniques described in this section are from *Fly Casting: A Systematic Approach* by Sheila Hassan.

The Grip • The thumb on top of the cork handle is the strongest grip for most people. With your thumb on top, the index finger is on the opposite side of the rod butt. You want the thumb and index finger to balance the rod, with your lower three fingers gently wrapped around the rod butt. A key feature of your grip is to be sure the heel of your hand sits on top of the cork grip. Your lower three fingers cradle the rod butt low in the fingers, like when you lift a suitcase handle. The primary points of pressure are your thumb and index finger, and your lower two fingers. Your middle finger is less important for controlling the rod, so it is available to help manage your fly line with shooting and stripping.

How to Use Fly Tackle *(continued)*

Wrist Action • The wrist can be very helpful in your casting, but must be used in moderation. The wrist has two positions: bent down, which is a zero-degree angle to your forearm *(left)*, and straight, which is a 45-degree angle to your forearm. This change in angle occurs when you stop and the rod unloads. It is useful for the forward cast stop. Every backcast starts with your wrist in the bent-down position and ends with your wrist in the straight position, with the rod butt at an approximately 45-degree angle to your forearm.

Basic Cast • The basic cast is the classic fly cast. It has both a backcast and a forward cast. Each cast is separate. Stand in a vertical stance with your feet, shoulders, and hips facing your target. Starting with your line straight on the water, use your rod hand and forearm as a unit to lift the line off the water. Remember that all casts start slowly and build acceleration gradually. Lift the line off the water with just enough speed so you lift inch by inch. If you lift too fast, you will see the water spray as it rips off the surface. If you lift too slowly, you will run out of stroke length. The correct speed is determined by watching your line and lifting inch by inch. You should see a small, V-shaped wake as you lift the line. This wake shows you have the right speed.

Next, you must focus on timing. Timing is the pause after the cast while the loop unrolls behind you but maintains the line under tension. Remember that the cast

must bend and unbend the rod. This can only happen when the line is under tension. When your backcast has unrolled, it is time for the forward cast. Look to your target and think of aiming the cast. Move your rod arm toward the target area, leading with the elbow and finishing with the hand. Start the forward cast slowly and build acceleration gradually to load the rod. With the line under tension and the rod loaded, you are ready for the forward cast wrist rotation to stop the rod. Push forward with your thumb and pull back with your lower fingers. Watch your loop unroll and follow through with the rod tip down to the water. The cast is complete.

False Cast • False casting is making a series of backcasts and forward casts without letting the line touch the water. False casting is used to dry your dry fly. Dry flies are designed to sit on top of the water, but can become waterlogged as you fish. False casting is also used to change direction, from downstream to upstream, and to measure the distance of your cast. Steps 1 through 5 show the sequence— elbow lifts and lowers, forearm moves back and forth. It's critical to maintain line tension between your rod and fly line in your left hand. Make sure there is no slack between the line hand and the stripping guide of the rod. False casting also allows you to add length to your cast by adding the technique of shooting line.

How to Use Fly Tackle *(continued)*

Shooting Line • After you learn to false cast, the next step is shooting line. Shooting line means you can extend the range of your fishing without having to carry that extra line in the air during your cast.

Before you get in the starting position, make sure you have enough line available to shoot. Start with a small amount, about 4 feet. You will have the rod in one hand and the line in the other hand. Make sure there is no slack between the line hand and the stripping guide of the rod. The extra line for shooting will be in a loose loop between your rod hand and line hand. Start by making two or three false casts. Watch for the casting loop to be formed after the stop on the forward cast.

When you see the loop has formed, you can release the line from your fingers and the loop will pull the extra line out.

When you are practicing shooting line, you may need to work on your timing of the shoot. If you release your line too soon, the loop will not have formed and you will not be able to shoot line. If you wait too long, your loop will unroll completely and there will be no energy left to shoot extra line. The rod must be stopped effectively, which means a smooth acceleration to an abrupt stop. This is what gives you a good loop with enough energy to shoot line. Practice shooting line on your third false cast and work on the timing until you can shoot all 4 feet.

Headwind • For most fly fishermen, wind is a challenge. In all wind situations, you will want high line speed to control your fly line. To handle a headwind, you will want a tight loop with more speed. To get a tighter loop, adjust your casting arc so it is only as wide as needed, and cast along a straight line, directly to the target. You will want to cast on a steeper downward angle and have your loop unroll inches above the water. Use a higher rate of acceleration and cast a little faster to get higher line speed. Crouching down low with your body may help you get that lower angle and greater speed. This combination of adjustments helps your loop cut into the wind better and helps you cast in headwinds.

Tailwind • A good technique for dealing with tailwinds is to make two forward casts. Turn to stand sideways to your target. Make a forward cast to your right side. While the cast is unrolling, rotate your hand and forearm to make a forward cast in the other direction, toward your left side. After the hand and forearm rotate, bring the elbow back in by your side and complete your forward cast to the left side. This is a very effective technique for tailwinds, as it uses the strength of your muscles in the forward direction to cast into the tailwind.

Single Haul • To learn the single haul, start with a single haul on the backcast. Move your line hand and rod hand in the same direction to start the casting stroke. When you reach the line leader connection, the rod hand will execute the stop, while the line hand accelerates in an opposite direction for the haul. Be sure to stop the line hand haul when the rod hand completes the stop.

As you lift the line off the water, if your rod hand is relaxed, you can feel the rod bending. The haul should feel like you are pulling into this bend, creating a deeper bend. Think of the backcast haul as helping to lift the fly off the water. Within the casting stroke, the loading move is the longest part. The stop and haul are relatively short in comparison. The wrist rotation and haul are very brief; they last just long enough to lift the fly off the water. As the fly leaves the water, your haul is complete and the rod is stopped. Your rod and line hands maintain their positions while the loop unrolls. On the next forward cast, as you move your rod arm forward, your line hand pivots to maintain its position relative to the rod hand. Make sure there is no slack between the line hand and rod hand and present the fly.

How to Use Fly Tackle *(continued)*

Double Haul • The key to the double haul is that it adds the power of the left hand to the work of the rod hand to increase the load in the rod. Start the backcast as usual with the rod hand and line hand moving in the same direction. When the rod hand is ready to execute the stop, the line hand accelerates in the opposite direction, with a crisp acceleration to a stop. While the line unrolls on the backcast, the line hand gives back the line it has just hauled out. The line hand will return to a position near the reel. It is crucial to be sure there is no slack in the line as the line hand gives back the line. When the loop has unrolled and the forward cast begins, the line hand and rod hand move forward. When the rod hand starts the forward cast wrist rotation for the stop, the line hand accelerates away from the rod hand. While the forward cast loop unrolls, the line hand gives back the line it has hauled out. You can either shoot the line or return the line hand to a position near the reel.

Roll Cast • The easily learned roll cast pays off heavily when the fisherman has some barrier behind him that prevents a normal backcast. In fact, the roll cast is a quick way to make a new cast under almost any circumstance. To execute this cast, tilt your arm at a slight angle away from your body as you lift your hand up toward your temple. Allow the line to slide behind the rod tip to create a D-shaped loop. Stop and allow the line to settle. Check your hand height and the angle of your rod butt to your forearm to be sure it is not greater than 45 degrees. Line

up your elbow with your target area. Execute the forward cast by slowly lowering your elbow to move your rod hand in line with your target area. Continue the acceleration to the target. When your thumb pad is opposite the target area, use hand movement to execute the forward cast wrist rotation and stop the rod. Lower the rod tip as the loop unrolls.

BAITCASTING

Baitcasting is a method of fishing distinguished by the use of a revolving-spool reel. Originally intended by its 19th-century creators as a means of casting live baitfish, baitcasting tackle today is used to present all sorts of offerings—from worms and minnows to spoons and huge jointed plugs—to game fish in both fresh and salt water. This method is also known as plugcasting.

Before the advent of spinning gear, baitcasting was the universally accepted tackle for presenting baits or lures. Even today, many anglers—especially those who grew up with a baitcasting outfit in their hands—prefer this method, even though the revolving-spool reel is more difficult to use than fixed-spool spinning and spincasting reels. The baitcaster feels that his gear gives him more sensitive contact with what is going on at the end of his line. He feels that he can manipulate a lure better on baitcasting gear and have better control over a hooked fish. Most fishermen agree that when the quarry is a big, strong fish such as a muskie, pike, or saltwater fish, baitcasting outfits get the nod over spinning or spincasting tackle.

Baitcasting tackle is often preferred for trolling, too, for the revolving-spool reel makes it easy to pay out line behind the moving boat, and the rod has enough backbone to handle the big, water-resistant lures used in many forms of trolling.

■ The Reel

The reel is by far the most important part of a baitcasting outfit, and the budding baitcaster would do well to buy the best reel he can afford.

The main distinguishing feature of baitcasting reels is that the spool revolves when line is cast out or reeled in, while in spinning and spincasting reels the spool remains stationary.

Baitcasting reels have a relatively wide, shallow spool, and most have multiplying gears that cause the

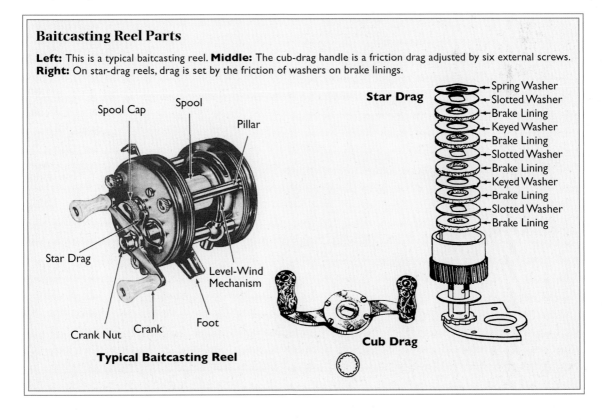

Baitcasting Reel Parts

Left: This is a typical baitcasting reel. **Middle:** The cub-drag handle is a friction drag adjusted by six external screws. **Right:** On star-drag reels, drag is set by the friction of washers on brake linings.

Spool Cap
Spool
Pillar

Star Drag

Level-Wind Mechanism

Star Drag

Crank Nut   Crank   Foot

Typical Baitcasting Reel

Star Drag
← Spring Washer
← Slotted Washer
← Brake Lining
← Keyed Washer
← Brake Lining
← Slotted Washer
← Brake Lining
← Keyed Washer
← Brake Lining
← Slotted Washer
← Brake Lining

Cub Drag

How to Match Up Baitcasting Tackle

This chart is meant only as a general guide aimed at helping you put together, in proper balance, the basic elements of a baitcasting outfit. Specific conditions—and your ability and personal preferences—should also be considered.

Species of Fish	Reel	Rod Action, Length (feet)	Line (pound test)	Lure Weights (ounces)
Panfish, small bass, pickerel, trout	Multiplying gear with level-wind	Ultralight, 6 to 6½	6 to 8	⅛ to ¼
Bass, pickerel, walleye, small pike, trout	Multiplying gear with level-wind	Light, 5½ to 6½	6 to 12	¼ to ½
Large bass, walleye, pike, lake trout, muskie, striped bass	Multiplying gear with star drag	Medium, 5 to 6	10 to 20	⅝ to ¾
Muskie, steelhead, lake trout, salmon, striped bass, bluefish, tarpon, snook	Multiplying gear with star drag	Heavy, 4½ to 7	18 to 25	¾ and up

Baitcasting Reels

▶ The Johnny Morris Signature Series Baitcast Reel is built on a solid aluminum frame with a carbon-titanium finish. This reel has an 11-bearing system and a carbon drag with up to 14 pounds of drag pressure. Five different models weigh from 8.3 to 9.6 ounces. The line capacity is 160 yards of 12-pound-test monofilament.

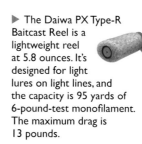

▶ The Daiwa PX Type-R Baitcast Reel is a lightweight reel at 5.8 ounces. It's designed for light lures on light lines, and the capacity is 95 yards of 6-pound-test monofilament. The maximum drag is 13 pounds.

▲ The Abu Garcia Revo MGX is a featherweight baitcasting reel for light-tackle freshwater fishing. Weighing only 5.4 ounces with a gear ratio of 7:1 and a maximum drag pressure of 24 pounds, the reel features 10 stainless-steel bearings and a line capacity of 115 yards of 12-pound-test monofilament.

▲ The Browning Midas Low-Profile Baitcast Reel has a one-piece aluminum frame, a V-shaped spool of forged aluminum, and nine stainless-steel bearings. It also has a magnetic cast control and heavy thumb-bar release. It will hold 120 yards of 12-pound-test line.

▲ The Abu Garcia 5600 is designed to handle most species of freshwater and inshore saltwater fish. A familiar reel for generations, the Abu Garcia Ambassadeur series features stainless-steel ball bearings, a carbon star-drag system, and line capacities up to 245 yards of 14-pound-test monofilament.

spool to revolve several times (usually four) for each complete turn of the reel handle. There is also some kind of drag mechanism, which is helpful in fighting big fish. These range from a simple click mechanism to a screw-down nut to a star drag. Some older reels have what is called a cub drag, which is adjusted by turning six screws on the base of the handle.

Almost all of today's good baitcasting reels have an important device called a level-wind. It usually takes the form of a U-shaped loop of heavy wire attached to a base that travels from one side of the spool to the other by means of a wormlike gear. The device permits line to be wound evenly on the spool and thus is a big help in preventing backlashes, which are often caused by line "lumping up" on the spool. A backlash occurs when the speed of the revolving spool is faster than that of the outgoing line, resulting in a "bird's nest."

Most baitcasting reels are being made with anti-backlash devices. These employ either centrifugal force or pressure on the spool axle or flange to slow down the spool during a cast. Some reels use magnets to accomplish this process. However, though these antibacklash devices are helpful, the user of a baitcasting reel must still learn to apply thumb pressure to the spool if he is to prevent backlashes under all conditions. Only experience can teach how much thumb pressure is needed under any given set of circumstances.

Another development in baitcasting is the free-spool reel. Without this feature, the cast lure not only pulls out line and turns the spool, but also turns the gears, the level-wind, and the reel handle. All these moving parts tend to shorten the cast. But in the free-spool reel, most of the gearing is disconnected from the spool before a cast is made, and only the spool (and sometimes the level-wind) turns. This makes it easier to start and stop the turning of the spool and so permits the use of lighter lures than can be cast with a standard baitcasting reel. Longer casts are also possible. A turn of the handle reengages the gears of the free-spool reel so that the retrieve can be made.

■ The Rod

Most baitcasting rods are now made of fiberglass or graphite. Rod lengths range from about 4 to more than 7 feet. Some, obviously, are more suitable for specific purposes. The most popular length—because it works well for many kinds of fishing—is about 6 feet. Manufacturers generally classify their rods according to their action, which refers to the lure weights that a rod handles efficiently. Generally, ultralight rods can handle lures weighing ¼ ounce or less. Light rods can handle ¼ to ½ ounce.

Typical Casting Rod Designs

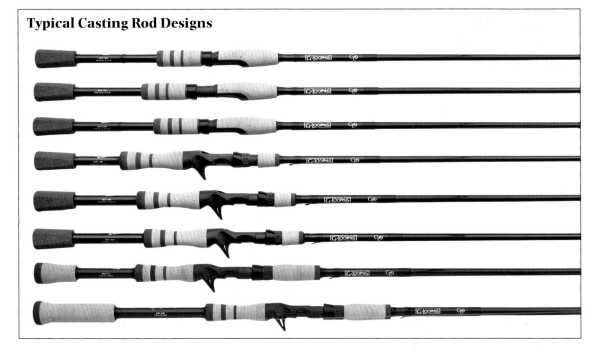

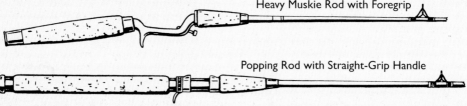

These are typical casting rod handles. The pistol grip (*top*) is for one-handed casting, while the straight grip (*bottom*) is for two-handed casting. The longer handle, originally built for bigger fish, is now finding favor with bass fishermen. Two-handed casting is less tiring and makes longer casts possible.

Heavy Muskie Rod with Foregrip

Popping Rod with Straight-Grip Handle

Medium rods are better at handling ⅝ to ¾ ounce, and heavy rods are for ¾ ounce or more.

Baitcasting rods have either a straight handle or a pistol-grip handle. No longer common is the double-offset handle, in which the reel seat is depressed and the butt grip is canted downward. Other features of baitcasting rods are a finger hook on the underside of the reel seat and a reel-holding screw lock.

Baitcasting rods are of one- or two-piece construction. Some have ferrules about midway up the rod, while others may have a detachable handle. The most popular baitcasting rods have a straight handle, a long butt section, a foregrip usually made of cork, and a rubber butt cap. These rods, sometimes called popping rods, have become so popular that lighter-action models are now commonly used for freshwater fishing. The longer straight handle makes it more comfortable and less tiring for casting and fighting fish. Well suited for freshwater and light saltwater use, these rods can also handle an extensive range of lure weights for various species of fish.

Fishing Pliers

For many years, the only tool on a fisherman's belt was a small pair of pliers with spring-loaded handles and a wire cutter on the side of the jaws. To make mine slip-proof, I put pieces of surgical tubing over the handles. The pliers measured only 4½ inches long, probably too short when dislodging big hooks from big fish with sharp teeth. I used mine mostly to pull knots tight, cut monofilament and wire, and rig baits. These pliers worked fine for one or two seasons, but then the cutters got dull and the spring-loaded handles always had to be oiled regularly to keep them working freely.

A lot has happened over the years! Today, fishermen now have a choice of dozens of fishing tools to hang on their belts, ranging from pliers made from titanium and aircraft aluminum to plastic. The new multipurpose pliers will also do a variety of jobs. Most models will crimp, cut braid and wire, and are totally corrosion proof. And those long-nose models will keep your fingers safely away from sharp teeth and hooks.

The price tags on some of these pliers are a real enigma. They range from $12 to more than $300. Are the inexpensive models good? Can fishermen justify dropping hundreds of dollars on a pair of pliers? Are they worth the money? Is it easier to buy $12 pliers and throw them away at the end of the season? Those expensive titanium pliers may well outlive you. These are tough questions to answer. Let your fishing budget be your guide.

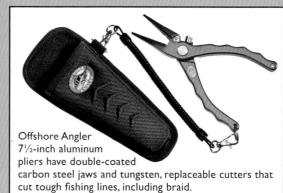

Offshore Angler 7½-inch aluminum pliers have double-coated carbon steel jaws and tungsten, replaceable cutters that cut tough fishing lines, including braid.

How to Use Baitcasting Tackle

How to Plug Cast • The grip should be relaxed and natural. The thumb on the reel spool controls the line during a cast. The reel is tipped so the spool is almost vertical with the handles up. This cuts down on spool friction.

Basic Forward Cast • Never take your eyes off your target. Let your rod tip whip down to a horizontal position behind you, and then drive it forward with speed and power. Thumb pressure used to hold the reel spool is released as the rod points toward the target. Very light thumbing on the spool will control the lure's flight and avoid a backlash. Most conventional reels have braking systems or magnetic cast controls to avoid backlashes.

Lure Retrieve • After the lure hits the water, assuming you are casting with your right hand, quickly move the rod to your left hand for the retrieve with your hand comfortably cupping the sideplate of the reel. Raise the rod to about 45 degrees and keep the butt against your body. This will keep the outfit steady and ready for a quick strike.

How to Use Baitcasting Tackle *(continued)*

Backhand Cast • The backhand cast is used to get your lure or bait out when some obstacle behind you prevents a routine backswing. Start with the rod horizontally in front of you. Bring the rod sharply rearward until you feel the weight of the lure and your rod loads. Immediately, with a strong snap of the wrist, bring your rod forward and release the line to complete the cast.

Sidearm Cast • The sidearm cast is a powerful toss that is good for long-range work and casting into the wind. It also saves the day when overhead foliage prevents a vertical backswing. The casting motion follows a one-two pattern. Sight the target, swing the rod back, and whip it forward. The casting arm remains straight and the rod tip points at the target until the lure is well on its way.

Silent-Dive Cast • The main purpose of the silent-dive cast is to drop the lure with a light splat rather than with a heavy splash. A small splat, like that made by a minnow surfacing, may attract fish that would be spooked by a loud splash. The forward cast is halted midair above the target by reel thumbing and hauling back on the rod. A braked lure hits the water more softly.

Underhand Lob • The underhand lob has a dual purpose. It will work where there is little room for a backcast, and it will drop the lure gently on the water. The rod tip is kept below parallel during the backswing. The forward swing is aimed slightly upward to loft the lure. A soft, underpowered lob is good for small pockets of water.

▨ Flipping

Flipping is an effective technique for bass fishermen. It's a simple but deadly approach for presenting a lure in and around brush, standing timber, grass, logs, lily pads, and heavy vegetation.

For flipping, most bass fishermen prefer 7- to 8-foot casting rods with 25- to 30-pound-test line. Lure selections are usually sparse—jigs and plastic worms. The fisherman ties on a black, blue, or brown ½-ounce "living rubber" jig. He protects the large hook with a fiber guard, and tips it with an Uncle Josh Pork Frog. This is especially deadly in the cooler springtime waters.

Flipping allows you to keep the lure close to cover constantly, thus allowing the fish to bite with very little

effort or movement. Start with about 8 to 9 feet of line from rod tip to lure. Then, strip off an arm's length of line. Using your wrist and not your shoulder or elbow, begin swinging the lure like a pendulum. Never let the lure come too far back. The swing should be smooth. When the lure reaches the back of its arc closest to you, a slight flick of the wrist (pretend you're only using the rod tip to do the work) will aim the lure toward the target. At this point, the line should be allowed to slide through your hand and the rod tip should be lowered to steer the lure to the desired spot.

A silent entry is essential. Never release the line until the lure reaches the water, because you want to control the lure. Once in the water, the jig or worm should fall freely to the bottom. Then, your task is to climb and wriggle the lure up and over every limb, root, and stem, carefully watching the line for the slightest nibble.

Flipping is simple yet deadly when fishing shorelines or heavy vegetation. Silent entry of your lure is essential.

SPINCASTING

Spincasting is a method of fishing that, in effect, combines a push-button type of spinning reel with a baitcasting rod. This tackle efficiently handles lures and baits of average weights from ¼ to ¾ ounce. With lighter or heavier lures, its efficiency falls off sharply. Spincasting is ideal for newcomers to fishing, for it is the easiest casting method to learn and is the ticket for lots of trouble-free sport.

▨ The Reel

Spincasting reels, like spinning reels, operate on the fixed-spool principle—that is, the weight of the lure or bait being cast uncoils the line from the stationary spool. Most spincasting reels are of the closed-face type, the spool and gearing being enclosed in a cone-shaped hood.

The major factor distinguishing the spincasting reel from the spinning reel is that spincasting action is controlled by a thumb-activated "trigger," a push button mounted on the reel. In operation, the spincaster holds his thumb down on the trigger until the rod is about halfway through the forward-cast motion. He then releases thumb pressure on the trigger, which frees the line and feeds it through a small hole in the center of the cone, sending the lure on its way.

There are two kinds of spincasting reels, those mounted atop the rod and those mounted below it. Most

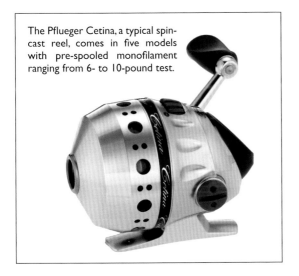

The Pflueger Cetina, a typical spin-cast reel, comes in five models with pre-spooled monofilament ranging from 6- to 10-pound test.

The grip for the spincasting reel is similar to the grip used for the baitcasting reel. The thumb depresses the control lever during the backcast, checking the line, and releases pressure as the rod whips forward.

spincasting reels are of the top-mounted type and are designed for rods having an offset reel seat. They can be mounted on straight-grip rods, but this combination is uncomfortable to use since the caster must reach up with his thumb to activate the reel trigger.

Below-the-rod spincasting reels are a much different design. They combine the balance of a spinning reel with the ease of a spincast reel. The line aperture in the cone is also larger than on a spincast reel. A lever activates the casting mechanism, much the same as on a push-button spincast reel.

Spincasting reels have various kinds of adjustable drag mechanisms. In one kind, the drag is set by rotating the cone that surrounds the spool. Other reels have star drags like those found on baitcasting reels. The drag in still other reels is activated by turning the reel handle.

Spincast reels are ideal for night fishing because of their trouble-free operation. However, besides the fact that they can handle a rather limited range of lure weights, if very light line is used on these reels, the line has a tendency to foul in the housing.

■ The Rod

Spincasting rods are basically the same as those designed for baitcasting, but there are a few differences. In general, spincasting rods average a bit longer than baitcasting rods. (The most popular lengths are 6 and 6½ feet.) They have flexible tips that are more responsive, and guides that are usually of the larger, spinning-rod type.

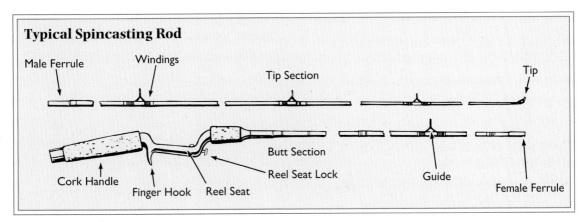

Typical Spincasting Rod

Male Ferrule
Windings
Tip Section
Tip
Cork Handle
Finger Hook
Reel Seat
Butt Section
Reel Seat Lock
Guide
Female Ferrule

How to Match Up Spincasting Tackle

This chart is meant only as a general guide aimed at helping you put together, in proper balance, the basic elements of a spincasting outfit tailored for fish of a particular weight category. Specific conditions—and your ability and personal preferences—should also be considered.

Species of Fish	Reel	Rod Action, Length (feet)	Line (pound test)	Lure Weights (ounces)
Panfish, small trout and bass, pickerel	Light	Light, 6½ to 7	4 to 8	⅛ to ⅜
Trout, bass, pickerel, pike, landlocks, walleye	Medium	Medium, 6 to 7	6 to 12	⅜ to ⅝
Pike, lake trout, steelhead, muskie, salmon, striped bass, snook, bonefish	Medium-Heavy, with star drag	Medium-Heavy, 6 to 6½	10 to 15	½ to ¾

CONVENTIONAL TACKLE FOR SALTWATER TROLLING AND CASTING

A host of saltwater game fish—from half-pound snapper bluefish to 40-pound yellowtails to bluefin tuna weighing nearly a ton—draws millions of fishermen to the briny each year. They stand in crashing surf and on jetties and piers, and they sail for deeper waters aboard boats of almost every description.

Because of the great differences in weights of saltwater fish, it is important for the fisherman to be armed with balanced tackle that is suited for the particular quarry he is after. Just as the freshwater muskie angler wouldn't use bluegill tackle, the person who is trolling for, say, blue marlin wouldn't use a jetty outfit designed for striped bass.

Balanced tackle—in which the rod, reel, line, and other items are all in reasonable proportion to one another—is important. A properly balanced outfit—for example, a 9-foot surf rod with a good casting reel and 15- to 25-pound-test line—is a joy to use. Conversely, if you substituted a 5-foot boat rod for the 9-footer in the above outfit and tried to cast, you would soon be turning the air blue. Besides the casting advantage, properly balanced gear makes hooking and playing a fish easier and more effective.

Let's take a detailed look at the various kinds of conventional saltwater gear and how to match up the component parts.

How to Match Up Saltwater Casting Tackle

This chart is meant only as a general guide aimed at helping you put together, in proper balance, the basic elements of a spincasting outfit tailored for fish of a particular weight category. Specific conditions—and your ability and personal preferences—should also be considered.

Species of Fish	Reel	Rod Type, Length (feet)	Line (pound test)	Lure Weights (ounces)
Small stripers, bluefish, weakfish, snook, bonefish, redfish, salmon, pompano, jacks	Light, with star drag	Popping, 6 to 7	8 to 15	½ to 1
Stripers, big bluefish, school tuna, albacore, bonito, salmon, dolphin, wahoo	Medium	Medium, 6½ to 8	12 to 30	¾ to 3
Channel bass, black drum, tarpon, dolphin, big kingfish, sharks	Heavy, with star drag	Heavy, 7 to 8½	15 to 40	1½ to 3
Surf species (bluefish, stripers, drum, channel bass, etc.)	Squidding (surf casting)	Surf, 7 to 10	15 to 45	1½ to 6

Trolling Reels

Trolling is a method of fishing in which a lure or bait is pulled along behind a moving boat. It is also a method in which the reel is of paramount importance.

At one time, saltwater trolling reels were designated by a simple but not completely reliable numbering system. This system employed a number followed by a diagonal (/) and then the letter O, which merely stood for "ocean." The numbers ran from 1 to 16, with each one representing the line capacity of the reel. The higher the number, the larger the reel's line capacity. It should be noted, however, that these numbers were not standardized—that is, one manufacturer's 4/O trolling reel may have had a smaller capacity than another maker's 4/O.

Trolling reels today are typically classified by line class and line capacity. For example, reels are classified as 12-pound test, 20-pound test, 50-pound test, 80-pound test, and so on. Weighing from 18 ounces up to nearly 10 pounds, these reels are designed primarily for handling the largest game fish (sailfish, marlin, bluefin tuna, and swordfish), but are also effective for bluefish, striped bass, channel bass, albacore, dolphins, and the like. Generally, 12- and 20-pound class is considered light tackle, 30- to 50-pound class is medium

weight, and 80- to 130-pound class is for the heaviest saltwater species.

These reels have no casting features (such as anti-backlash devices) since their sole function is trolling. Spools are smooth running, usually operating on ball bearings. The reels are ruggedly built and, of course, corrosion resistant. Unique features include lugs on the upper part of the sideplate for the attachment of a big-game fishing harness worn by the fisherman, a U-shaped clamp for a more secure union of rod and reel, and, in the largest reels, a lug-and-brace arrangement for extra rigidity.

By far the most important feature on a trolling reel is the drag. If a reel is to handle the sizzling runs and line-testing leaps of fish weighing hundreds of pounds, its drag must operate smoothly at all times. And the drag must not overheat or it may bind, causing the line to break.

Inexpensive reels of this type have the star type of drag consisting of a series of alternating metal and composition (or leather) washers. In some trolling reels, the drag is an asbestos composition disc that applies pressure directly to the reel spool.

Some expensive trolling reels have not one but two drag controls. One is a knob-operated device that lets you preset drag tension to a point below the breaking strength of the line being used. The other is a lever, mounted on the sideplate, that has a number of positions and permits a wide range of drag settings, from very light up to the safe maximum for the line in use. This lever, when backed off all the way, throws the reel into a free spool.

Trolling-reel spools are made of metal, usually either machined bronze or anodized aluminum, and range in width from 1⅝ inches to 5 inches (for the 80- to 180-pound-test outfits).

Some trolling reels are designed especially for wire and lead-core lines. They have narrow but deep spools and extrastrong gearing.

Other features of trolling reels include a free-spool lever mounted on the sideplate, a line-counting feature, a single oversize handle grip, and high-speed gear ratios ranging to as much as 40 inches of line retrieved for every single turn of the handle.

Trolling Rods

Big-game trolling rods have the strength and fittings to withstand the power runs and magnificent leaps of such heavyweights as marlin, sailfish, and giant tuna. The

Saltwater Reel Parts

The Daiwa Seagate is a typical saltwater conventional reel for general offshore fishing. Various models of the Seagate weigh from 14 to 21 ounces. The heaviest model will hold 630 yards of 50-pound-test braid line and 310 yards of 40-pound-test monofilament. For unlimited big-game fishing, reels get bigger and stronger to withstand powerful runs. They also cost more.

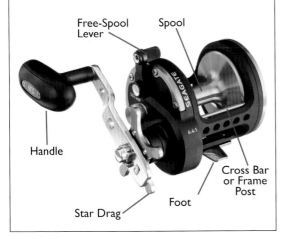

Free-Spool Lever

Spool

Handle

Cross Bar or Frame Post

Foot

Star Drag

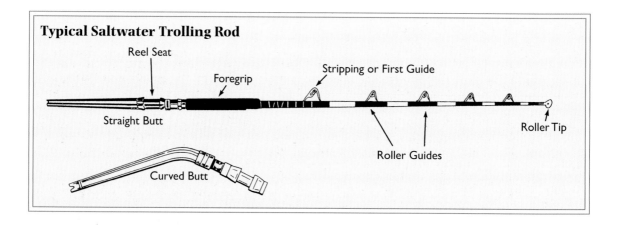

Typical Saltwater Trolling Rod

Reel Seat

Foregrip

Stripping or First Guide

Straight Butt

Roller Tip

Roller Guides

Curved Butt

great majority of these rods are of fiberglass and graphite composite construction.

Almost all blue-water rods have a butt section and a tip section—that is, they seldom have ferrules fitted midway along the working length of the rod. In most rods, the tip section is about 5 feet long, while butt lengths vary from 14 to 27 inches, depending on the weight of the tip. Tip sections are usually designated by weight, ranging from about 3 ounces to as heavy as 40 ounces, depending on the line that is being used and the fish that is being sought.

Trolling rods are rated according to the line-strength classes of the International Game Fish Association. The 11 IGFA classes are: 2-pound-, 4-pound-, 6-pound-, 8-pound-, 12-pound-, 16-pound-, 20-pound-, 30-pound-, 50-pound-, 80-pound-, 130-pound-, and 180-pound-test line. No rod used in catching a fish submitted for an IGFA record can have a tip length of less than 40 inches and the rod butt cannot exceed 27 inches in length. These measurements do not apply to surfcasting rods.

The fittings on trolling rods include strong, high-quality guides. The first guide above the reel (called the stripping guide) and the tip guide are of the roller type (either single-roller or double-roller). The middle guides, usually numbering four or five, are of the ring type and are made either of heavily chromed stainless steel or of tungsten carbide (carboloy), which is the most durable material. In some rods, all of the guides are rollers. Most roller guides have self-lubricating bearings that can be disassembled for cleaning.

Other features of trolling rods include extrastrong, locking reel seats, and gimbal fittings in the end of the butt that enable the rod to be fitted into a socket on a boat's fighting chair or into a belt harness worn by the fisherman.

Casting and Boat Reels

Conventional (revolving-spool) reels in this category are widely used by saltwater fishermen who cast lures and baits from piers, bridges, jetties, and in the surf, and by sinker-bouncers (bottom fishermen) in boats. Actually an outgrowth and refinement of freshwater baitcasting reels, these reels fill the gap between those freshwater models and big-game trolling reels.

Many surf and jetty casters, especially those who are after big fish, prefer a conventional reel (and rod) over a spinning outfit because the conventional rig is better able to handle heavy lures and sinkers. And a vast majority of experienced bottom fishermen lean toward the revolving-spool reel.

Conventional reels designed for casting, often called squidding reels, have wide, light spools (a heavy spool makes casting difficult) of either metal or plastic (metal is preferred for most uses), and gear ratios ranging from 2:1 to 6:1. Weights range from about 12 to 22 ounces. In most models, the drag is of the star type and there is a free-spool lever mounted on the sideplate. Some of these reels have level-wind mechanisms.

Depending on the model, line capacities can range from about 250 yards of 12-pound-test monofilament to 350 yards of 30-pound-test mono. Line capacity can also be dramatically increased with braided line. For most surf, jetty, and pier situations, 250 yards of line is sufficient.

Most of these reels have a mechanical brake, magnets, or a device to help prevent the spool from overrun-

Saltwater Casting and Boat Reels

◀ The Shimano Tiagra is a two-speed reel with a ratcheting drag lever. It is machined from 7-millimeter aluminum pipe stock for maximum strength. The Tiagra reels are built for the biggest saltwater fish. The smallest model weighs 38 ounces. The biggest Tiagra weighs 115 ounces and can hold 950 yards of 80-pound test.

▼ The PENN International VSX is a series of blue-water reels for big fish. Five models are available and will handle a range of lines from 300 yards of 4-pound-test mono-filament to 650 yards of 150-pound-test braid. Like most big-game reels, the Internationals have lever drag systems.

▶ The Ocean Master is a saltwater casting reel for both inshore and light offshore fishing. The six-disc drag handles up to 15 pounds of drag pressure. It weighs 10½ ounces and will hold 175 yards of 14-pound-test monofilament. Reels of this size are ideal for fishing from piers and jetties, as well as for surf and bottom fishing from boats.

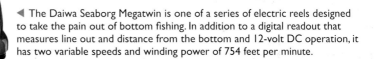

◀ The Daiwa Seaborg Megatwin is one of a series of electric reels designed to take the pain out of bottom fishing. In addition to a digital readout that measures line out and distance from the bottom and 12-volt DC operation, it has two variable speeds and winding power of 754 feet per minute.

---

ning during a cast and causing a backlash. In all models, however, as in freshwater baitcasting reels, thumb pressure against the spool is required to control the cast.

Conventional reels designed for deep-sea bottom fishing are quite similar to the casting models, but they are sometimes heavier and have deeper spools. They may also have larger capacities and take heavier lines.

■ Casting and Boat Rods

In choosing a conventional casting rod, more so than with a boat (bottom-fishing) rod, the type of fishing to be done and the fish being sought are critical factors. For casting in the surf, for example, the rod must be long enough so that the fisherman can make lengthy casts and hold the line above the breakers. A rod for jetty use, on the other hand, need not be so long. And if you'll be fishing mainly from piers and bridges, you'll need a rod with enough backbone to lift heavy fish from the water and up over the rail.

However, a beginning fisherman can get a casting rod that will handle most of the situations he'll be facing. A good choice would be one that is 8 to 9 feet in overall length and has a rather stiff tip. The stiff tip of a conventional rod lets the angler use a wide range of lure weights and enables him to have more control over big fish.

Conventional casting rods are available in lengths from 8 to 12 feet and even longer. Developments in graphite show that rods of this material can carry an exceptionally wide range of lure weights. In tests, weights of 18 ounces were cast with graphite rods. A majority of these rods are of two-piece construction, breaking either at the upper part of the butt or about midway up the working length of the rod.

These rods are distinguished by the number and arrangement of their guides. In most models, there are only three or four guides, including the tip guide, and all are located in the upper half of the tip section. Why this arrangement? Since these rods are stiffer than most others, fewer guides are required to distribute the strain along the length of the rod. The guides are bunched near the tip because that's where most of the bend occurs when a fish is being played.

Boat, or bottom-fishing, rods, as their name implies, are designed for noncasting use aboard boats—party

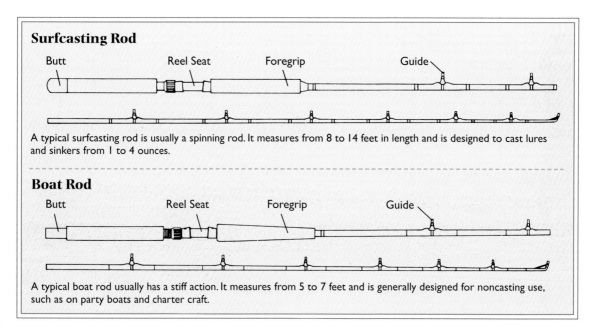

Surfcasting Rod

Butt   Reel Seat   Foregrip   Guide

A typical surfcasting rod is usually a spinning rod. It measures from 8 to 14 feet in length and is designed to cast lures and sinkers from 1 to 4 ounces.

Boat Rod

Butt   Reel Seat   Foregrip   Guide

A typical boat rod usually has a stiff action. It measures from 5 to 7 feet and is generally designed for noncasting use, such as on party boats and charter craft.

boats, charter craft, and private boats. They are also used on piers and bridges in situations in which a lure or bait is simply dropped down to the water.

Boat rods are considerably shorter than casting rods, running from about 5 to 7 feet in overall length, with a good average length being about 6 feet. Their shortness makes them highly maneuverable, a factor of more than a little importance aboard a crowded party boat, and makes it easier to handle, say, a 30-pound cod while trying to remain upright on a pitching deck.

As with most other modern rods, boat rods are mostly made of fiberglass or graphite. Most are one-piece or two-piece construction with a tip section and detachable butt. The number of guides on a boat rod depends on the length, but there are seldom more than six or eight. Some of these rods designed for large fish have a roller tip. Other boat-rod features are similar to those of casting rods.

Who Was Responsible for the First Circle Hook?

Circle hooks have been around since the turn of the century, but commercial longline fishermen brought them into worldwide use. It's ironic that the circle hook, developed for longline fishing because of its deadly hooking ability, would also become one of the most effective catch-and-release devices to come along in decades. Because of its unique design, fish will be hooked in the corner of the mouth, making release easy and without harm to the fish. What makes this hook so effective is the fact that fish will hook themselves, an important factor for longliners who leave their baited gear unattended. For recreational fishermen, it's important to remember not to try to set the hook when a fish takes the bait. Leaving your rod in a rod holder on a boat (dead sticking) is sometimes the best technique with circle hooks. Let the fish run and it will hook itself in the corner of the mouth. Circle hooks have proven effective for all species, including billfish.

How to Surf Cast

▼ **Fit of Rod and Reel** • This photo shows how the butt of a surf rod should just reach your armpit when held with your hand at the reel spool. A shorter butt section will lack the leverage to handle a long rod, while too long a butt adds needless weight. Proper butt length allows for comfortable and powerful two-handed casts.

▼ **The Casting Motion** • With feet set in a wide stance for balance, pull the rod butt powerfully with your left hand and push the grip behind the reel with your right hand, driving the rod tip forward. With both spinning tackle and conventional revolving-spool reels, the line is released when your rod is about 45 degrees in front of you.

▶ **"Fishing" the Cast** • When your lure or bait hits the water, the reel is engaged and you can begin your retrieve. If your lure comes in close to you without being hit by a fish, the rod is gradually angled to the right. This is to allow rod spring and a safe striking position if a fish hits in the final feet of a retrieve. The danger in striking at fish close in with the rod in front of you is that the lure may jerk loose and sail straight back into your face. The typical surf lure is heavy enough to do considerable damage with its sharp hooks. With your rod held to one side, a missed strike with a short line will only send the lure flying harmlessly back on the beach behind you.

▼ **Starting the Cast** • Start your cast from the stance shown. Your lure and bait should be dangling just above the sand as the rod is held parallel to the beach. If you are using a spinning reel, your index finger is extended to hold the line running between the spool and guides. When the rod snaps forward, the line is allowed to slip off your finger as the lure drives out over the water.

With a conventional revolving-spool reel, your thumb should be on the spool with firm pressure at the start of the cast to hold the spool during the casting motion. As the rod is powered forward, the thumb is lifted to let the weight of the lure or sinker take out line. Very light thumbing of the spool as the line goes out will prevent backlashes.

How to Surf Cast *(continued)*

▶ **Thumbing the Spool •** The angler's thumb is placed on the reel spool with firm pressure at the start of the cast to hold the spool during the back sweep of the casting motion. As the rod is powered forward, the thumb is lifted to let the weight of the lure or sinker take out the line. Very light thumbing as the line goes out will prevent backlash. Stop the spool from spinning the instant your lure or sinker hits the water. This takes practice. Many reels also have anti-backlash devices that help during a cast.

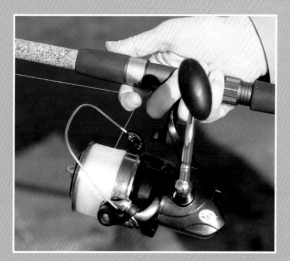

◀ **Proper Grip •** A spinning reel on a surf rod is gripped with two fingers on each side of the metal post that supports the reel. The forefinger of the right hand is extended to hold the line running between the spool and guides.

▶ **Retrieving the Lure •** The caster steadies the butt of the rod between his legs and reels in. Surf fishermen should angle their rods to the left or right as the lure enters the shallows. This allows a safe jerk at late-striking fish in case the hook breaks free and flies toward the caster. Fish will frequently follow a lure right into the white water of a breaking wave.

KITE FISHING

No one seems to know for sure where fishing with a kite originated. The best guess is that this unique technique was first used in China, and then in New Guinea and the Pacific Islands. The technique was also used in New Zealand, where surf fishermen flew kites to get their baits beyond the breakers. Regardless of where it was invented, kite fishing is now a well-established technique to fish live baits for tuna, billfish, king mackerel, dolphin, and any species that can be attracted to take a bait on the surface.

The concept is simple enough, but it takes a skilled captain and mate to fish live baits off one or two kites. The kites are generally made of ripstop nylon and flown on 80- or 100-pound-test line connected to a short kite rod. Kite rods are typically about 3 feet with one or two guides. Kites come in various models to handle winds up to 25 miles per hour. The kites can be flown at distances up to 100 feet or more, depending on wind conditions.

Attached to the kite are one or more release clips, the same as the clips used on outriggers. Each clip is assigned to a rod and reel baited with live pilchards, cigar minnows, goggle eyes, blue runners, or any other bait available. Dead baits can be used, but live baits are preferred. The line is passed through the release clips on the kite, fed out along the kite line, and lowered until the bait is literally dancing on the surface.

Two rods, rigged the same way, can also be fished off one kite. Some skilled captains and mates can actually launch two kites and simultaneously run as many as six baits, three off each kite. Styrofoam markers are sometimes used above the baits to keep track of them.

Generally, the kite rod and two fishing rods are placed in a three-way rod holder with the short kite rod in the middle holder. The mate must constantly monitor all three rods, keeping the kite flying and raising or lowering the baits to keep them active on the surface. Some mates use electric reels on the kite rod to make it easier to retrieve the kites.

Kite fishing is exciting and very productive. Under the right conditions, it is not uncommon for tuna and king mackerel to come completely out of the water to hit a bait skipped on the surface. Captain Bob Lewis played a major role in developing kite fishing in southern waters, especially Florida, where kite fishing often accounts for double-digit sailfish catches.

Left: Mate Sam Worden monitors a kite fishing setup. The middle rod flies the kite. The rods with live bait on either side are attached to the kite line with release clips. The baits are lowered and fished on the surface. Aggressive surface feeders will often jump clear of the water to hit a bait. **Right:** Mate Sam Worden gets a bait ready to attach to a release clip on the kite line. The red kite, already high in a blue sky, is clearly visible in this photo.

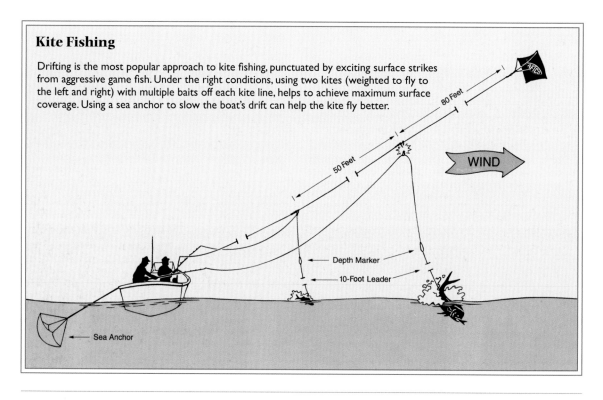

Kite Fishing

Drifting is the most popular approach to kite fishing, punctuated by exciting surface strikes from aggressive game fish. Under the right conditions, using two kites (weighted to fly to the left and right) with multiple baits off each kite line, helps to achieve maximum surface coverage. Using a sea anchor to slow the boat's drift can help the kite fly better.

80 Feet

50 Feet

WIND

Depth Marker

10-Foot Leader

Sea Anchor

HOW TO SET DRAG

Drag is what keeps a fish from breaking your line. That sounds simple, but fishermen sometimes lose big fish because they do not know or understand a few basic facts about the drag on their reel. Many anglers, for example, tighten their drag when a big fish makes a long run and strips off a lot of line. This is wrong. The drag should actually be lightened, because a lot of line in the water as well as a smaller spool diameter will increase the drag. Often the result is a lost trophy.

Drag is the resistance of a reel against the fighting pull of a fish, and it is set at a strain the line can endure without breaking. The drag mechanism usually consists of a series of metal (stainless steel, aluminum, or chromed brass) and composition (leather, cork, plastic, or fiber) washers. The washers are stacked, alternating metal and composition, and the friction between the surface areas of the washers creates "drag."

When an angler tightens the drag on his reel, he compresses these washers, creates more friction, and increases drag. Conversely, when he backs off the drag, he lessens friction and decreases drag.

If the size of a fish was the only factor in setting drag, the job would be easy. But there are other considerations, such as the friction of the line against the rod guides, resistance of the line being pulled through the water, and the amount of line remaining on the reel spool after a long run.

In addition, not all drags are created equal. They should be smooth, but many are sticky and jerky. In fact, it often takes as much as double the force of the drag setting to get the drag moving. For example, a drag set at 5 pounds may actually take up to 10 pounds of pull before the drag starts moving. It's obvious, therefore, that if you're using 8-pound-test line you should set your drag at about 2 pounds to allow for "starting your drag."

The amount of line on your spool is another factor. When the outside diameter of line on your spool is reduced by half, the drag tension is doubled. For example, if your drag is set at 2 pounds with a full spool, it will be increased to 4 pounds when a fish makes a long run and strips off half your line.

Long, fast runs will also generate friction and heat

between the drag washers. This will frequently tighten a drag and add even more tension.

It's also important to remember that a rod held at about 45 degrees will add about 10 percent to the drag you get with the rod pointed directly at the fish. This increased drag is due to friction between your line and the rod guides. If the rod is held at about 90 degrees, drag will increase to about 35 percent of the initial setting.

This is why it is important to lighten the drag and, when possible, point the rod at the fish when it is about to be netted or gaffed. If you hold your rod high and keep a tight drag, a sudden lunge by a fish could break your line. But if you point the rod tip at the fish, the line will run off the spool more easily, even with the same drag setting.

This technique of lowering the rod is also used when handling thrashing or jumping fish, such as tarpon and marlin. Lowering the rod will lighten drag tension and "cushion" the line from the shock of a jumping fish. This is called "bowing." It's part of the technique that makes it possible to land 100-pound tarpon on 10-pound-test line.

Taking all the above factors into consideration, how does an angler set his drag so that he can feel reasonably secure when he hooks a trophy fish? The first step is to determine the minimum and maximum range of drag for the various pound-test lines (see accompanying chart). By minimum drag, I mean "starting drag," the amount of pull needed to get the drag moving. If

Minimum and Maximum Range of Drag

Line	Minimum Drag (pounds)	Maximum Drag (pounds)
6-pound test	1½	4
8-pound test	2	5
10-pound test	3	6
12-pound test	4	8
20-pound test	6	12
30-pound test	8	15
50-pound test	12	25
80-pound test	20	40
130-pound test	30	50

the minimum drag seems light for the pound-test line, remember that there will be other factors increasing your drag beyond this setting, such as rod angle, spool diameter, and the amount of line in the water. Maximum drag means the heaviest setting you should use while fighting a fish. Never go beyond the maximum for your line class.

Let's take 12-pound-test line and see what factors come into play. Minimum drag is set at 4 pounds, but 8 pounds of pull will likely be required to get that

Left: Setting drag on your reel is easy with the help of a friend. The angler puts pressure on a 30-pound-test outfit while his friend checks the indicator on a fish scale. For 30-pound-test line, the drag should be set at a minimum of 8 pounds and a maximum of 15 pounds. **Right:** Any fishing scale can be used to set drag as well as weigh fish. The indicator and numbers should be large enough to read without getting close.

drag started. If the angler holds his rod at 45 degrees or higher, he can add another 10 percent, which brings the drag to 9 pounds. To this figure you also have to add water resistance or line drag, which varies according to the amount of line in the water, line diameter, and the speed of the fish. With 12-pound-test line and a fast fish, it can amount to as much as 2 pounds, which brings the total up to 11 pounds of drag on 12-pound-test line. With only 1 pound of drag to spare, a big fish would likely break the line. It's obvious that you're far better off with a very light drag setting.

The first step is to set your drag at the minimum setting. This is easily done at dockside with a reliable fish scale and the help of a friend. Run your line through the guides and tie it to the scale. Ask your friend to hold the scale and back off about 30 feet. Tighten your drag and begin to apply pressure as you would when fighting a fish. Now, adjust the drag so that it comes into play when the scale reads the correct minimum drag weight. For example, if you're using 12-pound-test line, the drag should begin to slip when you apply enough pressure to pull the scale indicator to the 4-pound mark.

Now, with your drag set at 4 pounds, slowly tighten your drag until it comes into play at 8 pounds, which is the maximum setting. Note how many turns of the star drag or spool cap are required to bring your drag to the maximum setting. Play with the drag, setting it back and forth from 4 to 8 pounds. Do this several times and get the feel of the resistance and pressure you're putting on the line. With enough practice, you'll be able to safely lighten and tighten the drag while fighting a fish.

An easier technique is to leave your drag set at the minimum setting and use your hand or fingers to apply more drag. This is a method many anglers use and it works well. You can practice with your buddy and the scale. With drag at the minimum setting, cup your hand around the spool (assuming you're using an open-face spinning reel), grip it so that the drag does not slip, and apply just enough pressure to pull the scale indicator to the maximum figure. Practice this technique and you'll soon be able to bear down on a fish and gain line without even touching the drag knob.

As mentioned above, you can also cup your hand around the spool of an open-face spinning reel to apply more drag. With conventional reels, use your thumb against the spool and hold the lines against the rod. Make sure you lift your finger when a big fish begins to run, or else you'll get a bad line burn.

Learn to combine this hand technique with "pumping" and you will be able to land big fish on light lines. Pumping a big fish in is not difficult. Let's assume you're using an open-face spinning reel with a light drag. Put your hand around the spool, apply pressure, and ease your rod back into a vertical position. Now, drop the rod tip and quickly reel in the slack. Repeat the process and you'll eventually have your fish at boatside. Always be ready, however, to lower the rod tip and release hand pressure from the spool when you think the fish is about to make a run. When it stops, you begin to pump once again.

One last point: At the end of the day, back off the drag and release all pressure on the washers, or they will lose their physical characteristics and take a set. If this happens, the drag will become jerky and unpredictable. If the washers do take a set, replacing them is the only solution.

ICE FISHING

Ice fishing differs greatly from open-water fishing, and it is a demanding sport. It requires an understanding of and an ability to cope with winter weather, knowledge of the cold-weather habits of the fish, and the use of an unusual assortment of gear, most of it unique to ice fishing.

There are two basic ice-fishing methods: tip-up fishing and jigging. In general, tip-ups are usually used on larger fish—pike, pickerel, walleyes, trout, and such—that prefer bait and require the angler to play the waiting game. Jigging is usually preferred for smaller fish that tend to school up—bluegills, perch, crappies, and the like. But these are merely generalizations, not hard-and-fast rules. For example, jigging (sometimes called chugging) is often quite productive on big lake trout and salmon in the Great Lakes.

▓ Tip-Ups

Also called tilts, these come in various styles, but they all perform two basic functions: they hold a baited line leading from a revolving-type reel spool, and they signal the bite of a fish. The most common type of tip-up consists

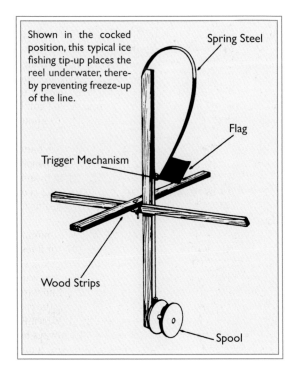

Shown in the cocked position, this typical ice fishing tip-up places the reel underwater, thereby preventing freeze-up of the line.

Spring Steel

Flag

Trigger Mechanism

Wood Strips

Spool

of three strips of wood, each about 18 inches long. Two are cross pieces that form an X as they span the hole. The third piece is an upright; at its bottom end is attached a simple line-holding spool, while the upper end holds the signaling device. The signal is usually a piece of very flexible spring steel with a red (some anglers prefer black) flag on the end. After the hook is baited and lowered to the desired depth, the steel arm is "cocked"—bent over and down and hooked onto a "trigger." When a fish strikes, an arm on the revolving spool releases the steel arm and it flies erect.

In this type of tip-up, the reel is positioned underwater. In other variations, the reel is positioned above the ice. Each type has its advantages. The above-the-ice reel can be more sensitively adjusted for light-biting fish, but the line tends to freeze on the reel once it gets wet. The underwater reel largely eliminates the problem of freezing, but the fisherman must remove the tip-up from the hole before he can grab the line.

Baits for tip-up fishing are usually live. In general, it pays to match the size of the bait to the size of the fish you're after. Baits range from tiny maggots (often called mousies) and grubs for panfish, to worms and small minnows for walleyes, and up to 6-inch baitfish for pike.

■ Jigging Rods

As done by ice fishermen, jigging is simply a method of imparting an up-and-down movement to a lure or bait. Jigging can be—and is—done with any sort of line-holding rod or stick.

Some jigging rods—more appropriately called sticks—are simply pieces of wood 18 inches or so long, with U-shaped notches in each end. The line—10-pound-test monofilament is very popular—is wound lengthwise onto the stick around the U-shaped notches and is paid out as needed. There are other types of jigging sticks of varying designs, and many ice anglers use standard spinning or spincast rods or the butt half of a fly rod.

Rods made specially for ice jigging are simple affairs consisting of a fiberglass tip section that is 2 or 3 feet long seated in a short butt. The butt may have a simple revolving-spool reel or merely a pair of heavy-wire projections around which the line is wound. The tip section may have two to four guides, including the tip guide. The shortness of such a rod lets the user fish up close to the hole and have better control over the lure or bait at the end of his line.

Jigging Rods

There are two types of ice-fishing jigging rods. The top rod uses two wire hooks on a handle to hold the line. The bottom rod uses an inexpensive reel on a short, baitcasting type of rod.

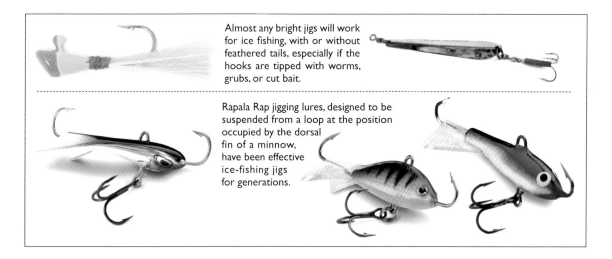

Almost any bright jigs will work for ice fishing, with or without feathered tails, especially if the hooks are tipped with worms, grubs, or cut bait.

Rapala Rap jigging lures, designed to be suspended from a loop at the position occupied by the dorsal fin of a minnow, have been effective ice-fishing jigs for generations.

Jigging Lures and Baits

There are many and varied jigging lures and baits, but flashiness is built into most of them. Others produce best when "sweetened" with bait. Two popular jigging lures are: an ungainly looking critter with a heavy body shaped and painted to resemble a baitfish, a hook at each end and a treble hook in the middle of its underside, and a line-tie ring in the middle of its upper surface; and a long, slim, three- or four-sided, silvery model with a treble hook at one end and a line-tie ring at the other.

Jigging methods vary with the fisherman and with the fish being sought. However, a productive way to fish many jigging lures, especially flashier types, is to twitch the lure slightly and then jerk it suddenly upward with a quick upward movement of the arm. The proper interval between jerks is learned with experience.

Popular jigging baits include a single perch eye (either impaled on a small hook or used to sweeten a tiny hair or rubber-bodied ice fly), worms, grubs, maggots, insect larvae, minnows, and cut bait (pieces of skin or flesh that are cut from the tail or body of such fish as smelt and perch).

Jiggers tend to move around more than tip-up fishermen, boring holes in different areas until they find a productive spot.

Other Equipment

Like most other forms of fishing, ice angling requires some auxiliary equipment. Most ice anglers prefer to keep such gear to a minimum, for they have to haul it with them wherever they go on the ice.

If you're going to fish through holes in the ice, you need something to make those holes. The ice auger is a popular tool for this job. Augers come in different designs. One has a long handle with a U-shaped bend at the top, and a rounded cutting blade at the bottom. The handle is turned much like that of a manual drill, and the blade cuts a round hole through the ice. Another type looks like a giant ice drill with sharp, widely spaced threads. It is used in the same way. Gasoline-powered ice drills are also available.

Then there's the ice spud or chisel. This is a heavy metal handle with a large, chisel-type blade at the bottom. The spud's weight helps the angler punch down through the ice, but the user must shape the hole once he has broken through.

An indispensable item of accessory gear is the ice skimmer, a ladle-type device that is used to keep the hole clear of ice chips and chunks and to skim ice.

Many ice anglers like to use an attached spring clip. It is attached to the fishing line and used to determine the water depth—an important factor because in winter most game fish are found on or near the bottom. A heavy sinker will serve the same purpose.

Ice Safety

Winter is the time of year when ice fishermen venture out onto frozen waters. Most will have fun, but a few will get into trouble because they don't know how to

Ice-Fishing Accessories

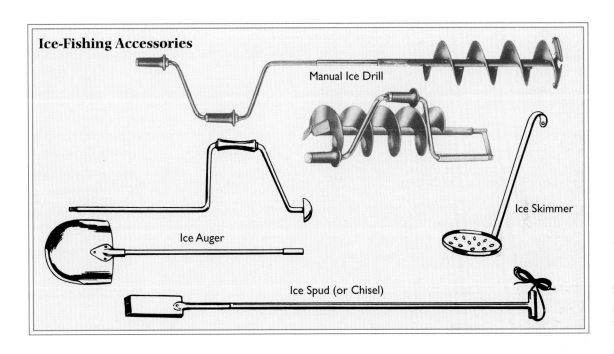

Manual Ice Drill

Ice Auger

Ice Skimmer

Ice Spud (or Chisel)

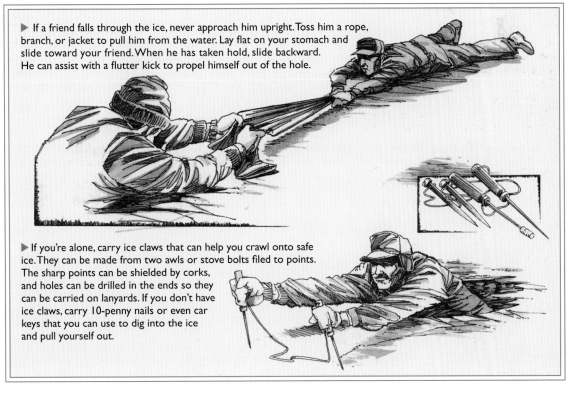

▶ If a friend falls through the ice, never approach him upright. Toss him a rope, branch, or jacket to pull him from the water. Lay flat on your stomach and slide toward your friend. When he has taken hold, slide backward. He can assist with a flutter kick to propel himself out of the hole.

▶ If you're alone, carry ice claws that can help you crawl onto safe ice. They can be made from two awls or stove bolts filed to points. The sharp points can be shielded by corks, and holes can be drilled in the ends so they can be carried on lanyards. If you don't have ice claws, carry 10-penny nails or even car keys that you can use to dig into the ice and pull yourself out.

Ice Safety Guidelines

These guidelines—courtesy of the Minnesota Department of Natural Resources—are for new, clear, solid ice only. White ice or "snow ice" is only about half as strong as new, clear ice. When traveling on white ice, double the thickness guidelines below.

Ice Thickness	Maximum Safe Load
2 inches or less	Stay off the ice!
4 inches	Ice fishing or other activities on foot
5 inches	Snowmobile or ATV
8 to 12 inches	Car or small pickup truck
12 to 15 inches	Medium truck

make sure that the ice is safe. The first rule is never take chances. There are two periods when accidents are likely to happen: early in the season when slush ice doesn't freeze uniformly and late in the season when ice melts at an uneven rate. It takes prolonged periods of freezing to make ice safe. Here are some rules to remember:

- Be cautious of heavy snowfalls while ice is forming. Snow acts as an insulator. The result is a layer of slush and snow on top of treacherous ice.

- Clear, solid river ice is 15 percent weaker than clear lake ice.

- River ice is thinner midstream than near the banks.

- River mouths are dangerous because currents create pockets of unsafe ice.

- When walking with friends, stay 10 yards apart.

- Lakes that have a lot of springs will have weak spots of ice.

LINES

No fisherman is stronger than the line that connects him and his quarry. Fishing lines are made of a wide variety of natural and synthetic materials and, as a result, differ widely in their characteristics and the uses to which they can be put. No two types of lines, for example, have the same degree of elasticity, abrasion resistance, water absorption, weight, and diameter.

Let's take a look at the physical characteristics of the various types of lines and the uses for which they are best suited.

MONOFILAMENT (SINGLE-STRAND NYLON): By far the most widely used fishing line today, monofilament is suitable for everything from blue-water trolling to surf-casting to freshwater spinning, and it is the universal material for leaders in both fresh water and salt because of its near-invisibility in water. It is extremely strong and light for its diameter, and it absorbs very little water (3 to 12 percent of its own weight). About the only drawback of monofilament is its relatively high rate of stretch (15 to 30 percent when dry, 20 to 35 percent when wet). For that reason, it is not the best choice for such uses as deep-water bottom fishing, during which large fish must be reeled up from considerable depths.

FLUOROCARBON: Fluorocarbon looks like monofilament, but it has different features. First, it's stiffer than monofilament and makes a better leader material. It also does not absorb water and is more resistant to oils, sunscreen, and other substances that may deteriorate monofilament. Fluorocarbon is actually a product of fluorine, carbon, and hydrogen. It's also tougher, sinks faster, and is more resistant to abrasion than monofilament.

DACRON: A DuPont trademark for a synthetic fiber that is made into a braided line, Dacron is nearly as strong as monofilament but does not stretch so much (about 10 percent). It has virtually the same characteristics whether wet or dry. Its visibility in water is greater than that of monofilament. Dacron's widest use is as trolling line.

LINEN: This is a braided line made from natural fibers and rated according to the number of threads, with each thread having a breaking strength of 3 pounds (six-thread linen has a breaking strength of 18 pounds, 15-thread linen has a breaking strength of 45 pounds, and so on). This material absorbs considerable amounts of water and is stronger when wet. Linen line is subject to deterioration and is heavy and bulky. Very little linen fishing line is made or used today.

CUTTYHUNK: This is a braided linen line originally created in the 1860s for the Cuttyhunk Fishing Club on Cuttyhunk Island, Massachusetts. The word cuttyhunk is often used to denote any linen line.

SILK: Before World War II, fly-fishing lines were made of silk and had an oily coating to make them water resistant. Modern materials have made the silk line obsolete, and very few are in use today.

LEAD-CORE: This type of line is made by sheathing a flexible lead core in a tightly braided nylon sleeve. It's suitable for deep trolling in both fresh and salt water, and is especially useful for quickly getting a bait or lure down deep without bulky, heavy sinkers or planers. It's color-coded in 10-yard segments for precise depth control.

WIRE: These lines, too, are designed for deep trolling in both fresh and salt water. They're made of stainless steel, Monel (nickel alloy), bronze, or copper. Wire is popular for downrigger fishing, but because it's heavy enough to sink on its own, it's also used without downriggers and in many cases eliminates the need for a cumbersome drail weight or planer. Since it has no stretch, the angler can jig the rod and give movement to a bait or lure. However, wire is somewhat tricky until a fisherman gets used to it. Kinks can develop, causing weak spots or possibly cutting an unwary angler's hand. Wire line is generally available in a wider range of test weights than lead-core line. Wire leaders, usually sleeved in plastic, are widely used to prevent line cutting when fishing for such toothy battlers as pike, muskellunge, and many saltwater species.

Fishing Line Troubleshooting

This chart was designed to help you quickly find and correct line troubles when you can least afford to have them—on the water. Copy this page and keep this handy chart in your tackle box.

Symptoms	Possible Causes	Recommended Cures
Unexplained line breaks under low-stress loads.	a. Nicks or abrasions. If the surface is smooth and shiny, failure may be line fatigue.	a. Strip off worn line or re-tie line more frequently.
	b. If surface is dull, faded, and fuzzy, failure is due to sunlight or excessive wear.	b. Replace line.
	c. Wear or stress points on guides or reel.	c. Replace worn guides.
Line is unusually sticky and stretchy.	Line stored in area of high heat or damaged by chemicals.	Replace line and change storage areas.
Line has kinks and flat spots.	a. Line spooled under excessive tension.	a. Use lower spooling tension. Make one final cast and rewind under low tension.
	b. Line stored on reel too long without use.	b. Strip out and soak last 50 yards in water.
Line has excessive curls and backlashes.	Using mono that is too heavy for reel spool diameter.	Use a more flexible mono or one with a lower pound test or smaller diameter.
Mono is stiff and brittle, and has a dry, powdery surface.	Improper storage in either wet or too warm conditions.	Replace line and change storage area.
Line looks good, but is losing too many fish.	Faulty or improperly set reel drag. Using too light a breaking strength for conditions.	Check reel drag. Lubricate or replace washers. Refill with line of higher breaking strength.
Reel casts poorly.	Not enough line on spool or line is too heavy for reel.	Fill spool with additional line. Use lighter, more limp monofilament.
Line is hard to see.	a. Line has faded due to excessive exposure to sunlight.	a. Replace line.
	b. Using wrong color line.	b. Switch to high-visibility line.

Braided Fishing Lines

Braided fishing line has a small diameter, minimum stretch, and a good knot strength. The new, high-tech synthetic braided lines get a high score on all counts. There are more than a dozen manufacturers of these new space-age braided lines, and they all claim their lines are three times as strong as monofilament lines of the same diameter. This means, of course, that you can get three times as much line on your reel, which is one of the biggest advantages of braided line. You no longer need big reels to make sure you have enough line, an important consideration for saltwater fishermen. The smaller diameter also means easier casting with lighter lures.

Braided lines have a stretch factor of less than 5 percent and some manufacturers even claim zero stretch. Monofilament has a stretch factor of about 25 percent, depending on the manufacturer. Minimal stretch is a big deal in fishing. It means sensitivity and fast hook-ups.

Braided lines have a lot going for them, including the sensitivity to transmit the slightest nibble. Braided lines are also sharp and hard. But they do present some problems. Nearly all braided lines float and easily get tangled in rigs and lures. In fact, many party or head boats prohibit braided lines because of tangles and the danger of cut fingers from these small-diameter, tough lines. If a caster gets a serious backlash and braided line digs into the spool, it may be nearly impossible to free the line.

Fly Lines

Ever since the time of Izaak Walton, anglers have been using special lines designed to present insect imitations to trout, salmon, and other fish. The earliest fly lines were made of braided horsehair. Then came oiled silk lines, which were standard until the late 1940s.

Today's fly lines are basically a synthetic coating over a braided core. They are made in various shapes and weights. Some are constructed so that they float (primarily for dry-fly fishing), and others are made to sink (for streamer and nymph fishing). Another development is the floating-sinking, or intermediate, line, the first 10 to 30 feet of which sinks while the rest of it floats. Several manufacturers offer fly lines designed with special tapers for various conditions and species. Tarpon, bonefish, and billfish anglers now have access to fly lines that make casting to these species easier.

It is impossible to overemphasize the importance to the fly fisherman of balanced tackle, and the most vital element in a fly-fishing outfit is the line. It must "fit" the rod if casting is to be accurate and efficient. A line that is too heavy for the rod causes sloppy casts, poor presentation of the fly, and lack of accuracy, and it makes it difficult to manipulate the fly once it is on the water. An angler who uses a line that's too light for his rod must flail the rod back and forth during repeated backcasts in order to get out enough line to make his cast, and even then his forward cast might not "turn over" and the line may fall onto the water in a jumbled mass of coils.

Before 1961, fly lines were identified by a system of letters—A to I—with each letter representing a line diameter. For example, an A line measured .060 inch in diameter, and an I line measured .020 inch. But when modern fly lines replaced silk after World War II, weight, rather than diameter, became the critical factor in matching a fly line with a rod. So, in 1961, manufacturers adopted a universally accepted fly-line identification code. Its three elements give a complete description of a fly line.

The first part of the code describes the line type: L means level, DT means double taper, and WF means weight forward. The second element, a number, denotes the weight of the line's first 30 feet. The third element tells whether the line is floating (F), sinking (S), or floating-sinking (F/S). Therefore, a DT6F, for example, is a double-taper, weight-6 floating line.

Many fly-rod manufacturers today are eliminating the angler's problem of proper line choice by imprinting on the rod itself, usually just above the butt, the proper line size for that particular rod. However, there are other general ways to pick the right fly line. The general recommendations in the accompanying chart may help.

Choosing the Correct Fly Line

Rod Length (feet)	Proper Line
7½	DT4F or WF4F to WF6F
8	DT5F or WF5F to WF8F
8½	DT6F or WF6F to WF9F
9 and 9½	DT8F or WF8F to WF12F

Type of Water	Suitable Line Weights
Very small streams	4 to 5
Small and medium streams	5 to 8
Large streams	7 to 11
Lakes (light outfits)	5 to 7
Lakes (heavy outfits)	8 to 11
Salt water	9 to 15

When making a cast with a fly rod, it's important to remember not to aim directly at the point where you want the fly to land. Aim a few feet above that point, so the fly will stop above the target and fall gently to the surface.

FLY LINE DESIGN: THE KEY TO CASTING PERFORMANCE

The fly line's shape, otherwise known as taper, determines how energy is transmitted and dissipated during the casting motion. By varying the lengths and diameters of the various parts of the line, specific performance attributes can be accentuated.

Parts of the Taper

Tip: This is the short (usually 6-inch) level front-end section of line primarily intended to protect the front taper. When changing leaders, a small part of the fly line is cut off. The level tip allows changes to be made without shortening the front taper and thus altering the way the line casts.

Front Taper: In conjunction with the diameter of the line's tip, the length of a line's front taper determines how powerfully or delicately a fly is delivered. Longer tapers dissipate more casting energy, enabling a more delicate presentation, while shorter tapers provide a much more powerful delivery.

Belly: The belly, the line section with the greatest diameter and length, carries most of the casting energy.

Rear Taper: This section decreases in diameter from the belly to the much thinner running section of the line in a weight-forward line. It is this transition that is the key to casting smoothness. Lines with short rear tapers cast quickly, but casting smoothness and control are sacrificed. Longer tapered lines cast more smoothly and are easier to control.

Head: This term is applied to the combination of the front taper, belly, and rear taper. Generally, the length of the head section dictates the effective casting and control range of a line. Short heads cast quickly but don't cast well for distance. Long heads cast and control well at longer ranges, but require more false casting to clear the head from the rod.

Running Line: This section exists primarily to make distance casting easier. The running line on a weight-forward line is small in diameter and creates less friction in the guides than a double-taper line. Running lines are also very lightweight. This is important because the energy stored in the head of the line during casting must pull the running line through the guides.

Taper Types

Fly lines are typically tapered so that they will deliver a leader and a fly appropriately. There are four basic taper types: level (L), double taper (DT), weight forward (WF), and shooting taper (ST).

LEVEL: These untapered lines are the same diameter from end to end. The lack of a taper makes them more difficult to cast accurately and control on the water.

DOUBLE TAPER: Best for short to medium casts in the 20- to 50-foot range, these lines have extralong bellies with identical tapers at either end. The tapers serve to dissipate casting energy, resulting in a delicate presen-

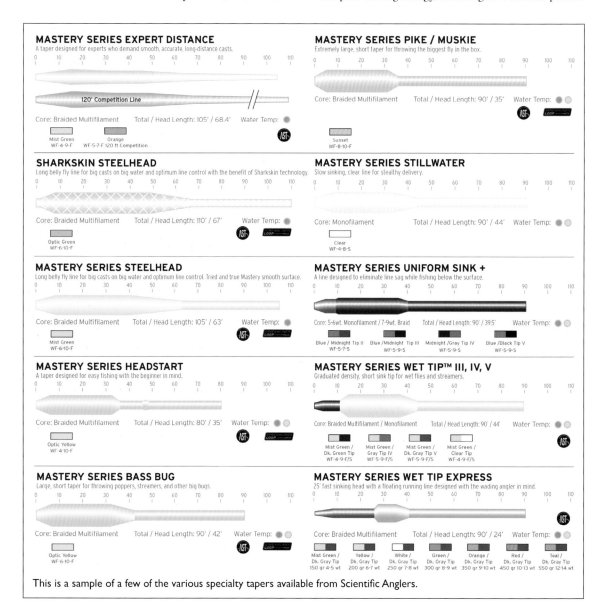

MASTERY SERIES EXPERT DISTANCE
A taper designed for experts who demand smooth, accurate, long-distance casts.
Core: Braided Multifilament   Total / Head Length: 105' / 68.4'   Water Temp:
120' Competition Line
Mist Green — WF-4-9-F
Orange — WF-5-7-F 120 ft Competition

MASTERY SERIES PIKE / MUSKIE
Extremely large, short taper for throwing the biggest fly in the box.
Core: Braided Multifilament   Total / Head Length: 90' / 35'   Water Temp:
Sunset — WF-8-10-F

SHARKSKIN STEELHEAD
Long belly fly line for big casts on big water and optimum line control with the benefit of Sharkskin technology.
Core: Braided Multifilament   Total / Head Length: 110' / 67'   Water Temp:
Optic Green — WF-6-10-F

MASTERY SERIES STILLWATER
Slow sinking, clear line for stealthy delivery.
Core: Monofilament   Total / Head Length: 90' / 44'   Water Temp:
Clear — WF-4-8-S

MASTERY SERIES STEELHEAD
Long belly fly line for big casts on big water and optimum line control. Tried and true Mastery smooth surface.
Core: Braided Multifilament   Total / Head Length: 105' / 63'   Water Temp:
Mist Green — WF-6-10-F

MASTERY SERIES UNIFORM SINK +
A line designed to eliminate line sag while fishing below the surface.
Core: 5-6wt. Monofilament / 7-9wt. Braid   Total / Head Length: 90' / 39.5'   Water Temp:
Blue / Midnight Tip II — WF-5-7-S
Blue /Midnight Tip III — WF-5-9-S
Midnight /Gray Tip IV — WF-5-9-S
Blue /Black Tip V — WF-5-9-S

MASTERY SERIES HEADSTART
A taper designed for easy fishing with the beginner in mind.
Core: Braided Multifilament   Total / Head Length: 80' / 35'   Water Temp:
Optic Yellow — WF-4-10-F

MASTERY SERIES WET TIP™ III, IV, V
Graduated density, short sink tip for wet flies and streamers.
Core: Braided Multifilament / Monofilament   Total / Head Length: 90' / 44'   Water Temp:
Mist Green / Dk. Green Tip — WF-4-9-F/S
Mist Green / Gray Tip IV — WF-5-9-F/S
Mist Green / Dk. Gray Tip V — WF-5-9-F/S
Mist Green / Clear Tip — WF-4-9-F/S

MASTERY SERIES BASS BUG
Large, short taper for throwing poppers, streamers, and other big bugs.
Core: Braided Multifilament   Total / Head Length: 90' / 42'   Water Temp:
Optic Yellow — WF-6-10-F

MASTERY SERIES WET TIP EXPRESS
25' fast sinking head with a floating running line designed with the wading angler in mind.
Core: Braided Multifilament   Total / Head Length: 90' / 24'   Water Temp:
Mist Green / Dk. Gray Tip — 150 gr 4-5 wt
Yellow / Dk. Gray Tip — 200 gr 6-7 wt
White / Dk. Gray Tip — 250 gr 7-8 wt
Green / Dk. Gray Tip — 300 gr 8-9 wt
Orange / Dk. Gray Tip — 350 gr 9-10 wt
Red / Dk. Gray Tip — 450 gr 10-13 wt
Teal / Dk. Gray Tip — 550 gr 12-14 wt

This is a sample of a few of the various specialty tapers available from Scientific Anglers.

tation. They don't, however, cast long distances as easily as weight-forward lines.

WEIGHT FORWARD: These lines are designed to fish well at short to long ranges. They cast farther and more easily than double-taper lines because their small-diameter running line offers less resistance in the rod guides.

SHOOTING TAPER: These tapers are best to use when maximum distance is needed, and control and accuracy are less important. Also called "shooting heads," they are commonly 30 to 35 feet long. They attach to a very small-diameter "shooting line" that offers less resistance in the rod guides. This results in maximum-length casts. The total length of the fly line ranges from around 100 to 120 feet.

■ Specialty Tapers

In addition to standard fly line tapers, there is a wide range of specialty tapers. These lines are designed to increase your effectiveness by providing performance characteristics to match situations you will encounter when fishing for specific species, ranging from trout and largemouth bass to tarpon and sailfish. Generally, when any large flies are used, more powerful tapers work best.

■ Leaders

There are three basic leader materials: wire, monofilament (single-strand nylon), and fluorocarbon.

Wire leaders—either piano wire (high carbon or stainless steel) or braided wire—are used generally to protect the line from sharp underwater obstacles and from the teeth, gill plates, and other sharp appendages of both freshwater and saltwater fish. Some wire leaders, particularly the braided type, are enclosed in a sleeve of nylon, which prevents the wire strands from fraying and eliminates kinking.

Some monofilament and fluorocarbon leaders perform a similar function. Called shock tippets, they are short lengths (6 feet or shorter in most cases) of strong monofilament or fluorocarbon testing up to about 100 pounds depending on the size of the fish being sought. Shock tippets protect the line from sharp objects and teeth, but they are also able to withstand the sledgehammer strikes of large fish. Shock tippets are especially important to fishermen targeting tarpon and billfish, such as sailfish and marlin.

The main purpose of most leaders, however, is to provide an all-but-invisible link between the end of the line and the lure, bait, or fly. Anglers using monofilament or fluorocarbon line might not need a leader, for the line itself is a leader material. But if highly visible braided line is sometimes used, a monofilament or fluorocarbon leader at least 6 feet long is a big advantage.

Fly fishing is perhaps the form of the sport in which the leader is most critical. Today's trout, salmon, and other fly-caught fish—both stocked and wild—are far more wise to the ways of the angler than they once were. When you go for these fish, a sloppy cast, a too-short leader, or an improperly presented fly will seldom bring a strike.

Though some fly fishermen feel that they can get by with a level leader (one with a diameter that is the same throughout its entire length), a tapered leader makes casting far more pleasant and efficient and brings far more strikes.

A tapered leader must be designed to transmit the energy of the cast from the line right down to the fly. But because the fly fisherman's offerings range from dry flies and wet flies to streamers and bucktails to bass bugs, tapered leaders differ, too. The proper leader is also determined by water conditions and the size of the fish.

The makeup of a tapered leader starts with the butt section, which is tied to the end of the fly line. The diameter of the tapered leader should be approximately one-half to two-thirds the diameter of the end of the line. The leader then proceeds through progressively lighter (and thinner) lengths down to the tippet, to the end of which the fly is itself tied.

The most popular leader lengths are 7½ and 9 feet, but under some conditions—such as when casting to trout in low, clear water—leaders of 12, 15, or more feet may be necessary.

You can buy tapered leaders, either knotless or with the various sections knotted together. Each time you change flies, however, you must snip off a bit of the tippet, so it pays to carry small spools of leader material in various strengths so that you can tie on a new tippet when necessary. You can also tie your own tapered leaders.

Leader material is classified according to X designations (1X, 2X, 3X, and so on), with the number sometimes representing the pound test of the line. The X designations, however, rarely indicate the exact pound test of the leader, and these labels vary among manufacturers. Always check labels for the exact pound test before making a choice. Tapered leaders are classified the same way.

Recommended Fly-Fishing Tippet Strength for Various Species

FRESH WATER

Species	Tippet	Species	Tippet
Bream, sunnies, other small fish	3-pound test	Sea-run brook trout	6-pound test
Smallmouth black bass	4- to 6-pound test	Cutthroat trout	3-pound test
Largemouth black bass	6- to 8-pound test	Sea-run cutthroat (bluebacks), harvest trout	4-pound test
Brown trout	3-pound test	Grayling	3-pound test
Brown trout (using streamers)	5-pound test	Rainbow trout	4-pound test
Sea-run brown trout	10-pound test	Steelhead (sea-run rainbow trout)	10-pound test
Brook trout	3-pound test	Winter steelhead	12-pound test
Brook trout (using streamers)	5-pound test		

SALT WATER

Species	Tippet	Species	Tippet
Mangrove or gray snapper	8-pound test	Jack crevalle	10-pound test
Bonefish	6- or 8-pound test	Horse-eye jack	10-pound test
Tarpon, baby (under 20 pounds)	8-pound test	Ladyfish	8-pound test
Tarpon, big (more than 20 pounds)	12-pound test	Snook	12-pound test
Channel bass (redfish)	10-pound test	Spotted seatrout	10-pound test
Striped bass (up to 10 pounds)	8-pound test	Barracuda	12-pound test
Striped bass (more than 10 pounds)	12-pound test		

SALTWATER FISH IN DEEP WATER, BY CHUMMING OR SIGHTING

Species	Tippet	Species	Tippet
Dolphin	10-pound test	Grouper	10-pound test
Mackerel	10-pound test	Yellowtail	10-pound test
False albacore	10-pound test	Bermuda Chub	10-pound test
Bonito	10-pound test		

SPECIAL LEADERS FOR FISH THAT MIGHT BITE OR FRAY THROUGH LEADER TIPPET

Species	Tippet and Leader
Bluefish	10-pound test with 12-inch, No. 4 wire leader added
Sailfish	12-pound test with 12-inch, 80-pound-test nylon added
Marlin	12-pound test with 12-inch, 100-pound-test nylon added
Tarpon	12-pound test with 12-inch, 100-pound-test nylon added
Tuna	12-pound test with 12-inch, 100-pound-test nylon added
Barracuda	12-pound test with 12-inch, No. 5 wire leader added
Sharks	12-pound test with 12-inch, No. 5 or No. 7 heavier wire leader added

FISHHOOKS

Modern hook design and manufacturing has come a long way since the first Stone Age bone hooks found by archaeologists and dating back to more than 5,000 BC. Today's fishhooks come in hundreds of sizes, shapes, colors, and special designs. They're made from carbon steel, stainless steel, or some rust-resistant alloy. They're hardened and tempered, then plated or bronzed to meet special specifications. Some are thin steel wire for use in tying artificial flies; others are thick steel for big-game fish that prowl offshore waters.

There is no such thing as an all-purpose hook. Fishermen must carry a variety of patterns and sizes to match both the tackle and size of fish being hunted. Let's start from the beginning by learning the basic nomenclature of a typical fishhook (see accompanying illustration).

Even the parts of a typical fishhook may vary in design to meet certain requirements. There are sliced shanks to better hold bait on the hook, forged shanks for greater strength in marine hooks, tapered eyes to reduce the weight of hooks used in tying dry flies, and so on.

▧ Hook Wire Size

The letter X and the designations "Fine Wire" or "Heavy Wire" are used to indicate the weight or diameter of a hook. For example, a 2X Heavy Wire means the hook is made of the standard diameter for a hook two sizes larger, and a 3X Heavy Wire is made of the standard diameter for a hook three sizes larger.

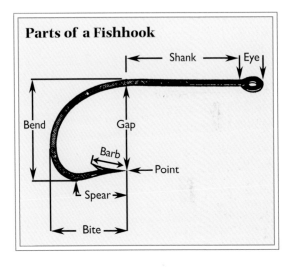

Parts of a Fishhook

For lightweight hooks, the designations are reversed. For example, a 2X Fine Wire means that the hook is made of the standard diameter for a hook two sizes smaller, and so on. These designations, however, vary from manufacturer to manufacturer.

Obviously, an angler seeking a big fish should lean toward the heavy hooks, which are not apt to bend or spring when striking the larger fish that swim the waters, particularly salt water.

Fishermen who use live bait will want to use fine-wire hooks, which will not weigh down the bait. The use of flies, particularly dry flies, also requires fine-wire hooks, since their light weight will enable a fly to float more easily.

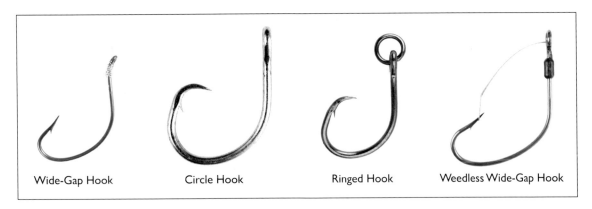

Wide-Gap Hook   Circle Hook   Ringed Hook   Weedless Wide-Gap Hook

▨ Shank Length

The letter X and the designations "Long" or "Short" are used to specify the shank length of a hook. One manufacturer lists shank lengths from extrashort to extralong. The formula for determining shank length is similar to that used for wire sizes. A 2X Long means the shank of the hook is the standard length for a hook two sizes larger, and a 4X Long is the standard length for a hook four sizes larger. A 2X Short has a shank as short as the standard length of a hook two sizes smaller, and a 4X Short for a hook four sizes smaller, and so on. Again, these designations might vary from manufacturer to manufacturer.

Picking a hook with the correct shank length depends on the type of fishing you plan to undertake. A short-shank hook is preferred for baitfishing, since it can be hidden in the bait more easily. A long-shank hook is at its best when used for fish with sharp teeth.

A bluefish, for example, would have a tough time getting past the long shank and cutting into the leader. Long-shank hooks are also used in tying streamers and bucktails.

▨ Hook Characteristics

In addition to size and shank length, there are other characteristics to consider when selecting a hook for a specific purpose. The barb, obviously, is a critical part of the hook. A short barb is quick to set in the mouth of a fish, but it also gives a jumping fish a greater chance of dislodging it. A long barb, on the other hand, is more difficult to set but it also makes it a lot tougher for a fish to shake it loose.

So what guidelines should an angler follow? Let's list some basic recommendations. The all-around saltwater

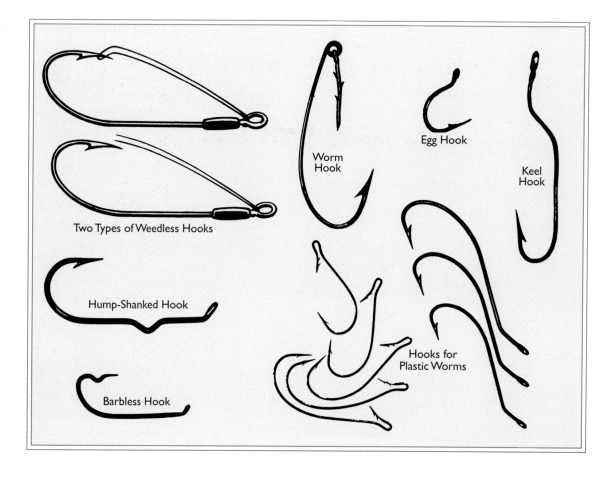

Two Types of Weedless Hooks

Hump-Shanked Hook

Barbless Hook

Worm Hook

Egg Hook

Keel Hook

Hooks for Plastic Worms

fisherman can't go wrong with the O'Shaughnessy, Kirby, Wide Gap, or Circle Hook patterns. And if you happen to have some salmon hooks, they're perfectly all right to use with a wire leader for barracuda and other toothy fish.

If you're a flounder fisherman, you'll find that the Chestertown and Carlisle patterns are your best bet. The long-shanked Chestertown makes it especially easy to unhook flounders.

If you're a bait fisherman, use the sliced-shanked Mustad Beak or Eagle Claw patterns. Those extra barbs on the shanks do a good job of keeping natural baits secured to the hook.

Fishermen can also become confused when they see hooks with straight-ringed eyes, turned-up eyes, and turned-down eyes. This should not present a problem. If you're replacing hooks on lures or attaching hooks to spinners, use a straight-ringed eye. If you're tying short-shanked artificial flies, pick the turned-up eye, which will provide more space for the hook point to bite into the fish. The turned-down eye is the best bet for standard flies and for baitfishing, since it brings the point of the hook closest to a straight line of penetration when striking a fish.

Curved shanks also lead to some confusion. A curved shank—curved right or left—has its place in

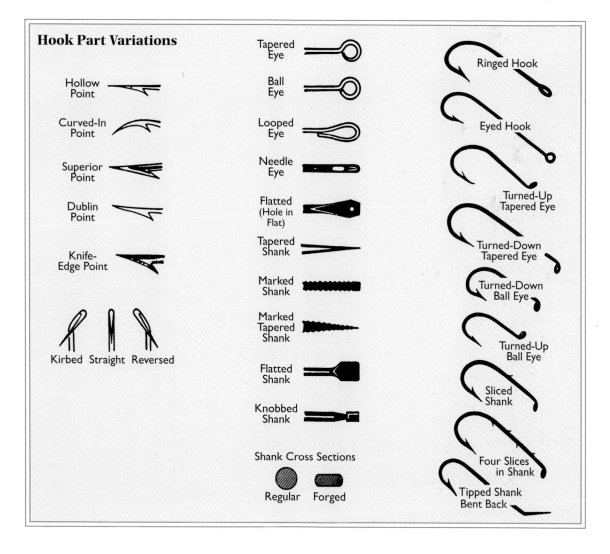

Hook Part Variations

Hollow Point

Curved-In Point

Superior Point

Dublin Point

Knife-Edge Point

Kirbed   Straight   Reversed

Tapered Eye

Ball Eye

Looped Eye

Needle Eye

Flatted (Hole in Flat)

Tapered Shank

Marked Shank

Marked Tapered Shank

Flatted Shank

Knobbed Shank

Shank Cross Sections

Regular   Forged

Ringed Hook

Eyed Hook

Turned-Up Tapered Eye

Turned-Down Tapered Eye

Turned-Down Ball Eye

Turned-Up Ball Eye

Sliced Shank

Four Slices in Shank

Tipped Shank Bent Back

baitfishing. The offset point has a better chance of hitting flesh when a strike is made. When you are casting or trolling with artificial lures or spinners, however, the straight-shanked hook is a better choice, since it does not have a tendency to spin or twist, which is often the case with curved-shanked hooks.

Hooks for Fly Fishing

HOOK EYES

Ball Eye: A strong, untapered eye, the ball eye is the simplest form. It is available turned up and turned down. Considered too heavy for dry flies, hooks with ball eyes are used for wet flies.

Tapered Eye: This type of eye is also produced turned up and turned down. The tapered eye is made to maintain a full inner diameter while at the same time featuring a reduced outer diameter. This is achieved by the diameter of the wire decreasing as the eye closes. The larger diameter makes for easier insertion of leader material in the eyes of the hooks. The tapered eye also lightens the weight of the hook and, when turned up, faces away from the point of the hook, leaving the gap clear and enhancing the chances of the small hook setting firmly and quickly when hit. Tapered eye hooks are used for dry flies, wet flies, and streamers.

Looped Eye: Properly referred to as the looped eye because of its construction, this eye is a traditional characteristic of salmon fly hooks. It is a strong fly hook, easily tied to leaders, and it is less likely to fray them than ball and tapered eyes. In addition to dry and wet salmon hook patterns, the looped eye is available in a barbless dry-fly pattern and in a long-shanked streamer hook. It is available turned up and turned down.

Oval Eye: This eye takes its name from its obvious shape. It is a characteristic found on many traditional salmon fly hooks as well as numerous treble hooks. The oval eye is used to achieve a slimmer profile than an eyed hook.

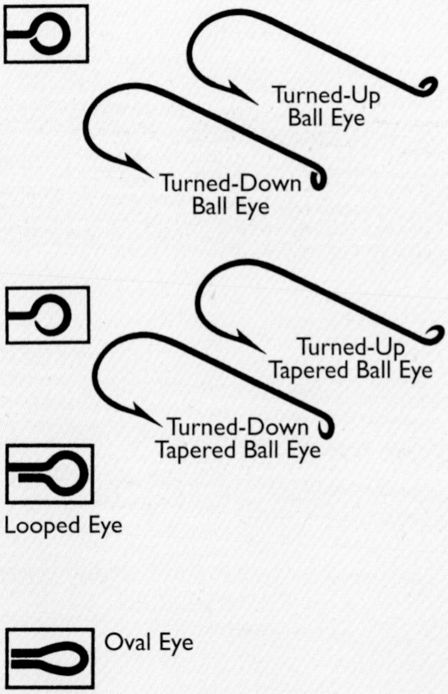

Turned-Up Ball Eye

Turned-Down Ball Eye

Turned-Up Tapered Ball Eye

Turned-Down Tapered Ball Eye

Looped Eye

Oval Eye

HOOK SIZES

Every fly has a size number that is determined by the hook pattern (name) and that is stated in terms of the width of the gap between the hook point and the hook shank. The gap width of the given size in one particular pattern or family of hooks (e.g., the Viking) for the most part does not vary. Between different hook families, however, there is little compatibility in gap width.

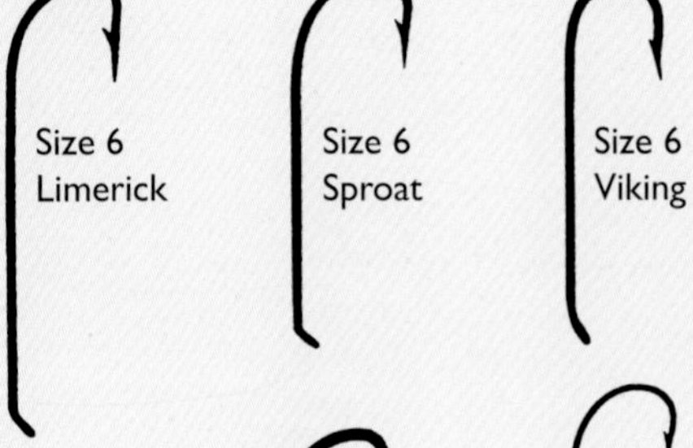

Size 6 Limerick

Size 6 Sproat

Size 6 Viking

HOOK SHAPES AND BENDS

Here are some examples of the variations in shapes and bends that help identify hook patterns used in fly tying.

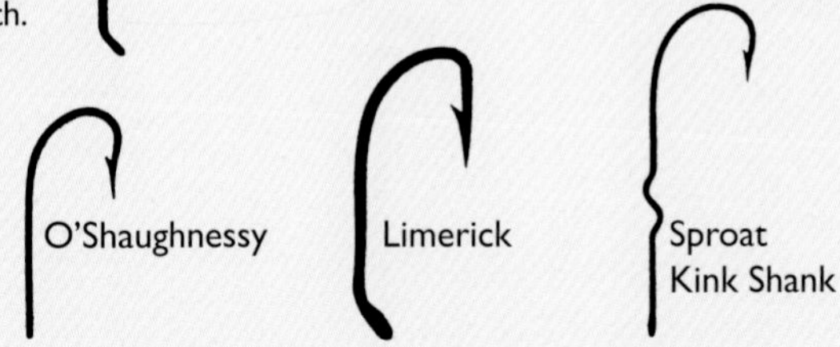

O'Shaughnessy

Limerick

Sproat Kink Shank

HOOK STYLES AND SIZES

The following pages illustrate the wide variety of hooks available. From live bait hooks to jig hooks to circle hooks to fly hooks, these styles and sizes are designed for various fishing techniques in fresh and salt water. The hooks included here are not shown at actual size, but the range of sizes available are indicated for each hook. The range of sizes may also vary from manufacturer to manufacturer. All illustrations in this section appear courtesy of O. Mustad & Son.

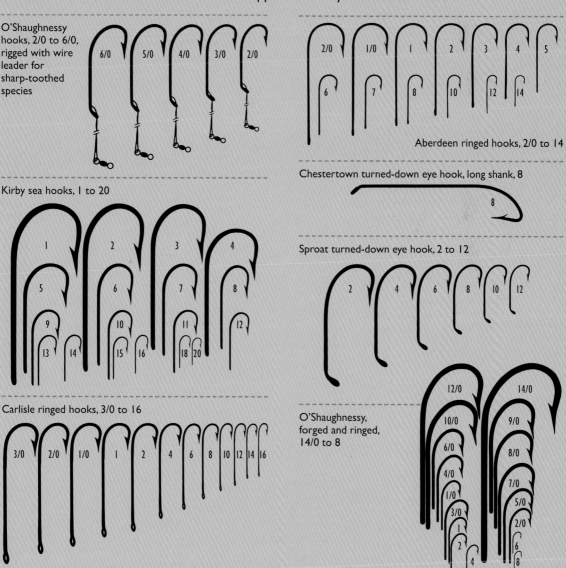

O'Shaughnessy hooks, 2/0 to 6/0, rigged with wire leader for sharp-toothed species

Aberdeen ringed hooks, 2/0 to 14

Kirby sea hooks, 1 to 20

Chestertown turned-down eye hook, long shank, 8

Sproat turned-down eye hook, 2 to 12

Carlisle ringed hooks, 3/0 to 16

O'Shaughnessy, forged and ringed, 14/0 to 8

Hook Styles and Sizes *(continued)*

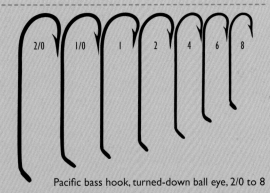

Pacific bass hook, turned-down ball eye, 2/0 to 8

Mustad treble hook, 12/0 to 20

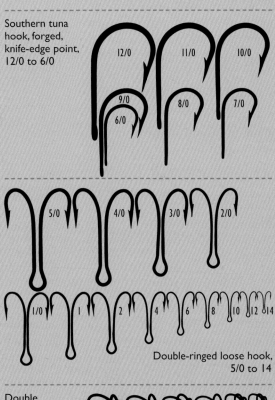

Southern tuna hook, forged, knife-edge point, 12/0 to 6/0

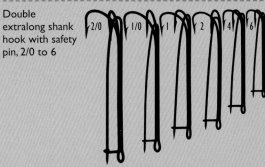

Double-ringed loose hook, 5/0 to 14

Double extralong shank hook with safety pin, 2/0 to 6

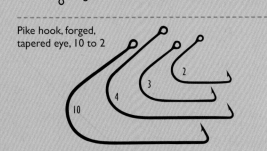

Pike hook, forged, tapered eye, 10 to 2

Limerick hollow-point hook, 2 to 20

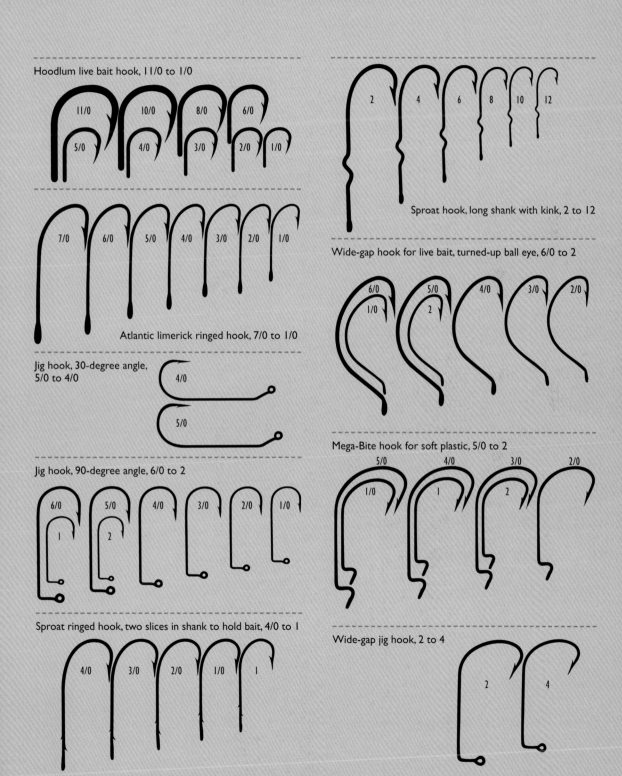

Hoodlum live bait hook, 11/0 to 1/0

11/0   10/0   8/0   6/0
5/0   4/0   3/0   2/0   1/0

7/0   6/0   5/0   4/0   3/0   2/0   1/0

Atlantic limerick ringed hook, 7/0 to 1/0

Jig hook, 30-degree angle, 5/0 to 4/0

4/0

5/0

Jig hook, 90-degree angle, 6/0 to 2

6/0   5/0   4/0   3/0   2/0   1/0
1   2

Sproat ringed hook, two slices in shank to hold bait, 4/0 to 1

4/0   3/0   2/0   1/0   1

2   4   6   8   10   12

Sproat hook, long shank with kink, 2 to 12

Wide-gap hook for live bait, turned-up ball eye, 6/0 to 2

6/0   5/0   4/0   3/0   2/0
1/0   2

Mega-Bite hook for soft plastic, 5/0 to 2

5/0   4/0   3/0   2/0
1/0   1   2

Wide-gap jig hook, 2 to 4

2   4

Hook Styles and Sizes *(continued)*

Big-Mouth hook, extrawide bend for plastic tube baits, 12/0 to 2/0

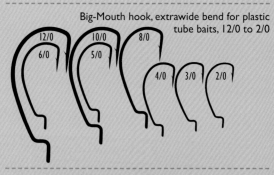

Beak bait hook, 9/0 to 8

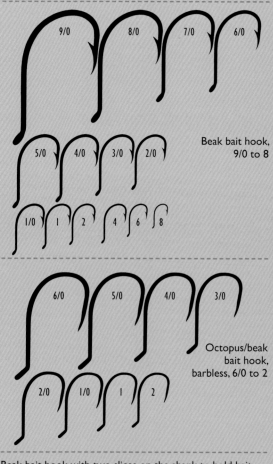

Demon perfect offset circle hook, 9/0 to 2/0

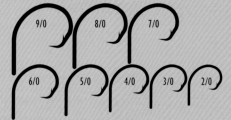

Impact swimbait hook with spring keeper that holds the bait, 9/0 to 2/0

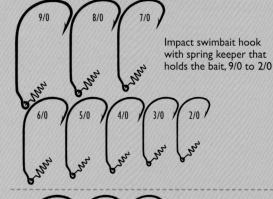

Octopus/beak bait hook, barbless, 6/0 to 2

Power Lock Plus weighted hook with gripper design to hold bait, 9/0 to 1/0

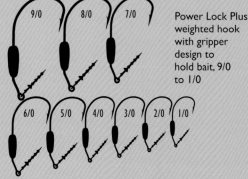

Beak bait hook with two slices on the shank to hold bait, 9/0 to 14

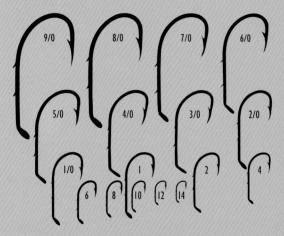

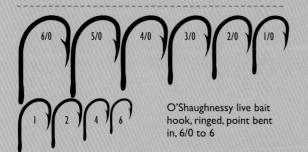

O'Shaughnessy live bait hook, ringed, point bent in, 6/0 to 6

Treble hook for doughball bait, 2 to 8

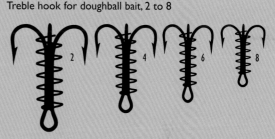

Demon circle hooks, ringed, offset, 9/0 to 1/0

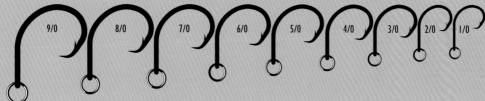

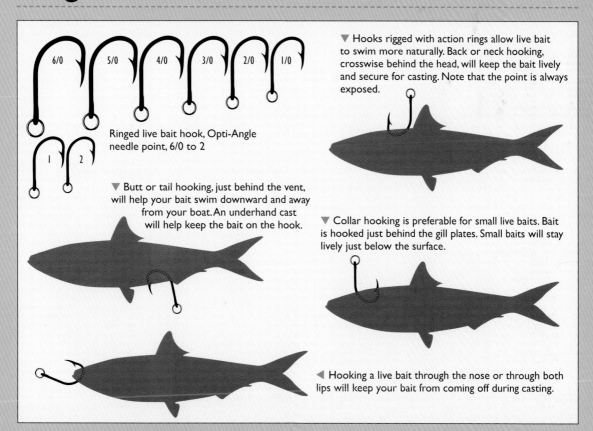

Ringed live bait hook, Opti-Angle needle point, 6/0 to 2

▼ Hooks rigged with action rings allow live bait to swim more naturally. Back or neck hooking, crosswise behind the head, will keep the bait lively and secure for casting. Note that the point is always exposed.

▼ Butt or tail hooking, just behind the vent, will help your bait swim downward and away from your boat. An underhand cast will help keep the bait on the hook.

▼ Collar hooking is preferable for small live baits. Bait is hooked just behind the gill plates. Small baits will stay lively just below the surface.

◄ Hooking a live bait through the nose or through both lips will keep your bait from coming off during casting.

Fly Hook Styles and Sizes

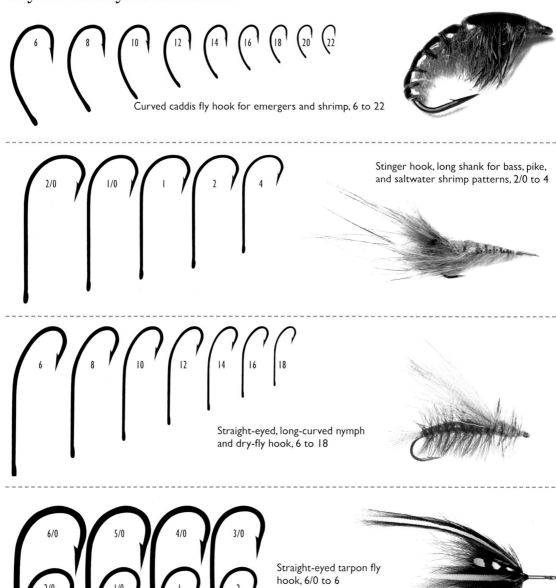

Curved caddis fly hook for emergers and shrimp, 6 to 22

Stinger hook, long shank for bass, pike, and saltwater shrimp patterns, 2/0 to 4

Straight-eyed, long-curved nymph and dry-fly hook, 6 to 18

Straight-eyed tarpon fly hook, 6/0 to 6

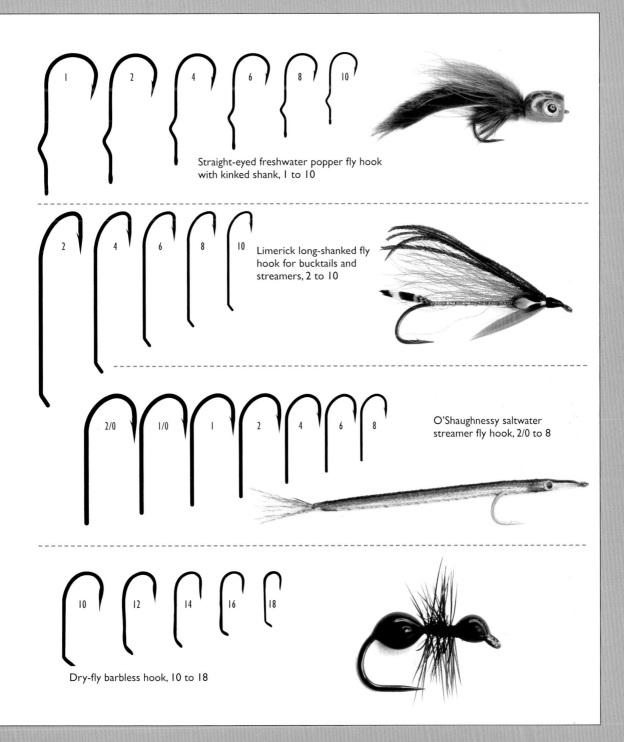

Straight-eyed freshwater popper fly hook with kinked shank, 1 to 10

Limerick long-shanked fly hook for bucktails and streamers, 2 to 10

O'Shaughnessy saltwater streamer fly hook, 2/0 to 8

Dry-fly barbless hook, 10 to 18

Fly Hook Styles and Sizes *(continued)*

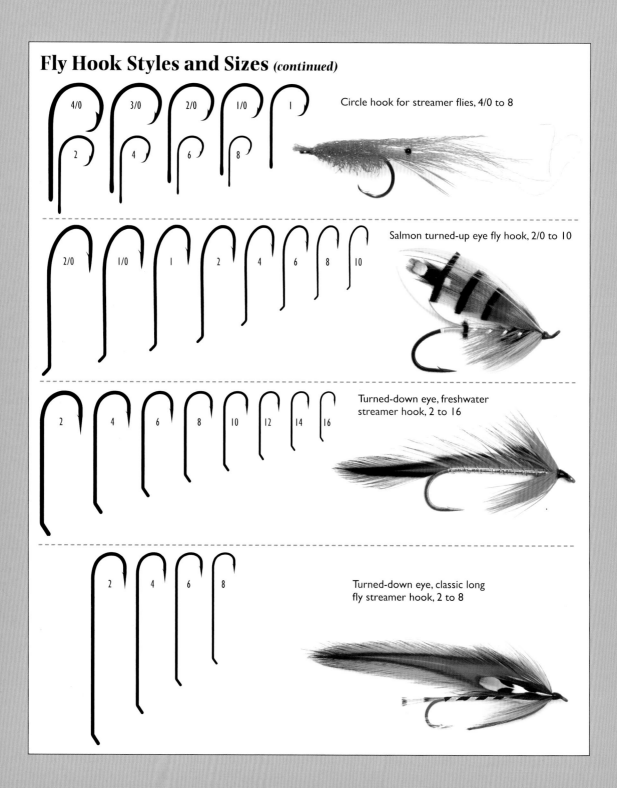

Circle hook for streamer flies, 4/0 to 8

Salmon turned-up eye fly hook, 2/0 to 10

Turned-down eye, freshwater streamer hook, 2 to 16

Turned-down eye, classic long fly streamer hook, 2 to 8

ARTIFICIAL LURES

Fishing with bait is enjoyable, certainly, but there's something about fooling a fish with an artificial lure that gives most anglers a special charge.

A neophyte fisherman who visits a well-stocked sporting-goods store or tackle shop is confronted with a bewildering array of plugs, spoons, spinners, jigs, flies, bugs, and others. Some artificials look like nothing that ever swam, crawled, or flew, and yet they catch fish.

Let's look at each type of artificial lure and see how and why it works and how it should be fished.

■ Plugs

Plugs are lures designed to imitate small fish for the most part, though some plugs simulate mice, frogs, eels, and other food on which game fish feed. Plug action—meaning the way the lure moves when retrieved by the angler—is important and is something on which manufacturers expend much money and time. These lures are called crankbaits because every crank of the reel handle imparts some sort of diving or darting action.

The type, size, and weight of the plug you select is determined by the fish you are after and the kind of fishing tackle you are using. The charts found at the beginning of this section on how to match up various kinds of fishing tackle will help the beginner choose the right weight plugs.

There are five basic types of plugs: popping, surface, floating-diving, sinking (deep running), and deep diving.

POPPING: These plugs float on the surface and have concave, hollowed-out faces. The angler retrieves a popping plug by jerking the rod tip back so that the plug's face digs into the water, making a small splash, bubbles, and a popping sound. Some make a louder sound than others. This sound is especially attractive to largemouth bass, pike, muskies, and some inshore saltwater species, such as striped bass and bluefish. Most popping plugs (and most other plugs) have two sets of treble hooks. Popping plugs are most productive when the water surface is calm or nearly so. They should usually be fished slowly.

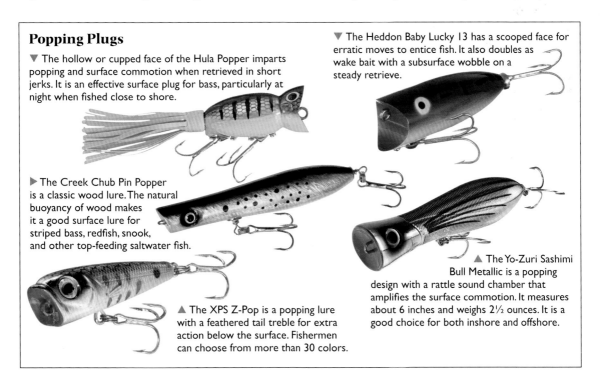

Popping Plugs

▼ The hollow or cupped face of the Hula Popper imparts popping and surface commotion when retrieved in short jerks. It is an effective surface plug for bass, particularly at night when fished close to shore.

▼ The Heddon Baby Lucky 13 has a scooped face for erratic moves to entice fish. It also doubles as wake bait with a subsurface wobble on a steady retrieve.

▶ The Creek Chub Pin Popper is a classic wood lure. The natural buoyancy of wood makes it a good surface lure for striped bass, redfish, snook, and other top-feeding saltwater fish.

▲ The Yo-Zuri Sashimi Bull Metallic is a popping design with a rattle sound chamber that amplifies the surface commotion. It measures about 6 inches and weighs 2½ ounces. It is a good choice for both inshore and offshore.

▲ The XPS Z-Pop is a popping lure with a feathered tail treble for extra action below the surface. Fishermen can choose from more than 30 colors.

Surface Plugs

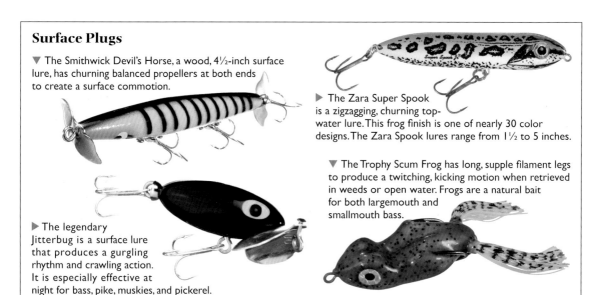

▼ The Smithwick Devil's Horse, a wood, 4½-inch surface lure, has churning balanced propellers at both ends to create a surface commotion.

▶ The Zara Super Spook is a zigzagging, churning top-water lure. This frog finish is one of nearly 30 color designs. The Zara Spook lures range from 1½ to 5 inches.

▼ The Trophy Scum Frog has long, supple filament legs to produce a twitching, kicking motion when retrieved in weeds or open water. Frogs are a natural bait for both largemouth and smallmouth bass.

▶ The legendary Jitterbug is a surface lure that produces a gurgling rhythm and crawling action. It is especially effective at night for bass, pike, muskies, and pickerel.

Deep-Diving Plugs

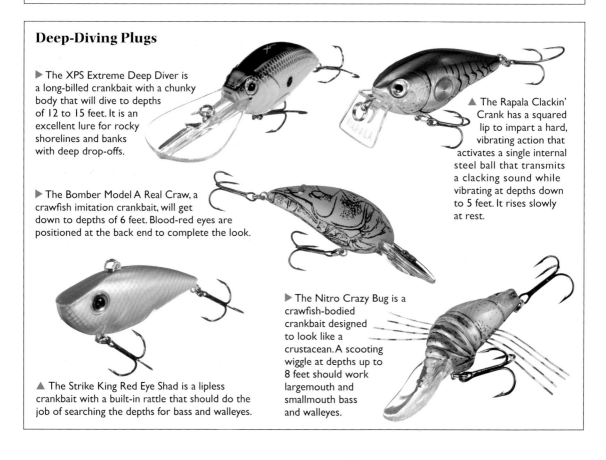

▶ The XPS Extreme Deep Diver is a long-billed crankbait with a chunky body that will dive to depths of 12 to 15 feet. It is an excellent lure for rocky shorelines and banks with deep drop-offs.

▲ The Rapala Clackin' Crank has a squared lip to impart a hard, vibrating action that activates a single internal steel ball that transmits a clacking sound while vibrating at depths down to 5 feet. It rises slowly at rest.

▶ The Bomber Model A Real Craw, a crawfish imitation crankbait, will get down to depths of 6 feet. Blood-red eyes are positioned at the back end to complete the look.

▶ The Nitro Crazy Bug is a crawfish-bodied crankbait designed to look like a crustacean. A scooting wiggle at depths up to 8 feet should work largemouth and smallmouth bass and walleyes.

▲ The Strike King Red Eye Shad is a lipless crankbait with a built-in rattle that should do the job of searching the depths for bass and walleyes.

Floating-Diving Plugs

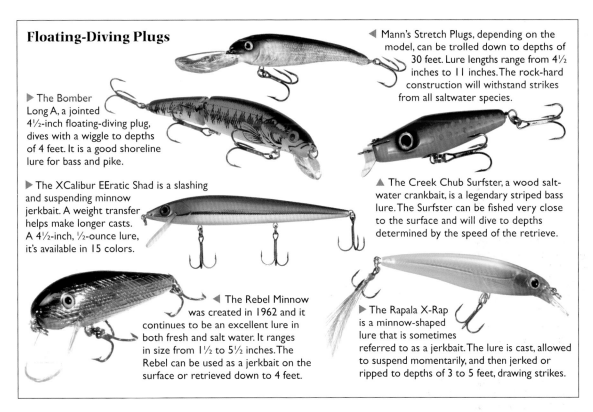

▷ Mann's Stretch Plugs, depending on the model, can be trolled down to depths of 30 feet. Lure lengths range from 4½ inches to 11 inches. The rock-hard construction will withstand strikes from all saltwater species.

▷ The Bomber Long A, a jointed 4½-inch floating-diving plug, dives with a wiggle to depths of 4 feet. It is a good shoreline lure for bass and pike.

▷ The XCalibur EEratic Shad is a slashing and suspending minnow jerkbait. A weight transfer helps make longer casts. A 4½-inch, ½-ounce lure, it's available in 15 colors.

▲ The Creek Chub Surfster, a wood saltwater crankbait, is a legendary striped bass lure. The Surfster can be fished very close to the surface and will dive to depths determined by the speed of the retrieve.

◁ The Rebel Minnow was created in 1962 and it continues to be an excellent lure in both fresh and salt water. It ranges in size from 1½ to 5½ inches. The Rebel can be used as a jerkbait on the surface or retrieved down to 4 feet.

▷ The Rapala X-Rap is a minnow-shaped lure that is sometimes referred to as a jerkbait. The lure is cast, allowed to suspend momentarily, and then jerked or ripped to depths of 3 to 5 feet, drawing strikes.

SURFACE: These plugs float on the surface, but they can be fished with various kinds of retrieves and create a different kind of surface disturbance than poppers do. Designed with an elongated, or bullet-shaped, head, they create surface disturbance by various means, including propellers (at the head or at both head and tail), a wide metal lip at the head, or hinged metal "wings" just behind the head. They can be twitched so that they barely nod, retrieved steadily so that they chug across the water, or skimmed across the top as fast as the angler can turn his reel handle. The proper retrieve depends on the lure's design and, of course, on the mood of the fish. It's best to try different retrieves until you find one that produces.

FLOATING-DIVING: These plugs are designed to float when at rest and dive when retrieved. Some float horizontally, while others float with the tail hanging down beneath the surface. They are made to dive by an extended lip at the head. The speed of the retrieve determines the depth of the dive. The faster the retrieve, the deeper the dive. Most of these plugs have a side-to-side

Freshwater vs. Saltwater Lures

A long time ago, I stopped labeling lures as "freshwater" and "saltwater." There is really no difference. Size no longer matters. I've caught 40-pound dolphin on 1-ounce bucktails and a 10-inch farm pond bass on a 7-inch Rapala. My favorite Creek Chub darter caught dozens of pike and so many bluefish that I retired the lure. The same is true for flies. My Clouser Minnows are equally productive on rainbow trout as they are on striped bass. Some lures have corrosion-resistant hooks and some have bronze hooks that will rust, but I never worry about hooks rotting away because they are easy to replace. With very few exceptions, all lures will work both in fresh and salt water.

wobbling action. An erratic retrieve—dive, surface, dive, surface—is often productive, and these plugs are also effective when made to swim just above a submerged weed bed, rock pile, and so on.

SINKING (DEEP RUNNING): These plugs sink as soon as they hit the water and are designed for deep work. Some

sink slower than others and can be fished at various depths, depending on how long the angler waits before starting his retrieve. Most of these plugs have some sort of wobbling action, and some fairly vibrate when retrieved. Some have propellers fore and aft.

These plugs are excellent fish-finders: the fisherman can start by bouncing them along the bottom, and

Saltwater Diving and Trolling Lures

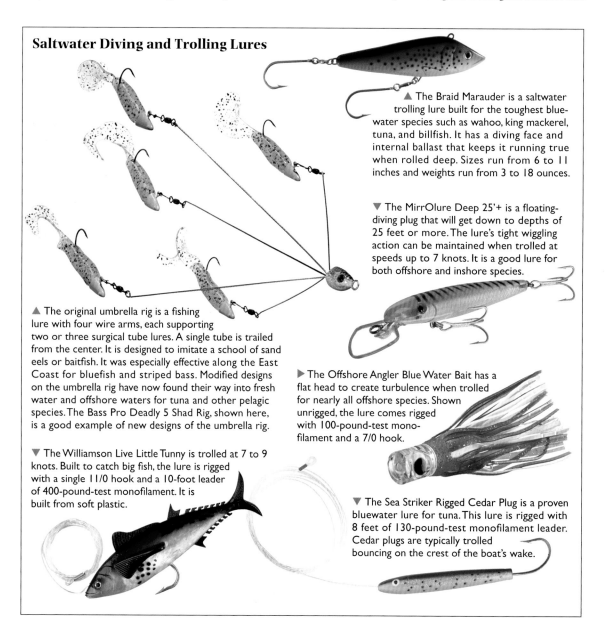

▲ The Braid Marauder is a saltwater trolling lure built for the toughest blue-water species such as wahoo, king mackerel, tuna, and billfish. It has a diving face and internal ballast that keeps it running true when rolled deep. Sizes run from 6 to 11 inches and weights run from 3 to 18 ounces.

▼ The MirrOlure Deep 25'+ is a floating-diving plug that will get down to depths of 25 feet or more. The lure's tight wiggling action can be maintained when trolled at speeds up to 7 knots. It is a good lure for both offshore and inshore species.

▲ The original umbrella rig is a fishing lure with four wire arms, each supporting two or three surgical tube lures. A single tube is trailed from the center. It is designed to imitate a school of sand eels or baitfish. It was especially effective along the East Coast for bluefish and striped bass. Modified designs on the umbrella rig have now found their way into fresh water and offshore waters for tuna and other pelagic species. The Bass Pro Deadly 5 Shad Rig, shown here, is a good example of new designs of the umbrella rig.

▶ The Offshore Angler Blue Water Bait has a flat head to create turbulence when trolled for nearly all offshore species. Shown unrigged, the lure comes rigged with 100-pound-test mono-filament and a 7/0 hook.

▼ The Williamson Live Little Tunny is trolled at 7 to 9 knots. Built to catch big fish, the lure is rigged with a single 11/0 hook and a 10-foot leader of 400-pound-test monofilament. It is built from soft plastic.

▼ The Sea Striker Rigged Cedar Plug is a proven bluewater lure for tuna. This lure is rigged with 8 feet of 130-pound-test monofilament leader. Cedar plugs are typically trolled bouncing on the crest of the boat's wake.

if that doesn't work, he can work them at progressively shallower depths until he finds at what depth the fish are feeding. It should be remembered that deep-running plugs don't have to be fished in deep water; for example, in small sizes they're great for river smallmouths.

DEEP DIVING: These plugs may float or sink, but they all are designed with long or broad lips of metal or plastic that cause the plugs to dive to depths of 30 feet or more as the angler reels in. As with other diving plugs, the faster the retrieve, the deeper the dive. Most of these lures have some sort of wobbling action. They are ideally suited for casting or trolling in deep lakes and at the edges of drop-offs, and they work best in most waters when the fish are holding in deep holes, as fish usually do during midday in July and August.

To Catch a Dolphin

Want to know how to hunt dolphins, especially big slammers? Brian Cone, a Florida Keys charter captain and a dolphin expert, showed me how he catches mahimahi. March is the unofficial start of dolphin season in the Keys, but it doesn't really get red-hot until April and then runs through the summer months.

"Earlier in the spring," Brian explained, "I look for sooty terns flying high over the water. These terns are usually over bigger dolphin and working into the current, feeding on flying fish and squid, a gourmet food for bull dolphin. That's the big difference. The birds need to stay high over bigger dolphin because they swim in smaller packs and the terns don't want to lose them. When you see birds swooping down on these larger baits, you can be sure big dolphin are in the area. If you see birds working closer to the water, they're usually feeding on small fish in the weeds and this means schoolies, dolphin running anywhere from 5 to 15 pounds. If I can't find birds, I'll look for scattered weed lines in 1,000 to 3,000 feet of water and troll it. I like scattered weed lines in heavily fished areas because those areas probably haven't been worked over by another boat. If you see bubbles in a weed line, it's also a good indication that another boat has already trolled the weeds."

With windless conditions, Brian trolled for his first fish. We put lures on the two flat lines, about 50 to 100 feet behind the boat. His favorite lures for attracting dolphin are a 5½-inch Moldcraft Super Chugger, a 4¼-inch Islander Tracker in blue and white, and a 4½-inch squid in a combination of pink, purple, and black. These favorite lures all have one thing in common: they are all small. None of them measure more than 6 inches.

On the outriggers, Brian put out two rigged ballyhoo without plastic skirts. He ran the dead baits out 150 to 200 feet. On his conventional trolling rods, Brian used 30-pound-class tackle with 6-foot, 80-pound-test leaders. Once we found fish, however, Brian preferred to switch to spinning tackle. His spinning rods were 15- and 30-pound class. He tied a 4-foot, 40- or 50-pound-test leader to a 4-foot bimini twist on the lighter spinning rods and a 60- or 80-pound-test leader on the heavier spinners.

When that first dolphin was hooked, Brian slowed the boat down to a slow idle, keeping it in gear but moving just fast enough to keep the school behind the boat. We had several ballyhoo cut in chunks and ready on the transom to start chunking when the school got close behind the boat. It's no secret that any kind of floating debris quickly attracts small baitfish and becomes a feeding station for many species of blue-water fish, especially dolphin. When we got that first fish close to the boat, we could see more dolphin. We tossed out chunks of cut ballyhoo to keep the school in range and feeding. These fish were ravenous and it took only seconds to get another hookup. We kept one dolphin in the water and gaffed it only when we had another near the transom. When we boated five or six dolphin, the school suddenly disappeared.

We used spinning tackle, which made it easier to cast baits to the ravenous school. But we had these dolphin so close, they almost appeared to be fighting over our chunks of ballyhoo.

Brian admitted that live bait may be better in certain situations, such as catching schoolies. Generally, however, Brian prefers to use dead bait, such as ballyhoo, flying fish, bonita, and squid chunks. He believes you get a better hookup with dead bait. Live bait may entice more fish, but dolphin will often feel the hook and tend to play with the bait rather than swallow it.

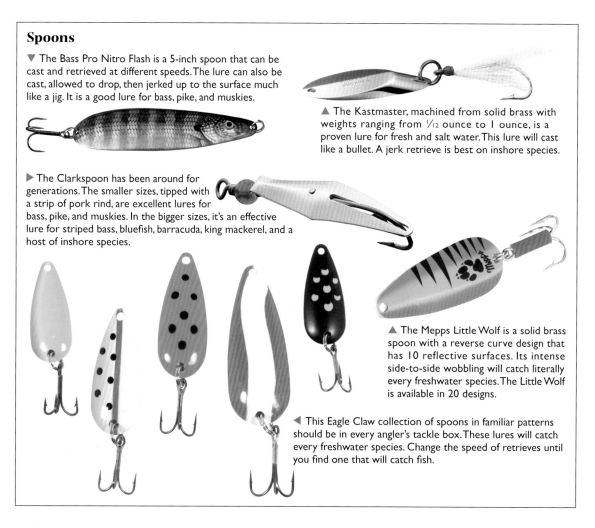

Spoons

▼ The Bass Pro Nitro Flash is a 5-inch spoon that can be cast and retrieved at different speeds. The lure can also be cast, allowed to drop, then jerked up to the surface much like a jig. It is a good lure for bass, pike, and muskies.

▲ The Kastmaster, machined from solid brass with weights ranging from $\frac{1}{12}$ ounce to 1 ounce, is a proven lure for fresh and salt water. This lure will cast like a bullet. A jerk retrieve is best on inshore species.

▶ The Clarkspoon has been around for generations. The smaller sizes, tipped with a strip of pork rind, are excellent lures for bass, pike, and muskies. In the bigger sizes, it's an effective lure for striped bass, bluefish, barracuda, king mackerel, and a host of inshore species.

▲ The Mepps Little Wolf is a solid brass spoon with a reverse curve design that has 10 reflective surfaces. Its intense side-to-side wobbling will catch literally every freshwater species. The Little Wolf is available in 20 designs.

◀ This Eagle Claw collection of spoons in familiar patterns should be in every angler's tackle box. These lures will catch every freshwater species. Change the speed of retrieves until you find one that will catch fish.

■ Spoons

Spoons are among the oldest of artificial lures. If you cut the handle off a teaspoon, you'd have the basic shape of this lure.

Spoons are designed to imitate small baitfish of one kind or another, so flash is an important feature in many of these lures. Most spoons have a wobbling, side-to-side action when retrieved.

Many spoons have a silver or gold finish, while others are painted in various colors and combinations of colors. Most have a single free-swinging treble hook at the tail; others have a single fixed hook. Weedless arrangements are becoming more and more popular on both types.

In general, the smaller spoons are better in streams and ponds, while the larger ones are a good choice for lakes. However, the angler must remember that with two spoons of equal weight but different sizes, the smaller one will cast easier in wind and sink faster, while the larger one will sink slower and swim at shallower depths.

What's the best retrieve for a spoon? Again, that depends on weather and water conditions and other circumstances, including the mood of the fish. But generally, an erratic retrieve, with twitches and jerks of the rod tip, is better than a steady retrieve because it makes the spoon look like an injured baitfish. Attaching a strip of pork rind to a spoon often adds to its fish appeal.

Spinners

Spinners, like spoons, are designed to imitate baitfish, and they attract game fish by flash and vibration. A spinner is simply a metal blade mounted on a shaft by means of a revolving arm or ring called a clevis. Unlike a spoon, which has a wobbling action, a spinner blade rotates around the shaft when retrieved.

Other parts of a simple spinner include a locking device to accommodate a hook at one end of the shaft, a metal loop to which the line is tied at the other end of the shaft, and a series of metal or plastic beads that separate the blade from the locking device and loop. In some spinners, notably the Colorado, the blade is mounted on a series of swivels instead of on a shaft.

Most spinners have either one or two blades. However, in some forms of fishing, particularly deep-water trolling for lake trout, eight or more spinner blades are mounted in tandem on a length of wire.

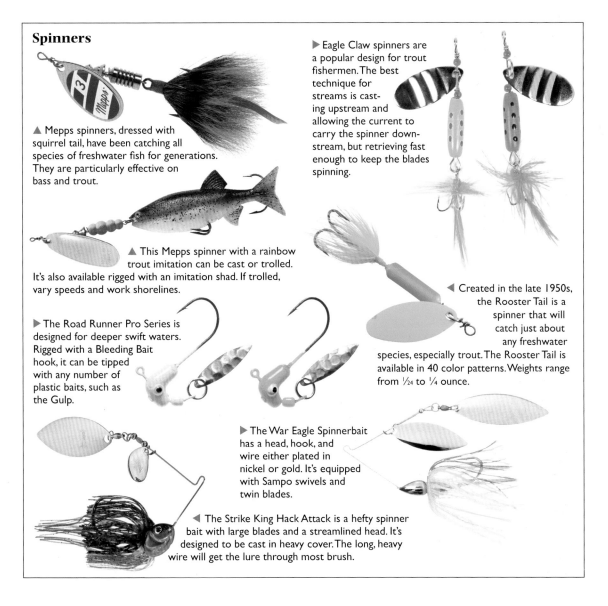

Spinners

▲ Mepps spinners, dressed with squirrel tail, have been catching all species of freshwater fish for generations. They are particularly effective on bass and trout.

▲ This Mepps spinner with a rainbow trout imitation can be cast or trolled. It's also available rigged with an imitation shad. If trolled, vary speeds and work shorelines.

▶ The Road Runner Pro Series is designed for deeper swift waters. Rigged with a Bleeding Bait hook, it can be tipped with any number of plastic baits, such as the Gulp.

▶ The War Eagle Spinnerbait has a head, hook, and wire either plated in nickel or gold. It's equipped with Sampo swivels and twin blades.

◀ The Strike King Hack Attack is a hefty spinner bait with large blades and a streamlined head. It's designed to be cast in heavy cover. The long, heavy wire will get the lure through most brush.

▶ Eagle Claw spinners are a popular design for trout fishermen. The best technique for streams is casting upstream and allowing the current to carry the spinner downstream, but retrieving fast enough to keep the blades spinning.

◀ Created in the late 1950s, the Rooster Tail is a spinner that will catch just about any freshwater species, especially trout. The Rooster Tail is available in 40 color patterns. Weights range from $1/24$ to $1/4$ ounce.

Buzz Baits

Booyah Counter Strike buzz baits have counter-rotating blades for stability and to create a distinct sound. Vary the retrieves with these lures to create a bubble trail.

Most spinner blades have either a silver or gold finish. Some, however, are painted in various colors, including black, yellow, and white, while others are striped and still others are made of simulated pearl. In general, the brighter finishes are best in shaded or discolored water and on overcast days, while the darker finishes are better in very clear water under bright skies.

Spinner blades have various shapes and other physical characteristics. Both shape and thickness determine how the blade reacts when retrieved. To illustrate this point, let's take a look at a few types of simple spinners, often used with bait, that have proven their worth over the years.

COLORADO: This spinner has a wide, nearly round blade that rotates well out from the shaft. Because it has considerable water resistance and spins relatively slowly, it is best suited for use in lakes and in streams with slow currents. A Colorado spinner used with a worm is a proven taker of trout, walleyes, and other fish.

WILLOW LEAF: This spinner has a long, narrow blade that spins fast and close to the shaft. Having minimum water resistance, it is well suited for use in fast-flowing water. A willow-leaf spinner is often used with a worm, minnow, or other natural baits.

JUNE BUG: Unusual in that the blade is attached directly to the shaft (there is no clevis), this spinner has a sort of "leg" that braces the blade against the shaft, and has a hole in the middle. A June Bug spinner with its hook sweetened by a night crawler is a potent combination for

trout, walleyes, and many other game fish. The June Bug comes in various designs.

Spinner-blade sizes are usually classified by numbers, but the numbers vary with the manufacturers and are not a reliable guide for the buyer. It's easy enough to simply look over a selection of spinners and select the size that seems right for your particular purpose.

Many spinner-type lures are produced today and are extremely popular, especially among freshwater fishermen. In all of them, the basic attracting element is a revolving spinner blade. Most have some sort of weight built in along the shaft and a treble hook at the tail. In many, the treble hook is hidden or at least disguised with bucktail, feathers, squirrel tail, or a skirt of rubber or plastic strands. Weedless hooks are also becoming increasingly popular on these lures.

Buzz Baits

Buzz baits are spinner baits that incorporate a wide propeller and jig that churn a substantial commotion as the bait is retrieved across the surface, leaving a bubble trail. Buzz baits can be fished fast or slow, depending on water conditions and the mood of the fish. Try various retrieves until you find one that catches fish.

Jigs

Generally speaking, a jig is any lure with a weighted head (usually lead), a fixed hook, and a tail of bucktail, feathers, nylon, or similar material. Jigs are made in sizes of

Jigs

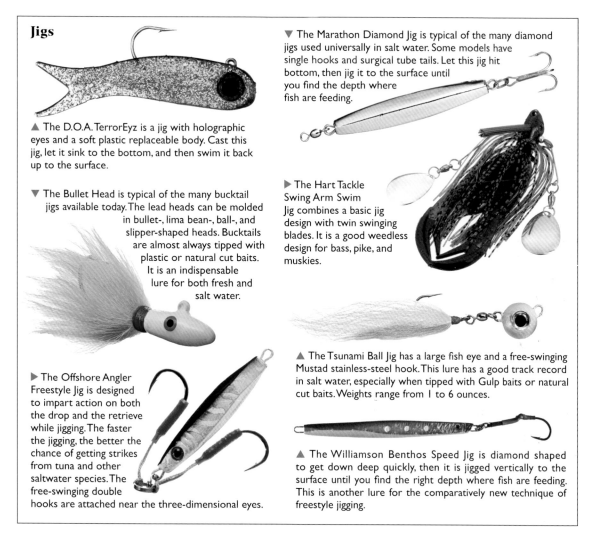

▲ The D.O.A. TerrorEyz is a jig with holographic eyes and a soft plastic replaceable body. Cast this jig, let it sink to the bottom, and then swim it back up to the surface.

▼ The Bullet Head is typical of the many bucktail jigs available today. The lead heads can be molded in bullet-, lima bean-, ball-, and slipper-shaped heads. Bucktails are almost always tipped with plastic or natural cut baits. It is an indispensable lure for both fresh and salt water.

▶ The Offshore Angler Freestyle Jig is designed to impart action on both the drop and the retrieve while jigging. The faster the jigging, the better the chance of getting strikes from tuna and other saltwater species. The free-swinging double hooks are attached near the three-dimensional eyes.

▼ The Marathon Diamond Jig is typical of the many diamond jigs used universally in salt water. Some models have single hooks and surgical tube tails. Let this jig hit bottom, then jig it to the surface until you find the depth where fish are feeding.

▶ The Hart Tackle Swing Arm Swim Jig combines a basic jig design with twin swinging blades. It is a good weedless design for bass, pike, and muskies.

▲ The Tsunami Ball Jig has a large fish eye and a free-swinging Mustad stainless-steel hook. This lure has a good track record in salt water, especially when tipped with Gulp baits or natural cut baits. Weights range from 1 to 6 ounces.

▲ The Williamson Benthos Speed Jig is diamond shaped to get down deep quickly, then it is jigged vertically to the surface until you find the right depth where fish are feeding. This is another lure for the comparatively new technique of freestyle jigging.

¹⁄₁₆ ounce to 6 ounces and even heavier, and they will take just about any fish that swims in fresh water or salt. Jigs imitate baitfish, crustaceans, and other game-fish forage. In some jigs, the hook rides with the point up to minimize the chance of snagging. Jigs, and related lures, take many forms. Here's a look at the most popular types.

FEATHERED JIG: Often called Japanese feathers, this jig is commonly used in saltwater trolling and casting. It consists of a heavy metal head with eyes. Through the head runs a wire leader, to the end of which the hook is attached. Running from the head down to the hook is a long tail, usually of feathers. A plastic sleeve covers the feathers for about half their length. This jig is typically used in trolling for tuna, billfish, dolphin, and other pelagic species.

BUCKTAIL JIG: This jig consists of a lead head, embedded hook, and trailing tail of bucktail. The head is painted, with the most popular colors being white, red, yellow, or combinations of these colors. The most popular member of the jig family, bucktail jigs are used on a wide variety of freshwater and saltwater game fish, especially largemouth and smallmouth bass, walleyes, pike, striped bass, bluefish, and many other bottom-feeders.

SHAD DART: This is a small jig (usually weighing about ¼ ounce) with a relatively long, narrow head, flat face, and short tail of bucktail or similar material. It is usually painted in two colors, with the most popular combi-nations being red and white, yellow and white, and red and yellow. It is an extremely popular lure for American (white) shad in East Coast rivers.

METAL (BLOCK-TIN) SQUIDS: Falling under the general category of jigs are these lures, which are used mostly in salt water for striped bass, bluefish, tuna, and the like. Made to resemble baitfish, they have a long, narrow body of block tin, stainless steel, chrome, or nickel-plated lead and either a single fixed hook or a free-swinging treble hook, with or without a tail of bucktail. Most metal squids range in length from 3 to 6 inches. All have bright finishes, usually silvery; in some, the finish is smooth, while others have a hammered finish that gives a scale-like appearance. Among the most popular metal squids are types such as the Hopkins (which has a hammered finish, a long, narrow, flat body, and a free-swinging tre-ble hook), the diamond jig (which has a four-sided body and a treble hook), and the sand eel (which has a long, rounded, undulating body). A strip of pork rind often adds to the effectiveness of metal squids.

JIG AND EEL: This jig consists of a small metal squid on which is rigged a common eel, either the real McCoy (usually dead and preserved) or a plastic artificial. These rigged eels range in length from about 6 inches up to a foot or longer. The jig and eel is a deadly combination for striped bass, big snook, redfish, and sea trout. The best retrieve depends on various conditions, but usually a slow, slightly erratic swimming motion is best.

Vertical jigging is a productive technique for a variety of species, especially in salt water. The most effective jigging method is to cast, let the jig drop to the bottom, and then begin retrieving with an up-and-down jigging motion. Once you determine where the fish are, concentrate on jigging at that depth. Most fish will strike when the jig is fluttering down to the bottom. Jigging speed will range from very rapid to slow and works best with braided line. Vertical jigging can be deadly on all species, especially striped bass, tuna, and grouper.

Plastic Lures

Hundreds of years from now the history books may refer to our era as the Age of Plastic. And fishermen haven't escaped the gaze of plastic manufacturers.

On the market today are soft-plastic lures that imitate just about anything a fish will eat. There are plastic worms, eels, snakes, crickets, crawfish, minnows, shrimp,

Hot Lures for Salmon

The most consistent key to catching salmon is color! Millions of salmon return each year to their birthplace to deposit billions of salmon eggs. Some of these eggs will eventually become salmon, but most will sink to the bottom and provide a food source for all Alaska game fish. Salmon eggs vary in color from pink to shades of red and orange. It's these reddish hues that trigger a feeding response.

What should be in your tackle box? A spin fisherman needs only spoons and jig heads with red or pink swimming plastic tails. Curly tails seem to work best. Cover the hook of the jig head and fish it slow with occasional twitches.

For fishermen who prefer to cast spoons, the same color rule applies. For several years, I've used Pixie spoons in weights from ¼ to ½ ounce. These chromed spoons have red or orange plastic insets molded to look like salmon egg clusters.

Alaska is a great proving ground for fly fishermen. Again, the color rule applies. When I arrived in Alaska, Chris Batin gave me a handful of his special flies. He calls them BBLs, which stands for Batin Bunny Leeches. The fly is a bright fuchsia-colored streamer with a barbell lead eye. Chris ties it on a 2X strong 1/0 hook with dyed rabbit fur. There's also enough weight with the barbell eyes to make it easy to cast with light spinning tackle. Chris's fly consistently proved deadly.

▲ Pixie Spoon
▼ Chris Batin's BBL

Rigging Plastic Worms

The plastic worm can be fished on the bottom, above the bottom, on the surface, and through thick weeds. It comes in different lengths, shapes, colors, flavors, and scents. The fake night crawler is so versatile it has spawned specialized hooks and a separate vocabulary. Here's how to tie the basic worm rigs, as well as when and where to fish them—and, just so there's no confusion, what they're called.

Floating Worm Rig: This is the simplest of all worm rigs. Thread a worm on a hook, push it up to the hook eye, and the rig is complete. You can buy floating worms (usually molded with air chambers), or you can make any worm a floater by threading a piece of cork on your line in front of the hook. You can also try "larding" the worm with bits of Styrofoam (cut from a plate or coffee cup). Some fishermen buy injectors—they look like miniature basketball pumps—to float worms, lizards, or any other soft-plastic lure. A floating worm works best at dusk or dawn. It's especially effective during spawning season, when bass are protective of their beds: cast the worm near a bass bed, swim it slowly, pause, and allow it to hang directly above the bed . . . and hang on.

Cork   3/0 Hook

Carolina Rig: This rig is designed to be fished deep, but not on the bottom. The principal difference between the Carolina and Texas rigs is that in the Carolina the sinker, usually a slip sinker, is placed 2 and 3 feet ahead of a floating worm. The sinker is held in position with a swivel (and often a bead). Use a bullet- or egg-shaped sinker; either will slide over most obstructions. The rig allows a bass to pick up the bait without immediately feeling the weight of a sinker, and it makes the worm more visible to suspended fish. The Carolina rig is another good summer lure for deep water. Depending on the amount of vegetation, the hook can be left exposed or buried in the worm.

Swivel   3/0 Hook

Slip Sinker (½ to 1 ounce)   Leader (2 to 3 feet)

Texas Rig: The Texas rig is a brush-buster. In its most common variant, a bullet-shaped sinker is threaded on the line just ahead of the worm, and the point of the hook is buried in it. This requires that the worm be carefully measured so it will hang straight when the hook point is inserted (it takes some practice). If the worm is "scrunched" on the shank of the hook, it won't be nearly as effective. The Texas rig is designed to be fished through weeds and brush and around stumps, and crawled along snag-infested bottoms. It's particularly effective on hot summer days when bass seek out brushy, shaded shorelines or hang very deep in cool water.

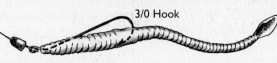

3/0 Hook

Slip Sinker (½ to 1 ounce)

Worm Hooks

This hook has a weighted shank with a free-swinging keeper at the eye to hold the worm.

This is a wide-gap hook with a weighted keeper. The worm is snugged against the eye; the point is buried.

The kink in the shank of this hook holds the worm securely and helps it hang straight.

The worm is threaded on the keeper. The ultrawide gap reduces the chance of a thrown hook.

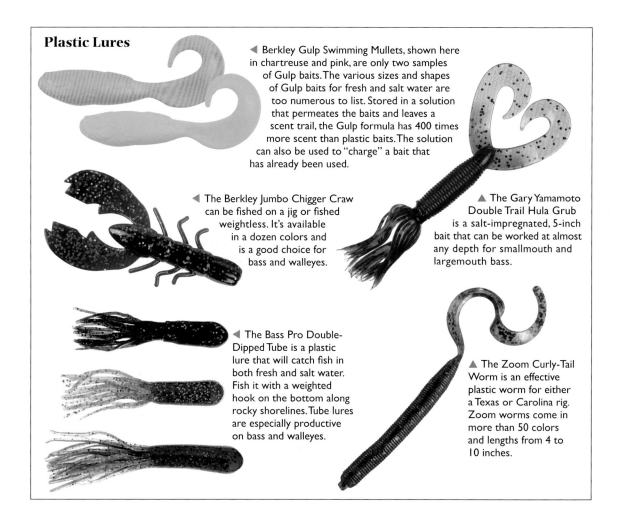

Plastic Lures

◄ Berkley Gulp Swimming Mullets, shown here in chartreuse and pink, are only two samples of Gulp baits. The various sizes and shapes of Gulp baits for fresh and salt water are too numerous to list. Stored in a solution that permeates the baits and leaves a scent trail, the Gulp formula has 400 times more scent than plastic baits. The solution can also be used to "charge" a bait that has already been used.

◄ The Berkley Jumbo Chigger Craw can be fished on a jig or fished weightless. It's available in a dozen colors and is a good choice for bass and walleyes.

▲ The Gary Yamamoto Double Trail Hula Grub is a salt-impregnated, 5-inch bait that can be worked at almost any depth for smallmouth and largemouth bass.

◄ The Bass Pro Double-Dipped Tube is a plastic lure that will catch fish in both fresh and salt water. Fish it with a weighted hook on the bottom along rocky shorelines. Tube lures are especially productive on bass and walleyes.

▲ The Zoom Curly-Tail Worm is an effective plastic worm for either a Texas or Carolina rig. Zoom worms come in more than 50 colors and lengths from 4 to 10 inches.

hellgrammites, mullet, flies, beetles, grasshoppers, frogs, and many, many more. Even salmon eggs! Many manufacturers impregnate these lures with secret formulas, attractants, and scents, claiming fish will strike these baits and not let go.

Surprisingly, a good many of these synthetic creations catch fish. A prime example is the plastic worm, which came into its own in the mid- and late 1960s. It has accounted for some eye-popping stringers of largemouth bass, especially in big southern lakes. A plastic worm threaded on a weedless hook and slithered through lily pads or an underwater weed bed is a real killer. Some plastic worms come with a weighted jig-type head or a spinner at the front.

▮ Pork Rind

Pork rind, as used by fishermen, is the skin from the back of a hog. It is sold in jars containing a liquid preservative to prevent spoilage and to retain the rind's flexibility.

It used to be that pork rind was used only as an addition to a spoon or other lure. For example, a single-hook spoon with a 2- or 3-inch strip of pork rind was—and still is—a popular combination for pickerel, pike, and the like.

Pork rind is still widely used that way today. It is sold in many shapes and sizes, from tiny half-inch V-strips for panfish up to 6-inch strips for muskies and saltwater game fish. Pork-rind baits come in many colors and shapes, such as lizards, frogs, worms, and eels.

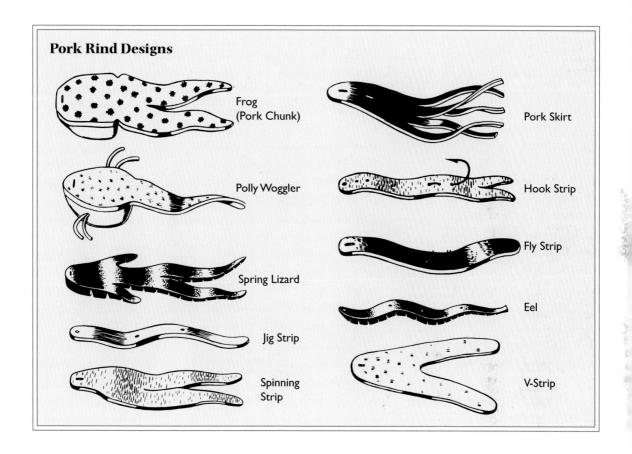

Pork Rind Designs

Frog (Pork Chunk)

Pork Skirt

Polly Woggler

Hook Strip

Spring Lizard

Fly Strip

Jig Strip

Eel

Spinning Strip

V-Strip

▨ Flies

An artificial fly is a combination of feathers, hair, floss, tinsel, and other materials tied to a hook to imitate a natural insect (dry and wet flies, including nymphs) or a baitfish (streamer flies and bucktails). Flies are used to take many freshwater and saltwater game fish, but most were originally designed for trout and salmon. There are four basic kinds of artificial flies: dry, wet (including nymph), streamer, and bucktail.

DRY FLIES: The dry fly, designed to imitate a floating insect, is tied so that the fibers of the hackles (feathers) stick out at approximately right angles to the shank of the hook. A properly tied dry fly sits high and lightly on the tips of its hackles, riding the surface of the water.

There are countless dry-fly patterns, but almost all of them fall into one of 10 basic types. Here is a brief description of each type:

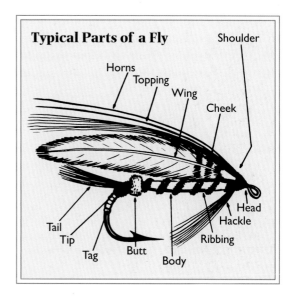

Typical Parts of a Fly

Shoulder
Horns
Topping
Wing
Cheek
Head
Hackle
Ribbing
Tail
Tip
Body
Tag
Butt

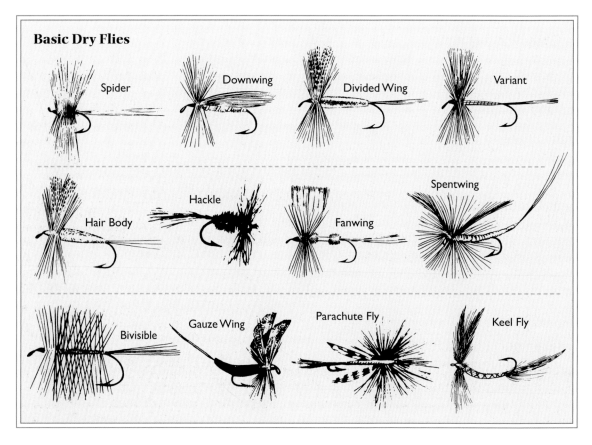

Basic Dry Flies

- **Downwing (or Sedge):** This fly has a built-up body, hackle, and wings lying flat along the shank of the hook. It floats with the hook underwater.

- **Divided Wing:** This is the standard dry-fly type. It has two erect separated wings of feather fibers, hackle, tapered body, and a stiff, slender tail. It floats with the hook above or partly underwater.

- **Hairwing:** This fly has upright wings made of deer hair, as well as hackle, a tapered body, and stiff tail. It floats with the hook above or partly underwater.

- **Fanwing:** This fly has large, flat, erect wings, hackle, body, and a stiff tail. It floats with the hook above or partly underwater. The large wings make this fly readily visible to an angler.

- **Bivisible:** This fly has no wings. White hackle is wound on the body at the fly's head, and hackle of another color (brown, gray, or black are the most popular) covers most of the remainder of the body. The

tail is stiff. It floats high, with the hook above water, and is highly visible to an angler.

- **Spentwing:** This fly has slender wings that stick out horizontally from the tapered body, hackle, and stiff tail. It floats on its wings and body with the bend of the hook underwater.

- **Spider:** This fly has no wings. The hackle is extralong and stiff. There is no body in the smaller sizes, a tinsel or herl body in the larger sizes. It has a stiff, extralong tail. It floats on its hackle tips and tail with the hook well out of the water.

- **Variant:** This fly has upright divided wings, extralong and stiff hackle, a very light body (or none at all), and a stiff, extralong tail. It floats on its hackle tips and tail with the hook well out of the water.

- **Hair Body:** This fly has upright divided wings, hackle, a body of clipped deer hair or similar material, and a stiff tail. It floats with the hook partly underwater.

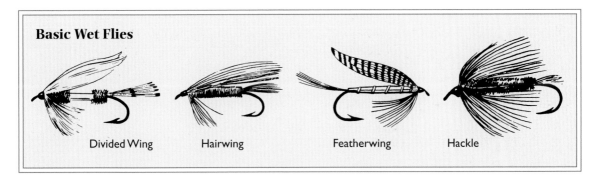

Basic Wet Flies

Divided Wing   Hairwing   Featherwing   Hackle

■ **Keel Fly:** The shank of the hook is weighted, causing the fly to ride upright in the water. The keel principle also has been applied to wet flies and streamers.

The budding fly fisherman who walks into a fishing-tackle store is sure to be overwhelmed by the display of artificial flies. Which patterns are best for his particular needs? Only experience can answer that question. However, here are 10 basic dry-fly patterns—and the most productive sizes—that should be found in every trout fisherman's fly box:

○ Light Cahill, Size 16
○ Gray Midge Hackle, Size 20
○ Black Flying Ant, Size 20
○ Red Variant, Size 14
○ Black Gnat, Size 12

○ Gray Wulff, Size 10
○ Blue Dun, Size 16
○ Adams, Size 12
○ Quill Gordon, Size 14
○ Jassid, Size 20

WET FLIES: Wet flies are tied to imitate submerged insects, either those that have fallen to the surface and drowned or those that are rising from the stream or lake bottom to the surface to hatch. Nymphs, which are classified as wet flies, are imitations of the larval or nymphal states of underwater insects that rise to the surface before hatching.

As with dry flies, there is a bewildering number of wet-fly patterns. However, most of them fall into one of four basic types. Here's a brief description of each type:

■ **Divided Wing:** Two prominent separated wings are tied at about a 30-degree angle from the shank of the hook. This type also has a wisp of hackle, body, and a stiff tail.

■ **Hairwing:** A wing of deer hair extends over the shank of the hook, a wisp of hackle, body, and a tail.

■ **Featherwing:** This type of fly has a swept-back wing of feather fibers, soft hackle, tapered body, and a sparse tail.

■ **Hackle:** This fly has soft hackle tied on at the head, which extends back over the built-up body all around the fly. It has a sparse tail.

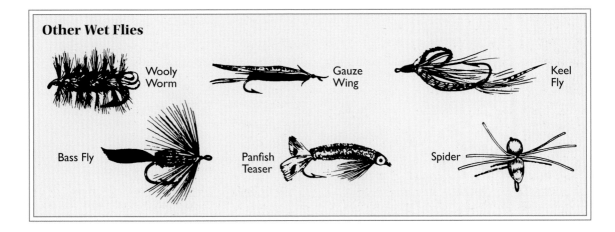

Other Wet Flies

Wooly Worm   Gauze Wing   Keel Fly

Bass Fly   Panfish Teaser   Spider

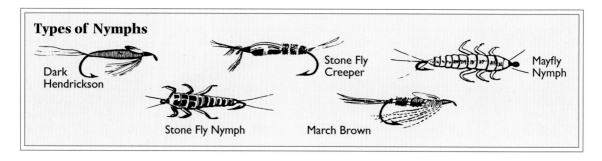

Types of Nymphs

Dark Hendrickson

Stone Fly Creeper

Mayfly Nymph

Stone Fly Nymph

March Brown

Here are 10 wet-fly patterns that should produce well for the trout fisherman:

○ Gray Hackle, Yellow Body, Size 10
○ Brown Hackle, Size 10
○ Coachman, Size 12
○ Royal Coachman, Size 12
○ Black Gnat, Size 14
○ Quill Gordon, Size 14
○ Blue Dun, Size 16
○ Light Cahill, Size 16
○ March Brown, Size 12
○ Ginger Quill, Size 16

NYMPHS: It is impossible to break down the various nymph patterns into broad classifications. However, most nymphs have the following basic characteristics: no wings, wisps of soft hackle at the head, a tapered body, usually of dubbed fur, and a sparse tail of a few feather fibers.

Here are 10 nymph patterns that no trout fisherman should be without:

○ March Brown, Size 12
○ Ginger Quill, Size 14
○ Yellow May, Size 12
○ Freshwater Shrimp, Size 8
○ Light Mossback, Size 6
○ Large Stone Fly, 2X long shank, Size 8
○ Large Mayfly, 2X long shank, Size 10
○ Caddis, 2X long shank, Size 10
○ Dark Olive, 2X long shank, Size 12
○ Montana, Size 4

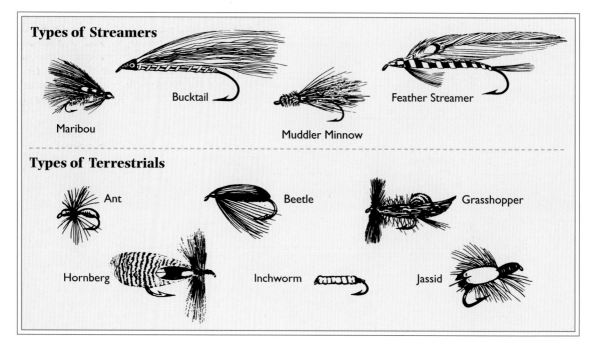

Types of Streamers

Maribou

Bucktail

Muddler Minnow

Feather Streamer

Types of Terrestrials

Ant

Beetle

Grasshopper

Hornberg

Inchworm

Jassid

STREAMERS AND BUCKTAILS: Streamer flies and bucktails are tied to imitate a minnow or other baitfish on which game fish feed. They are widely used in both fresh and salt water. Many saltwater streamers and bucktails, and some used in fresh water, have two hooks—the main hook, on which the dressings are tied, and a trailer hook. Streamers and bucktails are well known for producing big fish.

Streamers are tied with long wings of feathers. Bucktails are similar, but more durable, flies tied with wings of hair, usually deer hair. Most streamers and bucktails are tied on Size 8 and Size 10 long-shank hooks. Some have bodies that hide the shank of the hook, but in others the bare shank shows.

Here is a list of 10 of the most productive streamer patterns and 10 top bucktail patterns (best hook sizes are 6 to 12, unless otherwise noted):

Streamers
◦ Black Ghost
◦ Gray Ghost
◦ Supervisor
◦ Mickey Finn
◦ Black-Nosed Dace
◦ Red and Yellow
◦ Clouser Minnow
◦ Red and White
   Multiwing, Size 1
◦ Black Marabou
◦ White Marabou

Bucktails
◦ Black Prince
◦ Brown and White
◦ Black and White
◦ Red and White
◦ Mickey Finn
◦ Platinum Blonde, Size 1/0
◦ Strawberry Blonde, Size 1/0
◦ Brown Muddler Minnow,
   Sizes 1/0 to 10
◦ Black Woolly Bugger,
   Sizes 6 to 10
◦ White Marabou Muddler,
   Sizes 1/0 to 6

TERRESTRIALS: A class of artificial flies that is unique and deserves special mention is terrestrials—a group of flies, both wet and dry, that are tied to imitate insects that are born on land and then fly, jump, fall, crawl, or are blown into the water and become food for trout and other fish. Such insects include ants, grasshoppers, inchworms, beetles, houseflies, and others.

Among the most popular and productive terrestrial patterns are the Inchworm, the Black Ant (especially in very small sizes), and the Jassid, a fly that was developed in Pennsylvania and is particularly effective in limestone streams. It is tied on tiny hooks, with the best sizes being 18, 20, and 22.

BASS BUGS: If any form of fly fishing approaches the thrill of taking a wary trout on a dry fly, it is having a belligerent largemouth or smallmouth bass burst through the surface and engulf an enticingly twitched bass bug.

Bass bugs are fly-rod lures created to imitate such bass morsels as frogs, bees, dragonflies, mice, and anything else that looks like it would taste good to a bass or pike. Because of the size of a bass's mouth, these surface lures are tied on large hooks—size 4 to 2/0 in most cases. However, smaller versions of these bugs are made for panfish.

Most bass bugs fall into one of two categories: those with solid bodies (usually of cork, plastic, or balsa wood) and those with bodies of deer hair.

Many cork or balsa bugs have some hackle or bucktail at the tail to partly disguise the hook. Some have a perpendicular, hollowed-out surface so that when the angler jerks the rod tip the bug makes a popping sound that often brings a bass charging out of its lair. These bugs are called poppers. Others have a more streamlined body and are really designed to be twitched slowly rather than jerked.

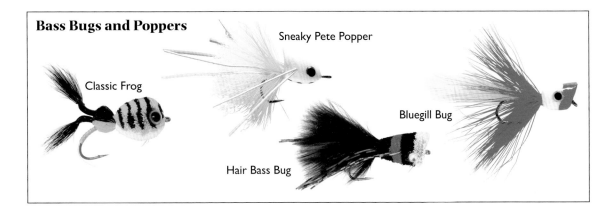

Bass Bugs and Poppers

Sneaky Pete Popper

Classic Frog

Bluegill Bug

Hair Bass Bug

NATURAL FOODS AND THEIR IMITATIONS

Fly tying is the art of imitating or suggesting numerous food forms—insects, minnows, crustaceans, and similar forage eaten by fishes—by dressing hooks with feathers, fur, wool, tinsel, latex, wire, and other suitable materials.

The following text provides a breakdown of the basic food forms fly tiers try to imitate. Get to know them, how they act in their own environment and for which fishes they form partial or principal diets. You don't have to be an entomologist to be a successful fly fisherman, but the more you know about these basic foods, the more fish you are going to find in your creel or live box.

Larva • A larva is the immature, wingless, and often worm-like form in which certain insects hatch from the egg, and in which they remain until the pupa or chrysalis stage. Grubs, caterpillars, and maggots are examples. Wet-fly larval imitations are fished underwater.

Pupa • A pupa is the intermediate, usually dormant, form assumed by insects after the larva stage, and is maintained until the beginning of the adult (dun or subimago) stage. Wet-fly pupa imitations are fished underwater.

Nymphs • The nymph, in the strictest sense, is the stage in the development of an insect when the rudimentary wings of the adult (imago or spinner) become visible. It is common practice, however, to use the word "nymph" to cover all forms of developing underwater insects. Normally fished below the surface as a wet fly, some nymph patterns are dressed to float.

Adult Insects • Imitations of adult insects (imagoes or spinners) generally have wings and are tied in dry-fly patterns for surface fishing and in wet-fly patterns for use underwater. Wets also are dressed to resemble small fishes and other natural foods.

Terrestrials • Among the lesser fish foods, terrestrials are land insects that, through one misadventure or another, wind up in the water to become forage for hungry fish. As a group, they include grasshoppers, beetles, ants, crickets, crane flies, inchworms, leafhoppers, and spiders. Imitations are fished on or in the surface film.

Midges • Entomologists use the word "midge" to identify a special order (*Diptera*) of minute, two-winged insects that include flies, mosquitoes, jassids, and gnats. To a fly fisherman, however, it refers to any very small artificial fly. Thus, it becomes a catch-all term for tiny caddis nymphs, mayflies, some of the terrestrials, and other minutiae. Midges are dressed in both wet and dry patterns.

Crustaceans • Since they form an important part of the diet of a number of fresh- and saltwater fish, these little creatures deserve attention. They include crabs, crayfish, prawns, scuds, sandbugs, shrimps, and sowbugs. Imitations are fished underwater.

Baitfish • Baitfish fall into the collective term "minnows," which include shiners, chubs, dace, silversides, darters, and sculpins. They are an extremely important source of food for sport and game fish. Bucktail and streamer imitations are built on hooks running from standard length to size 8 extralong shanks. Although some patterns can be worked on the surface with good results, they are normally fished underwater.

Other Fish Foods • This category is a smorgasbord of such goodies as mice, moths, frogs, eels, bloodsuckers, worms, dragonflies, and bees. Imitations are made of hollow deer, elk, and caribou hair, cork, balsa wood, pre-cast plastic, and Mylar tubing. For the most part, these are fished on the surface.

This Muddler Minnow streamer (*top*) was created to imitate a real live minnow (*bottom*). Normally fished underwater, the popular Muddler Minnow can also be worked on the surface.

Deer-hair bugs are, as you might expect, made of deer hair that is wound onto a hook and clipped to form the body shape of a mouse, large insect, and the like. These bugs are best fished very slowly. Weedless arrangements, usually stiff monofilament or light wire, are sometimes used.

CHOOSING THE RIGHT FLY: Selecting the correct fly to use at any given time is a problem that has both delighted and dumbfounded anglers since the dawn of this sport. Dry fly, wet, or streamer? What color? What size?

The answers to these questions can often be found in the water at your feet. Study it carefully, both at the surface and underneath. If insects are flying from the surface, you are in the middle of a hatch, and you should select a dry fly that imitates as closely as possible the color and size of the natural insects. If you see subsurface insects, choose a wet fly or nymph of similar size and color.

However, spotting and identifying natural insects may be difficult due to water conditions, the minute size of the insects, and the sparseness of the hatch. (A hatch occurs when aquatic insects rise from the stream or lake bottom and change from the larval stage to winged adult flies.) Also, the fisherman may not have the right size and color of artificials in his fly box.

There is also an easier way to pick the right flies. You

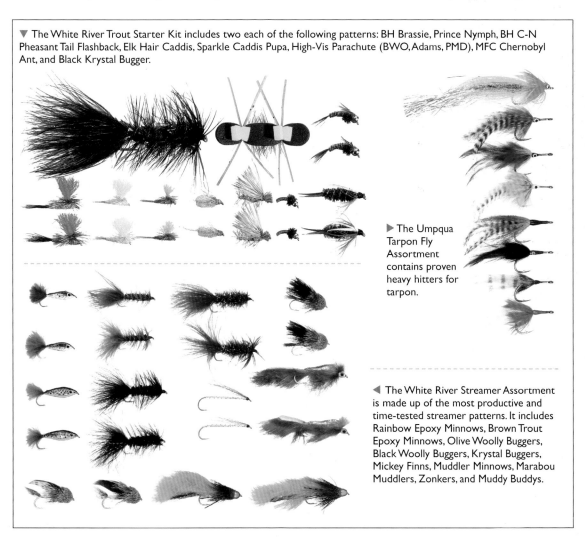

▼ The White River Trout Starter Kit includes two each of the following patterns: BH Brassie, Prince Nymph, BH C-N Pheasant Tail Flashback, Elk Hair Caddis, Sparkle Caddis Pupa, High-Vis Parachute (BWO, Adams, PMD), MFC Chernobyl Ant, and Black Krystal Bugger.

▶ The Umpqua Tarpon Fly Assortment contains proven heavy hitters for tarpon.

◀ The White River Streamer Assortment is made up of the most productive and time-tested streamer patterns. It includes Rainbow Epoxy Minnows, Brown Trout Epoxy Minnows, Olive Woolly Buggers, Black Woolly Buggers, Krystal Buggers, Mickey Finns, Muddler Minnows, Marabou Muddlers, Zonkers, and Muddy Buddys.

can let experienced fly fishermen make selections for you. It's an excellent way to get started with the right flies for either fresh or salt water. Several major outdoor outlets offer carefully selected assortments of flies for beginners as well as experienced fly fishermen. The accompanying fly assortments offered by Bass Pro, for example, have been recommended by veteran fly fishermen and will get you started with a good selection of the most productive flies.

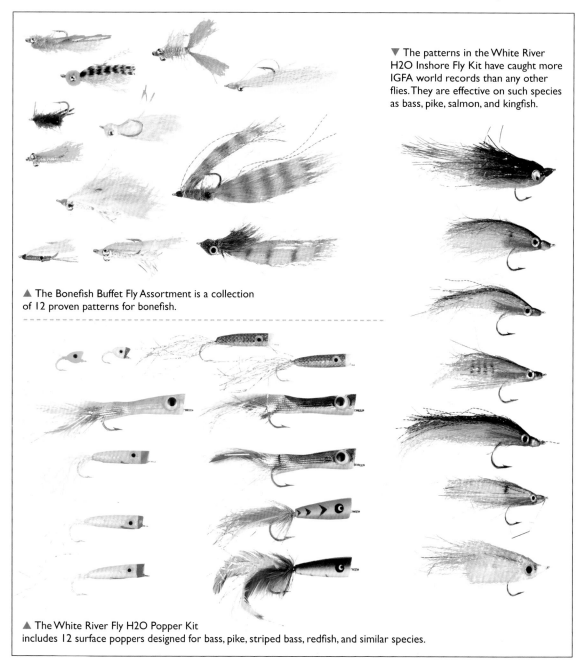

▼ The patterns in the White River H2O Inshore Fly Kit have caught more IGFA world records than any other flies. They are effective on such species as bass, pike, salmon, and kingfish.

▲ The Bonefish Buffet Fly Assortment is a collection of 12 proven patterns for bonefish.

▲ The White River Fly H2O Popper Kit includes 12 surface poppers designed for bass, pike, striped bass, redfish, and similar species.

Dolphin: A Fly-Fishing Favorite

Great opportunities for sight casting, vicious hits near the surface, and furious runs make the dolphin an exciting target for fly fishermen. You won't have time, however, to rig a fly rod when a school of dolphin suddenly explodes behind your boat. Rule No. 1: Always keep rigged fly tackle handy. An 8- or 9-weight rod and a reel with a good drag and at least 150 yards of 30-pound-test Dacron backing is an ideal outfit for dolphin. A floating weight-forward line with a 6- to 8-foot leader and a 20-pound-test tippet will round out the perfect fly tackle for dolphin.

Dolphin are not particularly fussy eaters. Almost any big streamer fly or popper cast to a dolphin will trigger a hit. The best flies, however, include Deceivers, Clouser Deep Minnows, Enrico's Pinfish, most tarpon flies, and any pattern that looks like a pilchard or ballyhoo.

How big a dolphin can you catch on fly tackle? In 2001, Nick Stanczyk—a 16-year-old high-school student from Islamorada, Florida—found out when he fought a 51½-pound bull for 5½ hours. Nick used a 9-weight rod and a 15-pound-test tippet. The dolphin shattered the old Florida state fly-rod record of 38 pounds set in 1995. Nick caught the dolphin on a pilchard imitation. The fish sounded several times in 600 feet of water and hovered on the bottom for more than 2 hours before the young angler was able to get it to the surface and within range of a gaff.

The heaviest dolphin ever landed on fly tackle was a 58-pounder caught on a 12-pound-test tippet by Stu Apte in Panama in 1964. The IGFA World Record dolphin is an 87-pounder caught in Costa Rica in 1976.

TYING FLIES AND BUGS

There are few pleasures in the sport of fishing that can match that of taking a trout, salmon, or other fish on a fly of your own creation. And there are other reasons for taking up this ancient art. On winter evenings, with the snow piled high outside and a bitter wind rattling the shutters, you can sit at the tying bench, reliving past fishing experiences and putting together the ingredients for future ones. And, of course, once you get the hang of it, you can tie respectable flies for a very small fraction of what you would pay for them in a store.

The following information from the late, well-known fisherman and expert fly tyer Tom McNally, and the accompanying illustrations, show the simple step-by-step procedures involved in tying the basic flies—streamers, wet flies, nymphs, and dry flies.

Writing of fly tying, a friend of mine described this ancient art as "the technique of fastening various materials on a hook to suggest real or fancied insects or food for the purpose of deceiving fish." That definition clears fly tying of the mysticism with which many would like to bury it. Actually, it's not difficult to turn out handsome, fish-catching flies. Anyone with a desire to learn can become a reasonably accomplished fly tyer. People with special aptitude can learn how to do it almost overnight.

Many years ago, I taught my wife to tie flies after three evening sessions at my worktable. Today, she shows me a trick or two. Some years ago, I taught my mother—who was looking for a hobby—to make shad flies and popping bugs. The ones she produced were sold in tackle stores. I don't know how many friends I've introduced to fly tying, and none failed to eventually turn out flies that were both attractive and fishable.

Fly tying was going on in Macedonia 2,000 years ago. A wasplike insect called hippuras was imitated by dressing a hook with purplish yarn and creamy hackles. The flies were floated, dry-fly fashion, on the Astraeus River. Ever since then, anglers have been using artificial flies—and many of those anglers have been tying their own. Judging from the growing interest in fly tying, fishermen will continue dressing their own hooks so long as there's fishing to be done. One doesn't have to be a watchmaker, surgeon, or engineer to tie flies. All that's needed is a little common sense and practice.

To become a professional or recognized fly tyer, of course, takes experience, and the intricacies of producing masterful flies would require a book-length treatise. But any beginner who absorbs the details here and studies the illustrations should be able to tie the simpler flies. Once big streamers and wet flies are mastered, and once you get the "feel" of the materials, the smaller and more complicated nymphs and dry flies can be attempted. The techniques are basically the same.

The Five Best Flies for Bass

We've all heard those familiar questions: If you were allowed only one book on a desert island, which would you pick? If you were allowed only one companion, who would you pick? Even more tragic, if you were allowed only five flies to use for bass, what would they be? Imagine the emotional consequences of such a question. In the event I was ever faced with such a terrible dilemma, I decided to ask several experienced fly-fishing dignitaries for their choices of the five best flies for bass. Their answers—especially now that two of them, Homer Circle and Nick Karas, have passed away—were priceless.

The first fisherman on my list was Jerry Gibbs, an old friend and longtime fishing editor of *Outdoor Life*. Here are Jerry's picks for five hot bass flies: Clouser Deep Minnow (Jerry likes the half-and-half, which is part Clouser and part Lefty's Deceiver); Sneaky Pete (one of Jerry's favorites for smallmouths); Gurgler (this Jack Gartside foam surface fly can be popped and softly gurgled, and it is deadly for both largemouths and smallmouths); Woolly Bugger (Jerry prefers his color combination, which is a maroon chenille body, black marabou tail, and grizzly hackle wound down on the hook shank to make the hackle fibers stick out at right angles); and Dahlberg Diver (which is Jerry's favorite, but he offers a tip: "Trim the deer or elk hair at the head to make it dive when you sharply pull the line, and then it will pop to the surface").

Next on my list was my friend John Randolph, editor emeritus and publisher of *Fly Fisherman* magazine. Wow, I thought, John has made fly fishing a lifetime career and his advice has to rank high on my list. While some experts are not too free with their secrets, John opened up for me with his choices: Clouser Deep Minnow (John's pick for both largemouths and smallmouths); Cup-Faced Yellow Popper (any brand will do, but John has a great modification—he attaches a No. 10 or 12 Zonker dropper rigged off the bend in the hook); Dahlberg Diver (he likes them all in various sizes and colors); Clouser Crayfish (a good producer for river smallmouths and largemouths); and Woolly Bugger (which is best with red-and-yellow rubber legs, and John uses it with and without the bead head, depending on water depth).

Jim Babb, editor emeritus and angling columnist for *Gray's Sporting Journal*, was my next call. Jim is one of the most knowledgeable fly fishermen I know. Here are Jim's picks: Tapply Hair Bugs (he likes them in yellow, red and white, and black, and uses sizes from No. 12 to 2/0); Dahlberg Divers (in full-dress frog colors and all black, usually fished on a sink-tip line); Gaines Frog Poppers ("Some of my Gaines poppers," says Jim, "are pretty chewed up, but still going strong after 30 years"); Big Woolly Buggers (he likes these flies with a Petitjean Magic Head in chartreuse, olive, or black); and Marabou Matuka Bullheads (this fly is most effective with lead eyes under the shank and Petitjean Magic Heads in mottled brown, olive, or black).

I thought I could see a pattern emerging in these choices until I recalled advice from Homer Circle, a familiar name to *Outdoor Life* readers. Homer got right to the point with an honest conclusion: "Having lived in Florida for 34 years, and tried fly fishing numerous times, I've found that the best way to conserve bass is to fly fish for them with wet flies! But, for catching the day's greatest total of smaller bass, I would not bet against a finger-size floating hair bug in black or yellow."

While remembering Homer's simple approach to selecting a fly for bass, I decided to visit Wendy Williamson, a fly-fishing guide in Hayward, Wisconsin. When not running rivers in her drift boat, Wendy and her husband run the Hayward Fly-Fishing Company. Wendy's specialties are smallmouths and muskies. Her top choices for bass started to sound familiar: Dahlberg Diver (green); Swimming Frog (green and black); Sneaky Pete (green head with black hackle); Craft Sculpin (rust color); and Tequeely (tinsel body with green legs).

At the time, I had never heard of a Tequeely, so I decided to check with a few more fishing guides. I called Nick Karas, a fly fisherman who had operated Saxatilis Charters in Orient Point, New York. Nick, a novelist who also wrote books on brook trout and striped bass fishing, went a step further and broke down his choices for both smallmouths and largemouths. For largemouths, Nick picked: Muddler Minnow (fished dry); Swimming Frog; Mickey Finn; Furry Hellgrammite; and Miller Moth

Bug. For smallmouths, he picked: Muddler Minnow (fished wet); Mickey Finn; Clouser Ultradeep Minnow; Clouser Crayfish; and Peck's Popper.

Did I have enough to boil down all this great advice into the five best flies for bass? Not yet. I wanted to ask one more fishing guide to be sure. I called Mike O'Brien, the editor of *Mid-Atlantic Fly-Fishing Guide* magazine and a Susquehanna River guide. "What are your best-producing flies for those Susquehanna bass?" I asked. Mike came back with a quick reply: Clouser Floating Minnow; Arbogast Fly Rod Hula Popper (weedless); Cramer Jailbait; Clouser Crayfish; and Gaines Skipping Bug.

Some of the same names kept popping up, but several of these flies were new to me. I had enough advice from the pros to come up with a list of their personal favorites, but what were the hot sellers in tackle shops? I had to know. I went a step further and contacted Bass Pro Shops and Cabela's. Katie Mitchell at Bass Pro responded quickly: "I checked with our product-development experts and here's the list of our best-selling flies." They include: Dahlberg Diver; Frog-Colored Popper (deer hair or cork); Bendback Minnow; and Clouser Deep Minnow.

David Draper at Cabela's called me and read a list of the best-selling flies for bass in that chain of stores: Enrico's Bluegill; Enrico's Perch; Peck's Popper Frog; Woolly Bugger; and Leadeye Leech.

I was finally satisfied with all the choices I could muster from these fly-fishing icons. I had uncovered a wealth of valuable advice for both novice and veteran fly fishermen. When I finished reviewing and tallying the choices, I definitely knew which flies could be called the five best flies for bass. Here are the winners:

Dahlberg Diver
Clouser Deep Minnow
Woolly Bugger
Clouser Crayfish
Swimming Frog

These five bass flies took top honors, but there were a lot of close second-place winners, including the Sneaky Pete, Muddler Minnow, and Peck's Popper. My best advice is to start using the top five flies, and then save your pennies to buy the rest of them, too.

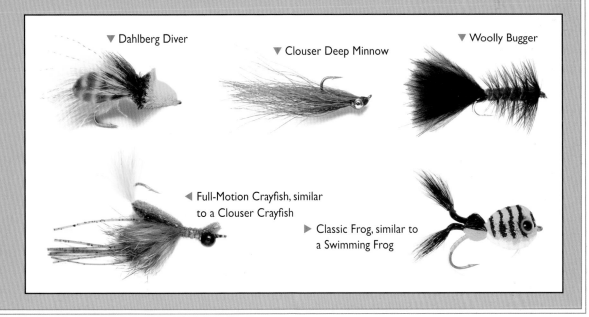

▼ Dahlberg Diver

▼ Clouser Deep Minnow

▼ Woolly Bugger

◄ Full-Motion Crayfish, similar to a Clouser Crayfish

► Classic Frog, similar to a Swimming Frog

FRESHWATER FLIES

▼ Woolly Bugger

▲ Tunghead
Soft Hackle
Pheasant Tail

▼ Sparkle Dun

▲ Royal Wulff

▼ Red Quill

▼ Schultzy's Red Eyes Leech

▶ Quill
Gordon

▶ Royal Coachman

▼ Mega Clouser

▼ Muddler Minnow

▼ Zonker

◀ Cone-Head
Muddler
Minnow

◀ Egg-Sucking
Hornberg

▶ Mosquito
Dry Fly

▶ Light
Hendrickson

▶ March Brown

▶ Black Gnat

▼ Gold-Ribbed
Hare's Ear Wet

▶ Light Cahill

▶ Gray Fox
Variant

▶ Hard Body
Ant Wet

▼ Bead-Head Zug Bug

▶ Blue Dun

▶ Adams

▶ Bully Bluegill
Spider

SALTWATER FLIES

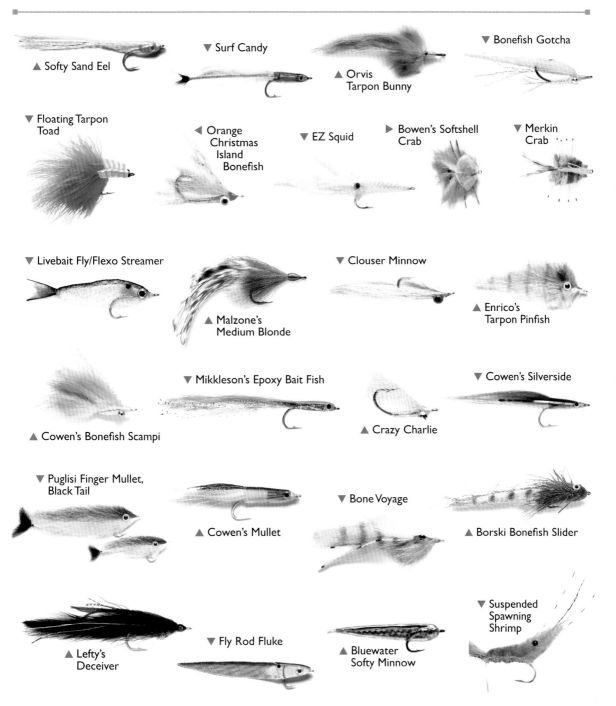

▲ Softy Sand Eel

▼ Surf Candy

▲ Orvis Tarpon Bunny

▼ Bonefish Gotcha

▼ Floating Tarpon Toad

◄ Orange Christmas Island Bonefish

▼ EZ Squid

► Bowen's Softshell Crab

▼ Merkin Crab

▼ Livebait Fly/Flexo Streamer

▲ Malzone's Medium Blonde

▼ Clouser Minnow

▲ Enrico's Tarpon Pinfish

▲ Cowen's Bonefish Scampi

▼ Mikkleson's Epoxy Bait Fish

▲ Crazy Charlie

▼ Cowen's Silverside

▼ Puglisi Finger Mullet, Black Tail

▲ Cowen's Mullet

▼ Bone Voyage

▲ Borski Bonefish Slider

▲ Lefty's Deceiver

▼ Fly Rod Fluke

▲ Bluewater Softy Minnow

▼ Suspended Spawning Shrimp

Why is fly tying growing in popularity? Because tyers save money? No, it's because fly tying is fun. Fishermen get more personal satisfaction out of gilling a bonefish or netting a trout with a hook they stuck into a vise and dolled up with feathers, tinsel, and fur.

That said, dollars can be saved by tying flies at home. A fly that would cost $4 at the tackle shop can be made for less than $1. You can get a start in the fly-tying game for less than $150. Your hunting friends will add duck, goose, turkey, pheasant, and grouse feathers to your stock of materials, as well as rabbit, fox, squirrel, and skunk fur. Deer, moose, elk, and bear skins are also useful. The hair or feathers from almost any wildlife can be used by a fly tyer.

The tyer's mainstay, however, is the common barnyard chicken. Its hackles are used in nearly every fly. The great bulk of fly-tying materials comes from material houses, but even direct purchase is inexpensive. If you wind up like most tyers, thoroughly wrapped up in the hobby, you'll take on enough materials in a few years to open your own supply house. But like other fly tyers, you wouldn't part with a hair of your motley assortment.

To begin, you'll need a few basic tools: a vise, hackle pliers, scissors, and a razor blade. In the early days, flies were tied by holding the hook between one's fingers, but in 1897, D. H. Thompson ended this by producing a lever-and-cam-type vise—the style most widely used and copied today. The vise is your single most important piece of equipment, and you should purchase a good one. Fine-pointed scissors will run about $10; the hackle pliers will be about $7. You may also want a bobbin to hold your spool of tying thread. It's inexpensive, frequently replaces hackle pliers, saves thread, and generally makes fly tying easier.

A beginner's basic materials should include thread (size 00 nylon), lacquer or head cement, hooks, hackles (neck, back, and breast feathers from roosters or gamecocks), duck-wing quills, mallard breast feathers, golden pheasant tippets, assortments of silk floss and chenille (a kind of tufted cord), tinsel, peacock herl from the "eyed" tail feathers of peacocks, and Mylar, a shiny metallic material that comes in narrow strips and in tube form. These materials, and more, usually are stocked by better sports and hobby stores. Some firms that deal in fly-tying materials supply catalogs, generally with photographs, that describe and price materials. The hook is the single most important factor in fishing, so tie your flies with the best.

■ Tools

A fly tyer needs only a few inexpensive tools. Let's take a look at each one and its use:

VISE: The most important device in the fly tyer's workshop, the vise is used to hold a hook securely and in the best position for the tyer to work around it. The most popular vise is the lever-and-cam type.

HACKLE PLIERS: These pliers are used to hold the tips

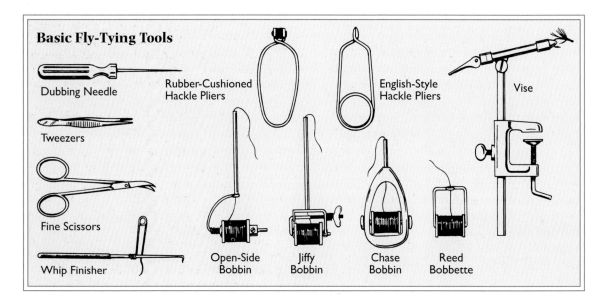

Basic Fly-Tying Tools

Dubbing Needle

Tweezers

Fine Scissors

Whip Finisher

Rubber-Cushioned Hackle Pliers

Open-Side Bobbin

Jiffy Bobbin

English-Style Hackle Pliers

Chase Bobbin

Reed Bobbette

Vise

of hackle feathers so that the tyer can wind the feathers onto the hook. Squeezing the sides of the pliers opens the jaws. There are two types: rubber cushioned and English style. Both work well. A surgeon's artery forceps also make adequate hackle pliers.

SCISSORS: Scissors are used to cut thread and other dressing materials and to perform other auxiliary duties. The best type is a pair of sharp, fine-pointed scissors with either straight or curved blades. Larger scissors are helpful for making hair bugs.

BOBBIN: A bobbin is a device that holds the spool of tying thread and hangs down from the hook, providing necessary tension on the thread while the tyer is at work. Most bobbins have a tube through which the thread is fed. The bobbin saves thread, and it is especially useful to tyers who have rough hands that tend to fray the thread.

DUBBING NEEDLE: A large, fairly heavy, sharp steel needle set in a handle of wood or plastic, a dubbing needle performs many duties, including picking out fur bodies to make them fuzzier, picking out wound-under hackle, dividing wings, separating strands of floss and the like, applying head lacquer, and making a whip finish.

Other helpful fly-tying tools and auxiliaries include tweezers, hackle gauge, magnifying glass, hackle cutter, hackle clip, hackle guards, whip finisher, head lacquer, and thread wax.

■ Streamers

Although you may have no use for large streamer flies, they are easy-to-tie jobs that are ideal for your first lessons in fly tying. Stick to streamers until you get the knack of handling the tools and materials. It won't be necessary to follow a standard pattern in tying one of these big streamers, so the need for specific materials is lessened.

Always prepare your working area, tools, and materials before starting a fly. Rig a bright lamp on your desk, and place a large sheet of white cardboard or white paper under your vise to provide a white background while you work on the fly. This makes the fly easier to see and the materials simpler to locate. You'll need a short length of chenille, floss, or wool for the body of your streamer. The preferred colors are black, white, yellow, or red. About six hackles 3 to 4 inches long will make the wing, which can be one of the colors mentioned, mixed colors, or natural brown or barred-grizzly feathers from Plymouth Rock chickens. Two or three extra hackles, colored differently than ones used in the wing, also will be needed.

Mount your vise at a comfortable height and clamp a size 2 hook on it. The tying thread must be started on the hook. Most tyers first wax the thread since this waterproofs it, helps it hold to the hook, and generally produces a stronger fly. However, waxing takes time, and I doubt that it's vital to the durability of a fly. I haven't waxed thread for years, and my flies stay together. I apply a generous portion of fly-tying cement to the hook shank, then wind the tying thread from the hook eye to the bend. The cement waterproofs the thread and locks it to the hook.

When you've reached the hook bend with your thread, cut off any excess, and then tie in one end of the chenille (floss or wool) by looping the tying thread over it tightly. Wind the thread back to the hook eye, and let the bobbin hang or attach hackle pliers to the thread to keep it taut. The body material can be wound to within $\frac{1}{16}$ inch of the hook eye, and tied off with the thread. The thread is looped in tight turns over the material to keep it in place. Be careful not to bring the body material all the way out to the hook eye or you'll have no room to tie off other materials or to form the fly's head. The excess body material is clipped off. Next comes the most difficult part of fly tying—attaching wings. Whether the fly is a streamer, nymph, wet, or dry, beginners usually have the most trouble with wings.

Choose from four to six hackles and use your fingernails to clean off some of the fuzzy fibers from the stems at the butt end of the feathers. Then, group the feathers in streamer-wing fashion and—holding them securely between two fingers of the left hand—place them in position on top of the hook, with the webby butts extending beyond the eye. Tie them in with tight loops of thread. Be sure to hold them tightly while tying. Otherwise, the hackles will turn on the hook and go in cockeyed. After making several tight turns over the butts, you can clip off the surplus.

The final step is hackling the head of the fly. The hackle feather (two or more may be needed to make a bushy fly) is wound around the hook so that the separate fibers flare outward like bristling hairs. This is the technique used in putting hackles on wet and dry flies. Good hackles are especially important on a dry fly because they make it float. Strip the web from the hackle feather, place it against the head of the fly at an angle, and secure with a few tight loops of thread. The hackle, gripped at the loose end by hackle pliers, should be turned around the fly two or three times. Then the thread can be wound over it once or twice, and the hackle tips can be cut off. The fly head is finished with several turns of tying

Tying a Streamer Fly

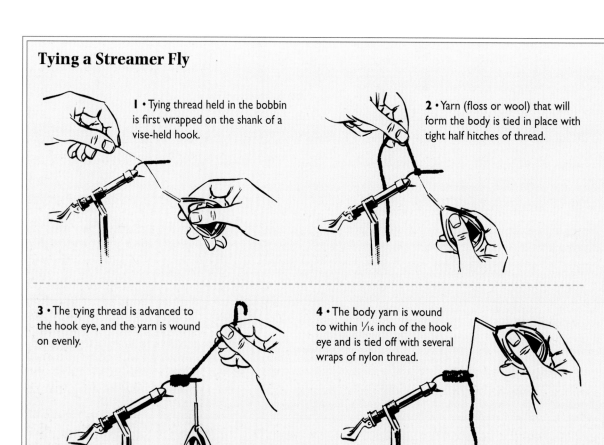

1 • Tying thread held in the bobbin is first wrapped on the shank of a vise-held hook.

2 • Yarn (floss or wool) that will form the body is tied in place with tight half hitches of thread.

3 • The tying thread is advanced to the hook eye, and the yarn is wound on evenly.

4 • The body yarn is wound to within 1/16 inch of the hook eye and is tied off with several wraps of nylon thread.

5 • After the thread tie-off, surplus yarn is snipped off close with fine-pointed scissors.

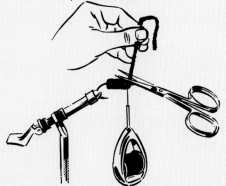

6 • Next, matched streamer feathers (four in this case) are tied in as shown here.

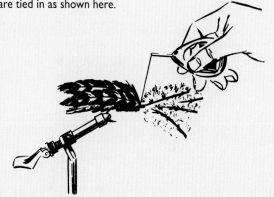

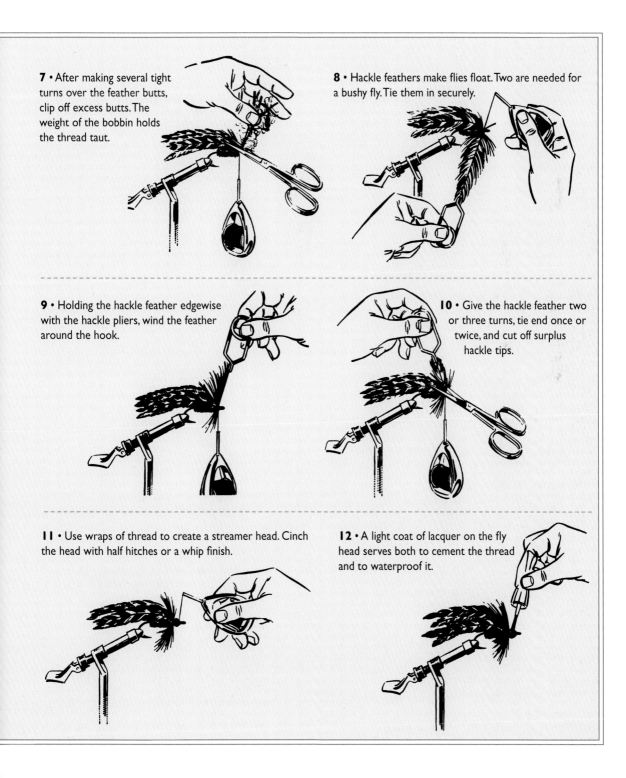

7 • After making several tight turns over the feather butts, clip off excess butts. The weight of the bobbin holds the thread taut.

8 • Hackle feathers make flies float. Two are needed for a bushy fly. Tie them in securely.

9 • Holding the hackle feather edgewise with the hackle pliers, wind the feather around the hook.

10 • Give the hackle feather two or three turns, tie end once or twice, and cut off surplus hackle tips.

11 • Use wraps of thread to create a streamer head. Cinch the head with half hitches or a whip finish.

12 • A light coat of lacquer on the fly head serves both to cement the thread and to waterproof it.

thread, and the thread is knotted off with a series of half hitches. Cement the head of the fly to waterproof it and keep knots secure. The whip-finish knot—identical to the one rod makers use in attaching guides—is better than half hitches, but it's a little beyond the beginner stage. Actually, half hitches, properly knotted and cemented, will keep a fly together indefinitely. The whip finish can be executed either manually or with the aid of a device called a whip finisher. For a look at both methods, see the end of this section.

The streamer is now finished, unless you'd like to paint "eyes" on it. This is easy to do with red, yellow, white, or black lacquer. You can buy small bottles of lacquer that have tiny brushes fixed to the caps. Most fly tyers paint their fly heads black. Lacquer dries in a few minutes. The fly's "eyes" are put on over the black base by dipping the blunt end of a fishing nail or wood match in light-colored lacquer and touching it to the head of the fly. As soon as that dries, a dark "pupil" is added. It's my opinion that such dolling up adds nothing to a fly's fish appeal, but it makes the fly more attractive to fishermen.

When you can tie one of these large streamers so it's proportioned correctly and won't come apart if you tug at a feather, you have mastered the fundamentals of fly tying. The methods you've learned in making this fly apply to any other pattern, including wets, nymphs, and dries.

The better streamers have tails, tinsel bodies, tinsel over chenille, wool, or floss, and perhaps colorful "cheeks" and "topping." The tying in of all these extras can be learned by following an advanced book on fly tying or watching an experienced tyer. Large streamers can be made with marabou feathers, bucktail hair, or saddle hackles. Either way, they're good for large trout, black bass, pike, walleyes, and saltwater species such as bonefish, striped bass, snook, and tarpon.

Wet Flies

A wet fly, whether bass- or trout-size, is tied much like a streamer, except that the wing material is usually cut from duck-wing quills or large turkey quills. (See step-by-step illustrations on next spread.) Other materials are red duck quill, silver tinsel, black silk floss, and red hackles.

Start your tying thread the same way you did when tying a streamer, only continue wrapping it around the hook to build up a tapered body. Cut a small section from the red duck quill and bind it down at the bend of the

hook with a few turns of thread. Be sure the tail is tied in tightly and is centered on top of the hook. Next, tie in a length of silver tinsel and several strands of black floss. The tying thread should be brought to the eye of the hook, and then the floss should be wrapped over the body, followed by the tinsel. The floss and tinsel are secured by thread at the head of the fly, and the surplus is trimmed off.

Attaching the wing is next. Select a pair of turkey quills and cut sections, one from each side of a feather, approximately half an inch wide. Place the two wing sections together, tips matched, curved sides facing. Grasp them firmly between your thumb and forefinger and place them on the shank behind the eye. (Pinching the wings firmly during the tying-on can't be overemphasized. When wings are poorly done, it's usually because they were not held firmly while being tied.) Bring the tying thread over the wings and down on the opposite side, sliding it slightly back between the fingers. Pinching the wings tightly, pull the thread down, following with several turns over the butts. The wing should appear, with the butts ready to be trimmed. The final step is tying soft red hackle behind the fly head, just like the big streamer.

Nymphs

Nymphs are the best flies for catching trout, and they're also good for smallmouth bass and panfish. One of the simplest nymphs to make is the "attractor" type, which doesn't imitate any particular live nymph but suggests several kinds of real nymphs.

Begin the nymph by tying a tail. Tail material can be fibers from a feather, sections of peacock herl or deer, or boar hairs. Pig bristle makes an excellent tail because it isn't broken easily by fish. A narrow section cut from a turkey feather, or olive or black duck quill, will serve to make the nymph's back or wing case. Tie it in just above the tail. A short length of tinsel and some wool yarn, chenille, or floss (drab colors) is put on next. Wind the tying thread back and forth over the shank, making a tapered body form, and then wind on the body material and tinsel, tying them off near the hook eye. The quill section is brought forward, covering the top half of the nymph's body, and is tied down at the hook eye with a few tight turns of thread. The surplus is trimmed. Spin a small, webby hackle around the head, tie off, and trim so fibers extend only from the underside of the nymph to simulate legs. I usually lacquer a nymph's head, but some tyers lacquer the body, too.

Tying a Nymph

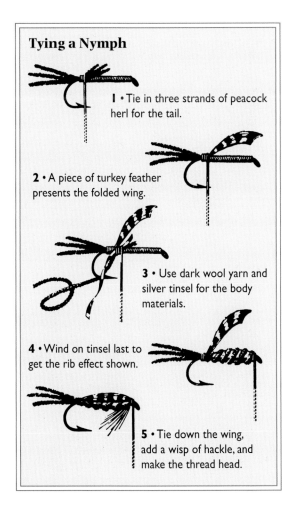

1 • Tie in three strands of peacock herl for the tail.

2 • A piece of turkey feather presents the folded wing.

3 • Use dark wool yarn and silver tinsel for the body materials.

4 • Wind on tinsel last to get the rib effect shown.

5 • Tie down the wing, add a wisp of hackle, and make the thread head.

▮ Dry Flies

The bivisible—invented by the late Edward R. Hewitt—is the easiest dry fly to build. The bivisible is made by winding stiff, dry-fly quality rooster neck hackles along the shank of a hook. Usually two or three hackles are needed to give a bivisible enough bulk to float well. The simplest way to start a bivisible is by tying the tip sections of a couple of hackles at the bend of a hook, allowing the tips to extend backward to form a tail. The tying thread is then brought forward to the hook eye, the hackles are turned around the hook tightly, and finally tied down at the hook eye. That's all there is to this all-hackle dry fly. You'll find that it's a fish-catcher, too.

Excluding salmon flies, dry flies with upright wings are the most difficult flies to tie. Don't attempt them until you've had experience at tying the other types, and then start by making simple patterns. If you concentrate on large dries, no smaller than hook size 6 or size 8, the work will come to you faster.

The materials used for dry flies are selected for flotation, and for resistance to water absorption. Chenille, for example, becomes heavy with water, so it's never used in a good dry fly. The hackles and tail are what float a fly, so the finest quality gamecock or rooster neck hackles should be used. Common dry-fly body materials include floss, raffia (fiber from the raffia palm), deer or moose hair, quill, peacock herl, and muskrat fur.

To make a basic Black Gnat dry fly, start the tying thread as usual. Cut a narrow section from each side of a matched, slate-colored, duck-wing quill. Place the wing sections together, curved sides out. Grasping them firmly

Tying a Dry Fly

1 • Wrap the hook shank with thread and then tie on the wings.

2 • Turns of thread anchor the wings. After that, tie on the tail.

3 • Next, tie in black yarn and wind it forward to the wings.

4 • Tie on the hackle feather and wind it on edgewise.

5 • Trim off the surplus hackle, and tie and lacquer the fly head.

Tying a Wet Fly

1 • Start the wet fly by wrapping the thread to build up a tapering, rounded body.

2 • The tail of the fly is cut from a duck's wing feather and tied centered on top of the hook.

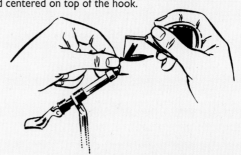

3 • The finished tail is shown here. The body material ready for use includes one strand of tinsel and three threads of black floss.

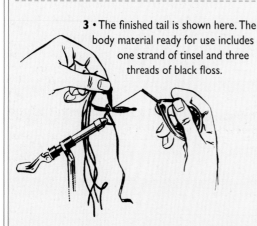

4 • After bringing the tying thread to the eye of the hook, wrap the floss and hold it by a thread loop while you wind the tinsel.

5 • Tie down the floss tinsel with thread near the hook eye. Then, snip off the surplus.

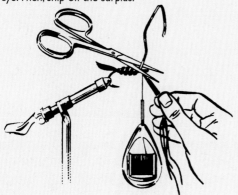

6 • For wings, cut two matched sections from each side of a turkey wing feather and then tie with the tips matched (hidden by thumb here).

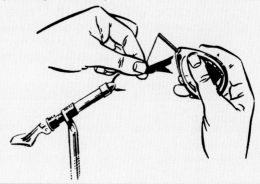

7 • After pinching the wings firmly, use several wraps of thread to cinch the fly wings in place.

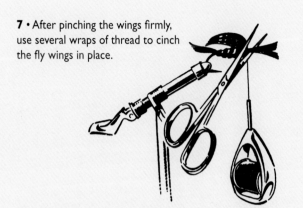

8 • Snip off the butt fragments of the turkey-feather wings close to the shank of the hook.

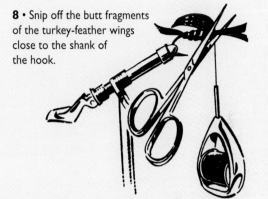

9 • Tie a soft, red hackle feather at the head and then wind it on edgewise as shown in the next illustration.

10 • Hackle pliers grip the feather tight for edgewise winding. Tie down the stem of the hackle feather and cut off the excess.

11 • Use wraps of thread to wind and tie off the head. Cinch with half hitches or a whip finish.

12 • A light coat of lacquer serves both to cement the thread and to waterproof it.

Tying a Cork Bug

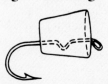

1 • Make a slit in the cork body, fill the slit with cement, and press the cork into position on the hook shank.

2 • Tie four to six neck hackles behind the cork body.

3 • Wind on two or three soft hackles to form the collar, tie them off, and cement the windings.

between the thumb and forefinger, place them on the hook over the eye and bring the thread over the sections and down, making several tight turns. Still holding the sections firmly between the fingers, raise them erect, bring the tying thread in front of them, and make enough turns against the wing bases to keep them upright. Spread the wings

Tying the Whip Finish

Budding fly tyers that are confronted with illustrations of how to tie a whip finish may be inclined to switch to golf. Though this knot looks complicated, it can be mastered in about 10 minutes of practice once the basic steps have been learned. The whip finish is undoubtedly the neatest way to finish off a fly. It is practically invisible, even on tiny dry flies.

There are two ways to make the whip finish—manually (that is, with the fingers alone) or with the aid of an ingenious little device called the whip finisher.

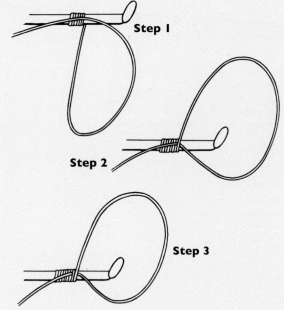

Without the Tool: Here's how to do it manually (for purposes of clarity, the accompanying illustrations show the knot itself, without the finger manipulations, which are impossible to show in detail and which the tyer will pick up with a bit of practice).

Grasp the thread (which is hanging down from the hook) with the last three fingers of the left hand, about 6 inches below the hook. Position the right hand so that its back is facing the tyer, and grasp the thread 2 inches down from the hook with the first two fingers and thumb. Twist the right hand to the right and forward so that the palm is facing upward. There is now a loop in the thread (Step 1).

With the left thumb and forefinger (which are free), grasp the left-hand side of the loop, and begin to wind it around both the hook and the return portion of the loop (Step 2). Use the right hand to help the left in making one complete turn around the hook (Step 3).

Make about six complete turns around the hook and the return part of the loop, making the first half of each turn with the left hand and the last half with the right hand.

After the last turn is completed, hold the loop

Step 1

Step 2

Step 3

apart and wrap thread between them to the opposite side of the hook, reversing to describe a figure eight between the sections. Tie in a few stiff black hairs or some suitable hackle fibers for a tail. Cut off the excess tail fibers, then tie in black silk floss and bring the tying thread forward to the front of the wings. A glossy black hackle feather (two may be needed) is tied in front of the wings. Secure the hackle feather with several turns of thread. Then, use hackle pliers to grasp the tip of the hackle and take a turn or two in front of the wings and two or three turns in back. Catch the hackle tip with tying thread and bind it down. Cut off the surplus end of the hackle feather. Finish the fly with a small, neat head made with the tying thread. Lacquer the head. That's all—your first winged dry fly is finished. Your second dry fly will be easier than the first, the third easier still, and so on until you begin to feel skilled.

■ Cork Bugs

You can buy cork bodies in many different shapes and sizes, or you can shape and size your own from a large piece of cork using a razor blade and an emery board or small file. Be sure to sand the body smooth so that you get a good finish when you paint it. Here are the basic steps in making a cork-bodied bug:

Place a hump-shanked hook (available at most tackle-supply outlets) in the vise, coat the shank with liquid cement, and wrap the part that is to be covered by the cork body with tying thread.

With a razor blade, make a slit in the cork body, fill the slit with cement, and press the cork into position on the hook shank. Give the cork body two coats of liquid cement, clear enamel, or wood sealer, and let it dry.

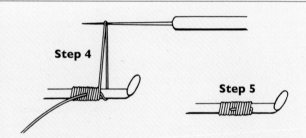

vertically taut with the left hand, and with the right hand insert into the loop, parallel to the hook, a dubbing needle (or a toothpick). Raise the dubbing needle until the loop is held taut by it (Step 4).

Then, with the left hand, pull on the free end of the thread, contracting the loop until the needle rests on the head of the fly. Remove the needle, pull the thread tight, and clip it off close (Step 5). The whip finish is now complete. The winding should be coated with head cement.

With the Tool: The whip finisher ties the same exact knot but eliminates the somewhat complicated finger manipulations. Here is how to use it:

Take the tool in the right hand, and place it near the hook and parallel to the hook shank. Run the thread from the hook around the spring retainer (Step 1).

Bring the end of the thread back near the fly, and with the tool's nose hook pick up the thread between the fly and the retainer (Step 2).

Now, keeping the thread taut with the left hand and in line with the fly, position the nose of the tool as close to the fly hook as possible—in fact, the fly hook can rest in the curve at the base of the tool's nose hook.

Rotate the tool clockwise around the hook shank, causing the thread to wind around both the hook and itself. Try to keep the windings tight up against one another. Make about six such turns (Step 3).

Keeping the thread taut, remove it from the tool's nose hook, and pull the thread with your left hand until the spring retainer is drawn up to the hook. Remove the retainer, pull the thread tight, and trim it off close to the windings. Apply head cement.

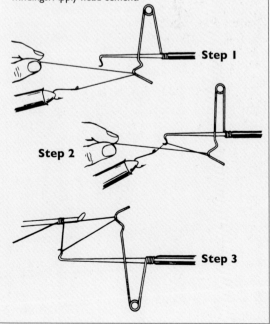

Tie to the shank of the hook, behind the cork body, four or six neck hackles (badger is a good choice) so that they flare out well and thus give a lifelike action when on the water.

Wind on two or three soft hackle feathers to form the collar, tie them off, and cement the windings. Paint the cork body with enamel of whatever color suits you, and paint on the eyes.

NATURAL FRESHWATER BAITS

Live bait is the real thing! Even the most avid purist would concede that live bait, when properly presented, is one of the deadliest of all lures. Many times, however, live bait is incorrectly rammed onto a hook. When this happens, the bait does not act naturally, may die quickly, and will likely turn away lunkers that grew big by learning how to recognize food that doesn't look right.

Live bait will only appear natural if placed on the hook correctly, and this depends on how you plan to fish it. You wouldn't, for example, hook a minnow behind the dorsal fin if you plan on trolling. Minnows just don't swim backward. Let's take a look at the popular baits and learn how to hook them.

Even though garden worms and night crawlers will take most species of fish, they must still be presented differently. A worm washed into a stream, for example, would drift with the current, so it should be fished that way. Hook it once through the collar or girdle with both ends free to drift naturally, fish it with no line drag, and let the current do the work. The worm should look strung out, bouncing along quickly through riffles and slowly through pools.

Using worms for panfish requires a different tack. Generally, the panfish angler is still-fishing, so natural presentation is less important. A single worm should be used and threaded about three times on the hook. If you're bothered by nibblers, use only a piece of worm and thread it on the hook, covering the point and barb completely.

Night crawlers are effective on bass, and many fishermen still-fish for bass with the big worms the same way they would for panfish. Actually, bass prefer a moving bait and anglers would catch more big bass if they cast and retrieved night crawlers slowly along the bottom. Hook the worm by running the point of the hook into its head, bringing the point and barb out an inch below the head. Rigged this way and retrieved slowly, a night crawler will appear to be crawling on the bottom.

Next on the list of most common live baits are minnows, from 1-inchers for panfish to 8-inchers for big fish.

There are two ways of hooking a live minnow, and how an angler intends to fish determines which one to use.

When trolling or fishing from a drifting boat, run the hook upward and through both lips of the minnow. The lip-hooked bait will move through the water on an even keel and look natural.

If you're still-fishing from an anchored boat or shoreline, hook the minnow just behind the dorsal fin. Be careful not to run the hook too deep or it will hit the spine and kill the bait. Hooked just behind the fin, a minnow can swim freely and for a surprisingly long time. There is no hook weight near its head or tail to throw off its balance.

Frogs rank as another excellent bait. Stick with the small frogs, however, such as leopard and green frogs. An old sock makes a fine frog carrier, and frogs are easy to find along any shoreline or riverbank during the summer. There is only one good way to hook a live frog and that is under the jaw and up through both lips. Cast it out and let the frog swim freely, or use a twitch-and-pause retrieve. A lip-hooked frog will stay alive for a long time. A frog can also be hooked through one of its hind legs. A hook through a frog's leg, however, will destroy some leg muscles, limiting its natural movement.

The crayfish, often called crawfish, is another top bait for bass and trout. The problem is that crayfish are often difficult to find. The best way to hunt them is at night in shallow water that has a rocky or gravel bottom. A crayfish's eyes will glow reddish in the beam of a flashlight. The light seems to freeze them and they can be easily picked up. The best way to hook a crayfish is to run the hook up, through, and out the top of its tail. Cast into rocky shorelines or streams, they'll account for big trout, bass, and walleyes.

Salamanders or newts also take bass, trout, and similar species. Finding salamanders isn't hard. They like small springs and streams. They're active at night and easily spotted with a flashlight. Salamanders are fragile and must be hooked carefully. Use a fine-wire hook and run it through the lips or the tail. Salamanders produce best when drifted along stream and river bottoms.

Natural Freshwater Baits

Natural Baits	Species of Fish
Minnows	Largemouth and smallmouth bass, trout, pickerel, pike, walleyes, perch, crappies, rock bass
Earthworms	Trout, white bass, rock bass, perch, crappies, catfish, sunfish, whitefish
Night crawlers	Largemouth and smallmouth bass, trout, pickerel, pike, walleyes, muskies, catfish, sturgeon
Crickets	Trout, crappies, perch, rock bass, sunfish
Grubs	Trout, crappies, perch, rock bass, sunfish
Caterpillars	Trout, largemouth and smallmouth bass, crappies, perch, rock bass, sunfish
Crayfish	Smallmouth bass, walleyes, trout, catfish
Hellgrammites	Trout, largemouth and smallmouth bass, walleyes, catfish, rock bass
Nymphs (mayfly, caddis fly, stone fly, and others)	Trout, landlocked salmon, perch, crappies, sunfish
Grasshoppers	Trout, largemouth and smallmouth bass, perch, crappies
Newts and salamanders	Largemouth and smallmouth bass, trout, pickerel, rock bass, walleyes, catfish
Frogs	Largemouth and smallmouth bass, pickerel, pike, muskies, walleyes
Wasp larvae	Perch, crappies, sunfish, rock bass
Suckers	Pike, muskies, smallmouth and largemouth bass
Mice	Largemouth and smallmouth bass, pike, muskies
Freshwater shrimp (scud)	Trout, smallmouth and largemouth bass, perch, crappies, rock bass, sunfish
Dragonflies	Largemouth and smallmouth bass, crappies, white bass, rock bass
Darters	Trout, largemouth and smallmouth bass, walleyes, pickerel, crappies, rock bass
Sculpins	Largemouth and smallmouth bass, walleyes, pickerel, rock bass
Salmon eggs	Trout, salmon
Cut bait (perch belly, etc.)	Pickerel, pike, muskies, largemouth and smallmouth bass, walleyes
Doughballs	Carp, catfish

The most popular live baits have been covered here, but there are still others worth mentioning. The hellgrammite, for example, ranks high with bass and trout. Water insects, hellgrammites average 1 to 2 inches long and can be caught in most streams by simply turning over rocks and holding a net just downstream from the rock. The hellgrammite has a hard collar just behind the head and this is where the hook should be inserted.

The nymph, an underwater stage of the aquatic fly, is still another top bait, particularly for trout. Nymphs differ in the way they behave. Some crawl on rocks, others climb shoreline growths, and still others float downstream. They will all eventually hatch into flies, but it is during this nymphal period that they can be effectively used as bait. There are two ways to put nymphs on a hook. They can be completely threaded—running the hook from the rear, through the body, and up to the head—or they can be simply hooked once just behind the head.

Grasshoppers also work well, and finding them is no problem. Most grassy fields are loaded with 'hoppers. Using a butterfly net, you should be able to fill a box quickly. It's easier to catch them at dawn and dusk. During midday, they are most active and spooky. There are several varieties of grasshoppers and nearly all of them take fish. It's best to use a fine-wire hook, running it down and through, behind the head.

Baiting Game

Worms, earthworms, and night crawlers are the most popular baits. Night crawlers come to the surface at night. They like warm and damp and dewy weather. Prowl around your lawn, a golf course, or a park after dark. Use a flashlight, but not one with a bright beam, which will spook worms. Cover the lens with red cellophane if necessary. Usually worms you will spot will only be partly out of their holes. Quickly press your finger at the spot where the tail enters the ground and grab the worm with the other hand.

Natural Freshwater Baits

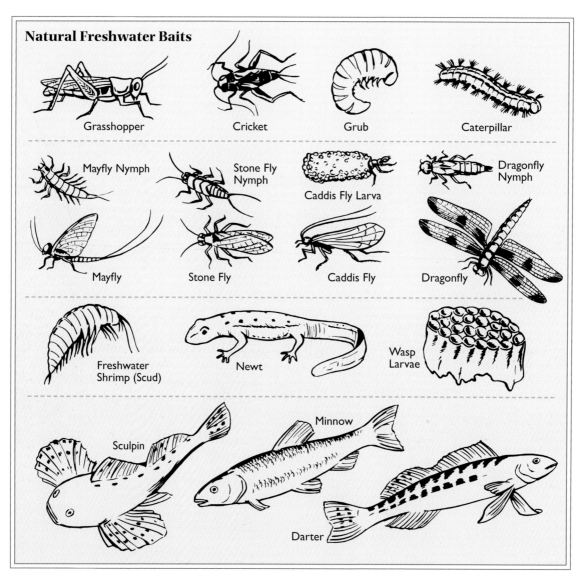

Grasshopper

Cricket

Grub

Caterpillar

Mayfly Nymph

Stone Fly Nymph

Caddis Fly Larva

Dragonfly Nymph

Mayfly

Stone Fly

Caddis Fly

Dragonfly

Freshwater Shrimp (Scud)

Newt

Wasp Larvae

Sculpin

Minnow

Darter

Crayfish and Hellgrammite Rigs

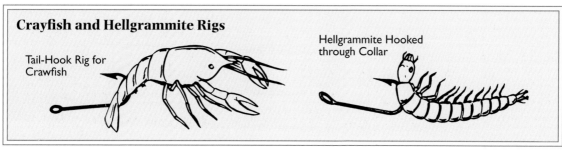

Tail-Hook Rig for Crawfish

Hellgrammite Hooked through Collar

Worm Rigs

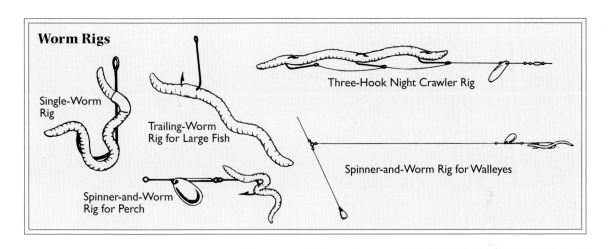

Single-Worm Rig

Trailing-Worm Rig for Large Fish

Three-Hook Night Crawler Rig

Spinner-and-Worm Rig for Perch

Spinner-and-Worm Rig for Walleyes

Minnow Rigs

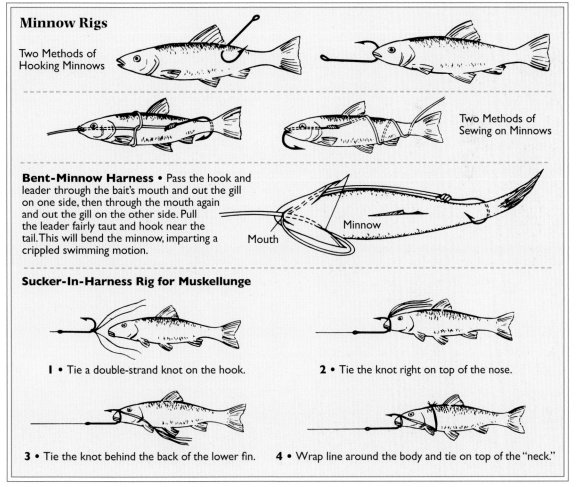

Two Methods of Hooking Minnows

Two Methods of Sewing on Minnows

Bent-Minnow Harness • Pass the hook and leader through the bait's mouth and out the gill on one side, then through the mouth again and out the gill on the other side. Pull the leader fairly taut and hook near the tail. This will bend the minnow, imparting a crippled swimming motion.

Mouth

Minnow

Sucker-In-Harness Rig for Muskellunge

1 • Tie a double-strand knot on the hook.

2 • Tie the knot right on top of the nose.

3 • Tie the knot behind the back of the lower fin.

4 • Wrap line around the body and tie on top of the "neck."

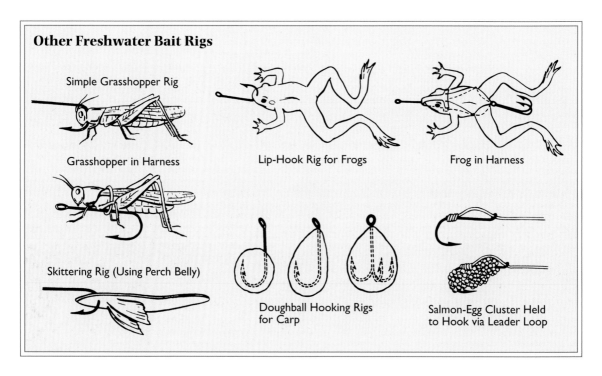

Other Freshwater Bait Rigs

Simple Grasshopper Rig

Grasshopper in Harness

Lip-Hook Rig for Frogs

Frog in Harness

Skittering Rig (Using Perch Belly)

Doughball Hooking Rigs for Carp

Salmon-Egg Cluster Held to Hook via Leader Loop

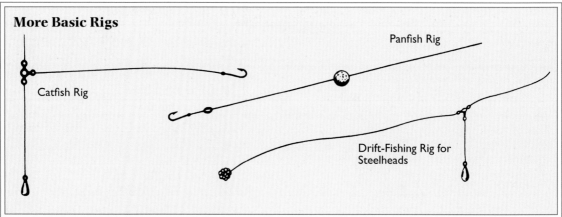

More Basic Rigs

Panfish Rig

Catfish Rig

Drift-Fishing Rig for Steelheads

▓ Big Shiners for Big Bass

Nearly all bass experts agree that fishing a live shiner is one of the most effective ways to catch the biggest bass of your life. Like most things, however, it's not as easy as it sounds.

Your first problem may be finding 10- to 12-inch shiners. If your bait shop doesn't have them, you'll have to catch them in back bays and river pools. You

can chum for shiners with oatmeal and bread crumbs and catch them with doughballs on a No. 12 or 14 hook. You'll need at least two dozen for a day of bass fishing.

Shiners are most productive when fished along shorelines or close to floating vegetation such as lily pads or hyacinths. The standard rig will have two hooks—a treble hook through the lips of the shiner, and a trailing single or treble hook in the tail of the bait or held along-

Get a Plan for Bass

Most of my bass fishing trips many years ago ended the same way. After an early morning burst of energy trying to find some big bass, I would get frustrated and turn to crappies and bluegills. I'd catch plenty of panfish, but never a bragging-size largemouth or smallmouth. My problem was a common one. I never fished with a plan.

The spring season can be the best time to fish for bass, but don't think you can just go out and flog the water and catch a big largemouth. Here's the plan that has worked for me. It's simple and will work every spring.

First, don't think spring is too cold for bass fishing. In fact, you can catch bass all winter long, but they really turn on when daytime temperatures hit the 50s. If it's early in the spring, use spinner baits and fish points and deeper shorelines in water 4 to 8 feet deep. You will find bass here before they move into the shallows.

It's also a good idea to concentrate on the weather fronts during the spring months. The best day will be the last day before a cold front. Check your weather forecast and plan to fish just before a storm. Once the cold front passes, go home. You will not likely have good fishing until it warms up again.

Invest in a water thermometer. You may occasionally catch a bass in 40-degree water, but you won't get consistent action until water passes the 50-degree mark. When water climbs to between 60 and 70 degrees, you will get some hot bass action. The key is to find the right water during spring. During summer, when water temperature rises, remember to use the reverse tactic. You will now have to look for cooler water.

There are other ways to find warmer water during spring. Fish the sunny side of the lake first, where water will warm up more quickly. You can also look for creek mouths, where the water running into a lake will sometimes be warmer. If you're picking a lake to fish, pick the smaller waters, which are likely to warm up first. It will also be easier to find the hot spots on a small lake where fishing pressure will probably be lighter.

Look for the right kind of bottom. If it's legal to fish for spawning bass in your state, look for them on sandy or gravel bottoms. Spawning bass don't spawn on soft muddy bottoms or solid rocks.

When the water warms up, you will start to find bass in the shallows. You should now begin to concentrate your fishing around flooded timber, brush, and stumps. If the bass are about to spawn, the big females will move into this kind of water first. Work the edges with spinner baits, weedless jigs, and plastic worms. Remember to check your state regulations, however, before you take bass off the beds.

If it's legal to fish for spawning bass, use a catch-and-release philosophy. Replace your treble hooks with single hooks and pinch down the barbs. You will be able to easily release all bass without harm. This is not the time to use bait, which will likely be swallowed and inflict injury. These tactics will work for both largemouth and smallmouth bass. On smallmouths, I've had good success with gold or silver spoons with a single hook. For largemouths, buzzbaits are especially effective. Cast them around cover and keep them moving.

Don't wait until the temperature climbs and bass begin to get lethargic and finicky. Fish for them now, when they're hungry.

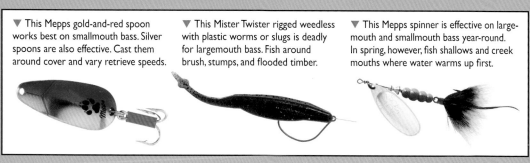

▼ This Mepps gold-and-red spoon works best on smallmouth bass. Silver spoons are also effective. Cast them around cover and vary retrieve speeds.

▼ This Mister Twister rigged weedless with plastic worms or slugs is deadly for largemouth bass. Fish around brush, stumps, and flooded timber.

▼ This Mepps spinner is effective on large-mouth and smallmouth bass year-round. In spring, however, fish shallows and creek mouths where water warms up first.

The Catfish Challenge

Catfish and .22-rimfire rifles have a lot in common. Both are great equalizers of sportsmen of all ages. Plinking with a .22 or catching a mess of catfish is just plain fun. It's apparent that the rest of the world has also discovered that catfish taste good. This ugly fish has become so popular that it is now raised commercially on catfish farms and it's rare to see a supermarket that doesn't sell Cajun-spiced catfish fillets. If you haven't gone catfishin' in a while, now may be the time to try it again.

You won't need a lot of expensive fishing tackle to catch a catfish. Just about any rod and reel will work fine. Where you fish and what you use on the end of your line is more important than the tackle in your hand. Nearly all rivers and lakes hold catfish, but there are certain places to look first.

Tailrace waters below dams where currents from two turbines collide, for example, are good spots to try for catfish. For this kind of water, tie a three-way swivel onto your line. On one swivel eye, attach a 6-inch length of line and a sinker. On the remaining eye, tie an 18-inch leader with a baited hook. Almost any kind of bait will catch a catfish, but live minnows might work best for this tailrace fishery, especially where the current will be the slowest. If you prefer a more relaxed fishing trip, find some small streams and rivers. Look for deep holes and drop-offs. Cast upstream and let your bait bounce off drop-offs and into the bottom of those holes.

You will also find catfish at the mouths of small feeder creeks, where worms, grubs, and other food wash into the river. Work the edges of muddy water with your bait. Catfish frequently feed better at night. Mark these hot spots with a jug so you can find them easier in the dark.

What makes a good catfish bait? Almost everything! I've heard of fishermen using small mice, diced laundry soap, rotten meat, hot dogs, and other strange baits. Fortunately, there are easier baits to find and use. If you prefer, you can use worms, hellgrammites, crayfish, small carp, minnows, and even small sunfish. If cut bait is your choice, you can use chunks of carp, sunfish, or almost any kind of meat. Oily fish attract catfish faster and more effectively than other baits.

You can also use commercially available blood baits, as well as chicken and beef livers. You can create stink baits for catfish. Cut baits and dead minnows, for example, can be left in the sun to rot. When they start to smell so bad that you don't even want to touch them, put them on a hook and you'll catch a catfish.

Catfish may be one of the ugliest fish that swims, but they make up for it at the dinner table. There is nothing better than fried catfish. Catfish have dorsal and pectoral spines that are as hard as nails, so handle them carefully. Getting punctured from a catfish can be a painful experience.

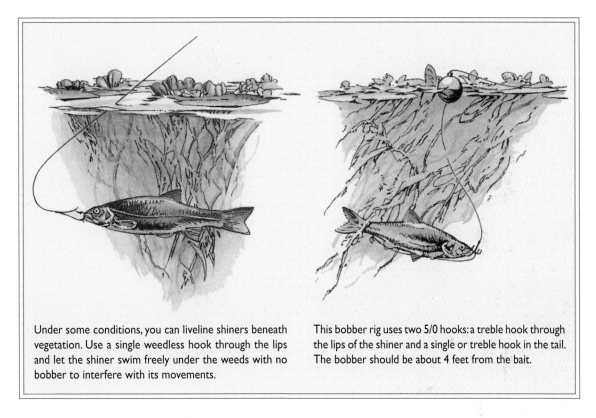

Under some conditions, you can liveline shiners beneath vegetation. Use a single weedless hook through the lips and let the shiner swim freely under the weeds with no bobber to interfere with its movements.

This bobber rig uses two 5/0 hooks: a treble hook through the lips of the shiner and a single or treble hook in the tail. The bobber should be about 4 feet from the bait.

side the tail with a rubber band. A bobber big enough to keep an active shiner from dragging it under water should be placed 3 to 4 feet above the bait.

Don't try to cast this half-pound bait overhand. Lob it underhand against shoreline vegetation and let the shiner take over. The fish will try to seek cover in the growth, and its movements will be telegraphed through the action of the bobber. When your shiner is motionless, jerk it back into action with a twitch or two of your rod tip.

The Best Tracking Line

Here's a neat trick: You may find it easier to track a shiner if you use a leader and a white level floating fly line with some backing on your conventional reel. The white fly line will be much more visible than monofilament. It will also be easier to track a bass when it picks up your bait.

If the bobber starts to bounce and jump on the surface, you'll know a big bass is after the shiner. Do nothing until that bobber goes down and stays down. A bass will grab the shiner around the middle and slowly swim away.

Begin counting as you watch your line move toward open water. As you count, slowly begin to reel in all slack until your rod tip is pointing in the direction the line is moving. Use your judgment here, but when your count is between 20 and 30 and all slack is out of your line, set the hook solidly.

Don't try to set the hook too quickly—you'll jerk the bait away from the bass. You have to allow enough time for the bass to pick up the shiner, swim away from the weed growth, and turn the shiner around in its mouth. Bass, like most other fish species, will swallow a live bait headfirst. You can also use circle hooks and you won't have to set the hook. As your line tightens, just lift your rod and the bass will hook itself.

You're after big bass, so leave your light tackle at home. Your best bet is a medium-weight rod with a conventional reel loaded with 20- to 30-pound-test line.

NATURAL SALTWATER BAITS

Natural baits are no less important in salt water than they are in fresh water. That fact is well known to anyone who has seen a school of bluefish slash viciously into a horde of mossbunkers or a tuna or sailfish ravaging a ballyhoo bait.

What natural saltwater baits should you use and when? Those are questions that only time and experience can help you answer accurately. Generally, you will find that it pays to use any bait that is prevalent when and where you are fishing. A few discreet questions at a bait shop in the fishing area will go a long way toward helping you choose a productive bait.

How you rig a saltwater bait can be a vital factor. The primary consideration in rigging most baits is to make them appear as lifelike as possible, whether they are to be trolled, cast out and retrieved, or bounced on the bottom.

The accompanying illustrations show proven ways to prepare and rig the most popular baits used in salt water.

Florida Bait Bomb

One of the most exciting and productive ways to fish the inshore waters of Florida is to chum the patches of coral for yellowtail snappers, groupers, or the dozens of other species that live and hunt for food in these reefs. Every catch is a colorful surprise.

Captain Glen Miller, a charter captain for more than 30 years in the Florida Keys, and his mate, Brooks Gregory, are masters at chumming these patches. Glen knows how to position and anchor his boat so that the current will carry his chum to the fish living on the coral. If the current is too strong, the chum might pass over the patch and might not get close enough to pull fish into the chum. Once Glen has his position and current figured out, he starts to chum with a mixture of sand, chum, and oats. Within 10 or 15 minutes, small fish begin to appear, darting in and out of the chum.

Glen cautions about over-chumming. Put out too much chum and you will end up feeding the fish instead of catching them. Ladle out a handful of chum, and then wait until all the chum is out of sight before tossing out more. You can also place a frozen chum block in a mesh bag and hang it near the transom. Wave action will gradually thaw and release the chum automatically.

Now is the time to use Florida bait bombs. Some Florida captains call them bait balls or chum balls instead. Call them whatever you want, but these bombs are deadly and catch fish. Once Glen has a good slick working, he puts a piece of cut bait on a hook and centers it in the mixture of water, sand, chum, and oats. The mix is now formed into a snowball shape and packed firmly. The bait bomb is ready for fish.

Glen strips off about 12 yards of line from the reel, so there is no drag when he tosses the bait ball into the slick. The ball is allowed to drop slowly back into the slick. The ball puts out a small cloud of chum with the piece of cut bait in the middle. The fish will follow the chum and find the bait when the ball finally breaks apart in the current. A fish, usually a yellowtail snapper or one of many species of grouper, will invariably hit the bait. These Florida reefs harbor a great variety of fish. It is not uncommon to catch a dozen different species on one coral patch.

The bait bomb is only one trick Florida captains use to bring fish to the boat. While building a chum slick, some fishermen will also have two live grunt baits on the bottom and two live pilchards, one off an outrigger and another on a kite rod. More often than not, a big grouper will take a grunt on the bottom rig near the surface and a kingfish will nail the live pilchards.

This technique for using bait or chum balls is a strategy that should work anywhere a fisherman is trying to entice fish into a chum slick. It's so effective that commercial yellowtail fishermen use it in Florida. In northern coastal waters, weakfish and bluefish are two good targets for the Florida bait bomb.

Natural Saltwater Baits

Species of Fish	Natural Baits and Lures	Recommended Methods	Hooks
Albacore	Feather lures	Trolling	7/0
Amberjack	Strip baits, feathers, spoons, plugs	Trolling, casting	6/0 to 9/0
Barracuda	Baitfish, plugs, feathers, spoons	Trolling, casting	1/0 to 8/0
Bass, channel	Mullet, mossbunker, crabs, clams, spoons, plugs	Casting, still-fishing, trolling	6/0 to 10/0
Bass, sea	Squid, clams, sea worms, crabs, killie	Drifting, still-fishing	1/0 to 5/0
Bass, striped	Sea worms, clams, eels, metal squids, plugs, jigs, live mackerel	Casting, trolling, drifting, still-fishing	2/0 to 8/0
Billfish (sailfish, marlin, swordfish)	Balao, mackerel, squid, bonito, strip baits, feathered jigs	Trolling	4/0 to 12/0
Bluefish	Rigged eel, cut bait, butterfish, plugs, spoons, feathers	Trolling, casting, drifting, still-fishing	3/0 to 8/0
Bonefish	Cut bait (mainly sardines and conch), flies, plugs, spoons	Casting, drifting, still-fishing	1/0 to 4/0
Bonito	Feather lures, spoons	Trolling	4/0 to 6/0
Codfish	Clams, crabs, cut bait	Still-fishing, drifting	7/0 to 9/0
Dolphin	Baitfish, feather lures, spoons, plugs, streamer flies	Trolling, casting	2/0 to 6/0
Eel	Killie, clams, crabs, sea worms, spearing	Still-fishing, drifting, casting	6 to 1/0
Flounder, summer	Squid, spearing, sea worms, clams, killie, smelt	Drifting, casting, still-fishing	4/0 to 6/0
Flounder, winter	Sea worms, mussels, clams	Still-fishing	6 to 12 (long shank)
Grouper	Squid, mullet, sardines, balao, shrimp, crabs, plugs	Still-fishing, casting	4/0 to 12/0
Haddock	Clams, conch, crabs, cut bait	Still-fishing	1/0 to 4/0
Hake	Clams, conch, crabs, cut bait	Still-fishing	2/0 to 6/0
Halibut	Squid, crabs, sea worms, killie, shrimp	Still-fishing	3/0 to 10/0
Jack Crevalle	Baitfish, cut bait, feathers, metal squid, spoons, plugs	Trolling, still-fishing, casting, drifting	1/0 to 5/0
Mackerel	Baitfish, tube lures, jigs, spinners, streamer flies	Trolling, still-fishing, casting, drifting	3 to 6
Perch, white	Sea worms, shrimp, spearing, flies, spoons	Still-fishing, casting	2 to 6
Pollack	Squid strip, clams, feather lures	Still-fishing, trolling	6/0 to 9/0
Pompano	Sand bugs, jigs, plugs, flies	Trolling, casting, drifting, still-fishing	1 to 4
Porgy	Clams, squid, sea worms, crabs, mussel, shrimp	Still-fishing	4 to 1/0
Rockfish, Pacific	Herring, sardine, mussels, squid, clams, shrimp	Still-fishing, drifting	1/0 to 8/0
Snapper, mangrove	Cut bait, shrimp	Trolling, still-fishing, drifting	1/0 to 6/0
Snapper, red	Shrimp, mullet, crabs	Trolling, still-fishing, drifting	6/0 to 10/0
Snapper, yellowtail	Shrimp, mullet, crabs	Trolling, still-fishing	4 to 1/0
Snook	Crabs, shrimp, baitfish, plugs, spoons, spinners, feathers	Casting, drifting, still-fishing	2/0 to 4/0
Sole	Clams, sea worms	Still-fishing	4 to 6
Spot	Crabs, shrimp, baitfish, sea worms	Still-fishing	8 to 10
Tarpon	Cut bait, baitfish, plugs, spoons, feathers	Trolling, casting, drifting, still-fishing	4/0 to 10/0
Tautog (blackfish)	Clams, sea worms, crabs, shrimp	Still-fishing	6 to 2/0
Tomcod	Clams, mussels, shrimp	Still-fishing	6 to 1/0
Tuna, bluefin	Mackerel, flying fish, bonito, squid, dolphin, herring, cut bait, feathered jigs	Trolling	6/0 to 14/0
Wahoo	Baitfish, feathered jigs, spoons, plugs	Trolling, casting	4/0 to 8/0
Weakfish	Shrimp, squid, sea worms	Still-fishing, casting, drifting, trolling	1 to 4/0
Whiting, northern	Sea worms, clams	Still-fishing, drifting, casting	4 to 1/0
Yellowtail	Herring, sardine, smelt, spoons, metal squids, feather lures	Trolling, casting, still-fishing	4/0 to 6/0

How to Rig Saltwater Baits

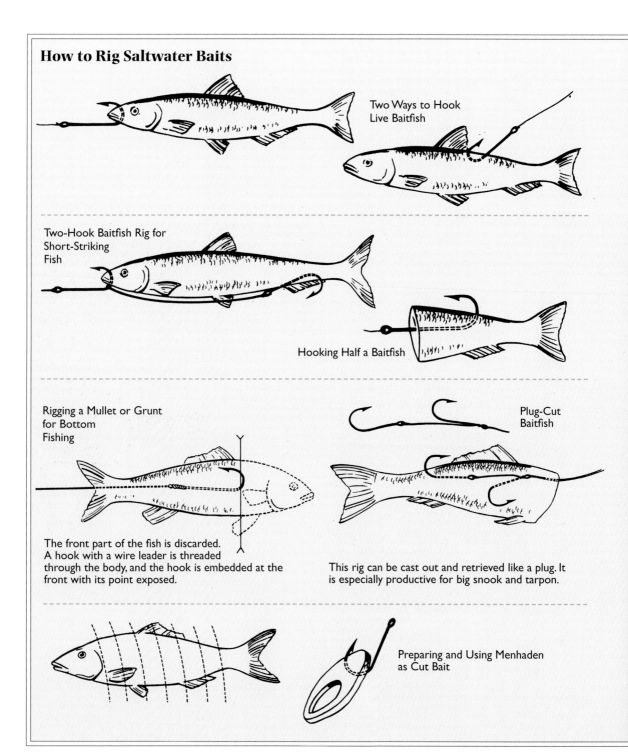

Two Ways to Hook
Live Baitfish

Two-Hook Baitfish Rig for
Short-Striking
Fish

Hooking Half a Baitfish

Rigging a Mullet or Grunt
for Bottom
Fishing

Plug-Cut
Baitfish

The front part of the fish is discarded.
A hook with a wire leader is threaded
through the body, and the hook is embedded at the
front with its point exposed.

This rig can be cast out and retrieved like a plug. It
is especially productive for big snook and tarpon.

Preparing and Using Menhaden
as Cut Bait

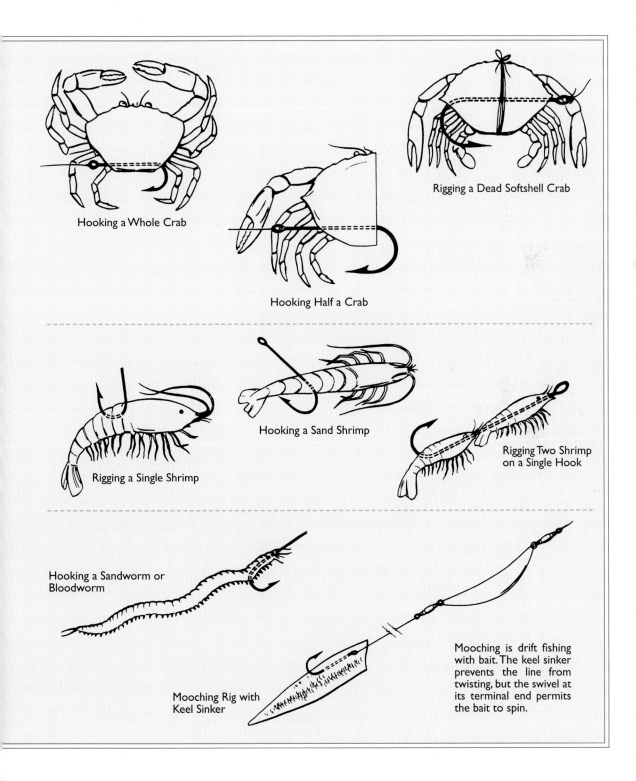

Hooking a Whole Crab

Hooking Half a Crab

Rigging a Dead Softshell Crab

Rigging a Single Shrimp

Hooking a Sand Shrimp

Rigging Two Shrimp
on a Single Hook

Hooking a Sandworm or
Bloodworm

Mooching Rig with
Keel Sinker

Mooching is drift fishing
with bait. The keel sinker
prevents the line from
twisting, but the swivel at
its terminal end permits
the bait to spin.

Saltwater Bait Rigs

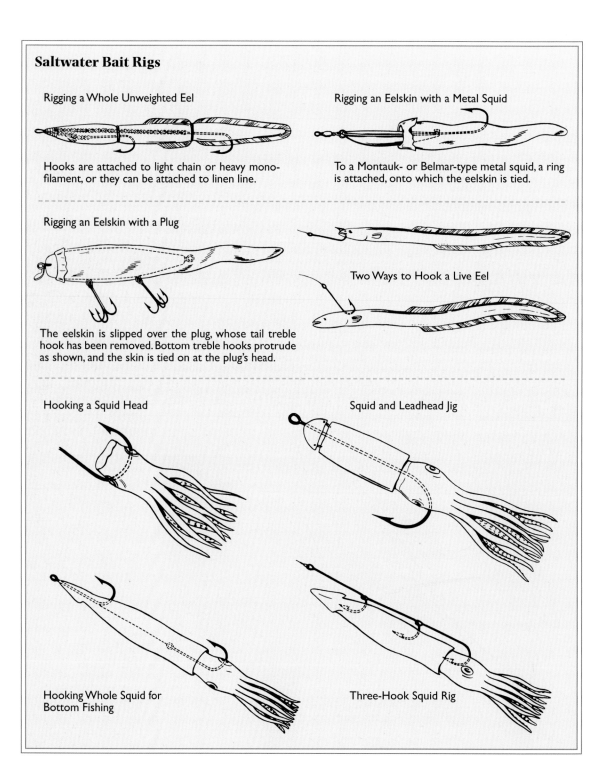

Rigging a Whole Unweighted Eel

Hooks are attached to light chain or heavy monofilament, or they can be attached to linen line.

Rigging an Eelskin with a Metal Squid

To a Montauk- or Belmar-type metal squid, a ring is attached, onto which the eelskin is tied.

Rigging an Eelskin with a Plug

The eelskin is slipped over the plug, whose tail treble hook has been removed. Bottom treble hooks protrude as shown, and the skin is tied on at the plug's head.

Two Ways to Hook a Live Eel

Hooking a Squid Head

Squid and Leadhead Jig

Hooking Whole Squid for Bottom Fishing

Three-Hook Squid Rig

Saltwater Trolling Rigs

Rigging a Mullet for Trolling

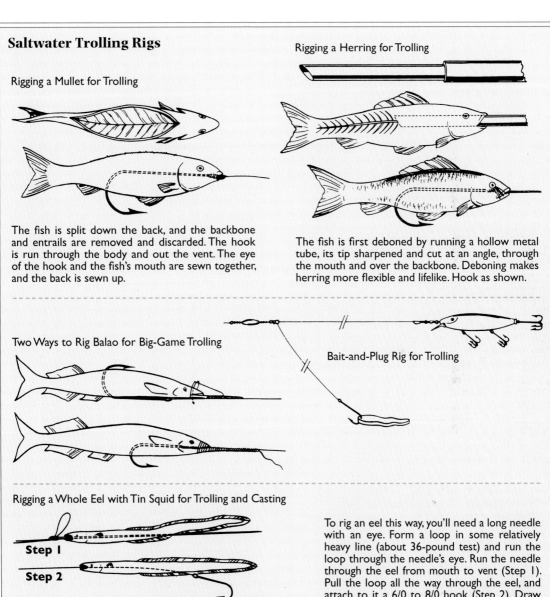

The fish is split down the back, and the backbone and entrails are removed and discarded. The hook is run through the body and out the vent. The eye of the hook and the fish's mouth are sewn together, and the back is sewn up.

Rigging a Herring for Trolling

The fish is first deboned by running a hollow metal tube, its tip sharpened and cut at an angle, through the mouth and over the backbone. Deboning makes herring more flexible and lifelike. Hook as shown.

Two Ways to Rig Balao for Big-Game Trolling

Bait-and-Plug Rig for Trolling

Rigging a Whole Eel with Tin Squid for Trolling and Casting

Step 1

Step 2

Step 3

Step 4

Step 5

To rig an eel this way, you'll need a long needle with an eye. Form a loop in some relatively heavy line (about 36-pound test) and run the loop through the needle's eye. Run the needle through the eel from mouth to vent (Step 1). Pull the loop all the way through the eel, and attach to it a 6/0 to 8/0 hook (Step 2). Draw the protruding line and hook shank into the eel (Step 3). Take a small block-tin squid, run its hook through the eel's head (or lips) from bottom to top, and tie the line to the eye on the flat surface of the squid (Step 4). With light line, tie the eel's mouth shut, make a tie around its head where the hook protrudes to prevent the hook from ripping out, and make a similar tie around the vent (Step 5).

Buoy Bouncing for Tripletail

It's a screwy way to catch a tripletail in Florida Bay, but then this is a screwy fish. It looks as if it belongs in a farm pond in Indiana, but it behaves like a dolphin in Florida's offshore waters.

This wasn't the first time I had fished for tripletail with Richard Stanczyk, so I knew enough to hold onto the pint-sized console of Richard's flats boat as we raced, slalom style, around the crab-pot buoys on Florida Bay. He was looking for the telltale shadow of a tripletail lurking under the buoys. I braced myself because I knew what was going to happen. When Richard spotted a tripletail, he would make a hairpin turn and throttle down so abruptly that an unsuspecting passenger would darn near get thrown out of the boat!

Richard Stanczyk owns Bud N' Mary's Marina in Islamorada in the Florida Keys and he's a pro at catching tripletail, a fish that actually has three tails and tastes so good that it's one of the few fish Richard will eat. Tripletail love floating structures and the only structures that float in Florida Bay are the crab-pot buoys from August to April, which is the crab season. Tripletail live in these waters year-round, but it's tough to find them without the buoys.

I had my grandson, Steven, with me on this fishing trip with Richard. We left Islamorada about 8:00 a.m. and made a long run across the flats to Sprigger Bank, where we caught lots of sea trout and mackerel. Running across the flats of the Florida Keys at 20 to 30 miles per hour in a couple of feet of water is always a unique experience. Richard seems to know when to swerve right or left without a jarring collision into a sandbar.

From Sprigger, we ran out to the crab pots to hunt tripletail. I don't want to mislead anyone into thinking that tripletail lurk under every pot. We usually look at 15 to 20 pots for every tripletail we find. I had to make several trips with Richard before I learned how to spot that telltale shadow of a tripletail. We always have at least two spinning rods rigged with live shrimp baits.

We got lucky that day and found several tripletail. One of them, in spite of some sloppy casting on my part, refused to spook and took my shrimp. As soon as I got the tripletail away from the pot, I gave the rod to my grandson and he finished the fight. These big, slab-sided fish can exert an unusual amount of pressure for their size. The fish was at least 7 pounds.

With much more casting accuracy, Richard caught several more tripletail. When a fish is located, you have to cast the shrimp as close as possible to the buoy and the tripletail without snagging the buoy or spooking the fish. This is not as easy as it sounds. The shrimp has to be close enough to the tripletail to lure it away from the buoy. If everything works, the tripletail will attack the shrimp and you will have a tough fight on your hands.

Steven Sparano, left, and Richard Stancyzk show off a good-size tripletail from Florida Bay. The key is to accurately cast a live shrimp close enough to a tripletail to lure it away from a buoy. There are no secret hot spots. Just look for the crab pots. Tripletail will almost always attack a shrimp.

Tackle requirements for tripletail are simple. All you need is a medium-weight spinning outfit with 10- or 12-pound-test line and a livewell full of live shrimp. Richard uses a 2/0 hook with some split shot just above the eye of the hook. He likes to break the tail off the shrimp to keep it from spinning when it's retrieved past the nose of a tripletail. Breaking the tail off a live shrimp also releases juices into the water, which act as an attractant. You can also leave the head on the shrimp or break it off. Richards prefers to leave it on.

On occasion, you can find tripletail under floating debris in offshore waters, but don't count on targeting this species in the ocean. When you find tripletail offshore, sometimes in a cluster of three or four fish, consider yourself very lucky.

In Florida Bay, tripletail can range up to 10 pounds, though the world record is 42 pounds, 5 ounces. The limit is two fish a day and the minimum size is 15 inches. There are no secret hot spots. Just look for the crab pots.

WHAT STRIPED BASS EAT

Striped bass are not fussy eaters and the list of baits that can be used is extensive. The following baits have all been used successfully to catch stripers: menhaden (bunker), herring, mullet, eels, sand eels, spearing, killies, clams, seaworms, squid, and crabs.

1 • Menhaden: Menhaden, more commonly called bunkers or mossbunkers, rank high on a striper's menu. In the Northeast, bunkers are usually found all spring, summer, and fall, especially inshore around inlets, rivers, and bays. As water temperatures drop in late fall, bunkers will migrate to more southerly waters. Bunkers can grow up to 16 inches and the big bunkers will attract and hold bigger striped bass than smaller bunkers or "peanut bunkers."

Nothing beats a live bait for stripers and live lining a frisky bunker is an exciting way to entice a bass into a strike. Rigging a bunker is easy. Run a 2/0 to 8/0 hook on a 4- or 5-foot, 40- to 50-pound leader through the nose of the bunker. A bass, like almost all fish, will swallow its prey headfirst. A nose-hooked bunker will generally get more hookups. But you have to allow enough time for a bass to turn the bunker around and eat it headfirst.

You can also run a hook just in front of or to the rear of the dorsal fin of the bunker. There are several schools of thought on the best place to hook a bunker. If you're drifting fast, the nose-hooked bunker is best. In calm water, hooking it near the dorsal fin may be a better option. You can also hook the bunker near the tail, but that generally keeps the bunker from swimming naturally. If you get a stubborn bunker that won't swim deep, use an egg sinker about 5 feet from the bait. A barrel swivel will keep the sinker from sliding down to the bunker. The weight of the egg sinker will depend on the size of the bunker and depth and current of the water you're fishing. A 3-ounce sinker will generally keep a bunker from swimming on the surface.

When an angler gets a pickup on a live bunker, it's important to let the striper run with the bait, giving it enough time to turn it in its mouth. It's best to count to 10 slowly, then reel in all slack until your line is taut and your rod tip is pointing toward the fish, and then strike hard. If you think you're missing too many strikes, rig a stinger hook near the bunker's tail. Some fishermen run the stinger hook through the bunker and near the anal vent. I think this keeps the bunker from swimming naturally. I prefer to hold the stinger hook along the bunker's body with a rubber band. The stinger hook should be a 1/0 or 2/0 treble hook.

If you're not getting enough hits on that 40- or 50-pound leader, try a 25-pound-test fluorocarbon leader. Fluorocarbon material is much less visible in the water and it's more durable and abrasion resistant than monofilament. If the stripers you are fishing for have been hammered all season, you might want to try a leader that won't be easily detected. When you use a lighter leader, such as fluorocarbon, make certain you constantly check it for frays and weak spots, especially if you're fishing around rock piles or jetties.

Never feel shortchanged if you can't get live bunkers. Dead or alive, bunkers are excellent baits for bass. Fresh-cut bunkers are always productive, but make sure it's fresh bunker and not old bait that has been refrozen several times. I never realized the importance of fresh bait until I fished the Cape May rips in New Jersey several years ago. Everything was right. The bass were there, the tide was right, and the water temperature was perfect. We were chunking with cut bunker and failing miserably. A nearby boat, however, was into stripers whenever I looked over. When the boat left the area, they came alongside and gave us the rest of their fresh bunker bait. The bunkers had never been frozen.

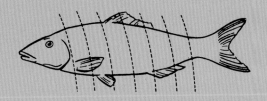

Preparing and Using Menhaden as Cut Bait

WHAT STRIPED BASS EAT (continued)

We started to catch stripers as soon as we baited up with fresh bait. I would never have believed it could make such a difference.

I also learned something else that day. When a buddy cuts up a fresh bunker and gives you any piece except the head, he is not your friend. If you want to catch a big bass, use the bunker head. Run your hook through the skin at the top of the head just over the eyes. Big bass will swallow the whole head. When you get a pickup, don't try to set the hook too quickly. Let him eat it. When you feel a steady pull, set the hook hard. Properly hooked, a bunker head will also stay on your hook longer.

Let's talk about hooks. Most bait fishermen have come to realize the value of circle hooks. It's no longer a secret that circle hooks are an effective catch-and-release phenomenon. Circle hooks will invariably hook fish in the corner of the mouth, making it much easier to release a fish with minimal handling and no harm.

What makes the circle hook different? First, and this is important, don't try to set a circle hook when a fish hits. In fact, don't try to set the hook at all. Let the fish chew on your bait until the hook does its job. A fish will take the bait into its mouth and start to swim off. At this point, if you try to set the hook, you will probably yank it right out of the fish's mouth because of the hook's design. Let the fish run and allow your line to tighten. When the line becomes taut, the eye of the hook will actually clear the mouth, but when the fish continues to swim away, the hook will rotate in the fish's mouth and the fish will hook itself in the corner of the jaw.

To overcome the urge to set the circle hook, try fishing "dead stick," which means leaving your baited rod in a holder and not touching it until there's a solid bend in the rod and it's time to reel the fish in. When the fish is landed, a simple twist with needlenose pliers on the shank will free the hook, or you can use a dehooking device. Releasing small fish over water means you won't even have to touch the fish with your hands.

The circle hook should prove effective for most bait-fishing situations, especially live lining big bunkers, herring, and eels for striped bass. Remember, however, that this dead-stick technique, which lets the fish hook itself, is only for circle hooks. With traditional hooks, I still recommend the 10-count technique.

2 • Herring and Mullet: The techniques for striper fishing with herring and mullet are pretty much the same as with bunkers. It's a matter of availability and the season. I would not feel shortchanged if herring was the only bait available. Quite the contrary, live lining a herring into a rip or off a jetty in the spring is almost a sure bet. The problem with herring is trying to keep them alive. They are not as tough as bunkers. Never discard those dead herring. Cut them into chunks and they will still catch stripers.

Mullet also makes an excellent striper bait. It's a baitfish that leaves its southern waters and reaches the Northeast during the fall months. Consider yourself very lucky when you're fishing an inlet or jetty and a school of bass or blue-fish drives mullet into the shallows or against the rocks. You'll experience a blitz that may be a once-in-a-lifetime event.

You can, of course, get your own bunkers, mullet, and herring if you learn to use a cast net, one of the most useful tools for the saltwater fisherman. You can use it to get the bait that you can't buy, and to net forage baitfish native to the water that you're fishing—which is the best bait to use under most circumstances.

3 • Eels: If I had but one live bait to use to catch a striper, it would have to be a live eel. Eels are also available along the entire Atlantic coast, and, fortunately, eels are not a difficult bait to find or catch. Eels are tough baits and stay alive on a hook for an amazingly long time. Two anglers can usually fish all night with about a dozen eels.

Though dead-rigged eels will also catch fish, I prefer to fish with live eels. There are several ways to hook and fish a live eel. I prefer live lining eels along sod banks, jetties, and through rips, where stripers are most likely to feed. Generally, eels work better at night, but I've caught stripers on eels from sunrise to sunset. Eels are slippery and slimy, so it

Two Ways to Hook a Live Eel

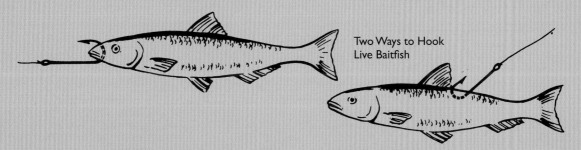

Two Ways to Hook
Live Baitfish

isn't always easy to get one on a hook. Holding an eel with a rough towel will help. Eels are also easier to handle if you keep them on ice, which makes them sluggish. Once they hit the water, however, they will bounce back to life.

Hooks from 2/0 to 6/0 are about right for live eels. I prefer 12-inch eels, but anything from 6 to 18 inches will produce. The bigger eels are preferable when there's a run of bigger bass. Almost any way you hook an eel will catch bass. If you're casting, run your hook through the lower jaw and out the nose. Eels are tough and will stay on the hook through repeated casts.

If you're live lining an eel, run the hook through the skin at the top of the head. Eel skin is like leather and your hook will not pull out. Your eel will also be able to swim more freely.

When you're live lining an eel, use a 5-foot leader of 40- or 50-pound test attached to your line with a barrel swivel. There's a reason for such a long leader. When a big bass picks up the eel and swims away with it, the line will brush back along its body and tail. A big bass might break a lighter line with its body or a swat of its tail. A 5-foot leader assures the angler that his line will drift behind the bass and only the heavy leader will be against the striper's body and tail. If you can't get your eel to go deep, use an egg sinker above the barrel swivel.

A striper might play with an eel before swallowing it, but many times it will hammer the bait without hesitation. As a rule, it's still wise to wait several seconds before setting the hook. If you are using a circle hook, however, allow the bass to run with the eel and hook itself.

Don't throw away a dead eel. It will still catch bass from a drifting boat. It can also be trolled or cast. Rigging a dead eel is not difficult, but it does take time and skill. Regardless of how and where you use a rigged eel, always remember that it is a lifeless piece of meat. You will have to impart action to the eel on the retrieve.

4 • Sand Eels, Spearing, and Killies: None of these small baitfish—sand eels, spearing, or killies—are prime striped bass baits, but all will catch stripers and almost any other saltwater species under certain conditions. I've caught more than my share of bass while drifting a lively killie on the bottom and along channel edges for fluke. When you find big schools of spearing and sand eels, you can also expect to find stripers feeding on them. Diving gulls will usually pinpoint these schools of baitfish and the stripers will be right under them in a feeding frenzy.

When you find this kind of condition, you can usually score by casting jigs, spoons, and bucktails. It's difficult to rig one of these small baits on a hook by itself, but I've learned to increase my chances by tipping my jigs with one or two spearing or sand eels. The scent of fresh bait on a hook is sometimes all it takes to trigger a hit.

5 • Clams: Clams are another staple for striped bass. Almost any size will work as a bait and you can dig up a clam almost anywhere in the surf or in bay waters. Just make sure you check state and local regulations before you start digging for clams. You may need a license.

Many anglers are convinced that the best time to use a clam for striper bait is just after a storm, when clams are washed ashore and the beach is littered with broken shells. This may be true and those broken shells on the beach are certainly a signal that stripers will start feeding on clams, but it would never prevent me from using clams at other times.

Rigging a clam is easy. Run your hook, usually a 2/0 to 4/0 barbed-shank baitholder style, through the hardest part of the clam. If the clam is not tough enough and tends to fly off during a cast, you might have to wrap it on the hook with sewing thread or the elasticized thread that most coastal tackle shops carry.

I use a fish-finder rig for all my surf fishing. Those nylon sliders make these rigs simple to tie. Tie the end of your

WHAT STRIPED BASS EAT (continued)

leader to a barrel swivel, thread the slider on your line, and tie it to the other end of the barrel swivel. The slider, which has a snap for your sinker, will now slide freely on your line. You can use as heavy a sinker as you wish. A fish will still be able to pick up your bait and swim off without feeling the weight of the sinker.

If you're having trouble with crabs, thread a cork about a foot above your baited hook. This will keep your bait away from most crabs and it will also make your bait more visible to a cruising bass. A striped bass will usually gobble up a clam with little hesitation, but I still suggest waiting until your line runs taut before setting the hook.

6 • Seaworms: To a saltwater fisherman, seaworms can only mean bloodworms and sandworms. Traditionally, these two seaworms are the first baits to be used when the early spring run of bass begins. Most often the first striper of the season is usually caught on a seaworm in bay waters or along the surf.

Bloodworms and sandworms are delicate and should be kept in damp seaweed. If they are to be kept for a week or so, spread them out in seaweed and keep them refrigerated. Bloodworms and sandworms are also natural enemies and should be kept separate.

Putting a bloodworm or sandworm on a hook is not difficult. Hook a sandworm, which will generally run bigger than a bloodworm, once through the head, bringing the barb out about an inch or so below the head. Hooking a bloodworm varies only slightly. Bloodworms tend to lose "body" after a few casts. When this happens, put two or three worms on the hook. Seaworms have a tendency to soften quickly and slide down a hook. Baitholder hooks with barbed shanks will help keep a worm up on the shank where it belongs. Seaworms are best fished in a current and allowed to drift naturally.

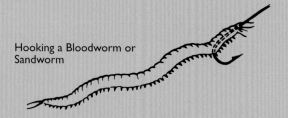

Hooking a Bloodworm or Sandworm

A word of caution about bloodworms and sandworms. They bite! There is absolutely no danger that these little worms will inflict an injury, but be aware that these worms have little pinchers that will pinch your skin.

7 • Squid: The fact that a huge squid will catch a striper has always been a puzzle to me. Stripers are inshore fish, where you are not likely to find big schools of squid, yet I have seen bass gobble up a whole squid or a squid head. A whole squid, usually more than 12 inches long, can be rigged with a single or double hook. Fish as you would an eel or sandworm, letting it drift with the current. Next time you cut a squid into strips for fluke baits, save the heads. Run a hook through both eyes and fish it as you would an eel or cut bunker, letting it drift along with the current in and around inlets or jetties.

8 • Crabs: Crabs rank high on a striper's menu, but not just any crabs. Bass prefer shedders or softshell crabs. Stripers will hit hard crabs, but it's the soft-shelled ones they prefer. A softshell crab, for fishermen who don't know, is a crab that has outgrown its hard shell and has shed it. A soft new shell is exposed and will harden very quickly. Before the new soft shell hardens, however, it makes an excellent striper bait.

A softshell crab may be difficult to hold on a hook and you may have to wrap it on the shank with sewing thread. Availability and cost are also important factors. Softshell crabs sold in a seafood market for human consumption can range from $3 to $5 each. Many fishermen prefer to eat softshell crabs for dinner rather than put them on a hook. But if you want to make the sacrifice, you will find no better striper bait.

When you use a hardshell crab, you can put the whole crab on your hook or cut it in half or quarters. Crabs can be fished in almost any manner, but the preferred technique is drifting a crab bait in any kind of tidal current.

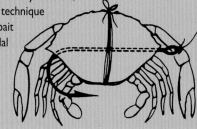

Rigging a Dead Softshell Crab

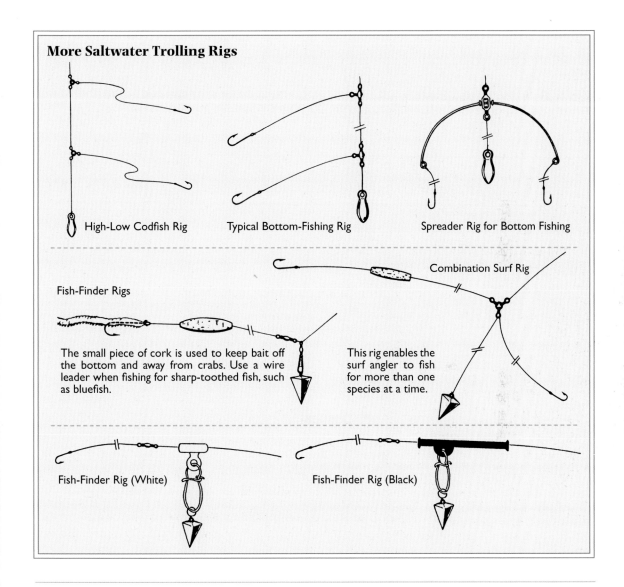

More Saltwater Trolling Rigs

High-Low Codfish Rig

Typical Bottom-Fishing Rig

Spreader Rig for Bottom Fishing

Combination Surf Rig

Fish-Finder Rigs

The small piece of cork is used to keep bait off the bottom and away from crabs. Use a wire leader when fishing for sharp-toothed fish, such as bluefish.

This rig enables the surf angler to fish for more than one species at a time.

Fish-Finder Rig (White)

Fish-Finder Rig (Black)

HOW TO CATCH BAIT AND KEEP IT FRESH

Anglers are often puzzled if they have to catch and keep something other than a dozen worms for a day's fishing. Catching the various baits and keeping them alive and kicking is not difficult, and sometimes catching bait is as much fun as the fishing. Only the popular baits are covered here. As you collect these, you'll soon discover that there are other baits available, such as grasshoppers, crickets, hellgrammites, lizards, and so on.

■ Worms

Worms, whether earthworms or night crawlers, are the most popular live baits. Night crawlers get their name from the fact that they come to the surface at night. They like warm and wet weather. Wait until it has been dark at least two to three hours, then prowl around your lawn, a golf course, or a park. Use a flashlight, but not one with a bright beam. If the beam is too bright, cover

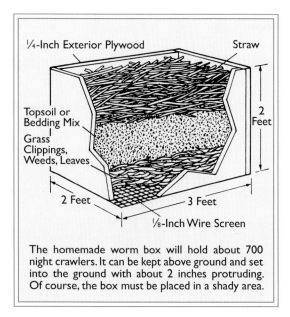

¼-Inch Exterior Plywood   Straw

Topsoil or
Bedding Mix

Grass
Clippings,
Weeds, Leaves

2
Feet

2 Feet   3 Feet

⅛-Inch Wire Screen

The homemade worm box will hold about 700
night crawlers. It can be kept above ground and set
into the ground with about 2 inches protruding.
Of course, the box must be placed in a shady area.

the lens with red cellophane. When you spot a worm, grab it by the head (the thicker end) with your fingers. If the worm tries to shoot back into the hole, hold onto one end until the worm releases tension and is free of the hole.

If you can't find night crawlers at night, it's probably too dry for them to come to the surface. You can wait for rain or water your lawn in the afternoon and go worm hunting that night.

If you're after the common earthworm, which is smaller than a night crawler, you'll have to dig for them. Concentrate on compost heaps, vegetable gardens, and stream banks.

A day's supply of worms can be carried in a few inches of damp soil in a coffee can from which both ends have been removed. Punch holes in the plastic lids that come with the cans. With two of these lids in place, it can be opened from either end for easy access to the worms on the bottom. If you keep this container in a burlap pouch and dip it occasionally in a cool creek, the worms will stay fresh all day.

Commercial boxes for worms, as well as other baits, are available. Most are made of porous fiberboard, which insulates the box and keeps the inside cool and humid.

If you want to keep a good supply of worms on hand, you can build a worm box. In a box of 2 feet by 3 feet by 2 feet, you can house 600 or 700 night crawlers. Sink the box in a shady spot, allowing 2 inches of it to be

above ground. Damp and cool are the key words in keeping worms fresh. A wet burlap bag over some straw will work well. You might also try spreading out a few handfuls of ice cubes on the straw every two or three days. The ice will keep the soil damp and cool as it melts. Food is no problem, since worms eat almost anything. You can feed them coffee grounds, breadcrumbs, and cornmeal.

Ice cubes, incidentally, can also be used effectively when transporting and keeping worms on an extended fishing trip. Try the following method on your next trip. In the center of your bait box, which should measure about 12 inches by 12 inches by 8 inches if you're carrying 400 or so worms, clear a space in the bedding. Next, fill a glass jar or plastic container with ice cubes, screw the cap back on, and put it in a plastic bag. Place the container in the center of the box and push the bedding or soil around it. The ice will keep the soil cool and damp and it will stay that way until the cubes melt. In hot weather, worms will actually crowd around the jar. The purpose of the plastic is to seal in condensation. Without the plastic, the soil would become too soggy for the worms.

▓ Sea Worms

Sea worms, such as bloodworms and sandworms, are delicate and should be kept in damp seaweed. If they are to be kept for a week or so, spread them out in seaweed and keep them refrigerated. Bloodworms and sandworms are enemies and should be kept separate. Use a wood partition to divide your bait box into two compartments.

▓ Minnows

Minnows rank as the second-most popular bait, and they can be caught almost as easily as worms. There are several ways to collect minnows: minnow traps, drop or umbrella nets, minnow seines, or cast nets.

Caution: A fishing license is usually required to take bait in fresh water, and many states set limits on the number of baitfish that may be kept. Check the fishing regulations of your state before netting or trapping.

The minnow trap requires the least skill to use. It works on the principle that a small fish will swim into the funnel-like openings after food and be unable to find its way out. For bait, you should wet oatmeal or cornmeal and roll it into balls the size of golf balls. The meal will break up gradually in the trap and provide bait for long periods. The best place to set the trap is in shallow water near a dock or boathouse. In streams, set it near the head or side of a pool where the current is slow.

The drop or umbrella net, which measures 36 by 36 inches, gets more immediate results but may be more difficult to use. Lower it into the water just deep enough so that you can still lift it fast. Sprinkle breadcrumbs over it and let them sink. When minnows begin to feed on the crumbs, lift the net fast. With practice, you'll make good hauls every time.

A minnow seine not only produces a lot of bait, but also is fun to use, especially in bays and tidal rivers. A seine is usually 4 feet high and anywhere from 10 to 50 feet long, with lead weights along the bottom and floats on top. A 20-footer is a good size for most purposes. Seining is easy. Two people carry the seine about 100 feet from the shore or until the depth hits 4 feet or so. Keeping the weighted end of the seine on the bottom, the people sweep toward shore. The seine will belly out, catching everything in its path and carrying bait up on shore, where it can be picked up.

The cast net is one of the most useful tools of both the freshwater and saltwater angler, because he can use it to get the bait that he can't buy and to obtain forage baitfish native to the waters that he's fishing—which is the best bait to use under most circumstances. Mono-filament nets, because their nylon strands are stiff, open better than nets made of braided threads. Mono nets also sink faster and are less visible after they're thrown into

the water. Generally, they catch more fish, but they're also more expensive. Cast nets are available in various sizes and types. Experts throw 16-foot and larger nets, but anglers who would only use them occasionally are better off getting one that measures 8 to 10 feet. Bridge nets, popular in the Florida Keys, are short nets with extra lead weights around the bottom. When the net is dropped off a bridge into deep water, its added weight allows it to sink quickly and hold baitfish before they dive and escape. A plastic bucket is the best storage container for a net. All nets should routinely be rinsed with clean, fresh water and cleared of debris.

The next problem is keeping the minnows alive and fresh. The water must be aerated to keep enough oxygen in the bucket for survival, and this can be done in several ways. Water can be aerated by battery-powered devices, or you can aerate the water manually with a tin can. Scoop up a canful of water and pour it back into the bucket from a height of 2 feet. Doing this a dozen times every 15 minutes should provide sufficient oxygen for a couple dozen minnows.

If you plan to troll, keep bait in a bucket designed for trolling. This bucket, built to float on its side, will take water at an angle and aerate it.

If you're still-fishing, use the traditional bucket, which is actually two buckets. The outer bucket is used when transporting minnows. When you start fishing, lift out the insert and lower it into the water. The insert, which floats upright, is vented so that water is constantly changed.

Bait water must be kept at a constant temperature. In summer, add ice cubes to the water before transporting it. As the ice melts, it will cool the water and add oxygen. Take care, however, not to cool the water too fast. It is important to avoid abrupt temperature changes, which will kill minnows.

Crayfish and minnow traps are easy to use. Minnows and crayfish swim into the funnel-like openings at either end, but can't find their way out. Place the trap near docks or wherever the current is weak. Bait it with a paste mix of oatmeal and water rolled into balls the size of golf balls.

A cricket basket is also handy for other baits, such as grasshoppers, lizards, and hellgrammites.

How to Throw a Cast Net

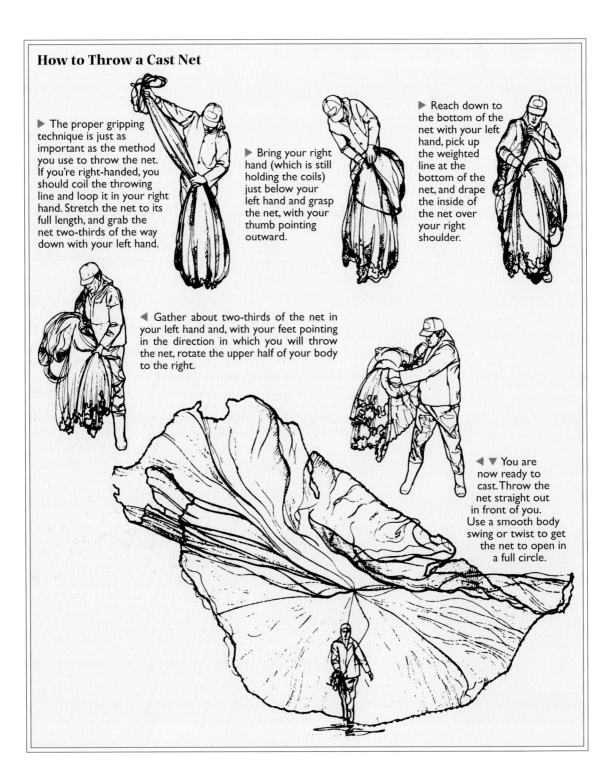

▶ The proper gripping technique is just as important as the method you use to throw the net. If you're right-handed, you should coil the throwing line and loop it in your right hand. Stretch the net to its full length, and grab the net two-thirds of the way down with your left hand.

▶ Bring your right hand (which is still holding the coils) just below your left hand and grasp the net, with your thumb pointing outward.

▶ Reach down to the bottom of the net with your left hand, pick up the weighted line at the bottom of the net, and drape the inside of the net over your right shoulder.

◀ Gather about two-thirds of the net in your left hand and, with your feet pointing in the direction in which you will throw the net, rotate the upper half of your body to the right.

◀ ▼ You are now ready to cast. Throw the net straight out in front of you. Use a smooth body swing or twist to get the net to open in a full circle.

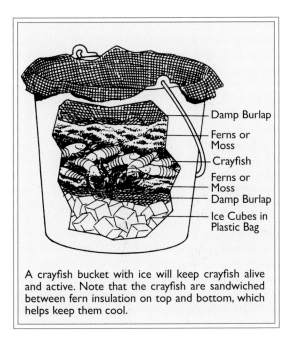

- Damp Burlap
- Ferns or Moss
- Crayfish
- Ferns or Moss
- Damp Burlap
- Ice Cubes in Plastic Bag

A crayfish bucket with ice will keep crayfish alive and active. Note that the crayfish are sandwiched between fern insulation on top and bottom, which helps keep them cool.

Crayfish

Crayfish make excellent bait, but they can sometimes be difficult to find. You'll do best at night along gravel shorelines. Crayfish feed in the shallows and you can spot them with a flashlight. Their eyes reflect reddish in the beam. When you locate one, hold a dip net behind it and touch its head with your hand or a stick. If you are lucky, it will swim backward into the net. If you are fast, you can try grabbing a crayfish from behind with your hand.

Keeping crayfish fresh in hot weather can be a problem. You can use an ice-bucket setup. In the bottom of a pail, place two dozen ice cubes in a plastic bag. Cover the ice with a layer of burlap, followed by a few inches of moss or ferns. Next, spread out the crayfish and cover them with another layer of moss or ferns. Cover this top layer with another piece of wet burlap. Crayfish will stay in fine shape in this insulated pail during the hottest weather. Keep the top piece of burlap wet.

Frogs

Few anglers will question the value of a lively frog as a bait. Look for frogs along the grassy banks of creeks, ponds, and lakes. Catching them is not hard. You can catch a fair number during the day, but you can collect more at night with a flashlight and a long-handled, small-mesh net. Frogs will remain still in the beam of a flashlight and you should have no trouble netting them. Keeping a day's supply of frogs is no problem. Commercial frog boxes are available, or you can make your own (see accompanying illustration).

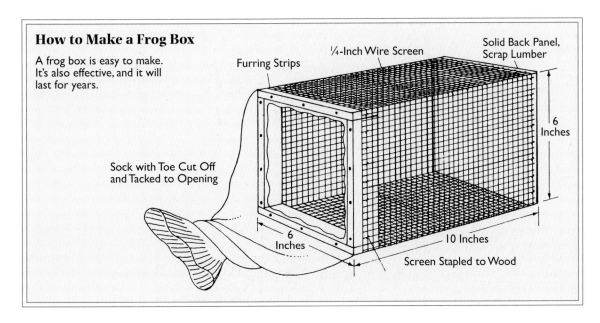

How to Make a Frog Box

A frog box is easy to make. It's also effective, and it will last for years.

- Furring Strips
- ¼-Inch Wire Screen
- Solid Back Panel, Scrap Lumber
- Sock with Toe Cut Off and Tacked to Opening
- 6 Inches
- 6 Inches
- 10 Inches
- Screen Stapled to Wood

KNOTS

Anyone who aspires to competence as a fisherman must have at least a basic knowledge of knots. Most anglers know and use no more than half a dozen knots. However, if you fish a lot, you are sure to run into a situation that cannot be solved efficiently with the basic ties. The aim of this section is to acquaint you with knots that will help you handle nearly all line-tying situations.

All knots reduce—to a greater or lesser degree, depending on the particular knot—the breaking strength of the line. Loose or poorly tied knots reduce line strength even more. For that reason, and to avoid wasting valuable fishing time, it is best to practice tying the knots at home. In most cases, it's better to practice with cord or rope; the heavier material makes it easier to follow the tying procedures.

It is important to form and tighten knots correctly. They should be tightened slowly and steadily for best results. In most knots requiring the tyer to make turns around the standing part of the line, at least five such turns should be made.

Now let's take a look at the range of fishing knots. Included are tying instructions, as well as the uses for which each knot is suited.

■ BLOOD KNOT

This knot is used to connect two lines of relatively similar diameter. It is especially popular for joining sections of monofilament in making tapered fly leaders.

1 • Wrap one strand around the other at least four times, and run the end into the fork thus formed.

2 • Make the same number of turns, in the opposite direction, with the second strand, and run its end through the opening in the middle of the knot, in the direction opposite that of the first strand.

3 • Hold the two ends so they do not slip (some anglers use their teeth). Pull the standing part of both strands in opposite directions, tightening the knot.

4 • Tighten securely, clip off the ends, and the knot is complete. If you want to tie on a dropper fly, leave one of these ends about 6 to 8 inches long.

■ STU APTE IMPROVED BLOOD KNOT

This knot is excellent for joining two lines of greatly different diameter, such as a heavy monofilament shock leader and a light leader tippet.

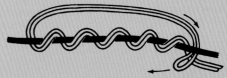

1 • Double a sufficient length of the lighter line, wrap it around the standing part of the heavier line at least five times, and then run the end of the doubled line into the fork thus formed.

2 • Wrap the heavier line around the standing part of the doubled lighter line three times in the opposite direction, and run the end of the heavier line into the opening in the direction opposite that of the end of the doubled line.

3 • Holding the two ends to keep them from slipping, pull the standing parts of the two lines in opposite directions. Tighten the knot completely, using your fingernails to push the loops together if necessary, and clip off the ends.

DOUBLE SURGEON'S KNOT

This knot is used to join two strands of greatly unequal diameter.

1 • Place the two lines parallel, with the ends pointing in opposite directions. Using the two lines as a single strand, make a simple overhand knot, pulling the two strands all the way through the loop, and then make another overhand knot.

2 • Holding both strands at each end, pull the knot tight, and clip off the ends.

IMPROVED CLINCH KNOT

This knot is used to tie flies, bass bugs, lures, and bait hooks to line or leader. This knot reduces line strength only slightly.

1 • Run the end of the line through the eye of the lure, fly, or hook, and then make at least five turns around the standing part of the line. Run the end through the opening between the eye and the beginning of the twists, and then run it through the large loop formed by the previous step.

2 • Pull slowly on the standing part of the line, being careful that the end doesn't slip back through the large loop and that the knot snugs up against the eye. Clip off the end.

DOUBLE-LOOP CLINCH KNOT

This knot is the same as the improved clinch knot except that the line is run through the eye twice at the beginning of the tie.

DOUBLE IMPROVED CLINCH KNOT

This is the same as the improved clinch knot except that the line is used doubled throughout the entire tie.

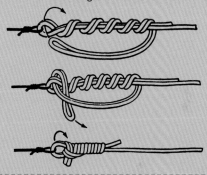

TRILENE KNOT

Used in joining line to swivels, snaps, hooks, and artificial lures, the Trilene knot is a strong, all-purpose knot that resists slippage and premature failures. It is easy to tie and retains 85 to 90 percent of the original line strength. The double wrap of monofilament line through the eyelet provides a protective cushion for added safety.

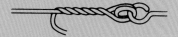

1 • Run the end of the line through the eye of the hook or lure and double back through the eye a second time.

2 • Loop around the standing part of the line five or six times.

3 • Thread the tag end back between the eye and the coils as shown.

4 • Pull up tight and trim the tag end.

SHOCKER KNOT

This knot is used to join two lines of unequal diameter.

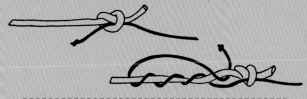

■ ARBOR KNOT

The arbor knot provides the angler with a quick, easy connection for attaching line to the reel spool.

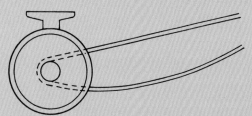

1 • Pass line around the reel arbor.

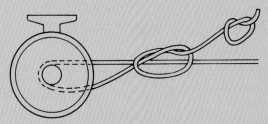

2 • Tie an overhand knot around the standing line. Tie a second overhand knot in the tag end.

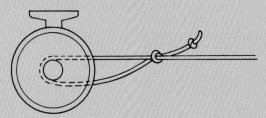

3 • Pull tight and snip off the excess. Snug down the first overhand knot on the reel arbor.

■ MULTIPLE CLINCH KNOT

This knot is used to join line and leader, especially in baitcasting. This knot slides through rod guides with a minimum of friction.

A loop is tied in the end of the line. Then, the leader is run into the loop, around the entire loop four times, and then back through the middle of the four wraps.

■ PALOMAR KNOT

This is a quick, easy knot to use when tying your line directly to a hook.

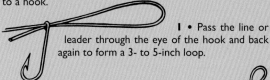

1 • Pass the line or leader through the eye of the hook and back again to form a 3- to 5-inch loop.

2 • Hold the line and hook at the eye. With the other hand, bring the loop up and under the double line and tie an overhand knot, but do not tighten.

3 • Hold the overhand knot. With the other hand, bring the loop over the hook.

4 • Hold the overhand knot. With the other hand, bring the loop over the hook.

■ PERFECTION LOOP KNOT

This knot is used to make a loop in the end of line or leader.

1 • Make one turn around the line and hold the crossing point with your thumb and forefinger.

2 • Make a second turn around the crossing point, and bring the end around and between loops A and B.

3 • Run loop B through loop A.

4 • Pull upward on loop B.

5 • Tighten the knot.

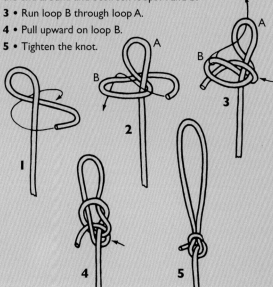

KING SLING KNOT

This knot offers the angler an easy-to-tie end loop knot that is used primarily as a connection for crankbaits. This knot allows the lure to work freely, making it more lifelike, and resulting in more strikes.

1 • Insert the tag end of the line through the artificial bait so that it extends 8 to 10 inches.

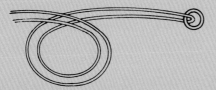

2 • Hold the tag end and the standing line in your left hand and form a loop.

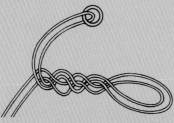

3 • With the bait in your right hand, make four turns around the tag end and the standing line above the loop.

4 • Bring the bait down and through the loop.

5 • To tighten, hold the line above the bait at the desired loop length and pull the tag end and the standing line at the same time. Trim the tag end.

DOUBLE SURGEON'S LOOP

This is a quick, easy way to tie a loop in the end of a leader. It is often used as part of a leader system because it is relatively strong.

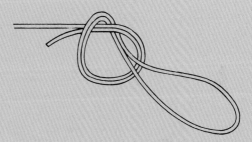

1 • Double the tag end of the line. Make a single overhand knot in the double line.

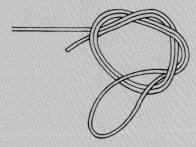

2 • Hold the tag end and standing part of the line in your left hand and bring the loop around and insert through the overhand knot again.

3 • Hold the loop in your right hand. Hold the tag end and standing line in your left hand. Moisten the knot (don't use saliva) and pull to tighten.

4 • Trim off the tag end.

WORLD'S FAIR KNOT

This is an easy-to-tie terminal tackle knot for connecting line to swivel or lure.

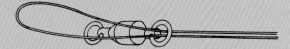

1 • Double a 6-inch length of line and pass the loop through the eye.

2 • Bring the loop back next to the doubled line and grasp the double line through the loop.

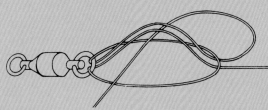

3 • Put the tag end through the new loop formed by the double line.

4 • Bring the tag end back through the new loop created by Step 3.

5 • Pull the tag end snug, and slide the knot up tight. Clip the tag end.

TUCKED SHEET BEND

This knot joins fly line and leader when the leader has an end loop.

1 • Run the fly line through the leader loop and around the loop as shown.

2 • Run the line back through the loops.

3 • Smoothly start to draw up the knots.

4 • Pull on both ends until the knot is tight.

DROPPER LOOP KNOT

This knot is frequently used to put a loop in the middle of a strand of monofilament.

1 • Make a loop in the line and wrap one end overhand several times around the other part of the line. Pinch a small loop in the middle and thrust it between the turns as shown by the simulated, imaginary needle.

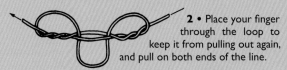

2 • Place your finger through the loop to keep it from pulling out again, and pull on both ends of the line.

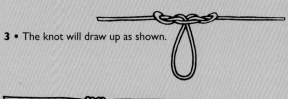

3 • The knot will draw up as shown.

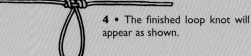

4 • The finished loop knot will appear as shown.

OFFSHORE SWIVEL KNOT

This knot is used to attach your line to a swivel.

1 • Slip a loop of double-line leader through the eye of the swivel. Rotate the loop a half turn to put a single twist between the loop and swivel eye.

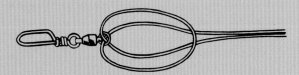

2 • Pass the loop with the twist over the swivel. Hold the loop end, together with both strands of double-line leader, with one hand. Let the swivel slide to the other end of the double loops now formed.

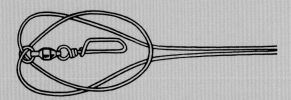

3 • Still holding the loop and lines, use your other hand to rotate the swivel through the center of both loops. Repeat at least five times.

4 • Continue holding the strands of double-line leader tightly, but release the end of the loop. As you pull on the swivel, loops of line will begin to gather.

5 • To draw the knot tight, grip the swivel with pliers and push the loops toward the eye with your fingers, still keeping the strands of leader pulled tight.

NAIL KNOT

This is the best knot for joining the end of a fly line with the butt end of a fly leader. The knot is smooth, streamlined, and will run freely through the guides of the fly rod. Caution: This knot is designed for use with modern synthetic fly lines; do not use it with an old silk fly line, for the knot will cut the line.

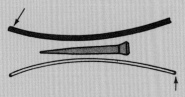

1 • Place the end of the fly line and the butt end of the leader—pointing in opposite directions—along the length of a tapered nail. Allow sufficient overlap.

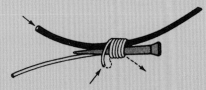

2 • Wrap the leader five or six times around itself, the nail, and the fly line, keeping the windings up against one another. Run the butt end of the leader back along the nail, inside the wraps.

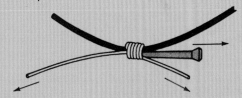

3 • Pull both ends of the leader tight, and then remove the nail and tighten again by pulling on both ends of the leader.

4 • Pull on both line and leader to test the knot, and clip off the ends, completing the knot.

■ NAIL KNOT (Alternate)

Tying procedures for this knot are the same as for the standard nail knot, except that in place of the nail, use an air-inflation needle like those used to inflate basketballs and footballs. The tip of the needle must be cut or filed off so that the tube is open at both ends. A large hypodermic needle with its point snipped off also works well. In tying Step 3 (third illustration from the top), the butt end of the leader—after having been wrapped five or six times around the fly line, leader, and tube—is simply run back through the tube (needle). Then, the knot is tightened, the tube is removed, and the final tightening is done.

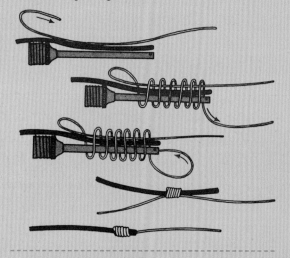

■ DOUBLE NAIL KNOT

This knot is used to join leader sections of the same or slightly different diameters. This is especially useful in saltwater fly fishing and in making heavy salmon leaders.

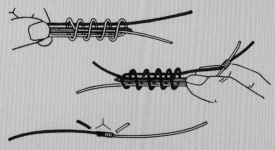

The tying procedure involves making two nail knots, one around each of the two leader sections. As each knot is formed, it is tightened only enough to prevent it from unraveling. When both are formed, each leader is pulled slowly so that the knots tighten together securely.

■ TURLE KNOT

This knot is used to tie a dry or wet fly to a leader tippet. It is not as strong as the improved clinch knot, but it allows a dry fly's hackle points to sit high and jauntily on the surface of the water.

1 • Run the end of the leader through the eye of the hook toward the bend, and tie a simple overhand knot around the standing part of the line, forming a loop.

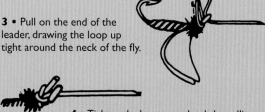

2 • Open the loop enough to allow it to pass around the fly, and place the loop around the neck of the fly, just forward of the eye.

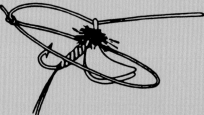

3 • Pull on the end of the leader, drawing the loop up tight around the neck of the fly.

4 • Tighten the knot completely by pulling on the main part of the leader.

■ LOOP KNOT

This knot is used to tie on a lure.

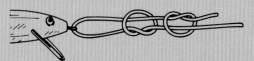

Tie an overhand knot in the line, leaving the loop loose and a sufficient length of line below the loop to tie the rest of the knot. Run the end through the hook eye and back through the loop in the line, and then tie another overhand knot around the standing part. Pull tight.

END LOOP

This knot is used to form a loop in the end of a line.

1 • Double the end of the line for about 6 or 8 inches.

2 • Wrap the double line around itself at least six times.

3 • Take the end of the doubled line and pass it through the first loop as shown.

4 • Now, tighten the knot by pulling on the loop and the tag end at the same time.

BUFFER LOOP

This knot is used to attach a lure to line or leader via a nonslip loop.

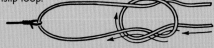

1 • Tie a simple overhand knot in the line, leaving the loop loose and leaving the end long enough to complete the knot, and then run the end through the eye of the lure.

2 • Run the end back through the loose loop and make another overhand knot, using the end and standing part of the line.

3 • Tighten the overhand knot nearest to the lure eye, and then tighten the second overhand knot, which, in effect, forms a half hitch against the first knot.

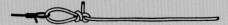

4 • The finished knot appears as shown.

KNOTTING BACKING LINE TO FLY LINE

This knot is used to join backing line to fly line.

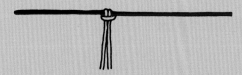

1 • Double the end of the backing line, make one wrap around the fly line, and pull all of the backing line through the loop at its doubled end so the lines appear as shown.

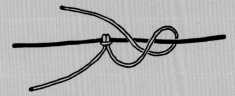

2 • With the end of the backing line, make a half hitch around the fly line, and pull it tight against the original knot.

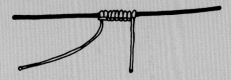

3 • Continue making such half hitches (eight or 10 should be enough) until the tie appears as shown.

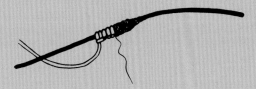

4 • Wrap the entire tie with nylon thread, including part of the end of the backing line. This step is simplified by placing the fly line in a fly-tying vise.

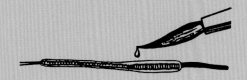

5 • Give the entire tie a good coat of lacquer.

ALBRIGHT KNOT (MONO TO MONO)

This knot is used to join lines of dissimilar diameter, such as a fly line to a leader or heavy shock leader to a finer leader tippet.

1 • Double the end of the heavier line, forming a long U shape. Bring the lighter line up into the U, and make about 10 wraps—in the direction of the bottom of the U—around the U and the standing part of the lighter line, bringing the end of the lighter line out of the bottom of the U.

2 • Pull slowly and evenly until the knot is tight.

ALBRIGHT KNOT (MONO TO WIRE)

This knot is used when a short length of wire leader is needed below monofilament leader tippet to prevent sharp-toothed fish from biting through the leader. The fly is attached to the wire leader with a brass crimping sleeve. It is also used to tie mono leader to wire or lead-core line so that the knot will pass through guides and tip tops smoothly. It eliminates the need for a swivel.

1 • Bend the end of a wire leader into a U or open-end loop. Run the end of monofilament into the tip of the U, make about seven wraps around the doubled wire, and run the end of the monofilament back out through the tip of the U.

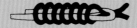

2 • Hold both leaders to prevent the knot from slipping, and slowly draw the wraps of monofilament tight.

3 • Clip off the ends, and the knot is finished.

FLY-LINE SPLICE

This splice is used to join two fly lines.

1 • Remove the coating from 2¼ inches of the end of each line, and fray about 1 inch.

2 • Enmesh the frayed ends of one line with those of the other, and wrap most of this joint with nylon thread.

3 • Make another series of wrappings over the entire splice. Finish the job with coats of varnish.

HAYWIRE TWIST

This knot is used to tie wire to the hook, lure, or swivel, or make a loop in the end of the wire.

1 • Run about 4 inches of the end of the leader wire through the eye of the hook, lure, or swivel, and then bend the end across the standing part of the wire.

2 • Holding the two parts of the wire at their crossing points, bend the wire around itself, using hard, even, twisting motions. Both wire parts should be twisted equally.

3 • Then, using the end of the wire, make about 10 tight wraps around the standing part of the wire.

4 • Break off or clip the end of the wire close to the last wrap so that there is no sharp end, and the job is complete.

BIMINI TWIST

This knot is used to create a loop or double line without appreciably weakening the breaking strength of the line. It is especially popular in bluewater fishing for large saltwater fish. Learning this knot requires practice.

1 • Double the end of the line to form a loop, leaving yourself plenty of line to work with. Run the loop around a fixed object, such as a cleat or the butt end of a rod, or have a partner hold the loop and keep it open. Make 20 twists in the line, keeping the turns tight and the line taut.

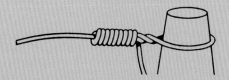

2 • Keeping the twists tight, wrap the end of the line back over the twists until you reach the V of the loop, making the wraps tight and snug up against one another.

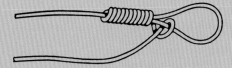

3 • Make a half hitch around one side of the loop and pull it tight.

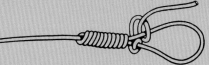

4 • Then, make a half hitch around the other side of the loop, and pull this one tight, too.

5 • Now, make a half hitch around the base of the loop, tighten it, clip off excess line at the end, and the bimini twist is complete.

SPIDER HITCH

This knot serves the same function as the bimini twist, but many anglers prefer the spider hitch because it's easier and faster to tie—especially with cold hands—and requires no partner to help, nor any fixed object to keep the loop open. Plus, it's equally strong.

1 • Make a long loop in the line. Hold the ends between your thumb and forefinger, with the first joint of the thumb extending beyond your finger. Then, use your other hand to twist a smaller reverse loop in the doubled line.

2 • Slide your fingers up the line to grasp the small reverse loop together with the long loop. Most of the small loop should extend beyond your thumb tip.

3 • Wind the doubled line from right to left around both your thumb and the small loop, taking five turns. Then, pass the remainder of the doubled line (large loop) through the small loop.

4 • Pull the large loop to make the five turns unwind off the thumb, using a fast, steady pull—not a quick jerk.

5 • Pull the turns around the base of the loop tight and then trim off the tag end.

The Uni-Knot System

The Uni-Knot System consists of variations on one basic knot that can be used for most needs in fresh water and salt water. The system was developed by Vic Dunaway, editor of *Florida Sportsman* magazine and author of numerous books. Here's how each variation is tied, step by step.

■ TYING TO TERMINAL TACKLE

1 • Run the line through the eye of the hook, swivel, or lure at least 6 inches and fold it back to form two parallel lines. Bring the end of the line back in a circle toward the eye.

2 • Turn the tag end six times around the double line and through the circle. Hold the double line at the eye and pull the tag end to snug up turns.

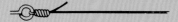

3 • Pull the running line to slide the knot up against the eye.

4 • Continue pulling until the knot is tight. Trim the tag end flush with the last coil of the knot. This basic Uni-Knot will not slip.

■ LOOP CONNECTION

Tie the same basic Uni-Knot as shown above—up to the point where the coils are snugged up against the running line. Then, slide the knot toward the eye only until the desired loop size is reached. Pull the tag end with pliers to tighten. This gives a lure or fly free, natural movement in the water. When a fish is hooked, the knot slides tight against the eye.

■ JOINING LINES

1 • With two lines of about the same diameter, overlap ends for about 6 inches. With one end, form a Uni-Knot circle and cross the two lines at about the middle of the overlap.

2 • Tie a basic Uni-Knot, making six turns around the lines.

3 • Pull the tag end to snug the knot.

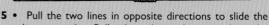

4 • Use the loose end of the overlapped line to tie a second Uni-Knot and snug it up in the same manner.

5 • Pull the two lines in opposite directions to slide the two knots together. Pull tight and snip the tag ends to the outermost coils.

■ JOINING LEADER TO LINE

1 • Using a leader no more than four times the pound test of the line, double the end of the line and overlap with the leader for about 6 inches. Make a Uni-Knot circle with the doubled line.

2 • Tie a Uni-Knot around the leader with the doubled line, but use only three turns. Snug up.

3 • Now, tie a Uni-Knot with the leader around the doubled line, again using only three turns.

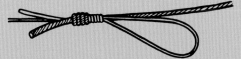

4 • Pull knots together tightly. Trim the tag ends and loop.

JOINING SHOCK LEADER TO LINE

1 • Using a leader of more than four times the pound test of the line, double the ends of both leader and line back about 6 inches. Slip the line loop through the leader loop far enough to permit tying a Uni-Knot around both strands of the leader.

2 • With doubled line, tie a Uni-Knot around the doubled leader, using only four turns.

3 • Put a finger through the loop of line and grasp both the tag end and running line to pull the knot snug around the leader loop.

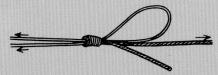

4 • With one hand, pull the long end of the leader (not both strands). With the other hand, pull both strands of line. Pull slowly until the knot slides to the end of the leader loop and slippage is stopped.

◼ DOUBLE-LINE SHOCK LEADER

1 • As a replacement for a bimini twist or spider hitch, first clip off the amount of line needed for the desired length of loop. Tie the two ends together with an overhand knot.

2 • Double the end of the running line and overlap it 6 inches with the knotted end of the loop piece. Tie a Uni-Knot with the tied loop around the double running line, using four turns.

3 • Now, tie a Uni-Knot with the doubled running line around the loop piece, again using four turns.

4 • Hold both strands of double line in one hand, both strands of loop in the other. Pull to bring the knots together until they barely touch.

5 • Tighten by pulling both strands of the loop piece, but only the main strand of running line. Trim off both loop tag ends, eliminating the overhand knot.

◼ SNELLING A HOOK

1 • Thread line through the hook eye for about 6 inches. Hold the line against the hook shank and form a Uni-Knot circle. Make as many turns as desired through the loop and around the line and shank. Close the knot by pulling on the tag end.

2 • Tighten by pulling the running line in one direction and the hook in the other. Trim off the tag end.

TERMINAL-RIG ACCESSORIES

The items of fishing gear covered in this section are various components of the rigs shown in previous sections. These accessories are as important as links in a chain, so buy the best you can afford. A well-constructed snap swivel of the correct size, for example, won't come apart at the seams under the surge of a big fish.

Swivels come in many forms and sizes, but basically a swivel consists of two or three round metal eyes connected in such a way that each eye can rotate freely and independently of the others. Swivels perform such func-

tions as preventing or reducing line twist, enabling the angler to attach more than one component (sinker and bait, for example) to his line, and facilitating lure changes.

Sinkers, like swivels, come in many shapes and weights. Usually made of lead, they are used to get a bait (or lure) down to the desired depth.

Floats are lighter-than-water devices that are attached to the line. They keep a bait at a predetermined distance above the bottom and signal the strike of a fish. Floats are usually made of cork or plastic and come in many forms.

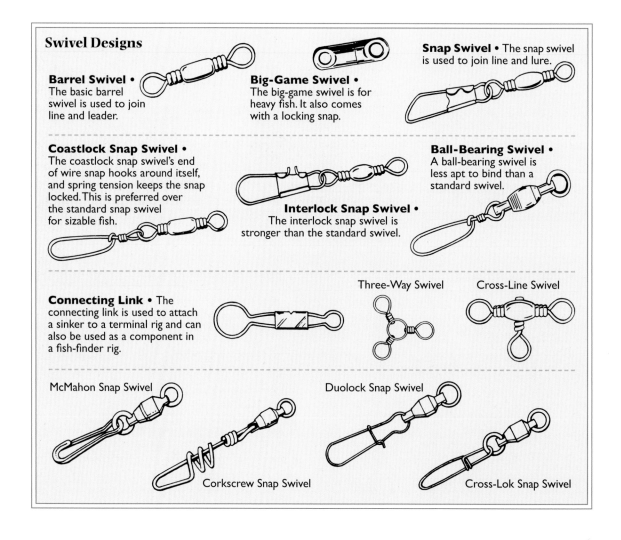

Swivel Designs

Barrel Swivel • The basic barrel swivel is used to join line and leader.

Big-Game Swivel • The big-game swivel is for heavy fish. It also comes with a locking snap.

Snap Swivel • The snap swivel is used to join line and lure.

Coastlock Snap Swivel • The coastlock snap swivel's end of wire snap hooks around itself, and spring tension keeps the snap locked. This is preferred over the standard snap swivel for sizable fish.

Interlock Snap Swivel • The interlock snap swivel is stronger than the standard swivel.

Ball-Bearing Swivel • A ball-bearing swivel is less apt to bind than a standard swivel.

Connecting Link • The connecting link is used to attach a sinker to a terminal rig and can also be used as a component in a fish-finder rig.

Three-Way Swivel

Cross-Line Swivel

McMahon Snap Swivel

Duolock Snap Swivel

Corkscrew Snap Swivel

Cross-Lok Snap Swivel

Sinker Designs

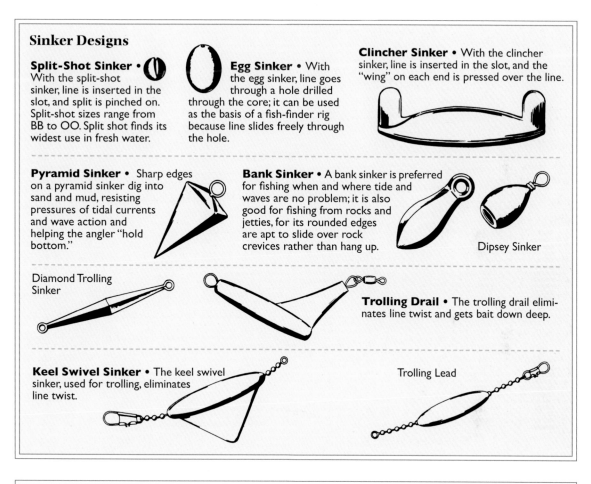

Split-Shot Sinker • With the split-shot sinker, line is inserted in the slot, and split is pinched on. Split-shot sizes range from BB to OO. Split shot finds its widest use in fresh water.

Egg Sinker • With the egg sinker, line goes through a hole drilled through the core; it can be used as the basis of a fish-finder rig because line slides freely through the hole.

Clincher Sinker • With the clincher sinker, line is inserted in the slot, and the "wing" on each end is pressed over the line.

Pyramid Sinker • Sharp edges on a pyramid sinker dig into sand and mud, resisting pressures of tidal currents and wave action and helping the angler "hold bottom."

Bank Sinker • A bank sinker is preferred for fishing when and where tide and waves are no problem; it is also good for fishing from rocks and jetties, for its rounded edges are apt to slide over rock crevices rather than hang up.

Dipsey Sinker

Diamond Trolling Sinker

Trolling Drail • The trolling drail eliminates line twist and gets bait down deep.

Keel Swivel Sinker • The keel swivel sinker, used for trolling, eliminates line twist.

Trolling Lead

Trolling Devices

The trolling planer is a heavily weighted device with metal or plastic "wings" that permit trolling at considerable depths. The bait-walker sinker keeps the bait moving near, but not dragging on, the bottom. The downrigger assembly shown has a terminal rig with a cable, cannonball, and release mechanism.

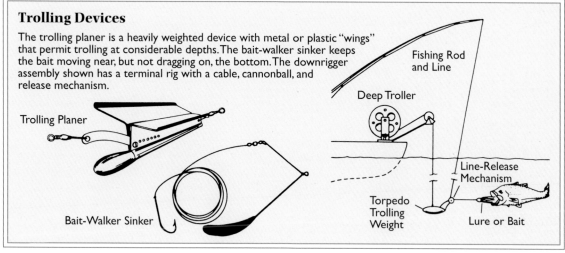

Trolling Planer

Bait-Walker Sinker

Fishing Rod and Line

Deep Troller

Line-Release Mechanism

Torpedo Trolling Weight

Lure or Bait

Float Designs

Cork Ball Float

Plastic Ball Float • In the plastic ball float, a spring-loaded top section, when depressed, exposes a small, U-shaped "hook" at the bottom into which line is placed. Releasing the top section reseats the "hook," holding the line fast.

Caro-line Cork Float • This float has a doubled length of line running through it lengthwise. The fishing line is run through the loop, and then the loop is pulled through the cork body, seating the line. The Caro-line float is generally used in surf fishing to keep a bait off the bottom and away from crabs.

Plastic Porcupine Float • The plastic porcupine float is light and highly sensitive to the strike of a fish.

Teeter Float • The teeter float has a slender section that floats perpendicular to the water and is highly sensitive to the strike of a fish.

Pencil Float • With the pencil float, line is attached at both ends. A strike causes one end to lift from the surface.

Panfish Are for Big People, Too

Every fisherman agrees that panfish are a perfect species for children. I agree, but I also think it's a great fish for big people, too. Bluegills and crappies are not difficult to catch and they are literally everywhere. In fact, many waters are overpopulated and overrun with stunted panfish. My favorite technique is with a fly rod and almost any kind of black or brown dry fly or small popper. Whether you're in a boat or fishing from shore, cast the fly as close as you can to the edge of a dock and twitch it a few times. If you don't get a hit, don't waste your time. Move to the next dock.

Not into fly fishing? You can do just as well with spinning tackle. You can catch panfish on small jigs and spoons, but, as a rule, bait works better than most lures. Worms and small minnows, especially for crappies, are the most consistent baits. Other baits that work include crickets, grubs, caterpillars, grasshoppers, and hellgrammites. Stick with ultralight tackle and 2- or 4-pound-test line. You can fish these baits deep with some split shot or with a bobber about 2 or 3 feet above your bait. With children, the bobber is probably more effective in shallow water close to shore. It's also fun for children to watch a bobber dance when a bluegill begins its attack.

Bluegills will eat just about anything you put in front of them, and you can find them in any shallow area of a lake or near structures such as docks and stumps. If you're looking for platter-size bluegills and crappies, there are a couple of factors to keep in mind. If you're fishing from shore, cast out a little farther and fish your bait deeper. Small bluegills will take bait anytime, but those bigger panfish concentrate their feeding at dawn and dusk.

Cleaning and cooking bluegills is easy. Fillet the two small slabs of meat from both sides of the fish. Dip the fillets in flour, egg, and bread crumbs, and then fry them golden brown in peanut or olive oil. It's that simple!

AVOIDING LINE TWIST

Winding new line on your reel is a fairly simple job, but if you do it wrong you'll end up with twists that will pose big problems from your first cast.

▨ Open-Face Spinning Reel

First, attach the reel to a rod. Any rod will do, but never try winding line on a spool by holding the reel in your hands. Next, string the line through the guides, open the bail, and knot the line to the spool. Finally, flip the bail closed.

The line should spiral off the supply spool in the same direction it is going onto the reel spool. Keep the rod tip several feet from the supply spool and maintain tension on the line by holding it between the thumb and forefinger of your rod-holding hand.

If you're alone, place the spool label side up on the floor and wind about 10 feet of line under tension on your reel. Now, drop the rod tip. If the slack line between the rod tip and reel immediately starts to twist, you're putting the line on wrong. Flip the spool label side down and start again. The line should now wind on your reel correctly.

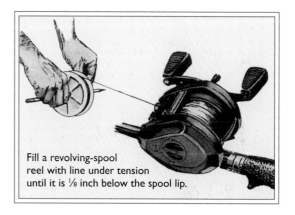

Fill a revolving-spool reel with line under tension until it is 1/8 inch below the spool lip.

You should fill an open-face spinning reel slightly below the spool lip. When the line drops more than 1/4 inch below the spool lip, it's time to put on new line.

▨ Revolving-Spool Reel

If you're filling a revolving-spool reel, start by pushing a pencil through the center of the supply reel. Have a friend hold both ends of the pencil and exert pressure

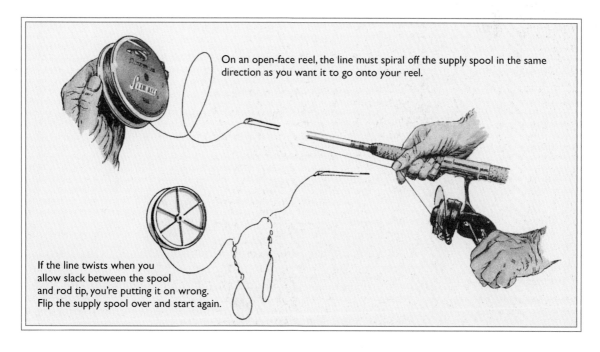

On an open-face reel, the line must spiral off the supply spool in the same direction as you want it to go onto your reel.

If the line twists when you allow slack between the spool and rod tip, you're putting it on wrong. Flip the supply spool over and start again.

inward on the supply spool with his hand to put tension on the line.

The line will go on evenly from side to side if the reel has a level-wind. If not, make sure you wind the line on evenly. You can also use your index finger and thumb of your holding hand to maintain additional tension. Fill the spool to within ⅛ inch of the spool lip.

Spincast Reel

With closed-face spincast reels, use nearly the same method as for open-face spinning reels, except remove the nose cone and hold it in front of the reel while winding on line. Most spincast reels have narrow, deep spools,

which means you'll lose casting distance if the line level drops below ⅛ inch on the spool.

When filling a spincast reel, slip the nose cone forward as you wind line, exposing the spool. Don't overfill the spool.

CARE AND REPAIR OF FISHING TACKLE

There's more than a germ of truth in the old saying, "A fisherman is no better than his tackle." It pays in more ways than one to keep your gear in good working order. For one thing, proper maintenance can add a good many years to the working life of rods, reels, and other tackle on which hard-earned money has been spent. And legions of fishermen have discovered, to their chagrin, that un-oiled reels can "freeze up," neglected rods can snap, and rusty lure hooks can give out—just when that record-breaking fish comes along. The following tackle-care tips should help to prevent such problems.

Care of Rods

Today's rods are designed for long life, but they still require some basic maintenance. The steps recommended below should keep any rod in good working order. How often they should be applied depends upon how often the rods are used and whether they are used in fresh or salt water. Remember that saltwater rods—in fact, all saltwater gear—require much more care than freshwater rods. Even the best of tackle cannot withstand the corrosive action of salt.

1. Wash the rod, including the guides, thoroughly with soap and fresh water, rinse it with hot water, and let it dry completely. If the rod is used in salt water, this step should be taken after each use.

2. If the rod is two pieces or more, thoroughly clean the ferrules. If the ferrules are metal, give them a very light coating of grease to help prevent oxidation.

3. Apply a light coating of wax (automobile wax does a good job) to the entire rod—excluding the cork handle, if the rod has one, and guides.

4. If your rod is starting to show signs of wear, you may want to varnish it. Two thin coats are better than one heavy coat. To avoid creating bubbles in the varnish, apply it with a finger or a pipe cleaner.

5. Store your rod in a dry, safe place. If the rod is bamboo, it must be placed so that it lays flat; if stored on end, it may develop a "set" or permanent bend. Caution: Never store a wet cork-handled rod in a rod case. Mildew will surely form on the cork.

Care of Lines

Check each line for cracking, aging, wear, and rot. If the entire line is no longer serviceable, discard it. If one end has taken all the use, reverse the line. Fly lines tend to crack at the business end after considerable use. If the cracking is confined to the last foot or so, clip off the damaged section or, if the line is a double taper, reverse it. If the damage is more widespread, replace the line.

Check particularly for nicks and other weak spots in monofilament and fluorocarbon, and test the line's breaking strength. If it's weak, replace it. With braided line, check for dark spots, which signify rot, and test the breaking strength. Replace if weak.

Care of Reels

Reels are the most important item of fishing gear and must be cared for properly. The following checklist should be followed:

1. Rinse the reel thoroughly with hot, fresh water. If used in salt water, do this after each trip and use soap. Let dry completely.

2. Oil sparingly.

3. Release drag tension to eliminate spring fatigue.

4. Check the reel's operation. Replace worn or missing parts, and send the reel to the manufacturer for repair if necessary.

5. Cover the reel with a very light coating of oil, and store it in a safe, dry place, preferably in a cloth bag (cloth permits air to enter and escape). Leather cases lock out air.

Care of Tackle Accessories

Accessory equipment deserves equal time from the fisherman. Saltwater lures, for example, are expensive, so take a few minutes to rinse them off with soapy, fresh water after each use so that they don't corrode. The same applies to swivels, hooks, and other saltwater accessories.

The following checklist covers a general overhaul of a tackle box and its contents:

1. Remove the contents of the box, and place the items in some kind of order on a table rather than simply dumping them in a pile. This will help you remember where everything goes when it's time to put your accessories away after cleaning.

2. Use a vacuum cleaner to remove dust and dirt and other loose particles. If the box is metal, wipe the inside with an oily rag, and lubricate the hinges. If it is plastic, wash it with soap and water.

3. Examine the hooks and lures, and discard rusty hooks and all lures that are beyond repair. Make a list of those lures you'll need to restock the box while they are fresh in your mind.

4. Repair salvageable lures. A soft-wire soap pad can be a great help in sprucing up dingy crankbait blades and spoons. Check for broken, rusty, or dull lure hooks, replacing the hooks if necessary or sharpening them with a small whetstone.

5. Sharpen all hooks, and give them a light coating of oil to prevent rust.

6. Wash the bag of your landing net with a mild detergent.

7. Patch all holes and weak spots in hip boots and waders, and store them in a dark, cool spot. The best way to store boots is to hang them upside down by the boot feet. A sturdy, heavy-wire coat hanger, cut in the middle of the bottom section and bent judiciously, makes an excellent and inexpensive boot-hanger.

Rod-Wrapping Tricks of the Trade

GUIDES AND TENSION: Guides should be purchased in matched sets to ensure uniformity. The feet of guides should be dressed with a file to a fine taper. Next, sight your rod. If you notice a slight bend or offset, apply guides opposite the bend; this will bring it into a straight position. Guides should be affixed with snug wrapping tension, so that you may sight after wrapping and make slight guide adjustments before applying the color preserver. Do not wrap guides to the absolute breaking point of the thread. Remember, 10 or 20 wraps of thread exert very heavy pressure on the feet of the guides. It is possible to damage a blank by wrapping too tight.

THREADS: Sizes 2/0 to E are the most commonly used threads. Sizes 2/0 or A are used for fly, casting, or spinning rods. Sizes D or E are used for the heavier freshwater spinning or saltwater rods. Naturally, the finer size 2/0 thread will make a neater job, but, being lighter, it is not quite as durable.

TRIM: You may trim the basic color of your wrap with five to 10 turns of another color of thread. This is done just as outlined in the instructions for a basic wrap.

COLOR PRESERVER AND ROD VARNISH: Good color preserver has plastic in it, and should be quite thin in order to penetrate the wrappings. Good-grade varnish is essential to the durability of the finish. Most custom rod builders prefer two-part rod finishes. A brush may be used to apply both the color preserver and rod varnish; however, air bubbles are usually present when a brush is used. To maintain a smooth finish, make certain these

How to Wrap Guides

1 • Start by wrapping over the end of the thread toward the guide so the thread end is held down by the wrapping. Using the tension from whatever type of tension device you are using to hold the wrapping tight, continue to turn the rod so that each thread lies as close as possible to the preceding turn.

2 • About five to eight turns from the finish of the wrap, insert the loop of the tie-off thread. (This can be 6 inches of heavier thread or a fine piece of nylon leader material.) Finish the wrap over this tie-off loop.

3 • Holding the wrap tightly, cut the wrapping thread about 4 inches from your rod. Insert this cut end through the tie-off loop. Still holding onto the wrapping thread, pull the cut-off thread under the wraps with the tie-off loop.

4 • With a razor blade, trim the cut-off end as close as possible to the wrap. With the back of a knife or your fingernail, push the wrapping up tight so that it appears solid, and none of the rod or guide shows through.

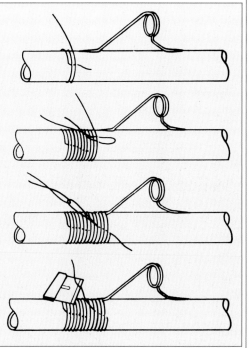

bubbles are out. A very satisfactory method of minimizing air bubbles is to apply both the color preserver and rod varnish with your index finger. This will prevent any shading of the wrapping color.

■ Selecting the Tip Top and Other Guides

The rod builder, like just about everyone else, gets what he pays for. It doesn't pay to skimp on rod guides, especially if the rod is to be used in salt water or for heavy freshwater fish such as pike, muskies, and salmon.

Guides are made of various metals, including hard-ened stainless steel, chrome (or chrome-plated Monel), Fuji Hardloy, agate, and tungsten carbide, with the carbide types being the most durable. Silicone carbide or titanium carbide are recommended for abrasive lines, such as braid or Dacron. Roller guides for heavy saltwater fishing are usually made of stainless steel, Monel, or nickel alloy. The rod builder should note that guides are available in sets tailored to particular rod types and lengths.

The tip top must fit snugly over the end of the rod, and so its selection is sometimes a problem. The accompanying chart will help the rod builder overcome this problem. It shows the actual sizes, in 64ths of an inch, of the inside diameters of a wide range of tip-top guides.

Rod Guide Diameters

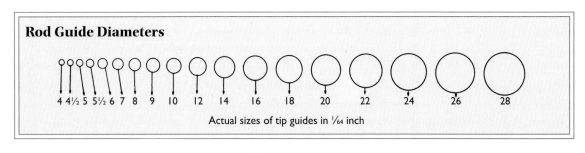

4 4½ 5 5½ 6 7 8   9   10   12   14   16   18   20   22   24   26   28

Actual sizes of tip guides in ¹⁄₆₄ inch

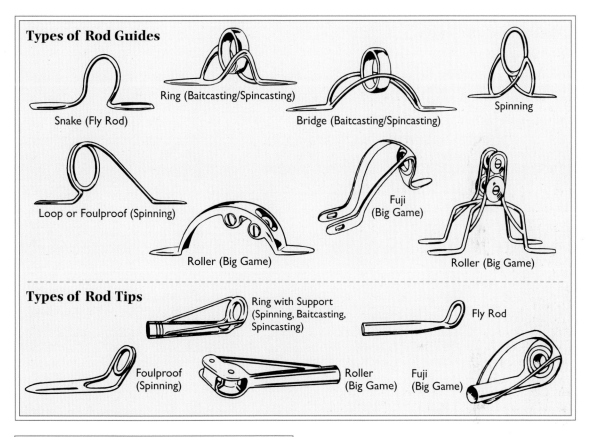

Types of Rod Guides

Snake (Fly Rod)

Ring (Baitcasting/Spincasting)

Bridge (Baitcasting/Spincasting)

Spinning

Loop or Foulproof (Spinning)

Roller (Big Game)

Fuji (Big Game)

Roller (Big Game)

Types of Rod Tips

Ring with Support (Spinning, Baitcasting, Spincasting)

Fly Rod

Foulproof (Spinning)

Roller (Big Game)

Fuji (Big Game)

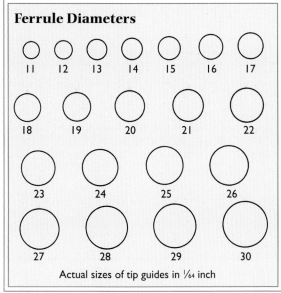

Ferrule Diameters

11 12 13 14 15 16 17

18 19 20 21 22

23 24 25 26

27 28 29 30

Actual sizes of tip guides in 1/64 inch

To determine what size tip top you need, simply place the end of the rod tip over the circles until you find the correct size.

■ Selecting Rod Ferrules

Most rods today that break down into two or more pieces avoid any kind of ferrule, preferring to use the tapers themselves to form a smooth integral connection and an action that comes close to a one-piece rod. Some rods, however, still use a ferrule system—joint-like devices inserted along the working length of a fishing rod that enables the rod to be dismantled into two or more sections. Ferrules are generally made of metal (nickel, brass, or aluminum), or a synthetic material. A ferrule set consists of two parts, the male ferrule and the female ferrule. The male section should fit snugly into the female section.

What size ferrule do you need for your rod? The accompanying chart will help you find out. It shows

Suggested Guide Spacing

All measurements are from the tip of the rod down. Figures indicate measurements at the guide ring.

	Rod Length	Lure-Weight Range (ounces)	Fly-Line Weights	Measurements at the Guide Ring (inches)							
				1st	2nd	3rd	4th	5th	6th	7th	8th
SPINCASTING, BAITCASTING	5½ ft.	⅛ to ⅓		4½	12	23	36				
	6 ft.	⅛ to ⅜		4	10	18	28	40			
	6 ft.	¼ to ¾		4	8¼	13	18	24½	32⅛	42	
	6 ft.	⅜ to 1¼		3½	7½	12	17⅜	23⅝	31⅞	42½	
	6 ft., 4 in.	1/16 to ¼		4	10	18½	28½	41			
	6 ft., 4 in.	⅜		4	10	18½	28½	41			
	6 ft., 4 in.	⅛ to ½		4	10	18½	28½	41			
	6 ft.	⅜ to ⅝		4	10	18	28	40			
	6 ft., 4 in.	¼ to ⅝		4	10	18½	28½	41			
FLY RODS	5 ft., 5 in.		5F, 6S	5	13	25	40				
	6 ft.		5F, 6S	3	7½	12	17¾	25	33	42½	
	7½ ft.		6F, 7S	6	13	21	30	41½	60		
	7 ft., 8 in.		6 or 7F, 7S	6	13	21	30	43	62		
	8 ft.		6 or 7F, 7S	6	13	21	30	41	52	66	
	8 ft.		7F, 7S	6	13	21	30	40	53	66	
	8 ft.		7 or 8F, 7 or 8S	6	13	21	30	41	53	66	
	8½ ft.		7 or 8F, 7 or 8S	6	13	21	30	40	56	73	
	8½ ft.		7F, 7S	6	13	21	30	40	56	73	
	8½ ft.		8 or 9F, 8 or 9S	6	13	21	30	40	56	73	
	9 ft.		7 or 8F, 7 or 8S	5	11	18	26	35	45	58½	73
	9 ft.		8 or 9F, 8 or 9S	5	11	18	26	35	45	58½	73
	10 ft.		9 or 10F, 9 or 10S	6	13	22	32	43	54½	66½	80½
SPINNING ROD	6 ft.	up to ¼		5½	15½	27½	40½				
	6 ft.	up to ⅜		3½	10	19	29¼	41½			
	6½ ft.	1/16 to ¼		3½	8½	15	23	33	46		
	6½ ft.	⅛ to 1		5	10⅜	16⅜	23⅜	31⅞	44		
	6½ ft.	⅛ to ⅜		3½	8½	15	23	33	46		
	6½ ft.	¼ to ⅝		3½	8½	15	23	33	46		
	7 ft. *	1/16 to ⅜	5 or 6F, 6S	4	10	18	27½	38½	52½		
	7 ft.	1/16 to ⅜		4	10	18	27½	38½	52½		
	7 ft.	up to 1½		4	10	18	27½	38	51		

KEY: F—FLOATING S—SINKING *—COMBINATION SPIN/FLY ROD

the actual sizes, in 64ths of an inch, of the inside diameters of a wide range of ferrules. To determine the correct ferrule for your rod, simply place the upper end of the butt section (if it is a two-piece rod) over the circles until you find the right fit.

Spacing of Rod Guides

Whether you are building a fishing rod from scratch (that is, taking a fiberglass blank and adding a butt, reel seat, and guides) or refinishing an old favorite, you must pay close attention to the placement of the guides along the working length of the rod.

Putting too many or too few guides on a rod, or placing them improperly along the rod, may detract from proper rod action and put undue strain on the line and the rod.

The accompanying chart gives the correct number of guides—and exact spacing measurements—for most spinning, baitcasting, spincasting, and fly rods.

Fishing Rods Are Not Poles

Some of my buddies insist on calling their fishing rods "poles." This is not a big deal and certainly cannot be compared to a disagreement about catfish baits or where to hook a minnow. But it gives me pause when someone refers to my $500 graphite fly rod as a "fishing pole." And it seems to make no difference whether you're fishing a small creek or ocean waters. I would have thought there would be some discreet discrimination among fishermen, but this aberration crosses all lines.

I can't imagine the staff members at the Orvis fly shop referring to the company's $900 Helios fly rod as a "fishing pole." But I guess it's just too late for most fishermen to alter this diminished perception of fishing tackle. As years pass, I am learning to accept this unfortunate label. This problem has even gone as far as the White House. A major outdoor magazine once awarded to a former president, who shall remain nameless, a beautiful monogrammed fly rod. He accepted it graciously, but he referred to it as "a good pole to fish live crickets." He was not reelected.

I will try to stop correcting fishermen. I will no longer say fishing rods are for fishing and poles are for flags! But next time I see a young child fishing for sunnies in a farm pond with a cane pole, I will say, "That's a fine-looking cane rod."

You should not lose any sleep over this nagging problem of mine. If you want to call them fishing poles, so be it. But if you ever see me double-hauling with my $500 fly rod, please be kind and don't call it a fishing pole.

ESTIMATING FISH WEIGHT

You've just caught a big pike. In fact, it measures 40 inches, according to the stick-on tape measure you received free from the bait shop. Now you want to know how much the pike weighs, but you don't have a scale.

Over the years, fishermen have come up with several ways to estimate fish weight without a scale. Some have proved to be fairly accurate; some didn't even come close. Eventually, the generally accepted formula became:

Length times Girth squared divided by 800 equals Weight,
or L x G² ÷ 800 = W

Using this formula is supposed to bring you within 10 percent of a fish's actual weight. The only problem is that the formula doesn't differentiate between fat fish (such as bass or tuna) and elongate fish (such as pike or barracuda).

Doug Hannon, a renowned Florida bass fisherman, has developed a more precise calculation specifically for bass and similarly shaped round fish. In addition to being more accurate, it requires only one measurement. Hannon's formula is:

Length cubed divided by 1,600 equals Weight,
or L³ ÷ 1,600 = W

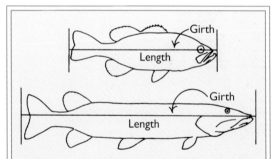

The traditional formula for determining the weight of a fish didn't take into account its shape—either elongate or round. The old equation could be off by as much as 10 percent.

If you caught a 20-inch bass, for example, the math would be 20 times 20 times 20 (8,000), divided by 1,600. Congratulations, that's a nice 5-pounder.

With the widespread adoption of catch-and-release fishing, fishermen have developed modifications of the length-cubed formula that work well with other species, too. For pike, muskies, and other elongate fish, use this formula:

$$L^3 \div 3{,}500 = W$$

In other words, that 40-inch pike that you caught would weigh about 18.3 pounds. (Actually, it's 18.28 pounds, but any fisherman is allowed to round up to the higher tenth.)

If you're a panfish specialist, the formula to use is:

$$L^3 \div 1,200 = W$$

An 8-inch bluegill, for example, would weigh 0.42 pounds. And if walleyes are your target, the formula changes slightly to:

$$L^3 \div 2,700 = W$$

This means the 22-inch walleye you boasted was a 10-pounder really only weighed about 4 pounds.

How to Hold a Fish

You want to release the fish you just caught unharmed, but do you know where to hold it without damaging any of its vital organs so that you can remove the hook safely?

It really depends on the fish. Some have sharp teeth, while others have gill plates that will cut you like a knife. Fin spines are other obstacles to avoid. Bass—including stripers and members of the black bass family—are the easiest to hold because their lower jaws make perfect handles. You should lift a bass with your thumb inside its lower lip, and your curled index finger pinching firmly against it from the outside. Big crappies also can be handled in the same manner.

Unlike bass and crappies, walleyes have very sharp teeth and sharp gill plates. Don't even think about trying a lip hold on a walleye—you'll regret it. Instead, grab it behind the head and across the back. Always start your grip in front of the dorsal fin and carefully slide your hand to the rear, pushing down the sharp dorsal spines with the heel of your hand.

Panfish and some varieties of perch likewise have sharp dorsal spines and should be held in the same manner as walleyes. The dorsal fin of a bluegill can inflict a painful puncture if it's not held down with your hand.

Trout and salmon might not have sharp dorsal fins, but they do have mouths full of teeth. When you hold a trout or salmon, first wet your hands and then cradle the fish in the palms of both hands. Trout are slippery, so you will need a firm grip. Don't squeeze too tight, however, if you plan to release the fish. Squeeze a trout too hard and you might rupture its organs, which is fatal.

Many species of freshwater and saltwater fish have sharp teeth and require special handling. Bluefish and barracuda, for example, can inflict painful bites if not handled carefully. The best way to hold one of these toothy critters is to get a firm grip behind the top of its head and hold on tightly while you remove hooks with needle-nose fishing pliers. You're holding the fish in an area of its body that is virtually impervious to injury. The same technique will work for muskies, pike, and pickerel.

Catfish have spines in the dorsal and pectoral fins that can puncture skin and inflict a nasty wound. When you hold a catfish, grip it from the front and slide your hand carefully toward the tail, pushing down the fins and sharp spines. Catfish are tough and can usually survive a firmer grip than might be employed for trout.

Barracuda

Bass

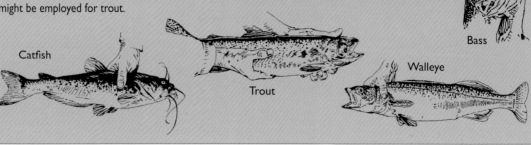

Catfish

Trout

Walleye

EASY FISH RELEASE

ffective catch-and-release fishing is a critical factor for the future of fish stocks in both fresh and salt water. A simple wire dehooker device is amazingly effective in releasing lip-hooked fish without harm and in a matter of seconds. The device, shown in the accompanying illustrations, is a wire with an L-shaped hook formed on the end. Using this type of dehooker, you can release a fish over water without touching it. The fish will drop safely back into the water.

If you must touch or net a fish, wear wet cotton gloves and always avoid touching the gills. If you regularly net your fish before release, use a smooth rubber mesh net, such as the nets used in fish hatcheries. Avoid nets with knots, which will break through the fish's protective coat of slime and make it vulnerable to fungus infection.

You can make your own catch-and-release device for lip-hooked fish from a length of heavy wire or you can buy one of the many inexpensive dehookers available from your local tackle dealer.

SKIN A FISH FOR MOUNTING

ou're on a remote river in Alaska and you've just caught a giant sockeye salmon that's perfect for your wall back home. Freezers are in short supply and the closest taxidermist is unknown to you, expensive, and may get around to your fish when things get slow at his day job. You've got a problem.

Here's the solution: If you decide you want a skin mount of your fish, you can preserve your trophy by skinning and salting it in the field. Once home, you'll have plenty of time to find a reputable taxidermist, since the salted skin can be frozen indefinitely.

Some planning is required. You'll need to pack a few plastic trash bags, some cotton, cardboard, and paper clips. Anything else you need—such as table salt (2 to 4 pounds) and scissors—can be found in most fishing camps.

It's a good idea to practice this method before you go. Lay the fish on a piece of cardboard and position it exactly as you want it mounted. Trace the

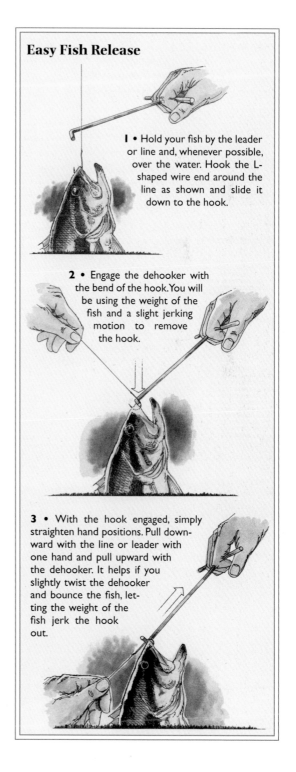

Easy Fish Release

1 • Hold your fish by the leader or line and, whenever possible, over the water. Hook the L-shaped wire end around the line as shown and slide it down to the hook.

2 • Engage the dehooker with the bend of the hook. You will be using the weight of the fish and a slight jerking motion to remove the hook.

3 • With the hook engaged, simply straighten hand positions. Pull downward with the line or leader with one hand and pull upward with the dehooker. It helps if you slightly twist the dehooker and bounce the fish, letting the weight of the fish jerk the hook out.

outline of the fish on the cardboard with a pencil. Then, at three spots along the length of the fish, measure its girth (or cut exact lengths of mono wrapped around it at these points). Save these dimensions with the outline. Also, take a few color photos of your catch as soon as possible, to help your taxidermist re-create true-to-life colors.

In these days of the catch-and-release mentality, most fishermen wisely opt to release their trophy fish unharmed and prefer to get a replica fiberglass mount of their fish instead. To ensure an accurate fiberglass replica, make sure you take a good color photo of the fish as well as an overall length measurement. The big advantage, aside from releasing your fish to fight another day, is that fiberglass mounts, which are hollow, are surprisingly lightweight, will never fade, and can also be hung outdoors.

Richard Stancyzk and Vin Sparano show off a good bone-fish, a species that is typically released. To make sure you get a good, accurate fiberglass replica, supply a taxidermist with length and girth measurements and a bright color photo of your fish.

How to Skin a Fish for Mounting

Step 1 • Make a lateral cut along the back side of the fish, where it will not show. Cut through the skin from the gill plate to the tail. Use scissors to cut cleanly through the bony substance at the gill plate.

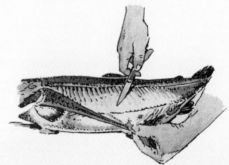

Step 2 • Using a small knife, pare the skin away from the body. Work slowly, being careful not to tear the skin. Be particularly careful in the area around the gills.

Step 3 • At the fins, working from the inside with the scissors, cut the meat free. At the base of the tail, turn the knife and cut directly through the flesh. Take care not to cut the skin on the other side.

Step 4 • Working back from tail to head, cut the skin away from the body on the other side. When the skin is completely freed, sever the backbone, leaving the head attached to the skin.

Step 6 • Free the gills and remove all flesh from inside the head, including the eyes. During the entire skinning process, make sure you don't break or split any fins.

Step 5 • Holding the skin with one hand, use a spoon to gently scrape the remaining meat from the skin. Remove all the cartilage from below and behind the gill plates.

Step 7 • Rub liberal amounts of table salt into the skin, inside the head, and into the base of all fins. Use plenty of salt and work it in thoroughly, but gently.

Step 8 • Wrap the fins in wet cotton. Place pieces of cardboard, held by paper clips, over the cotton. Wrap the fish in a plastic bag. Your trophy is now ready for the taxidermist.

WATER TEMPERATURE AND FISH

There is no doubt left in anglers' minds of the importance of water temperature and its direct bearing on the activities of fish. Water temperature will tell you where the fish gather and where they feed at various times of the year.

It is a scientifically proven fact that every species of fish has a preferred temperature zone or range and it will stay and generally feed in this zone. Smallmouth bass, for example, prefer water that is 65 to 68°F. During spring, this temperature range may be in shallow water, and in hot, midsummer weather, this range may be in depths of 30 feet or more. In other words, locate the depth that reads 65 to 68°F and you're sure to find smallmouths.

Taking temperature readings of water is not difficult, whether you use a sophisticated electronic thermometer or an inexpensive water thermometer lowered into the water on a fishing line. One electronic thermometer has a probe attached to a cable that is marked at regular intervals, so depth and temperature can be read simultaneously.

The inexpensive water thermometers can also do the job, and many also indicate depth by inserting a water pressure gauge in the thermometer tube. With these thermometers, allow at least 30 seconds to one minute for a reading. Also, the fishing line attached to it should be marked off in regular intervals, say 5 feet, so you can determine just how deep you are lowering the thermometer in the water.

The accompanying chart shows popular fresh- and saltwater game fish and baitfish and their preferred temperature zones. Look up the fish you are seeking and the water temperature it prefers. Then, begin taking temperature readings from the surface on down, at 5-foot intervals, until you locate the correct zone and depth. Concentrate your efforts at that depth and you'll soon come to discover how important this water temperature business is.

Preferred Temperature

Note: Celsius temperatures are rounded to the nearest degree.

FRESHWATER GAME FISH

Species	Lower Avoidance	Optimum	Upper Avoidance
American shad (*Alosa sapidissima*)		66°F (19°C)	86°F (30°C)
Atlantic salmon (*Salmo salar*)		62°F (17°C)	
Atlantic sturgeon (*Acipenser oxyrhynchus*)	56°F (13°C)	66°F (19°C)	70°F (21°C)
Black crappie (*Pomoxis nigromaculatus*)	60°F (16°C)	70°F (21°C)	75F° (24°C)
Bloater (*Coregonus hoyi*)	43°F (6°C)		50°F (10°C)
Bluegill (*Lepomis macrochirus*)	58°F (14°C)	69°F (21°C)	75°F (24°C)
Brook trout (*Salvelinus fontinalis*)	44°F (7°C)	59°F (15°C)	70°F (21°C)
Brown bullhead (*Ictalurus nebulosus*)		74°F (23°C)	
Brown trout (*Salmo trutta*)	44°F (7°C)	55–65°F (13–18°C)	75°F (24°C)
Buffalo species (*Ictiobus sp.*)	81°F (27°C)		94°F (34°C)
Burbot (*Lota lota maculosa*)		52°F (11°C)	
Carp (*Cyprinus carpio*)	75°F (24°C)	84°F (29°C)	88°F (31°C)
Chain pickerel (*Esox niger*)	60°F (16°C)	66°F (19°C)	74°F (23°C)
Channel catfish (*Ictalurus punctutatus*)	55°F (13°C)	82–89°F (28–32°C)	
Chinook salmon (*Oncorhynchus tshawytscha*)	44°F (7°C)	54°F (12°C)	60°F (16°C)
Chum salmon (*Oncorhynchus keta*)		57°F (14°C)	
Cisco (*Coregonus artedii*)		52–55°F (11–13°C)	
Coho salmon (*Oncorhynchus kisutch*)	44°F (7°C)	54°F (12°C)	60°F (16°C)

FRESHWATER GAME FISH (continued)

Species	Lower Avoidance	Optimum	Upper Avoidance
Flathead catfish (*Pylodictis olivaris*)	81°F (27°C)		90°F (32°C)
Freshwater drum (*Aplodinotus grunniens*)		74°F (23°C)	
Grass pickerel (*Esox americanus vermiculatus*)		78°F (26°C)	
Grayling (*Thymallus arcticus*)			64°F (18°C)
Green sunfish (*Lepomis cyanellus*)	73°F (23°C)	87°F (31°C)	91°F (33°C)
Goldeye (*Hiodon alosoides*)	72°F (22°C)		83°F (28°C)
Kamloops trout (*Salmo gairdneri*)	46°F (8°C)	47–54°F (8–12°C)	
Kokanee (*Oncorhynchus nerka*)		52–55°F (11–13°C)	
Lake trout (*Salvelinus namaycush*)	42°F (6°C)	50–59°F (10–15°C)	
Lake whitefish (*Coregonus clupeaformis*)	43°F (6°C)	51°F (11°C)	
Landlocked Atlantic salmon (*Salmo salar sebago*)		50–58°F (10–14°C)	65°F (18°C)
Largemouth bass (*Micropterus salmoides*)	60°F (16°C)	80°F (27°C)	
Longnose gar (*Lepisosteus osseus*)		92°F (33°C)	
Longnose sucker (*Catostomus catostomus*)		53°F (12°C)	
Mooneye (*Hiodon tergisus*)	72°F (22°C)		81°F (27°C)
Muskellunge (*Esox masquinongy*)	55°F (13°C)	63°F (17°C)	72°F (22°C)
Northern pike (*Esox lucius*)	56°F (13°C)	63°F (17°C)	74°F (23°C)
Pink salmon (*Oncorhynchus gorbuscha*)		49°F (9°C)	
Pumpkinseed (*Lepomis gibbosus*)		82°F (28°C)	
Rainbow trout (*Salmo gairdneri*)	44°F (7°C)	48–65°F (9–18°C)	75°F (24°C)
Redhorse suckers (*Moxostoma sp.*)	72°F (22°C)		79°F (26°C)
Rock bass (*Ambloplites rupestris*)		70°F (21°C)	
Round whitefish (*Prosopium cylindraceum*)		63°F (17°C)	
Sauger (*Stizostedion canadense*)	55°F (13°C)	67°F (19°C)	74°F (23°C)
Shortnose gar (*Lepisosteus platostomus*)	81°F (27°C)		94°F (34°C)
Smallmouth bass (*Micropterus dolomieui*)	60°F (16°C)	65–68°F (18–20°C)	73°F (23°C)
Sockeye salmon (*Oncorhynchus nerka*)		55°F (13°C)	
Spotted bass (*Micropterus punctulatus*)	71°F (22°C)	75°F (24°C)	80°F (27°C)
Steelhead trout (*Salmo gairdneri*)	38°F (3°C)	48–52°F (9–11°C)	
Sunfishes (*Centrarchidae*)	50°F (10°C)	58°F (14°C)	68°F (20°C)
Tench (*Tinca tinca*)			79°F (26°C)
Walleye (*Stizostedion vitreum*)	50°F (10°C)	67°F (19°C)	76°F (24°C)
White bass (*Morone chrysops*)	62°F (17°C)	70°F (21°C)	78°F (26°C)
White crappie (*Pomoxis annularis*)		61°F (16°C)	
White perch (*Morone americana*)		89°F (32°C)	
White sucker (*Catostomus commersoni*)		72°F (22°C)	
Yellow bass (*Morone mississippiensis*)		81°F (27°C)	
Yellow bullhead (*Ictalurus natalis*)		83°F (28°C)	
Yellow perch (*Perca flavescens*)	58°F (14°C)	65°F (18°C)	74°F (23°C)

FRESHWATER BAITFISH

Species	Lower Avoidance	Optimum	Upper Avoidance
Alewife (*Alosa pseudoharengus*)	48°F (9°C)	54°F (12°C)	72°F (22°C)
Bitterling (*Rhodeus sericeus*)		77°F (25°C)	

FRESHWATER BAITFISH (continued)

Species	Lower Avoidance	Optimum	Upper Avoidance
Bluehead chub (*Nocomis leptocephalus*)	50°F (10°C)	59°F (15°C)	63°F (17°C)
Bluntnose minnow (*Pimephales notatus*)	70°F (21°C)	84°F (29°C)	88°F (31°C)
Desert pupfish (*Cyprinodon macularius*)	71°F (22°C)		78°F (26°C)
Emerald shiner (*Notropis atherinoides*)		61°F (16°C)	
Fathead minnow (*Pimephales promelas*)	77°F (25°C)	84°F (29°C)	90°F (32°C)
Fourhorn sculpin (*Myoxocephalus quadricornis*)	39°F (4°C)		
Gizzard shad (*Dorosoma cepedianum*)		69°F (21°C)	
Golden shiner (*Notemigonus crysoleucas*)		70°F (21°C)	
Goldfish (*Carassius auratus*)		77°F (25°C)	
Guppy (*Poecilia reticulata*)		84°F (29°C)	
Lake chub (*Couesius plumbeus*)		48–52°F (9–11°C)	
Longjaw mudsucker (*Gillichthys mirabilis*)	48°F (9°C)	72°F (22°C)	
Moapa dace (*Moapa coriacea*)		85°F (29°C)	
Mosquitofish (*Gambusia affinis*)		81°F (27°C)	85°F (29°C)
Mottled sculpin (*Cottus bairdi*)		48–52°F (9–11°C)	
Mozambique mouthbrooder (*Tilapia mossambica*)		83°F (28°C)	92°F (33°C)
Ninespine stickleback (*Pungitius pungitius*)		48–52°F (9–11°C)	
Quillback (*Carpiodes cyprinus*)		72°F (22°C)	
Rainbow smelt (*Osmerus mordax*)	43°F (6°C)	50°F (10°C)	57°F (14°C)
River carpsucker (*Carpoides carpio*)	79°F (26°C)		94°F (34°C)
Rosyface shiner (*Notropis rubellus*)	70°F (21°C)	80°F (27°C)	88°F (31°C)
Slimy sculpin (*Cottus cognatus*)	39°F (4°C)		43°F (6°C)
Spotfin shiner (*Cyprinella spiloptera*)	79°F (26°C)	85°F (29°C)	95°F (35°C)
Spottail shiner (*Notropis hudsonius*)		54°F (12°C)	
Stonecat (*Notorus flavus*)		59°F (15°C)	
Stoneroller (*Campostoma anomalum*)	75°F (24°C)	84°F (29°C)	91°F (33°C)
Trout-perch (*Percopsis omiscomaycus*)	50°F (10°C)		61°F (16°C)
White River killfish (*Crenichthys baileyi*)		85°F (29°C)	

SALTWATER GAME FISH

Species	Lower Avoidance	Optimum	Upper Avoidance
Albacore (*Thunnus alalunga*)	59°F (15°C)	64°F (18°C)	66°F (19°C)
Amberjack (*Seriola dumerili*)	60°F (16°C)	65°F (18°C)	72°F (22°C)
Atlantic bonito (*Sarda sarda*)	60°F (16°C)	64°F (18°C)	80°F (27°C)
Atlantic cod (*Gadus morhua*)	31°F (-1°C)	44–49°F (7–9°C)	59°F (15°C)
Atlantic croaker (*Micropogon undulatus*)			100°F (38°C)
Atlantic mackerel (*Scomber scombrus*)	45°F (7°C)	63°F (17°C)	70°F (21°C)
Barracuda (*Sphyraena barracuda*)	55°F (13°C)	75–79°F (24–26°C)	82°F (28°C)
Bigeye tuna (*Thunnus obesus*)	52°F (11°C)	58°F (14°C)	66°F (19°C)
Blackfin tuna (*Thunnus atlanticus*)	70°F (21°C)	74°F (23°C)	82°F (28°C)
Black marlin (*Makaira indica*)	68°F (20°C)	75–79°F (24–26°C)	87°F (31°C)
Bluefin tuna (*Thunnus thynnus*)	50°F (10°C)	68°F (20°C)	78°F (26°C)
Bluefish (*Pomatomus saltatrix*)	50°F (10°C)	66–72°F (19–22°C)	84°F (19°C)
Blue marlin (*Makaira nigricans*)	70°F (21°C)	78°F (26°C)	88°F (31°C)

SALTWATER GAME FISH *(continued)*

Species	Lower Avoidance	Optimum	Upper Avoidance
Bonefish (*Albula vulpes*)	64°F (18°C)	75°F (24°C)	88°F (31°C)
Dolphinfish (*Coryphaena hippurus*)	70°F (21°C)	75°F (24°C)	82°F (28°C)
Fluke or summer flounder (*Paralichthys dentatus*)	56°F (13°C)	66°F (19°C)	72°F (22°C)
Haddock (*Melanogrammus aeglefinus*)	36°F (2°C)	47°F (8°C)	52°F (11°C)
Horn shark (*Heterodontus francisci*)		75°F (24°C)	
Kelp bass (*Paralabrax clathratus*)	62°F (17°C)	65°F (18°C)	72°F (22°C)
King mackerel (*Scomberomorus cavalla*)	70°F (21°C)		88°F (31°C)
Opaleye (*Girella nigricans*)		79°F (26°C)	86°F (30°C)
Permit (*Trachinotus falcatus*)	65°F (18°C)	72°F (22°C)	92°F (33°C)
Pollock (*Pollachius virens*)	33°F (1°C)	45°F (8°C)	60°F (16°C)
Red drum (*Sciaenops ocellatus*)	52°F (11°C)	71°F (22°C)	90°F (32°C)
Red snapper (*Lutjanus blackfordi*)	50°F (10°C)	57°F (14°C)	62°F (17°C)
Sailfish (*Istiophorus platypterus*)	68°F (20°C)	79°F (26°C)	88°F (31°C)
Sand seatrout (*Cynoscion arenarius*)	90°F (32°C)	95°F (35°C)	104°F (40°C)
Sea catfish (*Arius felis*)			99°F (37°C)
Skipjack tuna (*Euthynnus pelamis*)	50°F (10°C)	62°F (17°C)	70°F (21°C)
Snook (*Centropomus undecimalis*)	60°F (16°C)	70–75°F (21–24°C)	90°F (32°C)
Spotted seatrout (*Cynoscion nebulosus*)	48°F (9°C)	72°F (22°C)	81°F (27°C)
Striped bass (*Morone saxatilis*)	61°F (16°C)	68°F (20°C)	77°F (25°C)
Striped marlin (*Tetrapturus audax*)	61°F (16°C)	70°F (21°C)	80°F (27°C)
Swordfish (*Xiphias gladius*)	50°F (10°C)	66°F (19°C)	78°F (26°C)
Tarpon (*Megalops atlantica*)	74°F (23°C)	76°F (24°C)	90°F (32°C)
Tautog (*Tautoga onitis*)	60°F (16°C)	70°F (21°C)	76°F (24°C)
Weakfish (*Cynoscion regalis*)		55–65°F (13–18°C)	78°F (26°C)
White marlin (*Tetrapturus albidus*)	65°F (18°C)	70°F (21°C)	80°F (27°C)
White sea bass (*Cynoscion nobilis*)	58°F (14°C)	68°F (20°C)	74°F (23°C)
Winter flounder (*Pseudopleuronectes americanus*)	35°F (2°C)	48–52°F (9–11°C)	64°F (18°C)
Yellowfin tuna (*Thunnus albacares*)	64°F (18°C)	72°F (22°C)	80°F (27°C)
Yellowtail (*Seriola dorsalis*)	60°F (16°C)	65°F (18°C)	70°F (21°C)

SALTWATER BAITFISH

Species	Lower Avoidance	Optimum	Upper Avoidance
Atlantic silverside (*Menidia menidia*)			90°F (32°C)
Atlantic threadfin (*Polydactylus octonemus*)			92°F (33°C)
Bay anchovy (*Anchoa mitchilli*)		82°F (28°C)	92°F (33°C)
California grunion (*Leuresthes tenuis*)	68°F (20°C)	77°F (25°C)	93°F (34°C)
Gulf grunion (*Leuresthes sardina*)	68°F (20°C)	89°F (32°C)	98°F (37°C)
Gulf menhaden (*Brevoortia patronus*)			86°F (30°C)
Pacific silversides (jacksmelt and topsmelt) (*Atherinopsis sp.*)	72°F (22°C)	77°F (25°C)	82°F (28°C)
Rough silverside (*Membras martinica*)			91°F (33°C)
Skipjack herring (*Alosa chrysochloris*)	72°F (22°C)		84°F (29°C)
Spot (*Leiostomus xanthurus*)			99°F (37°C)
Tidewater silverside (*Menidia beryllina*)			93°F (34°C)

INTERNATIONAL GAME FISH ASSOCIATION RULES AND REGULATIONS

The following angling rules have been formulated by the International Game Fish Association (IGFA) to promote ethical and sporting angling practices, to establish uniform regulations for the compilation of world game-fish records, and to provide basic angling guidelines for use in fishing tournaments and any other group angling activities.

The word *angling* is defined as catching or attempting to catch fish with a rod, reel, line, and hook as outlined in the international angling rules. There are some aspects of angling that cannot be controlled through rule making, however. Angling regulations cannot ensure an outstanding performance from each fish, and world records cannot indicate the amount of difficulty in catching the fish. Captures in which the fish has not fought or has not had a chance to fight do not reflect credit on the fisherman, and only the angler can properly evaluate the degree of achievement in establishing the record.

Only fish caught in accordance with IGFA international angling rules, and within the intent of those rules, will be considered for world records. Following are the rules for freshwater and saltwater fishing and a separate set of rules for fly fishing.

INTERNATIONAL ANGLING RULES (Fishing in Fresh and Salt Water)

▨ Equipment Regulations

LINE

1. Monofilament, multifilament, and lead-core multifilament lines may be used. For line classes, see World Record Requirements.

2. Wire lines are prohibited.

LINE BACKING

1. Backing not attached to the fishing line is permissible with no restrictions as to size or material.

2. If the fishing line is attached to backing, the catch shall be classified under the heavier of the lines. Backing may not exceed the 130-pound (60-kilogram) line class and must be of a type of line approved for use in these angling rules.

DOUBLE LINE

The use of a double line is not required. If one is used, it must meet the following specifications:

1. A double line must consist of the actual line used to catch the fish.

2. Double lines are measured from the start of the knot, braid, roll, or splice making the double to the farthermost end of the knot, splice, snap, swivel, or other device used for securing the trace, leader, lure, or hook to the double line.

Saltwater species: In all line classes up to and including 20 pound (10 kilogram), the double line shall be limited to 15 feet (4.57 meters). The combined length of the double line and leader shall not exceed 20 feet (6.1 meters). The double line on all classes of tackle over 20 pound (10 kilogram) shall be limited to 30 feet (9.14 meters). The combined length of the double line and leader shall not exceed 40 feet (12.19 meters).

Freshwater species: The double line on all classes of tackle shall not exceed 6 feet (1.82 meters). The combined length of the double line and the leader shall not exceed 10 feet (3.04 meters).

Illustrated Guide to Equipment Regulations: Double Lines and Leaders

Double lines are measured from the start of the knot, braid, roll, or splice making the double line to the farthermost end of the knot, splice, snap, swivel, or other device used for securing the trace, leader lure, or hook to the double line. A double line must consist of the actual line used to catch the fish. For saltwater species, the double line shall be limited to 15 feet (4.57 meters) for all line classes up to and including 20 pound (10 kilogram), and shall be limited to 30 feet (9.14 meters) for line classes over 20 pound (10 kilogram). For freshwater species, the double line on all classes of tackle shall not exceed 6 feet (1.82 meters).

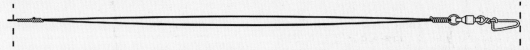

The leader shall be limited to 15 feet (4.57 meters) for saltwater species in line classes up to and including 20 pound (10 kilogram), and 30 feet (9.14 meters) for all line classes over 20 pound (10 kilogram). For freshwater species, the leader on all classes of tackle shall be limited to 6 feet (1.82 meters).

The length of the leader is the overall length including any lure, hook arrangements, or other device.

The combined length of the double line and leader shall not exceed 20 feet (6.1 meters) in line classes up to and including 20 pound (10 kilogram) and 40 feet (12.19 meters) in line classes over 20 pound (10 kilogram) for saltwater species. The combined length of the double line and leader shall not exceed 10 feet (3.04 meters) for freshwater species.

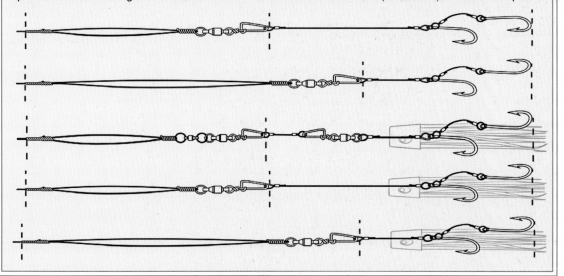

LEADER

The use of a leader is not required. If one is used, it must meet the following specifications: The length of the leader is the overall length including any lure, hook arrangement, or other device, and is measured to the bend of the last hook. The leader must be connected to the line with a snap, knot, splice, swivel, or other device. Holding devices are prohibited. There are no regulations regarding the material or strength of the leader.

Illustrated Guide to Hook Regulations: Natural and Artificial Baits

LEGAL, as the eyes of the hooks are no more than 18 inches (45.72 centimeters) apart in baits and no more than 12 inches (30.45 centimeters) apart in lures. ILLEGAL if eyes are further apart than these distances.

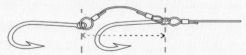

NOT LEGAL, as the second or trailing hook extends more than a hook's length beyond the skirt. See also two-hook rigs.

NOT LEGAL in bait or lures, as the eyes of the hooks are less than a hook's length (the length of the largest hook) apart.

LEGAL, as the eyes of the hooks are no less than a hook's length apart and no more than 18 inches (45.72 centimeters) in baits and 12 inches (30.45 centimeters) in lures.

LEGAL in baits and lures, as the point of one hook is passed through the eye of the other hook.

LEGAL, as the eyes of the hooks are no less than a hook's length apart and no more than 12 inches (30.45 centimeters) apart, and the trailing hook does not extend more than a hook's length beyond the skirt.

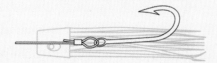

LEGAL, as the hook is contained within the skirt.

NOT LEGAL, as the single hook extends more than its length beyond the skirt.

NOT LEGAL, as the back hook is not firmly embedded in or securely attached to the bait and is a dangling or swinging hook.

LEGAL, as both hooks are firmly embedded in or securely attached to the bait. ILLEGAL if eyes of hooks are more than 18 inches (45.72 centimeters) apart.

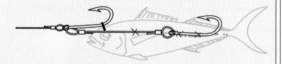

Saltwater species: In all line classes up to and including 20 pound (10 kilogram), the leader shall be limited to 15 feet (4.57 meters). The combined length of the double line and leader shall not exceed 20 feet (6.1 meters). The leader on all classes of tackle over 20 pound (10 kilogram) shall be limited to 30 feet (9.14 meters). The combined length of the double line and leader shall be limited to 40 feet (12.19 meters).

Freshwater species: The leader on all classes of tackle shall be limited to 6 feet (1.82 meters). The combined length of the double line and leader shall not exceed 10 feet (3.04 meters).

ROD

1. Rods must comply with sporting ethics and customs. Considerable latitude is allowed in the choice of a rod, but rods giving the angler an unfair advantage will be disqualified. This rule is intended to eliminate the use of unconventional rods.

2. The rod tip must be a minimum of 40 inches (101.6 centimeters) in length. The rod butt cannot exceed 27 inches (68.58 centimeters) in length. These measurements must be made from a point directly beneath the center of the reel. A curved butt is measured in a straight line. When the rod butt is placed in a gimbal, the measurement from the center of the reel seat to the pivot point of the gimbal can be no more than 27 inches (68.58 centimeters). (The above measurements do not apply to surfcasting rods.)

REEL

1. Reels must comply with sporting ethics and customs.

2. Power-driven reels of any kind are prohibited. This includes motor, hydraulic, or electronically driven reels, and any device that gives the angler an unfair advantage.

3. Ratchet-handle reels are prohibited.

4. Reels designed to be cranked with both hands at the same time are prohibited.

HOOKS FOR BAITFISHING

1. For live or dead baitfishing, no more than two single hooks may be used. Both must be firmly embedded in or securely attached to the bait. The eyes of the hooks must be no less than a hook's length (the length of the largest hook used) apart and no more than 18 inches (45.72 centimeters) apart. The only exception is that the point of one hook may be passed through the eye of the other hook. A hook may not precede bait, lure, or bait and lure combo by more than one hook's length.

2. The use of a dangling or swinging hook is prohibited. Double or treble hooks are prohibited.

3. A two-hook rig for bottom fishing is acceptable if it consists of two single hooks on separate leaders or drops. Both hooks must be embedded in the respective baits and separated sufficiently so that a fish caught on one hook cannot be foul hooked by the other.

4. A photograph or sketch of the hook arrangement must accompany all record applications made for fish caught on two-hook tackle.

OTHER HOOKS AND LURES

1. When using an artificial lure with a skirt or trailing material, no more than two single hooks may be attached to the line, leader, or trace. The hooks need not be attached separately. The eyes of the hooks must be no less than an overall hook's length (the overall length of the largest hook used) apart and no more than 12 inches (30.48 centimeters) apart. The only exception is that the point of one hook may be passed through the eye of the other hook. The trailing hook may not extend more than a hook's length beyond the skirt of the lure. A hook may not precede bait, lure, or bait and lure combo by more than one hook's length. A photograph or sketch showing the hook arrangement must accompany a record application.

2. Gang hooks are permitted when attached to plugs and other artificial lures that are specifically designed for this use. Gang hooks must be free swinging and shall be limited to a maximum of three hooks (single, double, or treble, or a combination of any three). Baits may not be used with gang hooks. A photograph or sketch of the plug or lure must be submitted with record applications.

3. Assist hooks or other such single hooks that are attached to a lure with a lead constructed of monofilament, multifilament, wire, or other such material must conform to the following: When using assist hooks on any artificial lure, other than a skirted lure, the lead cannot be more than 1½ hook's length and the bend of the hook may not be more than 4 inches (101 millimeters), whichever is less, from the closest point of attachment on the lure. Double and treble hooks may not be used as assist hooks.

Gaffs

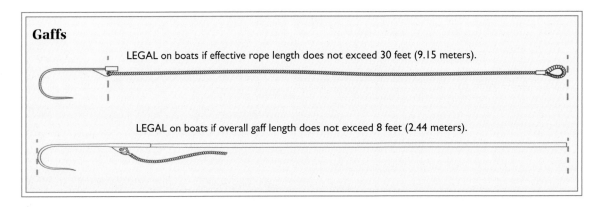

LEGAL on boats if effective rope length does not exceed 30 feet (9.15 meters).

LEGAL on boats if overall gaff length does not exceed 8 feet (2.44 meters).

OTHER EQUIPMENT

1. Fighting chairs may not have any mechanically pro-pelled devices that aid the angler in fighting a fish.

2. Gimbals must be free swinging, which includes gim-bals that swing in a vertical plane only. Any gimbal that allows the angler to reduce strain or to rest while fighting the fish is prohibited.

3. Gaffs and nets used to boat or land a fish must not exceed 8 feet (2.44 meters) in overall length. In using a flying or detachable gaff, the rope may not exceed 30 feet (9.14 meters). The gaff rope must be measured from the point where it is secured to the detachable head to the other end. Only the effective length will be considered. If a fixed-head gaff is used, the same limitations shall apply and the gaff rope shall be measured from the same location on the gaff hook. Only a single hook is permitted on any gaff. Harpoon or lance attachments are prohibited. Tail ropes are limited to 30 feet (9.14 meters). (When fishing from a bridge, pier, or other high platform or structure, this length limitation does not apply.)

4. Entangling devices, either with or without a hook, are prohibited and may not be used for any purpose, including baiting, hooking, fighting, or landing the fish.

5. Outriggers, downriggers, spreader bars, and kites are permitted to be used provided that the actual fishing line is attached to the snap or other release device, either directly or with some other material. The leader or double line may not be connected to the release mechanism either directly or with the use of a connecting device. Spreader bars are also acceptable when used strictly as a teaser.

6. Daisy chains, birds, floats, and similar devices may only be used if they do not unfairly hamper or inhibit the normal swimming or fighting ability of the fish, thereby giving the angler or crew an unfair advantage in fighting, landing, or boating the fish.

7. A safety line may be attached to the rod, reel, or har-ness provided that it does not in any way assist the angler in fighting the fish.

▓ Angling Regulations

1. From the time that a fish strikes or takes a bait or lure, the angler must hook, fight, and land or boat the fish without the aid of any other person, except as pro-vided in these regulations.

2. If a rod holder is used, once the fish is hooked, the angler must remove the rod from the rod holder as quickly as possible.

3. In the event of a multiple strike on separate lines being fished by a single angler, only the first fish fought by the angler will be considered for a world record.

4. If a double line is used, the intent of the regulations is that the fish will be fought on the single line most of the time that it takes to land the fish.

5. Use of a rod belt or waist gimbal is permitted.

6. When angling from a boat, once the leader is brought within the grasp of the mate, or the end of the leader is wound to the rod tip, more than one person is permitted to hold the leader. Anyone assisting a shorebound or wading angler must be within a rod's length of the angler before touching the leader or netting or gaffing the fish.

7. One or more gaffers may be used in addition to persons holding the leader. The gaff handle must be in hand when the fish is gaffed.

8. The equipment and angling regulations shall apply until the fish is weighed.

The following acts will disqualify a catch:

1. Failure to comply with equipment or angling regulations.

2. The act of persons other than the angler in touching any part of the rod, reel, or line (including the double line) either bodily or with any device, from the time a fish strikes or takes the bait or lure, until the fish is either landed or released, or in giving any aid other than that allowed in the rules and regulations. If an obstacle to the passage of the line through the rod guides has to be removed from the line, then the obstacle (whether chum, floatline, rubber band, or other material) shall be held and cut free. Under no circumstances should the line be held or touched by anyone other than the angler during this process.

3. Resting the rod in a rod holder, on the gunwale of the boat, or any other object while playing the fish.

4. Handlining or using a handline or rope attached in any manner to the angler's line or leader for the purpose of holding or lifting the fish.

5. Shooting, harpooning, or lancing any fish (including sharks and halibuts) at any stage of the catch.

6. Chumming with or using as bait the flesh, blood, skin, or any part of mammals other than the hair or pork rind used in lures designed for trolling or casting.

7. Using a boat or device to beach or drive a fish into shallow water in order to deprive the fish of its normal ability to swim.

8. Changing the rod or reel while the fish is being played.

9. Splicing, removing, or adding to the line while the fish is being played.

10. Intentionally foul hooking a fish.

11. Catching a fish in a manner that the double line never leaves the rod tip.

12. Using a size or kind of bait that is illegal to possess.

13. Attaching the angler's line or leader to part of a boat or other object for the purpose of holding or lifting the fish.

14. If a fish escapes before gaffing or netting and is recaptured by any method other than as outlined in the angling rules.

The following situations will also disqualify a catch:

1. When a rod breaks (while the fish is being played) in a manner that reduces the length of the tip below minimum dimensions or severely impairs its angling characteristics.

2. Mutilation to the fish, prior to landing or boating the catch, caused by sharks, other fish, mammals, or propellers that remove or penetrate the flesh. (Injuries caused by leader or line, scratches, old healed scars, or regeneration deformities are not considered to be disqualifying injuries.) Any mutilation on the fish must be shown in a photograph and fully explained in a separate report accompanying the record application.

3. When a fish is hooked or entangled on more than one line.

INTERNATIONAL FLY-FISHING RULES

▉ Equipment Regulations

LINE
Any type of fly line and backing may be used. The breaking strength of the fly line and backing are not restricted.

LEADER
Leaders must conform to generally accepted fly-fishing customs. A leader includes a class tippet, and, optionally, a shock tippet. A butt or taper section between the fly line and the class tippet shall also be considered part of the leader and there are no limits on its length, material, or strength. A class tippet must be made of nonmetallic material and either attached directly to the fly or to the shock tippet if one is used. The class tippet must be at least 15 inches (38.10 centimeters) long (measured inside the connecting knots). With respect to knotless, tapered leaders, the terminal 15 inches (38.10 centimeters) will also determine tippet class. There is no maximum length limitation.

A shock tippet, not to exceed 12 inches (30.48 centimeters) in length, may be added to the class tippet and tied to the lure. It can be made of any type of material, and there is no limit on its breaking strength. The shock tippet is measured from the eye of the hook to the single strand of class tippet and includes any knots used to connect the shock tippet to the class tippet. In the case of a tandem hook fly, the shock tippet shall be measured from the eye of the leading hook.

ROD
Regardless of material used or number of sections, rods must conform and cast according to generally accepted fly-fishing customs and practices. A rod shall not measure less than 6 feet (1.82 meters) in overall length and any rod that gives the angler an unsporting advantage will be disqualified. Overall butt length may not exceed 6 inches when measured from the center of the reel foot to the end of the butt. Overall butt length for two-handed or spey rods longer than 11 feet may not exceed 10 inches when measured from the center of the reel foot to the end of the butt.

REEL
The reel must be designed expressly for fly fishing. There are no restrictions on gear ratio or type of drag employed except where the angler would gain an unfair advantage. Electric or electronically operated reels are prohibited.

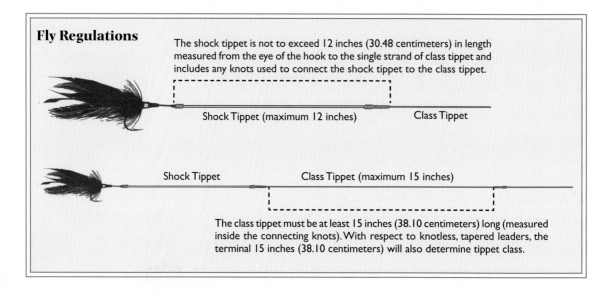

Fly Regulations

The shock tippet is not to exceed 12 inches (30.48 centimeters) in length measured from the eye of the hook to the single strand of class tippet and includes any knots used to connect the shock tippet to the class tippet.

Shock Tippet (maximum 12 inches)   Class Tippet

Shock Tippet   Class Tippet (maximum 15 inches)

The class tippet must be at least 15 inches (38.10 centimeters) long (measured inside the connecting knots). With respect to knotless, tapered leaders, the terminal 15 inches (38.10 centimeters) will also determine tippet class.

HOOKS

A conventional fly may be dressed on a single or double hook or two single hooks in tandem. The second hook in any tandem fly must not extend beyond the wing material. The eyes of the hooks shall be no farther than 6 inches (15.24 centimeters) apart. Treble hooks are prohibited.

FLIES

The fly must be a recognized type of artificial fly, which includes streamer, bucktail, tube fly, wet fly, dry fly, nymph, popper, or bug. The use of any other type of lure or natural or preserved bait, either singularly or attached to the fly, is expressly prohibited. Only a single fly is allowed. Dropper flies are prohibited. The fact that a lure can be cast with a fly rod is not evidence in itself that it fits the definition of a fly. The use of any lure designed to entangle or foul hook a fish is prohibited. No scent, either natural or artificial, is allowed on flies. The use of scented material in a fly is prohibited.

GAFFS AND NETS

Gaffs and nets used to boat or land a fish must not exceed 8 feet (2.44 meters) in overall length. (When fishing from a bridge, pier, or other high stationary structure, the length limitation does not apply.) The use of a flying gaff is not permitted. Only a single hook is permitted on any gaff. Harpoon or lance attachments are prohibited. A rope or any extension cannot be attached to the gaff.

■ Angling Regulations

1. The angler must cast, hook, fight, and bring the fish to gaff or net unaided by any other person. No other person may touch any part of the tackle during the playing of the fish or give aid other than taking the leader for gaffing or netting purposes. Anyone assisting a shorebound or wading angler must be within a rod's length of the angler before touching the leader or netting or gaffing the fish.

2. Casting and retrieving must be carried out in accordance with normal customs and generally accepted practices. The major criterion in casting is that the weight of the line must carry the fly rather than the weight of the fly carrying the line. Trolling a fly behind a moving watercraft is not permitted. The craft must be completely out of gear both at the time the fly is presented to the fish and during the retrieve. The maximum amount of line that can be stripped off the reel is 120 feet (36.57 meters) from the fly.

3. Once a fish is hooked, the tackle may not be altered in any way, with the exception of adding an extension butt. A harness cannot be attached to the fly rod.

4. Fish must be hooked on the fly in use. If a small fish takes the fly and a larger fish swallows the smaller fish, the catch will be disallowed.

5. One or more people may assist in gaffing or netting the fish.

6. The equipment and angling regulations shall apply until the fish is weighed.

The following acts will disqualify a catch:

1. Failure to comply with equipment or angling regulations.

2. The act of persons other than the angler in touching any part of the rod, reel, or line either bodily or with any device during the playing of the fish, or in giving any aid other than that allowed in the rules and regulations. If an obstacle to the passage of the line through the rod guides has to be removed from the line, then the obstacle shall be held and cut free. Under no circumstances should the line be held or touched by anyone other than the angler during this process.

3. Resting the rod on any part of the boat, or on any other object while playing the fish.

4. Handlining or using a handline or rope attached in any manner to the angler's line or leader for the purpose of holding or lifting the fish.

5. Intentionally foul hooking or snagging a fish.

6. Shooting, harpooning, or lancing any fish (including sharks and halibut) at any stage of the catch.

7. Chumming with the flesh, blood, skin, or any part of mammals.

8. Using a boat or device to beach or drive a fish into shallow water in order to deprive the fish of its normal ability to swim.

9. Attaching the angler's line or leader to part of a boat or other object for the purpose of holding or lifting the fish.

10. If a fish escapes before gaffing or netting and is recaptured by any method other than as outlined in the angling rules.

11. When a rod breaks (while the fish is being played) in a manner that reduces its length below minimum dimensions or severely impairs its angling characteristics.

12. When a fish is hooked or entangled on more than one line.

13. Mutilation to the fish, prior to landing or boating the catch, caused by sharks, other fish, mammals, or propellers that remove or penetrate the flesh. (Injuries caused by leader or line, scratches, old healed scars, or regeneration deformities are not considered to be disqualifying injuries.) Any mutilation on the fish must be shown in a photograph and fully explained in a separate report accompanying the record application.

WORLD RECORD CATEGORIES

Game-fish catches can only be considered for world-record status if they are caught according to the International Angling Rules. Following is information on world-record categories, requirements, and procedures for filing claims. An application fee of $40 for members and $65 for nonmembers is required for each claim. All materials submitted become the property of the IGFA. (See a sample application on page 179.)

▮ General Information

The IGFA maintains world records for both freshwater

Line Testing

The IGFA tests all line and tippet samples submitted with world-record claims in accordance with the metric line-class designations, which vary slightly from the standard U.S. customary designations. For example, the U.S. customary equivalent of 4 kilograms is 8.81 pounds. Thus, line designated by the manufacturer as 8-pound-class line may test up to 8.81 pounds (4 kilograms) to qualify for an 8-pound line-class record. The U.S. customary equivalents in pounds for the metric line classes are shown in the accompanying chart.

Line and tippet samples submitted with record claims are uniformly tested in accordance with government specifications, which have been modified and supplemented by the IGFA. (Note: The IGFA offers a line and tippet testing service for members only.)

U.S. Equivalent for Metric Line Classes

Metric (Kilograms)	U.S. Equivalent (Pounds)
1	2.20
4	8.81
6	13.22
8	17.63
10	22.04
15	33.06
24	52.91
37	81.57
60	132.27

and saltwater game fishes in all-tackle, line class, and tippet class categories. In order to qualify for a record, a catch must be a minimum of 1 pound (.453 kilogram) in weight, and must outweigh the existing record by the required amount or meet the minimum weight requirements, if any, for vacant records.

No applications will be accepted for fish caught in hatchery waters, sanctuaries, or small bodies of water stocked with fish for commercial purposes. The intent of this rule shall prevail and the IGFA retains the right to determine its applicability on a case-by-case basis. The catch must not be at variance with any laws or regulations governing the species or the waters in which it was caught.

When an additional species of game fish is made eligible for IGFA world records, the effective date will be announced. Fish caught on or after the effective date will be eligible for records. Announcement of an additional species in the *World Record Game Fishes* book or in other IGFA publications will be considered proper notification in lieu of any other notice.

▧ All-Tackle Category

All-tackle world records are kept for the heaviest fish of a species caught by an angler in any line class up to 130 pound (60 kilogram). Fish caught on lines designed to test over the 130-pound (60-kilogram) class will not be considered for record claims.

All-tackle record claims are considered for all species of fish caught according to IGFA angling rules.

Applications for species not currently included in the IGFA line class and tippet class listings must meet the following criteria:

1. The fish must represent a valid species with a recognized scientific name.

2. The fish must be a species commonly fished for with a rod and reel in the general area where the catch is made.

3. The fish must be identifiable based on photos and other supporting data presented with the application.

4. The fish must be considered trophy-sized. A rule of thumb is that the weight must fall within the top half of the estimated maximum weight of the species.

▧ Line Class and Fly Rod (Tippet Class) Categories

Line-class records are kept according to the strength of the line. Fly rod world records are maintained according to tippet strength. Each species recognized for line-class records is also recognized for tippet records. Records are kept in the following line and tippet classes:

Tippet Classes

Metric (Kilograms)	U.S. Customary (Pounds)
2	4
3	6
4	8
6	12
8	16
10	20

Line Classes

Metric (Kilograms)	U.S. Customary (Pounds)
1	2
2	4
3	6
4	8
6	12
8	16
10	20
15	30
24	50
37	80
60	130

With the exception of all-tackle claims, line classes are limited for many species. The following charts show the maximum line classes acceptable for world-record purposes for both freshwater and saltwater species.

Saltwater Species

Species	Maximum Line Class [in Kilograms (Pounds)]	Species	Maximum Line Class [in Kilograms (Pounds)]
Albacore / *Thunnus alalunga*	37 (80)	Jack, Pacific crevalle / *Caranx caninus*	24 (50)
Amberjack, greater / *Seriola dumerili*	60 (130)	Kahawai / *Arripis spp.*	15 (30)
Barracuda, great / *Sphyraena barracuda*	37 (80)	Kawakawa / *Euthynnus affinis*	15 (30)
Barracuda, Guinean / *Sphyraena afra*	60 (130)	Ladyfish / *Elops spp.*	15 (30)
Barracuda, Pacific /*Sphyraena argentea*	15 (30)	Leerfish (Garrick) / *Lichia amia*	24 (50)
Bass, black sea / *Centropristis striata*	15 (30)	Lingcod / *Ophiodon elongatus*	24 (50)
Bass, European /*Dicentrarchus labrax*	15 (30)	Mackerel, cero / *Scomberomorus regalis*	10 (20)
Bass, giant sea / *Stereolepis gigas*	60 (130)	Mackerel, king / *Scomberomorus cavalla*	37 (80)
Bass, kelp (calico) / *Paralabrax clathratus*	10 (20)	Mackerel, narrowbarred /*Scomberomorus commerson*	37 (80)
Bass, striped / *Morone saxatilis*	37 (80)	Mackerel, Pacific sierra / *Scomberomorus sierra*	10 (20)
Bluefish / *Pomatomus saltatrix*	24 (50)	Mackerel, Spanish / *Scomberomorus maculatus*	10 (20)
Bonefish / *Albula spp.*	15 (30)	Madai / *Pagrus major*	24 (50)
Bonito, Atlantic / *Sarda sarda*	15 (30)	Marlin, black / *Makaira indica*	60 (130)
Bonito, Pacific / *Sarda spp.*	15 (30)	Marlin, blue (Atlantic) / *Makaira nigricans*	60 (130)
Buri, Japanese Amberjack / *Seriola quinqueradiata*	60 (130)	Marlin, blue (Pacific) / *Makaira nigricans*	60 (130)
Cobia / *Rachycentron canadum*	37 (80)	Marlin, striped / *Tetrapturus audax*	60 (130)
Cod, Atlantic / *Gadus morhua*	37 (80)	Marlin, white / *Tetrapturus albidus*	60 (130)
Cod, Pacific / *Gadus macrocephalus*	24 (50)	Meagre / *Argyrosomus spp.*	60 (130)
Conger / *Conger conger*	60 (130)	Parrotperch, Japanese / *Oplegnathus fasciatus*	37 (80)
Corbina, California / *Menticirrhus undulatus*	10 (20)	Parrotperch, spotted / *Oplegnathus punctatus*	60 (130)
Dentex / *Dentex dentex*	15 (30)	Permit / *Trachinotus falcatus*	24 (50)
Dolphinfish / *Coryphaena hippurus*	37 (80)	Pollack, European / *Pollachius pollachius*	24 (50)
Drum, black / *Pogonias cromis*	37 (80)	Pollock / *Pollachius virens*	24 (50)
Drum, red / *Sciaenops ocellatus*	37 (80)	Pompano, African / *Alectis ciliaris*	24 (50)
Flounder, summer / *Paralichthys dentatus*	15 (30)	Pompano, Florida / *Trachinotus carolinus*	10 (20)
Grouper, black / *Mycteroperca bonaci*	60 (130)	Queenfish, doublespotted / *Scomberoides lysan*	15 (30)
Grouper, broomtail / *Mycteroperca xenarcha*	60 (130)	Queenfish, talang / *Scomberoides commersonnianus*	24 (50)
Grouper, gag / *Mycteroperca microlepis*	60 (130)	Rockfish, black/blue / *Sebastes melanops/mystinus*	15 (30)
Grouper, goliath / *Epinephelus itajara*	60 (130)	Rockfish, yelloweye / *Sebastes ruberrimus*	24 (50)
Grouper, red / *Epinephelus morio*	24 (50)	Roosterfish / *Nematistius pectoralis*	60 (130)
Halibut, Atlantic / *Hippoglossus hippoglossus*	60 (130)	Runner, rainbow / *Elagatis bipinnulata*	24 (50)
Halibut, California / *Paralichthys californicus*	37 (80)	Sailfish, Atlantic / *Istiophorus platypterus*	37 (80)
Halibut, Pacific / *Hippoglossus stenolepis*	60 (130)	Sailfish, Pacific / *Istiophorus platypterus*	60 (130)
Jack, almaco / *Seriola rivoliana*	60 (130)	Samson fish / *Seriola hippos*	60 (130)
Jack, crevalle / *Caranx hippos*	24 (50)	Seabass, blackfin / *Lateolabrax latus*	15 (30)
Jack, horse-eye / *Caranx latus*	24 (50)	Seabass, Japanese / *Lateolabrax japonicus*	15 (30)

Species	Maximum Line Class [in Kilograms (Pounds)]
Seabass, white / *Atractoscion nobilis*	37 (80)
Seabream, gilthead / *Sparus aurata*	24 (50)
Seatrout, spotted / *Cynoscion nebulosus*	15 (30)
Shark, blue / *Prionace glauca*	60 (130)
Shark, bonnethead / *Sphyrna tiburo*	15 (30)
Shark, blacktip / *Carcharhinus limbatus*	60 (130)
Shark, hammerhead / *Sphyrna spp.*	60 (130)
Shark, mako / *Isurus spp.*	60 (130)
Shark, porbeagle / *Lamna nasus*	60 (130)
Shark, thresher / *Alopias spp.*	60 (130)
Shark, tiger / *Galeocerdo cuvier*	60 (130)
Shark, tope / *Galeorhinus galeus*	37 (80)
Shark, white / *Carcharodon carcharias*	60 (130)
Sharks, whaler / *Carcharinidae* family	60 (130)
Skipjack, black / *Euthynnus lineatus*	15 (30)
Snapper (squirefish) / *Pagrus auratus*	24 (50)
Snapper, cubera / *Lutjanus cyanopterus*	60 (130)
Snapper, gray / *Lutjanus griseus*	15 (30)
Snapper, Guinean / *Lutjanus agennes*	60 (130)
Snapper, mullet / *Lutjanus aratus*	24 (50)
Snapper, mutton / *Lutjanus analis*	15 (30)
Snapper, Pacific cubera / *Lutjanus novemfasciatus*	60 (130)
Snapper, red / *Lutjanus campechanus*	24 (50)
Snapper, yellowtail / *Ocyurus crysurus*	10 (20)
Snook, Atlantic / *Centropomus spp.*	24 (50)
Snook, Pacific / *Centropomus spp.*	24 (50)
Spadefish, Atlantic / *Chaetodipterus faber*	10 (20)
Spearfish, Atlantic / *Tetrapturus spp.*	37 (80)
Spearfish, shortbill / *Tetrapturus angustirostris*	37 (80)

Species	Maximum Line Class [in Kilograms (Pounds)]
Swordfish / *Xiphias gladius*	60 (130)
Tarpon / *Megalops atlanticus*	60 (130)
Tarpon, oxeye / *Megalops cyprinoides*	10 (20)
Tautog / *Tautoga onitis*	15 (30)
Threadfin, giant African / *Polydactylus quadrifilis*	60 (130)
Threadfin, king / *Polydactylus macrochir*	15 (30)
Trevally, bigeye / *Caranx sexfasciatus*	37 (80)
Trevally, bluefin / *Caranx melampygus*	15 (30)
Trevally, giant / *Caranx ignobilis*	60 (130)
Trevally, golden / *Gnathanodon speciosus*	15 (30)
Tripletail / *Lobotes surinamensis*	24 (50)
Tuna, bigeye (Atlantic) / *Thunnus obesus*	60 (130)
Tuna, bigeye (Pacific) / *Thunnus obesus*	60 (130)
Tuna, blackfin / *Thunnus atlanticus*	24 (50)
Tuna, bluefin / *Thunnus thynnus*	60 (130)
Tuna, dogtooth / *Gymnosarda unicolor*	60 (130)
Tuna, longtail / *Thunnus tonggol*	37 (80)
Tuna, Pacific bluefin / *Thunnus orientalis*	60 (130)
Tuna, skipjack / *Katsuwonus pelamis*	24 (50)
Tuna, southern bluefin / *Thunnus maccoyi*	60 (130)
Tuna, yellowfin / *Thunnus albacares*	60 (130)
Tunny, little / *Euthynnus alletteratus*	15 (30)
Wahoo / *Acanthocybium solandri*	60 (130)
Weakfish / *Cynoscion regalis*	15 (30)
Yellowtail, California / *Seriola lalandi dorsalis*	37 (80)
Yellowtail, southern / *Seriola lalandi lalandi*	60 (130)

Freshwater Species

Species listed under the freshwater category are also eligible for world records if caught in salt or brackish water. The catch must be made in accordance with freshwater equipment regulations.

Species	Maximum Line Class [in Kilograms (Pounds)]	Species	Maximum Line Class [in Kilograms (Pounds)]
Arawana / *Osteoglossum bicirrhosum*	10 (20)	Drum, freshwater / *Aplodinotus grunniens*	37 (80)
Barramundi / *Lates calcarifer*	37 (80)	Gar, alligator / *Lepisosteus spatula*	60 (130)
Barbel / *Barbus barbus*	10 (20)	Gar, Florida / *Lepisosteus platyrhincus*	10 (20)
Bass, Australian / *Macquaria colonorum*	8 (16)	Gar, longnose / *Lepisosteus osseus*	37 (80)
Bass, largemouth / *Micropterus salmoides*	10 (20)	Gar, shortnose / *Lepisosteus platostomus*	10 (20)
Bass, rock / *Ambloplites rupestris*	6 (12)	Gar, spotted / *Lepisosteus oculatus*	10 (20)
Bass, shoal / *Micropterus coosae*	6 (12)	Grayling / *Thymallus arcticus*	10 (20)
Bass, smallmouth / *Micropterus dolomieu*	8 (16)	Grayling, European / *Thymallus thymallus*	10 (20)
Bass, spotted / *Micropterus punctulatus*	10 (20)	Huchen / *Hucho hucho*	60 (130)
Bass, striped (landlocked) / *Morone saxatilis*	24 (50)	Inconnu / *Stenodus leucichthys*	24 (50)
Bass, white / *Morone chrysops*	6 (12)	Kokanee / *Oncorhynchus nerka*	6 (12)
Bass, whiterock / *Morone saxatilis x Morone chrysops*	10 (20)	Muskellunge / *Esox masquinongy*	37 (80)
Bass, yellow / *Morone mississippiensis*	6 (12)	Muskellunge, tiger / *Esox masquinongy x E. lucius*	24 (50)
Bluegill / *Lepomis macrochirus*	6 (12)	Nembwe / *Serranochromis robustus*	10 (20)
Bowfin / *Amia calva*	15 (30)	Oscar / *Astronotus ocellatus*	6 (12)
Buffalo, bigmouth / *Ictiobus cyprinellus*	37 (80)	Payara / *Hydrolicus scomberoides*	10 (20)
Buffalo, smallmouth / *Ictiobus bubalus*	24 (50)	Peacock, blackstriped / *Cichla intermedia*	10 (20)
Bullhead, black / *Ameiurus melas*	6 (12)	Peacock, butterfly / *Cichla ocellaris*	10 (20)
Bullhead, brown / *Ameiurus nebulosus*	6 (12)	Peacock, speckled / *Cichla temensis*	10 (20)
Bullhead, yellow / *Ameiurus natalis*	6 (12)	Peacock, Orinoco / *Cichla orinocensis*	10 (20)
Burbot / *Lota lota*	10 (20)	Pellona, Amazon / *Pellona castelneana*	15 (30)
Carp, common / *Cyprinus carpio*	24 (50)	Perch, European / *Perca fluviatilis*	10 (20)
Carp, grass / *Ctenopharyngodon idellus*	37 (80)	Perch, Nile / *Lates niloticus*	60 (130)
Catfish, blue / *Ictalurus furcatus*	60 (130)	Perch, white / *Morone americana*	6 (12)
Catfish, channel / *Ictalurus punctatus*	37 (80)	Perch, yellow / *Perca flavescens*	6 (12)
Catfish, flathead / *Pylodictis olivaris*	60 (130)	Pickerel, chain / *Esox niger*	6 (12)
Catfish, redtail / *Phractocephalus hemioliopterus*	60 (130)	Pike, northern / *Esox lucius*	24 (50)
Catfish, sharptooth / *Clarias gariepinus*	60 (130)	Piranha, red / *Serrasalmus natterati*	10 (20)
Catfish, white / *Ameiurus catus*	10 (20)	Redhorse, shorthead / *Moxostoma macrolepidotum*	6 (12)
Char, Arctic / *Salvelinus alpinus*	15 (30)	Redhorse, silver / *Moxostoma anisurum*	6 (12)
Crappie, black / *Pomoxis nigromaculatus*	6 (12)	Salmon, Atlantic / *Salmo salar*	24 (50)
Crappie, white / *Pomoxis annularis*	6 (12)	Salmon, Atlantic (landlocked) / *Salmo salar*	15 (30)
Dolly Varden / *Salvelinus malma*	6 (12)	Salmon, Chinook / *Oncorhynchus tshawytscha*	60 (130)
Dorado / *Maxillosus spp.*	24 (50)	Salmon, chum / *Oncorhynchus keta*	15 (30)

Species	Maximum Line Class [in Kilograms (Pounds)]
Salmon, coho / Oncorhynchus kisutch	24 (50)
Salmon, pink / Oncorhynchus gorbuscha	15 (30)
Salmon, sockeye / Oncorhynchus nerka	15 (30)
Sauger / Stizostedion canadense	8 (16)
Shad, American / Alosa sapidissima	6 (12)
Shad, hickory / Alosa mediocris	10 (20)
Snakehead / Channa spp.	24 (50)
Snapper, Papuan black / Lutjanus goldiei	24 (50)
Sorubim / Pseudoplatystoma spp.	60 (130)
Splake / Salvelinus namaycush x S. fontinalis	15 (30)
Sturgeon / Acipenseridae family	60 (130)
Sunfish, green / Lepomis cyanellus	6 (12)
Sunfish, redbreast / Lepomis auritus	6 (12)
Sunfish, redear / Lepomis microlophus	6 (12)
Taimen / Hucho taimen	60 (130)
Tambaqui / Colossoma macropomum	60 (130)
Tench / Tinca tinca	10 (20)
Tigerfish / Hydrocynus vittatus	15 (30)
Tigerfish, giant / Hydrocynus goliath	60 (130)
Trahira / Hoplias spp.	24 (50)
Trout, brook / Salvelinus fontinalis	10 (20)
Trout, brown / Salmo trutta	24 (50)
Trout, bull / Salvelinus confluentus	10 (20)
Trout, cutthroat / Oncorhynchus clarki	10 (20)
Trout, golden / Oncorhynchus aguabonita	6 (12)
Trout, lake / Salvelinus namaycush	37 (80)
Trout, rainbow / Oncorhynchus mykiss	24 (50)
Trout, tiger / Salmo trutta x Salvelinus fontinalis	15 (30)
Walleye / Stizostedion vitreum	10 (20)
Warmouth / Lepomis gulosus	6 (12)
Wels / Silurus glanis	60 (130)
Whitefish, lake / Coregonus clupeaformis	8 (16)
Whitefish, mountain / Prosopium williamsoni	6 (12)
Whitefish, round / Prosopium cylindraceum	6 (12)
Zander / Stizostedion lucioperca	15 (30)

WORLD RECORD REGULATIONS

General Information

1. Protested applications or disputed existing records will be referred to the IGFA Executive Committee for review. Its decisions will be final. The IGFA reserves the right to refuse to consider an application or grant a claim for a record application. All IGFA decisions will be based upon the intent of the regulations.

2. Any and all claims and/or disputes regarding the IGFA International Angling Rules shall be governed by and construed and enforced in accordance with the laws of the State of Florida, without regard to such jurisdiction's conflict of laws principles. In the event that parties are unable to mutually resolve any dispute, controversy, or claim arising out of, in connection with, or in relation to the IFGA International Angling Rules, such dispute, controversy, or claim shall be resolved by litigation; in that connection, each of the parties to such dispute hereby:

(i) irrevocably and unconditionally consents to submit itself to the sole and exclusive personal jurisdiction of any federal or state court located within Broward County, Florida (the "Applicable Courts"),

(ii) waives any objection to the laying of sole and exclusive venue of any such litigation in any of the Applicable Courts,

(iii) agrees not to plead or claim in any such court that such litigation brought therein has been brought in an inconvenient forum and agrees not to otherwise attempt to deny or defeat such personal jurisdiction or venue by motion or other request for leave from any such court,

(iv) agrees that it will not bring any action, suit, or proceeding in connection with any dispute, claim, or controversy arising out of or relating to the International Angling Rules in any court or other tribunal other than any of the Applicable Courts. Nothing in this section shall prevent enforcement in another forum of any judgment obtained in the Applicable Courts.

In the event that it shall become necessary for any party to take action of any type whatsoever to enforce the terms of the IGFA International Angling Rules, the prevailing party shall be entitled to recover all its costs, including attorneys' fees, costs, and expenses, including all out-of-pocket expenses that are not taxable as costs, incurred in connection with any such action, including any negotiations, mediations, arbitrations, litigation, and appeal.

3. When a substantial award is specifically offered for a world-record catch in *any* line or tippet class, only a claim for an all-tackle record will be considered.

4. In some instances, an IGFA officer or member of the International Committee or a deputy from a local IGFA member club may be asked to recheck information supplied on a claim. Such action is not to be regarded as doubt of the formal affidavit, but rather as evidence of the extreme care with which the IGFA investigates and maintains its records.

Species Identification

1. Photographs must be submitted by which positive identification of the exact species can be made. Read the rules on photographs at the end of this section, and refer to the species identification section in the *World Record Game Fishes* book to determine which features must show to identify your fish. Applications without photographs will not be accepted.

2. If there is the slightest doubt that the fish cannot be properly identified from the photographs and other data submitted, the fish should be examined by an ichthyologist or qualified fishery biologist before a record application is submitted to the IGFA. The scientist's signature and title (or qualifications) should appear on the IGFA application form or on a separate document confirming the identification of the species.

3. If a scientist is not available, the fish should be retained in a preserved or frozen condition until a qualified authority can verify the species or until notified by the IGFA that the fish need no longer be retained.

4. If no decision can be made from the photographs and the angler can provide no further proof of the identification of the species, the record claim will not be considered.

Witnesses to Catch

On all record claims, witnesses to the catch are highly desirable if at all possible. Unwitnessed catches may be disallowed if questions arise regarding their authen-

ticity. It is important that the witnesses can attest to the angler's compliance with the IGFA International Angling Rules and Equipment Regulations.

Minimum Weight Requirements

MINIMUM WEIGHT REQUIREMENTS FOR VACANT RECORDS

The minimum acceptance weight for any record catch claim is 1 pound (.453 kilogram).

MINIMUM WEIGHT REQUIREMENTS NEEDED TO DEFEAT OR TIE EXISTING RECORDS

1. To replace a record for a fish weighing less than 25 pounds (11.33 kilograms), the replacement must weigh at least 2 ounces (56.69 grams) more than the existing record.

2. To replace a record fish weighing 25 pounds (11.33 kilograms) or more, the replacement must weigh at least one half of 1 percent more than the existing record. For example, at 100 pounds (45.35 kilograms), the additional weight required would be 8 ounces (226.7 grams); at 200 pounds (90.71 kilograms), the additional weight required would be 1 pound (.453 kilogram).

3. A catch that matches the weight of an existing record or exceeds the weight by less than the amount required to defeat the record will be considered a tie. In case of a tie claim involving more than two catches, the weight must be compared with the original record (first fish to be caught). Nothing weighing less than the original record will be considered.

4. Estimated weights will not be accepted (see Weighing Requirements). Fractions of ounces or their metric equivalents will not be considered.

Time Limit on Claims

With the exception of all-tackle records only, claims for record fish caught in U.S. continental waters must be received by the IGFA within 60 days of the date of catch. Claims for record fish caught in other waters must be received by the IGFA within three months of the date of catch.

Claims for all-tackle records only are considered for catches made in past years if the following conditions are met:

1. Acceptable photographs are submitted.

2. The weight of the fish can be positively verified.

3. The method of catch can be substantiated.

For catches made in the past, as much information as possible must be submitted on an IGFA world-record application form with any additional substantiating data.

If an incomplete record claim is submitted, it must be accompanied by an explanation of why certain portions are incomplete. An incomplete claim will be considered for a record if the following conditions are met:

1. The incomplete claim with explanations of why portions are incomplete must be received by the IGFA within the time limits specified above.

2. Missing data must be due to circumstances beyond the control of the angler making the record claim.

3. All missing data must be supplied within a period of time considered to be reasonable in view of the particular circumstances. The IGFA's Executive Committee will make final decisions on incomplete claims.

▓ Weighing Requirements

1. All record fish should be weighed on scales that have been checked and certified for accuracy by government agencies or other qualified and accredited organizations. Disinterested witnesses to the weight should be used whenever possible. All scales must be regularly checked for accuracy and certified in accordance with applicable government regulations at least once every 12 months. If at the time of weighing the fish the scale has not been properly certified within 12 months, it should be checked and certified for accuracy as quickly as possible. An official report stating the findings of the inspection prior to any adjustment of the scale must be included with the record application.

2. The weight of the sling, platform, or rope (if one is used to secure the fish on the scales) must be determined and deducted from the total weight.

3. At the time of weighing, the actual tackle used by the angler to catch the fish must be exhibited to the weighmaster and weight witness.

4. No estimated weights will be accepted. Fish weighed only at sea or on other bodies of water will not be accepted.

Conversion Formulas for Weights and Measures

Persons submitting world-record claims are required to provide the weights and measurements of the fish in the units in which they were taken. The following formulas are provided for your information:

Weights

Ounces	x	28.349	= Grams
Ounces	x	0.02835	= Kilograms
Pounds	x	453.59	= Grams
Pounds	x	0.45359	= Kilograms
Grams	x	0.0353	= Ounces
Grams	x	0.002	= Pounds
Kilograms	x	35.2736	= Ounces
Kilograms	x	2.2046	= Pounds

Measures

Inches	x	25.4	= Millimeters
Inches	x	2.54	= Centimeters
Feet	x	30.48	= Centimeters
Feet	x	0.3048	= Meters
Millimeters	x	0.03937	= Inches
Centimeters	x	0.3937	= Inches
Centimeters	x	0.0328	= Feet
Meters	x	39.37	= Inches

Miscellaneous

1 Pound Force	x	4.448	= Newtons
1 Kilogram Force	x	9.806	= Newtons
1 Fathom	x	6	= Feet

5. Only weights indicated by the graduations on the scale will be accepted. Visual fractionalizing of these graduations is not allowed. Any weights that fall between two graduations on the scale must be rounded to the lower of the two.

6. The IGFA reserves the right to require any scale to be recertified for accuracy if there are any indications that the scale might not have weighed correctly. (Note: The IGFA offers a scale-testing service for members only.)

Preparation of Claims

To apply for a world record, the angler must submit a completed IFGA application form, the mandatory length of line and terminal tackle used to catch the fish, and acceptable photographs of the fish, the tackle used to catch the fish, the scale used to weigh the fish, and the angler with the fish.

Application Form

The official IGFA world-record application form or a reproduction must be used for record claims. This form may be reproduced as long as all items are included. You can download a PDF of this form at www.igfa.org/Fish/World-Record-Application.aspx.

The angler must fill in the application personally. The IGFA also recommends that the angler personally mail the application, line sample or fly leader, and photographs.

When making any record claim, the angler must indicate the specified strength of the line or tippet used to catch the fish. In the cases of line class and tippet class records, this will place the claim in an IGFA line or tippet class category (see World Record Categories). All lines will be examined by the IGFA to verify the specified strength of the line. If the line or tippet over tests its particular category, the application will be considered in the next highest category; if it under tests into a lower line or tippet category, the application will not be considered for the lower line class. The heaviest line class permitted for both freshwater and saltwater records is 130-pound (60 kilogram) class. The heaviest tippet class permitted for fly-fishing records is 20-pound (10 kilogram) class. If the line or tippet over tests these maximum strengths, the claim will be disallowed.

Extreme care should be exercised in measuring the fish, as the measurements are often important for weight verification and scientific studies. See the measurement diagram on the record application to be sure you have measured correctly.

The angler is responsible for seeing that the necessary signatures and correct addresses of the boat captain, weighmaster, and witnesses are on the application. If an IGFA officer or representative, or an officer or member of an IGFA club is available, he or she should be asked to witness the claim. The name of a boatman, guide, or weighmaster repeated as witness is not acceptable.

The angler must appear in person to have his application notarized. In territories where notarization is not possible or customary, the signature of a government commissioner or resident, a member of an embassy, legation, or consular staff, or an IGFA officer or International Committee member may replace notarization.

Any deliberate falsification of an application will disqualify the applicant for any future IGFA world records and any existing records will be nullified.

Line or Tippet Sample

All applications for fly-fishing records must be accompanied by the lure, the entire tippet, and the entire leader. These components must be intact and connected.

All other applications must be accompanied by the entire leader, the double line, and at least 50 feet (15.24 meters) of the single line closest to the double line, leader, or hook. All line samples and the leader (if one is used) must be submitted in one piece. If a lure is used with the leader, the leader should be cut at the eye attachment to the lure.

Each line sample must be in one piece. It must be submitted in a manner that it can be easily unwound without damage to the line. A recommended method is to take a rectangular piece of stiff cardboard and cut notches in two opposite ends. Secure one end of the line to the cardboard and wind the line around the cardboard through the notched areas. Secure the other end, and write your name and the specified strength of line on the cardboard. Line samples submitted that are tangled or cannot be easily unwound will not be accepted.

Photographic Requirements

Photographs showing the full length of the fish, the rod and reel used to make the catch, and the scale used to weigh the fish must accompany each record application. A photograph of the angler with the fish is also required.

For species identification, the clearest possible photos should be submitted. This is especially important in the cases of hybrids and fishes that may be confused with similar species. Shark applications should include a photograph of the shark's teeth, and of the head and back taken from above in addition to the photographs taken from the side. Whether the shark has or does not have a ridge between the dorsal fins should be clearly evident in this photograph.

In all cases, photographs should be taken of the fish in a hanging position and also lying on a flat surface on its side. The fish should be broadside to the camera and no part of the fish should be obscured. The fins must be fully extended and not obscured with the hands, and the jaw or bill must be clearly shown. Avoid obscuring the keels of sharks and tunas with a tail rope.

When photographing a fish lying on its side, the surface beneath the fish should be smooth and a ruler or marked tape placed beside the fish if possible. Photographs from various angles are most helpful.

An additional photograph of the fish on the scale with the actual weight visible helps to expedite the application.

Photos taken by daylight with a reproducible-type negative film are highly recommended if at all possible.

(Note: The IGFA's bimonthly newsletter *International Angler* keeps anglers up to date on world-record catches. It's important that the IGFA has clear, publishable photographs of the fish and the angler. If you have action shots of the catch, please send those also.)

RULES AND REQUIREMENTS FOR ALL-TACKLE LENGTH WORLD RECORDS

General Information

Any fish entered for length records must be measured by anglers at the site of capture and released so that it swims away on its own and in good condition. A fish should be revived by moving it forward in the water to ensure a healthy release. Fish caught and entered for length records are not eligible for weighing and submission for other record categories.

Rules and Equipment Regulations

All IGFA rules and equipment regulations stipulated for fishing with conventional and fly tackle in fresh and salt water shall apply with the exceptions below. All angling and equipment regulations shall apply until the fish is measured and released alive.

GAFFS AND NETS

1. The use of gaffs to land a fish is prohibited.

2. Nets used to boat or land a fish must not exceed 8 feet (2.44 meters) in overall length. (When fishing from a bridge, pier, or other high stationary structure, this length limitation does not apply.)

3. The use of knotless, rubber-coated nets or similarly designed nets that minimize slime and scale removal is strongly recommended.

MEASURING DEVICE

1. All fish must be measured using an official IGFA measuring device. (You can order yours at store.igfa.org/IGFA-World-Record-Tool-s/1830.htm.)

2. The measuring device may be shortened by cutting it, but it may not be rejoined after it has been shortened.

Angling Regulations

The following acts will disqualify a catch:

1. Failure to comply with IGFA equipment or angling rules.

2. The fish dies during the documentation process, or does not swim away on its own accord after release.

Length Record Requirements

All fish entered for length records are subject to the same requirements stipulated for other record categories, with the following additions and exceptions:

MEASURING REQUIREMENTS

1. Fish must be measured using an official IGFA measuring device on a flat surface.

2. The fish's snout must be touching the nose stop, free of lures or lifting devices.

3. With the fish lying on top of the measuring device, measurements will be taken from the most forward part of the fish's snout with the mouth closed to the rear center edge of the tail.

4. All measurements will be made in centimeters.

5. Fish that measure between centimeter increments shall be recorded at the lower of the two increments. For example, a fish that measures between 45 and 46 centimeters will have a recorded length of 45 centimeters.

MINIMUM LENGTH REQUIREMENTS FOR VACANT RECORDS

Fish entered for vacant record categories must measure within the top half of that species' maximum recorded length, as shown in the eligible species list.

MINIMUM LENGTH REQUIREMENTS NEEDED TO DEFEAT OR TIE EXISTING RECORDS

1. To defeat an existing record, the fish must measure at least 2 centimeters longer than the existing record.

2. A catch that matches the length of an existing record or exceeds the length by less than 2 centimeters will be considered a tie. In the case of a tie claim involving more than two catches, the length must be compared with the original record (first fish to be caught). Nothing measuring less than the original record (first fish to be caught) will be considered.

PHOTOGRAPHIC REQUIREMENTS

Photographs included with applications must contain the following information:

1. The full length of the fish on the measuring device clearly showing the position of the mouth and tail. The fish may be held in position, but must be done in a manner that does not obscure the view of the fish on the tape.

2. A close-up showing the position of the fish's nose and tail on the measuring device.

3. The angler with the fish.

4. The rod and reel used to make the catch.

General Best Handling Practices

To remove your fish from the water to document it for record purposes, anglers should use either hands or a knotless, rubberized landing net to minimize slime and scale loss. Lip-gripping devices may be used to help subdue fish.

However, large fish should not be hoisted vertically out of the water, as this can cause damage to jaw muscle and bone as well as to internal organs. The best method for removing fish from the water by hand is to grip the fish or the lower jaw and support the fish's underside. Again, the point is always to hold fish horizontally and not vertically.

Documentation

The IGFA records require pictures, measurement, and/or weighing of the catch. All of this takes time, so you should have the necessary equipment ready before landing the fish. If the documentation process takes longer than several minutes, periodically place the fish back in the water or place in a livewell to allow it to breathe.

Releasing

Considerable time and care should be exercised when releasing fish. Fish should be placed in the water and held by the base of the tail. If the fish does not swim away from your grasp on its own, gently move it forward in the water to get water flowing over the gills.

For best results, move the fish in the forward direction only instead of back and forth. A fish's gills somewhat resemble the pages of a book and are designed for water flow in only one direction. Moving the fish in a slow circle or gently towing it behind the boat will accomplish this.

IGFA Record Application
FORM FOR RECORDING FRESHWATER AND SALTWATER GAME FISH CATCHES

Read all IGFA angling rules and world record requirements before completing and signing this application. The angler's signature on the completed form must be witnessed by a notary. This application must be accompanied by line or tippet samples and photographs as specified in the World Records Requirements. Hybrids and other species that may pose a problem of identity should be examined by an ichthyologist or qualified fishery biologist. IGFA reserves the right to employ verification procedures such as polygraph tests to determine the authenticity of record claims. **Materials submitted with application become property of IGFA and can be used at IGFA's discretion.**

I AM SUBMITTING THIS ENTRY FOR:

☐ An All-Tackle world record

☐ An All-Tackle Length record

☐ A world record in the following line class:

_____ lb / _____ kg

☐ A fly rod world record in the following tippet class:

_____ lb / _____ kg

☐ A state freshwater record in the following line class:

_____ lb / _____ kg

☐ A state freshwater fly rod record in the following tippet class:

_____ lb / _____ kg

☐ Junior Angler

☐ State Freshwater Junior Angler

| ☐ M-Smallfry (0-10) | ☐ M-Junior (11-16) |
| ☐ F-Smallfry (0-10) | ☐ F-Junior (11-16) |

SPECIES

Common name: _____

Scientific name: _____

WEIGHT: (Not applicable for length records)

Fish was weighed in: ☐ lbs ☐ kgs.

lbs: _____ oz: _____ kg: _____

Digital weight (if weighed on electronic scales, give weight exactly as shown): _____

DATE OF CATCH (MM/DD/YY): _____

PLACE OF CATCH: _____

_____

Was the fish released alive? ☐ Yes ☐ No

LENGTH (see measurement diagrams)

inches: x to x _____ xx to xx _____

cm: x to x _____ xx to xx _____

GIRTH (Not applicable for length records)

(measured completely around fish at thickest point)

inches: _____ cm: _____

METHOD OF CATCH (trolling, casting, fly fishing, etc.):

_____

FIGHTING TIME: _____

Was this catch recorded on video?   ☐ Yes ☐ No

ANGLER (Print name as you wish it to appear on your record certificate):

_____

Phone: _____

Email: _____

Permanent address- required for certificate mailing (include country and address code): ☐ New address

_____

_____

_____

Age/birthdate if 16 or under: _____

Fishing club affiliation: _____

EQUIPMENT

Rod

Make: _____

Tip length (center of reel to end of tip): _____

Butt length (center of reel to lower end of butt): _____

Reel

Make: _____ Size: _____

Main line or Fly tippet

Fly rod applications must include the entire leader still attached to the fly. **All other records** must include 50 feet of the main line **still attached to the double line and/or leader** (if used)

Make of line/tippet: _____ Stated size: _____

Make of fly line: _____

PAYMENT INFORMATION *(fees good through 12/31/14)*

☐ I am an IGFA member, enclosed is $50 (US) application fee. This fee pertains to all record categories.

☐ I am not an IGFA member, enclosed is $80 (US) for an annual membership and record application fees.

☐ Please send _____ extra copies of my record certificate at $5 (US) each.

Enclosed is $_____ check or money order for the world record application processing fee.

Or please charge to my:

___Visa ___MasterCard ___American Express ___Discover

Account No.

_____

Exp. date: _____ / _____ Signature: _____

For more information about the IGFA, and to download a PDF of the full, two-page IGFA record application form, visit www.igfa.org/Fish/World-Record-Application.aspx.

Eligible Species and Minimum Lengths for All-Tackle Length Records

Saltwater Species

Species	Length (in centimeters)
Albacore / Thunnus alalunga	61
Amberjack, greater / Seriola dumerili	92
Bass, black sea / Centropristis striata	33
Bass, European / Dicentrarchuslabrax	46
Bass, kelp (calico) / Paralabrax clathratus	33
Bass, striped / Morone saxatilis	67
Bluefish / Pomatomus saltatrix	59
Bonefish / Albula spp.	50
Bonito, Atlantic / Sarda sarda	42
Bonito, Pacific / Sarda spp.	49
Cobia / Rachycentron canadum	85
Corbina, California / Minticirrhus undulatus	33
Drum, black / Pogonias cromis	67
Drum, red / Sciaenops ocellatus	72
Grouper, black / Mycteroperca bonaci	77
Grouper, broomtail / Mycteroperca xenarcha	75
Grouper, gag / Mycteroperca microlepis	66
Grouper, red / Epinephelus morio	42
Halibut, California / Paralichthys californicus	66
Jack, almaco / Seriola rivoliana	80
Jack, crevalle / Caranx hippos	57
Jack, horse-eye / Caranx latus	50
Jack, Pacific crevalle / Caranx caninus	50
Kahawai (Australian salmon) / Arripis trutta	41
Kawakawa / Euthynnus affinis	47
Ladyfish / Elops spp.	39
Leerfish (Garrick) / Lichia amia	61
Mackerel, cero / Scomberomorus regalis	47
Mackerel, narrowbarred / Scomberomorus commerson	100
Mackerel, Pacific sierra / Scomberomorus sierra	49
Mackerel, Spanish / Scomberomorus maculatus	39
Madai / Pagrus major	40
Meagre / Argyrosomus spp.	30
Permit / Trachinotus falcatus	52

Species	Length (in centimeters)
Pollock / Pollachius virens	56
Pompano, African / Alectis ciliaris	58
Pompano, Florida / Trachinotus carolinus	28
Queenfish, talang / Scomberoides commersonianus	60
Rockfish, black/blue / Sebastes melanops	31
Roosterfish / Nematistius pectoralis	81
Samson fish / Seriola hippos	75
Seabass, blackfin / Lateolabrax latus	47
Seabass, Japanese (suzuki) / Lateolabrax japonicas	63
Seabass, white / Atractoscion nobilis	83
Seatrout, spotted / Cynoscion nebulosus	50
Shark, bonnethead / Sphyrna tiburo	50
Skipjack, black / Euthynnus lineatus	42
Snapper (squirefish) / Pagrus auratus	47
Snapper, African red / Lutjanus agennes	69
Snapper, cubera / Lutjanus cyanopterus	69
Snapper, grey / Lutjanus griseus	37
Snapper, mullet / Lutjanus aratus	58
Snapper, mutton / Lutjanus analis	45
Snapper, Pacific cubera / Lutjanus novemfasciatus	67
Snapper, red / Lutjanus campechanus	48
Snapper, yellowtail / Ocyurus chrysurus	34
Snook, Atlantic / Centropomus spp.	25
Snook, Pacific / Centropomus spp.	25
Tarpon, oxeye / Megalops cyprinoides	48
Threadfin, giant African / Polydactylus quadrifilis	100
Threadfin, king / Polydactylus macrochir	83
Trevally, bigeye / Caranx sexfasciatus	44
Trevally, bluefin / Caranx melampygus	58
Trevally, giant / Caranx ignobilis	76
Trevally, golden / Gnathanodon speciosus	48
Tripletail / Lobotes surinamensis	48
Tuna, blackfin / Thunnus atlanticus	52
Tuna, longtail / Thunnus tonggol	72
Tuna, skipjack / Katsuwonus pelamis	49

Species	Length
Tunny, little / *Euthynnus alletteratus*	53
Weakfish / *Cynoscion regalis*	48
Yellowtail, California / *Seriola lalandi dorsalis*	80
Yellowtail, southern / *Seriola lalandi lalandi*	78

Freshwater Species

Species	Length (in centimeters)	Species	Length (in centimeters)
Arawana / *Osteoglossum bicirrhosum*	41	Peacock, Orinioco / *Cichla orinocensis*	32
Barramundi / *Lates calcarifer*	62	Peacock, speckled / *Cichla temensis*	45
Bass, Australian / *Macquaria novemaculeata*	27	Perch, European / *Perca fluviatilis*	26
Bass, largemouth / *Micropterus salmoides*	48	Perch, Nile / *Lates niloticus*	100
Bass, smallmouth / *Micropterus dolomieu*	34	Perch, white / *Morone Americana*	21
Bass, striped (landlocked) / *Morone saxatilis*	65	Perch, yellow / *Perca flavescens*	18
Bass, white / *Morone chrysops*	24	Pickerel, chain / *Esox niger*	39
Bass, whiterock / *Morone saxatilis M. chrysops*	44	Pike, northern / *Esox lucius*	68
Bluegill / *Lepomis macrochirus*	19	Salmon, Atlantic / *Salmo salar*	64
Bowfin / *Amia calva*	45	Salmon, Atlantic (landlocked) / *Salmo salar*	46
Carp, common / *Cyprinus carpio*	55	Salmon, Chinook / *Oncorhynchus tshawytscha*	53
Carp, grass / *Ctenopharyngodon idella*	66	Salmon, chum / *Oncorhynchus keta*	48
Catfish, blue / *Ictalurus furcatus*	73	Salmon, coho / *Oncorhynchus kisutch*	53
Catfish, channel / *Ictalurus punctatus*	60	Salmon, pink / *Oncorhynchus gorbuscha*	39
Catfish, redtail (pirarara) / *Phractocephalus hemioliopterus*	69	Salmon, sockeye / *Oncorhynchus nerka*	35
Catfish, sharptooth / *Clarias gariepinus*	85	Shad, American / *Alosa sapidissima*	35
Char, Arctic / *Salvelinus alpinus*	51	Snakehead / *Channa spp.*	29
Crappie, black / *Pomoxis nigromaculatus*	24	Snapper, Papuan black / *Lutjanus goldiei*	50
Crappie, white / *Pomoxis annularis*	24	Sorubim / *Pseudoplatystoma spp.*	52
Dolly Varden / *Salvelinus malma*	50	Taimen / *Hucho taimen*	78
Dorado / *Salminus maxillosus*	55	Tigerfish / *Hydrocynus vittatus*	43
Gar, Florida / *Lepisosteus platyrhincus*	42	Tigerfish, giant / *Hydrocynus goliath*	64
Gar, shortnose / *Lepisosteus platostomus*	38	Trahira, giant / *Hoplias macrophthalmus*	26
Grayling / *Thymallus thymallus*	25	Trout, brook / *Salvelinus fontinalis*	34
Grayling, Arctic / *Thymallus arcticus*	37	Trout, brown / *Salmo trutta*	51
Kokanee / *Oncorhynchus nerka*	32	Trout, bull / *Salvelinus confluentus*	51
Muskellunge / *Esox masquinongy*	76	Trout, cutthroat / *Oncorhynchus clarki*	44
Nembwe / *Serranochromis robustus*	27	Trout, golden / *Oncorhynchus aguabonita*	35
Oscar / *Astronotus ocellatus*	19	Trout, lake / *Salvelinus namaycush*	74
Payara / *Hydrolicus scomberoides*	53	Trout, rainbow / *Oncorhynchus mykiss*	54
Peacock, blackstriped / *Cichla intermedia*	26	Walleye / *Stizostedion vitreum*	52
Peacock, butterfly / *Cichla ocellaris*	33	Zander / *Stizostedion lucioperca*	43

Note: To convert lengths to inches (U.S. standard), please see conversion formulas on page 175.

FRESHWATER GAME FISH

Section Two
FRESHWATER GAME FISH

Atlantic Salmon *(Salmo salar)*

DESCRIPTION: Atlantic salmon are anadromous fish, meaning that they are spawned in freshwater rivers and then migrate to the ocean to spend most of their lives before returning to fresh water to spawn themselves. When fresh from the sea, Atlantics are steel blue on top and silver on the sides and belly, and have dark spots on their sides. As their stay in fresh water lengthens, the colors become darker, with the sides taking on a pinkish hue as spawning time arrives. Very young salmon are called parrs. Parrs have distinctive dark vertical bars called parr markings. Unlike Pacific salmon, all of which die after spawning, about 15 percent of Atlantic salmon survive the spawning act and return to sea.

RANGE: The highly prized Atlantic salmon once ranged from Delaware north through Quebec and the Canadian Maritime provinces to Greenland, and in the western Atlantic Ocean to the British Isles and parts of Scandinavia. But today, because of "progress"—meaning dams, pollution, and urban and suburban sprawl—the range of the Atlantic salmon in the United States is restricted to a handful of rivers in Maine, though efforts are being made to restore this fine game fish to the Connecticut River and other northeastern rivers.

HABITAT: In fresh water, the Atlantic salmon must have clean, flowing, cold water. In upstream spawning areas,

Atlantic Salmon

fish can create "redds," or spawning beds. When in the ocean, these salmon range over vast areas but tend to concentrate on feeding grounds, which are only recently being discovered.

SIZE: Mature Atlantic salmon weigh from 9 to 75 pounds, with the average being 12 pounds. Their size depends on how many years they have spent in the sea, where their growth is fast. Salmon that return to fresh water after only one or two years at sea are called grilse and weigh up to about 6 or 8 pounds.

FOOD: These fish feed on small baitfish and the like when in the ocean, but upon entering fresh water, they stop feeding almost completely. And yet they can be induced to strike an artificial lure, particularly dry and wet flies.

FISHING METHODS: Casting from shore or boats, mostly in tidal waters of rivers and river mouths during spawning migration

BAITS: Artificial lures (especially spoons) and dry, wet, and streamer flies

Landlocked Salmon
(Salmo salar sebago)

COMMON NAMES: Landlocked salmon, Sebago salmon, landlock, and ouananiche

DESCRIPTION: The landlocked salmon is very similar in coloration and general appearance to the Atlantic salmon, of which the landlock is a subspecies. It is assumed that the subspecies descended from Atlantic salmon trapped in freshwater lakes thousands of years ago. As their name suggests, landlocks do not spawn in the sea. They either spawn in their home lakes or descend to outlet streams to spawn.

RANGE: Landlocks range over much of New England (they are most numerous in Maine), Quebec and other parts of eastern Canada, and north to Labrador. They have been introduced in New York and other eastern states and in South America.

HABITAT: The landlock survives best in deep, cold lakes that have a high oxygen content.

SIZE: Most landlocks average 2 to 3 pounds, but a 6-pounder is not unusual and an occasional 10-pounder is caught. The maximum weight is about 30 pounds.

FOOD: Landlocks feed mostly on small baitfish, particularly smelt.

FISHING METHODS: Casting and trolling

BAITS: Baitfish, smelt, artificial lures, and streamers

Chinook Salmon
(Oncorhynchus tshawytscha)

COMMON NAMES: Chinook salmon, king salmon, tyee salmon, and blackmouth (immature stage)

DESCRIPTION: The chinook, like all other Pacific salmon, is anadromous and seems to prefer the largest of Pacific coast rivers for spawning. Chinooks have a dark-blue back that shades to silver on the sides and white on the belly. Small, dark spots—barely noticeable in fish fresh from the sea—mark the upper part of the body.

RANGE: Chinook salmon range from southern California to northern Alaska, being more numerous in the northern part of that area. They often travel enormous distances upriver to spawn; in the Yukon River, for example, chinooks have been seen 2,000 miles from the sea.

HABITAT: Chinooks prefer large, clean, cold rivers, but often enter small tributary streams to spawn in shallow water over gravel bottoms.

SIZE: The chinook is the largest of the Pacific salmon, reaching weights of more than 100 pounds. Rarely,

Chinook Salmon

however, does a sportfisherman catch one of more than 60 pounds, and the average size is about 18 pounds.

FOOD: Chinook salmon eat ocean baitfish (herring, sardines, candlefish, and anchovies), freshwater baitfish, and fish roe.

FISHING METHODS: Casting and trolling

BAITS: Baitfish, egg sacks, spoons, spinners, and flies

Dog Salmon (Oncorhynchus keta)

COMMON NAMES: Dog salmon and chum salmon

DESCRIPTION: The dog salmon closely resembles the chinook salmon, but has black-edged fins and lacks the chinook's dark spots on the back, dorsal fin, and tail. During spawning, the male dog salmon often exhibits red or green blotches on its sides. The dog salmon is rarely taken by sportfishermen.

RANGE: One of five species of Pacific salmon, the dog salmon is found from central California north to Alaska,

Dog Salmon

Dog Salmon Spawning

but is far more numerous in Alaska than farther south. In their sea migrations, dog salmon travel as far as the Aleutians, Korea, and Japan.

HABITAT: Like all other salmon, the dog spawns in gravel in freshwater rivers, usually in the lower reaches of the parent streams, but occasionally far upstream.

SIZE: Dog salmon reach weights of 30 pounds or a bit more, but they average 6 to 18 pounds.

FOOD: The diet of dog salmon consists mainly of baitfish and crustaceans.

FISHING METHODS: Casting and trolling

BAITS: Baitfish, spoons, spinners, and flies, especially those in red

Sockeye Salmon
(Oncorhynchus nerka)

COMMON NAMES: Sockeye salmon, red salmon, and blueback salmon

DESCRIPTION: The sockeye is similar to the chinook, but it has a small number of gill rakers and tiny spots along its back. When spawning, sockeye males turn dark red, with the forward parts of their body being greenish. Females range in color from olive to light red. Sockeyes are more

Sockeye Salmon

often caught by sportfishermen than dog salmon, and they will take artificial flies and are good fighters.

RANGE: Sockeyes are found from California to Japan, but few are encountered south of the Columbia River. A landlocked strain of the sockeye (see Kokanee Salmon), originally found from British Columbia south to Oregon and Idaho, is being stocked in freshwater lakes in various areas of the United States.

HABITAT: This species spawns over gravel in freshwater lakes, especially those fed by springs.

SIZE: Sockeyes reach a maximum weight of about 15 pounds, but the average weight is 4 to 9 pounds.

FOOD: Sockeyes feed mainly on crustaceans, but also eat small baitfish.

FISHING METHODS: Casting and trolling

BAITS: Crustaceans, baitfish, spoons, and streamer flies

Humpback Salmon
(Oncorhynchus gorbuscha)

COMMON NAMES: Humpback salmon and pink salmon

DESCRIPTION: Similar to other salmon but smaller, the humpback has small scales and its caudal fin (tail) has large, oval, black spots. At maturity, or at spawning time, the males develop a large, distinctive hump on their backs. The humpback is among the most commercially valuable of the Pacific salmon and is becoming more popular with sportfishermen.

RANGE: The humpback is found from California to Alaska and as far away as Korea and Japan.

HABITAT: This species spawns over gravel in freshwater rivers, usually near the sea.

Humpback Salmon

Humpback Salmon Spawning

SIZE: The smallest of the Pacific salmon, the humpback averages 3 to 6 pounds, attaining a maximum weight of about 10 pounds.

FOOD: Humpbacks subsist largely on a diet of crustaceans, baitfish, and squid.

FISHING METHODS: Casting and trolling

BAITS: Crustaceans, baitfish, spoons, spinners, and flies

■ Coho Salmon *(Oncorhynchus kisutch)*

COMMON NAMES: Coho salmon, silver, and hooknose

DESCRIPTION: The coho is generally silvery with a bluish back and has small, dark spots along the upper part of the sides and tail. When the spawning urge takes hold, the males assume a reddish coloration, but when they enter fresh water they become almost black. The coho is highly prized as a sport fish, striking artificials readily and leaping breathtakingly when hooked.

RANGE: The coho is found from California to Alaska and as far from the West Coast of the United States as Japan. It has also been transplanted with unprecedented success in all of the Great Lakes and in many landlocked reservoirs throughout the United States.

HABITAT: This fish spawns in gravel in freshwater rivers, either near the sea or far upstream.

SIZE: Cohos reach weights approaching 30 pounds, but they average 6 to 12 pounds.

FOOD: A coho's diet is mainly baitfish, squid, crustaceans, and crab larvae.

FISHING METHODS: Casting and trolling

BAITS: Baitfish, squid, crustaceans, spoons, and flies

Kokanee Salmon

Kokanee Salmon Spawning

■ Kokanee Salmon
(Oncorhynchus nerka kennerlyi)

COMMON NAMES: Kokanee salmon, silver trout, blueback, little redfish, Kennerly's salmon, landlocked sockeye, redfish, and silversides

DESCRIPTION: The kokanee is a landlocked strain of the anadromous sockeye salmon. Biologically identical with the true sockeye (though much smaller), the kokanee is silvery on its sides and belly, but during spawning the males have reddish sides and the females have slate-gray sides. Kokanees resemble some trout, but differ from all trout in that they have more than 12 rays in the anal fin. The kokanee is the only Pacific salmon that matures in fresh water. It is much prized by fishermen.

RANGE: The kokanee's original range extended from Idaho and Oregon north to Alaska, but it has been introduced in recent years in lakes as far south as New Mexico and as far east as New England.

HABITAT: The kokanee spawns in gravel, both in lakes and in tributary streams, and ranges throughout lakes at other times.

SIZE: Much smaller than the true sockeye salmon, the kokanee reaches a maximum weight of about 4 pounds. The average length varies greatly, depending upon water and food conditions. In some places they never exceed 10 inches, while in other places—California's Donner Lake, for example—their average length is more than 18 inches.

Coho Salmon

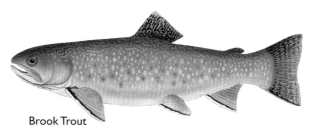
Brook Trout

FOOD: Kokanees feed almost exclusively on tiny forage—minute crustaceans and other plankton.

FISHING METHODS: Casting and trolling

BAITS: Small crustaceans, artificial lures, and flies

■ Arctic Char *(Salvelinus alpinus)*

COMMON NAMES: Arctic char, Arctic trout, alpine trout, and Quebec red trout

DESCRIPTION: The Arctic char is a far-north salmonid whose colors vary greatly. Sea-run char are quite silvery as they enter freshwater rivers, but their freshwater colors soon predominate, turning the char into a stunning fish with sides ranging in color from pale to very bright orange and red. Char are usually spotted in red, pink, or cream, and have the white-edged fins of brook trout, but they lack the brook trout's vermiculations (wormlike markings) on the back. There are both anadromous and landlocked strains of Arctic char.

RANGE: Arctic char are found in northern Canada, Alaska, Iceland, Greenland, Scandinavia, England, Ireland, Scotland, Europe, and the Soviet Union.

HABITAT: As its range indicates, the char thrives in very cold, clean water, preferring fast, shallow river water near the mouths of tributary streams. Relatively little is known about the nomadic movements of anadromous char, but they apparently spend the summer near the mouths of rivers, where they feed heavily before moving inland.

SIZE: Arctic char reach weights of nearly 30 pounds, but the average weight is 2 to 8 pounds.

FOOD: Char feed on a species of smelt called capelin and on sand eels, various baitfish, some crustaceans, and occasionally on insects.

FISHING METHODS: Casting

BAITS: Small baitfish, crustaceans, spoons, spinners, and flies

■ Brook Trout *(Salvelinus fontinalis)*

COMMON NAMES: Brook trout, speckled trout, speck, and squaretail

DESCRIPTION: This best-loved American native fish is not a true trout but actually a member of the char family. It is a beautiful fish, having a dark back with distinctive vermiculations (wormlike markings), sides marked with yellow spots and with red spots encircled in blue, a light-colored belly (bright orange during spawning), and pink or red lower fins edged in white. Wherever they are found, brook trout willingly take the offerings of fly, bait, and lure fishermen alike, a fact that has contributed to their decrease in many areas, though pollution has done far more to decimate populations of native brookies.

RANGE: Originally native only to northeastern North America from Georgia to the Arctic, the brook trout is now found in suitable waters throughout the United States, Canada, South America, and Europe. Stocking maintains brook trout in many waters, but true native brookies are becoming rare.

HABITAT: Brook trout must have clean, cold water, seldom being found in water warmer than 65°F. They spawn both in lakes and in streams, preferring small, spring-fed brooks.

SIZE: Though the rod-and-reel record for brook trout is 14½ pounds, fish half that size are a rarity today. In fact, a 5-pounder is an exceptional brook trout, and fish of that size are seldom found anywhere but in Labrador, northern Quebec and Manitoba, and Argentina. Native brook trout caught in streams average about 6 to 12 inches in length.

Arctic Char

Sunapee Trout

FOOD: Brook trout eat worms, insects, crustaceans, and various kinds of baitfish.

FISHING METHODS: Casting, trolling, and streamers

BAITS: Baitfish, worms, insects, spoons, spinners, and flies

■ Sunapee Trout *(Salvelinus aureolus)*

COMMON NAMES: Sunapee trout and Sunapee golden

DESCRIPTION: This attractive fish—which may be a member of the char family or a distinct species of trout (there is some disagreement on the subject)—has a dark-bluish back that lacks the wormlike markings of the brook trout. Its sides have spots of pinkish white, yellow, or red, and the yellowish or orange fins are edged in white.

RANGE: Originating in New Hampshire, principally in Sunapee Lake, the Sunapee trout is exceedingly rare, being found only in Sunapee Lake and in a few lakes and ponds in northern New England. The introduction of lake trout in Sunapee and other lakes has had a deteriorating effect on populations of Sunapee trout.

HABITAT: Little is known about the wanderings of this attractive fish, but it is known that in Sunapee Lake these trout move into the shallows in spring and fall, while in summer they are found in the deepest parts of the lake—way down to 60 to 100 feet, where the water is quite cold.

SIZE: Many years ago, 10- and 12-pound Sunapees were taken in the lake from which they derive their name, but today a fisherman is lucky to catch a 15-incher.

FOOD: Smelt makes up the majority of the Sunapee trout's diet.

FISHING METHODS: Casting

BAITS: Baitfish, smelt, spoons, spinners, and flies

■ Dolly Varden Trout *(Salvelinus malma)*

COMMON NAMES: Dolly Varden trout, Dolly, western char, bull trout, salmon trout, and red-spotted trout

DESCRIPTION: This member of the char family somewhat resembles the brook trout, but it lacks the brookie's wormlike back markings and is usually more slender. It has red and yellow side spots and the white-edged fins typical of all chars. In salt water, the Dolly is quite silvery. The Dolly, said to have been named after a Charles Dickens character, is not as popular in some parts of its range as other trout species, possibly because it is not as strong a fighter.

RANGE: Occurring from northern California to Alaska and as far from the United States as Japan, the Dolly is found in both fresh water and, in the northern part of its range, in salt water.

HABITAT: Dolly Vardens spawn in gravel in streams. At other times of the year, stream fish are likely to be found in places similar to those preferred by brook trout, such as under rocks, logs, and other debris and lying in deep holes. In lakes, they are likely to be found near the bottom near reefs and drop-offs. They are seldom found near the surface.

SIZE: Dolly Vardens reach weights of upwards of 30 pounds. The average size is 8 to 18 inches in some places (usually streams), and 3 to 6 pounds in other places (usually lakes).

FOOD: These fish are primarily bottom-feeders, though in streams they feed heavily on insects and may be taken on flies. Large fish feed heavily on baitfish, including the young of trout and salmon. It has been said that these

Dolly Varden Trout

trout will eat anything, which may be true considering that in some areas fishermen shoot ground squirrels, remove and skin the legs, and use the legs for Dolly Varden bait!

FISHING METHODS: Casting, trolling, and streamers

BAITS: Baitfish, spoons, spinners, and flies

▨ Lake Trout *(Salvelinus namaycush)*

COMMON NAMES: Lake trout, togue, mackinaw, gray trout, salmon trout, forktail, and laker

DESCRIPTION: More somberly hued than most other trout, the laker is usually a fairly uniform gray or bluish gray, though in some areas it is a bronze green. It has irregular, pale spots over its head, back, and sides and also has the white-edged fins that mark it as a char.

RANGE: The lake trout is distributed throughout Canada and in the northern United States, principally in New England, and New York's Finger Lakes, the Great Lakes, and many large western lakes. Stockings have widened the laker's range considerably and have restored the species to portions of the Great Lakes, where an incursion of lamprey eels decimated the laker populations in the 1950s and early 1960s.

HABITAT: Lake trout are fish of deep, cold, clear lakes, though in the northern part of their range they are also found in large streams. Lakers prefer water temperatures of about 45°F and are rarely found where water rises above 70°F. In the southern part of their range, they are usually found only in lakes that have an adequate oxygen supply in the deeper spots.

SIZE: The lake trout is the largest of the trout species, reaching weights of more than 100 pounds. Its average size often depends on the size, depth, and water quality of a given lake.

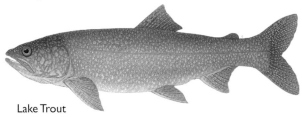

Lake Trout

Rainbow Trout

FOOD: Though the young feed on insects and crustaceans, adult lake trout eat primarily fish, such as smelt, small kokanee salmon, ciscoes, whitefish, and sculpin.

FISHING METHODS: Casting and trolling

BAITS: Baitfish, crustaceans, deep-running spoons, and plugs

▨ Rainbow Trout *(Oncorhynchus mykiss)*

COMMON NAMES: Rainbow trout, steelhead, Kamloops rainbow, Kamloops trout, and redsides

DESCRIPTION: This native American trout takes three basic forms: the nonmigratory rainbow, which lives its entire life in streams or lakes; the steelhead, which is spawned in freshwater rivers, migrates to the sea, and returns to the rivers to spawn itself (large rainbows that live in the Great Lakes and elsewhere in the eastern United States are also called steelheads but are not true members of the steelhead clan); and the Kamloops rainbow, a large subspecies found mostly in interior British Columbia. Though the rainbow's colors vary greatly depending upon where it is found, the fish generally has an olive or lighter-green back shading to silvery or white on the lower sides and belly. There are numerous black spots on the upper body from head to tail and a distinctive red stripe along the middle of each side. Sea-run and lake-run rainbows are usually quite silver, with a faint or nonexistent red stripe and few spots. The rainbow is an extremely important sport fish and will take flies, lures, and bait willingly. It usually strikes hard and is noted for its wild leaps.

RANGE: The natural range of the rainbow trout is from northern Mexico to Alaska and the Aleutian Islands, but stocking programs have greatly widened that range so that it now includes most of Canada, all of the northern and central states of the United States, and some of the colder waters in such southern states as Georgia, Tennessee, Arkansas, and Texas.

HABITAT: The rainbow, like all trout, must have cold, clean water, though it does fairly well under marginal conditions. It is found in shallow lakes and deep lakes, in small streams and large ones. It may be found at the surface one day, and feeding on the bottom the next. The rainbow's universality is due partly to the fact that it can do well in a wide variety of environments.

SIZE: The average nonmigratory stream rainbow runs from 6 to 18 inches in length, though some much larger specimens are occasionally taken. Nonmigratory lake fish tend to run considerably larger—up to 50 pounds or more. An average migratory steelhead runs from 8 to 12 pounds, but this strain reaches 35 pounds or so.

FOOD: Rainbows feed heavily on insect life, but they also eat baitfish, crustaceans, worms, and the roe of salmon and trout. The diet of the Kamloops rainbow is mainly kokanee salmon.

FISHING METHODS: Casting and trolling

BAITS: Baitfish, worms, salmon eggs, spoons, spinners, and flies

Cutthroat Trout *(Salmo clarki)*

COMMON NAMES: Cutthroat trout, coastal trout, cut, native trout, mountain trout, Rocky Mountain trout, black-spotted trout, harvest trout, Montana black-spotted trout, Tahoe cutthroat, and Yellowstone cutthroat

DESCRIPTION: Occurring in both nonmigratory and anadromous forms, the cutthroat trout gets its common name from the two slashes of crimson on the underside of its lower jaw. Its scientific name honors William Clark

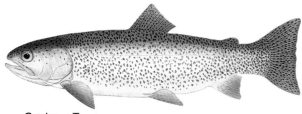

Cutthroat Trout

of the famed Lewis and Clark expedition. The cutthroat is often mistaken for the rainbow, but it lacks the rainbow's bright-red side stripe, and its entire body is usually covered with black spots, while the rainbow's spots are usually limited to the upper half of the body. The cutthroat usually has a greenish back, colorful gill plates, sides of yellow or pink, and a white belly. Coastal cutthroats are greenish blue with a silvery sheen on the sides and heavy black spots. The cutthroat is a fine sport fish, taking flies—particularly wet flies—readily and showing an inordinate liking for flashy spoons.

RANGE: The cutthroat is found from northern California north to Prince William Sound, Alaska, and inland throughout the western United States and Canada.

HABITAT: A fish of clean, cold water, the cutthroat frequents places like those preferred by the brook trout—undercut banks, deep holes, logs, and other debris. They prefer quiet water, generally, in streams. Unlike other trout that go to sea, anadromous cutthroats do not range widely in the ocean depths. Instead, they remain in bays at the mouths of their home streams or along the nearby ocean shores.

SIZE: Though cutthroats of up to 41 pounds have been caught by anglers, they seldom exceed 5 pounds and average 2 to 3 pounds. A fish weighing 4 pounds is considered large for a sea-run cutthroat.

FOOD: Young cutthroats feed mainly on insect life, while adults eat insects, baitfish, crayfish, and worms.

FISHING METHODS: Casting and trolling

BAITS: Insects, crayfish, worms, spoons, spinners, and flies

Golden Trout *(Salmo aquabonita)*

COMMON NAMES: Golden trout, Volcano trout, and Sierra trout

DESCRIPTION: This rare jewel of the western high country is the most beautiful of all trout. The golden trout has an olive back and crimson gill covers and side stripes, while the remainder of the body ranges from orangish yellow to gold. The dorsal fin has orange tips, and the anal and ventral fins have white edges. Each side

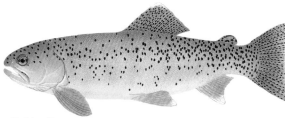

Golden Trout

contains about 10 black parr markings. The coloring differs from lake to lake. The golden is a rarely caught but highly prized sport fish.

RANGE: Originally found only in the headwaters of California's Kern River, the golden is now present in high-mountain lakes in many western states, including California, Wyoming, Idaho, and Washington. Modern fish-breeding and stocking techniques have extended the range of the golden—or, rather, a golden-rainbow trout cross—to the eastern states, including West Virginia and New Jersey.

HABITAT: The true golden trout is found in small, high lakes and their tributary streams at elevations of 9,000 to 12,000 feet. The water in these lakes is extremely cold, and weed growth is minimal or nonexistent. Because of the golden's spartan habitat, it can be extremely moody and difficult to catch.

SIZE: Golden trout are not large, a 2-pounder being a very good one, though some lakes hold fair numbers of fish up to 5 pounds. The maximum size is 11 pounds.

FOOD: Golden trout feed almost exclusively on minute insects, including terrestrial insects, but also eat tiny crustaceans and are sometimes caught by bait fishermen using worms, salmon eggs, and grubs.

FISHING METHODS: Casting and trolling

BAITS: Insects, worms, salmon eggs, spinners, and flies

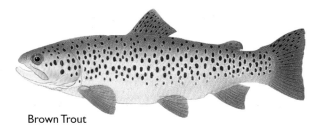

Brown Trout

▮ Brown Trout *(Salmo trutta)*

COMMON NAMES: Brown trout, German brown trout, and Loch Leven trout

DESCRIPTION: Introduced in North America in the 1880s, the brown trout is a top-notch dry-fly fish, and yet its daytime wariness and whimsy can drive fishermen to the nearest bar. The brown trout is generally brownish to olive brown, shading from dark brown on the back to dusky yellow or creamy white on the belly. The sides, back, and dorsal fin have prominent black or brown spots, usually surrounded by faint halos of gray or white. Some haloed red or orange spots are also present. Sea-run browns and those in large lakes are often silvery and resemble landlocked salmon.

RANGE: The brown is the native trout of Europe and is also found in New Zealand, parts of Asia, South America, and Africa. It is found in the United States from coast to coast and as far south as New Mexico, Arkansas, and Georgia.

HABITAT: The brown trout can tolerate warmer water and other marginal conditions better than other trout species can. It is found in both streams and lakes, preferring hiding and feeding spots similar to those of the brook trout. It often feeds on the bottom in deep holes, coming to the surface at night.

SIZE: Brown trout have been known to exceed 40 pounds, though one of more than 10 pounds is exceptional. Most browns caught by sportfishermen weigh ½ to 1½ pounds.

FOOD: Brown trout feed on aquatic and terrestrial insects as well as worms, crayfish, baitfish, and fish roe. Large specimens will eat such tidbits as mice, frogs, and small birds.

FISHING METHODS: Casting and trolling

BAITS: Baitfish, insects, worms, salmon eggs, spoons, spinners, and flies

▮ Grayling *(Thymallus arcticus)*

COMMON NAMES: Grayling, Montana grayling, and Arctic grayling

Grayling

DESCRIPTION: Closely related to trout and whitefish, the grayling's most distinctive feature is its high, wide dorsal fin, which is gray to purple and has rows of blue or lighter dots. Its back is dark blue to gray, and the sides range from gray to brown to silvery, depending upon where the fish lives. The forepart of the body usually has irregularly shaped dark spots. The grayling is a strikingly handsome fish and a fly fisherman's dream.

RANGE: The grayling is abundant in Alaska, throughout northern Canada from northern Saskatchewan westward, and northward through the Northwest Territories. It is less common in the United States, ranging in high areas of Montana, Wyoming, and Utah. Recently developed grayling-breeding procedures are extending the range of this fish into Idaho, California, Oregon, and other mountain states.

HABITAT: The grayling is found in both lakes and rivers, but is particularly at home in high and isolated timberline lakes. In lakes, schools of grayling often cruise near the shore. In rivers, the fish are likely to be found anywhere, but they usually favor one type of water in any given stream.

SIZE: The maximum weight of the grayling is 20 pounds or a bit heavier, but in most waters, even in the Arctic, a 2-pounder is a good fish. In U.S. waters, grayling seldom top 1½ pounds.

FOOD: The grayling's diet is made up almost entirely of nymphs and other insects and aquatic larvae. However, this northern fish will also readily eat worms and crustaceans.

FISHING METHODS: Casting

BAITS: Nymphs, insects, worms, and flies

Rocky Mountain Whitefish
(Prosopium williamsoni)

COMMON NAMES: Rocky Mountain whitefish, mountain whitefish, and Montana whitefish

DESCRIPTION: The Rocky Mountain whitefish resembles the lake whitefish, though its body is more cylindrical. Coloration shades from brown on the back to silver on the sides to white on the belly. The dorsal fin is large, but not nearly as large as that of the grayling. Where it competes with trout in a stream, the Rocky Mountain whitefish is considered a nuisance by many anglers, though it fights well and will take dry and wet flies, spinning lures, and bait.

RANGE: The Rocky Mountain whitefish is endemic to the western slope of the Rocky Mountains from northern California to southern British Columbia.

HABITAT: Found in cold, swift streams and in clear, deep lakes, these whitefish school up in deep pools after spawning in the fall and feed mostly on the bottom. In spring, the fish move to the riffles in streams and the shallows in lakes.

SIZE: Rocky Mountain whitefish reach 5 pounds, but a 3-pounder is an exceptional one. The average length is 11 to 14 inches and the average weight is 1 pound.

FOOD: These fish feed almost entirely on such insects as caddis and midge larvae and stone fly nymphs. They also eat fish eggs, their own included.

FISHING METHODS: Casting and fly fishing (not an important game fish)

BAITS: Insects, nymphs, fish eggs, and flies

Lake Whitefish
(Coregonus clupeaformis)

COMMON NAMES: Lake whitefish, common whitefish, Great Lakes whitefish, Labrador whitefish, and Otsego bass

Rocky Mountain Whitefish

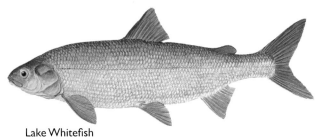

Lake Whitefish

DESCRIPTION: Similar in appearance—though only distantly related—to the Rocky Mountain whitefish, the lake whitefish has bronze or olive shading on the back, with the rest of the body being silvery white. It has rather large scales, a small head and mouth, and a blunt snout. Large specimens appear humpbacked. Lake whitefish, because they spend much of the year in very deep water, are not important sport fish.

RANGE: Lake whitefish are found from New England west through the Great Lakes area and throughout much of Canada.

HABITAT: These fish inhabit large, deep, cold, clear lakes and are usually found in water from 60 to 100 feet deep, though they will enter tributary streams in spring and fall. In the northern part of their range, however, lake whitefish are often found foraging in shallow water, and they will feed on the surface when mayflies are hatching.

SIZE: Lake whitefish reach weights of a bit more than 20 pounds, but their average size is less than 4 pounds.

FOOD: Lake whitefish feed primarily on small crustaceans and aquatic insects, but they will also eat baitfish.

FISHING METHODS: Casting (not an important game fish)

BAITS: Small baitfish, insects, and crustaceans

Cisco *(Coregonus artedii)*

COMMON NAMES: Cisco, herring, lake herring, common cisco, lake cisco, bluefin, Lake Erie cisco, tullibee, shortjaw chub, and grayback

DESCRIPTION: Though the cisco superficially resembles members of the herring family, it is not a herring but rather a member of the whitefish family. The cisco has a darker back (usually bluish or greenish) than the true whitefish. The body is silvery with large scales. There are more than 30 species and subspecies of ciscoes in the Great Lakes area alone, and all of them look and act alike. Ciscoes occasionally provide good sport fishing, particularly on dry flies, but they are more important commercially.

RANGE: The various strains of ciscoes occur from New England and New York west through the Great Lakes area and range widely through Canada. Their center of concentration seems to be the Great Lakes area.

HABITAT: Ciscoes prefer large, cold, clear lakes, usually those having considerable depth. Little is known of the wanderings of these fish; some species are found from the surface to several hundred feet down. They spawn in July and August over hard bottoms. In summer, ciscoes often come to the surface to feed on hatching insects, usually at sundown.

SIZE: The size of a cisco depends on its species. Some average only a few ounces in weight, while the largest attain a maximum weight of about 7 pounds. The average length is about 6 to 20 inches.

FOOD: Insect life—mainly bottom-dwelling types—is the blue-plate special of the cisco, though it sometimes feeds on surface insects and on minute crustaceans and worms as well.

FISHING METHODS: Fly fishing

BAITS: Insects, worms, and flies

American Shad *(Alosa sapidissima)*

DESCRIPTION: The American shad is an anadromous fish—meaning one that ascends coastal rivers to spawn but spends much of its life in salt water. A member of the herring family, the shad has a greenish back, with the remainder of the body being silvery. There are usually a few indistinct markings on the forebody. Shad put up a no-holds-barred battle on hook and line and are important sport and commercial fish, though pollution is putting a dent in their population in some areas.

RANGE: American shad were originally native only to the Atlantic, but they were introduced in the Pacific in

American Shad

the 1870s. On the Atlantic coast, they are found from Florida to the Gulf of St. Lawrence, while on the Pacific coast, they range from San Diego, California, to southern Alaska. They are also found in Scandinavia, France, Italy, Germany, Russia, and elsewhere.

HABITAT: American shad swarm up large, coastal rivers to spawn in the spring—from March to May, depending upon the location of the river. They are particularly susceptible to anglers below dams and in holes and slow runs just upstream of riffles, where they tend to rest before continuing upriver. They generally spawn in the main river.

SIZE: The average weight of an American shad is 3 to 5 pounds, while the maximum weight is 12 to 13 pounds. Egg-laden females are usually heavier than males.

FOOD: While in the ocean, American shad feed almost exclusively on plankton, so far as is known. After they enter fresh water on the spawning runs, these fish apparently do not feed at all. Curiously, however, they will strike at a small variety of artificial lures, including small, sparsely dressed wet flies and leadhead jigs tied on a gold hook and having a wisp of bucktail at the tail.

FISHING METHODS: Casting, jigs, and shad darts

BAITS: Artificial lures, small jigs, spinners, and spoons

Largemouth Bass
(Micropterus salmoides)

COMMON NAMES: Largemouth bass, bigmouth bass, black bass, green trout, Oswego bass, and green bass

DESCRIPTION: The largemouth bass is among the most important of this continent's freshwater game fish. In physical makeup it is a chunky fish, with coloration ranging from nearly black or dark green on the back, through varying shades of green or brownish green on the sides, to an off-white belly. The largemouth's most distinctive marking, however, is a horizontal, dark band running along its side from head to tail. In large, old bass particularly, the band may be almost invisible. There are two reliable ways to distinguish the largemouth from its close relative and look-alike, the smallmouth bass: the largemouth's upper jaw (maxillary) extends back behind the eye, while the smallmouth's does not; and the spiny part of the largemouth's dorsal fin is almost completely separated from the softer rear portion, while in the smallmouth the two fin sections are connected in one continuous fin.

RANGE: The largemouth is native to or stocked in every state in the Lower 48 and is found as far south as Mexico and as far north as southern Canada.

HABITAT: Largemouths are found in slow-moving streams large and small and in nonflowing waters ranging in size from little more than puddles to vast impoundments. They thrive best in shallow, weedy lakes and in river backwaters. They are warm-water fish, preferring water temperatures of 70°F to 75°F. Largemouths never venture too far from such areas as weed beds, logs, stumps, and other sunken debris, which provide both cover and food. They are usually found in water no deeper than 20 feet.

SIZE: Largemouth bass grow biggest in the southern United States, where they reach a maximum weight of a little more than 20 pounds and an 8- to 10-pounder is not a rarity. In the north, largemouths rarely exceed 10 pounds and a 3-pounder is considered a good catch.

FOOD: The largemouth's diet is as ubiquitous as the fish itself. These bass eat minnows and any other available baitfish, worms, crustaceans, a wide variety of insect life, frogs, mice, and ducklings.

Largemouth Bass

FISHING METHODS: Casting and trolling

BAITS: All baitfish, worms, crustaceans, frogs, artificial lures, and flies

Smallmouth Bass
(Micropterus dolomieui)

COMMON NAMES: Smallmouth bass, black bass, and bronzeback

DESCRIPTION: A top game fish and a flashy fighter, the smallmouth bass is brownish, bronze, or greenish brown in coloration, with the back being darker and the belly being off-white. The sides are marked with dark, vertical bars, which may be indistinguishable in young fish. (For physical differences between the smallmouth bass and its look-alike relative, the largemouth bass, see Largemouth Bass.) The smallmouth is not as common as, and is a wilder fighter than, the largemouth.

RANGE: The smallmouth's original range was through-out New England, southern Canada, and the Great Lakes area, and in large rivers of Tennessee, Arkansas, and Oklahoma. However, stocking has greatly widened this range so that it now includes states in northern and moderate climates from coast to coast.

HABITAT: Unlike the largemouth bass, the smallmouth is a fish of cold, clear waters (preferring water temperatures of no higher than 65°F or so). Large, deep lakes and sizable rivers are the smallmouth's domain, though it is often found in streams that look like good trout water—that is, those with numerous riffles flowing over gravel, boulders, or bedrock. In lakes, smallmouths are likely to be found over gravel bars, between submerged weed beds in water 10 to 20 feet deep, along drop-offs near shale banks, on gravel points running out from shore, and near midlake reefs or shoals. In streams, they often

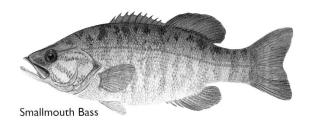
Smallmouth Bass

hold at the head of a pool where the water fans out, and in pockets having moderate current and nearby cover.

SIZE: The maximum weight attained by smallmouth bass is about 12 pounds. In most waters, however, a 4- or 5-pounder is a very good fish, and the average weight is probably 1½ to 3 pounds.

FOOD: Smallmouths eat baitfish and crayfish mainly, though they also feed on hellgrammites and other insect life, worms, small frogs, and leeches.

FISHING METHODS: Casting and trolling

BAITS: All baitfish, worms, crustaceans, crayfish, frogs, artificial lures, and flies

Redeye Bass *(Micropterus coosae)*

COMMON NAMES: Redeye bass, Coosa bass, shoal bass, and Chipola bass

DESCRIPTION: Given full status as a distinct species in about 1940, the redeye bass is a relative of the small-mouth. Though this fish is often difficult to identify positively, especially in adult form, the redeye young have dark, vertical bars that become indistinct with age and brick-red dorsal, anal, and caudal fins. This fin color and the red of its eyes are the redeye's most distinctive physical traits. The redeye is a good fighter and is good eating.

RANGE: An inhabitant of the southeastern states, the redeye bass is found mainly in Alabama, Georgia, and South Carolina. It is also found in the Chipola River system in Florida.

HABITAT: The redeye bass is mainly a stream fish, usually inhabiting upland parts of drainage systems. It often feeds at the surface.

SIZE: The maximum weight of the redeye bass is 6

Redeye Bass

pounds, but, in Alabama at least, the average weight is about 12 ounces.

FOOD: A large portion of the redeye's diet is insects, but it also feeds on worms, crickets, and various baitfish.

FISHING METHODS: Casting and drift fishing

BAITS: Worms, crickets, small baitfish, spinners, spoons, and flies

Spotted Bass
(Micropterus punctulatus)

COMMON NAMES: Spotted bass, Kentucky bass, Kentucky spotted bass, and Alabama spotted bass

DESCRIPTION: The spotted bass, recognized as a distinct species only since 1927, is quite similar in appearance to the largemouth bass and has characteristics of both the largemouth and the smallmouth. The spotted bass is olive green on the back with many dark blotches, most of which are diamond shaped. A series of short blotches form a horizontal, dark band along the sides that is somewhat more irregular than that of the largemouth. Spots below the lateral line distinguish the spotted bass from the largemouth, and that spotting, plus the lack of vertical side bars, distinguishes it from the smallmouth bass.

RANGE: The spotted bass is found in the Ohio-Mississippi drainage from Ohio south to the states bordering the Gulf of Mexico and western Florida, and west to Texas, Oklahoma, and Kansas.

HABITAT: In the northern part of its range, the spotted bass prefers large, deep pools in sluggish waters. Its preferred habitat in the southern part of its range is quite different, consisting of cool streams with gravel bottoms and clear spring-fed lakes. In lakes, spotted bass are sometimes found in water as deep as 100 feet.

SIZE: The maximum weight of spotted bass is 8 pounds, but few specimens top 4 or 5 pounds.

FOOD: Spotted bass, like most other members of the bass family, feed on various baitfish and insects, frogs, worms, crustaceans, grubs, and the like.

FISHING METHODS: Casting and drift fishing

BAITS: Baitfish, worms, frogs, artificial lures, and flies

Bluegill (Lepomis macrochirus)

COMMON NAMES: Bluegill, bluegill sunfish, bream, sun perch, blue perch, blue sunfish, copperbelly, red-breasted bream, copperhead bream, and blue bream

DESCRIPTION: Many fishermen cut their angling teeth on the bluegill, the most widely distributed and most popular of the large sunfish family. The color of the bluegill varies probably more than that of any other sunfish, ranging in basic body color from yellow or orange to dark blue. The shading goes from dark on the back to light on the forward part of the belly. The sides of a bluegill are usually marked by six to eight irregular, vertical bars of a dark color. A bluegill's prominent features are a broad, black gill flap, and long, pointed pectoral fins. Bluegills are excellent fighters, and if they grew to largemouth-bass size, they would break a lot of tackle.

RANGE: The bluegill's range just about blankets the entire 48 contiguous states.

HABITAT: The bluegill prefers habitat very much like that of the largemouth bass—that is, quiet, weedy waters, in both lakes and streams, where it can find both cover and food. In daytime, the smaller bluegills are usually close to shore in coves, under overhanging trees, and around

Spotted Bass

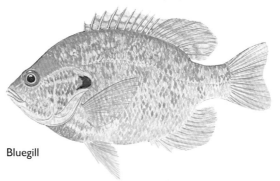

Bluegill

docks. The larger ones are usually nearby but in deeper water, moving into the shallows early and late in the day.

SIZE: The maximum size of bluegills is about 4½ pounds in weight and 15 inches in length, but the average length is 4 to 8 inches.

FOOD: A bluegill's food consists chiefly of insect life and vegetation. Other items on the menu include worms, grubs, small baitfish, crustaceans, small frogs, grass-hoppers, and the like.

FISHING METHODS: Casting, still-fishing, fly fishing

BAITS: Small baitfish, worms, insects, crickets, grass-hoppers, and flies

Redear Sunfish
(Lepomis microlophus)

COMMON NAMES: Redear sunfish, redear, shellcracker, stumpknocker, yellow bream, and chinquapin

DESCRIPTION: A large and very popular sunfish in the South, the redear has a small mouth, large and pointed pectoral fins, and a black gill flap with a whitish border (the bluegill lacks the white gill-flap border). The body color is olive with darker olive spots, and the sides have five to 10 dusky vertical bars. The redear is distinguish-able from the pumpkinseed—the member of the sunfish family it most closely resembles—by the lack of spots on the dorsal fin.

RANGE: The redear sunfish ranges from southern Illinois and southern Indiana south to Florida and the other Gulf states and westward to Texas and New Mexico. Its heaviest concentration is in Florida.

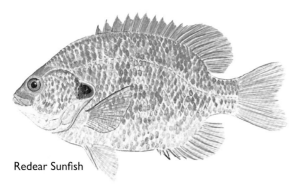

Redear Sunfish

HABITAT: The redear sunfish shows a definite liking for large, quiet waters, congregating around logs, stumps, and roots. It will, however, frequent open waters and seems to require less vegetation than other sunfish.

SIZE: The redear is more likely to run to a large size than most any other sunfish. The maximum weight seems to be 3 pounds, but 2-pounders are not uncommon.

FOOD: Redears depend mainly on snails for food, but will eat other mollusks, crustaceans, worms, and insects.

FISHING METHODS: Casting and still-fishing

BAITS: Small baitfish, worms, crickets, insects, artificial lures, and flies

White Crappie (Pomoxis annularis)

COMMON NAMES: White crappie, papermouth, bach-elor perch, papermouth perch, strawberry bass, calico, calico bass, sago, and grass bass

DESCRIPTION: This popular freshwater panfish is a cousin to the true sunfish. In coloration, its back is olive green and its sides silvery olive with seven to nine dark vertical bands, while the sides of the very similar black crappie have irregular dark mottling. Another, more reliable way to tell the white crappie from the black is the number of spines in the dorsal fin: the white has six while the black has seven or eight. The white is more elongated in general shape, while the black, by compari-son, has a high, rather arched back.

RANGE: The original range of the white crappie extended from Nebraska east to the Great Lakes, south through the Mississippi and Ohio River systems, and throughout most of the South as far north as North Carolina. Stock-ing has greatly extended that range, though the white crappie is still predominantly a southern species.

HABITAT: The white crappie can live under more turbid conditions than the black crappie—in fact, it prefers silty rivers and lakes to clear water and is common in south-ern impoundments and cypress bayous, warm and weedy ponds, and slow streams. The ideal home for these school-ing fish is a pile of sunken brush or a submerged treetop. In summer, crappies often seek such a spot in deep holes, moving into the shallows in the evening to feed.

How to Be a Crappie Expert

It doesn't take an angling wizard to catch a few crappies, but if you want to feed dinner guests, you have to learn a few tricks.

Location is the key to productive crappie fishing. When you're working at shoreline, look for brush piles or downed trees, especially if a structure is on the edge of deep water. Pilings and docks are also hot spots for crappies. These areas typically attract baitfish.

Crappies are also dedicated school fish. Find one and you will find many. When you catch one crappie, toss a marker over the side and mark the school. You can fish the spot until they stop hitting. If you catch one and still can't locate the school, tie a balloon to the crappie and turn it loose. It will try to get back to the school and give away its location.

You can use worms, grubs, crickets, and grasshoppers, but the best bait for crappies is a small live minnow. If you're trolling slowly to locate a school, hook the minnow through both lips. If you're still-fishing, hook your bait just behind the dorsal fin. If you can't find natural baits, try using small Gulp baits. Gulp baits come in so many sizes and shapes that you will have no trouble finding one of these ascended baits that will work for you.

If you don't want to use bait, try a small jig. Crappies seem to be more sensitive to color than other species. Keep changing jig colors until you find one that works consistently. The jig should weigh $\frac{1}{24}$ ounce, and don't use anything heavier than 6-pound-test line. In fact, 2- or 4-pound-test line is even better.

Crappies are also year-round fish. You can catch them right in the middle of football season. But remember that during the winter months, many lakes turn over, which means the coldest water will be on the top and the warmest water will be on the bottom. This is particularly true in the South. Because crappies always seek a comfort zone, they will look for that deeper, warmer water during the cold months.

Also remember that a crappie's metabolism drops during cold weather, so you will have to fish baits and jigs slower and deeper. Crappies will not chase a bait as fast or as far as they will during spring and summer. The reverse is true during the warm months, when the warm water is on top and the colder water is on bottom.

Don't worry about catching too many crappies and hurting the resource. Crappies are prolific and can handle the pressure. It's a good species to target when you're fishing for the freezer.

Crappies are also excellent eating. Cut the fillets into bite-size pieces. Mix cornmeal, flour, and pepper in a bowl. Beat some eggs in another bowl, and then dip the fillets in the eggs and coat with the cornmeal mix. Fry in vegetable oil until the fillets are golden brown. It's as simple as that!

Best Baits for Crappies

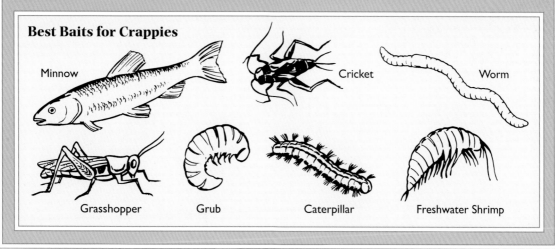

Minnow

Cricket

Worm

Grasshopper

Grub

Caterpillar

Freshwater Shrimp

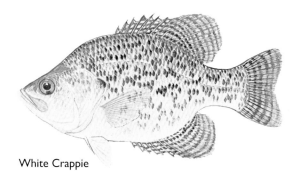

White Crappie

SIZE: White crappies average 6 to 10 inches in length and less than a pound in weight. However, individuals of more than 5 pounds have been caught by sportfishermen, and 2- or 3-pounders are not rare.

FOOD: White crappies eat baitfish for the most part—gizzard shad is their blue-plate special in southern lakes—but also feed on worms, shrimp, plankton, snails, crayfish, and insects.

FISHING METHODS: Casting and still-fishing

BAITS: Small baitfish, worms, crayfish, insects, jigs, and flies

Black Crappie
(Pomoxis nigromaculatus)

COMMON NAMES: Black crappie, calico bass, papermouth, and grass bass

DESCRIPTION: This near-identical twin of the white crappie is dark olive or black on the back. Its silvery sides and its dorsal, anal, and caudel fins contain dark and irregular blotches scattered in no special pattern. (For physical differences between the black and white crappie, see White Crappie.) Though it is a school fish like the white crappie, the black crappie does not seem to populate a lake or stream so thickly as does the white.

RANGE: The black crappie, though predominantly a northern United States fish, is found from southern Manitoba to southern Quebec, and from Nebraska to the East Coast and south to Texas and Florida. However, stocking has widened this range to include such places as British Columbia and California.

HABITAT: The black crappie prefers rather cool, clear,

weedy lakes and rivers, though it often shares the same waters as the white crappie. The black is a brush lover, tending to school up among submerged weed beds and the like. It occasionally feeds at the surface, particularly near nightfall.

SIZE: See White Crappie.

FOOD: See White Crappie.

FISHING METHODS: See White Crappie.

BAITS: See White Crappie.

White Bass *(Morone chrysops)*

COMMON NAMES: White bass, barfish, striped bass, and streak

DESCRIPTION: This freshwater member of the ocean-going sea-bass family has boomed in popularity among sportfishermen in recent years, thanks to its schooling habits, its eagerness to bite, tastiness of its flesh, and increase in its range. The white bass is a silvery fish tinged with yellow toward the belly. The sides have about 10 narrow, dark stripes, the body is moderately compressed, and the mouth is bass-like. The white bass may be distinguished from the look-alike yellow bass by its unbroken side stripes (those of the yellow bass are broken) and by its projecting lower jaw (the upper and lower jaws of the yellow are about even). The white bass is astonishingly prolific.

RANGE: White bass are found in the St. Lawrence River area and throughout the Mississippi and Missouri River systems, west into Texas, and in most of the other southern and southwestern states.

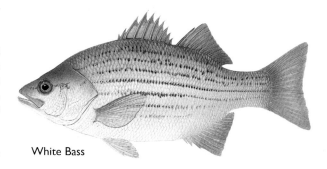

White Bass

HABITAT: The white bass lives in large lakes and rivers, but it appears to prefer large lakes containing relatively clear water. The burgeoning number of large, deep reservoirs constructed recently in the South and Southwest are tailor-made for the white bass. These fish like large areas of deep water and need gravel or bottom rubble for spawning. Schools of whites can often be seen feeding voraciously on or near the surface, particularly in the evening.

SIZE: The maximum size of the white bass is about 6 pounds, but the average size is ½ to 2 pounds. A 3- or 4-pounder is an excellent specimen.

FOOD: Baitfish, particularly gizzard shad, form the main part of the white bass's diet, though it will also eat crustaceans, worms, and insect life.

FISHING METHODS: Casting and still-fishing

BAITS: Small baitfish, worms, insects, and artificial lures

▧ Yellow Bass
(Morone mississippiensis)

COMMON NAMES: Yellow bass, barfish, brassy bass, stripe, striped bass, and streaker

DESCRIPTION: Quite similar in appearance to the white bass (for physical differences, see White Bass), the yellow bass has an olive-green back, silvery to golden-yellow sides with six or seven dark, horizontal, broken stripes, and a white belly. Like the white bass, the yellow bass is a member of the seabass family. It is a school fish, but its population levels tend to fluctuate drastically from year to year.

RANGE: The range of the yellow bass is quite restricted, being mainly the Mississippi River drainage from Minnesota to Louisiana and eastern Texas, plus the Tennessee River drainage, and Iowa. Even within its range, the yellow bass is found only in scattered lakes and streams.

HABITAT: One of the yellow bass's primary habitat requirements is wide, shallow, gravelly areas and rocky reefs. This fish prefers large lakes and large rivers, especially those with clear water. Yellow-bass schools tend to roam in deep water in daytime, coming into the shallows to feed late and very early.

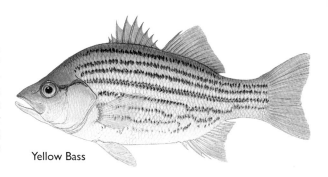
Yellow Bass

SIZE: Most yellow bass caught by sportfishermen range from 8 to 11 inches, and from ¼ to ¾ pound. The maximum size is probably about 3 pounds.

FOOD: Yellow bass feed almost exclusively on baitfish, but occasionally take crustaceans and insects.

FISHING METHODS: Casting and still-fishing

BAITS: Small baitfish, worms, insects, jigs, and spinners

▧ White Perch (Morone americanus)

COMMON NAMES: White perch, silver perch, and sea perch

DESCRIPTION: This fish is not a perch but rather a bass. And though it is often found in fresh water, it is not a freshwater bass. It is a member of the sea-bass family and superficially resembles one other member of that family—the saltwater striped bass—though it is much smaller. The white perch is greenish to blackish green on the back and silvery on the sides, particularly when living in salt water (freshwater individuals are usually darker). Young white perch have indistinct stripes on the sides, but adult fish lack them.

RANGE: In salt water, white perch range along the Atlantic coast from Nova Scotia to North Carolina. They are found inland as far as the Great Lakes and are especially abundant in New York State and New England.

HABITAT: In salt water, white perch are most likely to be found in brackish ponds and backwaters formed by coastal sandbars. Anadromous members of the clan run upriver to spawn. In inland lakes, these fish usually lie in deep water over a sand or gravel bottom during the day, sometimes at 50 feet or deeper, but often come into

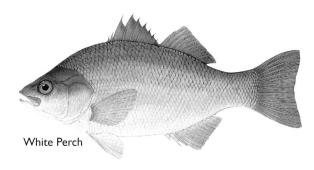

White Perch

shoreside shallows in the evening and at night to feed. At those times, and on dark days, schools of white perch may be seen breaking the surface.

SIZE: White perch seem to run larger in salt and brackish water than in fresh water. The average size, generally, is 8 to 10 inches. As for the weight, 2-pounders are not rare, but white perch seldom exceed 4 pounds.

FOOD: In salt water, white perch forage on small fish, shrimp, squid, crabs, and the like. In fresh water, their diet includes larval and other insect forms, crustaceans, baitfish, and worms.

FISHING METHODS: Casting

BAITS: Small baitfish, crabs, shrimp, crustaceans, spoons, and spinners

Yellow Perch *(Perca flavescens)*

COMMON NAMES: Yellow perch, ringed perch, striped perch, coon perch, and jack perch

DESCRIPTION: The yellow perch, in no way related to the white perch, is an extremely popular freshwater panfish. Though its colors may vary, the back is generally olive, shading to golden yellow on the sides and white on the belly. Six to eight rather wide, dark, vertical bands

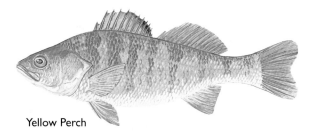

Yellow Perch

run from the back to below the lateral line. Though the body is fairly elongated, the fish has a somewhat hump-backed appearance.

RANGE: The yellow perch is a ubiquitous species, being found in most areas of the United States. It is most common from southern Canada south through the Dakotas and Great Lakes states into Kansas and Missouri, and in the East from New England to the Carolinas. Stockings have also established it in such places as Montana and the Pacific slope.

HABITAT: The yellow perch is predominantly a fish of lakes large and small, though it is also found in rivers. It prefers cool, clean water with plenty of sandy or rocky-bottomed areas, though it does well in a wide variety of conditions. As a very general rule, the best perch lakes are large and have only moderate weed growth. These fish feed at various levels, and the fisherman must experiment until he finds them.

SIZE: The average yellow perch weighs a good deal less than a pound, though 2-pounders aren't uncommon. The maximum weight is about 4½ pounds.

FOOD: Yellow perch eat such tidbits as baitfish (including their own young), worms, large plankton, insects in various forms, crayfish, snails, and small frogs.

FISHING METHODS: Casting and trolling

BAITS: Small baitfish, worms, crayfish, insects, jigs, spinners, and flies

Walleye *(Stizostedion vitreum)*

COMMON NAMES: Walleye, walleyed pike, pike, jack, jackfish, pickerel, yellow pickerel, blue pickerel, dore, and pikeperch

DESCRIPTION: The walleye is not a pike or pickerel, as its nicknames might indicate, but rather the largest member of the perch family. Its most striking physical characteristic is its large, almost opaque eyes, which appear to be made of glass and which reflect light eerily. The walleye's colors range from dark olive or olive brown on the back to a lighter olive on the sides and white on the belly. Here's how to tell the walleye from its look-alike relative, the sauger: the lower fork of the walleye's tail has a

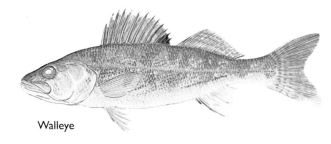
Walleye

milky-white tip, absent in the sauger; and the walleye's dorsal-fin foresection has irregular blotches or streaks, unlike the definite rows of spots found on the sauger's dorsal. The walleye isn't the best fighter among game fish, but it makes up for that shortcoming by providing delectable eating.

RANGE: The walleye is found in most of Canada as far north as Great Slave Lake and Labrador. Its original U.S. range was pretty much limited to the northern states, but stocking has greatly widened this range to include all of the East and most of the Far West and southern states.

HABITAT: The walleye loves clear, deep, cold, and large waters, both lakes and rivers, and prefers a sand, gravel, or rock bottom. It is almost always found on or near the bottom, though during evening and night hours it may move into shallow water to feed. Once you find a walleye hole, you should catch fish there consistently, for walleyes are schooling fish and are unlikely to move their places of residence.

SIZE: The top weight of walleyes is about 25 pounds, but a 6- to 8-pounder is a brag fish. Most walleyes that end up on fishermen's stringers weigh 1 to 3 pounds.

FOOD: Walleyes feed primarily on small fish and crayfish. Strangely enough, though they don't often eat worms, night crawlers are a real walleye killer, especially when combined with a spinner.

FISHING METHODS: Casting and trolling

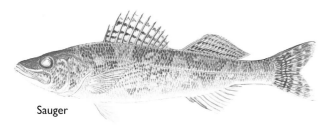
Sauger

BAITS: Baitfish, worms, frogs, crayfish, spinners, and spoons

▨ Sauger *(Stizostedion canadense)*

COMMON NAMES: Sauger, sand pike, gray pike, river pike, spotfin pike, and jack fish

DESCRIPTION: The sauger is very much like the walleye in all important respects, except that it is quite a bit smaller. It is olive or olive gray on its back and sides and has a white belly. Its large, glassy eyes are very much like those of the walleye. (For physical differences between the sauger and the walleye, see Walleye.)

RANGE: The sauger's range is generally a blueprint of the walleye's. However, sauger are most common in the Great Lakes, other very large lakes in the northern United States and southern Canada, and in large rivers (and their tributaries), such as the Mississippi, Missouri, Ohio, and Tennessee.

HABITAT: In this category, too, the sauger is much like the walleye, though the sauger can tolerate siltier or murkier water than the walleye and tends to stick to deeper waters. A good place to look for sauger is in tail-waters below dams.

SIZE: The sauger's maximum weight is about 8 pounds. Its average size is 1 to 2 pounds.

FOOD: See Walleye.

FISHING METHODS: See Walleye.

BAITS: Baitfish, worms, frogs, crayfish, jigs, and spinners

▨ White Sturgeon *(Acipenser transmontanus)*

DESCRIPTION: This huge, primitive throwback to geological history is one of 16 species of sturgeon in the world, seven of which occur in the United States. It is the largest fish found in this country's inland waters and the only member of the sturgeon family that is considered a game fish. The white sturgeon does not have scales but rather five rows of bony plates along its body. It has a large, underslung, sucking mouth, and its skel-

White Sturgeon

eton is cartilage rather than true bone. Sturgeon roe is better known as caviar. Though relatively few anglers fish for these behemoths, careful regulation of the fishery is necessary to prevent depletion of the populations of white sturgeon.

RANGE: The white sturgeon is found along the Pacific coast from Monterey, California, to Alaska. It is also found inland in the largest of rivers, including the Columbia and Snake.

HABITAT: Some white sturgeon are entirely landlocked, but many spend much of their lives at sea and ascend large West Coast rivers to spawn. In large rivers, they lie on the bottom in deep holes.

SIZE: The largest white sturgeon reported taken pulled the scales down to 1,800 pounds. The average size is difficult to determine.

FOOD: In fresh water, the white sturgeon uses its vacuum-cleaner mouth to inhale crustaceans, mollusks, insect larvae, and all manner of other bottom-dwelling organisms. Bait used by sturgeon anglers includes night crawlers, lamprey eels, cut bait, and even dried river moss.

FISHING METHODS: This species is not typically sought by fishermen (check regulations).

BAITS: Worms, eels, and baitfish

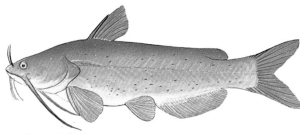

Channel Catfish

Channel Catfish
(Ictalurus punctatus)

COMMON NAMES: Channel catfish and fiddler

DESCRIPTION: This sizable member of the large catfish family (which includes bullheads) is undoubtedly the most streamlined, gamest, and most agile of the whole clan. In coloration, the channel cat is steely blue on top and shades to white on the belly, though young ones may be silvery even along the back. It is the only spotted catfish (it has dark speckles on the sides, though these spots may be missing in large specimens) with a deeply forked tail.

RANGE: The channel catfish occurs from the Saskatchewan River and entire Great Lakes area southward into Mexico. Stocking has transplanted this fish far west and east of its natural range.

HABITAT: Channel catfish are found in lakes, but they are more common in rivers, especially large ones. They are likely to be found in faster, cleaner water than other catfish and seem to prefer a bottom composition of sand, gravel, or rock. Like all other catfish, they are bottom-feeders and are especially active at night.

SIZE: Channel cats are among the larger members of the catfish family, attaining weights of up to 60 pounds. The average size is 1 to 5 pounds.

FOOD: The channel cat's varied menu includes just about anything it can get its jaws around—small fish, insects, crustaceans, worms, grubs, frogs, and many other aquatic food forms.

FISHING METHODS: Still-fishing and drift fishing in rivers

BAITS: Small fish, insects, worms, frogs, crustaceans, and stink baits

Blue Catfish (Ictalurus furcatus)

DESCRIPTION: The blue is the largest member of the catfish clan. It has a deeply forked tail, but lacks the spots of the channel catfish. In color, the blue catfish is pale blue on the back, a lighter silvery blue on the sides, and white on the belly. The most reliable way to tell the blue from

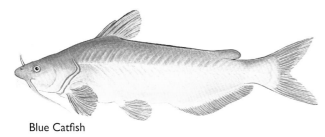

Blue Catfish

other catfish is by the number of rays on its straight-edged anal fin (there are 30 to 36 rays).

RANGE: The blue catfish is found mainly in the Mississippi River system, but it occurs south into Mexico and has been introduced into some rivers on the Atlantic coast.

HABITAT: The blue is a catfish of large rivers and is likely to be found below the dams creating large impoundments, especially in the southern United States. It prefers less-turbid waters than do most other catfish and seems to do best over bottoms of rock, gravel, or sand. It feeds in rapids or fast chutes.

SIZE: This heavyweight grows to more than 100 pounds. The average size, however, is 2 to 15 pounds.

FOOD: The blue catfish feeds primarily on small fish and crayfish. A favorite bait in some areas is a whole golden shad.

FISHING METHODS: Bottom fishing and drift fishing

BAITS: Baitfish, worms, crustaceans, and stink baits

▨ **Brown Bullhead** *(Ictalurus nebulosus)*

COMMON NAMES: Brown bullhead, horned pout, and speckled bullhead

Brown Bullhead

DESCRIPTION: Probably the most popular of the catfish—at least, it's the most often caught—the brown bullhead is a rather slender catfish with typical catfish features: sharp dorsal spine and sensitive barbels (the "feelers" projecting from the mouth area). The brown bullhead's chin barbels are dark brown or black. The tail has almost no fork, and the anal fin has 22 or 23 rays. The back is yellowish brown to light chocolate brown and has vague dark mottling, the sides are lighter, and the belly is yellow to milky white.

RANGE: Brown bullheads occur from Maine and the Great Lakes south to Mexico and Florida, but stocking has greatly expanded this range.

HABITAT: Brown bullheads prefer relatively deep, weedy waters in lakes and slow-moving streams. They may be found over sand and gravel bottoms and also over mud. They are almost exclusively bottom-feeders.

SIZE: The brown bullhead seldom weighs more than 3 pounds, with its average length being 6 to 16 inches.

FOOD: Insect larvae and mollusks constitute the majority of the brown bullhead's menu, but it will eat almost anything, from worms, small fish, and frogs to plant material and even chicken livers (a favorite catfisherman's bait).

FISHING METHODS: Still-fishing and drift fishing

BAITS: Baitfish, worms, frogs, and stink baits

▨ **Black Bullhead** *(Ictalurus melas)*

COMMON NAMES: Black bullhead and horned pout

DESCRIPTION: Quite similar in appearance to the brown bullhead, the black bullhead is black to yellow green on the back, yellowish or whitish on the sides, and bright yellow, yellow, or milky on the belly. Its chin barbels are dark or spotted, and its pectoral spines have no serrations. The body is chunky.

RANGE: The areas in which the black bullhead is most numerous are New York, west to the Dakotas, and south to Texas. However, the fish has been introduced into most other areas of the United States.

HABITAT: The black bullhead is a fish of muddy, sluggish,

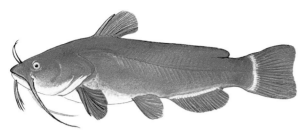

Black Bullhead

turbid streams and lakes. It seems to do well, in fact, in any kind of environment except cool, clear, deep water. It is a bottom-feeder.

SIZE: The largest black bullhead taken by sport fishing weighed 8 pounds, but this catfish seldom weighs more than 2 pounds.

FOOD: See Brown Bullhead.

FISHING METHODS: Bottom fishing and drift fishing

BAITS: Small baitfish, worms, crustaceans, and stink baits

Carp *(Cyprinus carpio)*

COMMON NAMES: Carp and common carp

DESCRIPTION: This big, coarse, much-maligned rough fish belongs to the minnow family and is related to the goldfish. In color, the carp is olive to light brown on the back, golden yellow on the sides, and yellowish white on the belly. At the base of each of its large scales is a dark spot. On each side of the upper jaw are a pair of fleshy barbels, and the dorsal fin has a serrated spine. Though the carp is cussed out by most sportfishermen and often poisoned out of lakes and streams, it is taken by rod and line, bow and arrow, spear, ice gig, and set line, and it can put up a whale of a battle.

RANGE: Introduced into the United States in 1876, the carp has found its way into just about every area in the nation. It is also widely distributed throughout Europe and Asia.

HABITAT: The carp can live almost anywhere and under almost any conditions—except cold, clear waters. It is almost always found on the bottom, except during spawning, when schools of carp are often seen slashing around on the surface.

SIZE: Carp reach a maximum size of about 60 pounds, but the average weight is 8 to 15 pounds.

FOOD: Carp are mainly vegetarians, feeding on aquatic plant life and plankton, though they also eat insects and are often caught by anglers on doughballs, cornmeal, and such.

FISHING METHODS: Bottom fishing

BAITS: Mostly doughball mixtures

Alligator Gar *(Lepisosteus spatula)*

DESCRIPTION: Exceeded in size in fresh water only by the western sturgeons, the alligator gar is the largest of the ancient gar family. It can be distinguished from its relatives by an examination of the teeth. Young alligator gars have two rows of large teeth on each side of the upper jaw; other gars have only a single row. The alligator gar has a long, cylindrical body that is olive green or brownish green along the back and lighter below. The sides and rear fins have mottling or large, dark spots. Gars are of minor importance as sport fish, though they wage a wild, no-holds-barred battle when taken on rod and line.

RANGE: The alligator gar is found mainly in the Mississippi and Ohio River systems as far north as Louisville, Kentucky, and St. Louis, Missouri, and as far south as northeastern Mexico.

HABITAT: Alligator gars prefer sluggish rivers, lakes, and backwaters over muddy, weedy bottoms. They often congregate in loose schools, usually near the surface, where they roll around.

SIZE: The largest reported alligator gar was 10 feet long and weighed 302 pounds. The average size, however, is undetermined.

FOOD: Various kinds of fish, notably the freshwater drum (or gaspergou), are the principal food of alligator gars, though anglers catch them on wire nooses baited with minnows and on bunches of floss-like material that tangle tenaciously in the gar's teeth.

FISHING METHODS: Bottom fishing and drift fishing

BAITS: Baitfish (though most fishermen catch this fish with any material that will tangle in the gar's teeth)

Muskellunge

Longnose Gar *(Lepisosteus osseus)*

DESCRIPTION: The longnose gar is the most common and most widely distributed of the entire gar family. Its name derives from its long, slender beak (nose). Other distinguishing characteristics are its overlapping diamond-shaped scales and the unusual position of its dorsal fin—far back near the tail and almost directly above the anal fin. The coloration is similar to that of the alligator gar.

RANGE: The longnose gar occurs from Quebec's St. Lawrence drainage west to the Great Lakes (excluding Lake Superior) and as far as Montana, south along the Mississippi River system, and down into Mexico.

HABITAT: The longnose lives in much the same habitat as the alligator gar, though it is more likely to be found swimming and feeding in flowing water—that is, where there is a moderate current.

SIZE: Smaller by far than the alligator gar, the longnose reaches a length of 4 to 5 feet.

FOOD: The longnose, like the alligator gar, feeds mostly on other fish, though it also eats plankton and insect larvae when young.

FISHING METHODS: Drift fishing

BAITS: See Alligator Gar.

Muskellunge *(Esox masquinongy)*

COMMON NAMES: Muskellunge, maskinonge (and a variety of other spellings), muskie, pike, blue pike, great pike, jack, spotted muskellunge, barred muskellunge, and tiger muskellunge

DESCRIPTION: Moody, voracious, and predaceous, the muskellunge, the largest member of the pike family, presents one of the greatest challenges of any freshwater fish. Its adherents probably catch fewer fish per

hour than do those who fish for any other freshwater species, and yet muskie fishermen are legion—and growing in number. The muskellunge—whose name means "ugly fish" in Ojibway dialect—is green to brown to gray in overall color, depending upon its geographical location. Side markings are usually vertical bars, though the fish may be blotched or spotted or lack any distinctive markings. The muskie has no scales on the lower part of its cheek and gill covers; other members of the pike family have scales in those areas. There are three subspecies of the muskellunge: the Great Lakes muskie, the Ohio (or Chautauqua) muskie, and the tiger (or northern) muskie.

RANGE: The Great Lakes muskie is generally a fish of the Great Lakes basin area. The Ohio (Chautauqua) muskie occurs in New York's Chautauqua Lake and through the Ohio River drainage. The tiger (northern) muskie is common in Wisconsin, Minnesota, and western Michigan. In overall distribution, the muskellunge is found as far north as the James Bay and Hudson Bay drainages in northern Canada, across the northern United States, from Wisconsin east to New York and Pennsylvania, and south into Tennessee, North Carolina, Georgia, and in much of the northern Mississippi drainage. Stocking and propagation methods are greatly widening the muskie's range.

HABITAT: Muskies live in rivers, streams, and lakes, usually only in clear waters, though they may inhabit discolored water in the southern part of their range. They prefer cold waters, but they can tolerate water as warm as 70°F to 75°F. Favorite hangouts for adult muskies are shoreline weed beds, particularly near deep water, and such items of cover as logs, stumps, and rocks. They are usually found in water shallower than 15 feet, though midsummer may find them as deep as 50 feet.

SIZE: Muskies can reach weights of more than 100 pounds. However, the biggest rod-caught specimen weighed just shy of 70 pounds, and the average is 10 to 20 pounds.

Northern Pike

FOOD: Muskies feed mainly on fish, including their own young, as well as suckers, yellow perch, bass, and panfish. They also eat crayfish, snakes, muskrats, worms, frogs, ducklings, squirrels, and just about anything else they can sink their ample teeth into.

FISHING METHODS: Casting and trolling

BAITS: Baitfish, small bass, panfish, worms, frogs, ducklings, big spoons, and plugs

Northern Pike (Esox lucius)

COMMON NAMES: Northern pike, pike, northern, snake, great northern, jackfish, and jack

DESCRIPTION: This baleful-looking predator of the weed bed is of great importance as a sport fish. In color, it is dark green on the back, shading to lighter green on the sides and whitish on the belly. Its distinctive side markings are bean-shaped light spots, and it has dark-spotted fins. The entire cheek is scaled, but only the upper half of the gill cover contains scales. The dorsal fin, as in all members of its family, is far to the rear of the body, almost directly above the anal fin.

RANGE: The pike is found in northern waters all around the globe. In North America, it occurs from Alaska east to Labrador, and south from the Dakotas and the St. Lawrence River to Nebraska and Pennsylvania. Stockings have extended this range to such states as Montana, Colorado, North Carolina, and Maryland.

HABITAT: Over its entire range, the pike's preferred living conditions are shallow, weedy lakes (large and small); shallow areas of large, deep lakes; and rivers of moderate current. In summer, pike are normally found in about 4 feet of water near cover; in fall, they are found along steep, stormy shores.

SIZE: In the best Canadian pike lakes, rod-caught pike average 5 to 25 pounds, but in most waters, a 10- to 15-pounder is a very good pike. The maximum weight is a little more than 50 pounds.

FOOD: Pike are almost entirely fish eaters, but they are as voracious and predacious as the muskie and will eat anything that won't eat them first.

FISHING METHODS: Casting and trolling

BAITS: Baitfish, small bass, perch, panfish, worms, frogs, spoons, spinners, plugs, and flies

Chain Pickerel (Esox niger)

COMMON NAMES: Chain pickerel, jack, and chainsides

DESCRIPTION: This attractive pike-like fish with chain-like markings is the largest of the true pickerels. Its body color ranges from green to bronze, darker on the back and lighter on the belly. Its distinctive dark, chain-like side markings and larger size make the chain pickerel hard to confuse with the other, less common pickerel (mud or grass pickerel and barred or redfin pickerel).

RANGE: The chain pickerel originally was found only east and south of the Alleghenies, but its range now extends from Maine to the Great Lakes in the north and from Texas to Florida in the south.

HABITAT: The pickerel is almost invariably a fish of the weeds. It lurks in or around weed beds and lily pads, waiting to pounce on unsuspecting morsels. It is usually found in water no deeper than 10 feet, although in hot weather it may retreat to depths of as much as 25 feet.

SIZE: Chain pickerel attain a maximum weight of about 10 pounds, but one of 4 pounds is bragging size. The average weight is 1 to 2½ pounds.

FOOD: Chain pickerel eat fish for the most part, although they will also readily dine on frogs, worms, crayfish, mice, and insects.

Chain Pickerel

FISHING METHODS: Casting and trolling

BAITS: Baitfish, worms, frogs, crayfish, spoons, spinners, plugs, and flies

Redhorse Sucker
(Maxostoma macrolepidotum)

COMMON NAMES: Redhorse sucker, redhorse, northern redhorse, redfin, redfin sucker, and bigscale sucker

DESCRIPTION: Many anglers look at the entire sucker clan—of which the redhorse is probably the best known and most widely fished for—as pests or worse. And yet countless suckers are caught on hooks, netted, trapped, and speared every year, particularly in the spring, when their flesh is firm and most palatable. The redhorse, like all other suckers, has a large-lipped, tubelike, sucking mouth on the underside of its snout. Its overall color is silver, with the back somewhat darker. The mouth has no teeth, and the fins lack spines.

RANGE: The redhorse is found east of the Rocky Mountains from the midsouth of the United States north to central and eastern Canada.

HABITAT: Unlike some of its relatives, the redhorse prefers clean, clear waters and is at home in large and medium-size rivers, even swift-flowing ones, and in lakes. These fish seem to prefer sandy shallows in lakes, and deep holes in streams. As spawning runs begin in the spring, the redhorse congregates at the mouths of streams.

SIZE: The redhorse sucker's maximum weight is about 12 pounds. Most of the redhorses taken by anglers weigh 2 to 4 pounds.

FOOD: This bottom-feeding species eats various small fish, worms, frogs, crayfish, various insects (both aquatic and terrestrial), and insect larvae.

Splake

FISHING METHODS: This species is not typically sought by fishermen.

BAITS: Small baitfish, worms, insects, and fish eggs

Splake
(Salvelinus namaycush x S. fontinalis)

DESCRIPTION: The splake is a trout hybrid created by crossing lake trout with brook trout. The name is a combination of *speckled* (brook) trout and *lake* trout. The first important crossing of these two trout species was done in British Columbia in 1946, and some of the new strain was stocked in lakes in Banff National Park in Alberta. The body shape of the splake is midway between that of the brook trout and lake trout—heavier than the laker, slimmer than the brookie. Like the true lake trout, the splake's spots are yellow, but its belly develops the deep orange or red of the true brook trout (see Brook Trout and Lake Trout). Splake mature and grow faster than lake trout. Unlike many other hybrids, the splake is capable of reproducing.

RANGE: The splake's range is quite spotty, including a number of lakes in western Canada, at least one of the Great Lakes, and a few lakes in the northern United States. Stockings are slowly increasing this range.

HABITAT: See Lake Trout.

SIZE: The world-record splake, caught in Georgian Bay, Ontario, Canada, was 20 pounds, 11 ounces.

FOOD: See Lake Trout.

FISHING METHODS: See Lake Trout.

BAITS: Baitfish, smelt, insects, crustaceans, spoons, spinners, and plugs

Tiger Trout
(Salmo trutta x Salvelinus fontinalis)

DESCRIPTION: This hybrid is a cross between the female brown trout and the male brook trout. The tiger's most prominent physical characteristic is the well-defined vermiculations (wormlike markings) on its back and sides. Its lower fins have the white edges of the true brook trout. The tiger is an avid surface-feeder and is considerably more aggressive than either of its parent species. Under hatchery conditions, only 35 percent of the tiger's offspring develop. The tiger occasionally occurs under natural conditions, but it does not reproduce.

RANGE: The tiger, being a hybrid, has no natural range, but stockings have introduced it into a few streams in the United States. At least one state, New Jersey, has stocked this trout in its waters on an experimental basis.

HABITAT: The tiger's habitat is undetermined, but it is probably similar to that of the brook trout.

SIZE: The world-record tiger trout, caught in Lake Michigan, Wisconsin, was 20 pounds, 13 ounces.

FOOD: The tiger's food is undetermined, but it is probably similar to that of the brook trout.

FISHING METHODS: Casting and drift fishing

BAITS: Spoons, spinners, and flies

▨ Rock Bass (*Ambloplites rupestris*)

COMMON NAMES: Rock bass, goggle eye, redeye, rock sunfish, black perch, and goggle-eye perch

DESCRIPTION: The rock bass isn't a bass—it's one of the sunfishes. And though it isn't much of a fighter, it is fun to catch and is sometimes unbelievably willing to gobble any lure, bait, or fly it can get its jaws around. The basic color of the rock bass is dark olive to greenish bronze, with a lighter belly. The sides contain brownish or yellowish blotches, and a dark spot at the base of each scale produces broken horizontal streaks. The mouth is much larger than that of most other sunfishes, and the anal fin has six spines, while the anal fin of most other sunfishes has only three spines. There is a dark blotch on the gill flap.

RANGE: The rock bass occurs from southern Manitoba east to New England, and south to the Gulf states. Stockings have somewhat widened this range in recent years.

HABITAT: Rock bass prefer large, clear streams and lakes and are often found in the same waters as smallmouth bass. As their name suggests, the more rocks and stones

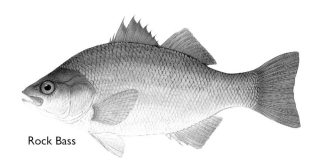
Rock Bass

on the bottom of the stream or lake, the better a fisherman's chances of finding rock bass. The species seems to prefer pools or protected waters to fast current or open waters.

SIZE: The top weight of the rock bass is a bit more than 2 pounds. Most of those caught by fishermen are 6 to 10 inches long and weigh about ½ pound.

FOOD: A voracious eater, the rock bass eats crawfish, minnows and other baitfish, worms, adult and larval insect life, and the like.

FISHING METHODS: Casting and drift fishing

BAITS: Small baitfish, worms, crayfish, spoons, spinners, and flies

▨ Hickory Shad (*Alosa mediocris* or *Pomolobus mediocris*)

DESCRIPTION: The hickory shad—like its larger relative, the American shad—is a herring. In color, it is gray green above, with silvery sides and underparts. Behind the upper part of the gill cover is a horizontal row of dark spots, usually numbering about six. Spots on the upper rows of scales form faint horizontal lines. It has a shallow-notched upper jaw, and the lower jaw projects prominently. The hickory shad is not so important a food or sport fish as is the American shad.

RANGE: The hickory shad is found along the Atlantic coast from the Bay of Fundy south to Florida.

HABITAT: An anadromous species (it lives in salt water but ascends freshwater rivers to spawn), the hickory shad's movements in the ocean are little known. But in the spring, it goes up the rivers, often the same rivers in which American shad spawn, though its runs usually precede those of the American shad.

SIZE: Though 5-pounders have been reported, the hickory shad seldom tops 2½ pounds in weight or 24 inches in length.

FOOD: The hickory shad feeds more on fish than does the American shad, and it is often caught by anglers using artificial flies and small spoons.

FISHING METHODS: Small jigs, shad darts, small spoons, spinners, and flies

BAITS: Artificial lures

Freshwater Drum
(Aplodinotus grunniens)

COMMON NAMES: Freshwater drum, sheepshead, gray bass, gaspergou, white perch, croaker, crocus, jewelhead, and grunter

DESCRIPTION: This species is the only freshwater member of the drum (croaker) family, which has about three dozen saltwater members. The freshwater drum has a blunt head, rounded tail, long dorsal fin, and a humped back. Colors are pearly gray on the back and upper sides, silver on the remainder of the sides, and milky white on the belly. A rather faint lateral line runs all the way into the tail. These fish make a weird "drumming" noise that, when they feed near the surface on calm evenings, seems to come from everywhere. It is caused by repeated contractions of an abdominal muscle against the swim bladder. Another oddity: the otoliths, or ear bones, of freshwater drum were used by Indians as wampum, as lucky pieces, and to prevent sicknesses.

RANGE: Freshwater drum are found from Guatemala north through eastern Mexico and the Gulf states to Manitoba, northern Ontario, Quebec, and the Lake Champlain area. East to west, they range from the Atlantic coast to the Missouri River drainage.

HABITAT: Found principally in large lakes and large, slow rivers, this species prefers modest depths (10 to 40 feet) and silty or muddy bottoms. It is a school fish, often congregating below large dams.

SIZE: Freshwater drum attain a maximum weight of about 60 pounds, but the average size is 1 to 5 pounds.

FOOD: Primarily a bottom-feeder, this species feeds almost entirely on mollusks—clams, mussels, and snails—which it "shells" with its large, strong teeth. Other foods include crawfish and some baitfish.

FISHING METHODS: Bottom fishing and drift fishing

BAITS: Clams, mussels, crawfish, snails, and baitfish

SALTWATER GAME FISH

Section Three
SALTWATER GAME FISH

Blue Shark *(Prionace glauca)*

DESCRIPTION: This large shark species, which has a reputation as a man-eater, is distinguished by its abnormally long pectoral fins and by its bright-cobalt color (the belly is white). It has the long snout of many members of the large shark family, and the dorsal fin is set well back on the back, nearly at the midpoint.

RANGE: Blue sharks are found throughout the tropical and temperate waters of the world.

HABITAT: Though often seen in shallow waters on the Pacific coast of the United States and on the surface in other northern areas, the blue shark is usually caught in deep water. It often roams in packs, while at other times it is found singly or in pairs.

SIZE: Blue sharks average less than 10 feet in length, but they have been reported to attain lengths of more than 20 feet. The largest rod-caught blue shark weighed 410 pounds.

FOOD: Blue sharks eat mainly mackerel, herring, squid, other sharks, flying fish, anchovies, and even such tidbits as seagulls and garbage deep-sixed from ships.

FISHING METHODS: Chumming and trolling from boats

BAITS: Whole or cut fish (and occasionally artificial lures)

Mako Shark *(Isurus oxyrinchus)*

COMMON NAMES: Mako shark and mackerel shark

DESCRIPTION: This huge, dangerous, fast-swimming, hard-fighting shark is closely related to the white shark.

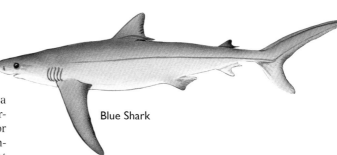

Blue Shark

It differs from the white mainly in the dorsal and pectoral fins, the tips of which are rounded in the mako, rather than pointed in the white. In color, the mako is dark blue to bluish gray above, shading to silver on the belly. The mako differs from the porbeagle shark in that its second dorsal fin is positioned a bit forward of the anal fin, while the porbeagle's second dorsal is directly above the anal fin.

RANGE: The mako is an inhabitant of the tropical oceans and the warmer areas of the Atlantic Ocean. In U.S. waters, it is found as far north as Cape Cod. It seems to be most numerous around New Zealand.

HABITAT: Makos tend to stay near the surface in open-ocean areas.

SIZE: Makos reach lengths of more than 12 feet and weights of more than 1,000 pounds.

FOOD: Staples of the mako's diet include tuna, mackerel, and herring. For some reason, it often attacks, but seldom kills, swordfish.

Mako Shark

FISHING METHODS: Trolling and chumming

BAITS: Whole or cut fish and scrap meat (and occasionally artificial lures)

White Shark *(Carcharodon carcharias)*

COMMON NAMES: White shark, great white shark, and man-eater

DESCRIPTION: The white shark—enormous, vicious, and incredibly powerful—is one of the largest of all fish. Its usual colors are grayish brown, slate blue, or gray, while the belly is off-white. Large specimens are sometimes a general off-white color. The white shark is built blockier than the look-alike mako, having a much deeper body. The white has a pointed snout, triangular serrated teeth, and a crescent-shaped caudal fin.

RANGE: The white shark is found throughout the world in tropical and temperate waters, though it seems to prefer warm to temperate regions over tropics. It is not numerous anywhere.

HABITAT: White sharks generally stay well offshore and seem to prefer relatively cool waters.

SIZE: The white shark is a true behemoth; one specimen 36½ feet long has been captured. The weight of that fish must have been astronomical, considering that a white shark just 13 feet long weighed 2,100 pounds! Whites that are 20 feet long are not at all uncommon.

FOOD: White sharks eat such things as other sharks that are 4 to 7 feet long, sea lions, seals, sturgeon, tuna, sea turtles, squid, and refuse.

FISHING METHODS: Chumming and trolling

BAITS: Whole fish or cut baits (and occasionally artificial lures)

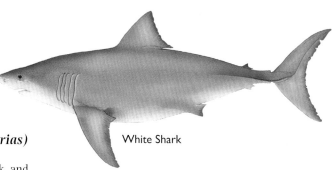

White Shark

Porbeagle Shark *(Lamna nasus)*

COMMON NAMES: Porbeagle shark and mackerel shark

DESCRIPTION: The porbeagle is a blocky-bodied shark that closely resembles the mako, though it is much less game. The best way to distinguish the porbeagle from both the mako and the white shark is the location of the second dorsal fin—the porbeagle is the only one whose second dorsal is directly above the anal fin. In color, the porbeagle shades from black to bluish gray on the back to white on the belly. Its anal fin is white or dusky.

RANGE: The porbeagle is found on both sides of the Atlantic as far south as the Mediterranean and Africa. On the Atlantic coast of the United States, it has been taken from South Carolina to the St. Lawrence Gulf. It is also found along most of the Pacific coast.

HABITAT: The porbeagle is a fish of temperate waters. In warm waters, it is found closer to shore and nearer to the surface, but when the water cools it may head for depths as great as 80 fathoms.

SIZE: The porbeagle apparently reaches a maximum length of about 12 feet, though the largest definitely recorded stretched 10 feet. The largest rod-caught porbeagle weighed 465 pounds.

FOOD: Porbeagles thrive on school-type fish such as mackerel and herring and on bottom-dwelling fish such as cod, hake, and flounders.

FISHING METHODS: Trolling and chumming

BAITS: Whole or cut baits

Thresher Shark *(Alopias vulpinus)*

DESCRIPTION: The thresher shark is nearly as large as the mako and is an excellent fighter, making breath-

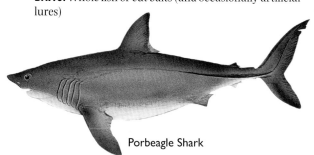

Porbeagle Shark

taking jumps and long runs. The thresher has one unique physical characteristic—its inordinately long upper lobe of the tail, or caudal fin, which is at least as long as the body. The thresher shark is dark gray, bluish, brown, or even black on the back and sides, while the belly is white, sometimes with a gray mottling.

RANGE: Threshers are found from Nova Scotia to Argentina and from Ireland to the Cape of Good Hope. They occur throughout the Mediterranean, in the Pacific from Oregon to Chile, and as far from the continental United States as Hawaii, Japan, and Australia.

HABITAT: The thresher is most at home at or near the surface in subtropical to temperate waters.

SIZE: Threshers reach lengths of 20 feet and weights of half a ton.

FOOD: The thresher shark uses its long tail to herd and injure such schooling fish as mackerel, menhaden, and bluefish.

FISHING METHODS: Chumming

BAITS: Whole or cut baits

Tiger Shark *(Galeocerdo cuvieri)*

DESCRIPTION: One of the so-called requiem sharks, the aptly named tiger is often the culprit in attacks on swimmers. In color, it is usually a general steel gray or brownish gray with a white belly, though the young have bars and spots on the back and upper sides. The upper lobe of the tail is long and slender, and it has a short and sharp-pointed snout.

RANGE: Tiger sharks are found throughout the world's tropical and subtropical regions.

HABITAT: Though sometimes caught offshore, the tiger seems to be largely a coastal fish, and it occasionally comes into quite shallow waters. It stays near the surface.

SIZE: Tigers are reported to reach lengths of 30 feet. The maximum weight is unknown, but 13- to 14-footers tip the scales at 1,000 to 1,500 pounds.

FOOD: Tiger sharks are omnivorous and cannibalistic. They eat their own kind, as well as fish of most species,

Tiger Shark

crabs, lobsters, and even sea lions and turtles. Examinations of their stomachs have revealed such things as tin cans, parts of crocodiles, and even human remains.

FISHING METHODS: Chumming and trolling

BAITS: Whole or cut baits (and occasionally artificial lures)

Hammerhead Shark *(Sphyrna mokarran)*

COMMON NAMES: Hammerhead shark, hammerhead, and great hammerhead

DESCRIPTION: There's no mistaking the hammerhead shark. Its small eyes are located at each end of its unique and grotesque head, which looks as if it had been modeled after the head of a huge mallet that had been pounded nearly flat. Gray or sometimes brownish gray on its back and sides and off-white on its underparts, the hammerhead's dorsal fin is less erect than that of any of its Atlantic relatives. Though not officially classified as a game fish, the hammerhead is a large and powerful adversary. Its hide makes fine leather, and its liver contains a high-grade oil.

RANGE: In the western Atlantic, the hammerhead occurs from North Carolina to Argentina. It is found elsewhere in the tropical and subtropical areas of the Atlantic, as well as in the eastern Pacific and the Indo-Pacific.

HABITAT: Hammerheads often travel in schools and may be found both near shore and far offshore.

SIZE: The average size is difficult to determine, but hammerheads apparently reach a maximum length of about 18 feet and a maximum weight of considerably more than 1,600 pounds.

FOOD: Voracious and cannibalistic, the hammerhead eats just about anything unlucky enough to get in its way, including big tuna, tarpon, and other sharks.

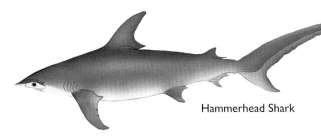

Hammerhead Shark

FISHING METHODS: Chumming and trolling

BAITS: Whole or cut fish (and occasionally artificial lures)

Swordfish *(Xiphias gladius)*

COMMON NAMES: Swordfish, broadbill, and broadbill swordfish

DESCRIPTION: The swordfish is one of the elite saltwater fish, much sought by both commercial and sportfishermen. It is distinguished from the other billfish (sailfish and marlin) by its much longer, flat bill (sword) and by its lack of scales and pelvic fins (the other billfish have both). The swordfish's dorsal and anal fins are sickle shaped. Its color is usually dark brown or bronze, but variations of black to grayish blue are common. The belly is usually white, but the dark colors sometimes extend right down to the fish's undersides.

RANGE: Swordfish are migratory and are found worldwide in warm and temperate waters. Their occurrence in the United States and adjacent waters extends in the Atlantic from Newfoundland to Cuba and in the Pacific from California to Chile.

HABITAT: Swordfish are open-ocean fish, usually feeding in the depths but often seen "sunning" on the surface.

SIZE: The maximum size of swordfish is a matter of some uncertainty, but specimens of nearly 1,200 pounds have been taken on rod and line. The average size is probably 150 to 300 pounds.

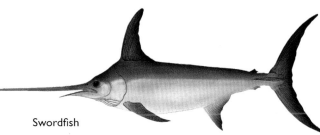

Swordfish

FOOD: Swordfish use their greatest weapon, the sword, to stun and capture such food as dolphins, menhaden, mackerel, bonito, bluefish, and squid.

FISHING METHODS: Night fishing was the standard technique, but now daytime methods regularly catch swordfish by placing baits at various depths from 100 feet to as deep as 1,500 feet.

BAITS: Whole squid, fish, or cut baits, such as mackerel fillets

Blue Marlin *(Makaira nigricans)*

DESCRIPTION: This king of the blue water is probably the most highly prized of the big-game fish, mainly because of its mammoth size and spectacular fighting abilities. In general coloration, the blue marlin is steel blue on the back, shading to silvery white on the belly. In most specimens, the sides contain light, vertical bars, which are not nearly as prominent as those of the white marlin. The dorsal and anal fins are bluish purple and sometimes have dark blotches. The blue marlin's distinguishing physical traits include a relatively short dorsal fin and a relatively long anal fin, and a body shape that is considerably rounder than other billfish.

RANGE: Blue marlin are found in warm and temperate seas throughout the world. In the United States and nearby waters, they occur from the Gulf of Maine to Uruguay in the Atlantic, and from Mexico to Peru in the Pacific.

HABITAT: Blue marlin are deep-water fish almost exclusively, and they are often seen cruising and feeding on the surface.

SIZE: The maximum size of the blue marlin is something more than 2,000 pounds, with the average being 200 to 500 pounds. Males seldom exceed 300 pounds, so those monsters often referred to as "Big Daddy" should really be called "Big Mama." Because the biggest blue marlin are thought to be in the Pacific, the International Game Fish Association separates these fish into two categories—Atlantic and Pacific.

FOOD: Blue marlin eat a broad range of fish life, including bluefish, mackerel, tuna, and bonito, as well as squid and octopus.

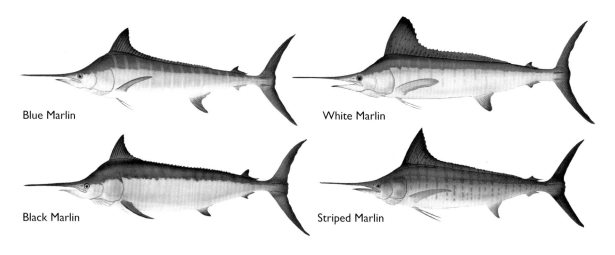

Blue Marlin

White Marlin

Black Marlin

Striped Marlin

FISHING METHODS: Trolling

BAITS: Feathers, lures, whole squid, and rigged ballyhoo

▓ White Marlin
(*Makaira albida* or *Tetrapturus albidus*)

DESCRIPTION: The white marlin is considerably smaller and less universal than the blue marlin. Its colors are a brilliant greenish blue on the back and upper sides, changing abruptly to white at the lateral line. The sides have an irregular number of vertical bands of light blue or lavender. A unique feature of the white marlin is the rounded tips of its dorsal and anal fins. The relatively flat-sided body is slender.

RANGE: The white marlin is limited to the Atlantic, occurring from Nova Scotia to Brazil and from the Azores to St. Helena Island and South Africa. Centers of concentration at differing times of year seem to be off the coast of Ocean City, Maryland, and near Venezuela.

HABITAT: Like the blue marlin, the white marlin is a fish of warm and temperate waters and is a migrant.

SIZE: Most white marlins caught by fishermen weigh 40 to 60 pounds, but the species apparently can reach 160 pounds.

FOOD: The white is mainly a fish eater, but it will dine on anything it can capture.

FISHING METHODS: Trolling

BAITS: Feathers, lures, squids, rigged ballyhoo, and mullet

▓ Black Marlin
(*Makaira indica* or *Istiompax indicus*)

DESCRIPTION: Possibly the largest of the marlins, the black is an ocean giant that is most easily distinguished from other marlins by the fact that its pectoral fins stick out at right angles from the body and are held rigidly in that position. The pelvic fins of the black marlin are shorter than those of other marlins, usually less than 1 foot long. The black marlin is seldom truly black, though its color varies greatly. Most are slate blue on the back and upper sides, shading to silvery white on the underparts. The sides occasionally exhibit pale-blue stripes.

RANGE: Black marlin seem to be found almost exclusively in the Pacific and Indian Oceans, being found as far north as southern California and Mexico. One area of abundance seems to be off the coast of Peru.

HABITAT: Little is known of the movements of the black marlin, though it is certainly a fish of the open oceans, and evidence indicates that it migrates only short distances if at all.

SIZE: The record rod-caught black marlin weighed 1,560 pounds, but specimens of up to 2,000 pounds have been taken commercially. The average size is probably 300 to 500 pounds.

FOOD: Various fish species (a tuna of 158 pounds was

found in a black marlin's stomach) and squid are the main items in the black marlin's diet.

FISHING METHODS: Trolling

BAITS: Whole fish, strip baits, whole squids, and artificial lures

Striped Marlin
(*Makaira audax* or *Tetrapturus audax*)

DESCRIPTION: Smaller than the blue and black marlins, the striped marlin, as its name suggests, is most easily distinguished by the stripes on its sides. These stripes vary both in number and in color, which ranges from pale blue to lavender to white. Body colors are steel blue on the back and upper sides, shading to white on the bottom areas. The striped marlin also has a high, pointed dorsal fin, which is usually taller than the greatest depth of its body. Like all other marlins, the striped variety puts up a breathtaking battle.

RANGE: Striped marlin are found in the Indian Ocean and in the Pacific from southern California to Chile.

HABITAT: Striped marlin are open-ocean fish. The fairly well-defined local populations seem to make short north-to-south migrations. Like all the other marlins, they are often seen feeding on the surface.

SIZE: The average rod-caught striped marlin weighs about 200 to 250 pounds, but the species grows to more than 500 pounds.

FOOD: Striped marlin feed on a wide variety of fish life (anchovies, bonito, mackerel, and many others), and on squid, crustaceans, octopus, and anything else that might get in their way.

FISHING METHODS: Trolling

BAITS: Whole fish, cut baits, whole squids, and artificial lures

Atlantic Sailfish (*Istiophorus albicans*)

DESCRIPTION: The uncommonly beautiful sailfish probably adorns more den and living-room walls than any other marine game fish. Sailfish are spectacular fighters, hurling themselves high out of the water time and time again. You can't mistake the sailfish for anything else that swims—thanks to its enormous purple (or cobalt-blue) dorsal fin, which it often seems to flaunt at fishermen. Body colors range from striking blue on the back and upper sides to silver white below the well-defined lateral line. Side markings usually consist of a variable number of pale, vertical bars or vertical rows of pale spots. The dorsal fin usually is marked with numerous black spots. A sailfish's pelvic fins are longer than those of other billfish.

RANGE: The Atlantic sailfish is commonly found in the Atlantic Ocean from Cape Hatteras to Venezuela, with winter concentrations off the east coast of Florida. This species is also found off England, France, Africa, and in the Mediterranean.

HABITAT: Sailfish are most often seen—and are almost always caught—on or near the surface. However, studies of their preferred diet indicate that they do much of their feeding in middle depths, along reefs, and even on the bottom.

SIZE: Most Atlantic sailfish caught by sportfishermen weigh 30 to 50 pounds, but the maximum size is probably a bit larger than the rod-and-reel record of 128 pounds, 1 ounce.

FOOD: According to studies made of the feeding habits of Atlantic sailfish in Florida waters, these fish feed mainly on a wide variety of fish life (tuna, mackerel, jacks, balao, needlefish, herring, and a few other species make up 83 percent of the Atlantic sailfish's diet). They also feed on squid and octopus.

FISHING METHODS: Trolling and sight casting

BAITS: Whole or cut baits, rigged ballyhoo, pilchards, and artificial lures

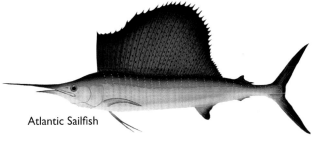

Atlantic Sailfish

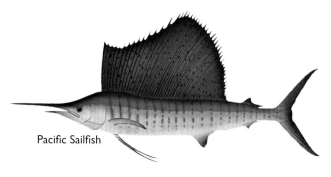

Pacific Sailfish

Pacific Sailfish *(Istiophorus greyi)*

DESCRIPTION: It is not known for certain whether the Pacific sailfish is truly a distinct species from the Atlantic sailfish, though it does grow considerably larger than the Atlantic variety. In most other important respects, the two fish are exactly alike. The only physical difference is that the Pacific sailfish's body colors tend to be somewhat more muted. It should be noted that in sport fishing for sailfish, marlin, and all other large pelagic game fish, the trend today is toward releasing all fish.

RANGE: Pacific sailfish are found in the Pacific Ocean from about Monterey, California, south to Ecuador, and also in the vicinity of the Hawaiian Islands and elsewhere in the South Pacific.

HABITAT: See Atlantic Sailfish.

SIZE: Pacific sailfish put on a good deal more weight than their relatives in the Atlantic. The maximum weight is about 240 pounds, but the average rod-caught Pacific sailfish weighs from 60 to 100 pounds.

FOOD: See Atlantic Sailfish.

FISHING METHODS: See Atlantic Sailfish.

BAITS: Whole or cut baits, rigged baitfish, and artificial lures

Bluefin Tuna *(Thunnus thynnus)*

COMMON NAMES: Bluefin tuna, bluefin, and horse mackerel

DESCRIPTION: The bluefin is the king of the tunas, all of which are members of the mackerel family. Bluefins—from those of school size (15 to 100 pounds) to giants of nearly half a ton—have incredible strength and tenacity, and they are much sought by both commercial and sportfishermen. The bluefin has the blocky, robust body of a typical heavyweight. The head is rather small, and the snout is pointed. The bluefin has shorter pectoral fins than any of the American tunas. It has two dorsal fins—the forward one retractable and the rearward one fixed—and a sickle-shaped tail. In color, the bluefin is steel blue on its back and upper sides, shading to light gray or creamy white on its lower parts. In small bluefins, the lower sides have vertical white lines.

RANGE: Bluefin tuna are found throughout the world, mostly in temperate and subtropical waters. In the western Atlantic, they occur in abundance from the Bahamas north to the Labrador Current. In the Pacific, they seem to be less abundant, being found in greatest numbers in the general area of Catalina Island.

HABITAT: The bluefin is generally a fish of the open ocean, though school-size bluefins occasionally come quite close to shore. In summer, bluefins show up in large numbers from New Jersey to Nova Scotia, the smaller fish showing up first and closer to shore. Atlantic areas where bluefins tend to congregate and provide good fishing include the New York Bight, New Jersey, Block Island to Rhode Island, Cape Cod Bay, Wedgeport and St. Margaret's Bay in Nova Scotia, and Conception Bay in Newfoundland.

SIZE: For all practical fishing purposes, bluefins can be grouped into two size categories: school fish (those weighing 15 to 100 pounds) and adult fish (those weighing more than 100 pounds). The average schoolie weighs 30 to 50 pounds, while the giant bluefins attain maximum weights estimated to be 1,500 pounds or more. The rod-and-reel record is 1,496 pounds.

FOOD: Bluefin tuna feed on whatever is available, including a wide variety of fish (including herring, sand lance, hake, and even dolphin), as well as squid and crustaceans.

Bluefin Tuna

FISHING METHODS: Trolling, chumming, and chunking

BAITS: Whole fish, cut baits, rigged baitfish, and artificial lures

■ Yellowfin Tuna (*Thunnus albacares*)

COMMON NAMES: Yellowfin tuna and allison tuna

DESCRIPTION: Considerably smaller than the bluefin, the yellowfin tuna is a top sport and commercial fish, particularly in the Pacific. In color, the yellowfin is steel blue or nearly black on the back and upper sides, silvery white on the lower parts. Characteristics that distinguish it from the bluefin are its much longer pectoral fins and the generous amount of the color yellow in most of the fins. The yellowfin is difficult to distinguish from some of the other tunas, but in large specimens the second dorsal fin and anal fin are much longer than those of any other tuna. The side markings of the yellowfin include a sometimes indistinct golden-yellow horizontal streak and white spots and vertical stripes on the lower sides.

RANGE: Yellowfins are found worldwide in tropical and subtropical waters. They are most numerous in the Pacific, where they are found widely off the coast of southern California and Baja California. They also range from the Gulf of Mexico north to New Jersey.

HABITAT: Yellowfin tuna are more southerly in general range than are bluefins. They are open-ocean fish, though there is some evidence that they do not make such long-range migrations as bluefins do.

SIZE: Yellowfins are thought to reach a maximum size of some 500 pounds. However, the rod-and-reel record is 405 pounds, and the average size is less than 100 pounds.

FOOD: See Bluefin Tuna.

FISHING METHODS: See Bluefin Tuna.

BAITS: Whole fish, cut baits, rigged baitfish, squid, and artificial lures

■ Bigeye Tuna (*Thunnus obesus*)

COMMON NAMES: Bigeye tuna, Pacific bigeye tuna, and Atlantic bigeye tuna

DESCRIPTION: Its eyes are not abnormally large, so it's difficult to determine how the bigeye tuna got its name. Its coloration is similar to that of its big brother, the bluefin, though its pectoral fins are longer. It is often hard to distinguish the bigeye from some of the other tunas. Its dorsal and anal fins are never greatly elongated (as in the large yellowfins), and the finlets running along the back and belly from the dorsal and anal fins to the tail are yellow with black margins. Though Atlantic and Pacific bigeyes are the same species, the International Game Fish Association separates them for record-keeping purposes.

RANGE: Bigeye tuna range throughout the world in tropical and subtropical waters.

HABITAT: Bigeyes are fish of the open oceans and deep water, as evidenced by the fact that many are caught by commercial longline fishermen.

SIZE: Bigeyes probably reach weights of 500 pounds and seem to grow somewhat bigger in the Pacific than in the Atlantic. The average size is about 100 pounds.

FOOD: See Bluefin Tuna.

FISHING METHODS: See Bluefin Tuna.

BAITS: Whole fish, cut baits, rigged baitfish, and artificial lures

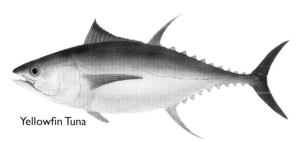

Yellowfin Tuna

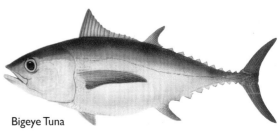

Bigeye Tuna

Blackfin Tuna

▨ Blackfin Tuna *(Thunnus atlanticus)*

DESCRIPTION: Far more restricted in range than any of the other popular tunas, the blackfin is also one of the smallest members of the family. It is darker in color than the other tunas and has fewer gill rakers. The finlets behind the dorsal and anal fins are totally dark—not marked with yellow like most of the other tunas.

RANGE: Blackfin tuna are found only in the western Atlantic Ocean, ranging from Cape Cod south to Brazil.

HABITAT: Blackfins are open-ocean, deep-water fish, like almost all the other members of the tuna family.

SIZE: The blackfin's top weight is probably not much more than 40 pounds or so. Most average 10 to 15 pounds. The world-record, rod-caught blackfin—weighing 49 pounds, 6 ounces—is an exceptionally big tuna for this species.

FOOD: The blackfin's diet is about the same as that of the other tunas, except that its prey is properly smaller.

FISHING METHODS: Trolling, chumming, and jigging

BAITS: Cut baits, live pilchards, cigar minnows, rigged ballyhoo, and artificial lures

▨ Albacore *(Thunnus alalunga)*

COMMON NAMES: Albacore and longfin tuna

DESCRIPTION: The albacore is what you are likely to get when you buy a can of all-white-meat tuna. It is one of the tunas, and thus a member of the mackerel family. The albacore's most outstanding physical trait is its abnormally long pectoral (side) fins, which extend from behind the gills well past the second dorsal fin, ending about even with the third dorsal finlet. The coloring is an iridescent steel blue above, shading to silvery white on the belly. The fins are generally blue and bright yellow.

RANGE: Albacore are found in tropical, subtropical, and temperate waters in most parts of the world. In U.S. and adjacent waters, they are primarily a Pacific species, being plentiful from southern British Columbia to southern California and Baja. In the Atlantic, quite a few are caught off Florida, and they are occasionally found as far north as Massachusetts.

HABITAT: Albacore almost never come close to shore. They haunt deep, open waters and often feed near or on the surface. When on top, they can be seen smashing wildly into schools of frenzied baitfish.

SIZE: Albacore of up to 90 pounds have been taken in nets, and the record rod-caught fish was 88 pounds, 2 ounces. The average weight is 5 to 25 pounds.

FOOD: Albacore feed on a wide variety of fish, as well as squid and crustaceans.

FISHING METHODS: Trolling and chumming

BAITS: Whole or cut baits, squid, and artificial lures

▨ Oceanic Bonito *(Euthynnus pelamis* or *Katsuwonus pelamis)*

COMMON NAMES: Oceanic bonito, bonito, skipjack, skipjack tuna, oceanic skipjack, and striped tuna

DESCRIPTION: The oceanic bonito is the most important member of the bonito group (which also includes the common, or Atlantic, bonito and the striped bonito, among others) and is the only bonito classified as a game fish by the International Game Fish Association. The oceanic bonito is striking blue above and silvery below,

Albacore

Oceanic Bonito

with some shadings of yellow and red. It is unique in having four or more well-defined dark stripes running from the area of the pectoral fin to the tail along the lower part of the body.

RANGE: Oceanic bonito are found in tropical and subtropical waters throughout the world. In U.S. and adjacent waters, they are most common off the southern coasts.

HABITAT: All the bonitos are fish of offshore waters, though they come relatively close to shore if that is where their favorite food is. They are school fish and generally feed on or near the surface.

SIZE: The average weight of the oceanic bonito is probably 10 to 18 pounds. The maximum is about 40 pounds.

FOOD: All the bonitos feed on a wide variety of fish, plus squid and crustaceans.

FISHING METHODS: Trolling and chumming

BAITS: Cut baits, jigs, and artificial lures

King Mackerel
(Scomberomorus cavalla)

COMMON NAMES: King mackerel, kingfish, cavalla, and cero

DESCRIPTION: Fast, strong, and good to eat is the king mackerel, the largest member of the Spanish-mackerel family in U.S. waters. Its streamlined body—colored in iridescent bluish green above and shading to platinum below—seems built for speed, which the fish exhibits both in the water and above in soaring leaps. The king's meandering lateral line and its lack of other side markings set it apart from most other fish. The lack of black in the rear part of the first dorsal fin distinguishes the king mackerel from other Spanish mackerels.

RANGE: Generally found from Brazil north to North Carolina and occasionally up to Cape Cod, the king mackerel is most numerous in the Gulf of Mexico and southern Atlantic Ocean.

HABITAT: King mackerel range in schools and usually stick to open water, though they sometimes hover near the outer reaches of bays, feeding on baitfish. March is the peak of the king-mackerel season for Florida anglers, while in the Gulf the fishing runs from spring into September.

SIZE: The average rod-caught king mackerel weighs 5 to 15 pounds, but the species apparently reaches a length of 5 feet and a weight of 100 pounds.

FOOD: King mackerel feed mostly on smaller fish.

FISHING METHODS: Trolling and kite fishing with live bait

BAITS: Most live baitfish, pilchards, cigar minnows, ballyhoo, and artificial lures

Wahoo (Acanthocybium solandri)

COMMON NAMES: Wahoo, queenfish, peto, and ocean barracuda

DESCRIPTION: It is probably good that wahoo are neither as numerous as striped bass nor as large as bluefin tuna, for they are one of the wildest things with fins. They smash a trolled lure or bait with incredible force, make blitzing runs, and hurl themselves far out of the water (reports have it that wahoo have leaped over a fishing boat lengthwise!). The wahoo resembles no other fish, though it is shaped generally like the king mackerel. Its iridescent colors include blue or blue green above, shading through coppery tints to silver below. The sides have narrow, wavy, dark, vertical bars. Older fish may lack the side markings.

RANGE: Wahoo range throughout the world in tropical

Wahoo

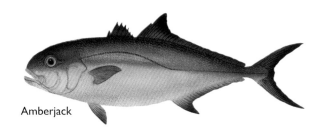

Amberjack

and subtropical waters. In the Atlantic, they stray as far north as the Carolinas, but they are most often caught off the Florida Keys, Mexico, and the West Indies.

HABITAT: Unlike most other mackerel-like fish, wahoos are loners—that is, they do not range in schools. They live in deep water, often staying near the edges of deep drop-offs or along reefs.

SIZE: The average wahoo caught by anglers weighs 10 to 25 pounds, but the species is reported to hit 150 pounds.

FOOD: Wahoos eat various fish, including flying fish, mackerel, mullet, and squid.

FISHING METHODS: Trolling

BAITS: Rigged baitfish, live baits, and artificial lures

Cobia *(Rachycentron canadum)*

COMMON NAMES: Cobia, crabeater, ling, coalfish, black salmon, lemonfish, black bonito, cabio, and cobio

DESCRIPTION: The cobia is something of a mystery. Little is known of its wanderings or life history, and the species has no close relatives. In color, the cobia is dark brown on the back and lighter brown on the sides and belly. A wide, black, lateral band extends from its snout to the base of its tail. Less distinct dark bands are found above and below the lateral. The first dorsal fin is actually a series of quite short, stiff, wide spines that look nothing at all like a standard dorsal.

RANGE: The cobia is found in many of the world's tropical and warm, temperate waters. It occurs in the western Atlantic from Massachusetts to Argentina, but its greatest abundance is from Chesapeake Bay southeast to Bermuda and in the Gulf of Mexico.

HABITAT: Young cobia are often caught in inlets and bays, but older fish seem to prefer shallower areas of

Cobia

the open sea. Cobias are almost invariably found around some kind of cover—over rocks, around pilings or bottom debris, and particularly under floating objects such as buoys, weeds, cruising rays, and flotsam.

SIZE: Cobia reach top weights of more than 100 pounds. The average size is 5 to 10 pounds in some areas, though in other areas, notably the Florida Keys and Gulf of Mexico waters, 25- to 50-pounders are not uncommon.

FOOD: Cobias feed largely on crabs, though they also eat shrimp and small fish of all kinds.

FISHING METHODS: Trolling and sight casting (typically found feeding under cruising rays)

BAITS: Live baits, especially grunts, cut baits, and jigs

Amberjack *(Seriola dumerili)*

COMMON NAMES: Amberjack, greater amberjack, and horse-eye bonito

DESCRIPTION: Amberjacks are related to pompanos and jacks, and more distantly to tunas and mackerels. The amberjack is a stocky, heavy-bodied fish with a deeply forked tail, the lobes of which are quite slender. Its body colors are blue green or blue on the back, shading to silvery on the underparts. The fins have some yellow in them. A well-defined dark band runs upward from the snout to a point behind the eye. Mostly a solitary wanderer, the amberjack sometimes gathers in small groups in preferred feeding areas.

RANGE: Though occasionally found as far north as New England, the amberjack is primarily a fish of southern Atlantic waters from the Carolinas south to Florida and nearby islands. In the Pacific, it is abundant from southern Mexico southward.

HABITAT: Reefs are the favorite habitat of amberjacks,

though these fish often cruise for food at moderate depths—approximately 20 to 40 feet.

SIZE: The average rod-caught amberjack probably weighs 12 to 20 pounds, though ambers of up to 50 pounds are far from rare. The maximum size is about 150 pounds.

FOOD: Amberjacks prey on many smaller fish, as well as on crabs, shrimp, and crustaceans.

FISHING METHODS: Bottom fishing

BAITS: Whole fish and cut baits

Pacific Yellowtail *(Seriola dorsalis)*

COMMON NAMES: Pacific yellowtail, yellowtail, and California yellowtail

DESCRIPTION: A member of the amberjack family, the Pacific yellowtail is probably the most popular sport fish on the Pacific coast. It is not, however, of great commercial value. The yellowtail has a horizontal swath, ranging in color from brassy to rather bright yellow, running from its eye to its tail. Above the stripe, the color is blue green to green; below it, the color is silvery. The fins are dusky yellow, except the caudal fin (tail), which is bright yellow. The yellowtail is a tremendously powerful fighter.

RANGE: Yellowtails have been caught from Mazatlan, Mexico, through the waters of Baja California, and north to the southern Washington coast. The world-record yellowtail was taken off the coast of New Zealand, but it is not known for sure whether it was of the same species as the Pacific yellowtail.

HABITAT: Yellowtails are fish of the mid-depths for the most part and are migratory. A preferred hangout is a kelp bed, and rocks often harbor yellowtails. Concentrations of yellowtails are around the Coronado Islands, Catalina Island, and off San Clemente, California.

SIZE: Yellowtails reach weights of more than 100 pounds, but the average size is 8 to 25 pounds.

FOOD: Like many other voracious marine species, the yellowtail usually feeds on whatever is available. It seems to prefer sardines, anchovies, mackerel, squid, and crabs.

FISHING METHODS: Casting live baits and trolling artificial lures

BAITS: Live sardines, anchovies, and artificial lures

Jack Crevalle *(Caranx hippos)*

COMMON NAMES: Jack crevalle, jack, cavally, cavalla, common jack, horse crevalle, and toro

DESCRIPTION: Probably the best-known member of a very large family, the jack crevalle is considered a fine game fish by some anglers but a pest by others. The crevalle is short, husky, and slab sided. It is yellow green on the back and the upper sides, yellow and silvery on the lower areas. There is a dark mark on the rear edge of the gill cover, and the breast is without scales except for a scaled patch just forward of the ventral fins.

RANGE: The jack crevalle is found from Uruguay to Nova Scotia in the western Atlantic, and from Peru to Baja California in the eastern Pacific. It is most numerous from Florida to Texas.

HABITAT: The crevalle seems to prefer shallow flats, though large, solitary specimens are often taken in deep offshore waters. It is a schooling species.

SIZE: Jack crevalles of more than 70 pounds have been caught, and 45-pounders are not uncommon in Florida waters. The average size is probably 2 to 8 pounds.

FOOD: Smaller fish are the main course of the jack crevalle, but shrimp and other invertebrates are also occasionally on the menu.

FISHING METHODS: Casting, live lining, chumming, and bottom fishing

BAITS: Live baits, cut baits, shrimp, and artificial lures

Jack Crevalle

Rainbow Runner
(Elagatis bipinnulatus)

COMMON NAMES: Rainbow runner, rainbow yellowtail, runner, skipjack, and shoemaker

DESCRIPTION: The rainbow runner, an excellent game fish, is a member of the jack family, but it doesn't look like most of the others. It is streamlined, not deep bodied and chunky, and its coloration is striking. The back is a vivid blue or green blue, while the lower areas and the tail are yellow. Along the upper sides is a broad dark-blue stripe, and below that are other, less prominent blue stripes. The fins are greenish yellow. Finlets at the rear end of the dorsal and anal fins distinguish the rainbow runner from the amberjack, which it somewhat resembles.

RANGE: Occurring in tropical waters worldwide, the rainbow runner is found in the Atlantic from Colombia to Massachusetts; in the Pacific, it has been recorded from Peru and the Galapagos Islands to Baja California.

HABITAT: The wanderings of this fish, which are nowhere numerous, are little known. Trollers catch rainbow runners off the east coast of Florida and in the Gulf of Mexico.

SIZE: The maximum size is about 30 pounds. Most caught rainbow runners are about 15 inches in length.

FOOD: Rainbow runners feed on smaller fish.

FISHING METHODS: Trolling

BAITS: Small baitfish and artificial lures

Permit *(Trachinotus falcatus or Trachinotus kennedyi)*

COMMON NAMES: Permit, great pompano, round pompano, and palometa

DESCRIPTION: The shy and wary permit, a much-prized game fish, is the largest of the pompanos. Blocky and very deep bodied (sometimes nearly half as deep as total body length), the permit's coloration varies greatly, especially in the young. Adults are generally bluish or gray on the back, with the rest of the body being silvery.

Permit

Very large ones may be almost entirely silvery with a green-blue tinge. Permit are far more numerous than many anglers think, but while they are often seen, they are much less often hooked and boated, for they put up a fight that is much more powerful than that of a bonefish. It usually takes at least a half hour to tire a big permit.

RANGE: In the Atlantic, permit are found from Brazil to Massachusetts, in the West Indies, and in Bermuda. A Pacific variety is found from Ecuador to southern California. It is most abundant off southern Florida.

HABITAT: Permit are found from the surf out to deep water. They tend to stay in channels and deep holes, but they often come onto shallow tidal flats to feed, at which time their tails and backs can be seen above the surface.

SIZE: Permit reach weights of 50 pounds, but those caught by anglers probably average 15 to 25 pounds.

FOOD: Mainly bottom-feeders, permit prefer crabs and other invertebrates, plus small fish.

FISHING METHODS: Bottom fishing, casting, live lining, and chumming (a favorite species for fly fishermen)

BAITS: Crabs, baitfish, shrimp, jigs, clams, bucktails, streamer flies, and artificial lures

Bluefish *(Pomatomus saltatrix)*

COMMON NAMES: Bluefish, chopper, tailor, snapper, and jumbo

DESCRIPTION: Savage, cannibalistic, delicious, abundant, willing—all these adjectives fit the bluefish, the only member of the family *Pomatomidae*. In coloration,

Bluefish

the bluefish is a rather dark blue on the back, shading through blue gray and gray silver to silvery on the belly. A fisherman getting his first look at a pack of blues attacking a horde of baitfish finds the sight hard to believe. The water boils white and then turns red and brown with the blood of the frenzied baitfish and the regurgitated stomach contents of the savage blues. Once hooked, the bluefish makes the angler fervently thankful that these fish don't reach the size of tuna, for blues are among the most powerful fighters in the sea.

RANGE: Blues are found in the western Atlantic from Massachusetts to Argentina, off the northwest coast of Africa, the Azores, Portugal, and Spain, and in the Mediterranean and Black Seas. They are also found in the eastern Indian Ocean, the Malay Peninsula, Australia, and New Zealand.

HABITAT: Though primarily a deep-water species, particularly the large ones, bluefish often come right into the surf and sometimes go quite a distance up brackish-water rivers. Blues are rather erratic wanderers, though their general migration routes are fairly constant. They usually travel in large schools. In winter, they are most numerous in Florida. As the waters warm, they head north to such bluefishing hotspots as the Carolinas, New Jersey, and New England. Tidal rips are top spots to look for blues.

SIZE: Bluefish average 2 to 5 pounds, though 15- to 20-pounders are not uncommon, and there was a 45-pounder taken off the coast of North Africa.

FOOD: Bluefish will eat anything they can handle—and

some things they can't, as many fishermen who have been bitten by a just-boated blue will attest. Menhaden is a bluefish's blue-plate special, and other preferred foods are mullet, squid, and eels.

FISHING METHODS: Live lining, chumming, and trolling

BAITS: Cut baits, bunkers, mullet, eels, jigs, and spoons

Dolphin *(Coryphaena hippurus)*

COMMON NAMES: Dolphin, bull dolphin, dorado, and mahimahi

DESCRIPTION: The dolphin (a cold-blooded species that should not be confused with the warm-blooded dolphin, which is a mammal and a member of the porpoise family) is spectacular in both coloration and fighting ability. Purple and blue on the dorsal surface, and iridescent green and yellow on the sides and lower body, the dolphin's merging colors are enhanced by scattered blue dots. The head is extremely blunt, being almost vertical in large specimens (called bulls, though they may be either male or female). The dorsal fin extends from the head nearly to the tail. The dolphin is an explosive battler and an acrobatic leaper.

RANGE: Dolphins range widely in tropical and subtropical seas. In the western Atlantic, they are found in relative abundance from North Carolina (particularly in or near the Gulf Stream) south into the Gulf of Mexico as far west as Texas. In the Pacific, they range as far north as Oregon, but they are most numerous off the coast of southern California.

HABITAT: Dolphins are usually school fish, though large ones are often loners. They are fish of the open oceans, but they lie under and cavort near various patches or bits of flotsam—floating grass, pieces of driftwood, and the like.

SIZE: The largest dolphin on record weighed 87 pounds. However, most rod-caught dolphins are 5 to 15 pounds.

FOOD: The food of dolphins includes a wide variety of smaller fish, squid, and crustaceans. In many parts of the dolphin's range, the flying fish forms a large portion of its diet, and the dolphin can often be seen soaring far out of the water in pursuit of a flying fish.

Dolphin

Why Dolphin Are the Perfect Game Fish

- Dolphin are everywhere, ranging from Massachusetts to Florida and the Bahamas throughout the Gulf of Mexico and the Caribbean down to Brazil. A highly migratory species, dolphin have been known to travel as far as 800 miles in 10 days.

- Dolphin are probably the fastest growing game fish, growing nearly three inches a week and weighing as much as 40 pounds. Cows (females) grow to about 40 pounds, but the bulls regularly weigh in at 60 pounds. The world record, caught in Costa Rica in 1976, weighed 87 pounds. See accompanying chart for average length-to-weight ratios.

- Dolphin are prolific. They become sexually mature when they reach 14 inches in length. Females are in a constant state of egg production and spawn multiple times in a year. A single dolphin can produce about 555,000 eggs per spawn. Unfortunately, the annual mortality rate for juvenile dolphin runs about 98 percent. The dolphin is an important forage species and an easy target for all billfish and sharks. If that's not bad enough, if dolphin get hungry enough, they will eat one another.

Length (Inches)	Weight (Pounds)
22	4
28	8
32	12
38	22
42	27
48	37.8
54	57.7
55	67.4
64	73.2

- Dolphin, generally listed as mahimahi on restaurant menus, is a superb food fish. Easy to fillet and prepare, the meat is flaky and moist. It can be broiled, grilled, fried, smoked, or steamed. Its unique flavor even makes it a good choice for ceviche.

FISHING METHODS: Trolling and sight casting

BAITS: Mullet, ballyhoo, squid, cut baits, and artificial lures

Tarpon *(Megalops atlantica)*

COMMON NAMES: Tarpon, silver king, and sabalo

DESCRIPTION: The tarpon, considered the king of game fish by the majority of those who have caught it, is a leaper to end all leapers. Tarpon jumps of 8 feet above the surface and 20 feet long have been measured. Tarpon are related to herring and shad, and, oddly enough, to smelt and salmon. Usually blue or greenish black on the back, the tarpon's sides and underparts are sparkling silver. The scales are very large, and there is a bony plate between the branches of the bottom jaw. The dorsal fin has no spines, but its last (rear) ray is abnormally extended and whiplike. The pectoral fins are quite low on the body. The tarpon's spectacular fighting tactics and hard, bony mouth make it difficult to subdue—one fish boated out of 20 strikes is about average success for a

tarpon fisherman. The tarpon's only shortcoming is that it isn't much on the table. Most rod-caught tarpon are released.

RANGE: Tarpon are found on both sides of the Atlantic in tropical and subtropical waters. In the western Atlantic, they stray as far north as Nova Scotia and range well south in the Gulf of Mexico. Main concentrations seem to be off southern Florida, Texas, and eastern Mexico.

HABITAT: Except in winter, when they apparently retreat to deeper water, tarpon are schooling fish of shallow waters. They frequent such places as mangrove flats, shoals, brackish bayous, cuts, inlets, and the lower reaches of coastal rivers. Sometimes they travel many miles upriver into fresh water. They are seldom far from the shore in summer.

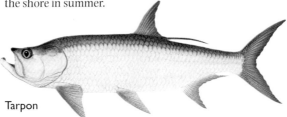

Tarpon

SIZE: Though the rod-and-reel record is 286 pounds, 9 ounces, tarpon reportedly attain weights in excess of 300 pounds. The average size of an adult tarpon is probably 30 to 100 pounds. Tarpon of more than 100 pounds are subdued each year on fly rods!

FOOD: Tarpon feed on a variety of marine life, including pinfish, mullet, needlefish, and other small fish, plus crabs and shrimp.

FISHING METHODS: Sight casting and fly fishing

BAITS: Whole baitfish, mullet, crabs, shrimp, and artificial lures

▨ Bonefish *(Albula vulpes)*

COMMON NAMES: Bonefish, ratfish, and banana

DESCRIPTION: What the tarpon is to leaping, the bonefish is to running. No one using sporting tackle can stop the blazing initial run of a hooked bonefish, which may tear 150 yards or more of line from a reel. The bonefish's body, built for speed, is shaped like a torpedo. The colors are bronze or blue green on the back, shading through bright silver on the sides to white on the belly. The sides occasionally have some dark mottling. The bonefish is sometimes confused with the ladyfish, but telling them apart requires only a look at the mouth. The bonefish's upper jaw—a snout, really—is far longer than the lower, giving the fish a sucker-like look. The ladyfish has jaws of about equal length. Bonefish are related to tarpon.

RANGE: Bonefish are found in all tropical marine waters, being caught in such widely separated places as South Africa, Brazil, and Hawaii, where the biggest ones are found. By far the largest concentrations of bonefish in North America are found around the Florida Keys and in the Bahamas.

HABITAT: Bonefish are a shallow-water species. They move onto very shallow tidal flats, sometimes in water only 6 inches deep, with the high tide to feed and then drop back into deeper water as the tide ebbs. On the flats is where fishermen—particularly fly fishermen—seek this ultrawary quarry.

SIZE: Bonefish probably reach a maximum weight of about 20 pounds or a bit more, but one of more than

Bonefish

8 pounds is worth bragging about. The average size is about 4 to 6 pounds.

FOOD: Bonefish are primarily bottom-feeders, preying on crabs (particularly the hermit crab), shrimp, squid, sand fleas, and other crustaceans and mollusks.

FISHING METHODS: Casting and sight casting (a favorite species for fly fishermen)

BAITS: Shrimp, crabs, artificial lures, and flies

▨ Striped Bass *(Morone saxatilis)*

COMMON NAMES: Striped bass, striper, linesides, rock, rockfish, squidhound, and greenhead

DESCRIPTION: The striped bass is one of the most popular coastal game fish. It fights well, and it "eats well." It is not likely to be mistaken for any other game fish in its range, primarily because of its general shape, side stripes (there are seven or eight horizontal dark stripes on each side), and the separation between the front and rear dorsal fin. The coloration is dark green to almost black on the back, silver on the sides, and white on the underparts. The striper is anadromous, living in the sea but ascending rivers to spawn.

RANGE: On the Atlantic coast, the striped bass is found from the Gulf of St. Lawrence south to the St. Johns River in Florida and in the Gulf of Mexico from western Florida to Louisiana. Introduced on the Pacific coast in the 1880s, the striper is found there from the Columbia River south to Los Angeles, California. The center of the striper's range in the Atlantic is Massachusetts to South Carolina; in the Pacific, it is in the San Francisco Bay area. Efforts to establish the striped bass in fresh water have been successful in such spots as the Santee-Cooper impoundment in South Carolina, Kerr Reservoir in North Carolina, some stretches of the Colorado River, and elsewhere.

Striped Bass

HABITAT: Striped bass are almost exclusively coastal fish, seldom ranging more than a few miles offshore. Among the striper's favorite haunts are tidal rips, reefs, rocky headlands, jetties, bays, inlets, channels, canals, and reedy flats in tidal marshes.

SIZE: Most striped bass caught by anglers probably fall between 3 and 15 pounds, but many fish of 40 to 60 pounds are caught each year, most of them by trollers in the Cape Cod to Delaware range. The rod-and-reel record is an 81-pound, 14-ounce fish caught in Long Island Sound, Connecticut, but there are reliable records of a 125-pounder having been caught off North Carolina in 1891.

FOOD: The striper is a voracious feeder that preys on a wide variety of fish and invertebrates. The list includes herring, mullet, menhaden, anchovies, flounders, shad, silver hake, eels, lobsters, crabs, shrimp, sea worms, squid, clams, and mussels.

FISHING METHODS: Casting, trolling, sight casting, and chumming

BAITS: Live and cut menhaden, eels, crabs, sandworms, bloodworms, and artificial lures

■ Snook *(Centropomus undecimalis)*

COMMON NAMES: Snook and robalo

DESCRIPTION: A fine fighter and excellent table fare, the snook is a much-sought prize of southern waters. In color, the snook is brown, green, or brownish gold on the dorsal surface (back), shading to greenish silver on the sides, and becoming lighter on the belly. Distinctive traits include a depressed upper jaw and a jutting lower jaw, a somewhat humped back, and, probably most distinctive of all, a prominent dark lateral line that usually extends to and into the tail. The snook strikes a fisherman's offering with a startling smash, but it is an unpredictable feeder.

RANGE: Snook are found throughout tropical waters on the Atlantic and Pacific coasts, though they have been known to stray as far north as Delaware. They are plentiful along the Florida coasts and along the Gulf Coast in the United States and Mexico.

HABITAT: Snook are shallow-water fish that frequent such spots as sandy shores, mangrove banks, tidal bayous, canals, flats, bays, bridges, and pilings, and sometimes go upstream into fresh water. In cold weather, they lie in deep holes.

SIZE: Snook probably average 2 to 5 pounds, but 10-pounders are not rare, and the top weight is more than 50 pounds.

FOOD: The voracious snook feeds on many varieties of fish, particularly mullet, but also eats crabs, shrimp, and crustaceans.

FISHING METHODS: Casting, live lining, and trolling

BAITS: Live shrimp, mullet, pinfish, crabs, artificial lures, and flies

■ Great Barracuda
(Sphyraena barracuda)

COMMON NAMES: Great barracuda, barracuda, and cuda

DESCRIPTION: This toothy warrior is the subject of misunderstanding by both anglers and swimmers. Proven records of barracuda attacks on swimmers are relatively rare, though this fish, apparently out of curiosity, often approaches quite close to swimmers. Many fishermen write the cuda off as a poor fighter, but it usually puts on a powerful, acrobatic battle when hooked on sporting tackle. Shaped much like the freshwater pikes, the great barracuda is bluish gray or greenish gray on the back, silvery on the sides, and whitish on the belly. Dark,

Snook

Great Barracuda

irregularly shaped blotches mark the sides, particularly toward the rear. The teeth are large and pointed. The cuda is a poor food fish and, in fact, may be poisonous.

RANGE: The great barracuda occurs in the American Atlantic from Brazil as far north as the Carolinas, though it occasionally strays north to Massachusetts. Centers of abundance are in Florida waters and in the West Indies.

HABITAT: Though barracuda are found in depths ranging from a couple of feet to 200 feet, they are mainly a shallow-water species. Preferred hangouts are reefs, flats, and around mangrove islands. The largest are usually found near offshore reefs.

SIZE: Known to reach weights of more than 100 pounds and lengths of 6 feet, the great barracuda probably averages 5 to 25 pounds. However, 50-pounders are not uncommon.

FOOD: Voracious in appetite, the barracuda feeds on a wide variety of smaller fish, preying largely on whatever is most numerous in any given area. A favorite prey is mullet, though it will eat everything from puffers to small tuna.

FISHING METHODS: Casting and trolling

BAITS: Almost any live baits and artificial lures

Channel Bass *(Sciaenops ocellata)*

COMMON NAMES: Channel bass, red drum, and redfish

DESCRIPTION: The name channel bass is actually a misnomer, for this species isn't a bass at all but rather a member of the croaker family. An important East and Gulf Coast game fish, the channel bass is copper or bronze in overall body coloration. It can be distinguished from the black drum, which it resembles, by its lack of chin barbels and the presence, at the base of the

upper part of the tail, of at least one large, black spot. Food value of the channel bass varies with size. Small ones—often called puppy drum or rat reds—are fine eating, but large specimens have coarse flesh and are only fair eating.

RANGE: Channel bass are found along the Atlantic and Gulf coasts from Massachusetts to Texas.

HABITAT: These coastal fish are found off sandy beaches for the most part, moving shoreward as the tide rises to feed in holes, behind sandbars, and on flats. They are also found in such spots as the lee of mangrove islands, sloughs, channels, and bayous.

SIZE: Channel bass reach weights of well more than 80 pounds, though those of 50 pounds or more are relatively rare.

FOOD: Channel bass are bottom-feeders, eating mainly crustaceans, mollusks, and sea worms, though they sometimes prey on smaller fish, particularly mullet and mossbunker.

FISHING METHODS: Casting and trolling

BAITS: Live baits, crabs, clams, cut mullet, and artificial lures

Weakfish *(Cynoscion regalis)*

COMMON NAMES: Weakfish, common weakfish, gray weakfish, squeteague, yellowfin, and tiderunner

DESCRIPTION: The weakfish gets its name not from its fighting qualities, which are excellent, but rather from its quite delicate mouth, which is easily torn by a hook. This popular, streamlined game fish is olive, green, or green blue on the back and silver or white on the belly. The sides are quite colorful, having tinges of purple, lavender, blue, and green, with a golden sheen. The back and upper sides contain numerous spots of various dark colors. The lower edge of the tail is sometimes yellow, as are the ventral, pectoral, and anal fins. The weakfish is excellent table fare.

RANGE: The weakfish occurs along the Atlantic coast of the United States from Massachusetts south to the east coast of Florida. Populations of the fish center around

Weakfish

the Chesapeake and Delaware Bays, New Jersey, and Long Island.

HABITAT: Basically a school fish (though large ones are often lone wolves), weakfish are a coastal species, being found in the surf and in inlets, bays, channels, and saltwater creeks. They prefer shallow areas with a sandy bottom. They feed mostly near the surface, but they may go deep if that is where the food is located.

SIZE: The average size of a weakfish seems to be declining. Today, most rod-caught fish are 1 to 4 pounds. Those early fall "tiderunners" of past decades, fish of up to a dozen pounds, are seldom seen nowadays. The biggest rod-caught weakfish was 19½ pounds.

FOOD: Weakfish eat sea worms, shrimp, squid, sand lance, crabs, and such small fish as silversides, killies, and butterfish.

FISHING METHODS: Casting, chumming, and jigging

BAITS: Shrimp, spearing, mullet, clams, crabs, and killies

Spotted Weakfish
(Cynoscion nebulosus)

COMMON NAMES: Spotted weakfish, spotted sea trout, speckled trout, trout, and speck

DESCRIPTION: This species is a southern variety of the common weakfish (see Weakfish), which it resembles. As its name might suggest, its markings (many large, dark, round spots found on the sides and back and extending onto the dorsal fin and tail) are far more prominent than those of the common weakfish. In general, body coloration of the spotted weakfish is dark gray on the back and upper sides, shading to silver below. Like the common weakfish, the spotted variety has a projecting lower jaw and two large canine teeth at the tip of the upper jaw. It is a top food fish.

RANGE: The spotted weakfish occurs throughout the Gulf of Mexico, in Florida waters, and north to Virginia, though it is found as a stray as far north as New York. It is most abundant in the Gulf of Mexico and in Florida.

HABITAT: See Weakfish.

SIZE: The average size of a spotted weakfish is somewhat smaller than that of a common weakfish. Most rod-caught spotted weaks fall in the 1- to 3-pound range. The maximum size is about 15 pounds.

FOOD: In many areas, spotted weakfish feed almost exclusively on shrimp. They may also eat various smaller fish, particularly mullet, menhaden, and silversides, as well as crabs and sea worms.

FISHING METHODS: See Weakfish.

BAITS: Cut baits, shrimp, worms, clams, killies, and artificial lures

California White Sea Bass
(Cynoscion nobilis)

COMMON NAMES: California white sea bass, sea bass, white sea bass, croaker, and white corvina

DESCRIPTION: Not a true sea bass, the California white sea bass is a relative of the weakfish of the Atlantic. It is a rather streamlined fish with front and rear dorsal fins that are connected. The body colors are gray to blue on the back, silvery on the sides, and white on the belly. The tail is yellow. The belly is somewhat indented from pelvic fins to vent. There is a dark area at the base of the pectoral fins.

RANGE: The California white sea bass has an extreme range of Alaska to Chile, but it is not often found north

Spotted Weakfish

of San Francisco. The population center seems to be from Santa Barbara, California, south into Mexico.

HABITAT: The white sea bass seldom strays far offshore and is most often found in or near beds of kelp. Night fishing is often very productive.

SIZE: The white sea bass averages about 15 to possibly 25 pounds, though specimens of more than 40 pounds are not uncommon. The maximum weight is a bit more than 80 pounds.

FOOD: White sea bass feed on a variety of small fish, as well as squid, crabs, shrimp, and other mollusks and crustaceans.

FISHING METHODS: Bottom fishing

BAITS: Baitfish, cut baits, crabs, shrimp, and clams

California Black Sea Bass
(Stereolepis gigas)

COMMON NAMES: California black sea bass, giant black sea bass, and giant sea bass

DESCRIPTION: This large, blocky fish is a Pacific version of the eastern sea bass. It is black or brownish black in general coloration, lighter on the underparts. Because of its size and color, the California black sea bass cannot be confused with any other species in its somewhat limited range.

RANGE: The California black sea bass is most numerous off Baja California and southern California, though it also ranges north to central California.

HABITAT: The California black sea bass is strictly a bottom-feeder, being found in deep water, usually over rocks and around reefs.

SIZE: The rod-and-reel record California black sea bass weighed 563 pounds, 8 ounces, which is probably about the maximum size for the species. The average size is 100 to 200 pounds.

FOOD: California black sea bass feed on a variety of fish, including sheepshead, and on crabs and other mollusks.

FISHING METHODS: Bottom fishing

BAITS: Baitfish, cut baits, crabs, clams, and shrimp

Black Drum *(Pogonias cromis)*

COMMON NAMES: Black drum, drum, and sea drum

DESCRIPTION: A member of the croaker family, the black drum is not as popular a game fish as the red drum. It is most easily distinguished from the red drum (channel bass) by the lack of a prominent dark spot near the base of the tail. The overall color of the black drum ranges from gray to almost silvery, usually with a coppery sheen. Young specimens usually have broad, vertical bands of a dark color. The body shape is short and deep, the back is arched, and the undersurface is somewhat flat. There are barbels on the chin.

RANGE: Black drums are an Atlantic species found from southern New England to Argentina, though they are rare north of New York. Centers of abundance include North Carolina, Florida, Louisiana, and Texas.

HABITAT: Usually found in schools, black drum prefer inshore sandy areas such as bays, lagoons, channels, and ocean surfs, and are also often found near wharves and bridges.

SIZE: The black drum is known to reach a maximum weight of nearly 150 pounds. However, the average size is 20 to 30 pounds.

FOOD: Black drum are bottom-feeders, preferring clams, mussels, crabs, shrimp, and other mollusks.

FISHING METHODS: Bottom fishing

BAITS: Clams, cut baits, and crabs

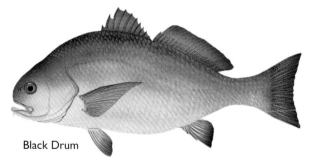

Black Drum

◼ Goliath Grouper *(Epinephelus itajara* or *Promicrops itajara)*

COMMON NAMES: Goliath grouper, giant sea bass, spotted jewfish, jewfish, spotted grouper, and guasa

DESCRIPTION: Probably the largest of the groupers, the goliath grouper is not the gamest of fighters, but its weight alone makes up for that shortcoming. The overall color of the goliath grouper ranges from black to grayish brown, and the back and sides are mottled. The upper sides contain dark spots. The tail is convex along the rear margin. The flesh of the goliath grouper is quite tasty. During World War II, it was sold as "imported salt cod."

RANGE: The precise range of the goliath grouper seems uncertain. However, it is found in warmer waters of both the Atlantic and the Pacific and is most abundant in Florida waters and off the coast of Texas.

HABITAT: Despite its large size, the goliath grouper is most often found in relatively shallow water along the coast. It is at home under ledges and in reefs, in rocky holes, around bridges, and in deep channels.

SIZE: Though the rod-and-reel record is a 680-pounder, goliath groupers reach weights of at least 750 pounds. The average is probably 100 to 250 pounds.

FOOD: Goliath groupers feed on a great variety of small reef fish, including sheepshead, and also feed on crabs and squid.

FISHING METHODS: Bottom fishing

BAITS: Live baits, grunts, and almost any fish found on the reefs

◼ Blackfish *(Tautoga onitis)*

COMMON NAMES: Blackfish, tautog, and oysterfish

DESCRIPTION: The blackfish is a member of the wrasse family, most of which are very brightly colored. The blackfish, however, is a drab gray or gray brown with irregular black mottling. Its body shape is relatively long and quite plump. The snout is blunt, the lips are thick, and the jaws hold powerful crushing teeth. The

edge of the tail is straight. The dorsal fin is quite long and spiny. The blackfish's flesh is very tasty, but for some reason it is not much used. The blackfish is an accomplished bait stealer.

RANGE: The blackfish is an Atlantic species found from Nova Scotia to South Carolina. It is most numerous from Cape Cod to Delaware Bay.

HABITAT: Blackfish are a coastal bottom-feeding species, preferring such lies as mussel beds, rocky areas both inshore and offshore, the outer edges of jetties and piers, and old wrecks. They are seldom found in water deeper than 60 feet.

SIZE: The average rod-caught blackfish weighs about 3 pounds, but 6- to 8-pounders are far from unusual, and the species can reach a maximum weight of about 25 pounds.

FOOD: Blackfish are bottom-feeders that eat such items as barnacles, mussels, crabs, snails, sea worms, shrimp, and even lobsters.

FISHING METHODS: Bottom fishing

BAITS: Crabs, shrimp, cut baits, and clams

◼ Sea Bass *(Centropristes striatus)*

COMMON NAMES: Sea bass, black sea bass, blackfish, humpback, and black will

DESCRIPTION: The sea bass, though small, is one of the most popular game fish in its somewhat restricted range. It has a rather stout body shape, with a high back and a moderately pointed snout. The apex of each gill cover holds a sharp spine. The overall color is gray to brownish gray to blue black, lighter on the fish's underparts. The sides are sometimes mottled and at other times appear to have light, horizontal stripes formed by rows of spots. The dorsal fin also has rows of spots. The most distinctive trait of the sea bass is the elongated ray on the upper edge of the tail—it sticks out far to the rear of the rest of the tail. Sea bass are fine eating.

RANGE: Sea bass are found from Maine to northern Florida, but they are most common from Cape Hatteras to Cape Cod.

HABITAT: Sea bass are bottom-dwellers of coastal areas. Their preferred depths seem to be 20 to 50 feet, though large sea bass are often found at depths of up to 100 feet, especially in winter. Sea bass like such spots as mussel beds, rocky areas, wrecks, pilings, bridges, offshore reefs and ledges, and rocky heads.

SIZE: Sea bass hit about 8 pounds maximum. The average weight is 1 to 3 pounds.

FOOD: Sea bass feed on smaller fish, but they prefer clams, mussels, crabs, shrimp, sea worms, and squid.

FISHING METHODS: Bottom fishing

BAITS: Cut baits, clams, crabs, shrimp, killies, and seaworms

Atlantic Codfish *(Gadus morhua)*

COMMON NAMES: Atlantic codfish, codfish, and cod

DESCRIPTION: This pot-bellied heavyweight of the northern Atlantic is the cause of many a runny nose among commercial and sportfishermen in the cold-weather months. The thick-bodied Atlantic cod seems to have two color phases: red and gray. In the red phase, the fish may vary from orange to reddish brown. The gray phase ranges from black to greenish to brownish gray. The underparts are lighter, and the sides have many dark spots. The pale lateral line distinguishes the Atlantic cod from the haddock. The cod differs from the look-alike pollock in its longer chin barbel and the fact that its upper jaw projects past the lower (the opposite is true of the pollock). The cod's dorsal fin is in three spineless sections, and the anal fin, also spineless, has two sections—an unusual fin makeup.

RANGE: In the western Atlantic, the cod is found from Greenland south to North Carolina. In the eastern Atlantic, it ranges throughout the Baltic Sea, from northern Scandinavia east to some parts of Russia, and south to the Bay of Biscay.

HABITAT: Atlantic cod are schooling fish for the most part, bottom-feeders, and lovers of cold water. Though the young may be found in shallow water, cod generally prefer depths of 60 feet or more and are sometimes found down to 1,500 feet. Sportfishermen usually catch cod at the 50- to 300-foot levels. Cod migrate north and south to some extent, but most movement is from relatively shallow water, where they are likely to be found in winter, to the deeps, where they go in summer. Cod seem to prefer areas with a rocky or broken bottom and such places as wrecks.

SIZE: The average Atlantic cod taken by sportfishermen probably falls into the 6- to 12-pound category, but the rod-and-reel record is more than 80 pounds, and the species is known to exceed 200 pounds. Cod of up to 60 pounds are not unusual in the New Jersey to southern New England area.

FOOD: Atlantic cod feed on a variety of bottom life, including various small fish (notably herring), crabs, clams, squid, mussels, snails, sea worms, and lobsters.

FISHING METHODS: Bottom fishing

BAITS: Cut baits, clams, squid, bunkers, and herring

Pollock *(Pollachius virens)*

COMMON NAMES: Pollock, Boston bluefish, green cod, and coalfish

DESCRIPTION: The pollock, in effect, lives under the shadow of its famous relative, the Atlantic cod. A better fighter than the cod (probably because it is generally taken from shallower water), the pollock has a shorter chin barbel than its relative, and its lower jaw projects beyond the upper jaw (the cod's upper jaw projects farther than the lower jaw). The pollock is not spotted, as is the cod, and its tail is more severely forked. A pollock's colors range from dark-olive green to brownish on the upper parts, yellowish to gray on the lower sides, to silvery on the belly. Like the cod, the pollock's flesh is excellent eating.

RANGE: Pollock range in the western Atlantic from the Gulf of St. Lawrence to Chesapeake Bay and in the eastern Atlantic from Iceland south to the Bay of Biscay.

HABITAT: In general, pollock are found in somewhat shallower water than are cod, and they are often caught at intermediate depths. Occasionally, usually during May at such points as Cape Cod's Race Point Rip, pollock come into shallow water near shore and can be taken on or near the surface.

SIZE: Most pollock caught by sport anglers weigh 4 to 12 pounds. However, the species has a maximum weight of 45 pounds.

FOOD: Pollock feed on a variety of fish—including herring and small cod—and on shrimp and some crustaceans and mollusks, as well as sea worms.

FISHING METHODS: Bottom fishing

BAITS: Live baits, cut baits, herring, clams, and seaworms

Summer Flounder
(Paralichthys dentatus)

COMMON NAMES: Summer flounder, fluke, and flatfish

DESCRIPTION: The summer flounder is one of about 500 members of the flatfish family, a curious group. They begin life in an upright position and have an eye on each side of the head. As they grow, however, the body begins to tilt, in some species to the right, in others to the left, and the eye on the downward-facing surface begins to travel to the upward-facing surface. Finally, the transformation is complete, and the fish spends the rest of its life on its side, with both eyes on the same side of the head (above and just to the rear of the point of the jaw). The summer flounder is white on the side that comes in contact with the ocean floor. The color of the upper surface depends on the physical makeup of the ocean floor, but is usually olive, brown, or gray, with prominent dark spots and some mottling. The body is flat and quite deep. The dorsal and anal fins are extremely long.

RANGE: The summer flounder occurs in the United States from Maine to South Carolina.

HABITAT: The summer flounder lives on the bottom of the ocean floor, often buried in sand or mud. In summer, it is found in shallow water, sometimes in depths of only a few feet, while in winter, it moves offshore into as much as 50 fathoms of water. It frequents bays and harbors, the mouths of estuaries, and is also often found around various bottom obstructions such as wrecked ships.

SIZE: Most summer flounders caught by sportfishermen weigh 1 to 4 pounds, but the maximum size is probably close to 30 pounds.

FOOD: Summer flounders eat a wide variety of small fish, as well as sea worms, crabs, clams, squid, and shrimp.

FISHING METHODS: Bottom fishing, drifting, and jigging (bucktails tipped with bait)

BAITS: Live baitfish, cut baits, squid, and spearing

Winter Flounder
(Psuedopleuronectes americanus)

COMMON NAMES: Winter flounder, flatfish, blueback, blackback, black flounder, and mud dab

DESCRIPTION: One of the smaller members of the vast flatfish family, the winter flounder differs from the summer flounder in its smaller size and weight and in the fact that it is "right-eyed" (that is, it has both eyes and the skin pigmentation on the right side of its head) while the summer flounder is "left-eyed." The winter flounder is white on the underside (the side on which it lies on the ocean floor), while on the other side the colors range from reddish brown to slate gray, usually with some dark spots. The mouth is small, and the lateral line is relatively straight. The winter flounder is widely sought for food by both commercial and sportfishermen.

RANGE: The winter flounder has an extreme range of Labrador south to Georgia, but it is most common from the Gulf of St. Lawrence to Chesapeake Bay.

HABITAT: The winter flounder is found mostly in shallow water—as shallow as 1 foot, in fact—but is occasionally found at depths of up to 400 feet. It lies on the bottom, preferring sand or mud, but accepting clay, gravel, or even a hard bottom. In the fall, this species tends to move toward the shallows, while in spring the movement is toward deeper water.

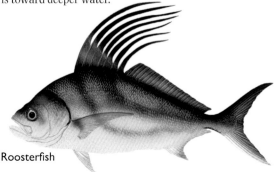

Roosterfish

SIZE: Winter flounders average from ½ to 1½ pounds in weight and 8 to 15 inches in length. The maximum size is about 8 pounds, and such heavyweights are often called snowshoes.

FOOD: Winter flounders eat such items as sea worms, crabs, shrimp, and minute crustaceans, as well as small fish and fish larvae.

FISHING METHODS: Bottom fishing and chumming

BAITS: Seaworms, clams, mussels, and squid

Roosterfish *(Nematistius pectoralis)*

COMMON NAMES: Roosterfish, papagallo, gallo, and pez de gallo

DESCRIPTION: The roosterfish—a relative of the jacks and pompanos, which it resembles at least in body shape—gets its name from the seven extremely long (far longer than the greatest body depth) spines of the forward dorsal fin, which vaguely resemble a rooster's comb. Its body colors are green to gray blue on the upper areas, white to gold below. Two black stripes curve downward and then rearward from the forward dorsal fin, which itself has a white, horizontal stripe. The roosterfish is a furious fighter and a fine table fish.

RANGE: Roosterfish are a Pacific species occurring from Peru as far north as southern California. They are particularly abundant in the Gulf of California.

HABITAT: Little is known of the movements and life history of the roosterfish. However, fishermen often catch them in sandy inshore bays and by trolling in open water. The fish are sometimes seen swimming on the surface, their dorsals erect and waving above the surface.

SIZE: The average size of a roosterfish is estimated at around 5 to 20 pounds. The maximum size is probably about 130 pounds.

FOOD: The dietary preferences of the roosterfish aren't known in detail, but these fish certainly feed on almost any small fish that is available. They strike artificial lures and plugs willingly.

FISHING METHODS: Casting and sight casting

BAITS: Live baits, cut baits, and artificial lures

Porgy *(Stenotomus chrysops)*

COMMON NAMES: Porgy, northern porgy, and scup

DESCRIPTION: The porgy (often called scup in some areas of its range) is what might be called a saltwater panfish. It has a somewhat ovate, high-backed body with a small mouth and strong teeth. The basic body color ranges from silvery to brown, and there are usually three or four dark, vertical bars on the sides. The dorsal fin is quite spiny. The porgy's flesh is highly palatable, and it is caught by both sport and commercial anglers, though in some areas rod fishermen consider the porgy a nuisance.

RANGE: The porgy (northern porgy) is found from Nova Scotia south to the Atlantic coast of Florida. In summer and fall, it is quite abundant off the coasts of New England, New York, and New Jersey.

HABITAT: Porgies seem to prefer some bottom debris, such as mussel beds. They live on or near the bottom in the middle depths of the continental shelf.

SIZE: Porgies average ½ to 2 pounds. The maximum size is about 4 pounds, and such individuals are often called humpbacks.

FOOD: Porgies feed mainly on small crustaceans, worms, mollusks, and occasionally on vegetable matter.

FISHING METHODS: Bottom fishing

BAITS: Cut baits, clams, squid, and crabs

Spanish Mackerel *(Scomberomorus maculatus)*

DESCRIPTION: This beautiful, streamlined fish—though of modest size as mackerels go—is a magnificent fighter, making sizzling runs and soaring leaps. Its body shape is rather compressed, and its colors range from iridescent steel blue or occasionally greenish on the dorsal surface to silvery blue below. The side markings are mustard or bronze spots, and are quite large. The dorsal fin is in two sections, and there are dorsal and anal finlets. Its side

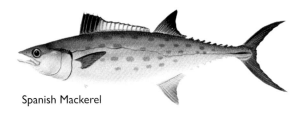

Spanish Mackerel

spots, lack of stripes, and absence of scales on the pectoral fins distinguish the Spanish mackerel from the king mackerel and the cero.

RANGE: Spanish mackerel occur from Cape Cod south to Brazil, but they are never numerous in the northern part of their range. They are most plentiful from the Carolinas into the Gulf of Mexico.

HABITAT: This warm-water species is usually found in open waters, cruising near the surface and slashing into schools of baitfish. They do, however, make occasional forays into the surf and into bays and channels in search of food sources.

SIZE: Spanish mackerel average 1½ to 4 pounds, but they can reach a maximum weight of about 20 pounds. A 10-pounder is a very good one.

FOOD: Spanish mackerel feed primarily on a wide variety of small baitfish and on shrimp. A favorite bait in some areas, particularly Florida waters, is a very small baitfish called a glass minnow.

FISHING METHODS: Casting, chumming, and jigging

BAITS: Live baits, cut baits, shrimp, and artificial lures

Sheepshead
(*Archosargus probatocephalus*)

COMMON NAMES: Sheepshead and convict fish

DESCRIPTION: Similar in shape and appearance to the porgy, the sheepshead is a high-backed, blunt-headed species whose bait-stealing abilities have frustrated countless fishermen. Its small mouth has a formidable set of rock-hard, close-coupled teeth that are capable of demolishing a crab and biting through a light-wire hook. The basic color is silvery, though the dorsal surface's color is closer to gray. The sides have five to seven

dark, vertical bands, and the spines of the dorsal fin are large and coarse. Sheepshead fight well and are excellent on the table.

RANGE: The sheepshead is found from Nova Scotia south to the northeastern Gulf of Mexico. It is far more numerous in the southern part of its range, particularly in Florida waters.

HABITAT: The sheepshead is a gregarious species that moves with the tides to wherever the food is plentiful. It is an inshore fish, taking up residence in bays and channels and around bridges, piers, pilings, and the like.

SIZE: The sheepshead averages about 1 to 5 pounds, but it may attain weights in excess of 20 pounds.

FOOD: Its teeth are a dead giveaway to the sheephead's dietary preferences, which include crabs, mollusks, barnacles, and the like, as well as shrimp.

FISHING METHODS: Bottom fishing and chumming

BAITS: Crabs, clams, shrimp muscles, sand bugs, and jigs

African Pompano (*Alectis crinitus*)

COMMON NAMES: African pompano, threadfish, Cuban jack, and flechudo

DESCRIPTION: The head profile in adult fish is slanted and almost vertical and the eyes are large. The body is flat with silver sides with an almost iridescent sheen. The forward rays of the dorsal and anal fins are long.

RANGE: The African pompano's range is from Brazil to Massachusetts. It is commonly caught in Florida waters.

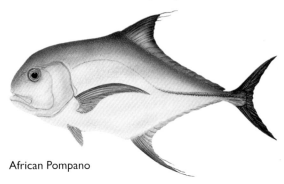

African Pompano

HABITAT: Young African pompano like shallow reefs. As the young Africans mature and become adults, they seek deeper reefs and wrecks.

SIZE: Adults can grow to lengths of 3 feet, and weights of 30 to 35 pounds are common. They are tough fighters, especially on light tackle. The record fish in Florida weighed 50 pounds, 8 ounces.

FOOD: Not a true pompano, the African feeds on small baitfish and can be caught by chumming over reefs. Drifting or trolling a rigged bait is the most common technique.

FISHING METHODS: Bottom fishing, chumming, drifting, and trolling

BAITS: Whole fish, cut baits, live baits, and squid

▉ Pompano *(Trachinotus carolinus)*

COMMON NAMES: Pompano, common pompano, and sunfish

DESCRIPTION: This high-strung, slab-sided character is the most abundant and most important member of the pompano family, which includes such fish as the much-prized permit. It has a small mouth, blunt head, and a relatively shallow body (its body depth decreases proportionally with growth). Dorsal-surface colors range from gray, silver, or blue to blue green, and the sides and underparts are silvery. The ventral surfaces are flecked with yellow. The dorsal fin is bluish, and most of the other fins are yellowish. The pompano is an epicurean's delight.

RANGE: The pompano is found from Brazil north to Massachusetts, and also in the West Indies and in Bermuda waters. It is particularly numerous in Florida and the Gulf of Mexico.

HABITAT: Pompano are inshore school fish, feeding on the bottom in shallow water in the surf, in channels and inlets and bays, and around bridges. They occasionally range well up into rivers with the tide.

SIZE: Pompano average about 2 pounds in weight, and the maximum size is thought to be about 8 pounds.

FOOD: Pompano feed mostly on bivalve mollusks and

Pompano

on small crustaceans, notably a small beetle-like crustacean called the sand flea.

FISHING METHODS: Bottom fishing, casting, and jigging

BAITS: Shrimp, sand bugs, cut fish, clams, jigs, and bucktails

▉ California Corbina *(Menticirrhus undulatus)*

COMMON NAMES: California corbina, corbina, corvina, whiting, and sea trout

DESCRIPTION: The wary and unpredictable corbina, a member of the whiting group, is among the most popular fish caught in inshore waters of the Pacific. The basic color is some shade of blue gray, and identifying characteristics include a blunt snout; a short, high, forward dorsal fin and a long, lower rear dorsal fin; and small barbels at the tip of the lower jaw. The corbina is a strong underwater fighter and an excellent food fish.

RANGE: The corbina is found from the Gulf of California north to Point Conception.

HABITAT: Primarily a target of surf fishermen, the corbina is an inshore species found mostly along sandy beaches and in shallow bays, moving into the surf line on the incoming tide.

SIZE: Corbina reach a maximum weight of about 8 pounds. The average size is 2 to 3 pounds.

FOOD: Crabs of various kinds are the favorite food of the corbina, but it also feeds on clams and sea worms.

FISHING METHODS: Bottom fishing and surf fishing

BAITS: Clams, squid, shrimp, and cut baits

Atlantic Croaker
(Micropogon undulatus)

COMMON NAMES: Atlantic croaker, croaker, hardhead, and golden croaker

DESCRIPTION: The most common and most prized of the eastern U.S. members of the huge croaker family, the Atlantic croaker is a strong fighter and makes for delicious eating. The croaker family gets its name from the sound it makes—audible for quite a distance—by repeated contractions of its swim bladder and a unique "drumming muscle." The Atlantic croaker has a small, tapered body; a short, high, forward dorsal fin and a long, lower rear dorsal fin; and small barbels on the chin. The colors are brassy gold and silver, and the upper parts of the body contain numerous dark spots that sometimes form slanting bars.

RANGE: The Atlantic croaker is found from Massachusetts south to Florida and west to Texas and eastern Mexico. In recent years, however, its numbers have declined in the northern part of the range. The center of abundance seems to be from the Carolinas to Florida and in the northern Gulf of Mexico.

HABITAT: Atlantic croakers are seldom found far from estuaries, preferring sandy shallows, shallow shell beds, sloughs, lagoons, and weedy flats. However, cold weather often sends the fish into deeper water.

SIZE: Atlantic croakers average ½ to about 2½ pounds and attain a maximum size of about 5 pounds.

FOOD: Predominantly bottom-feeders, Atlantic croakers feed on clams, crabs, sea worms, shrimp, snails, mussels, and sand fleas.

FISHING METHODS: Bottom fishing and chumming

BAITS: Shrimp, crabs, seaworms, clams, and cut baits

Red Snapper *(Lutjanus blackfordi)*

DESCRIPTION: Most widely known for its eating qualities, the red snapper is among the best known of the more than 200 species of snappers found in the world's warm seas. The red snapper's color pattern (rose red overall, though paler red on the underparts, with red fins

Red Snapper

and eyes, and a black spot on each side), long pectoral fin, and more numerous anal-fin rays distinguish this species from other snappers.

RANGE: The red snapper occurs from the Middle Atlantic and Gulf Coast of the United States southward throughout the tropical American Atlantic.

HABITAT: The red snapper's preference for deep waters—it is sometimes found as deep as 100 fathoms and seems most prevalent at 20 to 60 fathoms—detracts from its importance as a sport fish. It usually is found a few feet above a hard bottom.

SIZE: Most red snappers caught commercially run from 5 to about 30 pounds. The maximum size seems to be about 35 pounds.

FOOD: Red snappers eat baitfish and various deep-water mollusks and crustaceans.

FISHING METHODS: Bottom fishing, drifting, and chumming

BAITS: Squid, cut baits, crabs, and live baits

Yellowtail Snapper
(Ocyurus chrysurus)

COMMON NAMES: Yellowtail snapper, flag, and tail

DESCRIPTION: This fish is easily identified by the yellow stripe that runs the entire length of the body from the eye to the forked tail. It has a bluish tint above the yellow stripe and a silver underbelly. The colors become mottled as the yellowtail grows in size. Yellowtail are excellent eating and one of the best of the reef species.

RANGE: Yellowtail snappers range from Florida to the Bahamas and the Caribbean.

HABITAT: The yellowtail snapper is a popular school fish that lives on the coral reefs of southern Florida and the Florida Keys.

SIZE: The average weight is about 1 to 4 pounds. Yellow-tails that weigh more than 5 pounds are called "flags." The top weight is about 8 pounds.

FOOD: Yellowtail snappers eat mainly small baitfish and shrimp.

FISHING METHODS: Bottom fishing, chumming, and drifting baits (Yellowtail snappers are fussy eaters. Under clear water conditions, light leaders and 10-pound-test line are a must. A small jig baited with shrimp and drifted into a chum slick is the most produc-tive technique.)

BAITS: Small baitfish, cut baits, shrimp, and small jigs

Northern Whiting
(Menticirrhus saxatilis)

COMMON NAMES: Northern whiting, whiting, northern kingfish, and kingfish

DESCRIPTION: The northern whiting is one of four whitings (all members of the large croaker family) that inhabit the Atlantic and Gulf coasts of the United States. The basic color is silver gray or silver brown, and the upper part of the body contains rather indis-tinct dark, vertical bands. The mouth is small, and there is a single chin barbel. The northern whiting is the only one of the four U.S. whitings in which the third and largest spine of the forward dorsal fin, when laid flat, reaches well past the beginning of the long and soft rear dorsal fin. The northern whiting is an excel-lent food fish.

RANGE: The northern whiting is found on the Atlantic coast of the United States from Maine to Florida.

HABITAT: Northern whiting are usually found over a sandy bottom in the surf, shallow sloughs and bays, and, as the water temperature cools, in depths as great as 100 feet or more.

SIZE: Averaging about 1 pound, the northern whiting reaches a maximum size of about 3 pounds and 18 inches in length.

FOOD: The northern whiting feeds mainly on small bait-fish, sea worms, and small crustaceans.

FISHING METHODS: Bottom fishing, drifting, and surf fishing

BAITS: Baitfish, seaworms, crabs, and clams

Hogfish (Lachnolaimus maximus)

COMMON NAMES: Hogfish, hog snapper, hog wrasse, captain, perro perro, and pargo gallo

DESCRIPTION: The hogfish is unmistakable. It has a long snout with a purple band extending from its snout to its dorsal fin. The color is reddish, and the most notice-able features are the three long rays of the dorsal fin. Hogfish rank very high in taste and are one of the best of the reef species. They are sometimes called the captain's fish because this is one species captains prefer to keep for themselves.

RANGE: Hogfish can range from North Carolina to Bermuda, the Caribbean, and Florida, especially the reefs of the Florida Keys.

HABITAT: Hogfish are basically a reef fish. They are typi-cally caught by fishermen bottom fishing or chumming for snappers on patches of coral.

SIZE: Average hogfish run 1 to 6 pounds. Hogfish can grow to more than 20 pounds, but such fish are unusual. Some reports claim hogfish can reach 45 pounds.

FOOD: Hogfish eat mainly baitfish, shrimp, and crusta-ceans.

FISHING METHODS: Bottom fishing, chumming, and drifting baits (usually a bycatch of chumming coral reefs for snappers)

BAITS: Baitfish, cut baits, shrimp, and jigs

COOKING
TECHNIQUES
AND RECIPES

Section Four

COOKING TECHNIQUES AND RECIPES

FROM HOOK TO TABLE

There are certain species of fish that should be released unharmed after a good fight. Billfish, bonefish, and tarpon, for example, should be released to protect and ensure a healthy population of these great fighters. Fortunately, there are many other healthy species of fish that can be caught, cooked, and fed to millions of fishermen without hurting the species. Dolphin, for example, grow 3 inches a week and up to 40 pounds a year. A single dolphin produces 555,000 eggs several times a year. There are also many other species that can be harvested for the kitchen, including snappers, crappies, and some groupers. (Before taking any fish home, always consult local and state regulations on seasons, restricted species, size requirements, and limits.)

What happens to these species from hook to table, however, can make the difference between a delicious fish dinner and a culinary nightmare. In this chapter, I offer good advice on the proper field care and dressing of fish, as well as how to properly fillet, smoke, and freeze a fish.

Next comes the choice of a good recipe for your fish. The recipes included in this chapter will give you a good start toward making the right selection. Some recipes are based on a particular species. Trying to make dolphin ceviche out of a king mackerel, for example, would be a disaster. Follow the species recommendations as closely as you can, but if a recipe says "fish fillets," you are safe to use a fresh fillet from almost any other species. And don't be afraid to use fish that have been properly frozen and thawed.

The key word here is "fresh." Fish should smell fresh and not fishy. If it's a whole fish, the eyes should be clear and not cloudy and sunken. The flesh should be firm. Press your finger into the flesh; the flesh should spring back. Fresh fish will almost always produce a memorable dining experience.

FIELD CARE AND DRESSING OF FISH

If you sit down at the dinner table and bite into a poor-tasting bass or walleye fillet from a fish you caught, there's a good chance that the second-rate taste is your own fault. In all probability, the fish was not handled properly from the moment it came out of the water. Fish spoil rapidly unless they are kept alive or quickly killed and put on ice.

Here are the necessary steps involved in getting a fresh-caught fish from the water to the table so that it will retain its original flavor.

First, the decision to keep a fish dead or alive depends on conditions. For example, if you're out on a lake and have no ice in your boat, you'll want to keep all fish alive until it's time to head home. Under no circumstances should you toss fish into the bottom of the boat, let them lie there in the sun, and then gather them up at the end

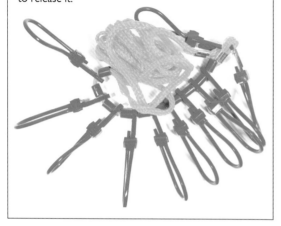

With safety-pin-type stringers, run the clip through the thin membrane behind the lower lip. This lets the fish swim freely and won't injure the fish should you decide to release it.

of the day. If you try that stunt, the fillets will reach your table with the consistency of mush and a flavor to match. Instead, put your fish on a stringer as quickly as possible and put them back into the water, where they can begin to recover from the shock of being caught.

Use the safety-pin type stringer and run the wire up through the thin, almost-transparent membrane just behind the fish's lower lip. This will enable the fish to swim freely, and the fish will recover from this minor injury should you decide to release it at the end of the day.

Do **not** shove the stringer under the gill cover and out of the mouth. This damages the gills and kills fish fast. Also, avoid cord stringers, where all fish are bunched in a clump at the end of the cord. This is perhaps acceptable on short trips for small panfish, which are generally caught in big numbers and quickly cleaned, but if you're after bigger fish and want to keep them alive and fresh— either for the table or release at the end of the day—use the safety-pin stringer. It does its job well.

If you're rowing or trolling slowly, you can probably keep the stringer in the water. If you have a big boat and motor, however, it's a good idea to take the stringer into the boat for those fast runs to other hot spots. If the run is fairly long, wet down the fish occasionally, but don't tow a fish in the water at high speed—you'll drown it.

If you're several miles from camp, use the following technique to get fish back alive. When returning to camp with a stringer of fish, stop your boat every half

mile or so and ease the fish over the side. Let the fish swim around for five minutes or so before hauling them back into the boat and continuing the trip to camp. This way, you should have no trouble reaching camp with lively walleyes to be put in your shoreline live box. Keeping fish alive is especially important on extended trips to remote areas, where ice in sufficient quantities isn't generally available.

On the subject of lengthy fishing trips to remote areas where ice is not available, you can still keep fish alive for a week or more. Your best bet is to use a homemade collapsible fish box, which can be weighted with a rock in a foot of water onshore or floated in deep water. Either way, the fish will stay alive until the end of the trip. Keeping fish alive for lengthy periods in remote areas is impossible without such a box. Keeping fish on a stringer at dockside will **not** work for long periods. With some wood and wire mesh, a fish box is easy to build. This assumes, of course, that a fish has been unhooked and is placed in the fish box in good condition. If it has been deeply hooked and appears to be dying slowly, however, it's best to kill the fish immediately, gut it, and keep it on ice.

Killing a fish quickly is simple. Holding the fish upright, impale it between the eyes with the point of your knife or rap it on the head with a heavy stick. The

A wicker creel still does its job well. Lined with wet ferns, grass, or newspapers, it will keep fish reasonably cool on the hottest days. Canvas creels are also readily available and simple to use. Occasionally dipping the entire creel in a stream, wetting it thoroughly, will keep the fish inside in good shape during a daylong trip. If you're a surf fisherman, you can also bury your fish in damp sand. This will keep your fish cool and out of the sun.

How to Field Dress a Fish

Step 1 • With the fish belly up, make a cut from the anal opening to the gills.

Step 2 • Make two cuts at the gills, one below and one above the gills where they form a V.

Step 3 • Next, stick a finger into the gullet as shown and begin to pull downward. The gills and entrails should come out easily.

Step 4 • With the entrails out, run your thumbnail along the backbone to break and clean the blood sac. Wash the fish. Once is enough—the less water coming into direct contact with the meat, the firmer the flesh will be when you eat it.

important factor is killing it quickly, since the more slowly it dies the more rapidly the flesh will deteriorate.

If you're a stream fisherman, it's wise to carry your catch in a canvas or wicker creel. The canvas creel works fine, so long as it is occasionally immersed in water. The traditional wicker creel will work just as well, but it should be lined with ferns, leaves, or wet newspaper.

If you're a surf fisherman, you can bury your catch in the damp sand. Just remember to mark the spot. A burlap sack occasionally doused in the surf also makes a practical fish bag. The important factor is to keep the fish cool and out of the sun.

Regardless of the various ways to keep fish cool, they should first be cleaned properly. With a bit of prac-

tice and a sharp knife, the job can be done in less than a minute.

Take a sharp knife and insert it in the anal opening on the underside of the fish. Slit the skin forward from there to the point of the V-shaped area where the forward part of the belly is attached to the gills. Put your finger into the gills and around that V-shaped area, and pull sharply to the rear. You will thus remove the gills and all or most of the entrails. Then, with the fish upside down, put your thumb into the body cavity at the anal opening, and press your thumbnail against the backbone. Keeping your nail tight against the bone, run your thumb forward to the head, thereby removing the dark blood from the sac along the backbone.

Electric Fillet Knives—When You Have More Than One Fish

If you're fishing for species where there is no bag limit and you're fishing for the freezer or you just want a fillet knife that's fast, you should shop for an electric fillet knife.

Those early electric fillet knives were too heavy and came with a 6-foot power cord. They worked fine, as long as you were within 6 feet of a power outlet. Today, electric fillet knives have seen big improvements. There are now cordless models with rechargeable batteries and models that can be plugged into your automobile's cigarette lighter or clamped to your boat's batteries. You can also buy electric fillet knives with interchangeable blades of different lengths and serrated stainless-steel blades.

Filleting a fish with an electric knife doesn't require drastic changes in technique. Lay the fish on its side, cut down just behind the pectoral fin until you hit bone, and then turn the blade sideways and run it flat against the backbone to the tail, but don't cut the fillet from the fish. Next, run the electric knife between the skin and flesh until the fillet is skinned.

The Berkley electric fillet knife has three power options. It can be plugged into your vehicle's cigarette lighter, into a 110-volt standard outlet, or into battery clips for a 12-volt vehicle battery. This model also comes with 6- or 8-inch stainless-steel blades.

One more tip: More good fish meat is probably ruined during the drive home than during any other point in the trip from the water to the plate. Take the time to ice the fish properly for the trip home. Don't pack the fish in direct contact with the ice. The ice is sure to melt, and the fish, lying in the water, might well deteriorate, becoming soft and mushy. It's far better to put the fish in plastic bags, seal the bags so that they are watertight, and then pack the bags in ice. The fish will stay cool—and dry—until you get home.

When you get the fish home, scale or skin them. If they are freshwater fish, wash them thoroughly, inside and out, in cool tap water. If they are saltwater fish,

prepare a heavy brine solution, and brush them thoroughly (a pastry-type brush works well) with the brine until they are clean.

Separate the fish into lots, each of which will make a meal for yourself or your family, and wrap each lot in freezer paper or plastic wrap. Then, package them in sealable plastic bags, sealing as tightly as possible to prevent freezer burn. Freeze the fish as quickly as possible.

Some fishermen prefer not to field dress their fish, but to fillet and skin them. This method, which appears difficult but is actually quite simple, is described in the next section.

HOW TO FILLET FISH

Filleting a fish is easy and doesn't have to be a messy chore. The two methods described here have a number of advantages. First, gutting the fish is not necessary since entrails are left intact and never touched with a knife. Second, scaling the fish is also eliminated because the fillet is skinned and the skin is discarded, scales and all. Finally, and perhaps most important, the

fillets are bone free, which is especially important when serving fish to children.

Filleting is also a good idea for fishermen on extended trips, where sizable quantities of fish are to be packed out or transported home. The head, entrails, fins, and skin are left behind and only the clean and meaty fillets are brought home.

How to Fillet a Fish

Step 1 • Using a sharp knife, make two initial cuts, one behind the gill plate (as shown) and another at the base of the tail down to the backbone or spine. The cut at the base of the tail is optional. Some fishermen prefer to extend the final fillet cut through the tail.

Step 2 • Next, make a cut on one side of the dorsal fin lengthwise from the first two initial cuts, starting behind the head and cutting down to the base of the tail. As you extend the cut, carefully begin to separate the fillet from the backbone.

Step 3 • Your slice downward will begin to separate the fillet from the backbone. A good fillet knife should have a 7- or 8-inch blade with some flex. A stainless-steel blade may be easier to maintain and will not rust, but carbon-steel fillet knives are easier to sharpen and will take an edge faster.

Step 4 • As you continue to separate the fillet, make sure you avoid the stomach and organs. Note that on this fillet there are no broken organs, digestive juices, or blood to taint the fillet.

Step 5 • Now, carefully begin to cut the fillet free from the fish. Keeping the blade as flat as possible will avoid damaging the fillets.

Step 7 • This is how the fillet should look when cut from one side of the fish. Next, turn the fish over and remove the fillet from the other side of the fish exactly the same way. The next step (not shown here) is to remove the pinbones, which are in the forward third of the fillet. You can feel them easily with your fingers. Using needle-nose pliers, pull them out of the fillet. With a slight wiggle, they should slide out easily.

Step 6 • The final cut will free the clean fillet from the fish. If you prefer to skin your fillets, place them flesh side up, flat on the table. Work your knife blade between the skin and the meat, holding the skin down with your fingers. With a sawing motion, holding the blade flat and down against the skin, cut the meat free of the skin. The fillet and skin will separate easily.

Step 8 • This is the final product—two clean salmon fillets. With the exception of flatfish, this technique will work on all other species with similar body types, such as striped bass, grouper, largemouth bass, and walleyes.

A word of caution: Check fish and game laws where you plan to fish. Some states and countries require that the skin be left on the fillets so the species can be identified at border crossings. Also, in some coastal states, fish with size limits cannot legally be filleted at sea.

There are two techniques to use when filleting a fish. The first, which requires an initial cut along both sides of the dorsal fin and a cut down to the backbone before slicing off the fillet, will salvage a bit more meat from the back of the fish. It is, however, more time consuming.

How to Fillet a Flounder

Step 1 • Filleting a summer flounder or fluke is a simple process. An 8- to 10-inch fillet knife with a flexible blade works best. The same technique can also be used on winter flounder, a much smaller flatfish. First, lay the flounder on a large cutting board.

Step 2 • Next, cut around the head and down along the lateral line to the tail, and then across the tail as shown. Make sure the cuts are down to the backbone. Some fillet knives have a serrated tip, which makes it easier to start that initial cut through the skin and scales.

Step 3 • Using your fillet knife, begin to cut between the flesh and the rib bones, starting at the base of the head and working toward the tail. It's important to keep the knife blade as flat as possible against the bones.

Step 4 • Use long, smooth strokes to separate the fillet from the bones. Gently hold back the fillet as you make the cut to make sure the blade is against the bones.

If you're filleting one or two big fish, use this technique.

If you are filleting a bunch of fish, however, take the shortcut technique, which is quick, easy, and clean. This method will work on any bass-shaped fish or walleye. Lay the fish flat and make a diagonal cut from behind the head to just behind the entrail sac, which holds the stomach. Next, turn the blade of the knife toward the tail and, holding the blade flat along the backbone, slice down to the tail until the fillet is cut clean off the fish. The little bit of waste along the top of the back is negligible.

Step 5 • Continue to use long, smooth strokes while cutting until the fillet is free from the body. Avoid using short strokes, which will make your fillet look like it has been chopped off.

Step 6 • The end result is a clean fillet. Each fillet will have a ribbon fin along the outside edge. Peel or cut it away from the fillet and save it for your next flounder trip. The ribbon fin makes an excellent bait.

Step 7 • The next step is to remove the skin. Hold the fillet skin down as shown, and, using a sawing motion with the blade flat against the skin, separate the skin from the fillet. You can use your finger to hold the fillet, but the tines of a fork may hold it more firmly to the cutting board.

Step 8 • Turn the flounder over, belly side up, and make the identical cuts to remove the fillets. Each flounder will produce four clean fillets ready for your favorite recipe.

How to Fillet Pickerel and Other Bony Fish

Too many fish in the pickerel family are being wasted because anglers do not know how to cope with the Y-bones. Bone-free fillets of pickerel, pike, and muskellunge are delicious. Give it a try!

To bake the fish whole, first scale the fish; then follow steps 1 through 4, but leave the fillets attached to the skin. Then, skewer or sew the skin together to form a pocket for stuffing.

For pan frying or baking, there's no need to scale the fish, just wet the scales and work scaleside down on dry newspapers. Don't slip. Follow steps 1 through 4; then with a thin, flexible knife, press the blade flat against the skin and, with a sawing motion, slide the knife along, freeing fillets from the skin. Your efforts should result in four bone-free fillets ready for the frying pan or for dusting with prepared baking mix before placing them in the oven.

The narrow strips along each side of the back can be rolled up in pinwheel fashion and held together with a toothpick inserted horizontally. If you like this system, strip the flank flesh and make pinwheels of all of it. The pinwheels come out with a handle for easy eating or dipping in sauces.

Caution: Cuts shown in the accompanying illustrations are made only down to the tough skin, not through it.

Notes on the Y-Bone Cuts: Until you have dressed a few, run the tip of an index finger along the fish to locate the line of the butts of the Y-bones. Ease the knife through the flesh on these cuts, slightly twisting the blade away from the bones. The knife is pushed through, as opposed to regular cutting action. It will follow the bone line easily. If it catches a bone, back up, increase the angle, and continue. The Y-bone strip and backbone will rip out in single strips if pinched between the thumb and index finger next to the skin to lift the head end from the skin. Grasp the lifted portion and rip out toward the tail.

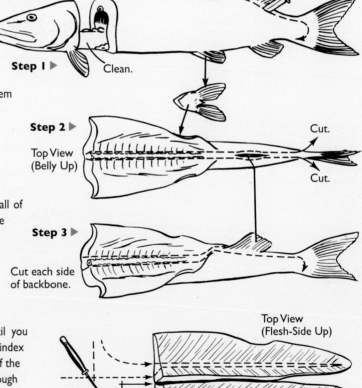

Cut off head.

Lift out dorsal fin.

Step 1 ▶

Clean.

Step 2 ▶

Top View
(Belly Up)

Cut.

Cut.

Step 3 ▶

Cut each side
of backbone.

Top View
(Flesh-Side Up)

End View
Angles for Y-Bone Cuts

Ribs

▲ **Step 4**

Fish Fillet Knives

Hold a knife in your hand. Do you like the way it looks and feels? If you do, you can probably do any cutting job with it, including filleting everything from a walleye to a 500-pound bluefin tuna. If you don't like the way a knife fits in your hand, you will never learn to use it effectively and it can literally be dangerous to use.

It's important to separate fish knives from hunting knives. I cherish my hunting knives and some of them may become family heirlooms. A hunting knife that may be used once a year to field dress a buck can cost hundreds of dollars. Fish knives are different. They rarely cost more than $15 to $35. Fillet knives are also work tools and designed for hard usage and abuse from the elements, especially salt water. I have even used sandpaper to remove rust from a knife left too long on a boat. It's not that difficult to put a good edge back on a fillet knife, even if it has a stainless-steel blade.

Choosing blade steel is actually a simple choice. I prefer stainless steel for fish knives. Carbon steel may be easy to sharpen, but, unfortunately, it will rust and require more care than stainless steel. If you prefer a knife that's easy to sharpen, but tougher to maintain, then buy a fillet knife with a carbon-steel blade. It's easy to put a razor edge on carbon steel with a whetstone. A good whetstone will last a lifetime with some care. Never use it dry. After you sharpen your knife, apply more oil to it and wipe it clean. Oil floats steel particles above the surface, so they do not clog the stone. Use a Washita stone, preferably mounted and clamped to your work surface so it does not move. It is very important that you maintain a 45-degree angle between the back of the blade and the stone as you draw the blade across the stone, as if you were taking a slice off the top.

On the other hand, if you want a fish knife that is nearly maintenance free, buy a knife with a stainless-steel blade. You can put a sharp edge on stainless steel with a whetstone, but if you're worried about maintaining that all-important 45-degree angle on the edge, an electric knife sharpener or a sharpening kit will ensure the correct angle and make the job easier.

The blade on a fillet knife should always have a slightly upturned tip. This design keeps the blade tip from accidentally tearing skin or flesh during filleting. If you can find one, buy a fillet knife with a serrated tip, which will make that initial cut into the fish skin easy. Blade length can vary, depending on the species of fish you usually fillet. A 4-inch blade makes an excellent trout knife, but an 8- to 10-inch blade is better for bigger fish and saltwater species.

Avoid fish knives with smooth, slick handles. Fish slime will make them dangerous to use. Fish knives should have rough, nonslip rubber or plastic handles. Many fillet knives on the market today have checkered polypropylene handles that are sanitary and easy to keep clean.

Most fishermen tend to be careless with fish knives because they are inexpensive and will invariably be lost long before they wear out. But that's not reason enough for letting a knife get rusty and dull. All knives should be kept sharp, clean, and coated with oil when not in use. Never store a knife in a sheath, especially a leather sheath, which will spot and corrode a blade from the acid in the leather. Remember, if a knife looks good and feels good in your hand, you probably picked the right knife.

This Dexter-Russell 8-inch fillet knife is a good size for nearly all fish species. The handle is slip-resistant polypropylene. Travel with the knife in a sheath, but never store it long-term in a sheath. Keep knives sharp, oiled, and stored with the blade wrapped in wax paper.

SMOKING YOUR FISH

Smoking your catch is simple, and you can easily turn out great-tasting smoked fish of a variety of species, from salmon to tuna. You can make your own smoker, but it may be more practical to buy a manufactured model. The method described here is "hot" smoking, which produces smoked fish that should be eaten within several days.

Before any fish is smoked, it must be brined. The brine solution will put salt in your fish to increase preservation, leech out blood, and intensify the smoke flavoring. Commercial brine solutions are available, or you can mix your own.

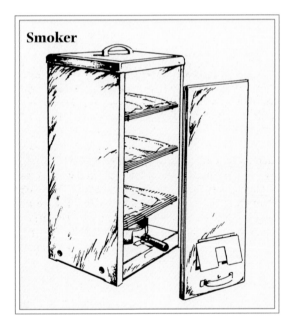

Smoker

Best Woods for Smoking

Alder: This is the sportsman's favorite. It is a good flavor for all fish and seafood.

Cherry: This type of wood is distinctive and delicious. It is excellent for all dark meats and game. Combine it with other woods for new flavors.

Apple: This is the sweetest and mildest of all flavors. It has a subtle, velvety flavor.

Hickory: The commercial favorite, hickory is famous for flavoring hams and bacons.

Mesquite: A Western favorite, mesquite has a hearty, clean, smoky flavor. It is especially good for meat and poultry.

Fish fillets are the easiest to smoke. Make sure all the bones are removed, cut the fillets into sections, and rinse them off with water. You can make a basic do-it-yourself brine solution with 1 gallon of water, 4 cups of salt, 2 cups of brown sugar, 2 tablespoons of crushed black pepper, and 2 tablespoons of crushed bay leaves. Next, soak the fillets in the brine for four to six hours in your refrigerator. If the fillets are thick, keep them in the brine for up to 10 hours. Use a glass, stainless-steel, or plastic bowl. Do **not** use aluminum, which will affect the flavor.

After brining, pat the fillets dry and let them air-cool for 30 minutes or so. When a glaze forms on the surface, the fillets are ready to smoke. Use good-flavored wood and keep your smoker at about 160°F to 180°F. Your smoked fish should be ready in six to eight hours.

HOW TO FREEZE FISH

The biggest problem in freezing fish is preventing "freezer burn." That's when all of the moisture has been drawn out of the flesh and you are left with dried-out fillets. It is more likely to occur in "frost-free" freezers because they are designed to pull moisture from the air inside the freezer.

One way to guard against freezer burn is to freeze your fish in a block of ice. When your fish is completely encased in ice, no air can get at it. Freezing fish in this manner ensures maximum storage life for your fish. You can keep fish frozen in ice for up to two years without much flavor loss. The only disadvantage of container

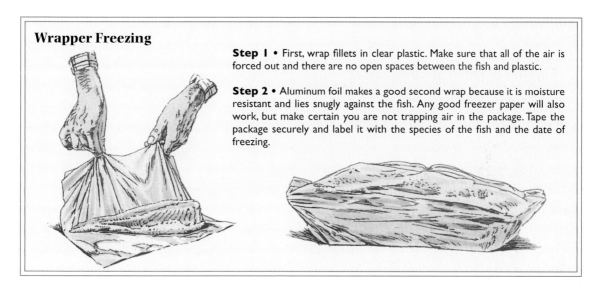

Wrapper Freezing

Step 1 • First, wrap fillets in clear plastic. Make sure that all of the air is forced out and there are no open spaces between the fish and plastic.

Step 2 • Aluminum foil makes a good second wrap because it is moisture resistant and lies snugly against the fish. Any good freezer paper will also work, but make certain you are not trapping air in the package. Tape the package securely and label it with the species of the fish and the date of freezing.

freezing is that it's bulky, awkward, and takes up more freezer space than wrapped packages. If freezer space is at a premium, double-wrap your fish tightly in plastic wrap and tightly wrap again in aluminum foil, which will maintain quality and flavor up to six months.

Unfortunately, trapped oxygen, which is virtually impossible to eliminate completely with traditional packaging, will promote bacteria that will spoil the quality of the fish and this will show up in odor and color. The best solution is vacuum packaging. Vacuum-packaging machines have proven their worth to sports-men, who can now safely freeze and preserve fish for longer periods of time than with traditional methods. Vacuum-packaging machines work on a simple principle. They literally suck all the oxygen out of a package before it is placed in a freezer. Freezer burn is virtually eliminated because the fish no longer comes in contact with cold, dry air. In an oxygen-free environment, such as vacuum packaging produces, the bacterium that causes spoilage does not multiply fast and loss of food quality is slowed down drastically. The major advantage, of course, is the length of time vacuum-packaged fish can be safely frozen in your freezer. Vacuum-packed fish, depending on the fish species, can be safely stored in a freezer for up to two years.

The Cabela's Pro Series Vacuum Sealer is an affordable solution to freezing quantities of fish. This machine will prevent freezer burn and extend freezer life. It will keep fish fresh for up to two years.

The Foodsaver Game Saver Deluxe is designed to vacuum seal food for long-term storage. Vacuum sealers literally suck all the oxygen out of a package before it is placed in a freezer. Freezer burn is eliminated because fish no longer come in contact with cold, dry air.

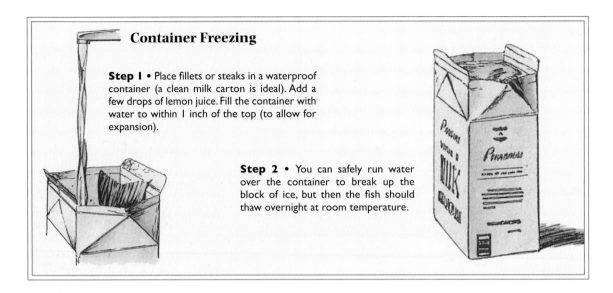

Container Freezing

Step 1 • Place fillets or steaks in a waterproof container (a clean milk carton is ideal). Add a few drops of lemon juice. Fill the container with water to within 1 inch of the top (to allow for expansion).

Step 2 • You can safely run water over the container to break up the block of ice, but then the fish should thaw overnight at room temperature.

RECICES

There is no better way to celebrate a successful fishing trip than with a delicious meal prepared from your catch. There are countless fish recipes out there to try, but this section includes a collection of my tried-and-true favorites. A few of my friends have also contributed their favorite recipes. These nationally known anglers are recognized experts in both catching and cooking fish. Bon appétit!

Recipe Contributors

Stu Apte is an International Game Fish Association Hall of Famer and holds 44 fishing records. You can learn more about him at www.stuapte.net.

James Babb is editor emeritus of *Gray's Sporting Journal*.

Chris Batin is editor and publisher of Alaska Angler/ Alaska Hunter Publications. The author of eight books, he has earned more than 120 national and regional writing awards and is a contributing writer for *Outdoor Life* and a fishing columnist for *Alaska Coast* magazine. You can learn more about him at www.alaskaangler.com.

J. Wayne Fears is the author of *Backcountry Cooking* and *The Complete Book of Outdoor Survival*. You can see more of his work at www.jwaynefears.com.

Jerry Gibbs is fishing editor emeritus of *Outdoor Life*.

John Phillips is the president of Night Hawk Publications and, along with his wife Denise, the author of *The Best Wild Game and Seafood Cookbook Ever*. You can see more of his work at www.nighthawkpublications.com.

Ken Schultz is the author of 19 books on sport-fishing topics, including *North American Fishing*, as well as the annual page-a-day calendar *Ken Schultz's Daily Fishing Tips*. You can see more of his work at www.kenschultz.com.

Jeremy Storm is the chef at Orca Adventure Lodge in Cordova Alaska.

Jim Zumbo is former hunting editor of *Outdoor Life*.

James Babbs's All-Purpose Fish Cakes
Serves 4

1½ to 2 cups cooked fish
1 cup mashed potatoes
2 tablespoons grated onion
    (or shallots, scallions, or chives)
2 tablespoons chopped herbs
    (such as parsley, thyme, or rosemary)
½ teaspoon grated lemon zest
½ teaspoon dry mustard
2 eggs
1 teaspoon mayonnaise
Salt and pepper
Old Bay seasoning
1 cup panko breadcrumbs
⅓ cup peanut oil, for frying

Fish cakes are a way of repurposing leftovers, or of making a meal from otherwise uninteresting fish. They're a centuries-old tradition along the hardscrabble coast of New England. Any fish works here, but the best is the most economical—made from meat scraped off fish frames with a spoon, or from bony fish (suckers, carp, chubs, whitefish, sea robins, small pollock, etc.) that you've skinned and roughly filleted, and then poached until done and flaked apart.

Combine the fish and potatoes with your fingers, feeling for bones. Add the onion, herbs, lemon zest, and dry mustard. In another bowl, beat the eggs together with the mayonnaise. Add to the fish mixture and work with your fingers until fully combined. Season with salt, pepper, and Old Bay to taste. With a ¼-cup measure, scoop out balls and flatten them into patties, and then press the patties into the breadcrumbs. Arrange the patties on a baking sheet lined with waxed paper, and freeze for 20 minutes. Heat oil (I prefer peanut oil mixed with bacon grease, but use what you like) in a heavy skillet, and fry in batches over moderate heat until golden on each side. ▓

Seared Tuna with Wasabi
Serves 4

2 (1-inch-thick, ½-pound) tuna steaks
    (bluefin and yellowfin are best)
Black pepper
1 tablespoon olive oil
1 teaspoon wasabi powder
2 ounces soy sauce

Coat steaks completely with black pepper. In a cast-iron skillet, add enough olive oil to coat the bottom and heat until the oil bubbles. Sear the tuna steaks on both sides, counting to 10 for each side. Place the steaks in a refrigerator for 10 minutes to chill and firm the tuna. Slice the steaks about ¼ inch thick and 2 inches long. Except for the seared surface, the tuna should be nearly raw. Put a teaspoon of wasabi powder in a small dish or cup. Add cold water and mix to form a paste. Allow the wasabi paste to strengthen for about 15 minutes, and then add the soy sauce and mix thoroughly. For an extra spicy mixture, use 2 teaspoons of wasabi powder. Serve the seared tuna on a platter with toothpicks for dipping into the wasabi and soy sauce mixture.

Striped Bass with Lemon and Onion
Serves 4

½ cup olive oil
½ cup lemon juice
½ teaspoon salt
½ teaspoon pepper
1 teaspoon oregano
1 tablespoon parsley flakes
4 (½-pound) striped bass or bluefish fillets,
    skinless
1 Spanish onion, sliced
2 lemons, sliced

Preheat oven to 400°F. Mix the oil, lemon juice, salt, pepper, oregano, and parsley together. Dip the fillets in this mixture (reserve ¼ cup). Place the fillets in a baking pan and top with the sliced onions and lemons. Pour the reserved oil mixture over the fillets. Bake for 25 minutes or until the fish flakes. Note: Largemouth and smallmouth bass can also be used, but freshwater bass will never be as tasty as saltwater bass.

Grilled Rainbow Trout
Serves 2

2 rainbow trout, whole, gutted
Olive oil
Butter
Salt and pepper
Sage or parsley (optional)
Lemon wedges

Coat the entire bodies of the rainbow trout with olive oil. Put several pats of butter inside the cavities, and then season with salt and pepper. Additional spices can also be used, such as sage or parsley. With a grill set at 350°F, a whole trout, depending on size, should take about 10 to 12 minutes on each side to cook. When the meat is firm and flakes easily, the trout is done. Serve with lemon wedges. Brook and brown trout can also be substituted.

Flounder with Mornay Sauce
Serves 4

4 flounder fillets
1 lemon
1 stick butter
½ cup cornstarch
4 cups milk
⅔ cup cream sherry
½ cup Parmesan cheese
½ cup Swiss cheese
½ cup finely chopped pimiento
Paprika, for garnish
Lemon wedges, for garnish

Preheat oven to 350°F. Place the flounder fillets on a baking pan. Sprinkle with the juice from 1 lemon. Bake until the flounder flakes with a fork, about 8 to 10 minutes. Melt the butter in a 2-quart saucepan. Slowly blend in the cornstarch. Gradually stir in the milk and cook, stirring constantly, over medium heat until the mixture comes to a boil and thickens. Reduce heat, and then add the sherry, Parmesan cheese, Swiss cheese, and pimiento. Stir until the cheese melts. Remove from heat. Spoon the sauce over the flounder. Garnish with paprika and lemon wedges.

Stu Apte's Ceviche
Serves 10 to 12

2 pounds red snapper fillets, cut into small chunks
1 pound of bay scallops (can be frozen)
1 pound of Key West pink shrimp, cut into small chunks
1½ pounds of conch, rough ground if possible
5 jalapeño peppers, cut into large chunks (minus the seeds)
3 medium Walla Walla or other sweet onion, diced
1 sweet red pepper, diced
1 sweet yellow pepper, diced
16 ounces key lime juice
16 ounces vinegar
Salt and pepper
Garlic, diced or chopped

Combine the first eight ingredients in a large bowl. Add key lime juice and vinegar (about half and half to cover all the ingredients). Add salt, pepper, and garlic to taste. Let the mixture marinate for 5 to 7 hours in the refrigerator, until the seafood turns opaque. The ceviche will stay fresh for about 2 weeks if stored in the refrigerator. ▪

Fast and Easy Walleye Shore Lunch
Serves 2 to 4

2 to 4 walleye fillets, skinned
Flour
Vegetable oil
Salt and pepper
4 potatoes, sliced
2 onions, sliced
Lemon wedges

Coat the fillets completely with flour and fry in vegetable oil until the fillets are golden brown. Season with salt and pepper to taste. In another skillet, fry the sliced potatoes and onions. Serve together with the fillets and lemon wedges. Note: If you can't catch walleye, use panfish, perch, or bass.

The Wonderful Shore Lunch . . . or Is It?

There are two schools of thought about traditional shore lunches. Are they wonderful wilderness eating experiences? Or the worst mess of greasy food you can ever imagine? I've had both.

Many years ago, I was fishing a lake in Canada with several friends in June. We decided to have a classic shore lunch, but we couldn't catch walleyes, which are the most common fare for a shore lunch. We had to settle for a skinny 3-foot pike, a species that is normally released because most fishermen can't stand eating it. Yeah, I know. You have some secret formula to blow up the bones in oil and make pike delicious. Sorry, I'll pass.

We picked a brushy spot to beach our boats, clean the pike, and start a fire. We lasted about three minutes. Hordes of black flies descended on us and the pike. It got so bad that we raced for the boats and the safety of a breeze out on the lake. We left the pike . . . bones and all. I didn't try a shore lunch again for many years.

I've learned a lot since that bad experience and my shore lunches get better and better. On a trip to Alaska, I smoked a silver salmon fresh from the ocean. My guide used a small smoker with pine boughs. We ate it for lunch with lemon juice, tomatoes, and onion slices. Shore lunches can't get much better than that.

A silver salmon shore lunch may be out of reach for most of us, but my grandson Joey and I also had a shore lunch in Canada that any fisherman can duplicate wherever the law will allow an open fire or camp stove on a shoreline. We were fishing on Lake Mistassini in Quebec. Our guide Stanley, an Ojibway, did all the cooking.

We caught plenty of walleyes, almost one on every cast. When it was time for lunch, Stanley found a small, sandy shoreline. Joey gathered enough wood and started a small fire. Stanley used two frying pans. From our boat, he took a can of beans and two small bags of potatoes and onions, which he cut into bite-size pieces. He rolled the walleye fillets in flour and fried them in one pan with the onions and potatoes. The beans went in the other pan. All the frying was done in vegetable oil. The only seasonings Stanley carried were flour, salt and pepper, and a lemon.

Watching Stanley cook a shore lunch over an open fire was a lesson in culinary simplicity. Cleanup was equally as simple. He wiped the frying pans clean with moss and stashed them in two plastic bags. It proved to be one of the finest shore lunches I have ever enjoyed.

You can make shore lunches as simple or as complicated as you wish. This is not like tailgating at a football game, and you don't need fresh walleye fillets or a silver salmon. A shore lunch will taste just as good with bass, yellow perch, or bluegill. If you don't like beans, try something else. Truth is, a shore lunch with good friends will always taste good, even if it doesn't.

Stanley, right, an Ojibway guide, and my grandson, Joey Andelora, cook a walleye shore lunch in Quebec.

The Tastiest Fish

I live on the New Jersey shore, where the striped bass is king. But I don't like eating stripers because they are one of the blandest fish I've ever eaten. Unless you cover a striper fillet with some fancy sauce or dressing, it will have nearly zero taste. You don't agree? Maybe you have different taste buds. I love to catch stripers; I just don't like to eat them. In the Northeast, I'll swap a striper any day for a fluke or sea bass.

I'm also convinced that where you eat your fish makes a difference. A fried grouper sandwich in the Florida Keys will always taste better than the same sandwich in New York. So, with that geographic disclaimer, just what is the tastiest fish? Let's get started by listing what I believe are the top 10 tastiest fish in salt water. Some of these species can't be found in all parts of the country, but I'm still going to try to rate the species regardless of where they are found.

1 • Hogfish — This species is sometimes called the captain's fish because some charter captains will take it home for dinner.

2 • Yellowtail Snapper —There are more than 100 species of snappers all over the world, but the yellowtail gets the highest rating, followed by the red snapper, mutton snapper, and then mangrove snapper. Admittedly, all snappers taste great.

3 • Summer Flounder (Fluke) — My Northeast favorite, the summer flounder is great breaded and fried golden brown with a touch of lemon juice.

4 • Grouper — Like the snapper, there are many species of groupers and they all taste good. The 5- to 15-pounders are preferred for the dinner table. Stay away from the heavyweight groupers. Fish biologists claim these older fish may have consumed too many smaller fish that feed on toxin-producing algae. There is always the risk of ciguatera poisoning. Ciguatera toxin is harmless to fish, but poisonous to people.

5 • Salmon (Wild) — Only wild salmon get a top rating. Farm-raised salmon are sometimes tasteless.

6 • Tripletail — Maybe because they hide under crab pots and are hard to catch, tripletail are excellent eating. Or maybe it's because they look so much like freshwater black crappies, which are superb eating.

7 • Dolphin — Encrusted with coconut, fried, and flambéed with Grand Marnier, you would be hard put to find a better fish dinner than dolphin.

8 • Yellowfin and Bluefin Tuna — The best way to eat tuna is sushi, or coated with black pepper, seared 10 seconds on each side, and served with lots of wasabi.

9 • Cobia — Beer-battered and deep-fried chunks are delicious, but cobia is also a favorite on the grill. Look for cobia feeding under huge rays in clear water.

10 • Mako Shark — I actually prefer mako to swordfish, and it's a lot cheaper, too.

Runners-up are cod, wahoo, striped bass, halibut, snook, and weakfish. Of this group, cod and wahoo are the best. Wahoo may look a bit like a king mackerel, but that's where the similarity ends. Wahoo meat is white and tastes great.

Here are a few fish that will never make my list of tasty fish: amberjack, king mackerel (unless smoked), grunts, bluefish (unless they are small 2- to 4-pounders), bonito, pickerel, or pike.

For freshwater fishermen, I have a short list and I can only come up with five species that I rate high for the table. Here they are in order of taste:

1 • Walleye	**4 • Trout**
2 • Black Crappie	**5 • Yellow Perch**
3 • Catfish	

I suspect that at least half of the fishermen who read this will not agree with my choices. I will also admit that fish preparation may be a critical factor, but I will still stick to my guns. These species are my top choices.

Fish Creole
Serves 2

½ cup chopped onion
1 clove garlic, finely chopped
¼ cup chopped green pepper
Butter
1 pound fish fillets
*   (such as striped bass, grouper, or cod)*
2 tablespoons salad oil
1 bay leaf
1 teaspoon salt
2 teaspoons sugar
½ teaspoon chili powder
1 (28-ounce) can tomatoes
1 tablespoon chopped parsley
1 teaspoon celery seed

In a medium saucepan, sauté the onion, garlic, and green pepper in butter until soft (about 5 minutes). Add the remaining ingredients, and simmer uncovered for 45 minutes, stirring occasionally, until the mixture has thickened.

Quick and Easy Fried Panfish or Crappie
Serves 2

½ pound panfish or crappie fillets
Salt, for sprinkling
Lemon-pepper seasoning, for sprinkling
1 to 2 cups dry pancake mix
Fat or oil, for frying
Tartar sauce

Wash and dry the fish. Dip the fish into clean, cool water, and then sprinkle lightly with salt and lemon-pepper seasoning. Coat the fish lightly with pancake mix. In a frying pan, fry in deep fat or 1½ inches of hot oil at 350°F for 4 to 5 minutes on each side. (Fish is done when browned on both sides and it flakes easily when tested with a fork. Be careful not to overcook.) Remove fish from the pan and drain on a paper towel. Serve with tartar sauce. If desired, fish may also be panfried over medium to low heat in just enough fat or oil to keep it from sticking until done as described above.

Jerry Gibbs's Baked Rainbow Smelt
Serves 4

20 rainbow smelt
Shortening or nonstick spray
2 tablespoons butter
Chopped shallots
¼ cup breadcrumbs
Old Bay seasoning
Tartar sauce (optional)

Preheat oven to 350°F. Gut the smelt and remove the heads, but leave the tails on. Pat the fish dry with a paper towel. Rub the interior of a shallow baking dish with shortening or use nonstick spray. When smelt are dry, line them up in this dish. Melt the butter in a saucepan, sauté the chopped shallots briefly, add the breadcrumbs, and then shake in the Old Bay seasoning to taste. Mix together. Sprinkle this mixture over the smelt. Bake the smelt until the smelt and crumb are brown, about 20 minutes. On your plate, address the smelt like trout, holding the tail, slicing the flesh horizontally along the body midline, and knifing the flesh away from the backbone and ribs. Then, grab the backbone at the tail and peel forward. All or most of the bones will come away. A side of tartar sauce is also nice.

Butter-Broiled Snapper
Serves 4

1½ pounds snapper fillets
2 tablespoons unsalted butter, melted
¼ cup lemon juice
½ cup whole-grain breadcrumbs
1 teaspoon herbal seasoning
¼ teaspoon freshly ground pepper

Brush the fillets with the melted butter and lemon juice. Mix the breadcrumbs with the herbal seasoning and pepper, and then coat the fish with the mixture. Broil for 5 to 8 minutes, or until the fish flakes easily with a fork.

Chris Batin's Alaska Wild Salmon in Green Curry
Serves 6

3 cups jasmine rice
2 tablespoons Aroy-D green curry paste
    (available from Asian food stores)
1 tablespoon garlic, minced
1 tablespoon Nature's Way coconut oil
2 cans Chaokoh coconut milk
1 tablespoon Bragg liquid aminos
2 tablespoons chopped fresh cilantro
1 green onion, chopped
1 cup zucchini, diced
1 red bell pepper, sliced in long half strips
1 cup green peas, frozen
6 small broccoli florets
1 wild Alaska sockeye salmon fillet, skinned,
    bones removed, sliced 2 inches long, 1 inch
    wide, and ½ inch thick
1 red Thai chili pepper, seeds removed and
    sliced lengthwise, for garnish
1 handful of Thai basil, washed and stems
    removed, for garnish

Start jasmine rice in a rice cooker about 10 minutes prior to starting the main course. In a rice cooker pot, rinse the rice under cold water until the cloudy water disappears. Allow the rice to settle to bottom of the bowl. Add 4 cups of water, cover, and cook on high. When done, open the cooker to allow the rice to air and cool slightly before serving. In a large non-stick stockpot, add the curry paste and garlic to the coconut oil. Blend and heat until fragrant, but avoid overheating. Add coconut milk and aminos. Blend into the oil and bring to a boil. Add the cilantro, green onion, zucchini, red bell pepper, green peas, and broccoli. Stir, place the lid on the pot, and continue boiling for 8 minutes. Add the salmon strips and continue boiling for 2 to 3 minutes, until the fish is nearly cooked. Remove from the heat and set aside with the lid on. Allow the fish to finish cooking. Add sliced red chili pepper and basil as a garnish. Place a cup of the cooked rice on individual plates and serve. Allow guests to add as much curry as they desire to the rice. ▪

▪ Baked Swordfish Steaks
Serves 6

2 pounds swordfish steaks
1 teaspoon salt
¼ teaspoon pepper
¼ cup all-purpose flour
Oil, for frying
1½ cups peeled, seeded, and diced tomatoes
1 cup sliced fresh mushrooms
¼ cup dry vermouth
1 clove garlic, minced
½ cup soft breadcrumbs
2 tablespoons butter, melted

Preheat oven to 350°F. Sprinkle both sides of the fish with salt and pepper, and then roll in flour. In a single layer in a 10-inch frying pan, place the fish in hot oil (360°F) for 4 to 5 minutes or until brown. Turn carefully and repeat. Place the fish in a single layer in a well-greased baking dish, approximately 12 by 8 by 2 inches, and set aside. Combine tomatoes, mushrooms, vermouth, and garlic in a 1½-quart saucepan. Bring to a boil, stirring constantly. Pour the hot sauce over the fish. In a small bowl, combine breadcrumbs and butter, and then sprinkle the crumbs over the top of the fish. Bake for 15 to 20 minutes or until crumbs are brown and the fish flakes easily when tested with a fork.

▪ Old-Fashioned Baked Bluefish
Serves 6

2 pounds bluefish fillets
½ teaspoon salt
⅛ teaspoon pepper
⅛ teaspoon paprika
2 tablespoons butter, melted
⅓ cup dry white wine
1 tablespoon soy sauce

Preheat oven to 350°F. Cut the bluefish fillets into serving-size pieces. Place in a well-greased baking dish. Sprinkle with salt, pepper, and paprika. In a small dish, melt the butter and then add wine and soy sauce. Pour some sauce over the fish. Bake for 15 to 20 minutes or until the fish flakes easily when tested with a fork. Serve with the remaining sauce poured over the fish.

Vin Sparano's Spicy Garlic Crab Sauce

This basic recipe for my blue claw crab sauce really comes from my mother, Agnes. As a small boy, I would watch her make the sauce from crabs my father and uncles would bring back from trips to Newark Bay in New Jersey. That was back in the mid-1940s, when I suspect no one bothered to check the edibility of those crabs in the ship channels. But we all survived. In fact, my mother and father both lived to their early 90s. I can't prove it, but maybe the crab sauce had something to do with their longevity!

Today, I run a few crab pots in Barnegat Bay and I enjoy making a batch of crab sauce for the family. I make a mess in the kitchen, but the end product is well worth it. My crab sauce is admittedly a bit hotter, for my mother never really made it hot or spicy enough for me. I fixed the problem by introducing massive doses of garlic and Old Bay seasoning into the recipe. Now it's just right!

My ingredients are on the heavy side. My wife, Betty, and I have four children and eight grandchildren. If you cook for smaller groups, cut the ingredients proportionately. My recipe will feed 10 to 12 people.

Here's what you will need to get started:

12 cloves chopped fresh garlic
1 tablespoon oregano
1 teaspoon salt
1 teaspoon black pepper
½ bunch of chopped fresh parsley
½ cup virgin olive oil
2 (12-ounce) cans tomato paste
3 (28-ounce) cans crushed tomatoes
3 (28-ounce) cans whole tomatoes
½ can Old Bay seasoning
12 to 15 blue claw crabs, cleaned*
Linguine, cooked

In a large pot, fry the garlic, oregano, salt and pepper, and parsley in olive oil. When the garlic is browned, add the tomato paste and blend with a wooden spoon. Stir continuously to keep the paste from sticking to the bottom of the pot. Next, add the crushed tomatoes and whole tomatoes. It may be messy, but the best way to add the whole tomatoes is to hold them over the pot and crush them with your hand. Stir until all ingredients are thoroughly mixed and the sauce is on the brink of simmering.

Now comes the important part: add the Old Bay seasoning. How much? How much can you stand? I stir in Old Bay until I can taste it in the sauce, about half a can. But I must caution you—this is usually too spicy for most people.

Finally, add the crabs and simmer at least 3 hours. Pour the sauce over a plate of linguine and you're all set. When you finish with the linguine, you can start eating the crabs. Just make sure you're wearing a lobster bib. This dish is great served with garlic bread and Chianti.

Crabs can be killed quickly by pouring boiling water over them. Once they are dead, rinse them with cold water to stop the cooking process. Next, break off the backs and rinse them clean with cold water. The sauce will have more crab flavor if you break the bodies in half before putting them in the sauce.

A typical crab trap has four doors that open and close with a hand line. Bait the trap with chicken backs, bunkers, or fish carcasses. Drop the trap in any bay or tidal marsh and wait for 10 to 15 minutes before pulling the trap, closing the doors, and checking for trapped crabs. You can also use a drop line with attached bait. When you feel a light tug on the line, a crab is eating your bait. Carefully lift the crab to just below the surface and scoop it into a net.

Codfish Maine Style
Serves 4 to 6

1½ cups cooked, flaked codfish
2 hard-cooked eggs
¼ teaspoon paprika
Celery salt, for sprinkling
Salt
Pork fat
Diced pork scraps (bacon fat and bacon bits
   may be substituted)
2 cups cooked rice
Parsley, for garnish

Combine flaked fish, chopped egg whites, paprika, and celery salt. Add salt to taste. Heat this mixture in melted fat with the pork scraps, tossing frequently in the pan to prevent burning. Pile hot cooked rice on a platter, toss the seasoned hot fish over the rice, and garnish with egg yolks and parsley.

Stu Apte's Coconut Oven-Fry Fish
Serves 4 to 6

1 teaspoon salt
½ teaspoon coarse black pepper
1 cup milk
1 egg
1 package Oven Fry (extra-crispy pork variety)
½ cup finely shredded coconut
2 fresh fish fillets, approximately 1½ pounds
   each

Preheat oven to 450°F. Mix salt, black pepper, milk, and egg together. Open the package of Oven Fry and put it in a large ziplock bag. Spread the shredded coconut on wax paper. Cut the fish fillets into 2- or 3-inch pieces. Moisten the fish by dipping into the milk and egg mixture and then shake off the excess. Lightly press the moistened fish on the shredded coconut, and then shake two or three pieces at a time in the ziplock bag with the Oven Fry. Fry or bake for 10 to 12 minutes or until the fish flakes easily when tested with a fork. ■

Creole Halibut
Serves 4

1½ pounds halibut
2 tablespoons fat
1 small onion, minced
½ clove garlic
2 cups canned tomatoes
1 bay leaf
1 teaspoon salt
1 pinch cayenne pepper

Preheat oven to 350°F. Arrange the fish on a greased baking pan and sprinkle with salt. Melt the fat in a pan and simmer the onion and garlic until tender. Remove the garlic, and then add the canned tomatoes, bay leaf, salt, and cayenne pepper and boil. Pour this sauce over the fish and bake in the oven for about 35 minutes (it is done when the fish flakes), basting several times with the sauce.

Hearty Fisherman Stew
Serves 6

2 pounds white, lean fillets
1½ cups sliced celery
½ cup chopped onion
1 clove garlic, minced
¼ cup butter
1 (28-ounce) can tomatoes, undrained
1 (8-ounce) can tomato sauce
2 teaspoons salt
½ teaspoon paprika
½ teaspoon chili powder
¼ teaspoon pepper
2 cups boiling water
1 (7-ounce) package spaghetti, uncooked
¼ cup grated or shredded Parmesan cheese

Skin the fillets and cut into 1-inch pieces. In a 5-quart Dutch oven, cook the celery, onion, and garlic in butter until tender. Add the tomatoes, tomato sauce, salt, paprika, chili powder, and pepper. Bring to a simmer. Cover and cook slowly for 15 to 20 minutes. Add the boiling water and uncooked spaghetti; stir and cover. Cook slowly about 10 minutes or until the spaghetti is almost tender. Add the fish; cover. Cook slowly about 10 minutes more or until the fish flakes easily when tested with a fork. Serve hot with Parmesan cheese sprinkled on top.

John Phillips's Favorite Fish Chowder
Serves 10 to 12

*1 pound catfish or crappie fillets, cut
    into 1-inch pieces*
1 cup cut green beans
1 cup shredded zucchini
1 cup thinly sliced onion
1 cup sliced or grated carrots
1 cup thinly sliced celery
1 cup thinly sliced yellow squash
3 cups skim milk
*2 cans (10¾ ounces) or 2 pints
    chicken broth*
1 cup grated cheese
⅛ teaspoon pepper
8 ounces egg noodles
1 tablespoon salt

In a large pot, combine the fish, vegetables, milk, and chicken broth. Cover and bring to a boil. Lower heat and simmer for 15 minutes. Stir in the cheese and pepper. In another pot, gradually add noodles and salt to rapidly boiling water. Cook uncovered, stirring occasionally, until tender. Drain in colander. Add the noodles to the vegetable mixture. Simmer about 5 minutes more or until thoroughly heated. After it's prepared, I also like to put this dish in my crockpot on low or warm to allow the flavors to combine before serving later for dinner. ▨

▨ Weakfish a la Pepper
Serves 4

1½ pounds weakfish or seatrout fillets
1 teaspoon garlic salt
½ teaspoon lemon-pepper seasoning
½ teaspoon instant chicken broth
½ cup boiling water
2 tablespoons vegetable oil
¼ cup tomato sauce
1 teaspoon capers
½ medium green pepper, cut into rings
½ medium red pepper, cut into rings

Cut the fish into 4-inch pieces and sprinkle with garlic salt and lemon-pepper seasoning. Dissolve instant chicken broth in boiling water. Cook the fish in vegetable oil in a 12-inch nonstick frying pan over moderate heat for 5 minutes, turning often. Add the tomato sauce and capers to the frying pan. Reduce heat; cover and simmer for 10 minutes. Top with the pepper rings and cook 5 minutes longer or until the fish flakes easily when tested with a fork and the peppers are tender.

▨ Grouper and Pineapple
Serves 2

2½ cups crushed pineapple, drained
1 cup cooked rice
1 cup breadcrumbs
1 small onion, minced
⅛ teaspoon pepper
1 teaspoon paprika
1 teaspoon salt
1 teaspoon poultry seasoning
2 large grouper fillets
1 cup pineapple juice

Preheat oven to 350°F. Mix the crushed pineapple, cooked rice, breadcrumbs, onion, pepper, paprika, salt, and poultry seasoning in a large bowl. Spread the mixture over the fish fillets arranged in a baking pan. Pour the pineapple juice over the fish and bake until tender, about 30 minutes.

▨ Fish Newburg
Serves 4 to 6

2 tablespoons butter
1½ tablespoons flour
¾ cup milk
1 pinch cayenne pepper
1 pinch nutmeg
¼ teaspoon salt
2 tablespoons fresh parsley, finely chopped
1 pound fish fillets, cooked
½ cup grated Cheddar cheese
2 egg yolks, beaten
¼ cup sherry
2 cups cooked rice

In a large skillet, melt the butter and then add the flour. Stir until smooth. Add the milk and stir until thick. Add the cayenne pepper, nutmeg, salt, and parsley and stir. Then, add the cooked fish, Cheddar cheese, egg yolks, and sherry. Keep on low heat. Serve with cooked rice.

Baked Grouper with Cheese Sauce
Serves 4 to 6

1 ½ pounds ¾-inch-thick grouper fillets
3 tablespoons butter
3 tablespoons all-purpose flour
1 tablespoon salt
½ teaspoon dry mustard
¼ teaspoon dried dill weed
1 pinch cayenne pepper
1 ½ cups half-and-half
1 ½ cups shredded Cheddar cheese
1 (4-ounce) can mussels, drained
¼ pound small shrimp, cooked and peeled
1 (4-ounce) can diced clams, drained

Preheat oven to 400°F. Cut the grouper fillets into serving-size pieces and place in a greased baking dish. In a 2-quart saucepan, melt the butter. Stir in the flour and cook until bubbling. Add the salt, dry mustard, dill weed, and cayenne pepper. Remove from heat and gradually stir in the half-and-half. Return the sauce to the heat and cook, stirring constantly, until thickened. Mix in one cup of Cheddar cheese, stirring until melted. Mix in the mussels, shrimp, and clams. Pour the cheese sauce evenly over the fish and sprinkle with the remaining cheese. Bake for about 20 minutes or until the top browns and the fish flakes easily when tested in the thickest part with a fork.

Yellowtail Tropical
Serves 2

½ cup raspberries
½ cup diced pineapple
½ cup white seedless grapes, halved
½ cup diced mangoes
1 tablespoon sugar
1 ounce white rum
1 pound yellowtail snapper fillets
Egg wash (egg mixed with milk or water)
Panko breadcrumbs
Oil, for frying

In a bowl, mix the raspberries, pineapple, grapes, and mangoes, and then add the sugar and white rum. Let the bowl sit for 1 hour. Pat the fillets dry, dip in the egg wash, and then roll in the panko breadcrumbs. Pan fry in light oil until golden brown. Spoon the fruit mixture over the fillets and serve immediately. Strawberries, blueberries, kiwis, and mandarin oranges are other potential fruit selections.

Jeremy Storm's Horseradish-Crusted Salmon
Serves 4

1 tablespoon horseradish
1 tablespoon mayonnaise
2 teaspoons sour cream
4 (6-ounce) salmon fillets, pin bones
*   removed, skin on*
1 tablespoon olive oil
Salt and pepper
¾ cup breadcrumbs
2 tablespoons chopped parsley

Preheat oven to 325°F. Mix the horseradish, mayonnaise, and sour cream in a small bowl. Brush the salmon fillets with olive oil and season with salt and pepper. Spoon the horseradish mixture over each fillet. In a separate bowl, mix the breadcrumbs and parsley and then sprinkle over the horseradish. Bake the fillets in the oven for 8 to 10 minutes.

Savory Baked Mako Shark
Serves 6

2 pounds skinless mako shark steaks
2 teaspoons lemon juice
⅛ teaspoon pepper
6 slices bacon, chopped
½ cup soft breadcrumbs
2 tablespoons chopped parsley
¾ cup thinly sliced onion

Preheat oven to 350°F. Place the fish in a single layer in a greased baking dish, about 12 by 8 by 2 inches. Sprinkle with the lemon juice and pepper. Fry the bacon until crisp and remove from the drippings; drain and crumble. In a small bowl, combine the crumbled bacon, breadcrumbs, and parsley. Cook the onion in the bacon drippings until tender, and then spread the onion over the fish. Sprinkle the crumb mixture over the top of the onion. Bake for 25 to 30 minutes, or until the fish flakes easily when tested with a fork.

▧ Batter-Fried Mako or Thresher Shark
Serves 6

2 pounds skinless mako or thresher
   shark fillets
1 cup all-purpose flour
1 tablespoon salt
1 teaspoon baking powder
1 cup water
1 tablespoon vinegar
Oil, for frying

Cut the fillets into 1-inch cubes. Combine the flour, salt, and baking powder. Slowly add the water and vinegar; mix well. Dip the fish cubes into the batter and then drop into hot oil (425°F). Cook the fish cubes about 2 to 3 minutes or until golden brown, and then drain on absorbent paper.

▧ Spanish Mackerel Paysanne
Serves 6

2 pounds Spanish mackerel fillets
½ teaspoon salt
¼ teaspoon white pepper
1 (4-ounce) can sliced mushrooms,
   drained
½ cup sliced green onions
¼ cup ketchup
2 tablespoons butter, melted
½ teaspoon liquid smoke

Preheat oven to 350°F. Cut the fillets into serving-size portions. Place the fillets in a well-greased baking dish, about 12 by 8 by 2 inches. Sprinkle with salt and white pepper. Combine the remaining ingredients and spread over the top of the fish. Bake for 25 to 30 minutes or until the fish flakes easily when tested with a fork.

J. Wayne Fears's Baked Halibut on Grits
Serves 4

BAKED HALIBUT
Oil
1½ pounds halibut steaks
½ cup milk
½ cup flour
½ cup cornmeal
½ teaspoon rosemary
½ teaspoon garlic salt
½ teaspoon black pepper
½ teaspoon mustard
Onion, thinly sliced (enough to cover halibut)
½ stick butter
Green onion tops, chopped
8 ounces grated Parmesan cheese

GRITS
4 cups water
1½ teaspoons dried minced onion
¼ teaspoon salt
2 tablespoons chicken broth
2 tablespoons butter
1 cup Aunt Jemima quick grits
¼ cup half-and-half
5 ounces sharp Cheddar cheese, shredded
Lemon wedges, for garnish

Preheat oven to 350°F. Oil the bottom and sides of a pan to a point above the height of the halibut. Add the milk to a shallow dish, and then combine flour, cornmeal, rosemary, garlic salt, black pepper, and mustard in another shallow dish. Dip the halibut in milk, and then dredge in the flour mixture. Arrange the dredged halibut, skin side down, to completely cover the bottom of the pan. Cover the halibut with thinly sliced onion and butter cut into pieces. Sprinkle with green onion tops, and then cover with Parmesan cheese. Bake for about 30 minutes, or until the halibut flakes easily. For grits, combine water, onion, salt, chicken broth, and butter in a heavy saucepan and bring to a boil. Add grits and reduce heat to low. Stir often until the grits soften, about 5 minutes. Stir in half-and-half. Add Cheddar cheese and stir until it melts. Serve the halibut on a bed of hot grits garnished with lemon wedges. ▧

Jim Zumbo's Trout with Capers
Serves 4 to 6

3 pounds trout fillets, skinned
6 tablespoons butter
½ cup dry vermouth
1 teaspoon Dijon mustard
3 tablespoons capers, chopped
2 tablespoons shallots, chopped
2 tablespoons parsley, chopped
1 tablespoon lemon juice
Zest of 1 lemon
Salt and pepper

Slice fish at an angle into ½-inch cutlets. Cook fish in 2 tablespoons of the butter in a skillet, 2 minutes per side. Lift out and place on a platter; keep warm. Add the vermouth to the skillet and bring to a boil. Reduce a little, and then put in the remaining butter, mustard, capers, shallots, parsley, lemon juice, and lemon zest. Add salt and pepper to taste. Cook 1 or 2 more minutes, and then spoon over the fish. ▨

Manhattan Striped Bass Chowder
Serves 6

1 pound striped bass fillets
¼ cup chopped bacon or salt pork
½ cup chopped onion
2 cups boiling water
16 ounces canned tomatoes
1 cup diced potatoes
½ cup diced carrots
½ cup chopped celery
¼ cup ketchup
1 tablespoon Worcestershire sauce
1 teaspoon salt
¼ teaspoon pepper
¼ teaspoon thyme
Parsley, chopped

Cut the striped bass fillets into 1-inch pieces. In a frying pan, fry the bacon or salt pork until crisp. Add the onion and cook until tender. Add the boiling water, tomatoes, potatoes, carrots, celery, ketchup, Worcestershire sauce, salt, pepper, and thyme. Cover and simmer for 40 to 45 minutes or until the vegetables are tender. Add the fish. Cover and simmer about 10 minutes longer or until the fish flakes easily when tested with a fork. Sprinkle with the parsley.

Marinated King Mackerel
Serves 6 to 8

1 teaspoon dried marjoram leaves, crushed
¼ cup lime juice
2 pounds king mackerel steaks
2 tablespoons butter, melted
1 teaspoon salt
1 pinch black pepper

Combine the marjoram and lime juice in a shallow dish. Add the steaks, turning to moisten both sides with the lime juice. Cover and place in the refrigerator. Marinate for 1 hour, turning once. Place the fish in a single layer on a well-greased 15-by-10-by-1-inch baking pan. Brush the fish with melted butter. Sprinkle with salt and pepper. Broil about 4 inches from the heat source for 10 or 15 minutes or until the fish flakes when tested with a fork. Fish need not be turned during broiling.

Jamaican Jerk Fish
Serves 4 to 6

1 onion
½ cup green onion
2 teaspoons dried thyme
1 teaspoon salt
1 teaspoon allspice
½ teaspoon nutmeg
½ teaspoon cinnamon
2 tablespoons hot red pepper flakes
1 teaspoon Tabasco sauce
1 teaspoon black pepper
2 tablespoons soy sauce
1 whole snapper or grouper, 3 to 5 pounds

Place all seasonings into a food processor, and then run at a high setting until liquefied. Then, place the mixture in a plastic bag with the fish and marinate at least 4 hours. Grill the fish slowly over hot coals; the fish is done when it flakes easily with a fork.

▧ Red Snapper with Vegetable Sauce
Serves 4 to 6

2 pounds red snapper fillets
2 tablespoons olive oil
½ cup chopped onion
¼ cup chopped celery
¼ cup chopped green pepper
¼ cup sliced carrots
1 tablespoon chopped parsley
1 clove garlic, minced
1 (15-ounce) can tomato sauce with tomato bits
½ cup pale dry sherry
1 teaspoon dried dill weed
½ teaspoon salt
1 pinch black pepper
1 tablespoon lemon juice

Preheat oven to 400°F. Cut the fillets into six portions. In a saucepan, combine the olive oil, onion, celery, green pepper, carrots, parsley, and garlic; cover and cook until tender. Stir in the tomato sauce, sherry, and dill weed. Bring to a boil and simmer for 10 minutes. Ladle about ½ cup of the tomato-vegetable sauce into a 12-by-18-by-2-inch baking dish. Place the fish portions on the sauce in the baking dish. Sprinkle with the salt, pepper, and lemon juice. Pour the remaining sauce over the fish. Bake for about 20 minutes or until the fish flakes easily with a fork.

▧ Pan-Fried Tuna
Serves 4

1½ pounds tuna fillets
4 tablespoons olive oil
2 cloves garlic, crushed
¼ stick butter
3 tablespoons fresh chopped herbs (such as winter savory, rosemary, or thyme)
Parsley or lemon balm, for garnish

Slice the fillets very thinly (about ⅛ inch thick). In a bowl, add 2 tablespoons of olive oil to the garlic and then coat the fillets with it. Heat the remaining olive oil and the butter in a large frying pan and toss in the fresh herbs, sautéing lightly for 1 minute. Turn up the heat, add the fillets, and fry for about 3 minutes, turning them gently from time to time. Serve with the pan juices and garnish with parsley or lemon balm.

Ken Schulz's Fish Ceviche
Serves 1

1 large or 2 small fish fillets, chopped
Juice from 1 lime
1 large or 2 small tomatoes, seeds removed and chopped
3 tablespoons chopped red onion
1 clove garlic, finely chopped
1 tablespoon cilantro, finely chopped
1 jalapeño pepper, seeds removed and finely chopped
2 tablespoons olive oil
Sea salt

Chop the fish, place it in a nonreactive bowl, and then squeeze the lime over the fish. Remove any pits and mix together. Add the tomatoes, onion, garlic, cilantro, pepper, and olive oil and mix thoroughly. Then, cover the bowl with plastic wrap and refrigerate for 2 hours. (Resist eating it sooner; a shorter length of time doesn't allow the citric acid in the lime juice to fully work on the fish.) When ready to eat, add sea salt to taste. Add or subtract to these ingredients as you like. Really fresh fish work the best. Make ceviche the day you catch the fish, or no more than a day after. ▧

▧ Fried Catfish
Serves 6

6 (½- to 1-pound) catfish fillets, skinned
2 teaspoons salt
¼ teaspoon black pepper
2 eggs, beaten
2 tablespoons milk
2 cups cornmeal
Oil, for frying

Sprinkle both sides of the catfish fillets with salt and pepper. In a shallow dish, mix the eggs and milk. Add the cornmeal to another shallow dish. Dip the fillets in the egg mixture and then roll in the cornmeal. Place the fillets in a frying pan with ⅛ inch of hot oil and fry to a golden brown on both sides. Drain on paper towels and serve.

FIRST AID FOR FISHERMEN

Section Five
FIRST AID
FOR FISHERMEN

• EMERGENCY MEDICAL TREATMENT •
• BITES AND SNAKE BITES • SUNBURN • INJURIES •
• SEASICKNESS • FIRST-AID KIT •

EMERGENCY MEDICAL TREATMENT

When a fisherman heads for the water, he will always be confronted with a special bunch of hazards. Rocking boats, seasickness, slippery rocks, or sharp fishhooks may turn his day into an accident or a trip to the emergency room. This special section on first aid for anglers is designed to help fishermen avoid some of those inherent dangers, as well as suggest treatments for accidents and illnesses that would otherwise ruin a day of fishing. It is important to remember, however, to seek medical attention as quickly as possible for serious injuries and attacks.

This chapter will give detailed step-by-step procedures for every first-aid situation the fisherman is likely to encounter. It should be remembered, however, that these procedures, though vitally important, aren't the only forms of first aid. The victim's mental distress also needs treatment. A reassuring word, a smile, your obvious willingness and ability to help—all will have an encouraging effect.

The knowledgeable first-aider also knows what not to do and thereby avoids compounding the problem by making errors that could be serious.

The procedures and instructions that follow reflect recommendations of the American Red Cross, the American Medical Association, the U.S. Department of Agriculture, and, of course, respected physicians.

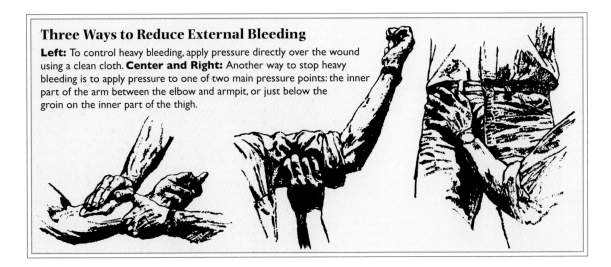

Three Ways to Reduce External Bleeding

Left: To control heavy bleeding, apply pressure directly over the wound using a clean cloth. **Center and Right:** Another way to stop heavy bleeding is to apply pressure to one of two main pressure points: the inner part of the arm between the elbow and armpit, or just below the groin on the inner part of the thigh.

Bleeding

EXTERNAL BLEEDING: If a large blood vessel is severed, death from loss of blood can occur in three to five minutes, so it is vital to stop the bleeding at once. Always do so, if possible, by applying pressure directly over the wound.

Use a clean cloth—a handkerchief, an item of clothing, or whatever else is near at hand. Use your bare hand if nothing else is available, and then, once the bleeding is under control, apply a cloth. Put on additional layers of cloth, and when the covering is substantial, bandage snugly with strips of cloth cut from a bedsheet, neckties, or similar materials. Don't remove the bandage. If it becomes saturated with blood, put on more layers of cloth, and perhaps tighten the dressing directly over the wound.

If you are sure that no bones are broken, try to raise the bleeding area higher than the rest of the body.

If extremely quick action is needed, or if the above method fails to stop the flow of blood, you may be able to diminish the flow by pressing your fingers or the heel of your hand at one of two pressure points. One of these is located on the inner half of the arm midway between the elbow and armpit; pressure applied here will reduce bleeding in the lower area of the arm. Pressure on the other point, located just below the groin on the front, inner half of the thigh, will reduce bleeding on the extremity below that point.

INTERNAL BLEEDING: Often caused by a severe fall or a violent blow, bleeding within the body can be difficult to diagnose, though it may be revealed by bleeding from the nose or mouth when no injury can be detected in those organs. Other symptoms may include restlessness, nausea, anxiety, a weak and rapid pulse, thirst, paleness, and general weakness.

The first treatment procedure is to use pillows, knapsacks, folded clothes, or something similar to raise the victim's head and shoulders if he is having difficulty breathing. Otherwise, place him flat on his back.

Keep him as immobile as possible, and try to have him control the movements caused by vomiting. Turn his head to the side for vomiting.

Do not give the victim stimulants, even if the bleeding seems to stop.

If the victim loses consciousness, turn him on his side, with his head and chest lower than his hips.

Medical care is a must. Get the victim to a doctor or hospital as soon as possible.

Applying a Tourniquet

Since a tourniquet can cause the loss of the affected limb, it should be applied only when no other means will reduce blood flow enough to prevent the victim from bleeding to death. **Left:** Wrap strong, wide cloth around the limb above the wound, and tie a simple overhand knot. **Center:** Place a short stick on the knot, tie another overhand knot over the stick, and twist the stick to stem bleeding. **Right:** Bind the stick with the ends of the tourniquet, but be sure to loosen it every 15 minutes.

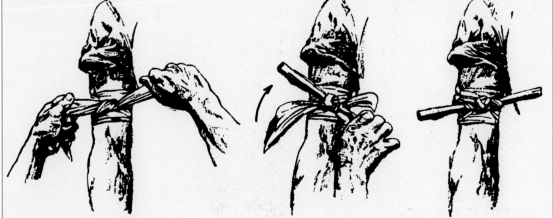

NOSEBLEED: Nosebleeds often occur for no reason, while at other times they are caused by an injury. Most of them are more annoying than serious. It occasionally happens, though, that the bleeding is heavy and prolonged and this can be dangerous.

The person should remain quiet, preferably in a sitting position with his head thrown back or lying down with his head and shoulders raised.

Pinch the victim's nostrils together, keeping the pressure on for five to 10 minutes. If the bleeding doesn't stop, pack gauze lightly into the bleeding nostril and then pinch.

Sometimes the application of cold, wet towels to the face will help.

USE OF A TOURNIQUET: According to the American Red Cross, the use of a tourniquet to stop bleeding in an extremity is "justifiable only rarely." Because its use involves a high risk of losing a limb, a tourniquet should be applied only if the bleeding seems sure to cause death.

Use only a wide, strong piece of cloth—never a narrow strip of material such as rope or wire. Wrap the cloth around the upper part of the limb above the wound, and tie a simple overhand knot (half a square knot). Place a short stick on the knot, and tie another simple overhand knot (that is, complete the square knot) over the stick. Twist the stick just enough to stop the bleeding. Loosen the binding (untwist the stick) for a few seconds every 15 minutes. (See illustrations on previous page.)

Once the bleeding has been controlled, keep the victim quiet and warm. If he is conscious and can swallow easily, give him some water or maybe some weak tea— no alcoholic drinks. If he is not conscious, or if abdominal or other internal injuries are suspected, do not give him any fluid.

▓ Artificial Respiration

Artificial respiration, now commonly called resuscitation, is the technique of causing air to flow into and out of the lungs of a person whose normal breathing has stopped. Causes of stoppage of normal breathing include inhalation of water, smoke, or gas, electric shock, choking, or drug overdose. In most instances, death will result within six minutes unless artificial respiration is administered.

The treatment may also be needed if breathing does not stop completely but becomes slow and shallow and the victim's lips, tongue, and fingernails turn blue. If you're in doubt, give artificial respiration—it is seldom harmful and can save a life.

Before beginning the artificial-respiration methods described below, check the victim's mouth and throat opening for obstructions; remove any foreign objects or loose dentures.

MOUTH TO MOUTH: Place the victim on his back. Put one hand under the victim's neck. At the same time, place the other hand on his forehead and tilt the head back.

Using the hand that was under the neck, pull the victim's chin up, thereby ensuring a free air passage. Take a deep breath, place your mouth over the victim's mouth, trying to make the seal as airtight as possible, and pinch the victim's nostrils closed. Blow into the victim's mouth until you see his chest rise.

Lift your head from the victim, and take another deep breath while his chest falls, causing him to exhale. Repeat the process. For the first few minutes, do so as

Mouth-to-Mouth Resuscitation

Remember the ABCs: airway, breathing, and circulation, in that order.

Airway. If there are no head, neck, or back injuries, gently tilt the victim's head and raise the chin. This will lift the tongue and ensure a clear air passage. Check for breathing by placing your ear over the victim's mouth and feeling for any exhalation.

Breathing. If the person is not breathing, pinch his nose, take a deep breath, and place your mouth over his. Breathe into his lungs two times slowly—one and a half to two seconds each time. If the victim's chest does not rise, re-tilt the head and repeat the cycle at a rate of 12 times per minute, until the victim can breathe on his own.

Circulation. Check for a pulse. Keeping the victim's head tilted, place your index and middle fingers on the victim's Adam's apple, and then slide your fingers down to the next "ridge" on the neck. This is where you'll find the carotid artery. Press firmly to determine if there's a pulse. If there isn't, proceed with chest compressions.

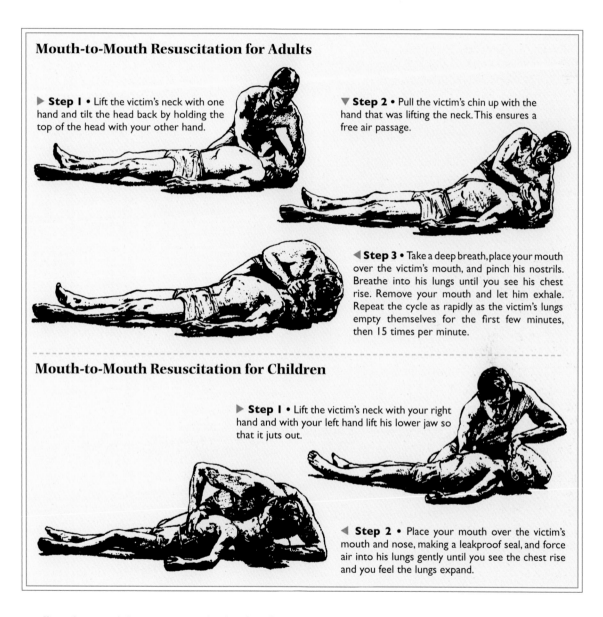

Mouth-to-Mouth Resuscitation for Adults

▶ **Step 1** • Lift the victim's neck with one hand and tilt the head back by holding the top of the head with your other hand.

▼ **Step 2** • Pull the victim's chin up with the hand that was lifting the neck. This ensures a free air passage.

◀ **Step 3** • Take a deep breath, place your mouth over the victim's mouth, and pinch his nostrils. Breathe into his lungs until you see his chest rise. Remove your mouth and let him exhale. Repeat the cycle as rapidly as the victim's lungs empty themselves for the first few minutes, then 15 times per minute.

Mouth-to-Mouth Resuscitation for Children

▶ **Step 1** • Lift the victim's neck with your right hand and with your left hand lift his lower jaw so that it juts out.

◀ **Step 2** • Place your mouth over the victim's mouth and nose, making a leakproof seal, and force air into his lungs gently until you see the chest rise and you feel the lungs expand.

rapidly as the victim's lungs are emptied. After that, do it about 12 times per minute.

If the victim is an infant or small child, use the same procedure, but place your mouth over both the mouth and nose, and force air into his lungs gently.

HEART STOPPAGE (CPR): If artificial respiration produces no response in an injured person, it may mean that his heart has stopped beating. You can make a fairly certain diagnosis by checking his pulse at the wrist and holding your ear to the victim's chest. If you feel no pulse and hear no heartbeat, you will have to use external heart massage (Cardiopulmonary Resuscitation, or CPR) in addition to artificial respiration.

Here are the warning signs of a heart attack:

■ Pressure; feeling of "fullness"; squeezing or pain in the center of the chest lasting more than two minutes

Chest Compressions

For heart stoppage, employ extended chest compressions (CPR) using the weight of the upper part of your body.

- Pain radiating to shoulders, neck, jaw, arms, or back; tingling sensation down left arm
- Dizziness, weakness, sweating, or nausea; pale complexion and shortness of breath

If the victim's heart and breathing have stopped, begin CPR. The technique involves mouth-to-mouth resuscitation, which delivers air to the lungs, and chest compressions, which help circulate the blood.

CHEST COMPRESSIONS: Positioning yourself perpendicular to the victim, place the heel of one hand on the lower third of the victim's sternum (breastbone). Place your other hand on top of the first one. Press down firmly with both hands about 1½ to 2 inches and then lift both hands to let the chest expand. Repeat at a rate of 80 to 100 compressions per minute. The mouth-to-mouth breathing should continue at a rate of two steady lung inflations after every 15 chest compressions.

▓ Choking

More than one person has died from choking on a fish bone, an inadvertently swallowed hard object, a piece of food that went down the "wrong pipe," and the like. Anything that lodges in the throat or air passages must be removed as soon as possible. Here's how to do it.

If the victim is conscious, give him four back blows between the shoulder blades. If the victim is lying down, roll him on his side, facing you with his chest against your knee. If the victim is sitting or standing, you should

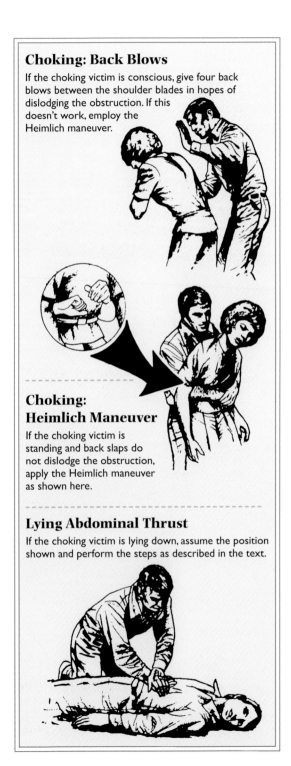

Choking: Back Blows

If the choking victim is conscious, give four back blows between the shoulder blades in hopes of dislodging the obstruction. If this doesn't work, employ the Heimlich maneuver.

Choking: Heimlich Maneuver

If the choking victim is standing and back slaps do not dislodge the obstruction, apply the Heimlich maneuver as shown here.

Lying Abdominal Thrust

If the choking victim is lying down, assume the position shown and perform the steps as described in the text.

be behind and to one side of him. If the victim is an infant, place him on your forearm, head down. Make sharp blows with the heel of your hand on the spine, directly between his shoulder blades.

If this doesn't remove the object, and the victim is standing or sitting, employ the Heimlich maneuver:

1. Stand behind the victim and wrap your arms around his waist.

2. Place the thumb side of your fist against the victim's upper abdomen, just below the rib cage.

3. Grasp your fist with your other hand and press into the victim's abdomen with two or three quick upward thrusts.

If the victim is in a lying position, do this:

1. Place him on his back and kneel close to his side.

2. Place your hands, one on top of the other, with the heel of the bottom hand in the middle of his abdomen, just below the rib cage.

3. Rock forward so that your shoulders are directly over the victim's abdomen and press toward the victim's diaphragm with a quick forward thrust.

4. Don't press to either side.

If the victim is unconscious, tilt his head back and attempt to give him artificial respiration. If this fails, give the victim four back blows in rapid succession. If the object has still not been forced out of the air passage, then stand behind the victim, put both of your fists into his abdomen, and give eight upward thrusts.

Finally, if none of these methods work, you should insert your index finger deep into the victim's throat, using a hooking action to try to dislodge the object.

FOR A SMALL CHILD: Put one arm around the youngster's waist from behind, and lift him up so that his head and upper torso are leaning toward the ground. With your free hand, give him several sharp taps between the shoulder blades. When the object has been dislodged, clear his throat with your fingers, and pull the tongue forward.

FOR AN INFANT: Hold him up by the ankles, head hanging straight down. Open his mouth, pull his tongue forward, and the object will likely fall out. If not, give him a tap or two on the back.

BITES AND POISONOUS PLANTS

▨ Snakebites

It is doubtful whether any other first-aid situation is more feared and less understood than snakebites, and there is little agreement, even among leading authorities, about their treatment.

About 6,500 people are bitten by venomous snakes in the United States each year. Of those, only about 350 are hunters or fishermen. And the death rate is very low, an average of 15 persons annually in the entire country. Most of those bites occur south of an imaginary line drawn from North Carolina to Southern California. More than half occur in Texas, North Carolina, Florida, Georgia, Louisiana, and Arkansas.

There are four kinds of venomous snakes in the United States. Three are of the pit-viper variety: rattlesnakes, copperheads, and cottonmouth moccasins. The fourth, the coral snake, is a member of the cobra family. The pit vipers are so named because they have a small, deep depression between the eyes and the nostrils. The coral snake has broad, red and black bands separated by narrow yellow bands, giving rise to the saying, "Red on yellow, kill a fellow."

The bite of a venomous snake—except for the coral snake, which chews rather than bites—is in the form of fang punctures of the skin. If you are bitten by a snake that leaves two U-shaped rows of tooth marks on your skin, relax—it is almost certainly a nonvenomous snake. The bite of a nonvenomous snake produces little pain or swelling.

Symptoms of the bite of a venomous snake include immediate pain, swelling and discoloration in the area of the wound, general weakness, nausea and vomiting, a weak and rapid pulse, dimming of vision, faintness, and eventually unconsciousness.

Most medical authorities now agree that the preferred treatment for a snakebite is antivenin administered as quickly as possible after the bite. If a snakebite victim is within a two-hour drive of a medical facility,

North American Venomous Snakes

Cottonmouth • Eastern cottonmouths as well as Florida and western cottonmouths are frequently confused with non-venomous water snakes. Cottonmouths have dark blotches on an olive body and broad, flat heads.

Eastern Diamondback • The body has dark diamonds with light borders along a tan or light-brown background. The diamonds gradually change to bands in the tail. The habitat is lowland thickets, palmettos, and flatwoods.

Coral Snake • This snake is dangerously venomous, but its small mouth prevents it from biting most parts of the body. It has red and black rings wider than the interspaced yellow rings. The habitat is open woods in the East and loose soil and rocks in the West.

Copperhead • This snake has large, chestnut-brown cross bands on a pale pinkish or reddish-brown surface with a copper tinge on the head. The habitat in the North is wooded mountains and stone walls; in the South, it is lowland swamps and wood suburbs.

Western Diamondback • This snake has light brown to black diamond-shaped blotches along a light gray, tan, and sometimes pink background. It also has black and white bands of about equal width around the tail. The habitat includes woods, rocky hills, deserts, and farmland.

Timber Rattler and Canebrake Rattler • In the South, there is a dark streak from the canebrake's eye to mouth, and dark chevrons and a rusty stripe along the midline. In the North, the timber rattler has a yellowish body and dark phase in parts of its range. The habitat for the canebrake is lowland brush and stream borders. The timber rattler prefers rocky wooded hills.

get the person there as fast and as calmly as possible. Keep the bite location immobile, even if you have to splint it. Also keep the bitten body part below the level of the heart. A snakebite victim may walk up to a half hour before symptoms start. If the distance is longer to transportation, the victim should be carried. If you are alone, you should still be able to walk for several hours before symptoms start.

Most bites, however, occur in the field, often many miles from a road, so the victim cannot always get antivenin quickly enough. Survival in such cases depends upon the first-aid steps taken by the victim and his companions. And here is where the disagreement among medical authorities is most prevalent.

Proper treatment for a snakebite continues to confuse sportsmen, but the most reliable medical opinions today agree that the old treatments did more damage than good. There are still snakebite kits on the market and they may make you feel better if you have one in your first-aid kit, but the best advice is don't use it. The use of a scalpel and making incisions is no longer recommended and may cause further injury. Suction devices used without incisions are of questionable value. Some tests indicate that such suction devices may only remove about 1 to 2 percent of the venom.

Here's the currently recommended treatment for a snakebite. Call 911 or get to a hospital where you can get antivenin as quickly as possible. Properly treated with antivenin, snakebites are rarely fatal. If you can't get to a hospital within 30 minutes, immobilize the bite and, if possible, keep it lower than the heart. Wrap a bandage 2 to 4 inches above the bite. The bandage should not cut off blood flow from a vein or artery. Make the bandage loose enough so that a finger can slip under it. Do not put ice on the bite. Avoid exertion and excitement. Sit down and try to calm yourself. Panic could bring on shock. Do not eat or drink alcohol. Do not remove any dressings until you reach a hospital. If possible, kill the snake and take the head for identification later. Use caution: The head of a snake can still bite through reflex action up to one hour after it is killed. Get to a hospital or doctor as soon as possible with a minimum of exertion.

Coping with Bugs

The outdoors is a great place, but bugs can turn a pleasant day into a nightmare. You can fight back! There are five bugs that will give you the most trouble: mosquitoes, black flies, no-see-ums, deerflies, and ticks. Mosquitoes,

the worst of the bunch, are most active at dawn and dusk. Mosquitoes are attracted to dark colors, so wear light-colored clothing. Black flies draw blood. Male black flies use blood for food, and the female needs blood to complete her breeding cycle. Common throughout Canada and the northern United States, black flies bite as soon as they land and they zero in on the face, hairline, wrists, and ankles. The peak period is spring and early summer. Aside from using a repellent, you should wear a hat, tuck pants into socks, tape cuffs around ankles, and wear long sleeves. No-see-ums are so small you can't see them, but they hurt when they bite. You'll find no-see-ums along lakes, beaches, and marshes. The deerfly is another painful biter and will attack the face, legs, arms, and neck. Once again, wear light-colored clothing. The tick, because of the threat of Lyme disease, is the most dangerous pest. Wear light-colored clothing, tuck pants into socks, avoid wooded areas and high grass, and use a tick repellent. The most effective repellent against these bugs contains DEET.

Bee Stings

Stinging insects are seldom more than an annoyance, even if they hit the target on your hide. Some people, however, are highly allergic to the stings of certain insects. If you or a member of your party has had a severe reaction to a bee sting in the past and is stung, take the following steps:

1. Use a tight, constricting band above the sting if it is on the arm or leg. Loosen the band for a few seconds every 15 minutes.

2. Apply an icepack or cold cloths to the sting area.

3. Get the victim to a doctor as soon as possible.

For the average bee-sting victim, these procedures will suffice:

1. Make a paste of baking soda and cold cream (if it is available), and apply it to the sting area.

2. Apply cold cloths to help ease the pain.

3. If there is itching, use calamine lotion.

Chigger and Tick Bites

The irritation produced by chiggers, which are the larval stage of a mite, results from fluid the tiny insects inject. Chiggers do not burrow under the skin, as is often suggested.

How to Battle the Bugs

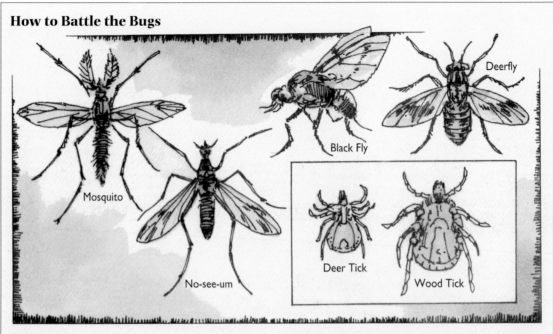

Mosquito

No-see-um

Black Fly

Deerfly

Deer Tick

Wood Tick

Mosquitoes home in on warmth, carbon dioxide, and the odor of human skin. Your best weapon is a repellant on your skin that will set up a barrier that will confuse the mosquito's sensors.

Black flies are inactive at night but a problem during the day. You will rarely feel the bite. The first thing you may notice is the blood. If you get bitten and begin to itch, coat bites with alcohol or witch hazel.

Deerflies are found anywhere in the northern woods, and both sexes can inflict painful bites. Use a headnet and tape cuffs, but be aware that deerflies can also bite through clothing.

No-see-ums are troublesome because it is difficult to protect yourself from them. They can fit through headnets, screens, clothing—almost anything. A repellant helps, but the only sure cure is a stiff wind.

Deer ticks pose a Lyme disease threat. They are half the size of the common wood tick and are orangish brown with a black spot near the head. Symptoms of Lyme disease include a red, ring-shaped rash, fever, chills, headache, stiff joints, and fatigue. Learn how to identify ticks and remove them from your body with tweezers. Don't burn, twist, or crush a tick on your body.

Since chiggers do not usually attach themselves to the skin until an hour or more after they reach the body, bathing promptly after exposure, using a brush and soapy water, may eliminate them. Once the bites have been inflicted, the application of ice water may help. The itching and discomfort can be relieved by applying calamine lotion or a paste made of baking soda and a little water.

Ticks—flat, usually brown, and about ¼ inch long—attach themselves to the skin by making a tiny puncture, and they feed by sucking blood. They can thereby transmit the germs of several diseases, including Rocky Mountain spotted fever and Lyme disease. A new strain, granulocytic ehrlichiosis, has flu-like symptoms nearly identical to Lyme disease. Protecting yourself from granulocytic ehrlichiosis is the same as with Lyme disease.

If you have been in a tick-infested area, be sure to examine your clothes and body for the insects, paying particular attention to hairy areas. Removing ticks promptly is insurance against the transmission of any germs they may be carrying since that process seldom begins until six hours or so after the insect attaches itself and begins to feed.

The Fisherman and Lyme Disease

A deer tick is a speck of a bug, but unnoticed on your body its bite can infect you with spirochete bacteria, which produces the crippling Lyme disease. Deer ticks are found on a wide variety of wild and domestic animals, but about 75 percent of deer ticks live on whitetail deer. This means that fishermen in deer country have a greater risk of contracting Lyme disease than most other sportsmen.

Fishermen hiking in the woods along streams and lakes should tuck in the bottoms of their pant legs. If you prefer to wear your pants outside your boots, so that your pants shed rain outside your boots rather than inside, use masking tape to close off your cuffs. Before you go into the woods, spray yourself with a good tick repellent. There are several on the market that will do the job well, especially if they contain the ingredient DEET.

After a day of fishing, check your body for ticks. The bite of a deer tick is painless, so you may never know you've been bitten unless you look for a tick or signs of a bite. Look wherever you have hair. Check your scalp, and the back of your neck and head. Two favorite spots of ticks are your armpits and groin. It's important to check everywhere.

If you find a tick, don't panic. Grab the tick as close to the skin as possible and pull outward slowly and steadily with firm force. Don't twist or jerk the tick out, which may break off parts of the tick in your skin. Squeezing it is also risky because you may release bacteria into your body.

It takes at least several hours for a deer tick to release its bacteria into your bloodstream, so it's critical to remove the tick as quickly as possible. When the tick is out, wash and disinfect the bite area thoroughly. If you see signs of redness or a rash, call a doctor immediately.

Use tweezers to remove a tick, but don't yank—that may cause the tick's head or mouth parts to break off and remain in the flesh. Pull it gently, taking care not to crush the body, which may be full of germs. If it can't be pulled off gently, cover the entire tick with heavy oil, which closes off its breathing pores and may make it disengage itself.

▨ Spider and Scorpion Bites

Scorpions are most common in the southwestern United States and are found in such spots as cool and damp buildings, debris, and under loose banks. Most species of scorpions in the United States are nonvenomous; few of their stings are dangerous.

The biting spiders in the United States include the black widow, brown widow, and tarantula. The brown widow—its abdomen has a dull-orange hourglass marking against a brown body—is harmless in almost all cases. The tarantula is a large (up to 3 inches long, not including the legs) and hairy spider, but despite its awesome appearance its bite is almost always harmless, though it may cause allergic reactions in sensitive people. The black widow—the female's body is about ½ inch long, shiny black, usually with a red hourglass marking

on the underside of the abdomen—has a venomous bite, but its victims almost always recover.

The symptoms of these bites may include some swelling and redness, immediate pain that may—especially with a black-widow bite—become quite severe and spread throughout the body, much sweating, nausea, and difficulty in breathing and speaking.

First-aid procedures are as follows:

1. Keep the victim warm and calm, lying down.
2. Apply a wide, constricting band above the bite, loosening it every 15 minutes.
3. Apply wrapped-up ice or cold compresses to the area of the bite.
4. Get medical help as quickly as possible.

▨ Poison Ivy, Poison Oak, and Poison Sumac

You cannot escape from poison ivy, poison oak, and poison sumac. There are virtually no areas in the United States in which at least one of these plants does not exist. Poison ivy is found throughout the country, with the possible exception of California and Nevada. Poison

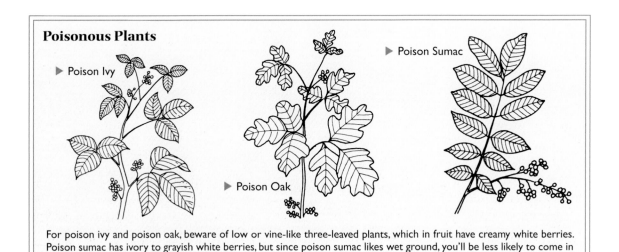

Poisonous Plants

▶ Poison Ivy

▶ Poison Oak

▶ Poison Sumac

For poison ivy and poison oak, beware of low or vine-like three-leaved plants, which in fruit have creamy white berries. Poison sumac has ivory to grayish white berries, but since poison sumac likes wet ground, you'll be less likely to come in contact with it if you keep your boots dry.

oak occurs in the southeastern states, and a western variety exists in the West Coast states. Poison sumac grows in most of the states in the eastern third of the country.

If you're lucky, you may be among the 50 percent of the population that is not sensitive to these poisonous plants. If you are not lucky, however, and you've already had a few run-ins with poison ivy, oak, or sumac, you better know how to identify these plants and learn where they grow. Poison ivy grows along streams, lakes, and on sunny hillsides. It can also grow as a shrub, a small tree, or a vine.

If you want to avoid poison ivy and poison oak, beware of low or vine-like three-leaved plants, which in fruit have creamy white berries. Poison sumac has ivory to grayish white berries. Poison sumac likes wet ground, so you are less likely to come in contact with it if you keep your boots dry.

Urushiol is the sticky, colorless oil that comes from the leaves and stems of poison ivy that, when it gets on your skin, causes the irritation. Urushiol in poison ivy is nearly the same in poison oak and poison sumac. If you're sensitive to one, you're sensitive to all of them.

If you don't wash the poison sap off your skin quickly, you will develop a rash within a couple of days. The rash will eventually produce swollen patches with blisters that will break and ooze.

Healing will take about two weeks, no matter what you do, but here is some advice to ease the intense itching and promote healing. The best medicine against poison ivy is cortisone, if given within the first 24 hours. Oral

prednisone will also help. If you are sensitive to poison ivy, take a supply of cortisone along on your trips.

Here are other remedies that will at least relieve some of the symptoms:

1. Cool compresses with Burow's solution will ease itching and speed up the drying process. Apply them for 15 minutes three or four times a day.

2. Calamine lotion will also relieve the itching.

3. Oatmeal baths are helpful. Add a cup of Aveeno oatmeal to the tub and soak in it for 15 minutes two or three times a day.

4. Aloe vera will aid in skin healing. Apply the lotion twice a day.

5. Oral antihistamines will help eliminate the itching, but antihistamine lotions don't help. Don't use anesthetic sprays or lotions, which may actually sensitize the skin and irritate the rash.

6. If you're very sensitive to poison ivy, try Ivy Shield, an organic clay barrier that will give 95 percent protection to the skin.

7. If you come in contact with poison ivy, shower with soap and water immediately.

The best protection is learning how to identify these plants and avoid them. The shiny leaves grow in groups of three, so try to remember the saying, "Leaves of three, beware of me."

SUNBURN

Not everyone is aware of the genuine health hazard from the solar system. The National Cancer Institute estimates 600,000 malignancies a year are a direct result of careless exposure to the sun. Of that number, close to 7,000 people will die from malignant melanoma, the most deadly skin cancer.

The sun is the bad guy, causing at least 90 percent of all skin cancers. Fortunately, the sun warns its victims with early symptoms. Those symptoms include those fashionable tans you see around town and usually ignore.

The sun produces two different types of ultraviolet rays, both harmful to the skin. Beta rays (UVB) can cause skin cancer. Alpha rays (UVA) can cause both skin cancer and premature wrinkling of the skin. The easiest and most effective way of protecting yourself from these rays is through the use of a good sunscreen that is rated with an SPF (sun protection factor) of at least 15.

There are sunscreens with ratings of SPF 35 and higher, but in most cases, a rating of SPF 15 is all that is necessary for daily use. With an SPF 15, a person can stay in the sun 15 times longer than without any protection at all. Some doctors claim that regular use of an SPF 15 for the first 18 years of life may reduce the risk of skin cancer by 78 percent. For this reason, it's extremely important for parents to remember to keep small children out of direct sunlight, especially between 10:00 a.m. and 3:00 p.m., when the sun is the strongest and can do the most damage to the skin. Choose a waterproof sunscreen. Apply it liberally an hour or two before you go out in the sun, and reapply it every two or three hours, especially after swimming and sweating. Some newer sunscreens are formulated to last all day, even after swimming.

Your skin type is also an important factor. If you're a Type I or II, which means fair skin, blond hair, and blue eyes, you will need more skin protection and a doctor should check you for skin cancer at least once a year. At the other extreme is Type V or VI, which includes people of Middle Eastern and African descent, who will burn only after heavy exposure.

If you spend a lot of time in the sun, you should know about the types of skin cancers and how to detect them early. There are three kinds of skin cancers: basal cell carcinoma, squamous cell carcinoma, and malignant melanoma.

Basal cell carcinoma is the most common skin cancer (about 80 percent) and is seldom deadly. It usually appears on the neck, head, face, and hands. It may be as small as a pinpoint or as large as an inch. It may also crust and bleed.

Squamous-cell carcinoma is the second-most common and looks like a raised pink wart. If left untreated, it can spread to other parts of the body.

Malignant melanoma is the least common, but it is the most deadly skin cancer. It usually appears quickly on the upper back or legs. It can be brown, black, or multicolored. Malignant melanoma grows fast and spreads to other organs.

If you spend a lot of time in the sun, check your skin regularly. Look at the back of your hands and your face. Look for scaly, rough patches of skin. Are there any white spots or red nodules with scales? If you see anything that looks suspicious, see your doctor. Most of the time, skin cancers are easily and successfully removed.

SURVIVING HEAT AND COLD

■ Sunstroke

Sunstroke is extremely dangerous. Aged people are the most susceptible. The usual symptoms are headache, dry skin, and rapid pulse. Dizziness and nausea may occur, and in severe cases the victim may lapse into unconsciousness. The body temperature soars, sometimes as high as 109°F.

Medical help, as soon as possible, is a must. Until it arrives, do the following:

1. Undress the victim, and sponge the body freely with cool water, or apply cold cloths, the objective being to reduce body temperature to a tolerable level of 103°F or below. If you have no thermometer, check the victim's pulse; a pulse rate of 110 or below usually means a tolerable body temperature.

2. When the body temperature lowers to 103°F, stop the sponging or cool-cloth treatment for about 10 min-

utes. If the temperature again starts to rise, resume the sponging.

3. If the victim is conscious and can swallow, give him as much as he can drink of a saltwater solution (1 teaspoon of salt to 1 quart of water).

4. Later, cover according to the victim's comfort.

Hypothermia

Hypothermia is one of the major causes of death among outdoor people, and it will strike anyone who is not prepared to handle extreme weather conditions. Hypothermia is caused by exposure to high winds, rain, snow, or wet clothing. A person's normal core (inner body) temperature is 98.6°F. When the body begins to lose heat, early stages of hypothermia will be apparent. The person will start to shiver and stamp his feet.

If these early signs of hypothermia are ignored, the next stage of symptoms will be uncontrollable spells of shivering, fumbling hands, and drowsiness. If not treated quickly, hypothermia will likely kill its victim when the body temperature drops below 78°F and this can happen within 90 minutes after shivering begins.

If you're outdoors and detect any of these symptoms

Hypothermia's Effects on the Body

When extreme cold causes the body to lose its interior heat, these symptoms occur as your temperature drops:

99 to 96 degrees • Shivering becomes intense; ability to perform simple tasks is slowed

95 to 91 degrees • Skin tone pales; shivering turns violent and speech is impaired

90 to 86 degrees • Muscular rigidity replaces shivering; thinking is dulled considerably

85 to 81 degrees • Victim becomes irrational and may drift into a stupor; pulse is slow

80 to 78 degrees • Unconsciousness occurs; reflexes cease to function

Below 78 degrees • Condition may be irreversible; death is likely at this point

in yourself or a friend, start treatment immediately. First, get to shelter and warmth as soon as possible. If no shelter is available, build a fire. Get out of wet clothing and apply heat to the victim's head, neck, chest, and groin. Use chemical heat packs if you have them. If not, use body heat from another person. If you have a sleeping bag, the victim should be placed in it with another person.

As the victim begins to recover, give him warm liquids, chocolate, or any other high-sugar-content foods. Never give a hypothermia patient alcohol. It will only impair judgment, dilate blood vessels, and impair shivering (the body's way of producing heat).

If you're in a boat and capsize into cold water, don't take off your clothing; it will help trap heat. If you are wearing a life jacket, draw your knees up to your body, which will reduce heat loss. If there are several people in the water, huddle together so you can conserve heat. Survival in cold water depends on the water temperature. If the water temperature is 32.5°F, survival time may be under 15 minutes. If the water is more than 80°F, survival time is indefinite.

Preventing hypothermia is a lot easier than treating it. First, stay in shape and get a good night's sleep before going outdoors. Always carry candy, mixed nuts, or some other high-energy food. Stay as dry as possible and avoid getting overheated. Wet clothing will lose 90 percent of its insulating qualities and will rob the body of heat.

Stop and rest often, and, most important, dress properly. This means wearing several layers of clothing to form an insulating barrier against the cold. Carry rain gear and use it when the first drops fall. Wear a wool hat with some kind of ear protection. Several manufacturers now make wool knit caps with a Gore-Tex lining, which will keep your head and ears dry in a downpour. It's a fact that an uncovered head can lose up to 50 percent of the body's heat.

You should also carry a survival kit with a change of clothing, waterproof matches, and candy bars or other high-energy snacks.

Frostbite

Frostbite is the freezing of an area of the body, usually the nose, ears, cheeks, fingers, or toes.

Just before the actual onset of frostbite, the skin may appear slightly flushed. Then, as frostbite develops, the skin becomes white or grayish yellow. Blisters may develop later. In the early stages the victim may feel pain, which later subsides. The affected area feels intensely cold and numb, but the victim is often unaware of the problem until someone tells him or he notices the pale, glossy skin. First-aid treatment is as follows:

1. Enclose the frostbitten area with warm hands or warm cloth, using firm pressure. Do not rub with your hands or with snow. If the affected area is on the fingers or hands, have the victim put his hands into his armpits.

2. Cover the area with woolen cloth.

3. Get the victim indoors or into a warm shelter as soon as possible. Immerse the frostbitten area in warm—not hot—water. If that is not possible, wrap the area in warm blankets. Do not use hot-water bottles or heat lamps, and do not place the affected area near fire or a hot stove.

4. When the frostbitten part has been warmed, encourage the victim to move it.

5. Give the victim something warm to drink.

6. If the victim must travel, apply a sterile dressing that widely overlaps the affected area, and be sure that enough clothing covers the affected area to keep it warm.

7. Medical attention is usually necessary.

Snow Blindness

The symptoms of this winter malady include a burning or smarting sensation in the eyes, pain in the eyes or in the forehead, and extreme sensitivity to light. First-aid steps include the following:

1. Get the victim into a shelter of some kind, or at least out of the sun.

2. Apply cold compresses to the eyes.

3. Apply mild eye drops to the eyes. Mineral oil is a suitable substitute.

4. Have the victim wear dark glasses.

Sun and Eyes

If you're a fisherman or a boater, you are probably already aware of the punishing effects of the sun's glare on your eyes. In fact, the effect of glare on the surface of the water can be 25 times brighter than the light level indoors. For most activities, sunglasses should be able to absorb about 60 percent of the sun's rays. For fishing or boating, however, sunglasses should be darker, absorbing up to 95 percent of the sun's rays. Bausch & Lomb suggests this simple in-store test for lens darkness: Look in a mirror with the sunglasses on. If the lenses are dark enough, you will have some difficulty seeing your eyes. This test does not work for photochromic sunglasses because they would be at their light stage indoors. If you are a fisherman, you should select sunglasses with polarizing lenses, which are usually made by sandwiching polarizing film between layers of dark glass or plastic. They eliminate reflections on the surface of the water and allow fishermen to see beneath the surface. Sunglasses come in a variety of lens colors, but most eye-care professionals recommend green, gray, or brown for outside activities.

Effects of Sun Rays

Ultraviolet (UV) rays, hidden in the sun's rays, can be irritating and dangerous, causing both short- and long-term harmful effects on the eyes. Industry standards require that sunglasses designed for water sports should absorb up to 95 percent of UV rays. Make sure that the sunglasses you select are ones that afford UV protection.

Ultraviolet Rays

Visible Spectrum

Ultraviolet Rays

Lens

SPRAINS

Sprains are injuries to the soft tissues that surround joints. Ligaments, tendons, and blood vessels are stretched and sometimes torn. Ankles, wrists, fingers, and knees are the areas most often affected.

Symptoms include pain when the area is moved, swelling, and tenderness to the touch. Sometimes a large

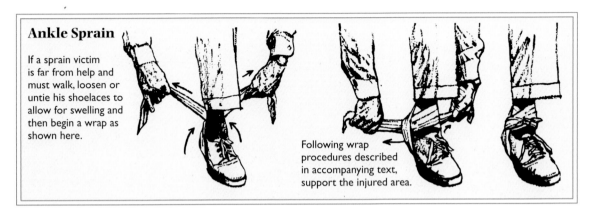

Ankle Sprain

If a sprain victim is far from help and must walk, loosen or untie his shoelaces to allow for swelling and then begin a wrap as shown here.

Following wrap procedures described in accompanying text, support the injured area.

area of skin becomes discolored because small blood vessels are ruptured.

It is often difficult to tell whether the injury is a sprain or a fracture. If in doubt, treat as a fracture. Otherwise, take the following steps:

1. Elevate the injured joint, using pillows or something similar. A sprained ankle should be raised about 12 inches higher than the torso. For a wrist or elbow sprain, put the arm into a sling.

2. Apply an ice pack or cold cloths to reduce swelling and pain. Continue the cold treatment for a half hour.

3. Always have a sprain X-rayed. There may indeed be a fracture or a bone chip.

If the victim of a sprained ankle is far from help and must walk, make the following preparations:

1. Untie the shoelaces to allow for swelling, but do not take off the shoe.

2. Place the middle of a long bandage (a folded triangular bandage is best) under the shoe just forward of the heel.

3. Bring the ends of the bandage up and back, crossing them above (at the back of) the heel.

4. Bring the ends forward around the ankle, and cross them over the instep.

5. Bring the ends downward toward the heel, and slip each end beneath the wrap that comes up from each side of the heel.

6. Bring the ends of the bandage all the way around the ankle again, pull on the ends to produce the desired tension, and then tie a square knot in front.

OTHER INJURIES

▨ Eyes Injuries or Foreign Body in Eye

For first-aid purposes, eye injuries fall into three categories: injury to eyelids and soft tissue above the eye, injury to the surface of the eyeball, or injury that extends into the tissue beneath the eyeball surface.

In Category 1, treatment involves putting on a sterile dressing and bandaging it in place. If the injury is in the form of a bruise (the familiar "black eye"), the immediate application of cold cloths or an ice pack should halt any bleeding and prevent some swelling. Later, apply warm, wet towels to reduce discoloration.

Injuries in Category 2 usually occur when a foreign body lodges on the surface of the eyeball. To remove the object, pull the upper eyelid down over the lower one, and hold it there for a moment, instructing the victim to look upward. Tears will flow naturally and may wash out the object.

If that doesn't work, put two fingers of your hand on the skin just below the victim's lower eyelid, and force the skin gently downward, thereby exposing the inner area of the lower lid. Inspect the area closely, and if the object is visible, lift it out carefully, using a corner of a clean handkerchief or a small wad of moistened sterile cotton wrapped around the end of a toothpick.

Foreign Body in Eye

▶ **Step 1** • Pull the upper eyelid down over the lower eyelid and hold it there, instructing the victim to look upward.

◀ **Step 2** • If Step 1 doesn't work, have the victim force the lower lid skin downward as shown and inspect for the foreign object. Remove the object as described in text.

◀ **Step 3** • Flush the eye with sterilized salt water as described in text.

If the foreign object can't be seen, it can sometimes be flushed out. Boil some water, add table salt (¼ teaspoon to an average glassful), and let the salt water cool to about body temperature. With the victim lying down, tilt his head toward the injured side, hold his eyelids open with your fingers, and pour the liquid into the inner corner of his eye so that it runs across the eyeball and drains on the opposite side.

Eye injuries in Category 3 are extremely serious. Never attempt to remove an object that has penetrated the eyeball, no matter how shallow. Apply a sterile compress or clean cloth, cover it with a loose bandage, and get the victim to a doctor at once.

Cuts, Abrasions, and Bruises

Minor mishaps frequently involve one of these three injuries. With abrasions (the rubbing or scraping off of skin) and small cuts, the emphasis should be on preventing infection.

Immediately clean the cut or abrasion and the surrounding area with soap and warm water. Don't breathe on the wound or let fingers or soiled cloth contact it.

If there is bleeding, put a sterile pad over the wound and hold it there firmly until the bleeding stops. Then apply an antiseptic, if available, and apply a fresh sterile pad, bandaging it in place loosely.

A bruise results when small blood vessels under the skin are broken, causing discoloration of the skin and swelling, which is often painful.

First aid may be unnecessary if the bruise is minor. If it is more severe, apply an ice pack or cold cloths to reduce the swelling and relieve the pain. Bruises on an extremity can be made less painful if the limb is elevated.

Puncture Wounds

A puncture wound results when a sharp object—knife, needle, branch end, or the like—penetrates the skin and the tissue underneath. The first-aider's primary objectives here, and with all other wounds, are to prevent infection and control bleeding.

Puncture wounds are often unusual in that they may be quite deep but the bleeding, because of the small opening in the skin, may be relatively light. The lighter the bleeding, generally, the lesser the chance that germs embedded by the penetrating object will be washed out. This means that the danger of infection is greater in puncture wounds than in other wounds. The danger of tetanus (lockjaw) infection is also greater in puncture wounds. First-aid procedures are as follows:

1. If the bleeding is limited, try to increase the flow by applying gentle pressure to the areas surrounding the wound. Do not squeeze hard, or you may cause further tissue damage.

2. Do not probe inside the wound. If a large splinter or a piece of glass or metal protrudes from it, try to remove it, but do so with extreme caution. If the sliver cannot be withdrawn with very gentle pressure, leave it where it is, or you may cause further damage and severe bleeding.

3. Wash the wound with soap and water.

4. Apply a sterile pad, and bandage it in place.

5. Get the victim to a doctor for treatment, including a tetanus shot if necessary.

Fishhook Removal

A doctor's care—and a tetanus shot, if needed—are recommended for anyone who has had a fishhook embed-

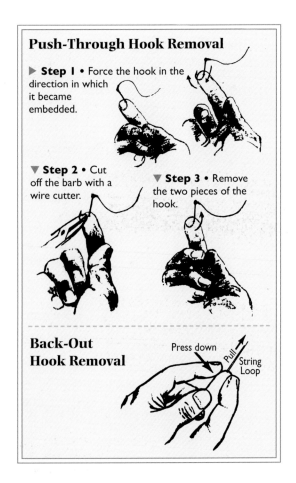

Push-Through Hook Removal

▶ **Step 1** • Force the hook in the direction in which it became embedded.

▼ **Step 2** • Cut off the barb with a wire cutter.

▼ **Step 3** • Remove the two pieces of the hook.

Back-Out Hook Removal

Press down

Pull

String Loop

sible. This can be quite painful, so the victim should anchor the affected part as solidly as possible before beginning the process. Using wire cutters or a similar tool, cut the hook in two at a point on the shank just before the bend. Remove the two pieces.

2. Have the victim anchor the affected part solidly. Take a 12- to 18-inch piece of strong string (30-pound-test fishing line is ideal), and run one end around the bend of the hook as if you were threading a needle. Bring the two ends together, and tie them in a sturdy knot. With the thumb and forefinger, push down (toward the affected part) on the shank of the hook at the point where the bend begins. This disengages the barb from the tissue. Maintaining that pressure, grasp the line firmly at the knotted end, and give a strong yank. The finger pressure on the shank should reduce flesh damage to a minimum as the barb comes out the same way it went in. Do not use this method if the hook is large.

If bleeding is minimal after either of these procedures, squeeze the wound gently to encourage blood flow, which has a cleansing effect. Put on a sterile dressing, and get medical help.

If the hook is a large one and is deeply embedded, or if it is in a critical area, do not try to remove it. Cover the wound, hook and all, with a sterile dressing, and get the victim to a doctor.

▓ Blisters and Foot Care

There was a time when you were told, "Never take brand-new boots on a hunting trip." That's no longer a hard-and-fast rule. Leather boots still require a break-in period, but composite boots that are synthetic do not require extensive breaking in.

Opinions vary, but most sportsmen prefer 8-inch-high boots for hunting, while 6-inch boots are the favorite for hiking.

Besides boots, there are other ways to protect your feet in the field. You should always wear two pairs of socks. The first pair to go on your feet should be lightweight, preferably polypropylene to wick away perspiration. The second should be heavyweight, to warm and cushion your feet. In addition to providing warmth, two pairs of socks rub against each other—not against your feet.

Finally, give your feet a break. On your next trip, occasionally take off your boots and socks and rest your feet on a log.

ded past the barb in the flesh. In many cases, however, medical help is not within easy reach. The severity of the injury and the size of the hook determine what action the first-aider should take.

If the hook has penetrated only up as far as the barb or slightly past it—and if it is not in a critical spot such as the eye—you should be able to pull or jerk it out. Then clean the wound, and treat it as you would any other superficial wound (see Cuts, Abrasions, and Bruises section for more information).

If the hook has penetrated well past the barb and is not in a critical area, there are two recommended methods of removal:

1. Force the hook in the direction in which it became embedded so that the point and barb exit through the skin. Try to make the angle of exit as shallow as pos-

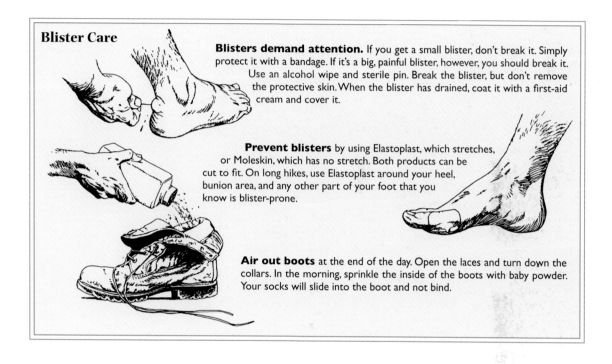

Blister Care

Blisters demand attention. If you get a small blister, don't break it. Simply protect it with a bandage. If it's a big, painful blister, however, you should break it. Use an alcohol wipe and sterile pin. Break the blister, but don't remove the protective skin. When the blister has drained, coat it with a first-aid cream and cover it.

Prevent blisters by using Elastoplast, which stretches, or Moleskin, which has no stretch. Both products can be cut to fit. On long hikes, use Elastoplast around your heel, bunion area, and any other part of your foot that you know is blister-prone.

Air out boots at the end of the day. Open the laces and turn down the collars. In the morning, sprinkle the inside of the boots with baby powder. Your socks will slide into the boot and not bind.

ILLNESS

▧ Appendicitis

The principle symptom is pain in the lower right part of the abdomen and sometimes over the entire abdominal region. Nausea and vomiting may be present, as may a mild fever. Constipation often occurs and is sometimes thought to be the cause of the victim's discomfort. Do not give a laxative if appendicitis is suspected—it will increase the danger that the appendix will rupture.

1. Have the patient lie down, and keep him comfortable.

2. Do not give him any food or water.

3. An ice pack placed over the appendix area may relieve pain. Do not apply heat to the appendix area.

4. Get medical help as soon as possible.

▧ Diarrhea

Diarrhea is a common malady among outdoorsmen. Its causes are often associated with change: during an extended fishing trip, for example, the sportsman's eating and drinking habits are often much different than what they are at home. Attacks of diarrhea usually subside once the body adapts to those changes.

Paregoric is helpful in combating diarrhea, as are many of the products designed for that purpose and sold in drugstores. If you or your companions are particularly prone to attacks of diarrhea, see a doctor and ask him to prescribe a drug, preferably in tablet form, that will combat the problem during trips afield.

▧ Toothache

First-aid procedures are as follows:

1. Inspect the sufferer's mouth under the strongest light available.

2. If no cavity is visible, place an ice pack or cold compress against the jaw on the painful side. If that doesn't provide relief, try a hot-water bottle or hot compress.

3. If a cavity can be seen, use a piece of sterile cotton wrapped on the end of a toothpick to clean the cavity as thoroughly as possible.

4. Oil of cloves, if available, can give relief. Pack it gently into the cavity with a toothpick. Do not let the oil touch the tongue or the inside of the mouth—the stuff burns.

How Not to Get Seasick

I haven't been seasick in the last 25 years or so. The night before a trip, I stay away from alcohol and get a good night's sleep. The following morning, I sip a cup of black coffee before I get on the boat. If I still feel good by 10:00 a.m., I'll start to eat . . . but never before. Will this simple formula work for you? To be quite honest, I don't know.

Finding a cure for seasickness is often a matter of trial and error. Everyone has a different approach. Some fishermen are convinced that a full stomach before a fishing trip is the best way to avoid seasickness, and that may work for some people. It doesn't work for me. I can, however, tell you what doesn't work for anyone—stay out late, overindulge, get on a boat tired and hungover, and I can guarantee that you will get sick in even a small chop.

In the simplest terms, seasickness is the inability of your body to adjust to motion. Your body has a built-in gyroscope to keep you on even keel, much the way a gyroscope keeps a rocket upright as it travels in space. This system works on solid ground, but on a rocking boat or a bumpy airplane, the mechanism sometimes fails and you get seasick.

This means, of course, that when you start feeling seasick, you should try to reduce movement as soon as possible. If you are on a boat, sit in the center and at the stern, where movement will be minimized. It also helps to keep your eye on a stationary object, such as a bridge or tower on the shoreline. You are trying to send a message to your brain that you are not really rocking and have no reason to be seasick. It sometimes works.

Fight the urge to go into the cabin. There is nothing stationary in a cabin; you have no fixed object, and you will likely get sicker. In fact, if you get seasick and head for the cabin, you will probably be there the rest of the day.

Over the years I've heard of dozens of concoctions to cure seasickness. Some may be effective for some people, but most wacky formulas don't work. A doctor once suggested cold stewed tomatoes and saltines, a formula that originated aboard an oil tanker. I suggested it to a friend and he still got sick. It could, however, work for you.

Fortunately, modern medicine has made great strides in helping people cope with an illness that will make you feel like you're dying. These seasickness drugs fall into two categories: antihistamines and scopolamine. These drugs are designed to inhibit the flow of nerve impulses from the vestibular system to the brain. Which drug will work for you? You may have to try them all until you find the one that works best for you.

Antivert and Bonine are nonprescription antihistamines that you take every 24 hours. They will make you drowsy. Marezine is another antihistamine, but it is taken every four to six hours.

Dramamine is the old standby. If the weather forecast calls for rough seas, I will take a Dramamine tablet the night before and another one hour before I get on a boat. It works for me. An antihistamine that is taken every four hours, Dramamine is a nonprescription drug and it will make you drowsy unless you get the "less drowsy" formula.

Transderm Scop is perhaps the most effective drug in fighting and preventing seasickness. It's a patch you put on the skin behind the ear that slowly releases scopolamine into your system for days. The side effects can sometimes be severe, however, and should be discussed with your doctor.

There's a lot you can do to protect yourself from getting seasick, but first, accept the fact that everyone will eventually get seasick. When someone brags that he doesn't get seasick, don't believe him. His time at the rail has not yet arrived! There is also no reason to be apologetic or embarrassed about getting seasick. Finally, never poke fun at someone who is seasick, especially a youngster. You may get paid back on your next trip!

FIRST-AID KIT

Improvisation is an ability that most outdoors people seem to develop naturally. But an improvised dressing for a wound, for example, is a poor second-best for a prepackaged, sterile dressing. Any first-aider can function more effectively if he has the proper equipment. A first-aid kit—whether it is bought in a pharmacy or is put together by the individual—should meet the following requirements:

- Its contents should be complete enough for the purposes for which it will be used.

- The contents should be arranged so that any component desired can be located quickly and without removing the other components.

- Each component should be wrapped so that any unused portion can be repacked and thereby prevented from leaking or becoming soiled.

- How and where the kit will be used are the main factors to consider when assembling a first-aid kit. The two kits described below should fill the needs of most outdoor situations.

■ POCKET KIT

Suitable for one-day, overnight, or short-term trips in areas not far from medical help.

- 1-by-1-inch packaged sterile bandages (2)
- 2-by-2-inch packaged sterile bandages (2)
- 2-by-2-inch packaged sterile gauze pads (2)
- Roll of adhesive tape
- Band-Aids (10)
- Ammonia inhalant (1)
- Tube of antiseptic cream
- Small tin of aspirin (or 12 aspirins wrapped in foil)

■ ALL-PURPOSE OUTDOORS FIRST-AID KIT

Suitable for general outings.

- 4-inch Ace bandages (2)
- 2-inch Ace bandages (2)*
- 2-by-2-inch sterile gauze pads (1 package)*
- 5-by-9-inch combine dressing (3)
- Triangular bandage (1)
- Sterile eye pads (2)
- ½-inch adhesive tape (5 yards)
- Assorted Band-Aids (1 package)*
- Betadine liquid antiseptic
- Yellow mercuric oxide ointment (for eyes)*

- Bacitracin (ointment)
- Tylenol (aspirin substitute)
- Dramamine (for motion sickness)
- Sunscreen
- Insect repellent
- Single-edge razor blade
- Tweezers (flat tip)
- Small scissors
- Eye patch
- Needle
- Matches in waterproof container
- Needle-nose pliers with cutting edge
- First-aid manual

Add these items if you are going into a remote area for an extended period of time:

- Tylenol with codeine (painkiller)**
- Tetracycline (antibiotic)**
- Lomotil, 2.5 milligrams (for cramps, diarrhea)**
- Antihistamine tablets
- Phillips Milk of Magnesia (antacid, laxative)

* Items, in fewer quantities, are recommended for a small first-aid kit for day trips. ** Requires a prescription.

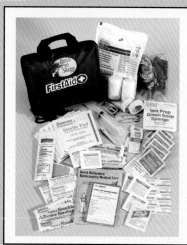

The Bass Pro Family First-Aid Kit is tailored specifically for outdoor activities and includes everything most families would need for a six-day trip. If you're not sure how to assemble a first-aid kit, a professionally packaged kit is a safe and sensible choice.

BOATING

Section Six
BOATING

• FISHING BOATS • BOATING ELECTRONICS •
• PREPARING FOR STORAGE AND LAUNCHING •
• BOAT KNOTS • BOATING SAFETY •
• HANDLING WIND, WEATHER, AND WATER •

HULL DESIGN

The shape of a boat's hull is the biggest factor in how it will do its job for you. Hull design has always been the most intriguing subject among people who know boats and keep up with new developments, for changes in hull lines—skillfully conceived—have brought about some dramatic developments in how boats perform.

There are really just two types—displacement and planing hulls—but boat hulls in common use today are far from simple. In some, characteristics of the two types have been combined in order to get the best of both. Also, a variety of specific shapes have been designed to do certain things well that another shape cannot do. And there remain several traditional hull shapes that have changed little in the midst of a marine-design revolution, continuing to do a modest job well, and often at minimum cost.

Displacement Hulls

Displacement hulls push through the water rather than planing on top of it, and therefore speed is limited. A round-bottomed, full-keeled displacement hull rides comfortably down in the water where wave and wind action have relatively little effect. The Indian canoe, the Viking ship, and the Great Banks fishing dory (a flat-bottomed boat) were all displacement-type hulls. They were narrow beamed and pointed at both ends—for excellent reasons. They could be moved through the water more easily with only oars or a sail for power; they could be maneuvered in either direction; following seas had much less effect on them than on a flat stern; and a pointed trailing end dissipated suction created by the water displacement. Today, there are squared-off sterns

to provide useful space for the motors and deck, but the displacement hull is probably tapered back from a wide point amidships.

The sea-kindliness of a displacement hull is due principally to its low center of gravity. It rises with the swells, and a surface chop has little effect. A full-displacement hull with round quarters is less affected by beam seas (waves rolling in from one side or the other), while its full keel gives a good bite in the water, helping you hold a course through winds and current. Because weight in a displacement hull is much less critical than in a planing hull, it can be sturdily, even heavily, built to take the worst punishment. Good examples of displacement hulls are present-day trawlers.

Small displacement hulls are excellent for passing rocky river rapids and surviving the worst chop on a lake. In large boats, cabin space is lower in the water, where it is more comfortable and feels more secure, especially on long cruises. On big water, you might be annoyed

The 38-foot Sabre Salon Express is a classic example of a seaworthy displacement hull. With a 13-foot beam, it is powered by a Volvo Penta pod propulsion drivetrain.

Boat Hulls

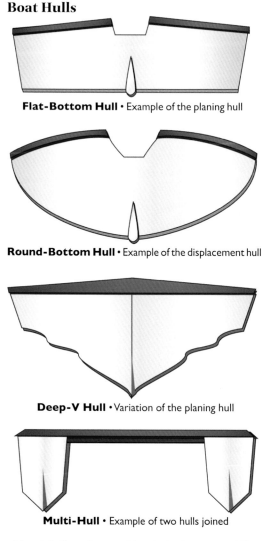

Flat-Bottom Hull · Example of the planing hull

Round-Bottom Hull · Example of the displacement hull

Deep-V Hull · Variation of the planing hull

Multi-Hull · Example of two hulls joined

A boat's hull may be one of four basic shapes: round, flat, V, or multi-hull. Some designs may also be a combination of these hull shapes and each shape has its advantages and disadvantages. For example, the flat hull has a shallow draft and is stable. It is good for fishing small waters, but a flat hull also means a rough ride, and it will pound in choppy water. A deep-V hull is stable and will not pound, but it may roll or bank in sharp turns. A round-bottom hull offers a slow but comfortable ride. Unfortunately, it has a tendency to roll. A multi-hull has great stability because of its beam, but needs more room to turn and maneuver.

at first by the constant roll, but the roll period is slower than the chop-chop surface banging of a planing hull on the same water and never as sharp. What's more, the displacement hull will keep you dry in wave action that would soak you continually in a planing hull.

Just how limited is a displacement hull's speed? There is an actual formula. The square root of the waterline length times 1.5 equals possible speed. For example, an 11-foot lake fishing boat might measure 9 feet at the waterline. Thus, the square root of 9 is 3, which is then multiplied by 1.5, and then you get 4.5. That boat's probable maximum speed is 4.5 miles per hour. Load it deeper so the waterline is extended and you increase the possible top speed slightly. But there's no point in loading it down with more power, for you won't increase the speed significantly above the formula figure. How narrow is the hull width? Designers work on ratios from 3.5:1 up to 5:1, length to width. To some, this describes a "tippy" boat, tender when you step in or lean over.

While a small displacement hull, such as a canoe, can dump you and then skitter away high and dry on top of the water while you try to grab it, a bigger displacement hull, say from 18 feet up, is as safe, even for novices, as anything in the water. And since speed is inherently limited, a small motor is in order. This makes for a safe, economical way to cruise or fish all day. You just move along at a modest, steady rate, dry and comfortable in big water (though not as comfortable in a small displacement-type boat on calm water, where tippiness is tiresome). You conserve your resources and enjoy the boat's natural action, and the boat is always under control. That's the portrait of boating with a displacement hull.

Modified displacement hulls and semi-planing hulls are made so that the after-third or more of the bottom is flattened. A flat bottom toward the stern rides higher as speed is applied, instead of digging in and pushing the bow up, as will happen in a full-displacement hull. The flat section aft also reduces the tendency to roll. These boats have wider transoms, and can use bigger motors and run faster. You'll find modified round-bottomed hulls in small aluminum fishing boats, as well as in offshore fishing boats, with a wide range of variations in design.

ROUND-BOTTOMED CARTOPPERS: Small aluminum fishing boats and fiberglass dinghies are often modified hulls that have round-bottom characteristics, yet they can move at high speed. You need a displacement hull for sitting on a choppy lake all day; nothing else will do. Using a motor of up to 25 horsepower, put the boat

Cruisers

Cruisers are generally more seaworthy and comfortable than runabouts. Size can range from 20 to more than 100 feet. Cruisers usually have overnight accommodations.

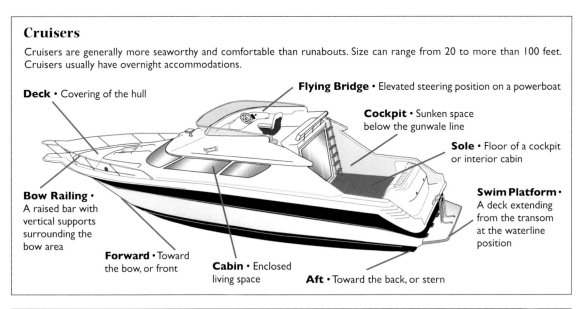

Deck • Covering of the hull

Flying Bridge • Elevated steering position on a powerboat

Cockpit • Sunken space below the gunwale line

Sole • Floor of a cockpit or interior cabin

Bow Railing • A raised bar with vertical supports surrounding the bow area

Swim Platform • A deck extending from the transom at the waterline position

Forward • Toward the bow, or front

Cabin • Enclosed living space

Aft • Toward the back, or stern

Runabouts

Most runabouts range in size from 16 to 25 feet and can be either outboard or inboard powered.

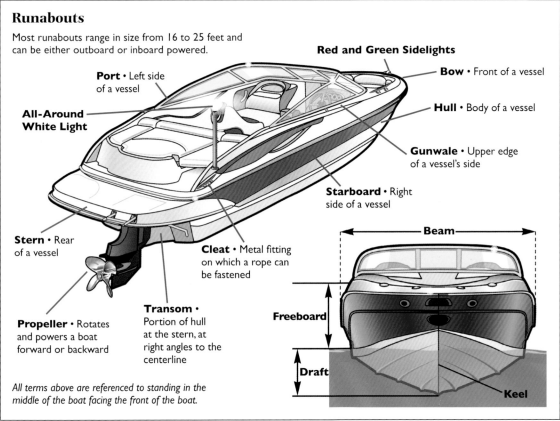

Red and Green Sidelights

Port • Left side of a vessel

Bow • Front of a vessel

All-Around White Light

Hull • Body of a vessel

Gunwale • Upper edge of a vessel's side

Starboard • Right side of a vessel

Stern • Rear of a vessel

Cleat • Metal fitting on which a rope can be fastened

Beam

Propeller • Rotates and powers a boat forward or backward

Transom • Portion of hull at the stern, at right angles to the centerline

Freeboard

Draft

Keel

All terms above are referenced to standing in the middle of the boat facing the front of the boat.

in the water and give it full speed. If the bow goes up and the stern digs in until you are depressed in a bowl the prop action makes in the water, reduce speed; it's a displacement hull, and your power is beyond the safe hull speed.

These boats have a rather full bow entry in relation to the beam, and there is a small keel. The middle and aft sections will be distinctly rounded, in contrast to the V-shaped cartop hull. If the sides taper toward the stern, you will find it better for rowing.

PUNT, PRAM, JOHNBOAT: Anyone can build and care for a flat-bottomed boat. This is the least complicated and least costly hull shape, and the amateur can build a large craft on simple lines at low cost. Flat-bottomed hulls pound more than others, but while newcomers dislike their clumsy appearance and strictly functional design, serious boaters continue to choose them for fishing on quiet waters, for they make an excellent platform.

The punt, pram, and johnboat are often indistinguishable except in name. What might be called a pram Down East and a punt on England's Thames River could be called a johnboat in Missouri. These square-ended, flat-bottomed hulls are the most stable and best load carriers of all little boats. They are rather heavy handling, and are designed for use in quiet water, where their low sides and flat bottoms come into their own.

The true punt is made to be poled. The sides are straight, and both ends are identical, rising flat at about 45 degrees. The bottom slopes up slightly toward the ends. The pram has bowed sides, tapering forward, and the bottom rises toward the bow. The bow end rises at a rather shallow angle, and the stern end is broader. The pram is usually rowed or sailed, but may be powered with a small outboard or electric motor.

The johnboat, the most popular with sportsmen, is made by a number of aluminum and fiberglass boat manufacturers. The hull figure has nearly as many variations within the basic plan as the number of regions in which it has been built and used. For instance, in marshy country, a coffin-shaped johnboat was built with a stern wide enough only for one person; it tapered toward a slight flare forward, then in again toward a narrow bow. Sometimes the bow was decked over to cover gear. The bottom sloped up from the flare both fore and aft, easing the push through vegetation and making it easy to maneuver in open water. This version continues to be a useful fishing boat in marshland and bayous.

Modern aluminum johnboats have riveted or welded hulls and range from 12 to 20 feet long. The bottom slopes up a bit forward from a low point directly in the midsection, and is rockered aft. The sides may be bowed somewhat forward and slope in toward the bottom. Three or four seats, with a wide bow seat, provide reinforcement in a broad-beamed hull that can carry a big load. Johnboats are rowed, poled, or powered.

Fiberglass johnboats are a better choice for saltwater fishermen. Saltwater corrosion will eventually take its toll on riveted aluminum hulls. Fiberglass johnboats can be molded in a variety of designs and are virtually maintenance free. Some manufacturers, such as Carolina Skiff, will custom design the interior, starting with the basic hull. These skiffs are also unsinkable and can be left in the water indefinitely with the scuppers open.

FLAT-BOTTOMED SKIFF: Put a pointed bow on a flat-bottomed shape and you have a hull that gives sharper entry to oncoming waves and reduces the tendency to pound that is characteristic of the square-ended johnboat or pram. It does, however, reduce stability.

For good rowing qualities, a skiff is built with a relatively narrow stern; the sides curve upward both fore and aft so that the tip of the bow and stern both clear the water slightly. The "active" bottom is the broad midsection. Such a boat is relatively easy to control and safe. For outboard power, the stern is built wider and lower. Flat-bottomed skiffs 12 to 16 feet long are common in all parts of the country. In shorter lengths, this hull is unstable, for the bow is too light.

THE DORY: This hull is fun to handle and is also very competent. You can take it through the surf or into fast, shallow rivers, for its two pointed ends and narrow bottom make it easy to row and control. Flaring, tall sides keep it dry inside, but this shape is somewhat tender, especially in small sizes. For use with an outboard, the design is modified by squaring off the stern. This presents a V-shaped transom, far from ideal for handling an outboard. Modern dory hulls have wider and lower sterns to improve handling with a motor. Mounting a small inboard engine amidships is the solution to powering the traditional double-end dory.

Planing Hulls

Planing hulls are built for speed. Given enough acceleration (called planing speed), the hull rises to the water's surface, levels off, and planes along the top. Design efficiency and possible power impose the only limits on its speed. The objective is to reduce wetted surface

Planing-Hull Designs

▲ The MAKO Pro Skiff is a 17-footer with an inverted-V hull. Rated for outboards up to 60 horsepower and with a weight capacity of 1,400 pounds, this is an ideal utility craft for sportsmen.

▲ The G3 Angler V172C is a typical side-console planing hull runabout. It's a 17-footer with a 92-inch beam and a 115-horsepower rating. The double-plated bow makes it a good choice for shoreline fishing.

▲ The Yellowfin 42, a 42-footer, is a good example of progress made in center consoles built to get offshore quickly with four 300-horsepower outboards totaling 1,200 horsepower.

▲ The G3 Eagle 166 SE is a 16½-foot rigged johnboat with a welded hull. Rated for a maximum of 60 horsepower, this model is ideal for most freshwater fishing. It comes with a 19-gallon livewell.

▲ The Viking 82 Convertible represents the ultimate in offshore fishing. The overall length is 87 feet and the beam measures 22 feet. With fuel options, it holds 6,750 gallons of fuel and 450 gallons of water. It is capable of bluewater big-game fishing all around the world.

▲ The MAKO 284 CC, a 28-footer with a 10-foot beam and deep-V hull, will handle nearly all offshore waters. This center console is rated for 600 horsepower with a fuel capacity of 228 gallons.

◀ Maverick's Mirage 18 HPX-V is a typical well-equipped flats boat. This 18-footer has a 150-horsepower rating, draws only 9 inches, and has both a poling tower and a bow casting platform.

(friction) and the weight of the bow wave that a nonplaning hull pushes before it. To achieve this, a lightweight hull is important, but weight is related to power. A planing hull can have a wider beam, with length-to-width ratios ranging from 2.5:1 to 3.5:1. A wider beam, especially in the aft section, makes more space for the power plant. In relation to power carried, the hull is lightweight.

On plane, this hull is more nimble in handling, since a substantial part of it is airborne and steering action is quicker. The wider beam and hard chines (where the bottom and sides meet) make for a more stable boat in calm water, though less so in a big roll.

But advantages in speed and handling bring penalties. A planing hull is more subject to wind and wave action—a surface chop can sometimes feel like a rock-strewn road at high speed. The lack of a useful keel on some planing hulls makes it hard to hold a course in heavy going. Aggravating these effects is the tendency of the bow to lift as more power is applied; the "active" hull on plane is aft, where the greatest weight is located in the broad beam and power plant. Power trimming the outboard engine may adjust the planing angle to level. Or, trim tabs may be added at the stern. These are metal power-operated tabs installed at the bottom of the hull at the transom that adjust the stern and bow up and down at planing speeds. Trim tabs are also used to adjust the boat's ride to compensate for passengers and gear that may be off center or when running in a rough sea to avoid spray and a wet ride. When a planing boat holds a horizontal angle at plane, it is easier to steer, gives a drier ride, and rides better.

But it goes without saying that much boating is on quiet water, where the planing hull has few if any serious problems. In any case, not many planing hulls now made are the pure type—flat bottoms or simple Vs. Manufacturers have adapted planing advantages to practical conditions, and come up with combinations that are safe, fast, comfortable, and still easy to handle.

CABIN DORY: This is one flat-bottomed boat that is still being made in sizes of 20 feet or more. The explanation is that the dory hull's sloping sides and narrow bottom give it some of the features of a deep-V hull in handling rough water. On the Gulf and the northwestern and northeastern coasts, you will see cabin boats with dory hulls made locally that have high bows running back to a flat, low stern, which is also wider than the stern of a displacement dory hull. The wide, flat section of the bottom aft makes this a planing hull. But even at low speed, it draws less water than a V-shaped hull and can be run in rough surf and shoal water where no other boats of this size would be safe.

V-BOTTOMED SKIFF: The first design aimed to combine planing ability with the kinder qualities of the displacement hull was the simple V bottom, with flat planes rising from the keel to hard chines. V-bottomed skiffs under 20 feet have slightly rounded chines to improve turning and reduce the slap of beam waves; the bottom aft is flattened; and the bow is deeper, with a sharp forefoot section. This makes a hull that is comfortable for all-day use on big lakes and bays, and can still plane off for a fast trip there and back. The bow deck line often has a wide flare overhanging the fine pointed bow. As the bow cuts the waves, the flare casts the spray aside, keeping passengers dry in moderate waves.

V-BOTTOMED CARTOPPER: Most cartop boats have planing hulls. To be light enough to qualify as a cartop boat, construction must be so light that you can lift it to a rack on top of a car. A planing hull is the logical type. Cartoppers that plane are usually modified-V hulls, though they may look round bottomed at a glance. The bow is sharp, molding to a flat aft bottom with rounded chines and a broad stern. If the shape tapers back to a narrower stern for easy rowing, you'll pay for it in reduced planing ability. Depending on the physical strength of the fisherman, 100 pounds seems to be the upper limit for a manageable cartop boat. There are racks designed for one-man loading and unloading.

DEEP-V BOTTOM AND CENTER CONSOLES: From a performance standpoint—when big demands are put on a hull—the best combination of displacement- and planing-hull traits is the deep V. Invented by designer Ray Hunt, the deep-V bottom extends from a slightly rounded forefoot all the way to the stern. The V shape at the stern works well with single or multiple outboards.

In a well-designed deep-V hull, the rounded, deep forefoot and full keel enable it to perform well in big waters, rising with the seas and rounding off a chop even at high speed. But how does such a hull rise on plane? With the help of longitudinal strakes, or steps in the bottom. As power is poured on, the strakes help the hull step up onto plane, while the V shape and flared bow part the wave tops and keep you reasonably dry. World ocean-racing records have been broken again and again with deep-V hulls.

Tough seagoing center-console boats ranging up to 42 feet with multiple outboard motors have created a brand-new category of offshore boats. It is not unusual to see these tough offshore boats with three and even four 300-horsepower outboard engines totaling up to 1,200 horsepower mounted on their transoms. In some respects, this breed of boat is safer than the big inboard-powered sportfisherman. It can run faster with less horsepower to offshore grounds on less fuel and get back to port more quickly in case of bad weather. It is exceptionally seaworthy in all but extremely rough and dangerous waters. These center consoles are also excellent fishing machines, giving fishermen 360 degrees of space to fight big fish. Smaller center consoles, say up to 26 feet, are trailerable with 8-foot beams. Bigger models, up to 42 feet, feature beams of nearly 12 feet, creating huge cockpit space for fishermen, tackle, and gear. Added advantages are that the engines can be replaced and there are no smelly and oily bilges to worry about. If an outboard-powered boat runs aground or hits underwater debris, it is less likely to incur serious damage, whereas an inboard risks damaging rudders and shafts.

FLATS AND BAY BOATS: There was a time when flats boats were made by a handful of local builders. The boats weren't big and the hulls weren't very user-friendly in rough water. Those early boats just didn't perform well north of the bonefish flats. A lot has happened since those early years, and constantly evolving flats-boat designs have now migrated north and west of the Florida flats.

What is a flats boat? Essentially, it's a boat designed for shallow-water fishing, usually for bonefish, permit, and tarpon. It also has low freeboard, which means the wind won't blow it around and the low profile won't spook fish. A flats boat has a wide beam, which makes it exceptionally stable for two standing fishermen. The casting decks are flat fore and aft. The decks are also uncluttered, as gear is stored out of sight in hatches. Boat cleats and hardware are minimal to avoid line snagging. A poling platform is usually mounted over the outboard engine. Before the time of poling platforms at the stern, guides poled their boats from the bow, which proved a tiring task.

Flats boats are also fast. Some 18-footers are rated for outboards up to 150 horsepower. Flats boats can run at speeds of 50 miles per hour or more and maneuver like sport cars. Typical sizes range from 16 to 18 feet.

Take a close look at a flats boat and its special features, and you'll suddenly realize that it could also make an acceptable bass boat. But a flats boat is perfectly designed for saltwater anglers stalking tidal flats, rivers, and barrier islands for striped bass, bluefish, weakfish, bonefish, and tarpon.

Bay boats are designed for fishermen who prefer to fish inshore waters, including bays, rivers, and sounds. Most bay boats are built to handle bigger waters than a flats boat. Bay boats are also bigger, ranging up to 25 feet with 8½-foot beams, and are powered with outboards up to 250 horsepower. Even the bigger models will have a draft of only 11 inches. On good weather days, some bay boats can also handle inshore waters. Typical bay boats are center consoles, though dual-console designs are becoming more popular and practical as family boats.

SEA SKIFF: This boat is often described as round bottomed, but in fact it is usually a combination of a V-hull and displacement-hull design. Forward, a rounded bilge helps it rise with waves and pound less in a chop. The bottom, with rounded chines, slants to a shallow V to form a keel, and flattens aft. The Jersey sea skiff, a remarkably practical and able hull for fishing in bigger waters, will taper to a narrower stern than many planing hulls. This raises the planing speed, but makes it a safer boat for getting home and running inlets when following seas may present the most trouble. Sea skiffs are usually planked with lapstrake. The strakes help lift the hull to reach plane when power is applied, and reduce roll in big water. But this also increases the total wetted surface or drag on the hull. Wood lapstrake hulls have great pliability and shock resistance, which admirably suits fishing the coasts. Today, nearly all wood skiffs of this design are custom built.

Multiple Hulls

You've heard them called tri-hulls, cathedral, trihedral, gullwing, and more. The basic principle is the catamaran, adding stability to a hull by means of a secondary hull. In the catamaran, the secondary hull is called an outrigger. A trimaran has two outriggers—one on each side of the load-bearing hull.

This idea, applied to modern fiberglass and aluminum boat design, has just about taken over boat manufacturing in the 15- to 35-foot class. First, it has brought unbelievable stability to small boats, even in rough water. Second, it has made the entire deck usable; you can fight a big fish standing on the gunwale or bow of such a boat without rocking it dangerously. The deck area is actually increased up to 100 percent, since a much wider beam in the same length is possible, with a bowline topside that is more square than pointed. This makes a boat that is useful all over. For families and fishermen who tend to concentrate on matters other

Multiple-Hull Designs

▲ The G3 LX 22, a 22-foot pontoon boat with a beam of 8½ feet, has a horsepower range from 40 to 115. Pontoon boats are a good choice for a variety of water sports. Under most water conditions, they are stable, safe, and easy to operate.

▲ The Boston Whaler 19-foot Montauk is a good example of a multiple-hull design. This popular unsinkable Montauk design is also available in 15-, 17-, and 21-foot models. With a 96-inch beam and a 115-horsepower outboard, this Montauk is a good choice for lakes, bays, and inshore waters.

▲ The World Cat 330TE is a 34-foot center-console catamaran built for offshore waters. A 10½-foot beam makes it a stable fishing platform. This World Cat is rated for twin 300-horsepower outboards. The twin-hull design affords stability and handles rough water very well.

than boat handling when the fun and action warms up, it has great value.

You can see why the multiple-hull design has brought about a revolution in small boats. Naturally, the hulls are unified—built in a single structure—while the Polynesian and East Indian catamaran and trimaran boats had hulls joined with wood poles bound at each hull. Between keel points are sculptured hollow spaces, where air is trapped when the boat is on plane, making a cushion against the chop and providing a lifting effect. In a tri-hull design, the middle hull is deepest (often with a deep-V bow and forefoot line), and the side hulls are minor points interrupting the rise of the V toward the waterline, sometimes acting as deep chines.

This hull is slower to plane than the other V hulls, for the multiple points tend to push a bow wave ahead of the boat until planing speed is reached. Also, the wetted area is greater, holding the hull off plane until considerable power pushes it up. It's also a heavy hull compared to others of the same length. Obviously, it takes more gas to operate. You have to reckon the greatly increased useful deck area and stability against these drawbacks.

A second revolution that has become as big as the multiple-hull takeover is the continuous boom in bass boats with multiple-hull characteristics. These bass boats, made of fiberglass, aluminum, or Kevlar, are mostly 14- to 20-foot boats with two- or three-point molded hulls. The difference is that the beam is narrow, requiring less power and making them practical in weedy waters and in the brush-filled shorelines of reservoir lakes. This hull is potentially very fast, but that's hardly the purpose in a bass boat.

■ Canoes and Kayaks

A fisherman who has never used a canoe or kayak to reach backwater havens is missing a rare wilderness experience. These silent boats can take you deep into remote areas that are hardly ever reached by most people.

Most canoes in the 16- to 17-foot range will work fine. Aluminum canoes are noisy, but they are also tough. Some space-age canoes made of Kevlar or Royalex ABS material are so tough that they can take as much abuse as aluminum.

For most canoe fishing, pick out a 17-footer. It will weigh 60 to 80 pounds and hold roughly 1,000 pounds of gear and people. Don't plan on putting more than two passengers in a canoe this size.

If you're new to canoeing, pick a model with a keel, which will make it easier to paddle in a straight line for

The Ocean Kayak Hands-Free model is motorized with a Minn Kota 36-pound thrust electric motor. It measures 14 feet and weighs 86 pounds with the motor.

long distances. White-water models that have no keel (or a very shallow keel) are designed for fast maneuverability and not suitable for cruising. A good cruising canoe should have a beam of at least 36 inches and a center depth of 12 to 14 inches. The beam should be carried well into the bow and stern, so it can carry the maximum amount of gear and food.

Wood canoe paddles may look pretty, but you're better off with tough resilient fiberglass paddles. If you insist on wood, always carry a spare. For both the bow and stern paddler, pick a paddle that reaches between your chin and eyes.

The kayak is a direct descendant of the seagoing kayaks of the Eskimos of the Far North. The basic kayak is a slender, closed-decked craft with a body-fitting cockpit and a waterproof skirt that seals the hatch around the paddler, who feels that he is "wearing the boat."

A two-bladed paddle propels the boat and a small rudder at the stern assists in steering, making the kayak track straight, or holding the craft in position. The kayak is light, fast, and easy to handle in nearly all types of water.

Various models are designed for touring, fishing, white-water, and sea kayaking. White-water kayaks are nearly always single-cockpit crafts designed for high maneuverability and minimal effort in paddling upriver or downriver. White-water models are usually 13 to 15 feet long with beams of 23 inches or so. Skilled paddlers

can run white water forward, backward, or even broadside in a kayak.

Touring kayaks, sometimes called expedition kayaks, are designed to carry one or two paddlers and range from 16 to 18 feet. Sea kayaks are bigger crafts with exceptional load capacities, as much as 900 pounds, and range from 18 to 22 feet in length with 30-inch beams. Some sea kayaks can accommodate three paddlers, and several manufacturers build collapsible and inflatable kayaks for ease of storage for traveling kayakers. Some inflatables feature multi-chambered bodies and aluminum-frame reinforcements. One touring model for two paddlers measures 12 feet with a beam of 34 inches. It weighs only 37 pounds and has a capacity of 350 pounds. It will store into a package that measures 35 by 19 by 7 inches.

PADDLING A KAYAK: If you have a paddled a canoe, paddling a kayak may come easier to you. The first mistake beginning kayakers make is that they spread their hands either too far apart or too close together. Either hand position will tire you out quickly. Gripping the double-paddled paddle, your hands should be no wider than your shoulders. Never grip the paddle tightly. Keep your hands a bit loose and your fingers slightly separated. Your knuckles should be pointing upward.

Basically, there are only four strokes you will have to learn: forward stroke, sweep stroke to turn, draw stroke

Canoes and Kayaks

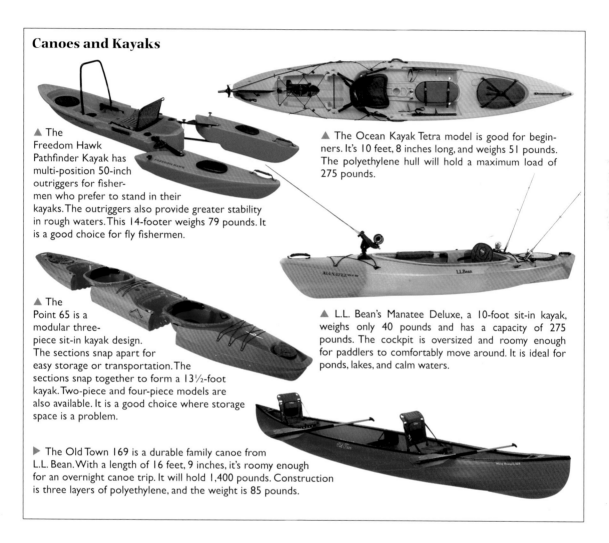

▲ The Freedom Hawk Pathfinder Kayak has multi-position 50-inch outriggers for fishermen who prefer to stand in their kayaks. The outriggers also provide greater stability in rough waters. This 14-footer weighs 79 pounds. It is a good choice for fly fishermen.

▲ The Ocean Kayak Tetra model is good for beginners. It's 10 feet, 8 inches long, and weighs 51 pounds. The polyethylene hull will hold a maximum load of 275 pounds.

▲ The Point 65 is a modular three-piece sit-in kayak design. The sections snap apart for easy storage or transportation. The sections snap together to form a 13½-foot kayak. Two-piece and four-piece models are also available. It is a good choice where storage space is a problem.

▲ L.L. Bean's Manatee Deluxe, a 10-foot sit-in kayak, weighs only 40 pounds and has a capacity of 275 pounds. The cockpit is oversized and roomy enough for paddlers to comfortably move around. It is ideal for ponds, lakes, and calm waters.

▶ The Old Town 169 is a durable family canoe from L.L. Bean. With a length of 16 feet, 9 inches, it's roomy enough for an overnight canoe trip. It will hold 1,400 pounds. Construction is three layers of polyethylene, and the weight is 85 pounds.

to move the kayak sideways, and reverse stroke to stop or move the kayak backward.

The forward stroke is simple. Put your paddle in the water to one side of the kayak and draw it past you, and then repeat the stroke on the other side of the kayak. The sweep stroke will turn your kayak. Put the paddle near your feet and sweep the blade in a wide arc toward the stern, turning the kayak. The draw stroke will move the kayak sideways. Place the paddle about 2 or 3 feet from you, depending on your reach, and draw it toward you, moving your kayak sideways. The reverse stroke simply means you paddle backward, which will slow down or stop your kayak. These basic strokes sound simple, but it will take practice to do them all comfortably.

FISHING KAYAKS: Almost any kayak can be used for fishing, but beginning around 2010, kayaks designed specifically for fishing literally stormed the outdoor market. Today, kayaks are used to fish all waters, from farm ponds to offshore waters for billfish. Kayaks can now take anglers into remote backwaters of fresh and salt water that were previously inaccessible.

There are at least a dozen kayak manufacturers producing models suitable for fishermen. First, a fisherman must decide whether he wants a sit-in or a sit-on model. Sit-in kayaks have a cockpit in which you sit, which is the traditional kayak design. Sit-on models have no cockpit, but are molded with exposed seat arrangements on top of the kayak, a design most fishermen seem to prefer. The

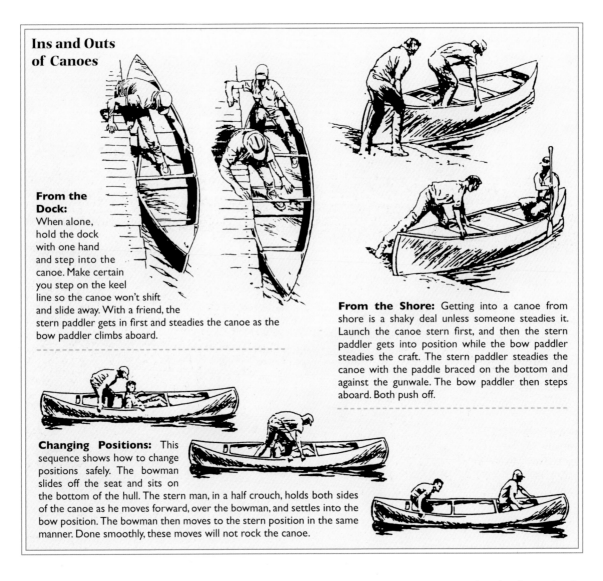

Ins and Outs of Canoes

From the Dock: When alone, hold the dock with one hand and step into the canoe. Make certain you step on the keel line so the canoe won't shift and slide away. With a friend, the stern paddler gets in first and steadies the canoe as the bow paddler climbs aboard.

From the Shore: Getting into a canoe from shore is a shaky deal unless someone steadies it. Launch the canoe stern first, and then the stern paddler gets into position while the bow paddler steadies the craft. The stern paddler steadies the canoe with the paddle braced on the bottom and against the gunwale. The bow paddler then steps aboard. Both push off.

Changing Positions: This sequence shows how to change positions safely. The bowman slides off the seat and sits on the bottom of the hull. The stern man, in a half crouch, holds both sides of the canoe as he moves forward, over the bowman, and settles into the bow position. The bowman then moves to the stern position in the same manner. Done smoothly, these moves will not rock the canoe.

sit-in models may be drier and warmer in some waters and allow you to keep more gear covered and dry, but the sit-on kayaks are easier to get on and off, an important factor for fishermen who also like to wade.

There are additional advantages to sit-on models. Some newcomers to kayaking harbor a fear of capsizing and getting trapped upside down underwater. If you capsize with a sit-on kayak, you simply roll the kayak over and climb back on. Sit-on kayaks are also more comfortable if you are big with long legs. Most sit-on models have watertight hatches, which make them a good choice for divers and photographers. Sit-on kayaks also tend to be more stable than the traditional sit-in models.

Good fishing kayaks should measure 12 to 14 feet with a beam of about 30 inches and weigh 60 to 80 pounds. Stability in a fishing kayak is a key factor. Those long, slender kayaks may be faster, but short, beamier models will be more stable and a better choice for fishing. For extra stability, some models offer removable outriggers.

INS AND OUTS OF CANOES: The cardinal rule for fisher-

Unswamping a Canoe

◄ **Step 1** • The man overboard holds on to your canoe and steadies it as you roll the swamped canoe and simultaneously lift one end onto your gunwale.

▼ **Step 2** • Work the canoe so it's entirely out of the water, resting upside down across the gunwales of your canoe. Allow the water to drain out.

▼ **Step 3** • Making certain the canoe is balanced across your gunwales, roll it over slowly. The swamping victim should still be in the water, steadying your canoe.

► **Step 4** • Slide the empty canoe back into the water. Now it's ready to go. Steady the craft against your canoe, allowing the person in the water to pull himself aboard.

men who use canoes is don't stand! Learn to cast, fight fish, and haul an anchor from a sitting position. Standing is one of the most common causes of people falling out of, or capsizing, canoes. Rule No. 2 is never swim away from your canoe if you get dumped. Most canoes have enough flotation to keep afloat until help arrives. Never be afraid of your canoe. I did some testing several years ago and I was amazed at how difficult it was to intentionally capsize or tip a canoe over from a sitting position. Getting in and out of a canoe, however, can be tricky unless you follow some basic procedures (see accompanying illustrations).

UNSWAMPING A CANOE: As mentioned, the most important rule in canoeing is don't stand! Standing is the most common cause of people falling out of canoes, but the rule is often violated by sportsmen who are casting, fighting fish, or hauling an anchor. Equally important, if your canoe swamps, is to never leave it to try to swim toward shore. Most modern canoes will keep you afloat, even when full of water. In fact, you can sometimes paddle a swamped canoe to shore with only your hands.

If another canoe swamps, you can use your canoe as a rescue craft to get the swamped canoe back into service without having to beach it (see accompanying illustrations).

▧ Paddleboarding

Fishermen who are interested in kayaks and canoes are also likely to be interested in paddleboarding, and this is especially true for shallow-water anglers. Paddleboarding is a water sport dating back to 1926, when some boards were made of redwood. The big comeback of paddleboarding started around 1996 and this water sport is still growing. Paddleboarders can lie down or kneel on a paddleboard, but standing has become the new norm. Most manufacturers recommend paddleboards that are 10 to 12 feet long with a fixed rudder and a weight capacity of about 250 pounds. The boards, which look like surfboards, are usually constructed of a polyethylene outer shell over a watertight polyurethane inner core. Paddles should be 8 to 10 inches taller than the paddler. Some paddles have an angle built in for better efficiency.

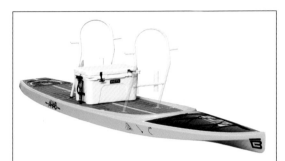

BOTE's 14-foot Ahab is a paddleboard rigged for fishing with rod holders, a cooler, and two holes for push-pole anchoring. The Ahab has a load capacity of 500 pounds.

Backcountry anglers will find paddleboards can reach some waters that might be inaccessible to all other boats, including kayaks. Paddleboards also have the added advantage of allowing anglers to stand to cast, which may be difficult in some kayaks.

Most paddleboards are designed for use in calm or light surf conditions. As a beginner, you should start out by kneeling on the paddleboard first. When you feel comfortable with the balance and stability, place your hands on the sides of the paddleboard and try to stand up, placing your feet where your knees were. Falling is part of the learning process. If you fall, aim for the water on either side of the paddleboard. Never fall on the board, which could cause injury.

It didn't take long for fishermen, especially shallow-water anglers, to recognize the potential of paddleboards. With a paddleboard, anglers can reach waters that even kayaks and canoes have trouble navigating. Or maybe it's the simplicity of fishing from a paddleboard that attracts anglers. Several paddleboard manufacturers have also recognized the potential of a fishing paddleboard. BOTE offers the Ahab Classic, which is specially designed for fishermen. The Ahab is a 14-footer with a 34-inch beam. The construction is of EPS foam core with a fiberglass skin. Weighing 45 pounds, it has a maximum weight capacity of 500 pounds. This fish-

ing paddleboard has a large, flat deck and is fitted with rod holders, a cooler, and two through holes for stakeout push poles.

The designers of the Ahab have obviously focused on shallow-water fishermen, particularly anglers who fish backcountry flats for bonefish, permit, trout, and similar species that inhabit the shallow waters of the southern states. During spring and summer in the northern states, fishermen may find paddleboarding an exciting way to fish back-bay waters and tidal flats for striped bass, flounder, weakfish, bluefish, and similar species. For freshwater anglers, a light and easily transported paddleboard allows easy access to small ponds and lakes for bass, trout, crappies, and panfish.

The BIC ACE-TEC Stand-Up Paddleboard is 11 feet, 6 inches long, and will support paddlers up to 260 pounds. The construction is multiple layers of styrene polymer and fiberglass with a foam core. It's designed for ponds, lakes, bays, and calm ocean waters.

The Pelican Surge Stand-Up Paddleboard is 10 feet, 4 inches long, and weighs 33 pounds. It's made of a polyethylene outer shell over a polyurethane inner core. The EVA deck is skidproof. A removable fiberglass fin helps tracking.

Sailboats

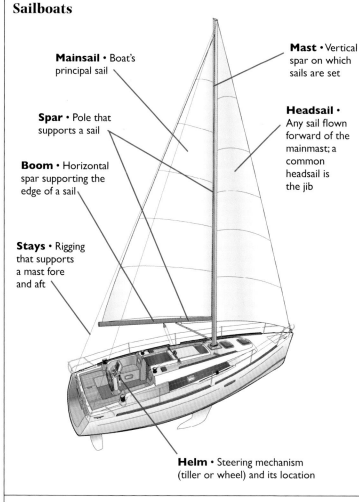

Mast · Vertical spar on which sails are set

Mainsail · Boat's principal sail

Headsail · Any sail flown forward of the mainmast; a common headsail is the jib

Spar · Pole that supports a sail

Boom · Horizontal spar supporting the edge of a sail

Stays · Rigging that supports a mast fore and aft

Helm · Steering mechanism (tiller or wheel) and its location

Wind is the oldest form of power for boats. There are many types and sizes of sailboats, but most of the components are the same. Regardless of size, all sailboats use a rudder to steer and wind for power. Here are the parts and types of popular sailboats.

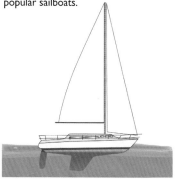

Sloop · A single-masted sailboat with the mast less than 40 percent of the boat length aft of the bow with a mainsail and normally one headsail

Cutter · A single-masted sailboat with a mainsail and usually two headsails, with the mast closer to amidships than for a sloop

Catboat · A sailboat with a mast near the bow, and no headsail

Yawl · A two-masted sailboat with the rear mast aft of the rudderpost

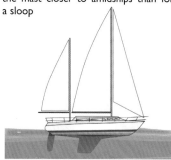

Ketch · A two-masted sailboat with the after mast forward of the rudderpost

MARINE MOTORS

Naturally, your choice of power should be matched to the boat you select. Don't feel limited, however, to what you see already mounted. The great variety of motor designs and horsepower ratings available, and the versatility of these motors, give you options that boaters have never had before. You can customize your boat-motor rig precisely to your own preferences—if you inform yourself before you buy.

An offshore fishing boat up to 40 feet and longer, for instance, doesn't have to be powered by inboard engines. It's common now to see unusually seaworthy deep-V hulls in the 25- to 42-foot range heading offshore with two, three, or four outboard engines totaling up to 1,200 horsepower.

Similarly, a 14-foot bass boat doesn't necessarily "take" a 10-horsepower trolling motor; depending on the boat's power rating, you can mount a much bigger outboard for covering distance, plus a small electric trolling motor. And for that matter, you don't have to paddle your own canoe; a 2-horsepower gas or electric motor will do it for you handsomely.

The motor to buy is the one that you particularly want and that is safe and sensible for your use. Power your boat adequately, but take care not to overpower it. Check the Boating Industry Association (BIA) plate and the maker's specs for the recommended and maximum power rating for that boat.

▮ Outboard

The outboard is a self-contained power unit that, happily, does not require through-hull fittings. It is lightweight in relation to the horsepower produced and it can be installed or removed quickly and inexpensively.

Mounted outside the boat, its fuel and vapor can be kept safely out of bilges and the cabin; deck space is clear of engine boxes or hatches. You have positive steering with outboard power—the whole motor turns, and the propeller thrust is in the direction that will help turn the boat, instead of at an angle to a rudder. The outboard tilts up for shallow running, beaching, or trailering. There are no underhull fittings that have to be protected at all costs.

A large outboard presents something of an obstacle to fishing lines, and the propeller, out from the hull, can be a hazard to divers and skiers. Mounted on the transom, the outboard is an unbalanced weight that is

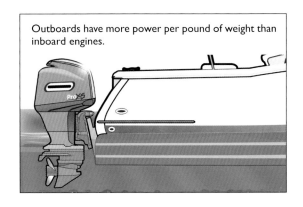

Outboards have more power per pound of weight than inboard engines.

trimmed by adjusting the position of its thrust relative to the plane on which the boat is moving—but it can be trimmed, whereas an inboard-powered boat must have its load trimmed instead.

Trim is easy to understand if boaters remember that at normal running speeds the outboard propeller shaft should be parallel to the surface. Some boats, however, obtain optimum planing attitude with the motor trimmed out slightly past this point. When trimmed out too far, the boat will not operate efficiently. The bow may plane too high or too low.

Boaters should have their outboards "tucked" under (trimmed in) when starting. This forces the bow down and the stern up, and the boat pops up on plane much quicker. As the engine is trimmed out, the bow rises and more of the boat clears the surface. With reduced drag (less friction between the boat and water), the boat gains speed. Once on plane at wide-open throttle, the outboard should be running in the middle of the recommended revolutions-per-minute range.

On bigger outboards, the power trim control button is on the end of the throttle control. With one finger, the boater can trim the engine for the best performance. The operator can easily adjust the engine for optimum boat attitude as boat load or water conditions change. Power trim improves acceleration and helps get a boat on plane quicker. It also means top-end speed advantages.

Outboard manufacturers now produce four-stroke engines up to 350 horsepower. Surprisingly enough, these big outboards with V6 engines are more fuel efficient per horsepower than smaller motors. A 250-horsepower outboard, for example, burns less gas at cruising speed than twin 150s. Some manufacturers used to

Outboard Motors

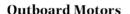

▶ The Mercury Verado 250 horsepower is a six-cylinder, four-stroke outboard engine. Mercury's Verado series ranges from 150 to 300 horsepower. The 150-, 175-, and 200-horsepower motors have four cylinders.

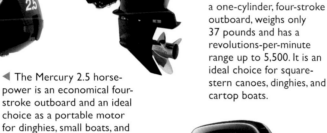

◀ The Mercury 2.5 horsepower is an economical four-stroke outboard and an ideal choice as a portable motor for dinghies, small boats, and inflatables.

▶ The Yamaha F2.5, a one-cylinder, four-stroke outboard, weighs only 37 pounds and has a revolutions-per-minute range up to 5,500. It is an ideal choice for square-stern canoes, dinghies, and cartop boats.

▶ The Suzuki 9.9 horsepower is a two-cylinder, four-stroke outboard with an electric starting system. The weight is 95 pounds with a short shaft and 100 pounds with a long shaft. It is a good portable outboard for waters with horsepower limitations.

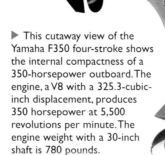

◀ The Suzuki 300-horsepower four-stroke outboard is a V6 engine with electronic fuel injection. This model weighs 615 pounds. With V6 power, Suzuki also offers 200-, 225-, and 250-horsepower engines.

▶ This cutaway view of the Yamaha F350 four-stroke shows the internal compactness of a 350-horsepower outboard. The engine, a V8 with a 325.3-cubic-inch displacement, produces 350 horsepower at 5,500 revolutions per minute. The engine weight with a 30-inch shaft is 780 pounds.

Trimming In (Down)
- Lowers the bow
- Results in quicker planing, especially with a heavy load
- Improves the ride in choppy water
- Increases steering torque or pull to the right

Neutral Trimming
- Levels the bow
- Normally results in greater efficiency

Note that the propeller shaft, which connects the propeller to the drive shaft, is parallel to the surface of the water.

Trimming Out
- Lifts the bow
- Increases top speed
- Increases clearance in shallow waters
- Increases steering torque or pull to the left
- In excess, causes the boat to bounce

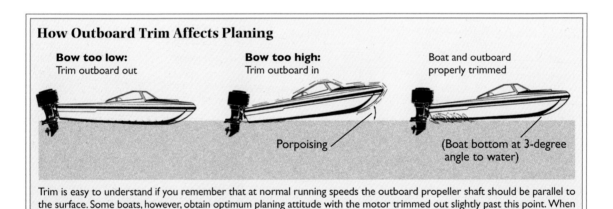

How Outboard Trim Affects Planing

Bow too low:
Trim outboard out

Bow too high:
Trim outboard in

Boat and outboard properly trimmed

Porpoising

(Boat bottom at 3-degree angle to water)

Trim is easy to understand if you remember that at normal running speeds the outboard propeller shaft should be parallel to the surface. Some boats, however, obtain optimum planing attitude with the motor trimmed out slightly past this point. When trimmed out too far, the boat will not operate efficiently.

produce special outboard engines for saltwater use. Today, however, nearly all outboard motor manufacturers build engines up to 350 horsepower that handle salt water and its corrosion problems.

▓ Electrics

The small, silent electric trolling motor purred along unnoticed by all but the most devoted fishermen until a decade ago, when it took off. Why? Better designs have

made electric motors more versatile, there are more models to match boats that people buy, and the new motors are more efficient—that is, they run longer on a battery charge. These motors are also slimmer, more powerful, saltwaterproof, and they pass through water and weeds with less resistance.

Because models and characteristics are changing rapidly, partly due to the developing popularity, a detailed discussion about how they work and what features are important is included here. All electrics are easy to start

Electric Motors

▶ The MotorGuide Digital Tour Electric has a bow mount with a foot control and thrust ratings up to 109 pounds. Some models have a bow mount with a transducer. Digital variable-speed control also maximizes fishing time.

▶ A bow-mounted electric outboard allows two anglers hands-free casting along a shoreline. New electric motors with sealed lower units are equally at home in salt water.

and operate. Endearing traits include low cost, light weight, and near-silent running. Electric is the ideal power for quiet waters, where silence and small movement are important to the careful fisherman.

Electric motors are powered with one of three systems. Motors listed as 12-volt models are powered with one 12-volt battery; 24-volt motors require two batteries; and 36-volt motors require three batteries. It's also best to use deep-cycle marine batteries. Obviously, the bigger electrics will provide more power (thrust) and will allow you to stay out on the water longer. Always use a model with a built-in battery gauge.

Nearly all electric motors are rated in pounds of thrust ranging from 8 to 109 pounds. If you have a 14-foot aluminum boat, motors with 30 to 40 pounds of thrust will be adequate. Bigger and heavier bass boats and flats boats, however, might need 75 to 100 pounds of thrust to handle the weight and bigger waters.

The penalty of electric motors? Slow speed (about 3.5 miles per hour with a canoe and one man and gear, 2.5 miles per hour with a cartop boat), and the storage battery, which gives you about four hours of continuous trolling time on one charge. But it's unlikely that you'll ever run an electric continuously for that long. In the careful sport it suits, your electric will be turned off frequently, and with experience, you'll learn how to conserve a battery charge. If you are casting or staked out with decoys, it's not hard to get a full day's use from one battery with a full charge. Trolling is another

matter; then, a second battery and your own battery charger are good investments.

How much current a motor draws, of course, determines how many hours of running time you can get on a battery charge. Several things affect this. First, always use a deep-cycle marine battery; some are specially designed for electric motors. Speed is also a big factor in current draw—electrics are most efficient at low speed settings. If your motor draws six amps to move your boat at 1.5 miles per hour, it might draw 16 to 18 amps to go 2.5 miles per hour. Also, some motors are designed with a higher speed range than others and will take more from your battery throughout the range.

Most models house the motor in a pod underwater, connected to the propeller by direct drive. A sturdy control shaft from 20 to 50 inches long mounts to the boat's transom or bow, and the controls are located at the top. This motor position eliminates transmission gears, gives quieter operation, and leaves only the control head at the top to get in the way of action. Waterproof shaft seals and tough motor housings take care of the once-important problem of a wet motor resulting from hitting rocks and logs.

For regular use in water that is filled with weeds and obstructions, some boaters prefer electrics that have the motor on top of the shaft, with the tiller and controls attached to the motor housing.

The ultimate convenience is a remote foot-pedal control that's available with many top-of-the-line models. All remotes give you no-hands steering and an on-off motor. Depress the pedal and the motor goes. Roll the ball of your foot over the pedal and three switches can activate a servomotor on the shaft that will give you right, middle, or left "rudder." A variable-speed control, which comes with remote-controlled models, is realized to full advantage only if you can control it from a remote box placed on the seat beside you.

Remote controls radically change the weight and cost features of electrics, however. Weight is increased by two or three times; price is increased drastically. Plug-in remotes, which let you detach the controls from the mounted motor unit, keep it a manageable package to tote to the car. Remote digital controls are also available for some models, as well as GPS control systems.

Most electrics can be mounted on the transom, on either side of the boat, or at the bow. Canoes give you an even choice, but most boats handle best with the electric attached to the transom. It's hard to hold a true course when it's attached on a midship gunwale, and at the bow—unless you have a remote control—you have to sit in the most uncomfortable place in the boat in order to run it. Many experienced hands prefer bow mounting because they can see the direction of steering while looking ahead, and because this gives them more exact steering since the motor leads the boat. With a foot control, it also leaves both hands free for casting.

Other things to look for on electrics: Make sure the shaft length fits the freeboard of your boat, especially at the bow. The prop should be 6 inches down in the water for its best bite. Brackets and tilt-control hardware must be well designed, so that the unit does not wobble or shift. Also, it should permit you to swing or bring the motor inside the boat readily for moving out fast with your regular outboard power.

▧ Inboard (Gasoline)

The typical inboard engine's similarity to an auto engine brought it to popularity and keeps it there. Inboard engine blocks are manufactured by car or truck engine makers, and then are converted to marine use. It is always possible to make repairs locally because it's the most common type of engine available.

The four-cycle inboard is heavier than a comparable outboard, requires permanent installation, and keeps fuel and vapor inside the boat. It also occupies a lot of space. But it's lighter on gas and oil, the lubricating oil system puts out less smog and takes less maintenance, and muffling and insulation can control its noise.

A major advantage is the inboard motor's location amidships, where the hull is capacious and weight is best handled. With a fixed, through-hull propeller shaft and separate rudder, however, an inboard installation presents rather delicate bottom gear that must always be protected. Since the shaft runs at a downward angle to clear the prop action, its thrust is less efficient, pushing at an upward angle.

The V drive helps to beat these drawbacks. It may also permit a lower engine location right against the stern, an advantage on some smaller inboard boats. Penn Yan boats, no longer in production, had improved this design with its tunnel drive section in the hull to protect the propeller. The Shamrock boat company features models with a pocket drive system in its hull. Another solution is the popular stern drive or inboard/outboard.

The first and last word about inboards is to the skipper: keep critical attention on good ventilation and fuel fixtures, and on the quality and condition of fuel lines.

▧ Diesel

You'll see diesels now in many sport-fishing boats under 50 feet that could not have accommodated this heavy machinery years ago. Compact designs and lighter metals in the high-compression cylinder walls have put them in hearty competition with gasoline engines in some categories.

Diesel Engine

The Yanmar Stern Drive diesel is a four-stroke water-cooled engine. Eight cylinders produce 370 horsepower at 3,800 revolutions per minute. Stern-drive engines are also available in gasoline models. This design places the weight of the engine in front of the stern.

While the diesel burns only half as much fuel as its gasoline counterpart, the diesel doing the same job weighs a third more, and the initial cost is twice as much. But with a diesel, you can increase your cruising range with the same gallons, or reduce the fuel carried to save weight. Because this fuel is less volatile, you have a safer boat. On a still day, however, diesel exhaust odor will not be pleasant. This engine makes sense if you use your boat hundreds of hours each year for extended cruising, chartering, and chasing game fish.

Stern Drive

The stern drive, or inboard/outboard, as you might know it, is an inboard four-cycle engine mounted at the stern with an outboard drive. The propeller of a stern drive drives parallel with the boat, and the lower unit of the outdrive turns, giving positive prop steering as with an outboard motor. There is no separate rudder. A power lift is much favored, as is an automatic kickup release that may save the lower unit when it hits an obstacle.

A stern drive is popular on smaller cruisers and open boats, for it is a compact inboard power arrangement that is feasible even where there is insufficient space for underdeck installation. The stern drive is a heavy machine to be located at the transom on small boats. It is a successful match with fast, deep-V hulls, for the point of the V helps to protect the propeller, and prop

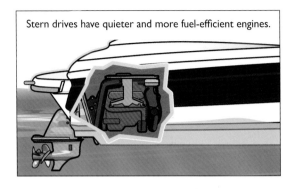
Stern drives have quieter and more fuel-efficient engines.

steering combines with the keel action of the V bottom to reduce sideslip in turns and maneuvers. It is more expensive than a straight inboard engine, but obviously more versatile. It is also the choice power for most racing boats.

Jet Drive

The jet drive is another exciting design that is a practical buy for some boaters. Water-jet propulsion is most efficient at high speeds, and it's an attractive choice for water skiers and personal watercraft (PWCs), also called jet skis.

Any inboard engine can be used with a jet pump. The engine is linked by direct drive to a high-speed impeller, and a water jet is forced out a nozzle to propel the boat. With the nozzle gate raised, the jet pushes the

Stern-Drive Engine

The Mercury MerCruiser 4.3L stern-drive package shows typical stern-drive construction. These engines are typically water cooled.

Jet-Drive Engine

The Yamaha F90 is a 90-horsepower, four-stroke, propeller-free jet drive. With no gear case or propeller below the hull, a jet-drive outboard allows boaters to pass over obstructions that would not be possible with a conventional outboard motor. Models are also available from 40 to 150 horsepower.

boat forward. With the gate down, the jet is deflected downward and forward to reverse the boat.

Jet boats used to spin out at high speeds. To improve directional stability, manufacturers have put a small rudder under the jet nozzle and keels 1 inch deep on either side of the impeller screen on the boat's bottom.

Any jet intake can be clogged eventually by thick weeds, but the impeller shrugs off sand, and passes small gravel without harm. One innovation incorporates water-jet drives into conventional outboard fishing

motors to permit operation in water too shallow for a prop. Initially, a jet-conversion unit had to be purchased, but now it's a standard propulsion system in most models. A crankshaft-driven impeller draws water through an intake grill, and the water is jetted rearward at high pressure, like the compressed air in a jet aircraft engine. When the motor is put in reverse, a cup swings over the jet stream, channeling it in the opposite direction. The throttle, shift, and, of course, steering are conventional.

BOATS FOR FISHING

You'll catch more fish and enjoy it more if you suit your boat and motor combination to the type of fishing you do. A good rule is small boats for sheltered waters and big, beamy boats for big waters. But that is only the beginning. Most people want a boat that will handle more than one type of fishing, so they look for the best combination of qualities. If you analyze your needs and preferences and decide what is really important, you'll be able to select a boat-motor combination with confidence.

■ Boats for Sheltered Waters

Trout ponds, little bass lakes, and such are not called quiet waters because nothing happens there. They are truly quiet, and the noise you make there will be the loudest heard all day unless it's moose country. Therefore, it is sensible to use the quietest boat you can find. If you stay within the 12- to 14-foot range, the size of your shadow will be reduced, and boat action will be in scale with the surroundings. Inflatables, canoes, kayaks, and

12-foot cartop boats fit quiet waters perfectly. You can launch these boats into the water soundlessly, with little more than a ripple. If you want to catch fish and keep the fishing good, make your outfit as simple as possible. Leave the outboard at home, bring only a paddle or pole, and be proud of your inexpensive rig. You've matched nature, and that is the sportsman's art.

For small rivers and streams, canoes, kayaks, light-weight johnboats, or cartop boats are time-honored choices and cannot be beat. They move easily against the current. Add a small outboard and you're in clover. The johnboat is probably more comfortable for two fishermen and gear when casting and moving for long hours, but experience with a canoe or kayak will win you over with its easy movement, light weight, and silence. A length of 15 feet or more offers enough space for two fishermen.

When you fish lakes only a few miles across, many types of boats will do the job. First, observe the wave action, wind, and depth; then, take a good look at the boats commonly used there. They probably suit those conditions remarkably well.

Small aluminum boats in the 12- to 14-foot range are ideal for ponds, lakes, and rivers. In the 12-foot length, they can be cartoppers.

Bass Boats

The Nitro ZV 21 is a classic bass-boat design. At 21 feet, 7 inches, with a 100-inch beam, the Nitro has a maximum rating of 350 horsepower. The maximum weight capacity is 2,500 pounds. The dual console and deep-V hull are designed for rough-water running.

The Ranger RT188C is an 18-foot crappie/bass boat rated for 115 horsepower. Built with a 92-inch beam, this aluminum model has an all-fiberglass console and comes with a custom-fitted trailer.

The Stratos 186 VLO, a fiberglass bass boat, measures 18 feet, 9 inches, and is rated for 115 horsepower. The bow is rigged with a Minn Kota trolling motor and foot pedal. Stratos offers this model factory rigged with its own custom-built trailer.

If the surface is usually quiet, consider a boat that will give you platform space with shallow draft, such as the johnboat or pontoon boat. If your sport is fishing for bass and crappies in brush and weeds, look for a boat that is easy to push and pry loose; the canoe, kayak, or johnboat works well.

The most popular boat in America today may well be the bass boat. The phenomenal boom in this new breed is well deserved because it fits the sport so well. The hull, developed on southern lakes, is a cross between the johnboat and tri-hull. Forrest L. Wood, founder of Ranger Boats, is credited with the creation of the first bass boat. It is very stable, yet rises quickly to the top of the water and moves fast when you want to cross the lake. With its shallow draft, you can get in almost anywhere there is water that holds fish. The seats are designed for all-day fishing, rod holders are located where you want them—it's all thought out. The typical bass boat today is built of fiberglass or Kevlar or a combination of both materials. These boats can range from 15 to 21 feet and can handle outboard motors up to 300 horsepower. The hulls are designed to handle almost any

kind of water and speeds. There are only two drawbacks: weight and price. Both are big. You'll also need a trailer for these rigs.

The favorite all-arounder, however, is the aluminum fishing boat. Successful makes are designed to adapt to the widest variety of conditions. With flotation built in, they are good in fairly rough water, are lightweight and easy to handle, can be stored anywhere, and certainly cost little for the service they give. You see them on all inland waters, whatever the area and fishing sport. They come in sizes from 12 feet up; probably the most serviceable length is 14 feet. A 10-horsepower outboard is the common power match, but they will take huskier pushers if that's what you need.

For remote waters where the approach is on foot, check out inflatables. You can backpack in, and then inflate at the water's edge with a CO_2 cartridge or foot pump. Inflatables handle rather badly, but they are very stable and surprisingly tough, and are a lot of fun. They can also handle small outboard motors and electrics. Other candidates for these backwaters are canoes and kayaks, but most of those take two persons to tote.

▨ Float-Trip Boats

Several schools of thought about boats for float trips are all cogent and tend to follow regional custom—not for custom's sake, but because water conditions vary considerably. A broad, fairly slow river without rapids will usually see shallow-draft boats that maneuver slowly but offer comfort and convenience in their broad-beamed stability. Johnboats, large inflatables, pontoon boats, and river-style houseboats fit these conditions. Such boats have broad front ends that are inefficient in meeting waves or cutting much speed, but those aren't the needs. All you need is enough power to push a heavy bow wave upstream when you return. Knowing your stream, the weight and size of the boat will help you determine how much power you need.

For fast rivers with rapids and white water, the needs are more demanding. First, you need a hull that will withstand a lot of punishment; it must be built strong to survive bumping hard into rocks, logs, and gravel bottoms without damage. Flotation must be positive—sufficient to support the craft, occupants, and load if swamped. Maneuverability is very important, as is a bow design that will lift and throw off white water. Light weight is necessary so that portages will be easy. The choice is usually a canoe or kayak for rivers where narrow bends and fast water between rocks make maneuverability essential. Expert white-water canoeists prefer craft under 15 feet, with round bottoms and no keel for quicker handling. However, since a canoe of this design won't hold much, the choice for float trips is usually a bigger canoe with high ends. Kayaks are another excellent choice when you will encounter some white water. Kayaks in the 12- to 14-foot range designed for fishing are more than adequate for float trips.

Open boats are good equipment carriers for extended float trips. Some can even be rigged to carry a couple of kayaks for exploring backwaters.

Inflatables are usually chosen for big, fast rivers. A big inflatable has great stability and is forgiving when you bounce it off banks and obstructions, and it's roomy enough to let you relax when the going is straight. But maneuvering a big inflatable is a real problem. Some experienced float men add a broad, shallow tiller for steering. On some rivers, this is essential. Don't plan on powering your boat on fast streams, but arrange for transport at the lower end of your float trip.

▨ Boats for Open Waters

On big lakes, river estuaries, coastal bays, inlets, and inshore waters, size and seaworthiness are absolutely essential. The bigger the water, the greater the potential dangers—and the need for a capable hull that will bring you safely back through all weather yet serve you comfortably in routine use and help you catch more fish. Open waters are not the places for a flat-bottomed, 12-foot skiff. Look at what is being used. You will see deep-V bow points, rounded chines on smaller boats, probably with flat planing surface aft, and enough freeboard to keep dry when the wind comes up. If your waters commonly have a sharp chop, as in many Great Lakes locations, you will need more freeboard, and the hull shape should ride comfortably in those conditions. Too much freeboard can be a curse, however, making fish handling difficult and presenting a big profile to the wind, causing eternal drifting.

Fishermen who run out to the reefs on the Great Lakes to anchor and drop a line for perch want a boat that gives a comfortable seat for hours on end, riding the waves without slapping and shipping water. The man who trolls for lake trout or coho salmon prefers a competent running boat that also provides a good platform for fighting and landing the fish, with a bow shape that will handle the waves when they rise, and that can move off fast to change locations and make the run home.

Calm days on open waters—and many big lakes a fraction of the size of the Great Lakes fit the case—are deceptive. The water looks calm when you start out in the morning. By noon, you are occupied with sunburn and poor fishing, so that when the wind and big waves come up at 3:00 p.m., you're taken by surprise. Getting back to shore can be dangerous if you are out in a 12- or 14-footer with a 10-horsepower motor. Think in terms of 16 feet or more length, with plenty of beam in relation to length. For big inland lakes and coastal bays, you will need a motor of 25 horsepower and up. For trolling the ocean beaches, a motor or twin motors from 100

The Boston Whaler 345 Conquest is designed for offshore waters. The length is 34 feet with a beam of nearly 12 feet. The Conquest has a maximum horsepower rating of 900. The fuel capacity is 391 gallons. A big, comfortable cabin makes this a good choice when fishing in unpredictable ocean waters.

The World Cat 330TE, a catamaran-hulled offshore boat, will handle twin outboards totaling 600 horsepower. A 34-footer with a beam of nearly 11 feet, the hull is designed to cushion impact when running in a rough ocean. The fuel capacity is 300 gallons.

horsepower up are necessary. If you plan to troll, choose a boat with a broad, clear stern for handling the lines. For casting, you should consider a boat that also provides a good casting platform both fore and aft.

▤ Offshore Outboard-Powered Boats

Perhaps the most versatile boats available are the center-console, deep-V boats. A deep bow permits them to handle the seas, but this slopes into a moderately flat mid and stern bottom that permits them to plane easily and ride over the flats without scraping. This design is also very stable for its seaworthiness. These boats are best described as inshore-offshore boats, great for fishing coastal bays and reefs, for running the inlets, and for going offshore—weather permitting—into really big-water country.

It is increasingly common to see these boats, some of them powered with up to three and four outboard engines, running to far offshore waters. Typical rigs are in the 28- to 40-foot range and are usually powered by twin 300- to 350-horsepower four-stroke outboard engines. Some boats, however, can range up to 45 feet with four 300-horsepower outboard engines for power. Some of these boats have beams exceeding 12 feet, weigh 24,000 pounds, and can carry about 500 gallons of fuel. Digital technology makes synchronizing revolutions per minute and trimming multiple outboard engines easy. With the right preparations, these boats are canyon ready.

▤ The Sportfisherman

The sportfisherman is a well-designed fishing machine with all the comforts of home that can sail in nearly all kinds of weather and offshore seas. It is, indeed, a breed apart from all other fishing boats. Until you have handled a boat on the ocean, following fish on really big water, it's hard to imagine what is required of a boat in these conditions. Not only are these boats bigger (typically 35 to 82 feet), with deeper hulls and more beam, but they are built to take tremendous force. Big power is needed, as well as great reliability and fuel economy, and a frequent choice is twin diesels. For example, an 82-foot sportfisherman has a 22-foot beam and a fuel capacity of 3,000 gallons. Cockpit space measures a huge 255 square feet. This boat would likely be powered by twin diesel engines putting out more than 2,000 horsepower each.

Fortunately, there are more economical choices if a fisherman is interested in a sportfisherman. Much more common and affordable to serious bluewater fishermen are sportfisherman boats in the 38- to 54-foot range. Regardless of size, in any sportfisherman layout and cockpit space is critical. Captains, mates, and fishermen must be able to handle the boat efficiently when baiting and hooking a big fish, so that it is not broken off or lost due to a slack line or pulled hook. With an inadequate boat or inept skipper, it can take hours to boat a good billfish. In that time, tackle and equipment break down, people have accidents brought about by fatigue, and the boat itself can be endangered. The steering

The Sun Tracker Fishin' Barge 20 DLX, a 20-foot pontoon boat, is a good choice for overnight fishing on big lakes and bays. With an economical 40-horsepower four-stroke outboard, this pontoon boat can easily hold anglers and gear.

station, whether it is from the bridge or tuna tower, should give the captain a clear view of the cockpit and stern as well as forward. The cockpit should be clear of all equipment except the fighting chair and tackle with a clean and unobstructed transom. The sportfisherman should be built with engine hatches under the cabin floor for easy access. Several staterooms, a galley, air-conditioned salon, extensive electronics, a generator, bait wells, and refrigerated fish boxes are typical features on most sportfisherman models.

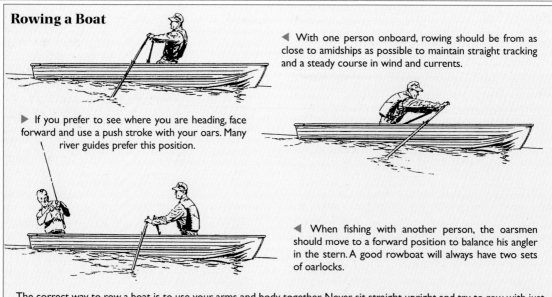

Rowing a Boat

◄ With one person onboard, rowing should be from as close to amidships as possible to maintain straight tracking and a steady course in wind and currents.

▶ If you prefer to see where you are heading, face forward and use a push stroke with your oars. Many river guides prefer this position.

◄ When fishing with another person, the oarsmen should move to a forward position to balance his angler in the stern. A good rowboat will always have two sets of oarlocks.

The correct way to row a boat is to use your arms and body together. Never sit straight upright and try to row with just your arms. Use your shoulders and the strength of your trunk. Long, strong strokes with oars are more efficient and less tiring than short strokes. With a little practice, you will be able to maintain a course by pulling a little harder on one oar than the other. You can pivot or turn a boat by pulling on one oar and pushing on the other. A pull on the right oar and a push on the left oar will turn the bow clockwise. Reverse the strokes to turn the bow counterclockwise. You can slow down and stop a boat by dropping both oar blades in the water and holding them stationary. When rowing with outboard power, tilt the engine up and keep the weight forward to reduce transom drag.

BOATING ELECTRONICS

Once you have selected your boat, you will need to rig it. And this means learning the basics of marine electronics. Basic electronic gear ensures the safety of your boat and passengers. A radio will summon help in case of an accident, and a depthsounder will help keep you out of trouble in unfamiliar waters. Once you've met the basic safety requirements, however, you'll quickly discover that electronics can be interesting and useful—whether cruising or fishing.

It's easy to pick out rod holders and similar accessories, but electronic equipment is a different story. If you make the wrong choice there, you could be out hundreds of dollars and stuck with something that doesn't perform as needed. Let's look at some of the electronics to consider.

▧ Depthsounders

How does a sounder work? The word "sonar" is an acronym for SOund, NAvigation, and Ranging. It was developed during World War II as a means of tracking enemy submarines.

With sonar, an electrical impulse is converted to a sound wave and transmitted into the water. When this sound wave strikes an obstacle, it rebounds. Sound transmitted through water travels at approximately 4,800 feet per second, compared with 1,100 feet per second through air. And since the speed of sound in water is a known constant, the time lapse between the transmitted signal and the received echo can be measured and the distance to the obstacle determined. An electronic sonar unit can both send and receive sound waves, as well as time, measure, and record them.

A depthsounder's transducer sends a high-frequency sound wave through the water. This sound wave is inaudible to fish as well as humans. When the echo returns, the transducer picks it up and reconverts it to electrical energy. The unit times the interval and puts a signal on the screen of your depthsounder. The signal identifies the distance between the transducer and the obstacle that returned the echo.

Some of the early depthsounders were called flashers and used a dial with a high-intensity neon bulb whiling at a constant speed. The biggest disadvantage of these early flashers was that they had no recording features. If a fisherman did not constantly monitor his flasher, he could pass over fish and not see them.

TYPES OF DEPTHSOUNDERS: There are three main types of depthsounders: chart recorder, liquid-crystal recorder, and video sonar.

- **The Chart-Recorder Depthsounder:** When a chart recorder is operating, an electronically regulated motor drives a lightweight belt at the edge of the recording paper. A stylus is attached to this belt. When the stylus is at the top of the paper, a small mark is burned onto the paper. This is called the zero mark, and represents the water surface. The stylus continues to move down the edge of the paper while the second pulse is traveling through the water. When an echo is detected, the stylus burns another mark on the paper. The depth of the object that reflected the echo can be read in feet by comparing its location on the paper to the depth scale printed on the paper.

  The paper speed is controlled by a variable-speed motor. During one revolution of the stylus belt, a very narrow mark will be made by the flexible stylus, but the paper will move a small amount before the next revolution. Each mark will blend into the one before so that a composite "picture" of the target will be made, one tiny mark at a time.

- **The Liquid-Crystal-Recorder Depthsounder:** In principle, the liquid-crystal recorder, or graph, works like a paper recorder, except that these "paperless recorders" use liquid-crystal squares, called pixels, on a display screen. When an impulse or electronic signal

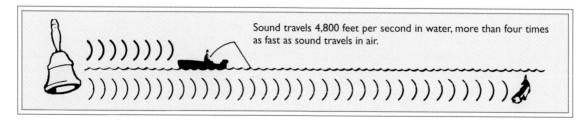

Sound travels 4,800 feet per second in water, more than four times as fast as sound travels in air.

Depthsounders

The Hummingbird 1158c DI Combo will show detailed views of the bottom and structures below your boat on a 10.4-inch color screen. This unit has chart-plotting capabilities and readings down to 1,500 feet.

The Hummingbird DI has a 5-inch grayscale display and is a good basic affordable unit that will give readings down to 500 feet.

The Lowrance HDS-12 Gen2 is a touch-screen fish finder and chart plotter. With its 12-inch widescreen color display, this unit has built-in Insight USA mapping, Broadband Sounder, and StructureScan high-definition imaging. It is a good choice for an all-in-one electronics package.

is sent to the screen, it hits the liquid and turns it so the tiny square shows black on the screen. A continuing series of signals will literally draw a picture of the bottom or any object or fish between the bottom and the boat. Some of the latest liquid-crystal recorders, or graphs, have features that border on the amazing. Some have memories with playback. Others have a split screen that shows two segments of the water. And many have optional fish alarms and water-temperature readouts.

- **The Video-Sonar Depthsounder:** Instead of using chart paper or liquid-crystal squares, an underwater video sonar produces a sharp clear black-and-white or color picture on a cathode ray tube (CRT) screen. The imaging principle is the same as that of a television picture. With color video sonar, the screen shows signal intensity by color difference, making it easier to distinguish individual fish from structures and the bottom. With black-and-white video sonar, the unit provides a constant view of the bottom, underwater structures, drop-offs, schools of fish, and even single fish in distinct, easy-to-identify shades of gray.

USES FOR DEPTHSOUNDERS: Though most fishermen believe the primary use for a depthsounder is to find fish, there are many other uses. Since a depthsounder tells depth accurately, it can be used for making contour maps of lakes, bays, saltwater areas, or large streams. It is useful in navigation because it warns you when you are approaching shallow water. It will find the deep holes in rivers. It is useful in salvage operations because

it will accurately show a sunken boat on the bottom. It even tells what kind of bottom your boat is passing over. Divers use it to study the depths before descending.

It tells the depth of the water accurately, but since everything it reports is shown by signals on a screen, the amount it can tell is limited by your ability to interpret the signals. The more skillful you become at reading the signals, the more your depthsounder will tell you about the mysterious world beneath the surface.

Marine Radios

In times of serious boating emergencies, the ability to summon help quickly can make the difference between life and death. If you don't already own one, consider purchasing a Very High Frequency (VHF) marine radio. VHF radios have channels that are reserved for distress calls and are continuously monitored by the U.S. Coast Guard. You may legally use your VHF radio for distress, safety, operational, and public correspondence communications. Distress and safety communications include calls relating to danger to life and property, safety bulletins, weather warnings, and talking with other boats to avoid a collision.

If you have a life-threatening emergency, issue a MAYDAY signal on Channel 16 (the calling and distress channel). This is a call to ask for assistance if there is immediate danger to life or property. A MAYDAY call has priority over all other radio calls. Use a MAYDAY call only for life-threatening medical emergencies or if your boat is sinking or on fire.

Marine Radios

◀ The Standard Horizon HX851 Floating VHF is a 12-channel VHF radio with a built-in GPS with waypoint navigation and compass distress calling. It receives all channels and NOAA weather alerts. It operates more than seven hours on a rechargeable lithium-ion battery. It is a good handheld choice for a marine radio and GPS.

▲ The Standard Horizon Eclipse GX1150 VHF marine radio will pick up all NOAA channels and U.S. and Canadian marine channels. It also includes a time and GPS display. For boaters who prefer a permanently mounted marine radio, this would be a good choice.

▶ The Uniden Atlantis 250 Handheld VHF radio will handle U.S., Canadian, and international channels, including 10 NOAA weather channels. This compact unit has a 10-hour battery life on a rechargeable NiMH battery pack. VHF handheld units are a must-have investment for all boaters.

If you hear a MAYDAY call, remain silent, listen, and write down the information being given by the boat in distress. If the U.S. Coast Guard or other rescue authority does not respond, try to reach the Coast Guard while traveling toward the boat. If you cannot reach the Coast Guard, try to assist the other boat to the best of your ability while not placing yourself or your passengers in danger.

Channel 16 is a calling and distress channel only. It is not to be used for conversation or radio checks. Penalties exist for misuse of a radio; hoax MAYDAY calls are felonies.

Be aware that the distance of sending and receiving messages is limited by the height of the antenna and the power of the radio.

▨ Global Positioning System (GPS)

The Global Positioning System (GPS) is a constellation of satellites that orbit the earth twice a day, transmitting precise time and position (latitude, longitude, and altitude) information. With a GPS receiver, users can determine their location anywhere on earth. Position and navigation information is vital to a broad range of professional and personal activities, including boating,

fishing, surveying, aviation, vehicle tracking and navigation, and more.

The complete system consists of 24 satellites orbiting about 12,000 miles above the earth, and five ground stations to monitor and manage the satellite constellation. These satellites provide 24-hour-a-day coverage for both two- and three-dimensional positioning anywhere on earth.

Development of the GPS satellite navigation system began in the 1970s by the U.S. Department of Defense,

The Garmin GPS-MAP 546s is a GPS/digital sonar with a 5-inch color screen. Sonar readings can go to depths of 2,000 feet. This unit is preloaded with U.S. coastal marine charts. It also has split-screen options.

which continues to manage the system to provide continuous, worldwide positioning and navigation data to U.S. military forces around the globe. However, GPS now has an even broader civilian and commercial application. The GPS signals are available to an unlimited number of users simultaneously.

HOW GPS WORKS: The basis of GPS technology is precise time and position information. Using atomic clocks (accurate to within one second every 70,000 years) and location data, each satellite continuously broadcasts the time and its position. A GPS receiver receives these signals to determine the user's position on earth.

By measuring the time interval between the transmission and the reception of a satellite signal, the GPS receiver calculates the distance between the user and each satellite. Using the distance measurements of at least three satellites in an algorithm computation, the GPS receiver arrives at an accurate position fix.

The position information in a GPS receiver may be displayed as longitude and latitude, military grid, or other system coordinates. Information must be received from three satellites in order to obtain two-dimensional (latitude and longitude) fixes, and from four satellites for three-dimensional (latitude, longitude, and altitude) positioning.

Newer GPS units are now also equipped with either Differential Global Positioning System (DGPS) or Wide Area Augmentation System (WAAS) capabilities, which simply means a fisherman can return to a fishing hot spot with 3-meter accuracy.

GPS receivers provide positioning, velocity, and navigation information for a variety of purposes. Anyone who needs to know the precise time or the exact location of people or objects will benefit from a GPS. In turn, this information can be used in charting and mapping, plotting a course, navigating from point to point, tracking vehicle movement, locating previously identified sites, or any number of similar functions.

GPS/PLOTTER/SOUNDER: GPS/plotters/sounders are the ultimate in boating electronics for recreational boaters and fishermen. These combination split-screen units allow you to chart courses, mark waypoints, and record fishing hot spots while giving you a detailed picture of the depth, bottom structures, and the fish under your boat. With a GPS/plotter/sounder, you can return to a wreck or reef with an accuracy of 3 meters. These sophisticated units can cost several thousand dollars, depending on the features. They will help you find and catch fish, but bear in mind that GPS/plotter/sounders will also keep you and your boat safe in unfamiliar waters.

Radar

RADAR means RAdio Detection And Ranging. Basically, it's an electronic device that provides ranges and bearings as well as visual pictures of boats, planes, land, and so on. Radar is extremely valuable to boaters on the water in times of low visibility, such as fog and night.

Radar operates much the way a depthsounder does, except that the transmission is through air rather than water. A radar unit transmits pulses of super-high frequency radio waves that are reflected by objects in the distance. The time it takes for the radio wave to go out and the echo to return is the measure of the distance to the object.

There are four components to a radar set:

1. The transmitter, which transmits radio waves in brief impulses.

2. The antenna, which radiates the impulses and collects the returning echoes.

3. The receiver, which picks up the returning echoes.

4. The screen, which produces a visual display of the objects in the path of the radar signals.

Makers of modern radar units for small boats have managed to combine these four components into two units: the transmitter and antenna in one unit, and the receiver and screen in another.

The Furuno Radar is available in three models: the 1834, 1935, and 1945. Depending on the antenna used, these units have a range from 36 to 64 nautical miles. All units have a 10.4-inch color LCD display with crystal-clear presentation and automatic gain/sea/rain controls for noise-free radar. The radar allows you to see other boats and targets both at short and long range in the dark, fog, or any weather condition.

As with other marine electronics, stiff competition has driven down the price of radar. Radar, at one time, was found only on big private yachts or commercial vessels. Today, it is not uncommon to see radar on small fishing boats in the 25-foot range. There's no doubt that radar can give you a much greater edge of safety.

EPIRB

EPIRBs (Emergency Position Indicating Radio Beacons) are electronic devices that transmit signals that can guide rescuers to your disabled boat. If you regularly go far offshore, especially beyond 20 miles or so, where you will be stretching the range of your Very High Frequency (VHF) radio, it's wise to carry an EPIRB. In an emergency, this device will transmit a continuous international distress signal on 406 megahertz (MHz). High-flying aircraft can pick up these signals as far away as 200 miles. More important, Coast Guard planes are equipped with automatic direction finders for EPIRB frequencies. EPIRBs are classified as Category 1 or Category 2. Category 1 EPIRBs are automatically activated when the unit hits the water and the signal can be detected anywhere in the world. Category 2 EPIRBs are similar

to Category 1, except some models have to be manually activated. EPIRBs use a special lithium battery for long-term low consumption. EPIRBs must also be properly registered with the Federal Communications Commission (FCC) and Coast Guard.

The ResQLink Personal Locator Beacon is for use when all other rescue means have failed. Deploy the antenna and press the on button and the unit will relay your position to a worldwide network of satellites to help lead rescue teams right to you. The unit is also waterproof with a built-in strobe light. It is a must-have unit for boaters offshore and on remote waters.

ANCHORS, MOORINGS, AND ROPES

An anchor is essential to safe boat operation, yet some boat liveries where small fishing boats are rented put their boats out without either an anchor or lines. When you know the importance of having an anchor, you will insist on having an effective one aboard even on a normally calm lake, and enough anchor line to give safe scope. In addition to safety, an anchor is necessary to hold position in a breeze or current when fishing. For a boater, a boat is half useless without a good anchor.

The major misconception about anchors is that the heavier the anchor, the more it will hold. This is not the case. The key is the meaning of hold. An anchor does not function by weighing down, but by holding on to the bottom effectively. A concrete block weighing 20 pounds may roll on a sloping bottom and slide on a hard bottom as the wind tugs at the boat. In the same situation, a Danforth anchor weighing only 3 pounds will

probably hold the boat fast after kedging only several feet until its sharp flukes find a grip on the bottom.

Many small boats are equipped with mushroom-type anchors. These have a solid, weighty feel—even the small ones. Regardless of the direction in which they are pulled, the lip of the cup will drag in contact with the bottom and possibly hold. But when they hook a bottom snag or settle in mud, the weight of the cast-iron mushroom plus the weight of the bottom becomes a formidable load to haul up through the water.

A mushroom anchor may be adequate on a protected lake with a firm bottom, but on a fast-moving stream this anchor will be ineffective. On big open water, a concrete block or any other simple, heavy anchor can be a hazard. When the wind blows, the anchor will roll until the boat is in water deeper than the length of the anchor rope. The anchor then becomes a load on the bow, dipping deeper in the trough of waves than it should.

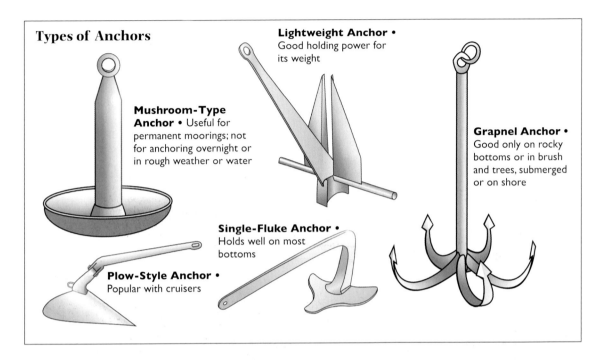

Types of Anchors

Mushroom-Type Anchor • Useful for permanent moorings; not for anchoring overnight or in rough weather or water

Lightweight Anchor • Good holding power for its weight

Grapnel Anchor • Good only on rocky bottoms or in brush and trees, submerged or on shore

Single-Fluke Anchor • Holds well on most bottoms

Plow-Style Anchor • Popular with cruisers

A number of anchor designs for pleasure boats have been developed that are effective by application rather than weight. One of the best is the Danforth. This anchor will hold on a hard bottom and can be retrieved on a rock-filled bottom. Most have trip features for releasing the anchor when it gets caught on the bottom.

Since anchor weight and size suitable for a boat of a given size vary widely according to the anchor design and to local conditions, no guidelines can be given that apply to all anchor types in common use. (Remember that concrete blocks and cans filled with concrete are among the most common small-boat anchors.) However, guidelines for mushroom-type and Danforth anchors are provided in the accompanying charts on the next page.

▶ If you fish in shallow water, you may never have to touch a rope or a muddy anchor again if you have a shallow-water anchoring system. These anchor systems, mounted on a boat's transom, can anchor your boat in waters up to 10 feet deep. Minn Kota's Talon Shallow Water Anchor is typical of these anchoring systems. Powered by a boat's battery, an anchoring spike is slightly driven into the bottom. These anchors can be lowered by a dash or foot switch. Protected from saltwater corrosion, these shallow-water anchors are ideal for flats boats and freshwater lakes and ponds where deep water is rarely encountered.

Mushroom Anchor Weights

Length of Boat (feet)	Power (pounds)	Sail: Racing (pounds)	Sail: Cruising (pounds)
25	225	125	175
35	300	200	250
45	400	325	400
55	500	450	550

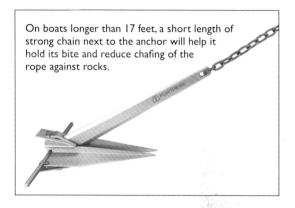

On boats longer than 17 feet, a short length of strong chain next to the anchor will help it hold its bite and reduce chafing of the rope against rocks.

The length of the anchor line is an important factor in effective anchoring. In calm waters, twice the depth of the water is enough line. This assumes you are in the boat and can bring it easily to shore if a sudden storm comes up or your motor gives out. In open waters, your anchor line should be three to five times the depth of the water. For riding overnight or when the boat is unattended, you need seven times the depth. Obviously the reason is holding power. If the length of the line plus the anchor design permit the pull to be applied horizontally against the anchor's purchase on the bottom, it will help it to hold. On boats 17 feet and longer, a short length of strong chain next to the anchor will help it hold its bite and reduce chafing of the rope against rocks and the anchor itself.

The best way to free most anchors that are stuck in the bottom is by pulling straight up. If you find you cannot do this, try snubbing the line until it runs vertically down to the snagged anchor. Take a bit around the cleat to hold the line tight, and then rock the boat fore and aft, or let the wave action do this until the anchor is worked free. The force of the boat's motion is greater than the force you can apply by hand.

When anchoring on large or windy waters, check the direction of the wind and wave action before setting anchor. If you have a choice of anchoring on a lee or windward shore, choose the lee. Then your boat won't be blown or washed onto the rocks by morning. In a popular mooring place, set your anchor so that you have several boat lengths between you and any other craft. Then, if a storm arises, even the worst fury won't cause damage.

Some fishermen like to drag or tow their anchor when drift fishing in windy, deep waters. This is a hazard to the anchor and line, and the anchor must be fully hauled to start the motor again to regain the best position. You might prefer instead to store a sea anchor or two for this purpose. This is a canvas bucket that acts as a drag. It is attached with a halter to a light nylon line that can be hauled in easily.

Suggested Danforth Anchor Sizes

Length of Boat (feet)	Beam		Standard Sizes		Hi-Tensile Sizes		
	Sail	Power	Working	Storm	Lunch	Working	Storm
10	4	4	2½	4	Hook	5	5
20	6	6	8	13	—	5	12
25	6½	7	8	13	5	12	12
30	7	9	13	22	5	12	18
35	8	10	22	22	5	18	18
40	9	11	22	40	5	18	28
50	11	13	40	65	12	28	60
60	12	14	65	85	12	60	90

Moorings

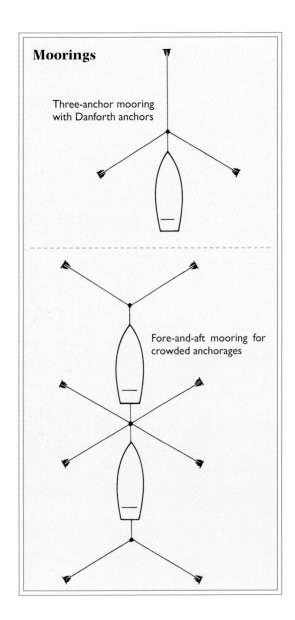

Three-anchor mooring with Danforth anchors

Fore-and-aft mooring for crowded anchorages

The Elusive Green Flash

Consider yourself very lucky if you witness the green flash. Not many boaters are so fortunate and some don't even believe it actually happens. The green flash is an amazing sunset phenomenon. Watch the red ball of the sun descend at sunset when you're on the water, especially if you're offshore in the southern half of the country. When the sun touches the horizon, it will turn orange, and then yellow. When the sun drops out of sight, you may instantly see a brilliant green flash. The color change is caused by the refraction of the sun's rays passing through layers of atmosphere. Your best chance of seeing the green flash is on a calm ocean with a clear view of the horizon. Look for this phenomenon when conditions are right. If you see the green flash, you are one of the lucky ones to witness this amazing end-of-day display.

As sunset approaches, these Florida Keys anglers might see the green flash.

▓ How to Set a Mooring

An anchored mooring is cheaper than a dock, and in many crowded public facilities it is the only choice. The authorities may stipulate the minimum mooring that is acceptable. You may want to improve on this, particularly if you have a valuable boat. In any case, remember that your boat might do damage if it drags its mooring or breaks loose—and the responsibility is yours.

On soft bottoms, heavy iron mushroom-type moorings are often used successfully. A chain is attached from the mooring anchor to a floating buoy, where the boat is tied, usually with a snap hook on a short line from the bow. Even a big mushroom mooring can be pulled through the mud if a really hard storm or hurricane blows, however, and it is for this occasional danger that you must prepare when setting a permanent mooring. A single mooring anchor assumes adequate scope on the line to hold in a blow, but scope of this length is impossible in crowded anchorages. Therefore, three anchors are sometimes used, set in an equilateral triangle with only one boat length of extra scope to the buoy (see accompanying illustrations). An alternative in the most crowded

Ropes: Minimum Tensile Strength (pounds)*

Circumference (inches)	Diameter (inches)	Ship Brand Manila	Yacht Manila	Linen Yacht	Nylon and Gold Line	Dacron	Poly-ethylene	Poly-propylene
9/16	3/16	450	525	600	1,100	1,050	690	1,050
3/4	1/4	600	688	1,020	1,850	1,750	1,150	1,700
1	5/16	1,000	1,190	1,520	2,850	2,650	1,730	2,450
1 1/8	3/8	1,350	1,590	2,090	4,000	3,600	2,400	3,400
1 1/4	7/16	1,750	1,930	2,700	5,500	4,800	3,260	4,300
1 1/2	1/2	2,650	2,920	3,500	7,100	6,100	4,050	5,300
1 3/4	9/16	3,450	3,800	4,350	8,350	7,400	5,000	6,400
2	5/8	4,400	4,840	5,150	10,500	9,000	6,050	7,600
2 1/4	3/4	5,400	5,940	7,100	14,200	12,500	9,000	10,000
2 3/4	7/8	7,700	8,450	9,400	19,000	16,000	12,000	13,000
3	1	9,000	9,900	12,000	24,600	20,000	15,000	16,500
3 1/2	1 1/8	12,000	13,200	——	34,000	21,500	18,500	19,500
3 3/4	1 1/4	13,500	14,850	——	38,000	24,500	21,000	22,000
4 1/2	1 1/2	18,500	——	——	55,000	36,000	29,000	31,500

*For the approximate average tensile strength, add 20 percent for Ship Brand, Yacht Manila, and Linen Yacht ropes.

Recommended Anchor Lines for Power Craft

	Anchor	Overall Length of Boat					
		Under 20 Feet	20–25 Feet	25–30 Feet	30–40 Feet	40–50 Feet	50–65 Feet
Length of anchor lines	Light	100 feet	100 feet	100 feet	125 feet	150 feet	180 feet
	Heavy		150 feet	180 feet	200 feet	250 feet	300 feet
Diameter if nylon	Light	3/8 inch	3/8 inch	1/2 inch	9/16 inch	3/4 inch	7/8 inch
	Heavy		1/2 inch	9/16 inch	3/4 inch	1 inch	1 1/8 inches
Diameter if first-class manila	Light	1/2 inch	1/2 inch	5/8 inch	3/4 inch	1 inch	1 1/4 inches
	Heavy		5/8 inch	3/4 inch	1 inch	1 3/8 inches	1 1/2 inches
Diameter if Plymouth bolt manila	Light	7/16 inch	7/16 inch	9/16 inch	5/8 inch	7/8 inch	1 inch
	Heavy		9/16 inch	5/8 inch	7/8 inch	1 1/8 inches	1 1/4 inches

locations is fore-and-aft anchoring, with two anchors to each buoy, and each boat tied to the buoy both fore and aft of it.

■ Anchor Lines and Strength

Synthetic fibers have produced ropes that are a blessing to boatmen. The new ropes are somewhat more expensive than manila, but they are stronger for their size, lighter, and more comfortable to handle. They also won't rot or mildew, and are easy to work with. One drawback is that they resist bite in tying; therefore, knots must be positive. Granny knots and loose knots are out.

Elasticity is always a factor to be considered when using any line for anchoring or tying a boat at a dock. Nylon rope is more than four times as elastic as manila when loaded repeatedly; Dacron is about 50 percent more elastic than manila, but it is more sensitive than nylon to abrasion.

BOAT KNOTS

Part of the fun of owning a boat is in learning and using boat knots. Here are ways to make the knots and splices needed for anchoring and mooring your boat.

SHORT SPLICE

This is the strongest of splices for joining ends of two pieces of rope, but it cannot be used to run through a pulley due to the bulk of the splice. This procedure also applies to splicing nylon and other synthetic ropes, but one additional full tuck should be used.

1 • Lash rope about 12 diameters from each end (A). Unlay the strands up to the lashings. Whip the strands to prevent untwisting and then put together as in illustration, alternating the strands from each end. Pull it up taut.

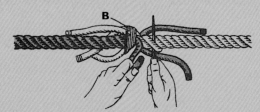

2 • Now, tie down all the strands temporarily (B). Take off the lashing from one side of the rope and raise one strand on this side, using a fid. Take the middle strand of the opposite side, and tuck it over one strand and under the raised strand. Pull it up taut.

3 • Tuck against the twist or "lay" of the rope. What happens is that the tuck goes over one strand, under the second, and out between the second and third.

4 • Roll the rope toward you. Pick up the second strand, and repeat the same operation. Then, do it again with the third strand. You have now made one full tuck.

5 • Take both lashings (which were applied in Steps 1 and 2) off the other side of the rope. Repeat the above operations.

6 • To finish, cut off the ends of the strands, leaving about 1 or 2 inches protruding.

Note • To taper the splice, first make one more tuck just like the first one. Then, make the third tuck the same way, but first cut off one-third of the yarn from the strands. For the fourth tuck, cut off half of the remaining yarn. For the untapered short splice, you do not cut the strands. You just make three more tucks, exactly like the first one.

LONG SPLICE

This knot is slightly weaker than the short splice, but it allows the rope to run freely through a properly sized pulley and causes less wear at the point of splicing.

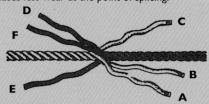

1 • Unlay the end of each rope about 15 turns and place the ropes together, alternating strands from each end as shown.

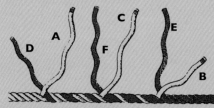

2 • Start with any opposite pair, unlay one strand, and replace it with a strand from the other part. Repeat the operation with another pair of strands in the opposite direction as shown.

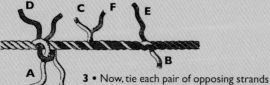

3 • Now, tie each pair of opposing strands (see B and E) with an overhand knot, tuck each strand twice, as in the short splice, and then twice more. Or, halve each strand (see A and D) and tie with an overhand knot before tucking. With this latter method, a smaller splice results—but at a considerable sacrifice of strength.

4 • Roll and pound well before cutting the strands off close to the rope.

EYE OR SIDE SPLICE

The side splice is also called the eye splice because it is used to form an eye or loop in the end of a rope by splicing the end back into its own side.

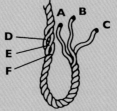

1 • Start by seizing the working end of the rope. Unlay the three strands—A, B, and C—to the seizing and whip the end of each strand. Then, twist the rope slightly to open up strands D, E, and F of the standing part of the rope as shown.

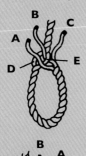

2 • The first tuck is shown. The middle strand is always tucked first, so strand B is tucked under strand E, the middle strand of the standing part.

3 • The second tuck is now made as shown. The left strand A of the working end is tucked under strand D, passing over strand E.

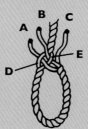

4 • This illustration shows how the third tuck is made. In order to make strand F easy to grab,

the rope is turned over. Strand C now appears on the left side.

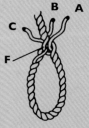

5 • Strand C is then passed to the right of and tucked under strand F as shown. This completes the first round of tucks.

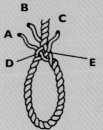

6 • This illustration shows the second round of tucks started, with the rope reversed again for ease in handling. Strand B is passed over strand D and tucked under the next strand to the left. Continue with strands A and C, tucking over one strand and then under one to the left. To complete the splice, tuck each strand in once more.

7 • The finished eye splice is shown. Remove the temporary seizing and cut off the strand ends, leaving at least ½ inch on each end. Roll the splice back and forth under your foot to even up and smooth out the strands.

FIGURE-EIGHT KNOT

This knot can be tied simply and quickly. Used in the end of a rope to temporarily prevent the strands from unlaying, it does not jam as easily as the overhand knot and is therefore useful in preventing the end of a rope from slipping through a block or an eye.

BOWLINE

The bowline is often used for temporary anchor knots. It never jams or slips if properly tied.

■ DOUBLE BOWLINE

Make an overhand loop with the end held toward you, exactly as in the ordinary bowline. The difference is that you pass the end through the loop twice—making two lower loops, A and B. The end is then passed behind the standing part and down through the first loop again as in the ordinary bowline. Pull tight. Used as a seat sling, the outside loop B goes under the person's arms, and the inside loop A forms the seat.

■ BOWLINE IN BIGHT

Here's a useful knot to know when you want to attach tackle to, say, the middle of a line when both ends of it are made fast. Grasp the rope where you want the new knot, shape it into a loop in one hand, and strike this against the two lines leading to the loop held in the other hand. Next, complete the first bight used in tying a regular bowline. Then, open up the loop after it has passed through the bight and bring the whole knot through it. Pull the loop tight over the standing part.

■ RUNNING BOWLINE

Tie the regular bowline around a loop of its own standing part. This makes an excellent slipknot, commonly used to retrieve spars, rigging, etc. And with lighter rope or twine, it's good for tightening to begin package tying.

■ SURGEON'S KNOT

This knot is usually tied with twine. It is a modified form of the reef knot, and the extra turn taken in the first tie prevents slipping before the knot is completed.

■ FISHERMAN'S BEND

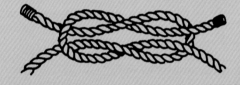

An important knot because of its strength and simplicity, it is used for making the end of a rope fast to a ring, spar, or anchor, or for a line to a bucket. It is more secure when the end is tied as shown.

■ REEF KNOT

Probably the most useful and popular of all knots, this is also known as the square knot. Used to join two ropes or lines of the same size, it holds firmly and is easily untied.

■ TIMBER HITCH

This knot is very useful for hoisting spars, boards, or logs. It is also handy for making a towline fast to a wet spar or timber. It holds without slipping and does not jam.

■ SHEET BEND

Used aboard a boat for joining small or medium-sized ropes, this knot is sometimes used for attaching the end of a rope to an eye splice.

FISHERMAN'S KNOT

This is probably the strongest known method of joining fine lines such as fishing lines. It is simple to tie and untie.

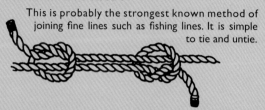

KNOTS FOR POLYPROPYLENE CORD

These are the knots to use for polypropylene cord.

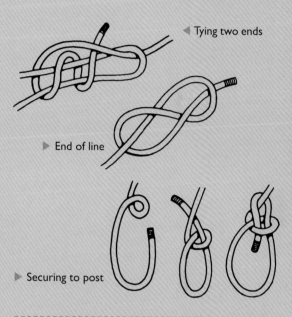

◄ Tying two ends

► End of line

► Securing to post

CLOVE HITCH

This is the most effective and quick way to tie a boat line to a mooring post. It can be tied in the middle or end of a rope, but it is apt to slip if tied at the end. To prevent slipping, make a half hitch in the end to the standing part.

TO PREVENT TWISTED ROPE FROM UNRAVELING WHEN CUT

For nylon, polyester, and polypropylene, tape the rope around the circumference as shown. Cut in the middle, leaving tape intact on either side. When cutting these synthetic fibers with a pocketknife or scissors, fuse the cut ends by match flame to prevent untwisting. Tape is unnecessary if a "hot knife" is used. Heat will melt and fuse the cut ends.

TYING LINE TO A CLEAT

This is the correct method for tying line to a cleat. The half hitch that completes the fastening is taken with the free part of the line. The line can then be freed without taking up slack in the standing part.

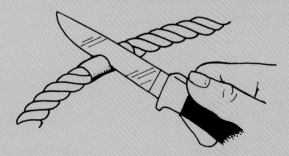

For manila and sisal, tape the rope as shown. Cut in the middle so that each end remains permanently taped. Natural fibers do not fuse with heat.

Easy Anchor Retrieval

This simple-and-easy method of pulling up your anchor is a boon to bad backs and big boats. Learn this technique and the hard work is done by an inflated net ball, the kind usually found on commercial fishing boats. The only equipment you will need is a stainless-steel anchor ring, heavy-duty stainless snap, 5 or 6 feet of nylon, and the net ball. The accompanying illustration shows all of the elements of an anchor-retrieval system properly rigged. This anchor-retrieval rig is available at all marina stores. The accompanying chart shows the suggested ball sizes.

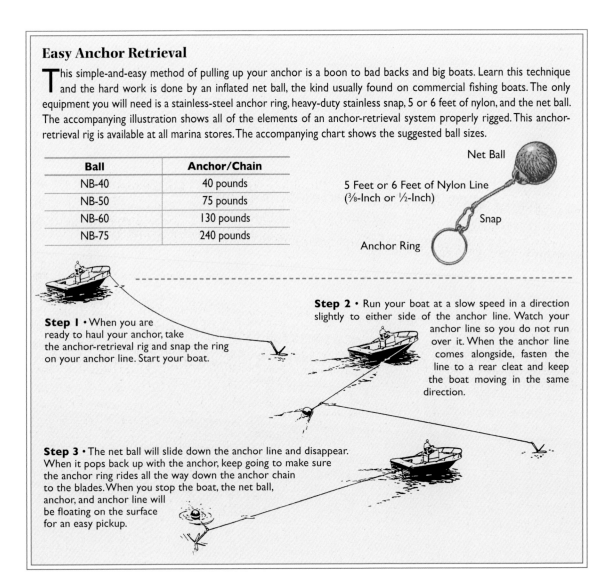

Ball	Anchor/Chain
NB-40	40 pounds
NB-50	75 pounds
NB-60	130 pounds
NB-75	240 pounds

Net Ball

5 Feet or 6 Feet of Nylon Line (⅜-Inch or ½-Inch)

Snap

Anchor Ring

Step 1 • When you are ready to haul your anchor, take the anchor-retrieval rig and snap the ring on your anchor line. Start your boat.

Step 2 • Run your boat at a slow speed in a direction slightly to either side of the anchor line. Watch your anchor line so you do not run over it. When the anchor line comes alongside, fasten the line to a rear cleat and keep the boat moving in the same direction.

Step 3 • The net ball will slide down the anchor line and disappear. When it pops back up with the anchor, keep going to make sure the anchor ring rides all the way down the anchor chain to the blades. When you stop the boat, the net ball, anchor, and anchor line will be floating on the surface for an easy pickup.

PREPARING FOR WINTER STORAGE

This work is necessary to keep your boat serviceable and to protect your investment in it. If you live where you can enjoy year-round boating, there are important semi-annual maintenance jobs that you will recognize. If you can store your boat at home, the job will be greatly simplified, but if you store it in a boatyard, you may have to work within the yard's schedule.

In deciding whether to store your boat outside or in a heated garage, for instance, there are two dangers that must be avoided: formation of ice on the boat and continual dry heat. Small aluminum boats are affected less than wood, fiberglass, or fabric ones. Hard freezing and ice can pop fastenings, open seams, split and check the surface, and cause permanent warp in straight lines.

Dry heat for long periods can destroy the resins in woods (including wood stringers and fittings in all boats) and dry out caulking and seam compounds. If you store your boat outdoors in natural humidity conditions, keep it covered so that water cannot collect and form ice. Indoors or out, free ventilation is essential so that condensation can evaporate. Here are the steps to preparing your boat for winter storage:

1. First, make sure your boat is properly cradled for storage. If you have a trailer that fits your boat, you have no problem. Level the trailer on chocks, wheels off the ground. If you own a small aluminum boat, it will store well turned facedown, resting on the strongly built gunwales. If you must build a cradle for a larger boat, make accurate templates and cut cradle supports for the transom, engine bed, construction center, and stem at least.

2. Clean the bottom and outside hull entirely of algae, fungi, and barnacles. This must be done immediately, before they harden and dry fast. At this time, you'll get a good look at the condition and know what repairs have to be made before spring launching.

3. Scrub down the entire boat inside, starting at the top. Flush and clean out bilges with bilge cleaner. Flush out freshwater tanks, fish and bait boxes, and freshwater lines with disinfectant solution and let them dry. Remove all traces of salt water, polish, clean, and spray with preservative.

4. Wash canvas tops, curtains, and rope lines with mild soap and rinse with fresh water. Spray with preservative before storing in a dry place. Whenever possible, have your boat entirely shrink wrapped for maximum protection. Make certain that several vent openings are in the shrink wrap to allow plenty of ventilation.

5. Treat serious rust at once. Clean down to the bare metal or remove and replace. Re-putty the fastenings, and spray fixed and moving hardware with light machine oil or WD-40.

6. Make sure every corner of the boat, every fitting and joint, is dry, clean, and free of fungi. Put desiccants wherever needed. Air the boat by opening all the hatches on a dry, bright day.

Follow motor-storage procedures in the owner's manual. Cover these points particularly:

1. Flush the cooling system with fresh water and a rust inhibitor, and then drain the system well.

2. Disconnect fuel lines and run idle until out of fuel.

3. Disconnect the battery, wipe the connectors and terminals clean, and then follow the maker's battery-storage procedures.

4. Clean the carburetor bowl with automotive carburetor cleaner or lacquer thinner. Slosh the cleaner fluid around in a portable gas tank and pour out through the fuel lines and drain it well. This removes the gummy substance left by fuel.

5. Remove the spark plugs with a spark-plug wrench, squirt lubricating oil into each cylinder, and then turn the crankshaft by hand to distribute the oil. Replace the spark plugs.

6. Leave the motor head and lower unit clean of heavy dirt, rust, and grease deposits. Wipe the head and lower unit with an oily cloth.

7. Make sure the lower unit grease reservoir is left full.

PREPARING FOR SPRING LAUNCHING

Most owners start too late, missing a month or two of good boating before they are ready to launch. Use the post-holiday season to do inside work you want to accomplish: build cabinets, a fish box, circulating baitwell, or do other basement or garage jobs. Keep your eye on the boat throughout the winter if it's stored outside. If the boat is stored at a marina, check the boat often head to foot. Make an estimate of jobs, tools, and materials you'll need. First, do the outside hull—everything it needs to give you a safe and trouble-free season. If you have a wood boat, the hull should be sanded down to clean, bare wood, whether you are restoring a few spots where needed or refinishing the complete hull. Peeling and cracking on top indicates trouble underneath. Down to bare wood, you may discover the source. Sand the wood smooth, fill in cracks and holes and over fastenings, replace damaged boards, and dust clean before starting to paint.

Proceed carefully until you know what to do. Get paint maker's recommendations and specifications for your hull. Polyester paints will give you an amazingly tough coat when properly applied, but you will probably do better with an epoxy-based paint over fiberglass. Talk to your dealer and other owners. If you want to paint an originally unpainted aluminum boat, get the boat maker's specifications; certain paints can't be used.

Before you paint a bare fiberglass hull or cabin, think twice. You will not be able to sand and strip as you would with a wood hull. To repaint, you have to leave the first coat of paint on or risk damaging the gel coat. Most owners for this reason try to bleach out discolorations and stains. Spots can be scoured and buffed. Ask for recommended materials at a marine store. Damaged spots can be patched with fiberglass. The best overall treatment is to wax well with a marine-grade wax and sail on. If you must paint, use steel wool, which will give tooth for the paint, and use paints recommended by the manufacturers. Any surface must be absolutely clean before repainting.

On cabin woods, spar varnish is usually used; it's tough and looks good. Whatever your choice, on high-wear areas that scuff and go bare quickly, use a good grade of marine spar varnish, preferably every season.

If you find mildew or water inside, note how they got in and repair the damage. Next fall, use more desiccants in some corners, buy a better tarp, or add weather stripping to your windows. Neutralize foul odors before you launch. It's easy; try the supermarket.

Flush out all freshwater systems again with disinfectant, fill the tanks, and turn on the pressure. A drip is a leak. Fix it before you sail and you'll have a drier, safer boat. Check all through-hull fittings. If you find any signs of leaking or rot, restore the watertight fit and get the best advice you can to make it permanent.

Here, from service experts, are some important steps to follow to get your outboard motor ready to go after winter storage:

1. Check the level of lubricant in the lower unit and make sure it's filled to the proper level. If it appears oil has been leaking, have a service expert check it out since it could indicate the lower seals and gaskets need replacing. And if you didn't do this before off-season storage, drain the gear case and refill it with the manufacturer's recommended lubricant.

2. If your motor has a power trim or power tilt unit, check the level of fluid in the system's reservoir, and refill it with the recommended fluid as needed.

3. Check your spark plugs. Your outboard can't start quickly and run efficiently if the plugs aren't sparking. Remove them, clean them, and make sure they are gapped to specification. Also make sure the spark-plug terminal connections and wiring are clean, unfrayed, and snug-fitting.

4. Check the boat's battery. Make sure it's fully charged. Clean the terminal posts and connectors so they are free of corrosion.

5. If there was unused fuel left in the tank and engine over the winter, it should have been treated with a fuel conditioner before storage. If the fuel was conditioned, all you need to do in the spring is make sure the fuel-system clamps and fittings are tight and not leaking. Also check for cracked, worn, or aged fuel lines and replace as necessary. However, if no fuel conditioner was added before storage, clean the fuel-pump filter before adding fresh fuel. Although they vary from brand to brand, most outboard fuel filters are designed for easy cleaning. Check your owner's manual for instructions. Of course, all the old, untreated fuel should be drained from the tank and disposed of properly before new, fresh fuel is added. If you have an outboard with an oil-injection system, check to make sure the oil tank is filled. Also, check your owner's manual for any special maintenance the oil-injection system might require.

6. Many boaters use a fuel conditioner for winter storage, but then neglect its in-season use. Used in much smaller quantities during the boating season, outboard fuel conditioners help keep the carburetor clean, reduce plug fouling, and reduce moisture in the fuel system. A note of caution: use only fuel conditioners designed for marine use in your boat, not automotive additives or conditioners, which can do your motor more harm than good.

7. Check your propeller. A little ding in the prop can make a big dent in your boat's performance. If the propeller is nicked, gouged, or bent, take it to your dealer or a prop shop for repair. If the prop is too far gone, invest in a new one. Stainless propellers offer much greater durability than most aluminum props. Here's a safety tip: before removing your propeller, always shift your motor to neutral and remove the key from the ignition switch to prevent the motor from accidentally starting. If you have trouble loosening the propeller nut, try wedging a piece of two-by-four between the prop blade and the antiventilation plate

to keep the prop from turning. Before replacing the propeller, lube the prop shaft with grease as specified in your owner's manual. Also, check around the base of the prop shaft for monofilament fishing line that may have become wrapped around the shaft. Look closely—old monofilament might look like a plastic washer. Be sure to check your owner's manual for any special instructions and torque specifications before installing the propeller.

8. While you're checking the prop, also check the bottom of the boat. For clean, efficient running, the hull must be clean and efficient, too. Now's the time to remove any leftover barnacles or dried-up marine algae or weeds.

9. Spring is also a good time to touch up any scrapes or scratches in your motor's paint job. Most manufacturers offer factory-matched colors in easy-to-use spray-paint cans. If you're touching up the lower unit, be careful not to clog the water intake screen with paint. This could lead to the motor overheating. Also, don't make the mistake of painting over the sacrificial zinc anodes on your motor. They won't work if they're covered with paint. While you're inspecting the motor, check the anodes. If they are more than 50 percent destroyed, replace them with new ones. If you boat in salt water or brackish water, the anodes are supposed to dissipate as they protect your motor.

10. After the mechanical work is done, give your motor (and boat) a good cleaning. Remove all the dirt and grime collected over the winter. Use an engine degreaser to clean up your outboard's power head. As a final touch, give the motor a coat of automotive wax or polish. This will help it sparkle and protect the finish from the sun and water.

11. After the motor's all cleaned up, consult the lubrication section of your owner's manual. Most motors require a shot of lubricant on the throttle linkage or other moving parts on the engine. On motors with remote steering, the steering cable ram should be greased before the start of each season and periodically thereafter. Once again, check the owner's manual for detailed instructions.

BOAT TRAILERS

What size boat is trailerable? That is really a conundrum. The answer depends on how much you are willing to put into trailering. Each year's new-boat announcements include a large cabin cruiser with the claim " . . . and it can be trailered!" The fact is that it actually can be trailered, but it may be a professional transport job. You will need a heavy-duty, custom-built trailer, and should have a heavy-duty truck to make it go. And then it might do the boat no good. It's not a consumer proposition.

Common boat sizes for regular trailering are 14 to 26 feet. It is true that some 12-footers weigh more than 120 or 130 pounds, more weight than can be lifted to the top of a car by two persons. On the other end of the range, boats longer than 20 feet commonly have a deep bow, broad beam, and big weight that cause all sorts of problems in trailering. For a start, most state and all federal highways have a width limit of 8 feet; beyond that, you'll need a special permit and arrangements to travel.

If you are going to buy a boat in the prime size range for trailering, should you get a trailer at the same time? You will probably get a better fit for your boat if you do. The maker can supply information about trailer specifications for current-model hulls, and the dealer will probably carry trailers that suit.

But if you live near the water, why have a trailer? First, you save on mooring fees and winter storage. Second, your boat will be a much bigger asset if you can take it along on vacations, trailering it to another water when you want to fish and hunt or camp away from home. Keeping a boat on its trailer in your yard, you can keep bottom fouling cleaned off instead of facing a big job once or twice a year. Make it part of your routine when washing and waxing the car, and you will have a hull that is always in good shape. Keep a tarp over the boat and motor when it's idle on the trailer. When it sits in your own yard, there's no worry about vandalism at a mooring or a marina dock.

▨ Choosing a Trailer

The best advice is to get a trailer one size bigger than your present boat requires. This will accommodate the occasional extra-heavy load you will pack in it. If you

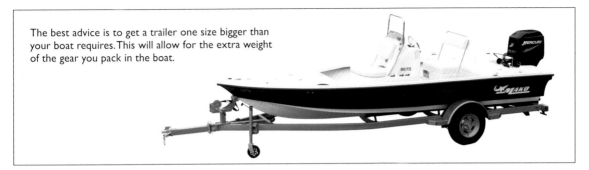

The best advice is to get a trailer one size bigger than your boat requires. This will allow for the extra weight of the gear you pack in the boat.

get a trailer larger than that, your boat will not be properly supported and the trailer will be awkward to tow, bouncing around because the boat is not heavy enough to hold it on the road.

Proper hull support is essential in a trailer. This is where the boat maker's advice is important. Three critical points are: full support at the transom, at the bottom forefoot, and at the construction center, either where the greatest weight is built in amidships or under the engine stringers in an inboard boat. You must avoid a trailer mismatch that will, over a period of time, cause the hull to hook or rocker. A well-engineered trailer for a boat of 500 pounds or more will have pairs of strong, securely set rollers on good bearings at frequent intervals for the entire bottom length.

Regardless of size, the trailer must enable you to back down to the water and launch your boat efficiently without getting the trailer-wheel hubs in the water. Winch quality is important for heavier boats. A wobbly or ill-fitting crank, wheel, and ratchet won't do. For a boat of 1,500 pounds or more, you might consider adding an electric winch. It saves a lot of knuckle busting.

Trailer suspension, wheel mounts, and general construction should be spelled out by the trailer maker. Study these and get full information from the dealer about use and maintenance. Leaf springs are good on a heavy trailer; a soft ride is not important, while good support is. If you trailer 3,500 pounds or more, tandem wheels are needed.

You will have to look up state laws on trailers for your region, and then equip your trailer and the tow vehicle according to those laws. The laws specify over what weights trailer brakes are required, but you may decide you want brakes even if your trailer is below the limit. In that case, look into brakes that operate in tandem with your car's foot pedal. Quality trailer brakes are practically foolproof, make driving safer and easier, and they reduce wear on the tow vehicle's rear suspension and tires.

Insist on a frame-mounted hitch, even though the salesman may try to give you a shallow hitch bolted to the body pan when you buy that new wagon. As for bumper-mounted hitches, they are dangerous. With a frame-mounted hitch, you will be able to step up in weight over a big range without additional expense, and you'll be able to trailer your present boat without worry. You will need an umbilical electric hookup to your car's electrical system for trailer lights and brakes and other accessories. The cable, clamps, and plugs come in a package at a reasonable price. On your car you'll need western-type rearview mirrors—big, rectangular ones mounted on arms on each side that let you see around the trailer. For a trailer load of 3,000 pounds or more, you should have an equalizing hitch that compensates for a big load in normal travel and substantially reduces danger in a crash stop.

■ Loading Your Boat and Trailer

Most makers recommend loading with 5 to 7 percent more weight ahead of the trailer axle. This prevents fishtailing and gives you good load control. If you are going on an extended trip with camping gear loaded inside the boat, watch the weight distribution. Weigh big items as they are loaded, and don't under any circumstances exceed the maker's maximum weight limit. Your trailer will be designed to haul your boat and motor with the correct load in front of the axle. Additional weight inside the boat should maintain this distribution, or the position of the boat on the trailer bed should be adjusted accordingly. A well-made trailer will let you do this.

■ Trailer Maintenance

Wheel bearings are the critical point. When traveling, stop every few hours to feel for excessive heat at the hubs. If the hubs are hot, let them cool off, and then drive slowly to the nearest service station and have them repack the wheel bearings. Have the bearings inspected before each trip, and have them repacked at the start of each season.

Keep the hitch and mount free of rust, repaint each season with metal paint on clean metal, and grease moving joints on an equalizing hitch only as the maker specifies. You'll find that a well-made boat trailer will last at least as long as the boat if it's well maintained. And you will be delighted when you learn how much extra gear you can take along in the boat.

■ On the Road and Launching

The U.S. Coast Guard makes the following recommendations for trailering a boat. Heeding their advice will ensure your safety on the road and also at the launch ramp.

Pre-Departure Checks

Make a complete check of the trailer and towing vehicle. Inspect tires for tread wear, inflation, and condition. Examine the hitch and associated safety devices, and check brakes on both vehicles.

■ Check the tightness of the wheel lugs. Repeat this periodically during the trip.

■ Equip the towing vehicle with large rearview mirrors on both sides. Check the inside rearview mirror. The boat and the load should be low enough so that it does not obstruct the view.

■ Check shocks and springs on both vehicles.

■ Load tools, emergency equipment, and foul-weather gear in a readily accessible location in the towing vehicle.

■ Check the load on the trailer. It must be loaded correctly from front to rear, and from side to side for the best balance.

■ Couple the trailer to the tow vehicle and observe the attitude of it. Check the trailer lights.

■ Check the wheel bearings on the trailer.

■ Check all tie-down straps.

UNDERWAY: Once underway, never forget that you have a boat behind you. This sounds foolish, but when you're wheeling along at highway speeds it is all too easy to lose a feel for the tow—until you have to pass, turn, or brake. Always start slowly, in low gear, and take the car up through the gears gently. Think twice about passing other vehicles—but if you decide to pass, don't delay. Be alert for signs restricting trailers. Remain sensitive to unusual sounds or handling factors, and if there's anything that seems at all strange, pull over immediately and check. In fact, you should pull over and check the entire rig every hour or so—check for high temperatures in the wheel bearings and slackening tie-downs, and make sure the lights, tire pressure, and car-engine temperature are OK. Here are some other safety tips to keep in mind when towing a trailer:

■ Never let anyone ride in the trailer while moving. It is dangerous, and illegal in many states.

■ Observe speed limits. In many states, the speed limit for a car towing a trailer is lower than for a car traveling by itself.

■ Maintain a greater following distance between your vehicle and the one in front of you. With the trailer, you need much more room to stop.

■ When traveling over bumpy roads or crossing railroad tracks, slow down. Going too fast may cause the tow vehicle to bottom out and the hitch to scrape, causing damage to both the car and the trailer.

■ Large trucks and buses create considerable turbulence, which may cause the trailer to fishtail. Keep a firm grip on the steering wheel and tension on the hitch ball. If there is a manual lever that will operate the trailer brakes separately from those on the car, a quick application of the trailer brakes may slow the trailer sufficiently to eliminate sway.

LAUNCHING: Launching will be the critical part of your trailer-boating expedition. It's embarrassing, as well as expensive, to safely travel many highway miles just to do something dumb at the moment of truth. Before going to the ramp, check with the marina operator or others to determine if there are any unusual hazards, such as a drop-off at the end of the ramp. You should prepare your boat for launching away from the ramp so that you don't hold up other boaters. This is known as "ramp courtesy." Preparations for launching should include raising the lower unit to avoid scraping, installing the drain plug,

When launching or recovering, never turn off the car's engine, and keep the parking brake set while you work the boat off the trailer.

releasing the tie-downs, and disconnecting or removing the trailer's stop and directional lights.

When launching or recovering, never turn the car's engine off, and keep the parking brake set while you work the boat off the trailer. Only the driver should be in the towing vehicle during launching and recovering. One or two observers can help the driver watch the trailer and traffic. Keep everyone else away from the launching ramp. It is also prudent to use a tire stop to avoid an unexpected dunking of trailer and car.

Many trailer-boat owners' worst moments have occurred at busy launching ramps because they have not practiced backing their rig. Before you attempt a launching, you should put in a couple of hours in a deserted parking lot learning how to back your rig through a maze of cardboard boxes. A helpful hint when backing is to place your hand on the bottom of the steering wheel and move the wheel in the direction you want the trailer to go. Do **not** oversteer.

If you have an unwieldy trailer, you may want to get an auxiliary front bumper hitch, which will make close-quarters maneuvering much simpler, as well as keep the drive wheels of the towing vehicle on higher, drier ground.

Make sure you **never, ever** cast off all the lines from the boat before launching. Someone on shore must have a line that is made fast to the boat. The line makes it easy to shove the boat off the trailer and then pull the boat to a dock or boarding platform or back to the trailer at a wide, busy launching ramp. Above all, take the time necessary to launch safely, but as soon as the boat is afloat, move the vehicle and the trailer to the parking lot and the boat to the dock for loading. Don't loiter.

Always try to avoid getting the trailer hubs in the water. If you cannot avoid dunking them, at least let them cool first. If you don't, the sudden cooling may crack or chip the bearings or suck them full of water. One way to pass the time, if you are a sailor, is to step the mast in the parking lot while waiting to launch. However, make sure that there are no low power lines or other overhead obstructions between you and the launching ramp. Unfortunately, a few boaters are electrocuted every year because their rigging comes in contact with overhead electrical wires.

BACKING A TRAILER: Backing a boat trailer down a tight, slick launch ramp can be tricky, and a busy ramp is not the place to learn. Practice in an empty parking lot on a Sunday morning. You'll be able to go at your own pace without an impatient audience.

When backing the trailer, keep in mind that you're pushing it, not pulling it. No big deal when you back straight up—you just have to keep the wheels of the tow vehicle perfectly straight. But when it's time to turn, everything is reversed: turning the steering wheel to the right will turn the rear end of the tow vehicle to the right, causing the trailer to turn left, and vice versa.

Steering Tip

Placing your hand on the bottom of the steering wheel simplifies the process of backing up. Pull the wheel to the right, the trailer heads right, and vice versa.

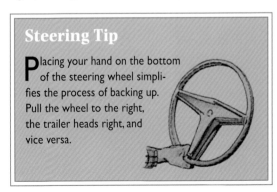

Backing a Trailer

Step 1 • Keep the tow vehicle and trailer straight and close to the ramp when getting into position. Remember that you will be steering in reverse.

Step 2 • When your trailer is in position to be backed onto the ramp, turn the steering wheel sharply in the direction opposite the intended path of the trailer.

Step 3 • As the trailer begins to move down the ramp, start to turn your steering wheel to the left (as shown), which will push your trailer to the right. If possible, have a second person outside to assist you with hand signals.

Step 4 • As soon as your trailer is lined up correctly on the ramp, straighten your wheels and follow the trailer as you back it down the ramp for your launch. While waiting your turn on the ramp, watch other launchings to gauge the effects of wind and current.

RETRIEVAL: Retrieving your boat is similar to launching and should be done with the same courtesy by reversing the procedures. Unload your boat at the dock and keep it there until the trailer is ready to move down the ramp. Move the boat to the trailer and raise the lower unit. Winch the boat on to the trailer and secure it. Finally, move the towing vehicle and trailer with the boat to the parking area for loading, housekeeping, and other general maintenance chores.

STORAGE: To prevent water from accumulating in the boat, remove the drain plug and tilt the trailer and the boat enough to allow drainage. This should be done for even short-term storage.

When storing the boat on its trailer for any length of time, get the weight off the wheels. Cinder blocks under the tongue and four corners of the frame of the trailer should be adequate support, shimmed up if necessary by boards. Once the trailer frame is jacked up, you should check to be sure that the boat itself is evenly supported. Be forewarned: the frame itself can easily be bent out of its normal shape by excessive jacking at a corner.

SAFE BOATING

Boaters don't have a clean record when it comes to accidents afloat. It has little to do with the perquisites of fishing, but much to do with neglecting to control the boat and guard personal safety aboard. A sportsman who has not schooled himself in basic boating safety and safe habits will forget about them in an emergency. Here's your chance to start right.

Basic Tool Kit

Every boat must be equipped to get home on its own. The exact selection of tools, spare parts, and supplies necessary must be suited to your boat and motor and to problems you are most likely to encounter. Here are the items that should be in a basic tool kit:

- Ordinary pliers
- Vise-grip pliers
- Diagonal-cutting pliers
- Long-nose electrician's pliers
- Screwdrivers
- Spark-plug wrench to fit
- Combination open-end and box wrenches in sizes ⅜ to ¾ inch
- Sharp knife

Spare Parts

Keep these spare parts on hand:

- Spark plugs of correct specifications
- Distributor cap, rotor, condenser, and point set
- Fuel pump and filter
- Oil filter
- Water-pump impeller
- V-belts to match each size used
- Spare fuel lines, cocks, and fittings
- Gaskets and hoses
- Bailing-pump diaphragm
- Fuses and bulbs to double for each used

All-Purpose Kit

For an all-purpose kit, include the following:

- 50-foot chalk line
- Nails, screws, bolts and nuts, and washers
- Hose clamps
- Electrical tape
- Insulated wire
- Cotter pins
- Elastic plastic bandage material and duct tape
- Machine oil

Outboard Motor Troubleshooting Checklist

Follow these steps to check the condition of your outboard motor:

- Check gas supply and tank pressure; squeeze the bulb several times.
- Check to be sure the propeller is not wrapped in weeds, line, or net. If line is wrapped around the prop, try to slow reverse to loosen it. Then, cut off pieces until you can pull the rest free.
- Look for loose wires and clamps at battery terminals.
- Remove ignition wire from any spark plug and crank the motor. A spark should jump from the wire end to the engine head; if there is no spark, check back to the ignition switch.
- If you have a hot spark, look into the fuel feed, pull the gas feed line off from the side of the outboard, and blow through the line until you hear bubbles in the tank.
- Clean the carburetor bowl and fuel filter.

Quartering a Following Sea

Quartering may be the only solution to crossing a following sea. Your speed, however, must be faster than the waves running at your stern. You'll have to make corrections with each wave you meet. As you cross the crest, wave action tries to turn a quartering boat broadside by pushing its stern into the trough between it and the next wave crest. You must power your boat into the direction of the trough to properly point your bow toward the next crest. (Note the direction of the outboard and prop in illustration.) Never allow wave action to push your boat parallel to the trough.

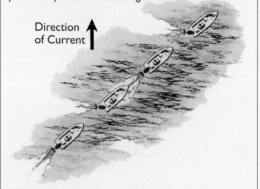

Direction of Current

Mouth of River or Inlet

Wherever a current enters a body of water—this is true for river mouths as well as ocean inlets—you can expect to find relatively calm water at the edge of the intruding flow. Usually this calm transition zone is marked by surface wave action. When running any inlet, always ride the back of the wave in front of you. Never power over its crest, or drift far enough back to be picked up by the crest of the following wave.

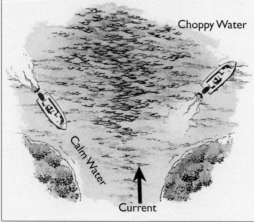

Choppy Water

Calm Water

Current

■ Safe Boating Procedures

First, it is important to know your boat. Get familiar with its equipment and discover its limitations. If it's a livery rental, check it over completely before you push off.

Make a habit of checking off safety equipment aboard. First, locate the safety items required by law. Then, compare your optional equipment with the Coast Guard's list of recommended equipment. Count the life preservers, and make sure that each passenger has one that will keep him afloat in the water.

Carry a proper chart, GPS, compass, VHF, and a fully charged cell phone.

Put tackle, guns, decoys, nets, and other gear where they are secure and won't clutter walkways and footing.

Check the fuel supply, and the condition of the tank and feed line. Make sure the spark is strong and regular. Take along at least 1½ times as much fuel as you estimate you will need. If you run into heavy waves, your boat will take more fuel to go the same distance.

Gasoline vapors are explosive and will settle in the low areas of a boat. During fueling, keep doors, hatches, ports, and chests closed, stoves and pilot lights off, electrical circuits off, and absolutely no smoking! Keep the fill nozzle in firm contact with the fill neck to prevent static spark. Don't spill, for you'll have to dry it up before starting the engine. Do not use gasoline appliances aboard—they're lethal risks. Use alcohol and other less volatile fuels.

After fueling, ventilate thoroughly before pressing the starter. One minute is the minimum safe ventilation time. Big boats should be ventilated longer, with effective blowers operating and all ports opened. Keep your fuel lines in perfect condition and the boat's bilges clean.

Electrical equipment, switches, and wiring are some prime sources of boat fires and explosions. Keep batteries clean and ventilated.

Do not overload your boat. Make sure you have safely adequate freeboard before casting off. Look ahead to water conditions and weather changes you may encounter.

Keep an alert lookout. If you have a boat longer than 20 feet, name your mate and agree that he'll keep lookout any time you can't. You have more to watch out for than other boats and shallow water. Watch for obstructions such as rocks and floating logs.

Swimmers are hard to see in the water. Running through swimmers or a swimming area is the most sensitive violation a boat can make. If in doubt, give beaches and rafts a wide swing.

Your wake is potent. You can swamp small craft such as canoes or rowboats, damage shorelines and shore property, disturb sleepers, and ruin fish and wildlife sport for hours by running fast through small passages and shallows. You are always responsible for any damage caused by your wake.

Learn the Coast Guard navigation rules and obey them at all times. Copies are available to download free on the Coast Guard website. Most collisions are caused by one-time violations.

Make sure at least one other person aboard knows how to operate the boat and motor in case you are disabled or fall overboard. Know a plan of action you will take in emergencies such as a man overboard, bad leak, motor that won't run, collision, bad storm, or troublesome passenger.

Storm signals and danger signs are often informal. Learn to read the weather, and keep alert to what passing boats are trying to tell you.

Wear your life preserver and make all your passengers, especially children, wear life preservers at all times. In a capsizing, remember that you are safer if you stay with the boat, where you can be seen. It will also help you stay afloat until help arrives.

Under Coast Guard legislation, it is illegal for anyone to build, sell, or use a craft that does not conform to safety regulations. Check with your dealer, and check yourself to make sure your boat measures up.

Small Boat, Big Water

The best way to stay out of trouble on open water is to learn how to read the wind and weather. The National Oceanic and Atmospheric Administration (NOAA) issues marine weather forecasts every hour with details of winds and seas. If you have a VHF-FM radio, NOAA weather radio broadcasts weather and warnings continuously on these frequencies: 162.400 MHz, 162.425 MHz, 162.450 MHz, 162.475 MHz, 162.500 MHz, 162.525 MHz, and 162.550 MHz. Matching the wind forecast with the accompanying chart will give you a good idea of the seas you can expect to encounter.

But such forecasts are regional, and local conditions can be radically different—thunderstorms, for instance. You can determine the distance in miles of an approaching thunderstorm by counting the interval between seeing a lightning flash and hearing its accompanying thunder in seconds, and then dividing by five. For example, if it takes 10 seconds to hear the thunder, the storm is 2 miles away.

Wind/Sea Relationships

	Velocity (knots)	Conditions
Calm Conditions	0–3	Sea like a mirror
	4–6	Ripples, less than 1 foot
	7–10	Smooth wavelets, 1 to 2 feet
	11–16	Small waves, 2 to 4 feet
Small Craft Warning	17–21	Moderate waves, 4 to 8 feet, whitecaps
	22–27	Large waves, 8 to 13 feet, spray
	28–33	High waves, 13 to 20 feet, heaped seas, foam from breaking waves
Gale Warning	34–40	High waves, 13 to 20 feet, foam blown in well-marked streaks
	41–47	Seas rolling, reduced visibility from spray, waves 13 to 20 feet
Storm Warning	48–55	White seas, very high waves, 20 to 30 feet, overhanging crests
	56–63	Exceptionally high waves, 30 to 45 feet
Hurricane Warning	More than 63	Air filled with foam, sea white, waves over 45 feet

But that knowledge won't help much if you don't have time to get to safety. Odds are you're going to get caught on the water eventually. Knowing how to handle difficult seas in a small boat is insurance all sportsmen should have.

Coast Guard–Approved Equipment

For safe boating under most conditions, you are required by federal law to carry Coast Guard–approved equipment aboard your craft. Coast Guard–approved equipment simply means that it has been approved by the Commandant of the U.S. Coast Guard and has been determined to be in compliance with U.S. Coast Guard specifications

Buoys

Buoys are traffic signals that guide boaters safely along waterways. They can also identify dangerous areas, as well as give directions and information. The colors and numbers on buoys mean the same thing regardless of what kind of buoy on which they appear.

Red colors, red lights, and even numbers • These indicate the right side of the channel as a boater enters from the open sea or heads upstream. Numbers usually increase consecutively as you return from the open sea or head upstream.

Green colors, green lights, and odd numbers • These indicate the left side of the channel as a boater enters from the open sea and heads upstream. Numbers will usually increase consecutively as you return from the open sea or head upstream.

Red and green horizontal stripes • These are placed at the junction of two channels to indicate the preferred (primary) channel when a channel splits. If green is on top,

the preferred channel is to the right. If red is on top, the preferred channel is to the left. The light color matches the top stripe. These are also sometimes referred to as junction buoys.

Nun buoys • These cone-shaped buoys are always marked with red markings and even numbers. They mark the right side of the channel as a boater enters from the open sea or heads upstream.

Can buoys • These cylindrical-shaped buoys are always marked with green markings and odd numbers. They mark the left side of the channel as a boater enters from the open sea or heads upstream.

1 • Red Colors and Lights

2 • Green Colors and Lights

3 • Red/Green Horizontally Striped Buoy

4 • Green/Red Horizontally Striped Buoy

5 • Nun Buoy (Red with Even Numbers)

6 • Can Buoy (Green with Odd Numbers)

Storm Warning Signals

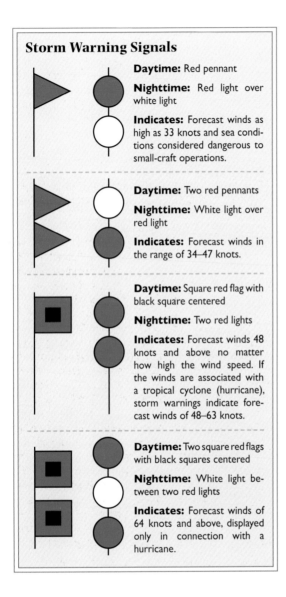

Daytime: Red pennant

Nighttime: Red light over white light

Indicates: Forecast winds as high as 33 knots and sea conditions considered dangerous to small-craft operations.

Daytime: Two red pennants

Nighttime: White light over red light

Indicates: Forecast winds in the range of 34–47 knots.

Daytime: Square red flag with black square centered

Nighttime: Two red lights

Indicates: Forecast winds 48 knots and above no matter how high the wind speed. If the winds are associated with a tropical cyclone (hurricane), storm warnings indicate forecast winds of 48–63 knots.

Daytime: Two square red flags with black squares centered

Nighttime: White light between two red lights

Indicates: Forecast winds of 64 knots and above, displayed only in connection with a hurricane.

A: Fires of ordinary combustible materials

B: Gasoline, oil, and grease fires

C: Electrical fires

Fire extinguishers must be carried on **all** motorboats that meet one or more of the following conditions:

- Inboard engines
- Closed compartments under thwarts and seats where portable fuel tanks may be stored
- Double bottoms not sealed to the hull or not completely filled with flotation materials
- Closed living spaces
- Closed stowage compartments in which combustible or flammable materials are stored
- Permanently installed fuel tanks

There is no gallon capacity to determine if a fuel tank is portable. However, if the fuel tank is secured so it cannot be moved in case of a fire or other emergency, or if the weight of the fuel tank is such that people onboard cannot move it in case of a fire or other emergency, then the Coast Guard considers the tank permanently installed.

Dry chemical fire extinguishers without gauges or indicating devices must be inspected every six months. If the gross weight of a carbon dioxide (CO_2) fire extinguisher is reduced by more than 10 percent of the net weight, the extinguisher is not acceptable and must be recharged. Check extinguishers regularly to be sure that the gauges are free and nozzles clear.

Fire-extinguisher requirements are classified by the size of the vessel:

1. Boats less than 26 feet in length with **no** fixed fire-extinguishing system installed in machinery spaces must have at least one approved Type B-I hand-portable fire extinguisher. When an approved fixed fire-extinguishing system is installed in machinery spaces, no Type B-I extinguisher is required. If the construction of the boat does not permit the entrapment of explosive or flammable gases or vapors, no fire extinguisher is required.

2. Boats 26 feet to less than 40 feet in length must have at least two approved Type B-I or at least one Type B-II hand-portable fire extinguishers. When an approved fixed fire-extinguishing system is installed, only one Type B-I extinguisher is required.

and regulations relating to materials, construction, and performance.

Here are the Coast Guard recommendations for the most essential lifesaving equipment you must have onboard under federal law.

FIRE EXTINGUISHERS: Each approved fire extinguisher is classified by a letter and a Roman numeral according to the type of fire it is designed to extinguish and its size. The letter indicates the type of fire:

3. Boats 40 feet to not more than 65 feet in length must have at least three approved Type B-I or at least one Type B-I and one Type B-II hand-portable fire extinguisher. When an approved fixed fire-extinguishing system is installed, one fewer Type B-I or one Type B-II extinguisher is required.

Note: Coast Guard–approved extinguishers carry the following label: Marine Type USCG Approved, Size —, Type —, 162.208/, etc. UL-listed extinguishers not displaying this marking are also acceptable, provided they are of the above sizes and types and carry a minimum UL rating of 5-B:C.

Fire Extinguishers

Extinguishers approved for motorboats are hand portable, of either B-I or B-II classification or their UL equivalents, and have the following characteristics:

Coast Guard Classes	UL Listing	Foam (gallons)	CO_2 (pounds)	Dry Chemical (pounds)	Halon (pounds)
B–I	5B	1¼	4	2	2½
B–II	—	2½	15	10	10
—	10B	—	10	2½	5

PERSONAL FLOTATION DEVICES (PFDS): All boats must be equipped with U.S. Coast Guard–approved life jackets called personal flotation devices, or PFDs. The quantity and type depends on the length of the boat and the number of people onboard or being towed. Each PFD must be in good condition, the proper size for the intended wearer, and, very important, must be readily accessible.

▪ Type I: Offshore Life Jacket

These PFDs provide the most buoyancy. They are effective for all waters, especially open, rough, or remote waters where rescue may be delayed. They are designed to turn most unconscious wearers to a face-up position.

▪ Type II: Near-Shore Vest

These vests are intended for calm, inland waters or where there is a good chance of quick rescue. This type will turn some unconscious wearers to a face-up position, but will not turn as many people to a face-up position as a Type I.

▪ Type III: Flotation Aid

These vests are good for calm, inland waters, or where there is a good chance of quick rescue. They are designed so wearers can place themselves in a face-up position. The wearer may have to tilt his head back to avoid turning facedown in the water. It is generally the most comfortable type for continuous wear.

▪ Type IV: Throwable Device

These cushions or ring buoys are intended for calm, inland waters where help is always present. They are not designed to be worn, but to be thrown to a person in the water and held by the victim until they are rescued.

▪ Type V: Special-Use Device

These PFDs are intended for specific activities and may be carried instead of another PFD only if used according to the label. Some Type V devices provide significant hypothermia protection. Type V PFDs must be used in accordance with their labels to be acceptable.

Note: U.S. Coast Guard–approved inflatable life jackets are authorized for use by people over 16 years of age. They must have a full cylinder and all status indicators on the inflator must be green or the device does not meet the legal requirements. Inflatable life jackets are more comfortable, which encourages regular wear.

VISUAL DISTRESS SIGNALS: All recreational boats, when used on coastal waters, the Great Lakes, territorial seas, and those waters connected directly to the Great Lakes and territorial seas, up to a point where a body of water is less than 2 miles wide, must be equipped with visual distress signals. Boats owned in the United States operating on the high seas must also be equipped with visual distress signals. The following are exempted from the requirements for day signals and only need to carry night signals:

- Recreational boats less than 16 feet in length

- Boats participating in organized events, such as races, regattas, or marine parades

- Open sailboats less than 26 feet in length not equipped with propulsion machinery

- Manually propelled boats

Pyrotechnic visual distress signals must be Coast Guard–approved, in serviceable condition, and stowed to be readily accessible. They are marked with a date showing the serviceable life, and this date must not have passed.

Personal Flotation Devices

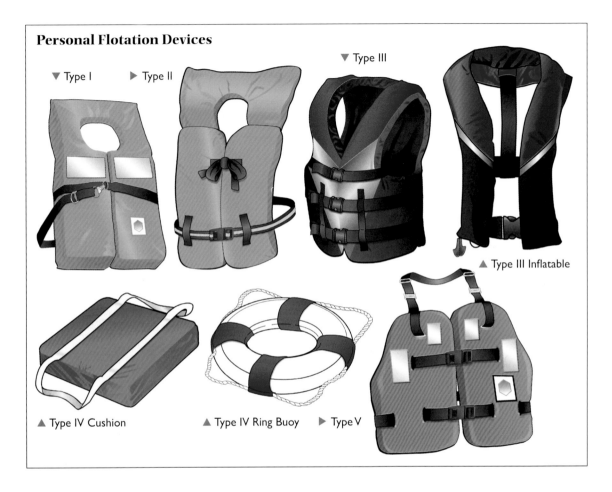

▼ Type I   ▶ Type II   ▼ Type III   ▲ Type III Inflatable

▲ Type IV Cushion   ▲ Type IV Ring Buoy   ▶ Type V

Coast Guard–approved pyrotechnic visual distress signals and associated devices include:

- Pyrotechnic red flares, handheld or aerial
- Pyrotechnic orange smoke, handheld or floating
- Launchers for aerial red meteors or parachute flares

Non-pyrotechnic visual distress signaling devices must carry the manufacturer's certification that they meet Coast Guard requirements. They must be in serviceable condition and stowed to be readily accessible. This group includes:

- Orange distress flags
- Electric distress flags

No single signaling device is ideal under all conditions and for all purposes. Consideration should there-fore be given to carrying several types. For example, an aerial flare can be seen over a long distance on a clear night, but for closer work, a handheld flare may be more useful.

HANDLING AND STORAGE OF PYROTECHNIC DEVICES: Pyrotechnic devices should be stored in a cool, dry location and must be readily accessible in case of an emergency. Care should be taken to prevent puncturing or otherwise damaging their coverings. A watertight container, such as a surplus ammunition box, painted red or orange and prominently marked "distress signals" is recommended.

If young children are frequently aboard your boat, careful selection and proper stowage of visual distress signals becomes especially important. If you elect to carry pyrotechnic devices, select devices that are in tough packaging and that would be difficult to ignite accidentally.

Coast Guard–approved pyrotechnic devices carry an expiration date. This date cannot exceed 42 months from the date of manufacture and at such time the device can no longer be counted toward the minimum requirements.

A wide variety of signaling devices, both pyrotechnic and nonpyrotechnic, can be carried to meet the requirements of the regulation.

Boats less than 16 feet long operating in coastal waters, and certain other exempted boats listed in the previous section, need only carry signaling devices when operating at night. All other recreational boats must carry both night and day signaling devices.

The following is an example of the variety and combinations of devices that can be carried in order to meet the requirements:

- Three handheld red flares (day and night)

- One electric distress light (night)

- One handheld red flare and two parachute flares (day and night)

- One handheld orange smoke signal, two floating orange smoke signals, and one electric distress light (day and night)

All distress-signaling devices have both advantages and disadvantages. The most popular, because of cost, are probably the smaller pyrotechnic devices. Pyrotechnics make excellent distress signals, universally recognized as such, but they have the drawback that they can be used only once. Additionally, there is the potential for both injury and property damage if pyrotechnics are not properly handled. Pyrotechnic devices have a very hot flame and the ash and slag can cause burns and ignite materials that burn easily. Projected devices, such as pistol-launched and handheld parachute flares and meteors, have many of the same characteristics of a firearm and must be handled with the same caution and respect.

Under the Inland Navigational Rules, a high-intensity white light flashing at regular intervals from 50–70 times per minute is considered a distress signal. Therefore, a strobe light used in inland waters should only be used as a distress signal.

The handheld and the floating orange smoke signaling devices are good day signals, especially on clear days. Both signals are most effective with light to moderate winds because higher winds tend to keep the smoke close to the water and disperse it, which makes it hard to see.

Sound-Signaling Devices for Vessels Less than 20 Meters (65.6 Feet) in Length

1 • Vessels 12 meters (39.4 feet) or more in length, but less than 20 meters (65.6 feet), must carry onboard a power whistle or power horn and a bell.

2 • Vessels less than 12 meters (39.4 feet) need not carry a whistle, horn, or bell. However, the navigation rules require signals to be made under certain circumstances, and you should carry some means for making an efficient signal when necessary.

The distress flag must be at least 3 by 3 feet with a black square and ball on an orange background. It is accepted as a day signal only and is especially effective in bright sunlight. The flag is most distinctive when waved on something such as a paddle or boat hook or flown from a mast.

The electric distress light is accepted for night use only and must automatically flash the international SOS distress signal (• • • – – – • • •). Flashed four to six times each minute, this is an unmistakable distress signal, well known to most boaters. The device can be checked anytime for serviceability if shielded from view.

Red handheld flares can be used by day, but are most effective at night or in restricted visibility, such as fog or haze. When selecting such flares, look for the Coast Guard approval number and date of manufacture. Make sure that the device does not carry the marking, "Not approved for use on recreational boats."

■ Navigation Lights

REQUIRED ON BOATS BETWEEN SUNSET AND SUNRISE: Recreational boats operating at night are required to display navigation lights between sunset and sunrise. Although most recreational boats in the United States operate in waters governed by the Inland Navigational Rules, changes to the rules have made the general lighting requirements for both the Inland and International rules basically the same. The differences between them are primarily in the options available.

1. A power-driven vessel less than 20 meters (65.6 feet) in length shall exhibit navigation lights as shown in

Range and Arc of Visibility of Lights

For Vessels Less than 20 Meters (65.6 Feet) in Length

Light	Visible Range in Miles		Arc in Degrees
	Less than 12 Meters	12 Meters or More	
Masthead light	2	3	225
All-around light	2	2	360
Side lights	1	2	112.5
Stern light	2	2	135

Figure 1. If the vessel is less than 12 meters (39.4 feet) in length, it may show the lights as shown in either Figure 1 or Figure 2.

2. On a vessel less than 12 meters (39.4 feet) in length, the masthead light must be 1 meter (3.3 feet) higher than the sidelights. If the vessel is 12 meters or more in length but less than 20 meters (65.6 feet), the masthead light must not be less than 2.5 meters (8.2 feet) above the gunwale.

3. A power-driven vessel less than 50 meters in length may also, but is not obligated to, carry a second masthead light abaft of and higher than the forward one.

4. A power-driven vessel less than 7 meters (23 feet) in length and whose maximum speed cannot exceed 7 knots may, in international waters **only**, in lieu of the lights prescribed above, exhibit an all-around white light, and shall, if practicable, also exhibit sidelights.

SAILING VESSELS AND VESSELS UNDER OARS:

1. A sailing vessel less than 20 meters (65.6 feet) in length shall exhibit navigation lights as shown in either Figure 3 or Figure 4. The lights may be combined in a single lantern carried at the top of the mast as shown in Figure 5.

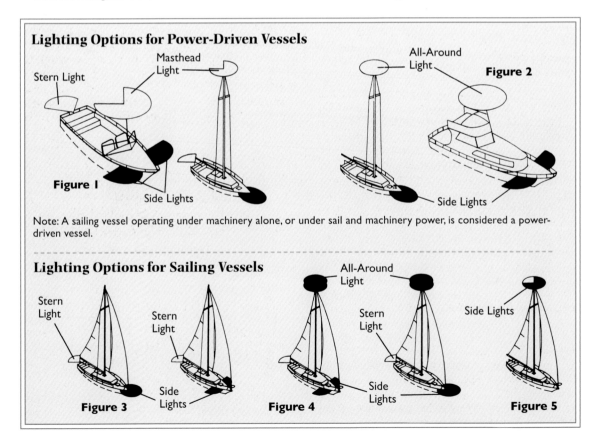

Lighting Options for Power-Driven Vessels

Stern Light — Masthead Light — All-Around Light — **Figure 2**

Side Lights

Figure 1   Side Lights

Note: A sailing vessel operating under machinery alone, or under sail and machinery power, is considered a power-driven vessel.

Lighting Options for Sailing Vessels

Stern Light — Stern Light — All-Around Light — Side Lights

Stern Light

Side Lights — Side Lights

Figure 3   **Figure 4**   **Figure 5**

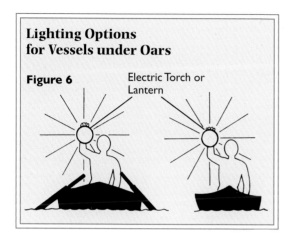

Lighting Options for Vessels under Oars

Figure 6

Electric Torch or Lantern

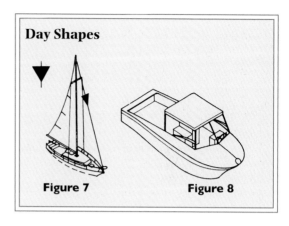

Day Shapes

Figure 7   **Figure 8**

2. A sailing vessel less than 7 meters (23 feet) in length shall, if practicable, exhibit those lights prescribed for sailing vessels less than 20 meters in length, but if it does not, it shall have ready at hand an electric torch or lighted lantern showing a white light that shall be exhibited in sufficient time to prevent collision (see Figure 6).

3. A vessel under oars may display those lights prescribed for sailing vessels, but if it does not, it shall have ready at hand an electric torch or lighted lantern showing a white light that shall be exhibited in sufficient time to prevent collision (see Figure 6).

LIGHTS USED WHEN ANCHORED: Power-driven vessels and sailing vessels at anchor must display anchor lights. However, vessels less than 7 meters (23 feet) in length are not required to display anchor lights unless anchored in or near a narrow channel, fairway, or anchorage, or where other vessels normally navigate.

An anchor light for a vessel less than 20 meters (65.6 feet) in length is an all-around white light visible for 2 miles exhibited where it can best be seen. A vessel less than 20 meters in length in inland waters, when at anchor in a special anchorage area designated by the Secretary of Transportation, does not require an anchor light.

DAY SHAPES: A vessel proceeding under sail when also being propelled by machinery shall exhibit forward, where it can best be seen, a conical shape, apex downward (see Figure 7), except that for Inland Rules, a vessel less than 12 meters in length is not required to exhibit the day shape (see Figure 8).

Loading Your Boat

There are several things to remember when loading a boat: distribute the load evenly, keep the load low, don't overload, don't stand up in a small boat, and consult the U.S. Coast Guard maximum capacity plate. On boats with no capacity plate, use the accompanying formula to determine the maximum number of people your boat can safely carry in calm weather.

The length of your vessel is measured in a straight line from the foremost part of the vessel to the aftermost part of the vessel, parallel to the centerline, exclusive of sheer. Bowsprits, bumpkins, rudders, outboard motors, brackets, and similar fittings are not included in the measurement.

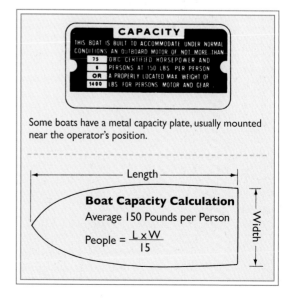

CAPACITY
THIS BOAT IS BUILT TO ACCOMMODATE UNDER NORMAL CONDITIONS AN OUTBOARD MOTOR OF NOT MORE THAN
75 OBC CERTIFIED HORSEPOWER AND
6 PERSONS AT 150 LBS PER PERSON
OR A PROPERLY LOCATED MAX WEIGHT OF
1400 LBS FOR PERSONS MOTOR AND GEAR

Some boats have a metal capacity plate, usually mounted near the operator's position.

Length

Width

Boat Capacity Calculation
Average 150 Pounds per Person

$$People = \frac{L \times W}{15}$$

HANDLING WIND, WEATHER, AND WATER

I recall a terrible boating tragedy years ago that could have been avoided. Eight men in a 28-foot pleasure craft got caught in 20-foot seas and 70-mile-per-hour winds about 30 miles off the East Coast of the United States. In a miraculous Coast Guard rescue, seven men were saved, but one man was never found.

The wife of a survivor told reporters, "I don't understand why the captain took the boat out. The captain didn't want to go. He said it was too windy."

I'll venture a guess why the captain took the boat out. It was probably a long-planned fishing trip, no one wanted to be disappointed, and the weather didn't look bad at the dock.

I remember that day and I also remember a weather forecast that would have kept me at the dock. I don't care how many friends showed up to go fishing, I would have treated them to breakfast at a local diner and sent them home. They would be disappointed, but alive. The open water is no place to prove that you have more guts than brains.

Never forget that if you own and run a boat, you are also the captain, and you are totally responsible for the safety of your passengers. If someone gets hurt on your boat, you have to take the blame.

I get scared when I see a boat pass me with young children sitting on the bow with their feet hanging over the side. One bumpy wake and a child could easily be killed by the prop. I get angry when I see a boater pulling a water skier in a channel with heavy boat traffic. I wonder what is going through the minds of small-boat operators who disappear in ground swells as they head offshore when a small-craft advisory flag is flying in plain view. I say a prayer when I see a family overload a rental boat and head out for a day of fishing with 2 inches of freeboard.

High winds and rough water can turn a pleasant day into a life-threatening nightmare. The best way to stay out of trouble is to learn how to read the weather, wind, and water. And it's equally important to know when to cancel a trip and stay home. This advice is even more important to fishermen who tend to use smaller boats and go out in marginal weather.

Rule No. 1: Check the weather. The National Weather Service issues marine forecasts every six hours with details of winds, seas, weather, and visibility. Heavy static on your AM radio may also indicate nearby storms. The National Weather Service also posts visible warnings at prominent locations along the shore, including Coast Guard stations, lighthouses, yacht clubs, and marinas.

One of the problems with weather forecasts is that they are not always right. Sometimes you may have to make judgment calls on your own. Learn to read simple weather signs. Watch for dark, threatening clouds, which nearly always indicate a thunderstorm or squall. Any steady increase in wind or sea is another sign of bad weather.

If you're on the water, don't wait too long to make a decision. Calm winds and water can turn into a gusty electrical storm in as little as 30 minutes. If you've taken all precautions and you still get caught in a storm, pinpoint your location or note your GPS location on a chart before heavy rain reduces your visibility. Watch for other boats, secure hatches, lower antennas and outriggers, stow all loose gear, and, most important, make sure everyone is wearing a life jacket.

Once the storm hits, try to take the first and heaviest gusts of wind on the bow of the boat. Approach waves at a 45-degree angle to keep the propeller underwater and reduce pounding. If there is lightning, unplug the radio and electrical equipment. Stay away from metal objects and order your passengers to stay low. If you don't lose power, you should be able to ride out almost any storm.

■ How to Forecast Weather

There are dozens of signs that will give you a hint of approaching weather patterns and a whole bunch of weather axioms that will prove true most of the time. Learning how to read some basic signs is fun and it can keep you out of trouble in the outdoors, but it's still important to remember that no weather forecasting system is 100 percent accurate.

There probably isn't a boatman alive who hasn't heard the axiom, "Red sky at night, sailor's delight. Red sky in the morning, sailors take warning." The red sky in the morning may well mean rain that day because there's enough moisture in the air to redden the sky at sunrise. Because of atmospheric conditions, that prediction may come true in the northern United States, but it won't work in tropical climates where red sunrises are common.

I've also heard the axiom, "A ring around the moon means rain." If you only look for a ring around the moon, you will get rain about 50 percent of the time.

You can get better odds, however, if you're more observant. If you notice a falling barometer along with that ring around the moon, you can be sure of rain within 24 hours about 80 percent of the time.

There are other weather signs to help you in the outdoors. Birds, for example, perch on wires, rooftops, and trees more often before storms because low-pressure air is less dense, making it a lot harder to fly. Waterfowl hunters also know that ducks and geese fly a lot higher in good weather than in bad. One reason, other than visibility, is that low pressure affects their ears.

Pay attention to most clouds. Generally, the high clouds will not rain on you, no matter how threatening they look. It's those low clouds that will pound you with rain. You can also forecast impending rain by observing smoke from any smokestack. If the smoke rises, you will get fair weather. If the smoke, however, is driven downward by low pressure, rain is on the way.

If you're in the woods and you sense that smells and scents are stronger around you, there's a good chance that you will get rain. Odors held captive by high pressure escape as the barometer drops, which nearly always means bad weather.

In coastal areas, rain is more likely at low tide than at high tide. A falling tide reduces atmospheric pressure. In the country, check the trees. Leaves show their backs or undersides before a rain. Vegetation grows to prevailing winds and a change of wind direction, which also means a change in weather, turns them over.

Well-designed center consoles, such as this unsinkable 38-foot Edgewater, can easily run in 6- to 8-foot seas, but safety depends on how knowledgeable the captain is on reading and handling rough water. The major concern must always be the safety of his passengers.

Listen to the sounds of boats, gunshots, distant voices, and so on. If the sounds are loud and hollow, you could get rain. A lowering cloud ceiling acts like a sounding board and will bounce noise back to you.

If weather starts to turn bad, note the direction of lightning. If it's in the west or northwest, the storm will probably reach you. Storms to the south or east, however, will usually go past.

When you leave your cabin in the morning, look at the grass. A heavy dew on grass at night and in early morning is a sign of fair weather. Dew forms at those times only when the air is dry and the skies are clear.

Are all of these weather signs true all of the time? Not on your life! But they work most of the time, which is about all you can say for any weather forecast.

■ Lightning and Your Boat

No other kind of foul weather will make a person feel as helpless as lightning. And there's good reason to be scared. Lightning is deadly, but there are certain precautions to take to minimize the risk of being struck.

Lightning is a discharge of static electricity from a charged cloud to earth or from one cloud to another. The electric charge is created when a cumulus cloud is formed in an updraft of warm, moist air. This combination results in a huge buildup of static electricity in a big cumulonimbus cloud. The top part of the cloud holds a positive charge and the bottom part holds a negative charge from the friction of the updraft. When a thundercloud passes overhead, the negative charge induces the earth to take on a positive charge, usually at the highest points, such as tall buildings, poles, or even humans. These charges in clouds and ground are normally kept apart by air, which acts as an insulator. When the static charge becomes strong enough, however, it overcomes the resistance of the air, and lightning occurs.

When a lightning bolt with a current of more than 100,000 amps passes through the atmosphere, the air is heated and expanded, creating a strong vacuum. It's this rapid expansion and collapse of air that creates the loud shock wave known as "thunder."

Thunder can also tell you how far you are from lightning. Count the seconds between lightning and thunder, and then divide by five. The answer is the distance between you and the lightning in miles. If there's a five-second lapse between lightning and thunder, for example, the lightning is a mile or so away.

If you're in a boat on a lake or offshore, lay fishing rods down and head for cover. If you're in a cabin boat and can't reach land ahead of the storm, stay in the cabin and close all the hatches. If you're running the boat, stay as low as possible at the controls. Lower all fishing rods, antennas, and outriggers. Don't hold any gear connected with the grounding system, and don't hold lifelines or rigging. Avoid acting as a bridge between conductive objects. Never touch outriggers, radio antennas, or electrical appliances until the storm has passed. Keep the boat's bow in the wind as much as possible and head for shore. Passengers should wear life jackets and stay in the cabin or as low as possible in the boat.

Get Ready for Hurricanes

Don't wait for a 12-hour warning to start preparing your boat for a hurricane. Do it now! You may need more time than you think to work out a plan of action that will secure and protect your boat in a storm. Now is the time to think about extra lines and special storm gear.

Even the best plan of action, however, cannot guarantee that your boat will survive a hurricane. Some hurricanes prove so violent that boats and people are helpless in their path. Fortunately, not all hurricanes are killers and there are some precautions you can take to keep storm damage to a minimum.

Most boaters believe their real threat of damage comes from winds and waves. This isn't so. Most boat damage comes from storm surge, which means high water. In fact, storm surge accounts for nine out of 10 hurricane-related deaths.

The safest place for your boat is out of the water. If you have a trailer, load your boat on it and take it home. If the boat and trailer fit in your garage, park it there and leave your car outside. Your boat is lighter than your car and can get blown off your trailer in hurricane winds. If you must leave your boat and trailer outside, put it where it will get the best protection from the wind, trees, and electrical lines. Let some air out of the trailer tires, block the wheels, and make sure the boat is strapped securely to the trailer.

You have two options when you leave your boat on a trailer. First, if it's a heavy boat, take out the drain plug to allow rainwater to drain quickly out of the hull. If your boat is light, however, and you are concerned that it may blow off the trailer, leave the drain plug in and fill the hull with water from a garden hose to add more weight. Don't put in too much water or you will damage the hull. Remember that rain will add more water and weight.

Don't trust a storage rack, even if your marina says it's a safe place. There may be other lighter boats that could be blown off their cradle and into your boat. Tell your marina to take your boat out of the rack and block it securely in a safe area. Your marina may balk at this, but be insistent.

If you are forced to leave your boat in the water, make sure it is tied securely, which means double lines. Most boats require five lines: two bow lines, two stern lines, and one spring line. If a hurricane is approaching, you will need 10 lines. It's also wise to go up one size larger than your normal dock lines. Line your boat with as many rubber fenders as you can find to protect the craft from the dock. Always give your lines chafe protection where they will come in contact with the boat or cleats. Neoprene hose is best, but canvas wrapped in place with duct tape will do in a pinch.

If your slip is a small one, look around for a bigger one that's empty and ask your marina if you can use it. The more distance you put between your boat and the pilings and bulkhead, the safer it will be.

Reading the weather is extremely important for all fishermen. High winds and rough water can turn a pleasant day into a life-threatening nightmare. Learn how to read the weather warnings, wind, and water. A calm inlet and offshore waters can turn into a turbulent and dangerous storm in a little as 30 minutes. It's important to know when to cancel a trip.

Mooring and anchoring in a protected harbor that is not crowded is a safe way to ride out a hurricane, but only if the mooring is a permanent installation and you back it up with two additional storm anchors.

When you leave your boat, take all loose gear and electronics with you and use duct tape to seal all hatches, windows, vents, and doors. When you feel your boat is ready for a hurricane, the next step is an important one: go home! When hurricane-force winds hit your boat at 100 miles per hour, there will be nothing you can do.

You can now track a hurricane by phone, which may give you enough warning to secure your boat. When a hurricane is headed your way, you can get official hurricane advisories issued by the National Oceanic and Atmospheric Administration (NOAA) or the Weather Channel.

■ Man Overboard!

Most fishermen will have their boats in the water before warm summer temperatures arrive. They will push the season and launch for trout, flounder, and other species that will start biting in early spring. One truth that is hard to accept is the fact that many fishermen are not dedicated boatmen. Fishermen are usually interested more in fishing than boating . . . and this means a potential danger to themselves and their passengers.

One distinct danger is falling overboard into cold water. Even if you are a good swimmer, the effects of cold water may be more than your body can handle. Cold water can rob your body of heat very quickly. When your body temperature drops, hypothermia becomes a very real threat to life.

Don't be misled into believing that water has to be 35 degrees to be dangerous to someone falling overboard. Cold water is anything below 70 degrees. When the water temperature drops to as low as 35 degrees, survival is usually based on the physical condition of the victim.

Panic and shock are the first and most dangerous hazards to a fisherman falling overboard. Cold water can shock the body and sometimes induce cardiac arrest. Remember how your breath is taken away when you dive into a pool? The same reaction happens when you fall headfirst into cold water. Your first gasp for air will fill your lungs with water. You may also become disoriented for a minute or two before you realize what is happening to you.

If at all possible, get back into your boat as quickly as possible. Your life may depend on it. Unless you have a big boat, this may not be as difficult as it sounds. The majority of fatal boating accidents involve small boats with outboard motors. Most small boats, even if capsized, can be righted and reentered.

Small boats are legally bound to have enough flotation to support all occupants. If you can, right the boat, climb back into it, and bail out the water. If you can't right the boat, climb onto the hull and hang on. It's critical that you get out of the cold water.

If the boat slips away and you can't reach it, there are certain precautions to take in the water until help arrives. Unless there is no chance for a rescue, do not try swimming. It will drain body heat and, if you're like most people, you will not be able to swim very far in cold water.

Your best bet is to remain still and get into a protective position to conserve heat and wait for a rescue. This means protecting your body's major heat-loss areas, such as your head, neck, armpits, chest, and groin. If there is more than one person in the water, huddle together to preserve body heat.

Treatment of cold-water victims varies. The first signs of hypothermia are intense shivering, loss of coordination, mental confusion, blue skin, weak pulse, irregular heartbeat, and enlarged pupils. If the victim is cold and only shivering, dry clothes and blankets may be all that is necessary.

If the victim is semiconscious, move him to a warm place and into dry clothes. Make him lie flat with his head slightly lower than his body, which will make more blood flow to the brain. You can also warm the victim with warm towels to the head, neck, chest, and groin.

Of course, it's always easier to avoid problems by taking a few simple precautions. First, wear a life jacket at all times, especially during cool weather. Whenever possible, wear several layers of wool for insulation. Wool, even when wet, will retain body heat.

If you suddenly find yourself in the water, make sure your life jacket is snug. Keep clothing buttoned up. The water trapped in your clothes will be warmed by your body heat and keep you warm.

■ Why Boats Sink

The mere thought of a boat sinking out from under its skipper and his passengers will send chills down the back of the toughest boater. Will he calmly handle the situation or will he go to pieces and panic? Why did it happen? What did he do wrong?

According to statistics, boaters should worry more about sinking at the dock than out on the water. Statistics show that three out of four recreational boat

Float Plan

File a float plan. Tell someone where you are going and when you plan to return. Tell them what your boat looks like and other information that will make identifying it easier should the need arise. Print a copy of the float plan from the Coast Guard website (www.uscgboating. org/safety/float_planning.aspx), fill it out, and leave it with a reliable person who can be depended upon to notify the Coast Guard, or another rescue organization, should you not return as scheduled. Do not, however, file float plans with the Coast Guard.

A PDF version of this form can be downloaded from the U.S. Coast Guard website.

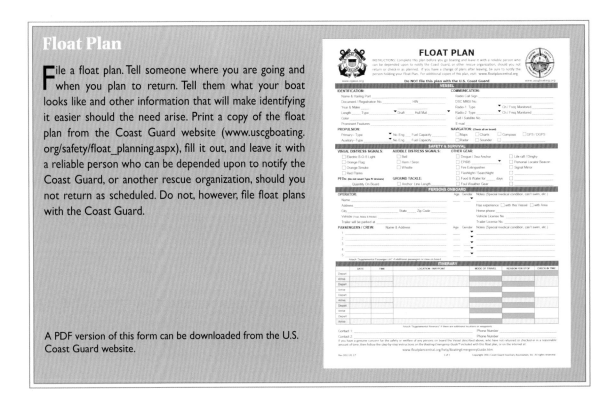

sinkings happen right at the dock. Fortunately, most dockside sinkings can be prevented.

First, never depend completely on an automatic float switch to turn on your bilge pump when water gets into your hull. Bilge pumps and switches, because of their location, get dirty and will sometimes jam in the off position and not turn on your pump at all or get stuck in the on position and kill your battery. Both cases are bad news and could sink an unattended boat. Check your bilge pump and switches before every trip. In fact, automatic float switches should be replaced every other year. These switches are inexpensive and easy to wire to a bilge pump.

Learn how to tie your boat correctly at the dock, especially in tidal water. If your boat swings or drifts too freely at the dock, it could get stuck under the dock and get pushed under the water when the tide rises. This kind of sinking happens all too often.

Make it a point of learning every through-hull underwater fitting on your boat. Draw the locations of the fittings on a piece of paper and check them every time the boat is out of the water. Look inside the hull. Do all

the fittings have seacocks? Do they all work? Do you close them when you leave the boat unattended? Do you keep them well lubricated? It's the kind of maintenance and attention that will keep your boat afloat.

Remember that your boat can take on water from above the waterline as well as from below. Check all deck fittings, fastenings, and hatches. Not all boat manufacturers use a good sealant on fastenings and some of them leak. Hose down your cabin and decks, and then look for leaks inside and in the hull. If you see a leak, fix it. You can sink from rainwater just as easily as from a leak below the surface.

Water from washings at the dock can sometimes get trapped in the hull. To get this water out, try this trick. When your bow lifts up, just before you get on a plane, manually switch on your bilge. If you have to, keep the bow high until all the bilge water rushes to the pump and gets pumped out.

Continually check all hoses and clamps. Clamps are cheap. If they look rusty, replace them. In fact, you should keep an assortment of different size clamps in your toolbox. Pay special attention to hoses that have sharp bends. If any look stressed or kinked, replace them. Replacing a hose when your boat is on a trailer is easy. It's a panic problem, however, if it happens 5 miles from shore. It's also a good idea to double clamp all hoses.

If you're shopping for a boat, look for designs with self-bailing cockpits. This means the deck is above the waterline. Any water coming into the boat will drain out the transom scuppers and not stay in the boat or hull. This is a comforting thought in a heavy sea. Most of the tough breed of small fishing boats built for offshore fishing have this feature. Many small, less expensive ski boats, however, do not have self-bailing cockpits. Stay away from them.

Make sure your transom drains, transom wells, and scuppers are clean and not clogged with dirt. Water must be allowed to drain out. The best time to check these drains and flush them out is when you're washing your boat with a hose and good water pressure.

Maintenance of through-hull fittings, seacocks, hoses, bilge pumps, and switches is easy. Make a checklist and do it often. This is especially important if you leave your boat unattended for long periods of time.

If you leave your boat in the water, you should also get a mooring cover that protects your boat from bow to stern. This kind of full cover will give you peace of mind the next time it storms and your boat is 50 miles away at the marina where it may not get any attention.

■ Why Boats Blow Up

A day on the water can be an exhilarating experience, but when things go wrong with your boat, it can also be a frightening experience. The thought of a fire or explosion on a boat is even more terrifying. If you're far from land, there is no safe place to run.

Fires and explosions can only come from faulty fuel systems or human error. Fortunately, both are avoidable if you take certain precautions. First, let's start with the deck. Is your gas cap clearly labeled "gasoline"? As far-fetched as it sounds, there are cases on record where a clueless gas attendant has pumped gasoline into a rod holder or into a water tank.

All boats must have an overside drain or tank vent for your fuel tank. Make sure that excess fuel or fumes at the gas dock will not find their way into your boat or bilge. Make sure your vent has a mesh screen in place, which could keep fumes from igniting in the fuel line.

If your fill hose is worn or frayed, replace it. But make certain you buy the right hose. It should be stamped "USCG Type A2," which is fire resistant. Your filler cap should also be grounded with an electrical wire from the fill opening to the tank, so that any static electricity from the dock hose will flow to the ground without causing a spark.

It's critical that you run your blower to clear your bilge of gas fumes before starting your engine. Check the blower hose and make sure it's not crushed or broken or twisted. After you've run your blower, sniff the bilge with your nose, which is probably the best fuel detector of all. If you have any doubts, don't start your engine. This is especially true at the fuel dock, where most explosions and fires occur.

If you're buying a new or used boat, check the fuel tanks. Any tank over 7 gallons should have a label with the manufacturer's name, date of manufacture, capacity, and material. It should also say, "This tank has been tested under 33 CFR 183.580." If you can't find this label, avoid the boat or have the tank replaced.

Even if you have all the right fittings and parts, you can still get into trouble if you are careless. Explosions are most likely to occur at the fuel dock, when a leak in the fill or vent system may not be discovered until the tank is topped off.

When you refuel, take certain precautions. First, close all hatches and turn off the battery switch and stove. Fill the tank yourself, if you can, and never fill it to the very top. If you do, and the gas expands, you could get spillage in your boat and bilge. After refueling, run the blower for a full five minutes or longer, and then sniff the bilge with your nose before starting the engine.

If you use outboard-motor tanks, take them out of the boat and do your refueling on the dock. This is the safest procedure. Unfortunately, most inboard and stern-drive boats don't have this option.

Let's suppose, for example, that you don't notice a fuel leak until it is too late and you're out on the water with a bilge full of gas. Do you know what to do? Here's the best and only procedure. Do not start the engine or use any electrical equipment other than your VHF radio or cell phone—and this should be only after you turn off all other electrical circuits. Next, turn off your battery switch and have all your passengers put on life jackets and stay on deck. Finally, call the Coast Guard and describe your problem and situation. They will instruct you on the next step.

If you find gas has leaked into your boat at the dock, order all guests off the boat. Turn off the battery switch and shore power. Notify the marina manager and call the fire department.

Don't wreck your day or endanger your guests because you don't know how to handle a gas emergency. Most of these procedures are simple common sense.

Index

Acknowledgments

The author would like to thank the following people, companies, organizations, and agencies for their permission, cooperation, and assistance in compiling information and photographs for this book:

Andy Anderson • Stu Apte • Joe Arterburn, Cabela's • James Babb • Chris Batin • David Blinken • Dean Corbisier, Suzuki • Chris Corey, L.L. Bean • James Daley, Orvis • Laura Davidson, Blogging Over Thyme • Brittney Dileo, BOTE Board • Daniel D. Dye II, Florida Backyard Snakes • Greg Eck, Yanmar America Corporation • J. Wayne Fears • Steve Fleming, Mercury Marine • Pete Frederickson, Viking Yachts • Jerry Gibbs • Christina Harris, WorldCat • William W. Hartley, Hartley Industries • Sheila M. Hassan • Jihan Hill, Rushton Gregory Communications • Jim Hutchinson, Recreational Fishing Alliance • Isaiah James, Windsor Nature Discovery • Andrea Jansen, Mercury Marine • Charlie Johnson, Maverick Boat Company • Jeff Kauzlaric, Furuno • Jenna Kendall, Bass Pro • Karen Kinser, Wright & McGill/Eagle Claw • Ben Lavely, Best Made • Jim Martinson, Sheldon's • Stephen Matt, G3 Boats • Mac McKeever,

L.L. Bean • Reid McKinstry, Mustad • Tom Mielke, Mercury Marine • Captain Glen Miller, Bud N' Mary's Marina • Stacy Miller, WorldCat • Katie Mitchell, Bass Pro • Gail Morchower, International Game Fish Association • Kellie Mowery, Cabela's • Peter Orlando, EdgeWater Boats • Jorge Oviedo, Mustad • Richard Pata, AFTCO • Martin Peters, Yamaha • John Phillips • Kim Phillips, Bass Pro • Cason Pilliod, Kalkomey • Tom Rosenbauer, Orvis • Tammy Sapp, Bass Pro Shops • Ken Schultz • Dusan Smetana • Captain Richard Stanczyk, Bud N' Mary's Marina • Sarah Stern, Sabre Yachts • Jeremy Storm • Mitch Strobl, Kalkomey Enterprises • Jack Vitek, International Game Fish Association • Josh Ward, Ranger and Stratos Boats • Bobby Wheaton, Yamaha Marine Group • Jeff Wieringa, Scientific Anglers • Greg Wollner, Rapala • Joan Wulff, Wulff School of Fly Fishing • Leslie Zlotnick, Yamaha • Jim Zumbo

■ ■ ■

Photography Credits

© Sheila Hassan: pp. 23–28 (all).

© Robert Holland/EdgeWater Boats: p. 351.

© Bob Krist Photo/Florida Keys News Bureau: p. 326.

Courtesy of L.L. Bean: pp. 245 (bottom), 303 (middle left, middle right, and bottom right), and 306 (bottom left).

Courtesy of Lowrance: p. 320 (right).

Courtesy of Maverick: p. 298 (bottom left).

Courtesy of Mepps: pp. 76 (bottom right), 77 (top left and second from top left), and 111 (left and right).

Courtesy of Mercury: pp. 309 (top left and middle left) and 313 (bottom left).

Courtesy of Mister Twister: p. 111 (middle).

Courtesy of Mustad: pp. 68–70 (all).

Courtesy of Ocean Kayak: p. 302.

Courtesy of Orvis: pp. 87 (all), 93 (all), and 94–95 (all).

Courtesy of Pflueger: p. 21 (top right).

Courtesy of Ranger: p. 315 (middle).

Courtesy of Rapala: p. 50 (bottom left, middle, and bottom right).

© Tom Rosenbauer: pp. 55 and 88.

Courtesy of Sabre Yachts: p. 294.

© Shutterstock.com/18042011: pp. 270–271 and back cover (middle row, center).

© Shutterstock.com/Kletr: p. 112.

© Dusan Smetana: pp. 12–13, 182–183, 212–213, 292–293, 352, and back cover (top row, all; middle row, right).

© Vin Sparano: pp. 45 (both), 47 (both), 80 (both), 120, 154, 246 (all), 248–249 (all), 259, and 368.

Courtesy of Standard Horizon: p. 321 (top left).

Courtesy of Stratos: p. 315 (bottom).

Courtesy of Suzuki: p. 309 (bottom left and middle right).

Courtesy of Viking: p. 298 (middle right).

Courtesy of World Cat: pp. 301 (bottom) and 317 (right).

Courtesy of Yamaha: pp. 309 (top right and bottom right) and 313 (bottom right).

Courtesy of Yanmar: p. 312.

Courtesy of Yellowfin: p. 298 (second from bottom left).

ILLUSTRATION CREDITS AND OTHER NOTES

Unless otherwise noted here, all black-and-white line art was picked up from the fourth edition of Vin Sparano's *Complete Outdoors Encyclopedia*.

Courtesy of AFTCO (American Fishing Tackle Company): p. 46.

© James Daley: pp. 14, 184, 214, 244, 272, and 294 (opener illustrations only).

Courtesy of IGFA (International Game Fish Association): pp. 161 (all), 162 (all), 164 (both), 166 (both), and 179.

Courtesy of Kalkomey.com: pp. 295 (all), 296 (all), 307 (all), 308, 310 (all color), 313, 324 (all), 343 (all), and 346 (all).

Courtesy of Mustad: pp. 63–70 (all).

Courtesy of Scientific Anglers: p. 56 (all).

Courtesy of Windsor Nature Discovery: pp. 184–198 (all), 200–210 (all), 214–233 (all), 236, and 238–240 (all).

Courtesy of the United States Coast Guard: p. 354.

• Photos and portions of the text for the How to Use Fly Tackle section (pp. 23–28) were excerpted from Sheila Hassan's book *Fly Casting: A Systematic Approach* and used with her permission. For more information, visit her website: www.cast90.com.

• All text and line art for the International Game Fish Association Rules and Regulations section (pp. 160–181) were provided courtesy of the International Game Fish Association.

• With the exception of recipes contributed by the individuals listed on p. 256, all recipes from pp. 257–269 are from Vin Sparano's personal collection.

• Illustrations and information on boat hulls, sailboats, marine motors, anchors, buoys, and personal flotation devices were provided courtesy of Kalkomey Enterprises (see page numbers listed above). For more information, visit the company's website at www.boat-ed.com.

About the Author

Vin T. Sparano has been an outdoor editor and writer for more than 50 years. He earned his B.S. degree in journalism in 1960 from New York University. Sparano is editor emeritus of *Outdoor Life* magazine, having served as editor-in-chief from 1990 to 1995 and previously as executive editor for more than 10 years.

In addition to his long career with *Outdoor Life*,

Sparano was a syndicated features writer for *USA Today* and Gannett Newspapers. He has written and edited 19 books—including Universe's *Complete Outdoors Encyclopedia*, the full-color fifth edition of the classic encyclopedia originally published in 1976—and has produced electronic software focusing on fishing techniques and hot spots through the use of navigational charts and satellite photos.

Sparano and his wife, Betty, live in Waretown, New Jersey, where he is a familiar sight fishing from his boat, *Betty Boop*. During the fall, his focus is on the great striped bass fishery off Barnegat Inlet. In the winter months, Sparano travels to Florida, where he fishes the famous Islamorada Flats for tarpon and bonefish, as well as the offshore waters for sailfish, tuna, and other bluewater game fish.

A certified NRA rifle, pistol, shotgun, and hunting safety instructor, Sparano has been a member of the Outdoor Writers Association of America, fulfilling a term on its board of directors, and is also a heritage member of the Professional Outdoor Media Association. Sparano was a recipient of a Lifetime Achievement Award from both the New York Metropolitan Outdoor Press Association and the Fisherman's Conservation Association.

In 1996, Sparano was awarded the United States Department of the Interior Conservation Award by Secretary of the Interior Bruce Babbitt for his extraordinary contributions to conservation and outdoor journalism. In 2013, he was enshrined in the Fresh Water Fishing Hall of Fame. Sparano is also listed in *Who's Who in America*.